CRITICAL SURVEY
OF
LONG FICTION

CRITICAL SURVEY
OF
LONG FICTION

English Language Series

REVISED EDITION

Wel-Z

Essays

8

Edited by
FRANK N. MAGILL

SALEM PRESS
Pasadena, California   Englewood Cliffs, New Jersey

SECOND PRINTING

Library of Congress Cataloging-in-Publication Data
Critical survey of long fiction. English language series/
    edited by Frank N. Magill. — Rev. ed.
        p.   cm.
    Includes bibliographical references and index.
    1. English fiction—Dictionaries. 2. American
fiction—Dictionaries. 3. English fiction—
Bio-bibliography. 4. American fiction—
Bio-bibliography. 5. Novelists, English—
Biography—Dictionaries. 6. Novelists, American—
Biography—Dictionaries.
I. Magill, Frank Northen, 1907-   .
PR821.C7   1991
823.009′03—dc20   91-19694
ISBN 0-89356-825-2 (set)   CIP
ISBN 0-89356-833-3 (volume 8)

PRINTED IN THE UNITED STATES OF AMERICA

LIST OF AUTHORS IN VOLUME 8

page

Weldon, Fay 3473
Wells, H. G. 3480
Welty, Eudora 3488
Wescott, Glenway 3501
West, Nathanael 3512
West, Paul 3520
Wharton, Edith 3530
White, Patrick 3543
Wideman, John Edgar 3560
Wilder, Thornton 3570
Wilson, A. N. 3580
Wilson, Angus 3587
Wilson, Ethel 3598
Wodehouse, P. G. 3608
Woiwode, Larry 3619
Wolfe, Thomas 3627
Woolf, Virginia 3641
Wouk, Herman 3663
Wright, Richard 3679

Yerby, Frank 3691
Yglesias, José 3699
Young, Al 3710

Origins and Development of the Novel Before 1740 3721
Origins and Development of the Novel from 1740 to 1890 3730
Origins and Development of the Novel Since 1890 3753
The English Novel 3779
The American Novel 3794
Picaresque Novel 3803
Epistolary Novel 3810
Gothic Novel 3823
Historical Novel 3835
Detective Novel 3842
Western Novel 3849
Fantasy Novel 3857
Science-Fiction Novel 3865
The Novella 3873
Terms and Techniques 3880

CRITICAL SURVEY
OF
LONG FICTION

FAY WELDON

Born: Alvechurch, England; September 22, 1931

Principal long fiction

The Fat Woman's Joke, 1967 (also known as . . . *And the Wife Ran Away*, 1968); *Down Among the Women*, 1971; *Female Friends*, 1974; *Remember Me*, 1976; *Words of Advice*, 1977 (also known as *Little Sisters*); *Praxis*, 1978; *Puffball*, 1980; *The President's Child*, 1982; *The Life and Loves of a She-Devil*, 1983; *The Shrapnel Academy*, 1986; *The Rules of Life*, 1987; *The Hearts and Lives of Men*, 1987; *The Heart of the Country*, 1987; *Leader of the Band*, 1988; *The Cloning of Joanna May*, 1989; *Darcy's Utopia*, 1990.

Other literary forms

Fay Weldon began her writing career with plays for radio, television, and theater, but she soon transferred her efforts to novels, for which she is best known. She has also published short stories, a biography of Rebecca West, and an introduction to the work of Jane Austen in fictional form, *Letters to Alice on First Reading Jane Austen* (1984).

Achievements

In addition to a successful career as an advertising copywriter, Fay Weldon has enjoyed a long career as a television scriptwriter, a playwright (for television, radio, and theater), and a novelist. Her play *Spider* (1972) won the Writers' Guild Award for Best Radio Play in 1973, and *Polaris* (1978) won the Giles Cooper Award for Best Radio Play in 1978. Weldon has earned growing acclaim for her humorous fictional explorations of women's lives and her biting satires that expose social injustice, and her novel *Praxis* was nominated for the Booker Prize, a prestigious literary award in England. Although her works often focus primarily on the lives of women, Weldon comments on a wide-ranging number of issues with relevance to all. Her work reveals a deep yet unsentimental compassion for all human beings, an understanding of their weaknesses and foibles, and a celebration of their continued survival and ability to love one another in the face of adversity.

Biography

Fay Weldon was born into a literary family in the village of Alvechurch, England, in 1931. Her mother, her maternal grandfather, and her uncle were all published novelists. While still a child, Weldon emigrated with her family to New Zealand, where she grew up. When she was six years old, her parents (Frank Thornton Birkinshaw, a doctor, and Margaret Jepson Birkinshaw) were divorced; Weldon continued to live with her mother and sister. This experience of being reared by a single mother in an era that did not easily accommodate single-parent families gave Weldon early insight into the lot of women who flouted social norms. When she was fourteen, Weldon, her mother, and her sister joined her grandmother in London. These were years of hardship in postwar England, but the strong and independent women of the family set a good example. Weldon was able to observe, at first hand, both the trials women faced and the importance of family and of humor in over-coming these difficulties.

In 1949, Weldon earned a scholarship to St. Andrew's University in Scot-land, and in 1952 she was graduated with an M.A. in economics and psychol-ogy. In 1955, she had her first son, Nicholas, whom she supported as a single mother. Weldon's literary ambitions had not yet crystallized—though she had begun writing—so she drifted into a series of writing jobs: propaganda for the Foreign Office; answering problem letters for a newspaper; and, finally, composing advertising copy. In this last career she was quite successful, producing many jingles and slogans that would become household sayings and honing her talent for concision, wit, and catchy, memorable phrasing.

In 1960, she married Ronald Weldon, a London antiques dealer, and to-gether they settled in a North London suburb, where they had three children: Daniel (born 1963), Thomas (born 1970), and Samuel (born 1977). Begin-ning in the mid-1960's, Weldon combined professional and family respon-sibilities with a burgeoning career as a writer. Her efforts were at first di-rected toward writing plays. Her one-act play "Permanence" was produced in London in 1969 and was followed by many successes. For British television networks, Weldon has written more than fifty plays, as well as other scripts, including an award-winning episode of *Upstairs, Downstairs*.

Writing for television led to fiction: Weldon's first novel, *The Fat Woman's Joke* (1967), had begun as a television play. Her third novel, *Female Friends*, solidified her reputation. In the 1970's, Weldon left her job in advertising. She was able to devote more of her time to writing, earning further acclaim for *Praxis* in 1978. *The President's Child*, in 1982, was an even bigger best-seller, thanks to its "thriller" quality, while *The Life and Loves of a She-Devil*, in 1983, introduced Weldon's work to a mass audience when it was made into a motion picture, *She-Devil* (1989), starring Meryl Streep and Roseanne Barr.

Analysis

In her fiction, Fay Weldon explores women's lives with wit and humor. She is caustic in her implicit condemnation of injustice but avoids preaching by satirizing both sides of every issue and by revealing the gulf between what characters say and what they do. Despite their realistic settings, her novels blend fable, myth, and the fantastic with satire, farce, and outlandish coincidence to produce tragicomedies of manners.

Weldon's admiration for writers such as Jane Austen (whose work she has adapted for television) is expressed openly in *Letters to Alice on First Reading Jane Austen*, but it is also evident from the parallels in Weldon's own work. In a typical Weldon novel, a limited cast of characters interact in a well-defined setting. A series of misunderstandings or trivial coincidences initiates the action, which then takes on a momentum of its own, carrying all along with it until an equally trivial series of explanations or coincidences bring closure and a resolution that restores all to their proper place. The theme is often a minor domestic drama, such as a marital crisis, rather than an epic upheaval, but such personal interactions are seen to represent in microcosm society as a whole and therefore have a universal appeal.

This structure is present even in Weldon's early work, no doubt because it is a formula that works well for television. In her first novel, originally entitled *The Fat Woman's Joke*, but renamed . . . *And the Wife Ran Away* for its American publication in 1968, Weldon takes as her subject the crisis in the marriage of a middle-aged, middle-class couple, Esther and Alan Wells, when Alan decides to have an affair with his young and attractive secretary, Susan. The beginning of Alan's affair coincides with Esther and Alan's decision to go on a diet, a symbolic attempt, Weldon suggests, to recapture not only their lost youthful figures, but also their youthful love, ambition, and optimism. Infidelity, the novel therefore subtly suggests, is related to aging and to a more deep-seated identity crisis. Weldon frequently uses hunger or the satisfaction of food as a metaphor for other, more metaphysical and intangible, needs, and this theme recurs in a number of her works (for example, in the short story "Polaris," 1985).

The influence of Weldon's background as a scriptwriter (and the novel's origin as a play) is also evident in its form. Esther, who has left her husband at the opening of the novel, recounts her version of events to her friend Phyllis, as she gorges herself on food to compensate for the self-denial she has suffered during the diet. Esther's narrative is intercut with scenes of Susan telling her version to her friend Brenda. The novel is thus almost entirely conveyed through dialogue describing flashbacks seen from the perspective of the female characters. This technique is evident elsewhere in Weldon's early work—for example, in *Female Friends*, where parts of the novel are presented in the form of a script.

The Life and Loves of a She-Devil stands as one of Weldon's most accomplished works. It represents the themes that are the hallmark of Weldon's fiction (a concern with women's lives and the significance of human relationships such as marriage) while encompassing her use of fantasy in one of her most carefully constructed and formally satisfying novels. The plot tells the story of a middle-class, suburban housewife, Ruth, whose accountant husband leaves her for a rich and attractive writer of romance novels. Unlike the typical wife, however, Ruth does not simply bow to the inevitable. When her husband calls her a "she-devil" in a moment of anger, this becomes her new identity, and she musters a formidable array of resources to live up to it. Through a series of picaresque adventures, she makes the life of her husband Bobbo and his new love Mary Fisher impossible, has Bobbo framed and then imprisoned for embezzlement, destroys Mary's ability and will to write, and finally undergoes massive plastic surgery so that she looks just like the now-dead rival Mary and can assume her place in Bobbo's broken life. The configuration at the end of the novel thus mirrors the beginning, but with the variation that power dynamics of the relationship have been inverted: Ruth is now in command, while Bobbo has been humiliated and accepts his fate like a downtrodden wife.

The tale not only presents a certain kind of symmetry reminiscent of fairy stories but also evokes a poetic magic in the telling of it. Many of the chapters begin with a variation on the opening line of the novel: "Mary Fisher lives in a High Tower, on the edge of the sea." These incantations, repeated with variations, have the hypnotic quality of a witch's spell, reinforcing both Ruth's supernatural power and her obsession with Mary Fisher (whose residence in a tower evokes a fairy-tale princess). This poetic refrain also unifies the narrative and gives a cyclical structure to the plot.

At first glance, *The Shrapnel Academy* appears to be a variation on the theme of the "country house weekend" plot, a staple of British literature. A group of characters, most of them unknown to one another, are seen arriving at the Shrapnel Academy, a military institute, for a weekend. Bad weather will ensure that they remain confined to the academy, cut off from the outside world and forced to confront one another and the problems that arise.

While many novelists fail to acknowledge the presence of the host of servants who make such country weekends possible, Weldon's novel takes the reader below stairs and into the lives of the hundreds of illegal immigrant servants and their extended families and camp followers. *The Shrapnel Academy* could thus be subtitled "Upstairs, Downstairs," like the television series about an upper-class Edwardian family and its servants (to which Weldon contributed an award-winning episode). *The Shrapnel Academy* strays far beyond the realist conventions of the television series, however, and by presenting the clash between shortsighted, class-based militarism and the struggle for survival and dignity in the microcosm of the Academy, Weldon succeeds in painting an apocalyptic allegory.

The Shrapnel Academy illustrates how Weldon avoids assigning blame by showing how character flaws and opportunity combine to create problems. Despite the black humor of this novel, Weldon's moral universe is not one of black and white. The reader is made to sympathize with the choices of the militarists and is shown the complicity of the victims so that simplistic judgments become impossible. As in most of Weldon's novels, no one villain is responsible for the misfortunes that befall the characters; instead, everyone bears some degree of responsibility for the accumulation of trivial choices and decisions that combine to make up the "frightful tidal wave of destiny." The theme of destiny increasingly preoccupies Weldon; it is one of the major themes in *The Cloning of Joanna May*, for example, in which the role of coincidence is the subject of mystical and metaphysical speculation.

Many thematic and stylistic elements of Weldon's work also recur in *The Shrapnel Academy*, such as the revenge fantasy theme, food symbolism, and the revision of mythology and fable. Since war affects everyone—increasingly, Weldon argues, women and children—the militaristic theme of *The Shrapnel Academy* should not be construed as belying a male-oriented narrative. Weldon uses the female characters in this novel to offer characteristic insight into the position of the various women above stairs—Joan Lumb, the officious administrator, the General's mistress Bella, Shirley the unquestioning and dutiful wife, Muffin the fluff-brained assistant—as well as the often anonymous women who are raped, die in childbirth, or become prostitutes in the "third world" below stairs.

Formally, too, the novel displays typical characteristics of Weldon's work (short narrative passages with aphoristic asides, the use of dialogue), as well as innovative and experimental qualities. Weldon interrupts the narrative at frequent intervals, sometimes to offer a satirical summary of military history, highlighting advances in warfare or giving accounts of famous battles. Weldon brings out the absurdity of celebrating such "progress" and uses her fine wit to draw the reader's attention to the Orwellian doublespeak and the underlying assumptions of military thinking. At other times, Weldon interpellates the reader directly, apologizing for the delay in getting on with the story or inviting readers to put themselves in the place of one of the characters—invitations that pointedly drive home the lesson that the reader is no better than the characters he is inclined to judge. Weldon even interrupts the story to offer a recipe for cooking pumpkin, only one of the ways Weldon breaks with the conventional codes of narrative (elsewhere she offers lists, timetables, and even a seating plan and a menu).

Weldon's fiction has developed from dialogue-based, scriptlike narratives to a style that resembles more conventional forms of the novel, although still with a characteristic lack of reverence for the conventions of storytelling. Her themes have expanded from domestic dramas and personal relationships to topical questions of national and international import, but without abandoning the belief that the personal remains the minimal unit of significance at the base of even the largest human networks. Humor has remained a constant feature of her work, her delicious wit and sharp irony the armor that protects her from charges of overseriousness, preaching, or doctrinaire political stances.

Melanie Hawthorne

Other major works

SHORT FICTION: *Watching Me, Watching You*, 1981; *Polaris and Other Stories*, 1985.

PLAYS: *Permanence*, pr. 1969; *Time Hurries On*, pb. 1972; *Words of Advice*, pr., pb. 1974; *Friends*, pr. 1975; *Moving House*, pr. 1976; *Mr. Director*, pr. 1978; *Action Replay*, pr. 1979 (also known as *Love Among the Women*); *I Love My Love*, pr. 1981; *After the Prize*, pr. 1981 (also known as *Wordworm*).

TELEPLAYS: *Wife in a Blonde Wig*, 1966; *The Fat Woman's Tale*, 1966; *What About Me*, 1967; *Dr. De Waldon's Therapy*, 1967; *Goodnight Mrs. Dill*, 1967; *The 45th Unmarried Mother*, 1967; *Fall of the Goat*, 1967; *Ruined Houses*, 1968; *Venus Rising*, 1968; *The Three Wives of Felix Hull*, 1968; *Hippy Hippy Who Cares*, 1968; *£13083*, 1968; *The Loophole*, 1969; *Smokescreen*, 1969; *Poor Mother*, 1970; *Office Party*, 1970; *On Trial*, 1971 (in "Upstairs, Downstairs" series); *Old Man's Hat*, 1972; *A Splinter of Ice*, 1972; *Hands*, 1972; *The Lament of an Unmarried Father*, 1972; *A Nice Rest*, 1972; *Comfortable Words*, 1973; *Desirous of Change*, 1973; *In Memoriam*, 1974; *Poor Baby*, 1975; *The Terrible Tale of Timothy Bagshott*, 1975; *Aunt Tatty*, 1975; *Act of Rape*, 1977; *Married Love*, 1977 (in "Six Women" series); *Pride and Prejudice*, 1980; *Honey Ann*, 1980; *Watching Me, Watching You*, 1980 (in "Leap in the Dark" series); *Life for Christine*, 1980; *Little Miss Perkins*, 1982; *Loving Women*, 1983; *Redundant! Or, The Wife's Revenge*, 1983.

RADIO PLAYS: *Spider*, 1972; *Housebreaker*, 1973; *Mr. Fox and Mr. First*, 1974; *The Doctor's Wife*, 1975; *Polaris*, 1978; *Weekend*, 1979 (in "Just Before Midnight" series); *All the Bells of Paradise*, 1979; *I Love My Love*, 1981.

NONFICTION: *Letters to Alice on First Reading Jane Austen*, 1984; *Rebecca West*, 1985.

EDITED TEXT: *New Stories 4: An Arts Council Anthology*, 1979 (with Elaine Feinstein).

Bibliography

Blodgett, Harriet. "Fay Weldon." In *Dictionary of Literary Biography*. Vol. 14, *British Novelists Since 1960*. Part 2, edited by Jay L. Halio. Detroit: Gale Research, 1983. The most comprehensive assessment of Weldon's career available, although incomplete. The article gives a biographical overview as well as critical assessment of Weldon's work from 1968 to 1982. The discussion includes considerations of theme and critical reception.

Chesnutt, Margaret. "Feminist Criticism and Feminist Consciousness: A Reading of a Novel by Fay Weldon." *Moderna Sprak* 73 (1979): 3-18. Chesnutt stresses materialist-feminist goals in her framework to this article, but in her discussion of Weldon's *Down Among the Women*, she employs a structuralist approach (based on the work of A. J. Greimas) to assess the novel's representation of female consciousness and its effectiveness as "emancipatory literature."

Krouse, Agate Nesaule. "Feminism and Art in Fay Weldon's Novels." *Critique: Studies in Modern Fiction* 20, no. 2 (1978): 5-20. An accessible overview that analyzes the feminist themes and structures of Weldon's first four novels (this limited scope is the only drawback), while stressing Weldon's artistic achievements and offering comparisons to other women writers. Krouse explains how Weldon's feminism avoids stressing only the problems of women's lives and instead becomes a force for positive change.

Weldon, Fay. "Towards a Humorous View of the Universe." In *Last Laughs: Perspectives on Women and Comedy*, edited by Regina Barreca. New York: Gordon and Breach, 1988. A short (three-page) article about humor as a protection against pain, with perceptive comments about class-related and gendered aspects of humor. Although Weldon herself does not draw the connections specifically, the reader can infer much from her comments about the role of humor in her own work.

Wilde, Alan. " 'Bold, But Not Too Bold': Fay Weldon and the Limits of Poststructuralist Criticism." *Contemporary Literature* 29, no. 3 (1988): 403-419. The author focuses primarily not on Weldon's work but on literary theory, using *The Life and Loves of a She-Devil* as an arena to pit poststructuralism against New Criticism. The argument is at times obscure, but Wilde offers some useful comments regarding moderation versus extremism in this novel.

H. G. WELLS

Born: Bromley, England; September 21, 1866
Died: London, England; August 13, 1946

Principal long fiction

The Time Machine: An Invention, 1895; *The Wonderful Visit*, 1895; *The Island of Dr. Moreau*, 1896; *The Wheels of Chance: A Holiday Adventure*, 1896; *The Invisible Man: A Grotesque Romance*, 1897; *The War of the Worlds*, 1898; *When the Sleeper Wakes: A Story of the Years to Come*, 1899; *Love and Mr. Lewisham*, 1900; *The First Men in the Moon*, 1901; *The Sea Lady*, 1902; *The Food of the Gods, and How It Came to Earth*, 1904; *Kipps: The Story of a Simple Soul*, 1905; *In the Days of the Comet*, 1906; *The War in the Air, and Particularly How Mr. Bert Smallways Fared While It Lasted*, 1908; *Tono-Bungay*, 1908; *Ann Veronica: A Modern Love Story*, 1909; *The History of Mr. Polly*, 1910; *The New Machiavelli*, 1910; *Marriage*, 1912; *The Passionate Friends*, 1913; *The Wife of Sir Isaac Harman*, 1914; *The World Set Free: A Story of Mankind*, 1914; *Bealby: A Holiday*, 1915; *The Research Magnificent*, 1915; *Mr. Britling Sees It Through*, 1916; *The Soul of a Bishop: A Novel—with Just a Little Love in It—About Conscience and Religion and the Real Troubles of Life*, 1917; *Joan and Peter: The Story of an Education*, 1918; *The Undying Fire: A Contemporary Novel*, 1919; *The Secret Places of the Heart*, 1922; *Men like Gods*, 1923; *The Dream*, 1924; *Christina Alberta's Father*, 1925; *The World of William Clissold: A Novel at a New Age*, 1926 (3 volumes); *Meanwhile: The Picture of a Lady*, 1927; *Mr. Blettsworthy on Rampole Island*, 1928; *The King Who Was a King: The Book of a Film*, 1929; *The Autocracy of Mr. Parham: His Remarkable Adventure in This Changing World*, 1930; *The Bulpington of Blup*, 1933; *The Shape of Things to Come: The Ultimate Resolution*, 1933; *The Croquet Player*, 1936; *Byrnhild*, 1937; *The Camford Visitation*, 1937; *Star Begotten: A Biological Fantasia*, 1937; *Apropos of Dolores*, 1938; *The Brothers*, 1938; *The Holy Terror*, 1939; *Babes in the Darkling Wood*, 1940; *All Aboard for Ararat*, 1940; *You Can't Be Too Careful: A Sample of Life, 1901-1951*, 1941.

Other literary forms

H. G. Wells's short stories appear in such collections as *The Stolen Bacillus and Other Incidents* (1895), *Tales of Space and Time* (1899), *The Country of the Blind and Other Stories* (1911), and *A Door in the Wall and Other Stories* (1911). *The Outline of History: Being a Plain History of Life and Mankind* (1920) and *Experiment in Autobiography: Discoveries and Conclusions of a Very Ordinary Brain Since 1866* (1934) extended his literary range. His sociological essays include *A Modern Utopia* (1905), and *Mind at the End of Its Tether* (1945).

Achievements

Wells is best known for his science-fiction novels, some having been adapted as popular films. A socialist and Fabian, he was a spokesman for women's rights and international peace movements, for which he wrote books of advocacy in essay and fictional form. He was also an effective novelist of social satire and comedy.

Biography

Herbert George Wells was born in 1866 at Bromley in Kent, England, to Joseph and Sarah Neal Wells. He attended a commercial academy from 1874 to 1880. Having run away from his apprenticeship in a drapery shop, he taught in a preparatory school. Then he attended the London Normal School of Science from 1884 to 1887, studying biology under T. H. Huxley. In 1891 he was married to Isabel Mary Wells, and he published "The Rediscovery of the Unique." *The Time Machine* brought him fame in 1895, the same year that he divorced Isabel to marry Amy Catherine Robbins.

In 1901, Wells's son George Philip was born; Frank Richard followed in 1903. In 1914, having visited Russia, Wells published a prophecy, *The War That Will End War*; that year his son Anthony West was born to Rebecca West. After visiting soldiers on front lines of World War I, Wells supported a "League of Free Nations," and he entered the propaganda effort against Germany. In 1920 he made another trip to Russia, to meet Vladimir Ilich Lenin, and published *Russia in the Shadows*.

Wells was defeated as a Labour candidate for Parliament in 1922, and Amy Catherine died in 1927. He coauthored a book on biology before visiting Russia and the United States in 1934 to meet Joseph Stalin and President Franklin Delano Roosevelt. In 1935 he wrote film scenarios for *Things to Come* and *The Man Who Could Work Miracles*. In 1938 Orson Welles's radio broadcast of *The War of the Worlds* frightened people in the United States, paving the way for Wells's successful lecture tour there in 1940. Wells died in London on August 13, 1946.

Analysis

H. G. Wells's early scientific romances begin with *The Time Machine* (1895) and conclude with *The First Men in the Moon* (1901). His social satire and comic romance commence with *Kipps* (1905) and end with *The History of Mr. Polly* (1910). Didactic fiction dominated his last decades, from *Ann Veronica* (1909) to *You Can't Be Too Careful* (1941). Throughout is a struggle between science and socialism. Visions of doom alternate with calls to reform and renewal; individuals acquire knowledge of science but lose control of their destinies.

Wells's early novels are journeys of ironic discovery. The enduring point of *The Time Machine* is in the Time-Traveller's frightening discovery in the year

802701. He encounters the Eloi, who have been terrorized by the Morlocks, molelike creatures who prey upon the flesh of the Upper-worlders. They are the fruits of an evolutionary process of separating capitalists from workers. Before he returns to his own time, the Time-Traveller accidentally moves even further into the future, to an Earth about to fall into a dying Sun.

Edward Prendick, narrator of *The Island of Dr. Moreau*, is a castaway, grateful to reach Moreau's island—until he realizes its horrors. He thinks that Moreau is turning people into animals, but when he finds the Beast-people, he realizes his mistake. Moreau explains that pain is animality, and he excises pain to humanize animals, but they kill him as they revert to their animal natures. Prendick barely escapes becoming an animal before he returns to civilization, where he has anxiety attacks about people's animality.

Pessimism is never far from the surface of Wells's writing. Losing faith in reason, he turned to prophetic satire, as in *The Invisible Man*. In this story, Griffin, having failed to anticipate the awful effects of losing visibility, has lapsed in ethical responsibility, because he had no training or economic opportunity to make better use of his knowledge. Lacking love, he lacks constructive purpose for his power. His invisibility represents knowledge itself, as either destructive or constructive. Knowledge and power combine without sympathy in *The War of the Worlds* to result in catastrophe. The narrator is a frightened man struggling to compete for survival of the fittest. He believes that the Martians are little more than brains, dispassionate reason threatening annihilation. All brain with no sympathy threatens civilization, but so does instinct with no brain. The Martians near success, when suddenly they die, ironically having succumbed to the tiniest life-form, bacteria.

Wells reverses the cosmic journey in *The First Men in the Moon*, as Bedford accompanies eccentric scientist Cavor to mine the Moon, adding private enterprise to science. The heroes find an intoxicating mushroom, which prompts Bedford to speculate his private motive for profit will produce public benefits—even for the Moon itself. This madly grandiose notion is subverted when Bedford and Cavor are captured by the antlike Selenites, who live under the surface of the moon. When Bedford escapes alone to Earth, Cavor sends messages that he is to be executed to prevent Earthmen from returning with their violent ways, to do to the Moon what Wells had envisioned in *The War of the Worlds*, where Earth was invaded by Martians.

The Food of the Gods, and How It Came to Earth edges beyond science and humor into socialism and satire. Experiments with Boomfood on a chicken farm cause mass destruction through the creation of giant chickens, rats, and wasps; human babies become giants, and ordinary mortals grow terrified. Wells is on the giants' side, because they can make a new world by destroying the faults of the old. People accommodate to preserve old ways, but they shut their eyes to truth, eventually causing a crisis of choice between old and new. The story ends as the giants prepare for a war with the little people.

With *In the Days of the Comet* Wells presents a more optimistic view of changes that can be made in the world. Willie Leadford describes life before the great "change," when a comet turned Earth into paradise. The power of the novel, however, is in the rhythm of rage and hate that accelerates as Willie pursues the woman he loved, to kill her and her new lover. This momentum is accented by other accelerating events, including economic crisis and war with Germany. The comet changes all, including Willie and his beloved, Nettie, who offers to live with both lovers. In a new world, people learn to accept polygamy as natural and right.

Kipps: The Story of a Simple Soul is a kind of *Great Expectations*. The aunt and uncle who reared Kipps expected him to become a store clerk; Kipps has not been very skilled at anything he has undertaken, and he proves no better at handling an unexpected inheritance. Kipps has a dreary existence: he gains no real pleasure from life, not even from reading. Life in lower-middle-class commercial and shopkeeping society is without substance, imagination, or purpose. Kipps's first thought is to buy a banjo, though he cannot play it. Thinking more seriously of his prospects, he asks his art teacher to marry him, and she proceeds to teach him to speak and dress properly. Kipps tries and hopes, until he encounters an old love, Ann Pornick, working as a maid. He snubs her and in his guilt asks her forgiveness; she not only forgives him but also marries him. Thus Kipps has stumbled through mistake after mistake, from education to apprenticeship to courtship and marriage. Finally, when he loses most of his fortune, he and his wife resign themselves to a restricted life and open a bookshop.

Wells's satire is directed at Kipps for trying to be more than he can be, for misplacing values in a system of manners; indeed, Wells intensely scorns the social superficialities. The protagonist of *Tono-Bungay*, George Ponderevo, has much in common with Kipps, but George is less simple and more reflective. His early life is like Kipps's (and Wells's) in that he resists training for trade, shows a talent for science, marries above his class, divorces, and rediscovers a childhood romance, through scenes of satirical analysis of the social snobs, religious bigots, and capitalist cutthroats of England. More sympathetic is ambitious Uncle Teddy, who makes a fortune with Tono-Bungay, a bogus medicine, and launches a disastrous career in the "romance of modern commerce." George Ponderevo is more a master of his destiny than is Kipps. After the collapse of his uncle's financial empire, George turns to engineering as a means of commitment to scientific objectivity. He is beyond society and governments, as he is alone in the world of love.

Science triumphs over socialism and capitalism in *Tono-Bungay*, while individual vitality triumphs over all ideas in *The History of Mr. Polly*, another of Wells's best comic novels from his middle period. This story begins with a discontented middle-aged shopkeeper, Mr. Polly, contemplating his boredom, indigestion, and proud misuse of English. He decides to burn his shop and cut his throat. Having succeeded in his arson but forgotten to cut his throat, he deserts his wife for happy obscurity as a fat woman's handyman, forgetting the life he detested. Although Mr. Polly is an absurd creature, surrounded by stupid, unambitious people, he is sympathetic because he rebels against that absurdity and stupidity. Wells rewards Mr. Polly well for his rebellion.

Wells also rewards the heroine of his infamous novel *Ann Veronica*, which takes up more fully themes of free love and women's rights. Ann Veronica Stanley rebels against her father's authority and flees to London, where she attends university lectures in biology. Having thrown herself into the cause of women's suffrage, she is arrested and imprisoned. Then she elopes with her biology instructor, a married man, to Switzerland. This unconventional woman, however, receives a very conventional reward: she marries her lover, has children, and becomes reconciled with her father.

Having put new ideas into old literary forms with *Ann Veronica*, Wells set the direction of his writing for the rest of his life. In his later novels, ideas, argument, debate, and intellectual analysis become prominent, often at the expense of literary form. Feminist causes give way to issues of world peace in books dealing with the world wars, the one that was and the one to come. *Mr. Britling Sees It Through* is one of the best, though it is a troubling confusion of political despair and comic resignation. Touches of good humor keep the book going with scenes of absurdity, as when Mr. Britling tries to drive his car or Mr. Direck tries to understand British manners. This good humor erodes, however, under the pressure of the events of World War I. Mr. Britling's son is killed, his children's German tutor also is killed, and his private secretary is terribly wounded. The war nearly destroys Mr. Britling, but he sees it through, clinging to a religious hope of divine struggle through human suffering. He commits himself to the cause of world peace, but in the course of writing a letter to the German parents of his children's tutor, he gradually gives way to outrage against Germany and finally collapses in grief. The novel ends when Mr. Britling gets up from his writing to look out his window at the sunrise.

Such an ending hints of an uncertainty in Wells's own commitment to hope. His novels analyze the dead end of civilization and call for redirection through peaceful applications of scientific discoveries. Wells's bitterness at the barbarism of World War I emerges again in *Mr. Blettsworthy on Rampole Island*, whose hero, driven by an unhappy love affair and a failing business, travels to forget. This is one of Wells's most interesting later works, combining anthropology and psychology with experimentation in form. Mr. Blettsworthy's experience with cannibals on Rampole Island may be a fantasy of his madness or an insight into reality, but his experience on the battlefield of World War I is a plunge into an all-too-real madness. Blettsworthy's romantic life of optimism finally yields to a cynical discontent with reality. His perspective is not, however, Wells's final word, since Blettsworthy's business partner, Lyulph Graves, speaks at the end for a philosophy of "creative stoicism," like the attitude which is assumed by Mr. Britling and, perhaps, by Wells himself. Certainly there were differing points of view in Wells's imagination. These differences may express intellectual confusion, but they gave substance to his fiction and saved it from succumbing utterly to his tendency to preach.

The opposition of Blettsworthy and Graves is repeated in the relationship of Mr. Parham with Sir Bussy Woodcock in *The Autocracy of Mr. Parham*, which envisions a time when humankind might destroy itself through another barbarous world war. Mr. Parham voices the Fascist call (by Benito Mussolini) to traditional discipline and order as a way to prevent self-destruction; Sir Bussy expresses suspicion of dictatorship, social discipline, and intellectual utopias. Wells employs an entertaining device for exposing the differences between his protagonists: he brings them into a fantasy of the future as the result of a séance.

Possessed by a Nietzschean force calling itself the "Master Spirit," Mr. Parham's ego is loosed upon the world as the British dictator Lord Paramount. He goes to war with the United States and Germany, aiming for Russia, but he cannot command the obedience of Sir Bussy, who refuses to use a powerful new gas to destroy the opposition. After the séance, Mr. Parham discovers that Sir Bussy has had a dream very much like his own fantasy. Wells's use of comic irony is very strong in the conclusion, as Mr. Parham is deflated by Sir Bussy's plans to preach peace through the very means by which Mr. Parham had hoped to reach the world himself: journalism. Mr. Parham is a smug intellectual who knows where the world ought to go, if it would only follow his instructions; Sir Bussy is a muddled businessman, limited by the contingencies of immediate events, and satisfied with the disorganized vitality that distresses Mr. Parham. This difference between creative capitalism and intellectual autocracy is imaged as a difference in personalities caught in a play of life's ironies.

Wells's scientific romances display an optimistic hope for a future made better by scientific discoveries, countered by the pessimistic doubt that humankind could make the necessary choices for social and political progress. Wells shows sympathy and scorn for the stunted characters of his middle novels, for Kipps, George Ponderevo, and Mr. Polly; he exposes their inadequacies, largely as products of a narrow, stultifying environment, but he also rescues them in life-affirming conclusions. Finally, between the great wars, H. G. Wells, like his Mr. Britling, "saw it through," exercised the "creative stoicism" of Lyulph Graves, and occasionally managed to rise above his pamphleteering style to produce entertaining novels of lives muddled by uncertainty, conflict, and contradiction.

Richard D. McGhee

Other major works

SHORT FICTION: *The Stolen Bacillus and Other Incidents*, 1895; *The Plattner Story and Others*, 1897; *Thirty Strange Stories*, 1897; *Tales of Space and Time*, 1899; *The Vacant Country*, 1899; *Twelve Stories and a Dream*, 1903; *The Country of the Blind and Other Stories*, 1911; *A Door in the Wall and Other Stories*, 1911; *The Short Stories of H. G. Wells*, 1927; *The Favourite Short Stories of H. G. Wells*, 1937.

NONFICTION: *Text-Book of Biology*, 1893 (2 volumes); *Honours Physiography*, 1893 (with Sir Richard A. Gregory); *Certain Personal Matters*, 1897; *A Text-Book of Zoology*, 1898 (with A. M. Davis); *Anticipations of the Reaction of Mechanical and Scientific Progress upon Human Life and Thought*, 1902 (also known as *Anticipations*); *The Discovery of the Future*, 1902; *Mankind in the Making*, 1903; *A Modern Utopia*, 1905; *Socialism and the Family*, 1906; *The Future in America: A Search After Realities*, 1906; *This Misery of Boots*, 1907; *New Worlds for Old*, 1908; *First and Last Things: A Confession of Faith and Rule of Life*, 1908; *The Great State: Essays in Construction*, 1912 (also known as *Socialism and the Great State*); *The War That Will End War*, 1914; *An Englishman Looks at the World: Being a Series of Unrestrained Remarks upon Contemporary Matters*, 1914 (also known as *Social Forces in England and America*); *God, the Invisible King*, 1917; *The Outline of History: Being a Plain History of Life and Mankind*, 1920; *Russia in the Shadows*, 1920; *The Salvaging of Civilization*, 1921; *A Short History of the World*, 1922; *Socialism and the Scientific Motive*, 1923; *The Open Conspiracy: Blue Prints for a World Revolution*, 1928; *Imperialism and the Open Conspiracy*, 1929; *The Science of Life: A Summary of Contemporary Knowledge About Life and Its Possibilities*, 1929-1930 (with Julian S. Huxley and G. P. Wells); *The Way to World Peace*, 1930; *What Are We to Do with Our Lives?*, 1931 (revised edition of *The Open Conspiracy*); *The Work, Wealth, and Happiness of Mankind*, 1931 (2 volumes); *After Democracy: Addresses and Papers on the Present World Situation*, 1932; *Evolution, Fact and Theory*, 1932 (with Julian S. Huxley and G. P. Wells); *Experiment in Autobiography: Discoveries and Conclusions of a Very Ordinary Brain Since 1866*, 1934 (2 volumes); *The New America: The New World*, 1935; *The Anatomy of Frustration: A Modern Synthesis*, 1936; *World Brain*, 1938; *The Fate of Homo Sapiens: An Unemotional Statement of the Things That Are Happening to Him Now and of the Immediate Possibilities Confronting Him*, 1939; *The New World Order: Whether It Is Obtainable, How It Can Be Attained, and What Sort of World a World at Peace Will Have to Be*, 1940; *The Common Sense of War and Peace: World Revolution or War Unending?*, 1940; *The Conquest of Time*, 1942; *Phoenix: A Summary of the Inescapable Conditions of World Reorganization*, 1942; *Science and the World Mind*, 1942; *Crux Ansata: An Indictment of the Roman Catholic Church*, 1943; *'42 to '44: A Contemporary Memoir upon Human Behaviour During the Crisis of the World Revolution*, 1944; *Mind at

the End of Its Tether, 1945.
CHILDREN'S LITERATURE: *The Adventures of Tommy*, 1929.

Bibliography
Bergonzi, Bernard. *The Early H. G. Wells: A Study of the Scientific Romances*. Manchester, England: University Press, 1961. Bergonzi examines Wells's *fin de siècle* milieu and analyzes the scientific romances to *The First Men in the Moon*; he concludes that the early writings deserve recognition. Includes a bibliography, an appendix providing texts of "A Tale of the Twentieth Century" and "The Chronic Argonauts," notes, and an index.
Costa, Richard Hauer. *H. G. Wells*. Rev. ed. Boston: Twayne, 1985. A sympathetic survey of Wells's career and influence, with an emphasis on the major novels in the context of literary traditions before and after Wells. A chronology, a review of contemporary trends in Wells criticism, notes, an annotated bibliography, and an index strengthen this helpful book.
Haynes, Roslynn D. *H. G. Wells: Discoverer of the Future*. London: Macmillan, 1980. This is a thorough study of the influence of science on Wells's fiction and sociological tracts. It shows how science helped Wells to achieve an analytical perspective on the problems of his time, from art to philosophy. A bibliography and an index follow notes for the text.
Huntington, John. *The Logic of Fantasy: H. G. Wells and Science Fiction*. New York: Columbia University Press, 1982. Demonstrates the logic of evolution and ethics in Wells's scientific romances, focusing on *The Time Machine*, *The Island of Doctor Moreau*, and *The First Men in the Moon*, to show how Wells converted indirect thought into direct thought, producing utopian and anti-utopian structures. An index follows helpful notes.
Williamson, Jack. *H. G. Wells: Critic of Progress*. Baltimore: Mirage Press, 1973. A study of Wells's science fiction mainly through *The First Men in the Moon*, with a concluding brief survey of Wells as a prophet of the world state in his writings from 1901 to 1946. Features a bibliography, notes, and an index in the appendix.

EUDORA WELTY

Born: Jackson, Mississippi; April 13, 1909

Principal long fiction

The Robber Bridegroom, 1942; *Delta Wedding*, 1946; *The Ponder Heart*, 1954; *Losing Battles*, 1970; *The Optimist's Daughter*, 1972.

Other literary forms

In spite of her success and acclaim as a novelist, Eudora Welty regards herself as essentially a writer of short stories. In an interview that appeared in the fall, 1972, issue of the *Paris Review*, she says, "I'm a short-story writer who writes novels the hard way, and by accident." In 1980, all of her previously collected short fiction and two uncollected stories were published in one volume, *The Collected Stories of Eudora Welty*. Another new collection, *Moon Lake and Other Stories*, was published in the same year, and *Retreat* in 1981. Prior to that, some had appeared in *Short Stories* (1950) and in *Selected Stories of Eudora Welty* (1954). Other early short-story collections are *A Curtain of Green and Other Stories* (1941); *The Wide Net and Other Stories* (1943); *The Golden Apples* (1949), regarded by some as a loosely structured novel, but considered by Welty to be a group of interconnected stories; and *The Bride of the Innisfallen, and Other Stories* (1955). Welty has also published numerous essays and reviews, some of which have been collected in *The Eye of the Story: Selected Essays and Reviews* (1978). In addition, she has published a book for children, *The Shoe Bird* (1964), and books of her own photographs, *One Time, One Place* (1971) and *Eudora Welty: Photographs* (1989). A memoir, *One Writer's Beginnings*, appeared in 1984.

Achievements

Although it was not until she wrote *Losing Battles* and *The Optimist's Daughter* that Welty's name began to appear on the best-seller lists, her work had long been recognized and appreciated by discerning readers. In five decades of writing and publishing, she has received nearly every major award for fiction offered in the United States. Among them are the prestigious William Dean Howells Medal of the Academy of Arts and Letters for "the most distinguished work of American fiction" for the years 1950 through 1955, the National Institute of Arts and Letters Gold Medal for the Novel in 1972, the Pulitzer Prize for Fiction in 1973, and the National Medal for Literature at the American Book Awards ceremony in 1980. In addition, she has been awarded several honorary doctorates, Guggenheim Fellowships, special professorships, and membership in the National Institute of Arts and Letters.

Disinterested in either fame or fortune, Welty has simply wanted the opportunity to write and the assurance that there are readers who enjoy her work. She repeatedly expresses gratitude to such writers and editors as Robert Penn Warren, Cleanth Brooks, Albert Erskine, Ford Madox Ford, and Katherine Anne Porter, who were among the first persons of influence to recognize her ability and to promote interest in her early stories. Warren, Brooks, and Erskine accepted some of her first stories for *The Southern Review* and thus opened the door for subsequent publication in such magazines as *The Atlantic*, *Harper's Bazaar*, and *The New Yorker*. This exposure to a national audience also facilitated the publication of her first volume of stories.

Regarded by Reynolds Price, Guy Davenport, and other distinguished readers as America's greatest living writer, Welty has only recently begun to receive critical attention commensurate with her achievements.

Biography

Eudora Alice Welty was born in Jackson, Mississippi, on April 13, 1909. She has lived there most of her life, and still lives in the family home in which she was reared. She was the only daughter of Christian Webb Welty and Mary Chestina Andrews Welty; she had two younger brothers. Soon after their marriage in 1904, Welty's parents moved to Jackson. Her father, who came from Ohio, where his father owned a farm, was president of the well-established Lamar Life Insurance Company. Her mother, a West Virginian, was descended from pre-Revolutionary War Virginia stock, engendered by country preachers, teachers, and lawyers. Welty, who claims that she would feel "shy, and discouraged at the very thought" of a biography about her, feels that a "private life should be kept private." Still, though she insists that it is the writer's work, not his or her life, that is important, she did finally write a memoir of her family history and her early years, *One Writer's Beginnings*, which was published in 1984 and received positive critical comment.

Perhaps one reason she suggested that her own biography would not "particularly interest anybody" is that she has lived for the most part in the mainstream of American society. As Katherine Anne Porter aptly observes in her introduction to *A Curtain of Green*, Welty is not the "spiritual and intellectual exile" that typifies the modern artist. She attended Central High School in Jackson, then went for two years to Mississippi State College for Women, in Columbus, before transferring to the University of Wisconsin in 1927. After graduating with a bachelor of arts degree in English in 1929, she enrolled in the School of Business at Columbia University, where she studied advertising for a year. By then, the country was in the throes of the Depression, and she returned to Jackson to seek work. During the next several years, she held a variety of jobs in advertising, radio scriptwriting, and part-time newspaper work. She also began writing stories. Possibly the most important of those early jobs was the position of "Junior Publicity Agent" with the

Works Project Administration from 1933 to 1936. In this position, Welty was required to travel extensively through Mississippi doing newspaper stories on various WPA projects. Her work involved taking photographs, talking with a great variety of people, and—perhaps most important—listening to them. As Welty herself confesses, she has a "good ear" and a visual imagination, qualities that enabled her to hear and observe things and people during those three years that she would use in her fiction throughout her life.

A number of the photographs she took while on her WPA assignment were displayed for a month in the Lugene Gallery in New York, a small camera shop. Later, some of them appeared in her published collection of photographs *One Time, One Place*. Only after several years of discouraging rejection slips did Welty finally publish a story, "Death of a Traveling Salesman," in a small magazine called *Manuscript* in 1936. Soon after that, her talent was discovered by Robert Penn Warren, Albert Erskine, and Cleanth Brooks. Then, John Woodburn of Doubleday, Doran, and Company became interested in her work, and with his support, her first collection of short stories, *A Curtain of Green and Other Stories*, was published in 1941. The next year, her first novel, *The Robber Bridegroom*, appeared. Two of her books have been successfully adapted for the stage, *The Robber Bridegroom* as a Broadway musical in 1974 and *The Ponder Heart* as a New York stage play in 1956.

Humane, thoughtful, and generous, Welty has modestly accepted the many honors that have come to her. Scarcely a year has passed since 1940 in which she has not received a major award of some kind. At the same time, she has given abundantly of her time to schoolchildren, scholars, interviewers, and aspiring writers. She has been active in community causes in Jackson, given scores of lectures and readings, assisted numerous charities, and even provided recipes for cookbooks. During the years of severe unrest over civil rights issues, her critics blasted her for not actively taking up that cause in her fiction. She answered those critics eloquently in a 1965 *The Atlantic* essay entitled "Must the Novelist Crusade?"

In her introduction to *The Collected Stories of Eudora Welty*, Welty expresses characteristic gratitude for the help and encouragement she received along the way. In her memoir she speaks of her good fortune in being reared in a family that encouraged the reading of books. She has a particular love for myths, fairy tales, and legends, and she counts it her good fortune to have grown up in a region where, as she says, people love talking and delight in a good yarn. Even though she was teased as a child for having a "Yankee" father, her work is deeply rooted, like its creator, in the South as a place. Still, neither she nor her fiction could be called "regional" in any narrow sense of the term. In fact, she balks at the regionalist title. Her work, for all its down-home Southern flavor, attests the universality of her vision and the capacity of her art to elude easy labels. Her subject is not the South, but humanity.

Analysis

Paramount in Eudora Welty's work is the sense of what "community," or group membership, means in the South and how it is expressed through manners, attitudes, and dialogue. Clearly, it provides a special way of seeing and responding. In Welty's published essays and interviews, certain concerns keep surfacing—the relationship between time and place and the artistic endeavor; the importance of human relationships in a work of fiction; the necessity for the artist to be grounded in real life and yet be aware of life's "mystery"; the value of the imagination; and the function of memory. These concerns find expression in her work principally in the tension between what is actual, what is seen and heard in a specific time and place, and what is felt or known intuitively. Welty uses the sometimes conflicting demands of the community and the self, the surface life and the interior life, to describe this tension in her novels. On the one hand is the need for community and order; on the other is the need for the separate individual life which often works against community and order.

Typically, a Welty novel swings between overt action, including dialogue, and individual contemplation. This is especially evident in *Delta Wedding*, where Welty almost rhythmically alternates dialogue and action with the inner musings of her principal female characters. In *The Optimist's Daughter*, only Laurel Hand's thoughts are set against the exterior action, but it becomes apparent that her father, as he lies unmoving on his hospital bed, is silently contemplating the mystery of life and human relationships for perhaps the first time in his life. Her mother, too, near the end of her life, had begun speaking out the painful things she must have harbored for many years in her dark soul. Even Edna Earle Ponder in *The Ponder Heart* seems to talk incessantly to keep the inner life from raising itself into consciousness. In *Losing Battles*, where Welty says she consciously tried to tell everything through speech and action—she had been accused of obscurantism in previous works—the pattern still emerges. Instead of swinging between action and cerebration, however, this novel swings between action and description. Still, the effect is surprisingly similar, though the pages of action and dialogue far outnumber the pages of description, and the transitions between the two modes of narration are very abrupt. Even so, the young schoolteacher who chooses love and marriage against her mentor's advice slips occasionally into Welty's meditative mode. The alternation of thought and action is also the basic structural pattern of the stories in *The Golden Apples*.

Thus, in Welty's novels, external order is established through speech and action that sustain community, either the social or family group. In fact, the novels are often structured around community rituals that reinforce the group entity against outside intrusions and shore up its defenses against its most insidious foe, the impulse to separateness in its individual members. *Delta Wedding* is set entirely in the framework of one of these community-perpetuating rituals. For the moment, the wedding is everything, and members of the group pay it homage by gathering, giving gifts, feasting, and burying their individual lives in its demands. *Losing Battles* is also framed by a community ritual, the family reunion. The threat from individual outsiders is felt constantly, and the family takes sometimes extreme measures to ward off influences that might undermine its solidarity. There are at least two rituals that provide structure for *The Ponder Heart*, the funeral and the courtroom trial. The first of these is conducted in enemy territory, outside the acceptable group domain; the second is conducted in home territory, and acquittal for the accused member of the group is a foregone conclusion. A funeral is also the major external event of *The Optimist's Daughter* and becomes the battleground in a contest for supremacy between two opposing groups or communities. Several of the stories or chapters in *The Golden Apples* are also structured around community rituals, including the June piano recital, the girls' summer camp, and the funeral.

In addition to these large, highly structured observances, there are the multitude of unwritten laws that govern the group. Welty's community members attach great importance to certain objects and practices: a treasured lamp given to the bride, a hand-crafted breadboard made for a mother-in-law, the establishment of family pedigrees, the selection of one male member of the community for special reverence and heroic expectation, the protection of the past from intrusion or reassessment, and, perhaps most important of all, the telling of stories as an attestation of the vitality and endurance of the group.

Underlying all of this attention to ritual and group expectation, however, is the unspoken acknowledgment that much of it is a game the participants have agreed to play, for their own sake and for the sake of the community. Some of the participants may be fooled, but many are not. Aware but fearful, they go through the motions of fulfilling community requirements in an effort to hold back the dark, to avoid facing the mystery, to keep their individual selves from emerging and crying for existence. They sense themselves to be at what Welty calls "the jumping off place," and are afraid to make the leap in the dark. They agree to pretend to be fooled. They tell stories instead of rehearsing their fears and uncertainties. The bolder ones defy the group and either leave it or live on its periphery. In every book, there are moments when a character confronts or consciously evades the dark underside of human personality and experience, and memory becomes a device for dealing with the effects of that confrontation or for evading it.

Paradoxically, storytelling, an important ritual for securing the past and bolstering community against passion, disorder, the intimations of mystery, and the erosive effects of individual impulses and yearnings, assists in the breakdown of the very group it was intended to support. The risk of indulging in rituals is that they sometimes set people to thinking and reevaluating their own individual lives and the lives of others close to them. The ritual is performed by the group, but it may stir the solitary inner being to life and to the kind of probing contemplation that jeopardizes the group's authority. Such a countereffect may be triggered by the storytelling ritual even though that ritual is meant to seal up the past for ready reference whenever the group needs reinforcement. Because storytelling relies on memory, it can become an exercise of the individual imagination. It tends to lapse, as one commentator observes, "into the memory of a memory" and thus shifts sides from the group's activities into the realm of mystery. The community's habit of setting up straw men for heroes can similarly erode community solidarity because it too relies upon imagination and memory. It glorifies the individual rather than the group spirit.

As Welty presents this conflict, then, between the self and the group, and between the intuitive and the actual, she writes into her work a sense of foreboding. The community, especially the traditional Southern community, is doomed. It cannot forever maintain itself on the old terms, for it is dependent upon the acquiescence of separate individuals who seem increasingly impervious to the efforts of the group to contain them. Welty's work also suggests that some of the things the community prizes and perpetuates are merely gestures and artifacts with little intrinsic value or meaning. When the meanings behind what a community treasures have been lost or forgotten, that community cannot long endure. In actively laboring to exclude others, the group works against its own best nature, its capacity for loving and caring. Threats to order and community may indeed come from the outside, but Welty insists that the more serious threats come from the inside, from that part of the human heart and mind that seeks to go its own way.

Welty's first novel, *The Robber Bridegroom*, is quite unlike her others. Its most noticeable differences are its setting in a much older South, on the old Natchez Trace in the days of bandits and Indians, and its fairy-tale style and manner. Even with these differences, Welty establishes what becomes her basic fictional stance. She achieves tension between the actual and the imaginary by freighting this very real setting with fabulous characters and events. The legendary characters are transformed by Welty's imagination and deftly made to share the territory with figures from the Brothers Grimm. Welty indicated the double nature of her novel, or novella, when in an address to the Mississippi Historical Society she called it a "Fairy Tale of the Natchez Trace." A favorite of William Faulkner, the book is a masterpiece, a delightful blend of legend, myth, folklore, and fairy tale that swings from rollicking surface comedy and lyrical style to painful, soul-searching explorations of the ambiguities of human experience. Although it deals with love and separateness—Robert Penn Warren's terms for the conflicting needs of communities and individuals in Welty's work—it does not deal with them in the same way that the later novels do. Clement Musgrove, a planter whose innocence leads him into marriage with the greedy Salome and an excursion into humanity's heart of darkness, learns what it is like to face the cold, dark nights of despair comfortless and alone. His daughter, Rosamond, is beautiful and loving, but she is also an inveterate liar who betrays her husband's trust in order to learn his "real" identity. Jamie Lockhart, who leads a double life as both bandit and gentleman, keeps his true identity hidden even from her whom he loves. Thus, like so many Welty characters, the principal actors in *The Robber Bridegroom* have interior lives that threaten the equilibrium of their exterior worlds.

In another sense, too, *The Robber Bridegroom* is closely linked with Welty's other novels. In writing the book, Welty testifies to the value of stories and the storytelling ritual that buttresses community, a theme that reappears in all her novels. She finds common ground with her readers in this novel by spinning a yarn full of their favorite childhood fairy tales. Then, too, fairy-tale worlds, imaginative though they are, sustain surface order, for they are worlds of sure answers, of clear good and evil, of one-dimensional characters, and of predictable rewards and punishments. As such, they confirm what the community collectively believes and perpetuates. Just as imagination, intuition, and the ponderings of the individual human soul jeopardize the codes a community lives by in other Welty novels, so do they undercut the basic assumptions of the fairy tale in this novel. Here, answers are sometimes permanently withheld, people are complex and unpredictable, the richest prize is found in human relationships rather than in kingdoms and gold, appearances are deceiving, and evil may lie in unexpected places. It is worthy of note that Welty began her novel-writing career with a book that delights in the fairy tale at the same time that it questions community assumptions about fairy-tale morality.

The tension between community expectations and individual yearnings and apprehensions is central to *Delta Wedding*. The narrative takes place in the Mississippi delta country, during the week of Dabney Fairchild's wedding. The Fairchild family, after whom the nearby town is named, is of the social elite and has moderate wealth, mostly in property. The wedding provides an occasion for the family to gather and exercise the rituals and traditions that bind them together and strengthen their sense of community. The wedding itself is the principal ritual, of course, with its attendant food preparation, dressmaking, rehearsal, and home and yard decorating. Welty's eye for manners and ear for speech are flawless as the Fairchilds deliberate over the consequences of George Fairchild's having married beneath him and Dabney's seemingly unfortunate repetition of her father's mistake. The Fairchilds still claim George, however, even though they have little use for his wife, Robbie Reid; and they will continue to embrace Dabney in spite of her choosing to marry an outsider, Troy Flavin. It is the habit of community to maintain order by defining and placing people and things in relation to itself. A person either does or does not have legitimate ties to the group.

The Fairchilds also repeat family stories in order to keep the past secure and give stability to the present. Their current favorite story is also one that makes a hero out of the male heir-apparent. George's dead brother was apparently more remarkable than he, but George is the one survivor, and the family's hopes rest with him. At least a dozen times in the book, some version is told of George's staying on the railroad track with his mentally retarded niece whose foot was caught in the rails. Instead of leaping to safety with the others, he stayed to face the oncoming train. Luckily, the engineer of the Yellow Dog was able to stop the train in time. By choosing to stay with Maureen instead of answering his wife's plea to save himself, George made a reflexive choice for honor and blood over marital obligation. Later, he again chooses family over wife when he comes for the pre-wedding activities instead of looking for his absent, heartbroken wife.

Running counter to the speech and actions that affirm order and community, however, is an undercurrent of threat to that order. Welty intersperses the overt actions and attitudes of the family, especially of the aunts, whose sole desire is to perpetuate the clan structure, with individual ruminations of other female characters who are part of that structure and yet somewhat peripheral to it. Ellen, who married into the Fairchilds and has never dared resist them, has moments of personal doubt that would be regarded as treasonous were they known by her aunts. Dabney also wonders, in a brief honest moment, about the homage paid to the wedding ritual for its own sake. Further, she accidentally breaks a treasured lamp, a family heirloom given her by the aunts as a wedding present. Little Laura, having lost her mother, has also lost her basic tie to the family. From her position on the edge of the Fairchild clan, she questions the community tenets that exclude her. Even George seems ready to violate community expectations by his apparent willingness to deprive two of the aunts of their home.

The novel's essential statement, then, is that the community is losing its hold. In an interview published in 1972 by *The Southern Review*, Welty is asked the question: "Is Shellmound [the home of the Fairchilds] with its way of life and its values doomed?" She replies, "Oh, yes. I think that was implicit in the novel: that this was all such a fragile, temporary thing. At least I hope it was." She adds, "Well, you're living in a very precarious world without knowing it, always." The community's position is inexorably altered in the face of individual yearning and independent action.

There are two large community rituals in *The Ponder Heart*: the funeral of Bonnie Dee Peacock and the trial of Uncle Daniel Ponder for her murder. Such narrative matter sounds ominous enough to one unfamiliar with Welty's capacity for comedy, but to the initiated, it promises a hilarious display of Southern talk and manners. Still, *The Ponder Heart* is troubled, as Welty's other novels are, by an ominous current running beneath its surface action.

Like the Fairchilds of *Delta Wedding*, the Ponders have social position and wealth—perhaps greater than that of the Fairchilds. They are on the decline, however, in spite of the efforts of Edna Earle Ponder, Welty's first-person narrator, to maintain the family and its image. Symbolic of the failing family or community image that Edna Earle seeks to perpetuate and protect are two buildings which the family owns, the Beulah Hotel, run by Edna Earle, and the Ponder home a few miles out of town. In the end, both buildings are virtually empty. The family has shrunk to two members, and the future holds no promise.

The storyline tells of middle-aged Uncle Daniel's taking to wife young Bonnie Dee Peacock, losing her, regaining her, losing her again, reclaiming her, and then finally losing her by tickling her to death in the aftermath of an electric storm. Uncle Daniel's mental age is considerably lower than his chronological age, but he is blessed with a generous nature. He gives away everything he can get his hands on, and has to be watched continually. Not that Edna Earle cares to restrain him very much, for he is the revered scion, like George in *Delta Wedding*, without whose approbation and presence the community would totter. Her duty is to protect and sustain Daniel, and she will not even permit herself private doubts over what that duty requires. The entire novel is the report of her conversation about Uncle Daniel with a visitor who is stranded at the Beulah. Clearly, Edna Earle's talk and actions are designed to maintain order and community as she has known them all her life. She believes that if she relaxes her vigil, the structure will collapse.

The ritual of the Peacock funeral is important because it is grossly inferior to the Ponder notion of what constitutes a funeral. The Peacocks are what the Ponders (except Daniel, who in his innocence would not know the difference) would call "country"; in other words, they are regarded as comically inferior beings who have no business marrying into the Ponder family. The trial is more to Edna Earle's liking, though it is threatened by the presence of the low-bred Peacocks and a prosecuting shyster lawyer who is an outsider. Edna Earle gets caught in a lie designed to protect Daniel, but the day is saved when Daniel begins passing out greenbacks in the courtroom. The jury votes for acquittal in record time, and Daniel cheerily dispenses the whole family fortune. He discovers to his sorrow afterward, however, that people who have taken his money can no longer face him. Thus, in the end, Daniel, who wanted nothing more than company and an audience for his stories, is left lonely and friendless. Though Edna Earle tries to inject new hope through the promise of a new audience—her captive guest at the Beulah—doom is on the horizon for the Ponders even more surely than it was for the Fairchilds. The collapse of community structure in this novel, as in *Delta Wedding*, can be laid partly to the failure of the community's rather artificial system of supports—rituals, traditions, family stories, pedigrees, and a family "hero." It must also be laid, however, to the fact that Uncle Daniel, in his innocence, breaks away and acts as an individual. He is not capable of the contemplation that undermines community in *Delta Wedding*, but neither can he be restrained to act as a member of the group instead of as himself.

In *Losing Battles*, Welty partially turns the tables on what she had done with the conflict between community and self in her previous two novels and in *The Golden Apples*. Here, she shows that community, though mildly ruffled by individual needs and doubts, can prevail when it is sustained by strong individuals who are also loyal group members. Welty indicates in a *Southern Review* interview that she deliberately chose as her setting the poorest section of Mississippi during the time of the Depression, so that her characters would be shown on a bare stage with themselves as their only resource, without "props to their lives." Thus, the artificial structures built of money and status that support community in *Delta Wedding* and *The Ponder Heart* are not available to the Vaughn-Beecham-Renfro clan in *Losing Battles*. Perhaps that is one reason for their greater durability.

The story is told almost entirely through dialogue and action, interlaced with occasional lyrical descriptions of setting and even less frequent ruminations of the story's principal outsider, Gloria Renfro, the hero's wife. The action takes place entirely in one day and the following morning, with details of the past filled in through family storytelling. Jack Renfro, the young grandson who has been exalted by family hope and expectations, bears some resemblance to George Fairchild and Daniel Ponder. On him lies the chief burden of sustaining the family, of guaranteeing its survival as a unit. He returns home from the state penitentiary to the waiting family reunion that is celebrating old Granny Vaughn's birthday. He finds there not only his bride, but a baby daughter he has never seen. The family has believed, has had to believe, that things will be better once Jack has returned home. Jack himself believes it and, as Welty indicates, the others take their faith from his. Through a series of wild, funny episodes—and more than a few tender moments—the family prevails. Welty says that in this comic novel she intended to portray the indomitability, the unquenchable spirit of human beings. Folks such as these may be losing the battles, but they are still fighting them, and that is what counts.

Welty describes "the solidity of the family" as "the strongest thing in the book." She also recognizes that, in a clan such as this, a character sometimes has to be himself before he can reinforce the unity of the group. Welty says that such a "sticking together" as is seen in *Losing Battles* "involves both a submerging and a triumph of the individual, because you can't really conceive of the whole unless you *are* an identity." The extended family of *Losing Battles* engages in rituals to maintain itself just as the Fairchild family does in *Delta Wedding*. It acknowledges milestones reached by its members, milestones such as weddings and ninetieth birthdays; it tells stories; it creates a hero; and it works painstakingly to establish and affirm blood relationships with any who might seek entrance into the group. All is done with the honor of the clan—or the individual as member of the clan—in mind, whether it is going to jail or rescuing a car from a cliff on Banner Top.

In spite of the prevailing unity and the optimistic conclusion to the novel's events, there are small rumblings of individual assertion against community. Gloria loves Jack, but she does not want to be a member of his family. She envisions a smaller community, made up of just her, Jack, and their baby, Lady May. The group, however, will not allow her to build a community of her own. Against her will, it tries to reconstruct a parentage for her that would make her a blood relation. The relatives perform a rather cruel ritual of pouncing on her and forcing her to eat watermelon, but she remains adamant. She also remains steadfast in her admiration for Miss Julia Mortimer, the schoolteacher who picked Gloria as her successor and who fought a losing battle all her life against the joyful ignorance of the likes of Jack's family.

Thus, there are several influences in the book that threaten, though not seriously, the sense of community. Gloria and her child, and Miss Julia, are the most obvious ones. It becomes apparent, though, in the very style of the narration, which repeatedly turns from family action and talk to brief imaginative description, that the ordering of the actual and the real according to community necessity does not entirely carry the day. There is another side to experience, the imaginative, the intuitive—a part of the individual soul that resists allegiance.

In *The Optimist's Daughter*, Welty returns to a more balanced combination of action and contemplation. The book's perceiving eye is Laurel Hand, daughter of Becky and Judge McKelva. The abiding question for Laurel is why, after the death of the intelligent, sensitive Becky, the Judge took for a wife a crass, tasteless woman half his age. Laurel helplessly watches her father's still form as he silently reviews his life in a hospital room, ironically set against the backdrop of the Mardi Gras festival. She repeats her helpless watch as he lies in his coffin at Mount Salus while his wife, Wanda Fay Chisom, performs her gnashing, wailing ritual of bereavement and his old friends perform their ritual of eulogy. The Chisom family, who nod appreciatively as Fay grossly mourns, are the same breed as the Peacocks in *The Ponder Heart*, entirely out of context in the McKelva home. Laurel, however, is equally uncomfortable with her own group's rites of community preservation—telling stories about the Judge that make a hero of him, despising the intrusive outsider, urging Laurel to stay and bolster the old relationship. Laurel's husband Phil was killed in military service many years ago and Laurel herself is working in Chicago, but the women who were bridesmaids at her wedding have kept that group intact and still refer to themselves as "the bridesmaids."

Laurel's last night at home is spent in anguish. Trapped by an invading chimney swift in rooms full of memories, she is caught hopelessly in the past. In the course of the night, she is forced to examine the protective structure she had built around her parents' marriage and her own. In doing so, she must allow memory and imagination to reinterpret the past which she had wanted to keep sealed away in the perfection of her own making, and she must relinquish her old idea of what constitutes group unity and loyalty. The Wanda Fays of the world will always claim their space, will always intrude. The secret for surviving their intrusion, Laurel discovers, is to withdraw one's protective walls so that the Fays have nothing to knock down. Laurel at last allows truth to dismantle the edifice of community as she had conceived it, and she finds, through the imagination and the heart, a new source of strength in watching the artificial construct tumble. Thus, the foreboding and pessimism arising from the impending doom of community in *Delta Wedding* and *The Ponder Heart*, diverted for a time in the paradoxical optimism of *Losing Battles*, are to some extent reversed in Laurel's final acceptance in *The Optimist's Daughter*. *The Golden Apples* had foretold such an outcome, for a number of its characters must also deal with the relationship between their individual lives and the group life.

The miracle of Welty's work is the skill with which she has brought her imagination to bear on the actual and made a reconciliation out of the conflicting demands of the community and the private life, out of that which can be perceived by the senses and that which can be known only intuitively. For Welty, the actual is mainly the realities of Mississippi life. In her work, however, the reality of Mississippi becomes a springboard rich with possibilities for an imagination that knows how to use time and place as doorways to the human heart.

Marilyn Arnold

Other major works

SHORT FICTION: *A Curtain of Green and Other Stories*, 1941; *The Wide Net and Other Stories*, 1943; *The Golden Apples*, 1949; *Short Stories*, 1950; *Selected Stories of Eudora Welty*, 1954; *The Bride of the Innisfallen, and Other Stories*, 1955; *The Collected Stories of Eudora Welty*, 1980; *Moon Lake and Other Stories*, 1980; *Retreat*, 1981.

NONFICTION: *Music from Spain*, 1948; *The Reading and Writing of Short Stories*, 1949; *Place in Fiction*, 1957; *Three Papers on Fiction*, 1962; *One Time, One Place: Mississippi in the Depression, A Snapshot Album*, 1971; *A Pageant of Birds*, 1974; *The Eye of the Story: Selected Essays and Reviews*, 1978; *Ida M'Toy*, 1979; *Miracles of Perception: The Art of Willa Cather*, 1980 (with Alfred Knopf and Yehudi Menuhin); *One Writer's Beginnings*, 1984; *Eudora Welty: Photographs*, 1989.

CHILDREN'S LITERATURE: *The Shoe Bird*, 1964.

Bibliography

Devlin, Albert J. *Eudora Welty's Chronicle: A Story of Mississippi Life*. Jackson: University Press of Mississippi, 1983. Devlin analyzes certain works, such as *Delta Wedding*, in great detail. He offers insightful criticism and suggests that Welty's writing contains a historical structure, spanning from the territorial era to modern times.

Evans, Elizabeth. *Eudora Welty*. New York: Frederick Ungar, 1981. Presents a reliable but not comprehensive overview of Welty's life and work.

Manning, Carol S. *With Ears Opening Like Morning Glories: Eudora Welty and the Love of Storytelling*. Westport, Conn.: Greenwood Press, 1985. An advanced book offering a critical interpretation of Welty's writing. Manning believes that the root of Welty's creativity is the Southern love of storytelling. Offers a select bibliography.

Vande Kieft, Ruth M. *Eudora Welty*. Rev. ed. Boston: Twayne, 1987. Vande Kieft offers an excellent critical analysis of Welty's major works, an overview of Welty's career, and an annotated secondary bibliography. A well written, useful study for all students.

Westling, Louise Hutchings. *Sacred Groves and Ravaged Gardens: The Fiction of Eudora Welty, Carson McCullers, and Flannery O'Connor*. Athens: University of Georgia Press, 1985. Westling examines the lives and works of Welty and the other authors in terms of their common concerns as women, such as their relationships with men and with their mothers. Offers a provocative and original viewpoint.

GLENWAY WESCOTT

Born: Kewaskum, Wisconsin; April 11, 1901
Died: Rosemont, New Jersey; February 22, 1987

Principal long fiction

The Apple of the Eye, 1924; *The Grandmothers: A Family Portrait*, 1927;
The Pilgrim Hawk: A Love Story, 1940; *Apartment in Athens*, 1945.

Other literary forms

Glenway Wescott's first published work was *The Bitterns: A Book of Twelve
Poems* (1920); another volume of poetry, *Natives of Rock: XX Poems, 1921-
1922* appeared in 1925. Two of his short stories were privately published in
France by friends as separate books: . . . *Like a Lover* (1926) and *The Babe's
Bed* (1930). A collection of stories with a long title essay, *Good-bye, Wis-
consin*, was published in 1928. Other books include a variety of forms: *Fear
and Trembling*, a collection of essays (1932); *Twelve Fables of Aesop, Newly
Narrated* (1954); and *Images of Truth: Remembrances and Criticism* (1962).
Several uncollected poems and stories appeared in literary journals over the
years, along with a number of personal and critical essays. Perhaps Wescott's
most imaginative work is "The Dream of Audubon: Libretto of a Ballet in
Three Scenes," in *The Best One-Act Plays of 1940* (1941), which holds the
key to Wescott's extensive use of bird imagery and symbolism.

Achievements

After his beginnings as a published poet, Wescott often reviewed books of
poetry and fiction. His critical pieces reveal that from the time of his earliest
experiments in prose fiction, he was forming his idea of the novel and the
aims of the art that it best embodied: to present images of reality and the
truth of experience.

Even after his first two novels were published, critics disagreed as to whether
Wescott *was* a novelist. The skepticism had several causes, mostly related to
form. The first section of his first novel, *The Apple of the Eye*, was published
separately as the story "Bad Han" in two parts in *The Dial*. Wescott then
expanded it with two more parts to make a novel. *The Grandmothers*,
accepted as a novel by the Harper's Prize judges, was a series of portraits of
individual characters. Today, these books are recognized as formally innovative: they focus on the process of self-discovery, and they are unified by
the relation of the parts to the experience of the protagonist.

The short stories in *Good-bye, Wisconsin* seemed to support the critics'
judgment that Wescott was essentially a short-story writer and their further
pigeonholing of him as a regional realist attacking the narrowness of culture
in the Midwest and as a typical expatriate writer. Doubts about Wescott's

capacities as a novelist were permanently laid to rest, however, with the triumph of *The Pilgrim Hawk*, which was hailed as a masterpiece of its genre and later reprinted in two anthologies of great short novels. *The Pilgrim Hawk*, set in France, and the next novel, *Apartment in Athens*, showed that Wescott could go beyond regional materials. The latter, however, although chosen by the Book-of-the-Month Club, was not a critical success, probably because its propagandistic aims were too obvious.

Wescott spent many years in service to literature. He was president of the National Institute of Arts and Letters, 1958-1961. He wrote and delivered a number of introductory and presentation speeches, later published in the Proceedings of the American Academy of Arts and Letters. He also became a member of the National Commission for the United Nations Educational, Scientific, and Cultural Organization (UNESCO). As a public man of letters, he gave many talks and readings, appeared on radio and television, participated in symposia and writers' conferences, and served on various committees for the Institute and the Authors' Guild. He edited *The Maugham Reader* (1950) and *Short Novels of Colette* (1951), writing the introduction for the latter.

Currently an unfashionable writer, Wescott should be read in any survey of the great decades of the American novel from 1920 to 1940. A revival of critical interest in his work is long overdue.

Biography

Glenway Wescott was born in Kewaskum, Wisconsin, on April 11, 1901, the first of six children. According to the autobiographical portrait of Alwyn Tower in *The Grandmothers*, he was a sensitive, imaginative, and solitary child. His nature was antipathetic to the physical and cultural poverty of the farm life in which he spent his boyhood. At age thirteen, because of difficulties with his father, he left home and lived with an uncle and others while going to high school.

In 1917, Wescott entered the University of Chicago, began writing poetry, and soon joined the Poetry Club. The following year, he became engaged, but he did not marry then or later; the engagement was broken in 1921. During this period, Wescott tried fiction, beginning the story "Bad Han," which became part of his first novel.

Because of ill-health, Wescott withdrew from the University of Chicago after a year and a half, thus ending his formal education. Shortly thereafter, he went to New Mexico for an extended visit with Yvor Winters, a period which he referred to as one of the happiest of his life.

In 1920, after a visit to his family, Wescott went to Chicago to stay with Monroe Wheeler, with whom he was to share his travels abroad and much of his life in the United States and to whom he dedicated his 1962 volume of essays. He traveled with Wheeler to New York City, then to England and

Germany, before returning to the United States and embarking on a career of serious writing.

In 1925, Wescott moved to France, beginning eight years as an expatriate but returning yearly for a visit to his family. He used the experience of an expatriate looking back at his pioneer family in Wisconsin as the framework for *The Grandmothers*, which was written during the first year of his stay abroad. Winning the prestigious Harper's Prize, the book was a critical and popular success. With the publication of a volume of short stories the following year, Wescott's position in the forefront of talented young writers seemed assured.

During his stay abroad, Wescott spent extended periods in Germany, leading him to write the essays in *Fear and Trembling*, and later during wartime to try to explain the German character in the novel *Apartment in Athens*. In 1933, Wescott moved back to the United States, dividing his time between New York City and the farm in New Jersey where his family had moved. He went to Europe with his brother and the latter's bride, Barbara Harrison, in 1935 and again traveled abroad in 1938, before finally settling in America.

The year 1940 marked a period of renewed creativity for Wescott with the appearance of his acclaimed short novel *The Pilgrim Hawk*, a ballet libretto, several lyrical essays, and, in 1945, *Apartment in Athens*, a war novel set in Greece (which Wescott had never visited). Thereafter, he produced less, leading the life of a public man of letters. Besides the distractions of that role, he suggested another reason for his diminished literary output in later life, saying, "I am an incorrigibly copious letter-writer, and doubtless have wasted time in that way."

His father, with whom he eventually became reconciled, died in 1953, and his mother, to whom he was extremely devoted, died in 1960. Wescott lived on the family farm in rural New Jersey until he died on February 22, 1987.

Analysis

When Glenway Wescott left his native Wisconsin, returned and left again, each time it was to move farther east, first to Chicago, then New York, then Europe. It was also to plunge into the major literary currents of the day: imagism in poetry, regionalism in fiction, criticism of American culture and society by the expatriates, focus on the self as a major theme, revolt against traditional forms and experiments with new ones. If he was typical of the young writers of the 1920's, then he was also—like F. Scott Fitzgerald, Ernest Hemingway, and William Faulkner—a distinctive voice whose contributions to this innovative period of American fiction should be studied along with those of his greater contempories.

Published when Wescott was twenty-three, *The Apple of the Eye* was considered an impressive, although not faultless, first novel by such reviewers as Kenneth Burke and Ruth Suckow. In content, it is a typical initiation story, following the self-discovery of the hero, Dan Strane, as he rebels against Midwestern puritanism, finds an affirmative meaning in life, and departs to live it his own way. In form, the novel is more original, with its tripartite structure. Its style reveals, even this early, the author's mastery of what Ira Johnson calls the "lyric, disciplined, imagistic prose of sensibility."

Book I elaborates on a sort of legend that Wescott's mother once told him about an old servant. Hannah Madoc, called "Bad Han," is a "secular saint" who accepts love and lives life as it comes, without the common tortures of guilt. Han's lover, Jules Bier, influenced by his father, leaves her to marry Selma Duncan, who represents puritanism, the "evasion of experience." Book II introduces Rosalia and tells of her love affair with Dan's new friend, Mike Byron. Mike begins Dan's initiation by explaining that while puritanism appeals to the imagination, it is unhealthy in its division of the flesh from the spirit. Dan turns away from his beloved mother and her religion, while Mike initiates in him an awareness of the pleasures of sensuality. Meanwhile, Mike's and Rosalia's affair gains momentum, then dies, and Rosalia is deserted by Mike. Maddened by sorrow and guilt, she dies in the marsh.

In Book III, Dan's uncle, Jules Bier, retells the story of Bad Han as an object lesson in what is wrong with the local religious views, which have brought Rosalia and others tragedy. Bad Han becomes a powerful symbol, leading Dan to feel he is her spiritual son. Completing his separation from the sterile, frustrating environment, he departs for college, at the same time realizing that he has been blessed by experiencing several kinds of love and has felt a "sense of awakening."

Dan Strane is the first of Wescott's several autobiographical portraits. The natural setting, the rural poverty, the roughness of farm life, the puritanism, all were elements of the author's boyhood against which he rebelled. Even some of the most intimate aspects of Dan are tied to Wescott's life: the devotion to the mother, the conflict with the father, the despair and thoughts of suicide (Wescott had attempted suicide when he was eighteen), the implied homosexual attachment.

Most striking for a first novel is Wescott's lyrical style, with its piling of images into central symbols with many facets. The meaning of a symbol such as the marsh changes with the season of the year and the perception of it by a character or the omniscient narrator. It appears variously fecund, barren, ominous, even sexual. Bad Han, herself a creature of the marsh, also assumes symbolic import. A natural symbolist from the beginning, Wescott grew ever more powerful in his control of this tool of meaning, reaching finally its near-perfect use in *The Pilgrim Hawk*.

Even in this first novel, bird imagery and symbolism are pervasive, with passages about bitterns, turkeys, pigeons, wild geese, and crows. Later, in his ballet libretto, "The Dream of Audubon," Wescott sums up the key to his bird symbolism: "We are all hunters; and our heart's desire, whatever it may be, is always somehow a thing of air and wilderness, flying away from us, subject to extinction in one way or another."

In addition to the search for self-knowledge, Wescott was preoccupied with the search for an organic form to fit his materials; in his second novel, *The Grandmothers* he found one of great originality. An expatriate poet, Alwyn Tower, puts together a series of individual histories to create a family portrait. As a third-person participant-narrator, looking back from the "tower" of Europe at his origins, Alwyn treats time as fluid, moving from the self-present to the self-past when as a child he heard fragments of stories from his paternal grandmother. His curiosity roused, he watched his grandparents' life, caught glimpses of their past life, and now as an adult is able imaginatively to re-create it, as he does the lives of his parents and of other relatives. The task the adult Alwyn sets himself, at his desk in a Riviera hotel, is a purposeful search for usable knowledge needed by the self, the "all" that he will "win": "For the personages in rocking-chairs, the questionable spirits leaning over his cradle, had embodied not only the past, but the future—his own wishes and fears; and he was not to be content until an everyday light had unveiled all their faces."

Devoting himself to the acceptance of life and the creation of art, once he has exorcised their spirits, Alwyn can find meaning where they failed. His close examination of the family, and all the misguided ambition, anxiety, pride, and stubbornness of its members, remembered and imagined with compassion, will result finally in the detachment needed for the full creation of the self.

The first chapter shows Alwyn as a small boy in Wisconsin, remembered by the adult Alwyn in Europe, sensing the rich, mysterious layers of family history in his grandmother's rooms, hearing hints and half-explanations, and being tantalized by curiosity about the whole of the stories. In the second chapter he sees the Towers as making up a "composite character, the soul of a race; something so valuable that one recognized it only as an atmosphere, a special brightness, or a peculiar quality of the temperaments and customs and fortunes of Americans; as if it were the god of place." Despite his affinity for Europe, Alwyn loves his country and his family; in fact, he feels they are one and the same.

In the next twelve chapters, the narrator reconstructs and reflects on the lives of family members in the two preceding generations. The reader learns snatches of their stories as the boy learns them. Such suspense as there is in the essentially plotless book comes from waiting with him to get the answers: Why did his grandmother Rose marry Henry Tower instead of his brother Leander, who was her sweetheart before he went off to war? What happened to their brother Hilary, who went with Leander and never came home? Why did his Aunt Flora look like "a girl of thirty" and die early? These questions and more are answered in relation to love, family, religion, and historical

Critical Survey of Long Fiction

context, although whether the answers are actually remembered or are imagined is always a guess.

Through this one family, Wescott explores the many ways of love and how it makes the Towers its victims. Henry and Rose, the grandparents, each lose their first, romantic love: Henry, when his first wife, Serena, dies; Rose, when Leander will not marry her and she has to settle for his brother. Rose marries her second choice, Henry, because she wants to escape from her own family of rough boys, and she wants "nothing in the world . . . but to be acceptable" to the Towers. Throughout the novel, events and their interpretation hinge on the family—its honor (the boys go to fight in the Civil War); its pride (the one who deserts cannot come home); its narrowness (James cannot choose a career in music); its prejudices (the spinster cannot marry a Catholic). For its members, love of family and of place are all-important and almost identical. Even though it means facing Rose, whom he jilted, Leander decides to return to Hope's Corner from California. The deserter, Evan, returns for visits, even though he knows his father will spurn him. Hope's Corner, poor as it is, symbolizes what has been the dream of the American pioneers, now changed: "The West, that point of the compass which had glittered with hope like a star, came to resemble the East—the light went out of it. . . . Every hope had a rendezvous with disappointment."

"Mother" and "home" are important themes in the novel. In its beginning, the author protagonist hears a drunken sailor on the quay below crying, "I want my mother!" While exploring memory, Alwyn discovers that, beginning with Rose and certainly including his own mother, the strong women who have married the Tower men have been their salvation, and he proclaims America a matriarchy. He finds in himself some of the characteristics of the Tower men and realizes that he will have to accommodate them somehow in his artist self.

Many kinds of love abound in these portraits, but in the conclusion, Wescott develops the theme of incest, making of it a complex metaphor for what Alwyn is doing. He looks back from the "tower" of Europe at his nineteenth year, when he spent many nights watching by the bed of his dying grandmother, Rose Tower. His other grandmother, Ursula Duff, in the confusion of age has called him by the name of her eldest son and also called him her sweetheart. He thinks of this as oracular, "a menace or a promise" that must be interpreted. In the effort, he meditates on the incest taboo, and he also recalls the tradition that the breaking of that law may sometimes create a legendary hero—or god. This idea, in turn, symbolizes his way of becoming self-created: "Memory was incest. . . . The desire to understand was, after all, desire." If the word *mother* "meant that which had produced one," then it included the wilderness, Wisconsin, the family, its "squalor, ideals, manias, regrets, sensuality, what consolations there had been." He had broken the law by going back to what had produced him, going back in imagination and going forward again: "Alwyn thought with rather unreasonable pride that he had become a man in as nearly as possible the way that men had become heroes or gods."

In his third autobiographical novel, *The Pilgrim Hawk*, Wescott again treats the themes of the self and love, again evokes their essences through symbolism, and for the second time places the development of the story inside the consciousness of a narrator, this one with a first-person viewpoint. Here the self is not, as in *The Grandmothers*, primarily a member of a family or an evolving artist but a practicing artist exploring the difficulties of his vocation and probing the extent of his talent as well as his own problems of love.

Geographically, there is a reversal: the narrator, Alwyn Tower, the protagonist of *The Grandmothers*, has been an expatriate in France but is now in America about ten years later, looking back at that other place and time. The historical context is the world on the verge of war; he visualizes gun emplacement in the idyllic countryside he once visited. Again, the structural framework makes possible a double layering of time. Tower remembers what happened on one May afternoon and how he speculated on the meaning of the events; in present time, he meditates and elaborates still further on those meanings.

On that day, Alwyn Tower is at the home of his friend Alexandra Henry (who later meets and marries his brother), when the Irish Cullens arrive. From the beginning, all attention is centered on Lucy, the pilgrim hawk Madeleine Cullen carries on her leather-encased wrist. The bird, along with the lore of falconry, is fascinating to Tower. Even more so is the conundrum of the triangular relationship of the two Cullens and the hawk. Tower sees the hawk, its needs and activities, as vastly symbolic, even of certain aspects of himself.

The events of that day, presented chronologically, can be summarized briefly as following the patterns established by the hawk. The account is interspersed with the reflective analogies drawn by the narrator. He first notes Lucy's "hunger," which can be a "painful greed, sick singlemindedness," it reminds Tower of "human hungers, mental and sentimental," for example, his own hunger to be a literary artist, which, because no one warned him that he did not have enough talent, "turned bitter, hot and nerveracking." Then, because his work has not been going well, he thinks of her as "an image of amorous desire," which would be a "natural consolation" to the weary artist.

The hawk bates—that is, throws herself headlong off her perch on the wrist and hangs helpless, upside down. While Mrs. Cullen brings her under control and soothes her, the narrator meditates on the woman's apparent need to dominate, and the group debates the value of independence. Larry Cullen, who is tethered to his wife as firmly as Lucy is, says that such yearning for freedom is the only human characteristic of hawks.

Later in the novel, Tower hears Cullen express embarrassingly frank sexual feelings toward his wife, as well as resentment at the way Lucy, constantly on his wife's arm, interferes with his embraces while traveling. These comments about sexual desire continue the hunger-imagery. Tower, also, has been thinking of his own need for love: "Old bachelor hungry bird, aging-hungry-man-bird, and how I hate desire, how I need pleasure, how I adore love, how difficult middle age must be!"

With his jealousy fully roused, Cullen goes to free Lucy, who has been left weathering in the garden. Thus he, in his own way, bates. Having observed the act, Tower quietly informs Mrs. Cullen, and she is able to recapture the bird.

Jealousy also erupts in a subtriangle: Jean, the cook, is enraged by the flirtation of his wife, Eva, with Ricketts, the Cullens' chauffeur. Disturbed by both episodes, the Cullens leave early, only to return immediately. Mrs. Cullen enters the house with the news that her husband has tried to shoot someone, whether the chauffeur—of whom he is also jealous—or himself is not clear. In other words, he has bated again. She goes to toss the gun into the pond in the garden and returns to make a final farewell. Tower and Alexandra linger on the scene, discussing what it all has meant, at the same time concluding from sounds in the garden that Jean and Eva have been reconciled.

The ridiculousness of Mrs. Cullen's appearance while she enacts this drama with Lucy still clutching her wrist makes the bird, too, seem funny to Tower; he begins to unload all the symbols he has piled on her and to see more realistically. The narrator is amused at "how often the great issues which I had taken this bird to augur come down in fact to undignified appearance, petty neurasthenic anecdote." The bird's—and Cullen's—"poor domestication" reminds him of "the absurd position of the artist in the midst of the disorders of those who honor and support him, but who can scarcely be expected to keep quiet around him for art's sake." So it goes, while brick after brick of the carefully built, towering symbol is pulled down.

In his final meditations, the narrator becomes ashamed of the intricate theories he has spun during the afternoon and dubious about their validity. They may be only projections of the artist's self. He calls them "guessing," "cartooning," "inexact and vengeful lyricisms," and says, "Sometimes I entirely doubt my judgment in moral matters; and so long as I propose to be a story-teller, that is the whisper of the devil for me." While Alex absents herself on household duties, he tries to "compress the excessive details of the afternoon into an abstraction or two," even though he knows that "abstraction is a bad thing, innumerable and infinitesimal and tiresome."

Abstraction—that is, the expression of truth in statement rather than in images—is what Wescott could not or would not give up. In William H. Rueckert's opinion, "Without absurdity, it can be said that Wescott slays himself as an artist in this work." The work itself remains a jewel of art.

Wescott, through the persona of Alwyn Tower in *The Pilgrim Hawk*, appeared to reject further attempts at the art of fiction. Meanwhile, however, he had thought about what the ideal novel should be like: objective, written "with precise equivalents instead of idioms, a style of rapid grace for the eye rather than sonority for the ear," one out of which the self, its prejudices, and its parochial origins "will seem to have disappeared." His next book, *Apartment in Athens*, is a traditional novel, and it suffers by comparison with his more original works.

The chief problem with the novel is its didacticism, arising from its design as propaganda. Since he was ineligible for the draft, Wescott said, he wanted to contribute to the war effort by embodying in a novel his understanding of the German mentality gained on several visits to Germany. He got the idea of setting the story in Athens in meetings with a hero of the Greek underground who was visiting in the United States.

When a Nazi officer, Captain Kalter, is billeted in the apartment of the Helianoses, a Greek family of four, they become his "slaves," constantly harassed and abused. Somehow, though, the parents, an aging couple, find their love renewed by the experience. After leave in Germany, Kalter comes back a changed man, and the Helianoses are baffled by his kindness. When he reveals that he has lost his whole family in the war, Mr. Helianos offers sympathy and blames Hitler, whereupon the Nazi flies into a rage, beats him, and has him arrested. With her husband in jail, Mrs. Helianos and her children, Alex and Leda, expect more abuse, but Kalter, although obviously declining in health, continues to be kind. When he commits suicide, he leaves a note to a friend in the military suggesting that his death may be charged against this Greek family and used to get information from them about the underground. His friend declines to pursue the suggestion. Helianos is executed anyway. His wife, who has refused to become involved in the Resistance, now joins it and resolves to dedicate her children also to the eventual freedom of Greece.

Told in plain style, from the omniscient point of view, thus without the voice and play of intellect of a participating narrator, *Apartment in Athens* is not an artistic success. Although Edmund Wilson praised this novel, and it was a Book-of-the-Month-Club selection, it lacks the rich imagery and symbolism of Wescott's previous novels, and it is also marred by long stretches of exposition and argument. One chapter amounts to a lecture by Kalter on the Nazi view of German superiority in all things; another is mostly given over to a letter from prison expressing the views of Helianos on the threat of Germany and the prospects of Greece.

Wescott found his materials in his own life, primarily among the people of the farms and small towns of Wisconsin, with their hard work, cultural poverty, and puritanical outlook, but he wrote of them with nostalgia and compassion rather than with the satiric venom of many Midwestern writers of the period. He dwelt on the themes of self, love, family, and home, showing how they interacted with one another and the environment to determine the fate of his characters. His major theme was the self-discovery of the artist, a participant-narrator in his two best novels who is also an expatriate. Because of the established distance in time and place, the narrator is able to reflect not only on the events he is recounting but also on himself as an artist. The memories are laden with rich imagery, often linked in a matrix of symbols in the narrator's mind. When Wescott abandoned his distinctively subjective, symbolic style, he seemed to have lost his impulse as a storyteller, although he continued to be active as a man of letters.

Eileen Tarcay

Other major works

SHORT FICTION: . . . *Like a Lover*, 1926; *Good-bye, Wisconsin*, 1928; *The Babe's Bed*, 1930.

POETRY: *The Bitterns: A Book of Twelve Poems*, 1920; *Natives of Rock: XX Poems, 1921-1922*, 1925.

NONFICTION: *Elizabeth Madox Roberts: A Personal Note*, 1930; *Fear and Trembling*, 1932; *A Calendar of Saints for Unbelievers*, 1932; *Images of Truth: Remembrances and Criticism*, 1962.

MISCELLANEOUS: *The Maugham Reader*, 1950 (edited); *Short Novels of Colette*, 1951 (edited); *Twelve Fables of Aesop, Newly Narrated*, 1954.

Bibliography

Beach, Joseph Warren. *The Twentieth Century Novel: Studies in Technique*. New York: Appleton-Century-Crofts, 1932. The entry on Wescott discusses his technique in *The Grandmothers* and likens this work to that of Joseph Conrad. Beach faults Wescott for his lack of visual information that characterizes "the born writer of fiction," although concedes other strengths in the book.

Cowley, Malcolm. *Exile's Return*. New York: Viking Press, 1951. A notable book on the expatriate movement of the 1930's, which explores writers who were once called the "lost generation." Helpful in placing Wescott in this movement and defining his relation to the times.

Johnson, Ira. *Glenway Wescott: The Paradox of Voice*. Port Washington, N.Y.: Kennikat Press, 1971. A full-length, valuable study of Wescott, with extensive critical commentary on his major works, complete with bibliography and plot summaries of his novels. The commentary on Wescott's fiction assesses his technique and evaluates the artistic merit of his works. Includes a discussion of his essays in *Images of Truth*. An indispensable guide for the Wescott scholar.

Kahn, Sy Myron. "Glenway Wescott: A Bibliography." *Bulletin of Bibliogra-*

phy 22 (1956-1959): 156-160. Part 1 presents an exhaustive bibliography of Wescott's writings up to 1954; part 2 is selective bibliography of critical commentary on Wescott, including major articles and noteworthy reviews. A valuable resource for the Wescott scholar.

Rueckert, William H. *Glenway Wescott*. New York: Twayne, 1965. A useful introduction to the works of Wescott—both poetry and fiction—chronicling his development as a writer. Includes commentary on the "dry years" between 1933 and 1939, during which time Wescott, having returned to America from Europe, wrote very little that was published. Largely a sympathetic study of Wescott but points out that his ideas on the novel are limiting and this has affected his work. Contains a selected bibliography.

NATHANAEL WEST
Nathan Weinstein

Born: New York, New York; October 17, 1903
Died: El Centro, California; December 22, 1940

Principal long fiction
The Dream Life of Balso Snell, 1931; *Miss Lonelyhearts*, 1933; *A Cool Million: Or, The Dismantling of Lemuel Pitkin*, 1934; *The Day of the Locust*, 1939.

Other literary forms
Nathanael West often used the short-story form for preliminary sketches of characters and themes that later appeared in his novels. Between 1930 and 1933 especially, he wrote stories with a broader focus and in a more sophisticated style than his first work, *The Dream Life of Balso Snell*. The stories include "The Adventurer," "Mr. Potts of Pottstown," "Tibetan Night," and "The Sun, the Lady, and the Gas Station," all unpublished. After the publication of *Miss Lonelyhearts* in 1933, West also worked as a scriptwriter in Hollywood for several years.

Achievements
Since West's death in a automobile accident in 1940, his work has steadily gained critical attention. His characters' hysterical pitch of loneliness, their frustration, and their inability to find a source of relief have gradually interested a wide audience, especially since World War II. Stripped of their professional masks, the people in West's novels reveal a talent for cruelty. They tease, exploit, or murder to ensure their own survival in a world reminiscent of T. S. Eliot's *The Waste Land* (1922), but their world is without Eliot's hint of redemption or spirituality. In *Miss Lonelyhearts*, the world is dead; in *The Day of the Locust*, it is corrupt and jaded, a modern Sodom which West symbolically destroys. This last novel was made into a film in the 1970's; although it never became a box-office hit, West would have approved of its powerful treatment of dreamers and misfits.

Biography
Nathanael West was born Nathan Weinstein in New York City on October 17, 1903. His father's and mother's families had known one another before they immigrated to the United States from Russia. His father's side used construction skills learned in the old world to become successful contractors in the new country, taking advantage of the building boom of the turn of the century. His mother's side was well educated, and Anna Wallenstein Weinstein wanted her son Nathan and her two daughters to have all the perquisites of an upwardly mobile, middle-class life. Soon after settling in New York

City, the Weinsteins learned to enjoy their comforts and to value them highly. They also assumed that their son would receive the finest possible education, pursue a professional career, or at least join the family business. West was an avid reader but a much less ambitious student. He attended a variety of grammer schools before his parents placed him in DeWitt Clinton High School. West, however, preferred exploring Central Park during the day and the theater district in the evenings. He was particularly attracted to the vaudeville shows, his first exposure to techniques such as slapstick and stereotypes which he later used in his fiction.

West was not very disciplined, but his clever and adventurous nature helped to get him into Tufts University without a high school diploma. After one unsuccessful year there, he attended Brown University. West's biographer attributes Brown's acceptance of West to a complicated mismatching of transcripts with another student whose name was also Weinstein, though whether this was planned or accidental is not absolutely certain. Whatever the case, West was graduated from Brown in 1924 with a degree in philosophy, which he earned in only two and a half years.

Neither West nor his parents had much nostalgia for their Jewish Lithuanian roots; instead, they concentrated on rapid assimilation. In 1926, he legally changed his name to Nathanael West. Even so, the subject of roots still appears in most of his work. The degree of corruption in Lemuel Pitkin's hometown in *A Cool Million* is nothing compared to what he finds elsewhere in the country. The protagonist in *Miss Lonelyhearts* suffers from acute isolation despite his efforts to communicate, and this seems to stem from his earliest memories of childhood; he is estranged from his Baptist upbringing and has only a single comforting memory of his youth. Tod Hackett in *The Day of the Locust* leaves the East Coast, where he was an undergraduate at the Yale School of Fine Arts, for Hollywood. He observes other new arrivals and decides that they have come to California to die in one way or another. Although he does not include himself in this category, it is clear that he too succumbs to the superficial glitter and wastefulness.

West's parents encouraged him to pursue a dependable career, but their son was not interested, and he convinced them to send him to Paris in 1926. He enjoyed the artistic and literary circles there, but signs of the coming Depression were being felt in the construction industry and West had to return to New York after three months. Relatives managed to find him a job as a night manager of a midtown hotel, providing West with an income, a place to write, and a steady flow of guests to watch. West found these people fascinating, and so it is not surprising that seedy hotels and their transient occupants find their way into *The Day of the Locust*. Working as a night manager also gave West time to revise *The Dream Life of Balso Snell*, which he had begun while in college. William Carlos Williams liked the manuscript and recommended that Moss and Kamin publish it; five hundred copies were printed in 1931.

S. J. Perelman, also a student at Brown, married West's sister Laura. Through Perelman, who worked at *The New Yorker*, West met other writers and artists. It was also through his brother-in-law that West conceived of the controlling idea for *Miss Lonelyhearts*. Perelman knew a writer named Susan Chester who gave advice to readers of *The Brooklyn Eagle*. The three of them met one evening in 1939, and she read samples of the letters. West was moved by them and eventually used an advice-to-the-lovelorn column and a tormented newspaper columnist for what is probably his most famous novel. *Miss Lonelyhearts* was published by Liveright in 1933.

West soon went to Southern California to work on film scripts. His experience with the less glamorous aspects of Hollywood and the film industry, with the masses of aspiring actors and actresses, with people who had little talent to begin with, but compensated for that with their dreams, helped provide the themes, landscapes, and characters of West's final novel, *The Day of the Locust*. In 1940, West married Eileen McKenney, the sister of Ruth McKenney, who worked with Perelman at *The New Yorker*. West's careless driving was known to all his friends, and a few months after his marriage, he and his wife were killed in an automobile crash.

Analysis

Although all of Nathanael West's fiction is concerned with certain recurring themes, it gradually matures in tone, style, and subject. *The Dream Life of Balso Snell*, his first novel, has a clever but sarcastic and ugly adolescent tone. *The Day of the Locust*, his last novel, is also satirical and sarcastic, but its greater maturity and empathetic tone make it both disturbing and profoundly moving.

West's Miss Lonelyhearts dreams that he is a magician who does tricks with doorknobs: he is able to make them speak, bleed, and flower. In a sense, this conceit explains all of West's work. His protagonists travel across dead landscapes which they try to revivify. In *The Dream Life of Balso Snell*, the landscape is mechanical, wooden, purely farcical; in *A Cool Million*, West shows one American town after another, all equally corrupt. *Miss Lonelyhearts* is set in the dirt and concrete of New York City, and *The Day of the Locust* is set in the sordid but irresistible Southern California landscape. West's typical protagonist is a quester, intent on bringing life wherever he travels; Miss Lonelyhearts especially is obsessed with the challenges of a savior. The task of making a dead world bloom, however, seems hopeless. Life may surface in a moment of communication or lovemaking, but something is likely to go awry, as the moment reverses itself into an unnatural distortion. For example, as Miss Lonelyhearts tries to comfort an old man he meets in Central Park, he suddenly has the urge to crush and destroy him. Shrike, his employer at the newspaper office, compares making love to his wife with sleeping with a knife in his groin. This dichotomy is at the heart of West's vision. Characters driven by benevolent ambitions are thwarted—by themselves, by those in need of their help, by cosmic and divine indifference—until they become grotesque parodies of their original selves. Innocence and success can be recalled only through dreams. At best, the world is passively dead; at worst, it is aggressively violent.

The quester of *The Dream Life of Balso Snell* does not take himself seriously, and the novel itself seems to be an extended literary joke. Balso Snell describes a dream in which he encounters the famous wooden horse of the Greeks in ancient Troy. A brash and distinctly modern tour guide leads him through the interiors of the horse, which quickly become the subject of numerous adolescent witticisms. The inside of the horse expands to a landscape that Balso explores for the rest of his dream. West's purpose is humor and parody, which he accomplishes mercilessly although unpleasantly, beginning even with the title of this first book. Following his "path," Balso meets a Catholic mystic, and West has the opportunity to mock the literary lives of saints. Then Balso meets a schoolboy who has just hidden his journal in the trunk of a nearby tree. Balso reads its entries, which serve as a parody of the nineteenth century Russian novel. Balso then meets the boy's teacher, Miss McGeeny, who has been busily writing a biography of a biographer's biographer; West parodies another literary genre.

The Dream Life of Balso Snell is not a significant work of fiction, but it is useful for readers to appreciate how quickly West's style and perspective deepened. His later novels have the same piercing quality, and West never lost his tendency to satirize, but the later novels are finely and precisely directed. West's later fiction also has the same motifs—quester, mechanical or obsessive journeys, dreams, and suffering humanity—but West examines them much more seriously in the later novels.

West is in superb control of his material in *Miss Lonelyhearts*, published only two years after *The Dream Life of Balso Snell*. The vituperative tone of the earlier work is balanced by greater development of plot and diversity of character. Following his preference for fast action and exaggeration, West uses comic-strip stereotypes: the meek husband and the bullying wife, Mr. and Mrs. Doyle; the bullish employer, Shrike, and his castrating wife Mary; and Miss Lonelyhearts' innocent but dumb girl friend Betty. Miss Lonelyhearts himself is only somewhat more developed, primarily because he is in almost every episode and because the third-person voice sardonically presents his private thoughts.

As in *The Dream Life of Balso Snell*, a central quester travels a barren landscape. Between the newspaper office and the local speakeasy is Central Park. As Miss Lonelyhearts walks across it, he realizes that there should be signs of spring but, in fact, there are none to be seen. Then he recalls that last year, new life seemed wrenched from the soil only in July. Miss Lonelyhearts' job as a newspaper columnist thrusts him into the position of a quester, and he makes a highly unlikely candidate. Simultaneously attracted to and repelled by his mission to assuage the grief of his readers, he makes attempts to get close to some of them, such as Mr. and Mrs. Doyle, but he then suddenly feels a compulsion to keep separate from them. This dichotomy keeps him in motion, reeling him like a puppet from one person's apartment to another, building a pressure that is released only when Miss Lonelyhearts has a final breakdown.

In each new location, the newspaperman tries to make a meaningful connection with another human being. Strict chronology becomes vague as the protagonist's state of mind becomes increasingly disturbed. He reaches toward Betty when they are sitting on the couch in her apartment but suddenly has no interest in her. He does remain sexually interested in Mary Shrike, but she refuses his advances as long as they stay in her apartment, and in the restaurant she teases him sadistically. He telephones Mrs. Doyle, a letter-writer, saying he will advise her in person. He exploits her unhappiness to satisfy his own need but, not surprisingly, is disappointed in the results. Rather than help others, the quester of this novel uses them as targets for venting his own anger. As he is increasingly frustrated in his task of bringing beauty and gentleness into the world, Miss Lonelyhearts takes to the isolation of his own room.

Another kind of quest occurs here, one that parodies the earlier quest. Rather than embark on further quests from one location to another in New York City, Miss Lonelyhearts hallucinates a journey; his bed serves as his mode of transportation. It appears to him a perfect world and a perfect journey, sanctioned by God, who finally communicates to him that he has chosen the right conclusion to his quest. Miss Lonelyhearts feels that he has become a rock, perfect in its design not because God has helped to create it, but because it is impenetrable to all but its own existence. It is ironic that the driven quester actually drives himself into a blissful delusion of isolation.

Reality intrudes. Mr. Doyle, incensed at being cuckolded, rushes up the stairs to the apartment. Miss Lonelyhearts rushes down the stairs, hoping to meet him and welcome what he assumes is Doyle's conversion. Instead, there is a scuffle and Doyle's gun fires. Only in dreams do doorknobs blossom and human beings turn into gentle and compassionate creatures—at least in West's novels. Miss Lonelyhearts dies, a victim of his own miscalculation.

The protagonist of *A Cool Million: Or, The Dismantling of Lemuel Pitkin*, is another miscalculating quester. Pitkin is an idealistic young man who leaves his hometown to seek his fortune. The fact that the immediate cause of his departure from Ottsville, Vermont, is the dishonest foreclosing of his mother's mortgage does not dampen his enthusiastic belief that his nation is the land of limitless possibilities. He has faith in himself and in those who insist they are using him for his own good.

Mr. Shagpole Whipple, ex-president of the United States and now director of the Rat River National Bank in Ottsville, becomes Lemuel's earliest supporter. He advises his young friend that America "is the land of opportunity," a land that "takes care of the honest and the industrious." Lemuel is inspired and sets out in what becomes a parody of the Horatio Alger myth. On the train to New York City, he enjoys a conversation with a Mr. Mape, who was left "a cool million" by his father. Lemuel is impressed, especially since, he explains, he must make his fortune starting with only the thirty dollars in his pocket. By the end of the trip, he has been divested of that thirty dollars. Lemuel is the fall guy for another scheme, so that he, and not the thief, is apprehended by the police, brought to trial, and declared guilty. Being sent to prison is only the first of a long series of misfortunes. Lemuel is always someone's dupe or prey, but he bounces back to try again, although he repeatedly gets nothing out of his adventures. In fact, the more he travels, the less he has. Lemuel loses his teeth, his scalp, his eye, part of a hand, one leg; each time there is someone close by who can benefit from his new loss. Lemuel is used by entrepreneurs and thieves of all varieties.

A Cool Million is fast-paced and episodic. Its characters are pure stereotypes—the ingenuous dupe, the patriot, the innocent young girl, the deceitful villain. Everyone and everything is satirized: Midwesterners, Jews, Southerners, capitalists, and socialists. *A Cool Million* shows how West was beginning to use his material for clearly defined purposes and to control his sharp-edged humor and black comedy in order to make a point. This novel, however, remains a minor work in comparison to *Miss Lonelyhearts* and *The Day of the Locust*. In these works, pathos emerges from West's stereotypes and seems all the more powerful because of its sources. *A Cool Million* is clever and biting but not poignant or profound.

West is at his best in *The Day of the Locust*. Tod Hackett, the central quester, comes to Hollywood from the East to learn set and costume designing. The people he gets to know are desperately in need of beauty, romance, and renewal, but, as in *Miss Lonelyhearts*, the harder they struggle to achieve these goals, the farther away they are.

The story is about dreamers who have traveled to what they believe is the dream capital of America, which West portrays as the wasteland of America. In addition to Tod, there is Faye Greener, beautiful but exploitative, making up in vanity what she lacks in intelligence. Homer Simpson is a thickheaded but sincere middle-aged bachelor from the Midwest. He has run from his one attempt to break through his dull-witted loneliness because the memory of failure is too painful. Characters such as Faye and Homer are particularly successful; although they are stereotypes, they still have something unpredictable about them. This quality usually manifests itself involuntarily by a spasm or quirk. For example, Faye is obviously a second-rate actress, but Tod sees through her tawdry facade to a deep archetypal beauty. Faye is unaware of any such quality; even if she knew, she would not appreciate it, because it has almost nothing in common with the self she has created. Homer Simpson has difficulty controlling parts of his body. He does not fall asleep easily because waking up is so arduous. His hands seem disassociated from his psyche; he has to put them under cold running water to rouse them, after which his fingers seem to follow their own rhythms. Like Faye, he has a structural purity without means to express it. Like Miss Lonelyhearts, his emotions swell in intensity, causing pressure that eventually must find release.

Faye becomes Tod's obsession. If he is a quester, she is his grail, and a most difficult challenge. Tod can neither support her nor further her acting career. Instead, he becomes a voyeur, watching her tease Earle Shoop, the cowboy from Arizona, and Miguel, the Mexican. He settles for simply painting Faye in a mural he calls "The Burning of Los Angeles." Tod observes that people come to California to die, despite their ambitions, and the mural reflects their disappointments. In the mural, a mob chases Faye, who seems oblivious to imminent danger and maintains a calm, detached expression. Those who realize they have failed need to express their anger, and those who think they have succeeded exist in a state of happy but dangerous ignorance. As in all of West's fiction, the challenge is as impossible as turning doorknobs into flowers. As the dreamers recognize the gap between their desires and accomplishments, thwarted ambition leads to frustration, and frustration to violence. The power of *The Day of the Locust* derives from the last few chapters, which describe the mindless and destructive product of such frustrated dreams.

It is the evening of a motion-picture premiere; violet lights run across the sky, and crowds of fans are kept under control by police barricades. The premiere provides the opportunity for fans to see face-to-face the "stars," the ones who have made it. The tension is too great, however, and the control too tenuous. The crowd begins to charge toward the theater, and Tod is caught in the pressure. *The Day of the Locust* is a tight, "pressured" novel, but all gives way at the end. As the crowd surges, it builds up strength from the people whose lives are filled with boredom and mistakes. There is mass pandemonium. Homer, moving like a robot, mechanically and swiftly murders a child who has been teasing him. Tod, submerged in the crowd, is hurt, but steadies himself at the base of a rail. In agony, he begins to think about his mural, "The Burning of Los Angeles," until reality and his thoughts merge. He thinks of the burning city, of mobs of people running into the foreground with baseball bats, and he and his friends fleeing from the mob. He actually believes he is painting the flames when policemen grab him from the rail and lift him into a police car. When the siren begins, Tod is not sure whether he or the siren has been making the noise. In effect, he succumbs to the chaos around him.

The Day of the Locust is a bleak novel, reflecting West's belief that recognizing limitations is difficult for humanity, which prefers to think that all things are possible. West shows limitations to be everywhere: within the masses; within the questers trying to save them; within the arid landscape itself. As the limitations prove insurmountable, natural ambitions and desires for harmony are inverted. Love becomes pantomime and compassion a veil for selfish and sadistic purposes. West's characters and settings desperately need to be renewed, but the job of salvation is difficult, one that West's protagonists fail to achieve.

Miriam Fuchs

Bibliography

Bloom, Harold, ed. *Nathanael West*. New York: Chelsea House, 1986. This useful collection includes essays on all of West's work in what Bloom hopes is a representative selection. S. E. Hyman's essay is a valuable introduction to West. Contains a bibliography.

_____, ed. *Nathanael West's "Miss Lonelyhearts."* New York: Chelsea House, 1987. This valuable collection offers nine essays from a variety of viewpoints on *Miss Lonelyhearts*. Includes a chronology and a bibliography.

Comerchero, Victor. *Nathanael West: The Ironic Prophet*. Syracuse, N.Y.: Syracuse University Press, 1964. Comerchero's study attempts to provide an overall introduction to West's work, concentrating on his general use of irony, the pessimism of his work, and the element of the grotesque in his characterizations. Contains notes.

Martin, Jay, ed. *Nathanael West: A Collection of Critical Essays*. Englewood Cliffs, N.J.: Prentice-Hall, 1971. This collection contains some brief critical commentaries by West himself as well as analyses by others. Martin's introductory essay is a useful summary; some of the others presuppose a fairly sophisticated reader. Includes a selected bibliography.

Widmer, Kingsley. *Nathanael West*. Boston: Twayne, 1982. Widmer's general introduction concentrates on "West as the prophet of modern masquerading, role-playing, and its significance" while offering useful analyses of West's work. Lengthy notes and an annotated bibliography are provided.

PAUL WEST

Born: Eckington, England; February 23, 1930

Principal long fiction

A Quality of Mercy, 1961; *Tenement of Clay*, 1965; *Alley Jaggers*, 1966; *I'm Expecting to Live Quite Soon*, 1970; *Caliban's Filibuster*, 1971; *Bela Lugosi's White Christmas*, 1972; *Colonel Mint*, 1972; *Gala*, 1976; *The Very Rich Hours of Count von Stauffenberg*, 1980; *Rat Man of Paris*, 1986; *The Place in Flowers Where Pollen Rests*, 1988; *Lord Byron's Doctor*, 1989.

Other literary forms

Paul West is a remarkably prolific novelist whose literary interests also include poetry, criticism, and other nonfiction. In addition to his books of verse, *Poems* (1952), *The Spellbound Horses* (1960), and *The Snow Leopard* (1964), West has published three memoirs: *I, Said the Sparrow* (1963), which recounts his childhood in Derbyshire; *Words for a Deaf Daughter* (1969), one of West's most popular works, which poignantly relates the experiences of his deaf daughter, Mandy; and *Out of My Depths: A Swimmer in the Universe* (1983), which describes the author's determination to learn to swim at middle age. His short stories were collected in *The Universe and Other Fictions* in 1988. Besides his numerous essays and book reviews in countless periodicals, journals, and newspapers, West has published *The Growth of the Novel* (1959), *Byron and the Spoiler's Art* (1960), *The Modern Novel* (1963), *Robert Penn Warren* (1964), *The Wine of Absurdity: Essays in Literature and Consolation* (1966), and *Sheer Fiction* (1987).

Achievements

When West arrived on the literary scene as a novelist, he was regarded as an author who possessed a compelling voice but also as one who wrote grotesque and verbally complex fictions. The unevenness of critical reaction cannot overshadow, however, the regard with which serious readers have approached his work, and a list of his fellowships and awards clearly indicates a writer of significant stature: He is the recipient of a Guggenheim Fellowship (1962), a *Paris Review* Aga Kahn Prize for Fiction (1974), the National Endowment for the Humanities Summer Stipend for science studies (1975), the National Endowment for the Arts Fellowship in Creative Writing (1980), the Hazlett Memorial Award for Excellence in the Arts (1981), the American Academy and Institute of Arts and Letters Award in Literature (1985), and a National Endowment for the Arts Fellowship in Fiction (1985). Besides teaching at Pennsylvania State University since 1962, West has been a visiting professor and writer-in-residence at numerous American universities. As his fiction has developed, West has shown himself to be a highly imaginative, experimental, and linguistically sophisticated writer. Critics usually commend him for his original style and note the striking diversity of his oeuvre.

Biography

Paul Noden West was born in Eckington, Derbyshire, on February 23, 1930, one of two children, into a working-class family. After attending local elementary and grammar schools, West went to Birmingham University, then to Lincoln College, Oxford, and in 1952 to Columbia University on a fellowship. Although profoundly attracted to New York life, West was forced to return to England to fulfill his military service in the Royal Air Force and there began his writing career. Once he concluded his service, West taught English literature at the Memorial University of Newfoundland, wrote a volume of poems, and did considerable work for the Canadian Broadcasting Corporation. In 1962 he was awarded a Guggenheim Fellowship and returned to the United States, where he took up permanent residence. He has been a member of the English and comparative literature faculties at Pennsylvania State University since 1962, dividing his time each year between teaching and writing in New York. His preference for the United States he has voiced many times, and he has, in fact, become an American citizen.

Analysis

Paul West has long insisted that what is most important to him as a writer is the free play of the imagination. What the imagination invents, he contends, becomes something independent and actual. West himself states the case most clearly when noting that "elasticity, diversity, openness, these are the things that matter to me most." Thus his fictions often revolve, both thematically and structurally, around the interplay between the individual and his or her imagination and an absurd, threatening universe. Often these fictions rely heavily upon dreams of one sort or another, with characters living in their dreams or living out their dreams or becoming confused about where dreams leave off and the world begins.

Consequently, West's fictions often abound with a sense of precariousness as characters who are constrained in one form or another struggle to free themselves and find their places in the world. Sanity frequently becomes the central issue in these lives, with protagonists taking on the forces of conventionality in their private wars with the drab and mundane. Typical West heroes are outsiders, often marginal or largely inconsequential figures, who will not or cannot conform to the forces about them and who, in striking out on their own, pay steep prices for their individuality.

A Quality of Mercy, West's first novel and a work which he largely disowns, deals with a collection of embittered and failed lives overseen by Camden Smeaton, the novel's central consciousness. The novel is otherwise unmemo-

Critical Survey of Long Fiction

rable except insofar as it anticipates concerns West more successfully developed in later novels: alienation, immersion in dream and illusion, the idea of an irrational universe, and the use of stylistic fragmentation.

On the other hand, *Tenement of Clay*, West's second novel, stands as a far more accomplished work, controlled, stylistically inventive, morally probing. Here West introduces the reader to the voices of two narrators, each of whom is compelling and unique. The work is divided into three chapters, the two shortest forming a frame offered by Pee Wee Lazarus, a dwarf wrestler whose direct idiom immediately assaults the reader and demands his attention. His desire is to "involve" the reader in his tale, a story that revolves around Papa Nick, narrator of the middle section, who along with Lazarus meets a taciturn giant he names Lacland. Lacland appears to have no home or clear destination, so Nick takes him back to his rooms, where Nick presides over a private flophouse for local bums. Kept in the darkened basement, Lacland soon develops, under Lazarus' perverse tutelage, a sexual appetite and his own abusive language. After a series of horrible misadventures, Lacland reverts to his despondency and silence and eventually becomes Nick's legal ward.

All these events, extreme and dramatic as they may appear, actually operate as a backdrop to Nick's personal turmoil. For years he has carried on a fitful relationship with Venetia, a former film actress, who exhorts him to abandon his altruism toward the derelicts and to run off with her to a life of leisure. When Nick physically collapses from the burden of Lacland and Lazarus' escapades, Venetia nurses him back to health, leaves him when he returns to his bums, and dies in a car crash in Florida.

The novel's soul comes in the form of Nick's constant ruminations, which offer a way of coping with and sometimes solving the dilemmas of his existence. Gradually the line between straight narration and Nick's hallucinations begins to dissolve; the two become one, and the reader learns something fundamental about this world: Dream and reality invade each other; there is no escaping one for the other.

The novel is furthermore important for the moral questions it raises. Perhaps the most telling of these involves one's responsibilities to other human beings; in particular terms, is Nick responsible for the lives he admits into his home? As Lacland and Lazarus demonstrate, Nick has assumed the role of a Dr. Frankenstein and created his own monsters, whom he has unwittingly unleashed upon the world. Is the answer to this dilemma incarceration? Lacland's temporary internment in the basement suggests that it is not.

For Nick, these are the questions that finally come with life itself, and his failure to arrive at any fixed solution suggests a form of authorial honesty about the complexity of modern existence. In this context, the epigraph from Samuel Beckett makes sense: "If there were only darkness, all would be clear. It is because there is not only darkness but also light that our situation becomes inexplicable."

The novel's title comes from a passage in John Dryden's *Absalom and Achitophel* (1681-1682), and certainly the images of tenements abound in the work: All the buildings in this metropolis Lazarus calls New Babylon, especially Nick's flophouse, the grave into which Venetia is lowered, and the human body itself, which contains and in many cases entraps the spirit. In their concerns with their corporeal selves, most of these characters miss the important questions Nick poses throughout. Life, then, amounts to inhabiting one vast tenement, and the point is never escape, but how one chooses to live that life.

With his next novel, *Alley Jaggers*, West moved even further into depicting a consciousness at odds with the rest of the world. Alley is as compelling a narrator as Lazarus or Nick, and like them he speaks in a language that is distinct and unique, an idiom that oddly combines Irish brogue, Midlands accent, and personal argot.

Alley is a profoundly frustrated little man who realizes that his job and marriage are unfulfilling but who has no idea how to remedy his situation. He spends his most satisfying moments dreaming of horses and the elaborate names owners concoct for them and creating airplanes in his attic retreat. Alley wants desperately to make an impression of some kind, and one of his creations, an androgynous, semihuman form emitting a silent scream, both intrigues his fellow workers and stands as an effigy of his own condition.

Eventually his boredom and frustration explode into violence when he accidentally kills a young woman during an unsuccessful sexual tryst. In fear and confusion, he wraps her body in plaster and makes a companion for his own statue. When the police inevitably discover the body, Alley has finally and inadvertently stumbled into prominence: In the police he finds his first willing audience in years.

West's purpose here is far more sophisticated than the old cliché of the criminal as artist or as misunderstood noble creature. Instead, Alley represents the alienated individual, the small person cut off from any meaningful existence who struggles in hopeless confusion to make his life somehow mean something. Unfortunately, Alley is locked in the prison of himself, both convict and jailer at once, and remains in fundamental confusion about what to do. Nevertheless, his most vital moments are spent in his imagination, which is infinitely more extravagant and vital than his quotidian existence.

The second novel in the Jaggers trilogy, *I'm Expecting to Live Quite Soon*, represents an entirely different turn in West's career. Here he not only shifts his attention from Alley to his much maligned wife, Dot, but also creates a more controlled, straightforward type of narrative. The real daring in this work comes in West's attempt to enter the consciousness of a woman, to take the same world of the first novel and shift the perspective to see through the eyes of another member of the family.

Where Alley was frustrated and irresponsible to anyone outside himself,

Dot lives a life of devotion and caring: attending to Alley's irascible mother, ministering to her dying father in a nursing home, and visiting Alley in the mental hospital. Like Alley, she needs a release from boredom and conventionality, which eventually she achieves through immersion in her sensual self. The measure of her change can be seen in her eventual decision to throw over her old life and run away to Birmingham with Jimsmith Williams, a black bus-driver.

Bela Lugosi's White Christmas, the final volume in the trilogy, finds Alley (now referred to as AJ) in analysis with Dr. Withington (With) in a state institution. Who is counseling whom becomes vague as With is drawn increasingly into AJ's fractured mind, and the two eventually reverse roles, thus effecting AJ's temporary freedom and With's incarceration.

More than any of the previous novels, this one dramatically stakes its claim to stylistic and linguistic experimentation. Attempting to enter AJ's mind as fully as possible, West fashions one of his densest, most verbally complex fictions. While the reader is often at a loss to understand the exact meaning of many passages, what one does comprehend is AJ's indefatigable desire to experience as much as he can as quickly as he can. The result is criminal melee with AJ commandeering a bulldozer and digging up graves in search of his dead father, threatening customers in a bar, sodomizing and murdering a cow, covering himself with the animal's blood and sawdust, and starting a fire in a factory near his mother's home.

AJ's immersion in his own mind becomes so complete that, like a Beckett character, he reaches a state of almost total silence by the end of the novel. Once again, West examines the line between madness and sanity, originality and convention, but like all of his fictions, the work is no polemic; AJ is neither saint nor hopelessly depraved misanthrope but a tortured human being who desperately wants "a bit of individuality." The work is also significant for the fact that West actually intrudes on the fiction in spots, first in a long footnote in which he explains the eccentricities of his characters' names and ends by noting that "in this text, optical illusion is empirically sound," and later in another footnote announcing his own presence throughout the narrative. The point in both cases is to assert artifice as a fictional construct: Fictions are both stories about people and about fiction itself.

West deals with some of these same concerns in *Caliban's Filibuster*, the novel that was published immediately before *Bela Lugosi's White Christmas*. This work represents West at his most experimentally extreme as he takes his deepest plunge into an individual's consciousness. Cal, the narrator, is yet another of West's profoundly frustrated protagonists, in this case a failed novelist-cum-screenwriter who chafes at bastardizing his talent for decidedly mercenary ends. As he travels over the Pacific Ocean with his companions Murray McAndrew, a ham actor, and Sammy Zeuss, a crass film producer and Cal's employer, voices representing various of Cal's divided selves carry on endless debates about his artistic aspirations. Thus the reader is not only taken fully into the character's mind but also given access to the dimensions of his troubled psyche.

To appease these voices and satisfy himself, Cal concocts three separate yet interdependent scenarios in which he and his companions play significant roles. In creating these tales, Cal attempts to convince himself of his abused talent and also to distance himself from his experience, like a viewer before a screen in a theater watching versions of his own life. Like Caliban, his Shakespearean namesake in *The Tempest*, Cal seethes with revenge, cursing those who control him. On his behalf, however, readers must regard his filibuster as an attempt to retain his individuality, which he sees as being eroded by the sterile conventions of his profession.

One way to view the novel is as West's paean to language itself, for it abounds in extravagant verbal complexities: anagrams, puns, malapropisms, acronyms, rhymes, and alphabet games. Language operates not only as Cal's professional tool but also as his saving grace; it literally keeps him sane, affording him the diversity of experience that the world denies. Like so many of West's heroes, Cal feels himself trapped, contained by forces which inexorably press against and threaten to destroy him. Language becomes his one potent defense.

In *Colonel Mint*, West operated from a seemingly straightforward, but by no means uncomplicated, premise: An astronaut in space claims that he has seen an angel. Whether he has or not is beside the point; instead, the fact that he *thinks* he has and that others want to disabuse him of this belief becomes the subject of this alternately humorous and morally serious work. For his comment Mint is shunted off to the hinterlands of Washington State and is forced to undergo endless hours of interrogation. If he recants he can go free; otherwise, he must indefinitely remain a prisoner of the space program.

The more Mint refuses to cooperate, the more clever and depraved the methods used against him become. After threats, physical beatings, and sexual sadism fail to make Mint waver, his tormentor, General Lew R., begins, like Dr. With in *Bela Lugosi's White Christmas*, gradually to assume Mint's point of view. He wonders what it would be like to see an angel, what exactly an angel is, and finally he accepts, though he cannot empirically confirm, that Mint has seen an angel.

When the two men escape from the interrogation compound for the wilds of the surrounding woods, it appears they have defeated the forces of conformity and conventional thinking. As is the case in so many of West's fictions, however, those forces track the characters down and exact payment: Lew R. is shot and Mint is frozen. Thus, in this novel, to assert one's individuality becomes tantamount to political treason, and the response of the state is swift, final, and utterly unforgiving.

Stylistically the novel is far more straightforward than *Caliban's Filibuster*, but in at least one important respect it recalls a feature of *Bela Lugosi's White Christmas*. The tone of the novel, for all of its physical and psychological horror, is remarkably level, often nonchalant and conversational. Here the narrator, not necessarily the author, addresses the audience directly a number of times. For example, early in the work, when the reader begins to doubt the plausibility of Mint's abduction, the narrator anticipates one's objections by remarking, "You might ask, now, where is the humanity in all this; where sweet reason went. . . ." The effect here and later in the work, when the intrusions continue, is one of complicity; the audience cannot remain at the safe distance of voyeur but must participate, psychologically and emotionally, in the events that transpire. The forces of conformity involve everyone, and the audience becomes uncomfortably aware of this throughout the narrative.

In *Gala*, West extends the range of his experimentation but also returns to some familiar territory as he develops fictionally the situation described in *Words for a Deaf Daughter*. Here, novelist and amateur astronomer Wight Deulius and his deaf child Michaela construct a model of the Milky Way in their basement. The reader takes a stellar journey through the universe, moving increasingly toward what appear to be the limits of the imagination.

What is especially intriguing about this work is the form West's experimentation takes. Recalling the practice of earlier novels, but especially *Caliban's Filibuster*, West fashions a unique structure for the fiction. Where in the latter work he relies upon the International Date Line and the color spectrum (different sections of the novel are devoted primarily to different colors), in *Gala* elements of physics and the genetic code symbols offer the pattern for the story. West explains this practice when remarking, "I am a compulsive exotic and structural opportunist. I have no idea what structures I will choose next—although I do feel that they will probably be from nature rather than from society."

In his ninth novel, *The Very Rich Hours of Count von Stauffenberg*, West once again shifted focus and style to re-create the details of one of Adolf Hitler's would-be assassins. The novel represents the best in historical fiction, a seemingly effortless blending of fact, elaboration, and pure fantasy, with the result that history becomes for the reader felt experience rather than a catalog of dry, distant details. As West points out in a preface, Stauffenberg is important not only for his public persona but also as someone whose military experience recapitulates, to greater or lesser degrees, that of West's father and all those who lived through World War II. Thus the reader comes to understand an important feature of this writer's fiction, which he expresses as follows: "Whatever I'm writing evinces the interplay between it and my life at the moment of writing, and the result is prose which, as well as being narrative and argumentative and somewhat pyrotechnical, is also symptomatic."

While the narrative, on the surface, seems markedly different from the novels which immediately precede it, one can also see characteristic West concerns emerging. For example, most of the novel places the audience squarely in Stauffenberg's mind as he copes with his war wounds, struggles to express the abiding love he feels for his wife and family, ponders the responsibilities that come with his social and military class, and rages increasingly at the psychopathic perversity of Hitler, the displaced paperhanger. West manages to avoid the obvious trap of the revisionist historian who might be tempted to make Stauffenberg into a martyr or saint. Instead, he emerges as a deeply committed, idealistic man but also one whose psyche is profoundly bruised and disturbed by the events of which he finds himself a part.

The structure of this novel is also just as experimental as that of earlier novels. West had been reading a number of medieval books of hours, lay breviaries that offer devotional prayers alongside richly illuminated paintings. Stauffenberg's rich hours are the last thirty-six of his life; the novel, however, does not stop with his execution. West imaginatively allows the count to speak to the audience from the grave, becoming, then, the most authoritative and omniscient of narrators describing those turbulent last months of the Third Reich.

Rat Man of Paris, his most popular novel, found West exploring yet again the effects of the Third Reich on the life of yet another alienated, marginal figure, in this case a boulevardier of modern Paris who spends his time accosting passersby with a rat he conceals in his overcoat. Étienne Poulsifer, the rat man, has survived the Nazi occupation and destruction of his childhood village, and carries about with him the emotional and psychological baggage of his horrifying past, as well as the rats which serve as metaphor for that growing legacy.

When he learns of Klaus Barbie's extradition to France, Poulsifer confuses him with the Nazi commander responsible for his parents' death and goes on a personal campaign to become the conscience of an entire nation. Watching all this is Sharli Bandol, Rat Man's lover, who desperately tries to bring some order and love into the chaos of his condition. The birth of a son appears to temper Poulsifer's extremism, but to the end he retains his eccentricity and thus his individuality.

Like *The Very Rich Hours of Count von Stauffenberg*, *Rat Man of Paris* carefully examines the interplay between personal and public trauma, and as West puts it, "Everybody who's born gets the ontological shock, and some people get the historical shock as well, and he has both. Because he has the historical shock, he has the ontological shock even worse, and this has blighted his life." Thus the rat man stands as a contemporary Everyman, radically imperfect, overwhelmed by the world in which he finds himself, but tenaciously determined to make something of his existence.

Also like other of West's protagonists, Poulsifer demonstrates the vitality of the creative imagination. Were it not for his wild musings, the delight he takes in yoking utterly disparate things together in his mind, he would be consumed by history and dreary conventionality. In many ways he is the last free man, an essential primitive who refuses the definitions and restrictions of others for a life created on his own terms.

Throughout his career, West has drawn criticism for his own stylistic eccentricities and rich verbal texturings, and the usual complaint holds that he is self-indulgent and willfully obscure. While indeed his fiction makes considerable demands of his audience, he is anything but deliberately perverse or obscure. In fact, West consistently attempts to reach and communicate with his audience, to involve them, in each of his rich fictional stories. His note at the beginning of *Tenement of Clay*, the interview appended to *Caliban's Filibuster*, the footnotes in *Bela Lugosi's White Christmas*, the moments of direct address in *Colonel Mint*, the announcement in the middle of *Gala* of the novel's particular structure, and the preface to *The Very Rich Hours of Count von Stauffenberg*—all demonstrate that West is fully aware of his audience and always desirous of its sympathetic participation in the fictional experience. West is committed to the proposition that writing matters, and that good writing must present its own unique experience. As he says in his essay "In Defense of Purple Prose," "The ideal is to create a complex verbal world that has as much presence, as much apparent physical bulk, as the world around it. . . . This is an illusion, to be sure, but art *is* illusion, and what's needed is an art that temporarily blots out the real."

David W. Madden

Other major works

SHORT FICTION: *The Universe and Other Fictions*, 1988.

POETRY: *Poems*, 1952; *The Spellbound Horses*, 1960; *The Snow Leopard*, 1964.

NONFICTION: *The Growth of the Novel*, 1959; *Byron and the Spoiler's Art*, 1960; *Byron: Twentieth Century Views*, 1963 (editor); *I, Said the Sparrow*, 1963; *The Modern Novel*, 1963; *Robert Penn Warren*, 1964; *The Wine of Absurdity: Essays in Literature and Consolation*, 1966; *Words for a Deaf Daughter*, 1969; *Out of My Depths: A Swimmer in the Universe*, 1983; *Sheer Fiction*, 1987.

Bibliography

Bryfonski, Dedria, and Laurie Lanza Harris, eds. *Contemporary Literary Criticism*. Vol. 14. Detroit: Gale Research, 1980. Contains extracts from reviews of West's works, including *Gala* and *Words for a Deaf Daughter*, from such sources as *The Washington Post*, *The New York Times Book Review*, and *The Nation*. Most of the reviews are favorable, addressing West's intelligent writing as both an advantage and a disadvantage. One reviewer praises *Words for a Deaf Daughter*, calling it a "sympathetic book for anyone who feels responsible for someone else." Another review describes *Gala* in terms of its "startling, dazzling meditations."

Lucas, John. "Paul West." In *Contemporary Novelists*, edited by James Vinson. London: St. James Press, 1976. Lucas discusses the Alley Jaggers sequence of novels, which "deservedly won his reputation as an original novelist," although he faults them for their lack of psychological study. Mentions West's highly acclaimed study of Lord Byron's poetry and *Bela Lugosi's White Christmas*. Lists West's works up to 1975 and includes a statement by West.

McLaughlin, Brian. "Paul West." In *British Novelists Since 1960*, edited by Jay L. Halio. Vol. 14 in *Dictionary of Literary Biography*. Detroit: Gale Research, 1977. McLaughlin cites West as a writer of "sheer energy and acrobatic intelligence." Likens him to experimental contemporaries such as William H. Gass and Gabriel García Márquez. Discusses his novels, in particular *Words for a Deaf Daughter* and *The Very Rich Hours of Count von Stauffenberg*, and examines the complex relationship between autobiography and fiction in his works.

Wakeman, John, ed. *World Authors, 1950-1970*. New York: H. W. Wilson, 1975. Includes a short piece by West in which he discusses his life and work, followed by a critical commentary on his work up to 1969. His writing is praised as "gifted, versatile, and prolific" and deserving of more attention.

West, Paul. "Paul West." In *Contemporary Authors: Autobiography Series*, edited by Mark Zadrozny. Vol. 7. Detroit: Gale Research, 1988. A beautifully written autobiography by West, filled with rich images and information about his early life, his ideas about writing, and other writers who became his friends. Includes a bibliography of his works.

EDITH WHARTON

Born: New York, New York; January 24, 1862
Died: St. Brice sous Forêt, France; August 11, 1937

Principal long fiction:
The Touchstone, 1900; *The Valley of Decision*, 1902; *Sanctuary*, 1903; *The House of Mirth*, 1905; *Madame de Treymes*, 1907; *The Fruit of the Tree*, 1907; *Ethan Frome*, 1911; *The Reef*, 1912; *The Custom of the Country*, 1913; *Summer*, 1917; *The Marne*, 1918; *The Age of Innocence*, 1920; *The Glimpses of the Moon*, 1922; *A Son at the Front*, 1923; *Old New York*, 1924; *The Mother's Recompense*, 1925; *Twilight Sleep*, 1927; *The Children*, 1928; *Hudson River Bracketed*, 1929; *The Gods Arrive*, 1932; *The Buccaneers*, 1938.

Other literary forms
In addition to her novels, of which several had appeared serially in *Scribners*, *The Delineator*, and *The Pictorial Review*, Edith Wharton published eleven collections of short stories and three volumes of poetry as well as a variety of nonfiction works. She wrote an early and influential book on interior decorating, *The Decoration of Houses* (1897, in collaboration with architect Ogden Codman, Jr.), a short book on the art of narrative, *The Writing of Fiction* (1925) published originally in *Scribner's Magazine*, and a delightful if highly selective autobiography, *A Backward Glance* (1934), which includes among other things an amusing account of Henry James's circumlocutory manner of speech. Wharton, an indefatigable traveler, recorded accounts of her travels in *Italian Villas and Their Gardens* (1904), *Italian Backgrounds* (1905), *A Motor Flight Through France* (1908), and *In Morocco* (1920). During World War I, she wrote numerous pamphlets and letters to inform Americans about French and Belgian suffering and to enlist sympathy and support. Articles she wrote to explain the French people to American soldiers were later collected in the volume *French Ways and Their Meanings* (1919), and accounts of her five tours of the front lines were published under the title *Fighting France from Dunkerque to Belfort* (1915). Wharton also published a great many short stories, articles, and reviews that have never been collected. A number of her stories and novels have been adapted for the stage, motion pictures, and television, and have also been translated into French, Italian, Spanish, German, Danish, Finnish, and Japanese.

Achievements
Unlike Henry James, whose readership was small and intensely discriminating, Wharton managed to attract a large audience of general readers and at the same time command the interest of critics and fellow writers as well. Among her admirers were Sinclair Lewis and F. Scott Fitzgerald; Bernard

Berenson, the art critic; and Percy Lubbock. Wharton's popularity remained high almost to the end of her career in the 1930's, but critical enthusiasm began to diminish after 1920, when the quality of her fiction declined. Even in the early years, 1905 to 1920, when Wharton's best fiction was being published, there were reservations expressed or implied by those who thought her a follower of and to some extent a lesser James, a charge easier to disprove than to eradicate. The truth is, that, though Warton learned from James—and a few of her novels, particularly *Madame de Treymes* reflect Jamesian themes as well as techniques—Wharton had her own manner as well as her own subject, and as she grew older, she continued to discover differences between her fiction and James's. It should also be pointed out (whether in praise or blame will depend on the critic) that James was a more dedicated artist than Wharton; his fiction had a finish and a coherence to be found in only a half-dozen of her novels; moreover, Wharton sometimes skated on the thin ice of superficiality, and in one novel, *The Glimpses of the Moon*, plunged through. Toward the end of her career, she also grew increasingly out of touch with life in the postwar world, much of which offended her. Her long residence in France, moreover, not only cut her off from the life of her fellow countrymen, but also—since she spoke French or Italian almost exclusively—loosened her grasp of English, so much so that a critic such as the young Edmund Wilson could complain that there were awkward phrases even in her masterpiece *The Age of Innocence*.

Wharton's major talent was for social observation. Unlike James, whose interest was ultimately metaphysical and whose novels were often invented from the slightest hints and employed few details, she filled her novels with precise accounts of the decoration of houses, of dress and of dinner parties, describing them often down to the cut of a waistcoat and the contents of the soup tureen. This is not to say that such details were signs of superficiality, but rather that Wharton's fiction depended heavily on the notation of manners and were the result of direct observation. Wharton tended to write—again, unlike James—out of her own direct experience. Even novels such as *Ethan Frome* and *Summer*—both set in provincial New England, and so different from the world she inhabited in New York and Paris—were created with remarkable attention to surface details, of which the famous cut glass, red pickle dish of Zeena's in *Ethan Frome* is a familiar example.

Wharton's fiction, it now appears, was (again, unlike James's) significantly autobiographical. Even the novels of provincial life, so different on the surface, treated issues that came out of the tensions of her own restricted upbringing and her unhappy marriage. Marriage was one of Wharton's principal subjects and provided her with a way of exploring and dramatizing her two main themes: the entrapment of an individual, as R. W. B. Lewis puts it in his *Edith Wharton: A Biography* (1975), and the attempt by an outsider, often a vulgar lower-class individual, to break into an old, aristocratic society. There is a sense in which these two themes are contradictory; the first one implies a point of view that identifies with the individual rather than with society; the second one judges from the point of view of society. The apparent contradiction, however, merely points up the range and boundaries of the author's sensibility. In some novels, *Ethan Frome* and *The House of Mirth*, for example, Wharton writes with sympathy of the trapped individual; in others, *The Custom of the Country*, and *The Children*, she writes from the standpoint of a traditional society. In her best novels, there is both sympathy for the trapped individual and the invocation of an outside claim—marriage vows, moral code, traditional manners—with the balance of sympathy tipped to the individual.

Wharton's major work was written between 1905, the year *The House of Mirth* was published, and 1920, when *The Age of Innocence* appeared. Interesting novels were still to come: *The Mother's Recompense*, *The Children*, and *The Buccaneers*, which has the best qualities of her earlier fiction; but the major works of the 1930's, *Hudson River Bracketed* and *The Gods Arrive*, betray a serious falling off of energy and of talent. In these novels, Wharton was attempting to judge the contemporary world by the values of the past, but was so out of sympathy with the life around her and so out of touch with its manners that her representation of it in these later books can hardly be taken seriously.

Despite this later decline, however, and despite the undeniable influence of James on some of her early work, Wharton produced a considerable body of original fiction, high in quality and superior to most of what was being published at the time. Her fiction also influenced other, younger American writers, notably Sinclair Lewis and F. Scott Fitzgerald. After a long decline in readership and a period of critical indifference, there now appears to be a renewal of interest in her writing, both by critics and scholars of the American novel and by feminist scholars interested in extraliterary issues.

Biography

Edith Wharton was born Edith Newbold Jones on January 24, 1862, in New York City. Her parents, George Frederic and Lucretia Rhinelander Jones, were descendants of early English and Dutch settlers and belonged to the pre-Civil War New York aristocracy, families whose wealth consisted largely of Manhattan real estate and who constituted in their common ancestry, landed wealth, and traditional manners a tightly knit, closed society. With the industrial expansion that occurred during and immediately after the Civil War, the old society was "invaded" by a new class of self-made rich men such as John Jacob Astor and Cornelius Vanderbilt. Whereas the old society had lived unostentatiously, observing, outwardly at least, a strict code of manners—the women presiding over a well-regulated social life and the men making perfunctory gestures at pursuing a profession—the new rich spent lavishly, built expensive, vulgar houses, and behaved in ways the old order found shockingly reprehensible. With its energy, its money, and its easier morality, the new order inevitably triumphed over the old, and this displacement of New York society constituted one of the chief subjects of Wharton's fiction, particularly in *The House of Mirth* and *The Custom of the Country*.

Wharton was educated at home by governesses, and later, tutors, and it was expected that she would assume the role young women of her class were educated to play, that of wife, mother, a gracious hostess. From an early age, however, Wharton showed intellectual and literary talents which, along with an acute shyness, kept her at the edge of conventional social life and later threatened to consign her at the age of twenty-three to a life of spinsterhood—the worst fate, so it was thought, that could befall a young woman of her class. After one engagement had been called off (because the young man's mother opposed it), and a promising relationship with a young lawyer, Walter Berry (who later became a close friend), had failed to develop romantically, Wharton married a man twelve years her senior, Edward ("Teddy") Robbins Wharton, a friend of her favorite brother.

Teddy Wharton was a socially prominent Bostonian without a profession or money of his own; Henry James and other friends in England were later incredulous that Wharton could marry a man so obviously her intellectual inferior and so incompatible in his interests; nevertheless, the marriage in the beginning must have been a liberation, both from the social pressure to marry and from her mother's domination. Wharton was close to her father, but there was a coolness between her and her mother that is frequently reflected in her fiction in the portrayal of mother-daughter relationships. By marrying Teddy, she was at last free to come and go as she pleased, to establish her own residence, which she did on a grand scale at Lenox, Massachusetts, and to travel abroad as often as she liked, In time, however, the marriage to Teddy became irksome, partly from lack of deep affection for him, but also because of his increasing bouts of depression and, later, his financial and sexual irresponsibilities. After revelations of his mismanagement of her estate and his adulterous affairs, she divorced Teddy in 1913. In his research for the biography of Wharton, Lewis uncovered the fact that she herself had had a brief but intense affair in 1908 with an American journalist named Morton Fullerton, and that that relationship had a profound influence on her fiction.

Wharton had lived and traveled in Europe as a child with her parents and after her marriage had visited abroad as often as possible, alternating the seasons between her house at Lenox and an apartment in Paris, with shorter visits to England and rural France. In 1903, when she met James in England, there began an important friendship, with frequent visits and exchanges of letters and motor trips in Wharton's powerful automobile. The Whartons always traveled in luxury, and their style and Edith's energy quite overwhelmed James at the same time he delighted in them. Like James, and for somewhat the same reasons, Wharton became in time an expatriate, giving up the newer, rawer life of America for the rich, deeply rooted culture of Europe. She felt at home in the salons and drawing rooms of Paris and London, where art and literature and ideas were discussed freely, where women were treated by men as equals, and where life itself was more pleasing to the senses and to the contemplative mind. Wharton also felt that in Europe, respect for the family, for manners, for learning, and for culture, even among the poorer classes, was very much alive.

Even before the final break with Teddy, Wharton had lengthened her frequent stays abroad and, finally, in 1911, allowed the house at Lenox to be sold. When World War I broke out, she remained in Paris and devoted her time, energy, and money to the relief of French and Belgian refugees; in 1916, she was officially recognized for her services to her adopted country by being made a Chevalier of the Legion of Honor. After the war, she bought a house just north of Paris and, later, another in the south of France. She made only one more trip home, in 1923, to receive an honorary degree at Yale. The remainder of her life was spent abroad.

According to those who knew her well, Wharton was a highly intelligent, well-read, brilliant conversationalist, somewhat remote at first, though the grand manner that many complained of was apparently a way of covering up her deep shyness. She read and spoke Italian and French fluently, and her salons in both Paris and Saint Claire were gathering places for literary, artistic, and social luminaries of the time, including such well-known figures as F. Scott Fitzgerald, Bernard Berenson, Jean Cocteau, Aldous Huxley, and Kenneth Clark. Despite the hectic pace of her social life and her frequent travels, Wharton continued to write regularly, turning out novels and short stories and articles, most of which sold well and brought her a great deal of money. She suffered a slight stroke in 1935, which for a time curtailed her activities; two years later, she was fatally stricken. After a short illness, she died at her home in St. Brice sous Forêt, August 11, 1937. Her body was buried in a cemetery at Versailles, beside the grave where the ashes of her old friend Walter Berry had been buried earlier.

Analysis

On a surface level, there is a surprising variety in the kinds of characters and the aspects of life with which Edith Wharton was familiar. In *The House of Mirth*, for example, one of her best novels, she was able to create characters such as the Trenors and the Van Osburghs, who belong to opposite ends of the upper level of old New York society, as well as Nettie Struther, the poor working-class girl who befriends Lily Bart when she has sunk from the glittering world of Fifth Avenue social life to a seedy, boardinghouse existence. In *The Fruit of the Tree*, she created not only the world of the fashionable Westmores, but also the factory milieu in which the foreman John Amherst attempts to bring industrial reform. In *The Reef*, she could treat life in a French chateau, as well as in a sordid hotel in Paris, and in her two brilliant short novels, *Ethan Frome* and *Summer*, she managed to depict a life in rural Massachusetts that she could only have known by observation, rather than by direct experience.

It must be admitted, however, that Wharton is at times less than convincing. Some critics consider her attempt to deal with factory life in *The Fruit of the Tree* inept, even ludicrous, though others believe it entirely adequate; and certainly the life of impoverished Nettie Struther is delineated with nothing like the thoroughness of Lily Bart's, whose upper-class milieu Wharton knew at firsthand. Still, the extent of Wharton's social range and her ability to create realistic characters from a background quite different from her own is impressive, unrivaled in American fiction of the time.

As for variety of character types, one might cite in particular those to be found in *The House of Mirth*, in the range of male characters—from the fastidious Selden to the rapacious Gus Trenor and the socially ambiguous and vulgar Simon Rosedale, all of them suitors for Lily's attention. Both *Ethan Frome* and *Summer* present a more limited range, but both contain sharply realized and distinctly differentiated characters, including the powerful Ethan, the pretty young Mattie, and Zeena, the neurasthenic wife of Ethan. In *Summer*, Charity Royall, the mountain girl, is vividly created, as is her feckless young lover and her elderly guardian and attempted seducer, Lawyer Royall.

Despite this surface breadth, this impressive range of social observation, Wharton's novels have a rather narrow thematic focus. It has been said that Edith Wharton's chief theme is entrapment. Blake Nevius, in *Edith Wharton: A Study of Her Fiction* (1953), points out how this theme is implicit in the principal relationships among characters in many of the novels, in which a superior nature is caught in a wasteful and baffling submission to an inferior nature. It was a situation that Wharton herself must have experienced, not only with a mother who was obsessed with fashion and propriety, but also in a society narrowly given up to the pursuit of pleasure. It was a situation in which she later found herself in her marriage to Teddy, who disliked and resented her interest in social and intellectual life. In novel after novel, one sees this same situation treated—superior individuals trapped in relationships with their inferiors and prevented from extricating themselves by a finer sensibility.

In *The House of Mirth*, Lily Bart is impoverished by the bankruptcy and later the death of her father and is obliged to recoup her fortune in the only way open to her, by attempting to marry a rich man. Lily's situation was not Wharton's, but the social pressures on her must have been similar: to make a suitable marriage, with social position certainly, and, if possible, money as well. In the novel, Lily is given a choice that Wharton apparently did not have: an offer of marriage from an emancipated young lawyer of her own class (though Walter Berry, a lawyer, was thought at one time to have been Wharton's suitor). Wharton chose a passionless marriage with Teddy; Lily was not allowed that solution. Selden deserts her at the crucial moment and she dies of an overdose of sleeping medicine.

In her autobiography *A Backward Glance*, Wharton stated that her subject in *The House of Mirth* was to be the tragic power of New York society in "debasing people and ideas," and Lily Bart was created in order to give that power dramatic scope. Lily's entrapment by society and her eventual destruction are not the final story. Lily overcomes the limitations of her upbringing and aspirations and acts on principle. She has in her possession a packet of letters which could be used to regain her social position, but the letters would involve the reputation of Selden. She also has a ten-thousand-dollar inheritance which could be used to establish herself in a profitable business, but she burns the letters and uses the money to repay a debt of honor. Lily dies, but in choosing death rather than dishonor, she has escaped entrapment.

In *The Age of Innocence*, published fifteen years after *The House of Mirth*, the underlying conflict is the same, though the tone of the novel and the nature of the entrapment are somewhat different. Here, the trapped individual is a man, Newland Archer, a young lawyer who is engaged to marry May Welland, a pretty and shallow young woman of respectable old New York society of the 1870's and 1890's. This is the world of Wharton's young womanhood, a society that is narrow and rigid and socially proper. Into this limited and self-contained world, she brings Ellen Olenska, a cousin of May, who belongs to this world by birth but left it years before and has since married a Polish count. Ellen has now separated from her husband, who has been notoriously unfaithful, and has returned to the bosom of her family for support and comfort. Archer is engaged by the family to help her in her quest for a divorce settlement. The inevitable happens. Archer and Ellen fall in love. Archer is attracted by Ellen's European sophistication, her freedom of thought and manners, and her refusal to take seriously the small taboos of New York society. Archer considers breaking with May and marrying Ellen. The family, sensing his defection, contrive with other members of the society to separate the lovers and reunite Archer with May, his conventional fiancée. Social pressure forces Ellen to return to Europe, and Archer is again thinking of pursuing Ellen; then May announces that she is expecting a baby. Archer is finally and permanently trapped.

As though to drive home the extent to which Archer has been defeated, Wharton takes him to Paris years later. His son is grown, his wife dead, and Ellen Olenska is now a widow living alone. Archer makes an appointment to see Ellen but gets only as far as a park bench near her apartment. At the last minute, he decides to send his son to see her, while he remains seated on the bench, telling himself that it would be more real for him to remain there than to go himself to see Ellen. The trap has done its work.

While one can see resemblances between Ellen and Wharton—the expatriation, the charm, the liberated views, perhaps even the slight French accent with which Ellen speaks—Archer is also Wharton, or that side of her that could never entirely escape the past. *The Age of Innocence* was thought by some reviewers to be a glorification of the past, which it clearly is not. Wharton does evoke with some nostalgia the old New York of her youth, but she also sets forth with delicate but cutting irony that society's limitations and its destructive narrowness. Archer has led an exemplary life, one is led to believe, but the happiness he might have had was gently but firmly denied him. Whereas a more popular novelist might have allowed Archer to be reunited with Ellen at the end of the novel, Wharton insists that that would be unreal; for her, personal happiness in the real world is the exception rather than the rule.

Two of Wharton's best novels—also two of her shortest; some critics prefer to call them novellas—both deal with protagonists trapped by passionless marriages. The earliest of these, *Ethan Frome*, is about a Massachusetts farmer married to an older, neurasthenic wife, whose pretty young cousin has come to work for her. The inevitable again happens. Ethan falls in love with Mattie and dreams about running away with her. Ethan's jealous wife, however, arranges for Mattie to be sent away, and Ethan is obliged to escort her to the train station. It is winter, and the lovers stop for a brief time together. They embrace, realize the inevitablity of separation, and decide to kill themselves by coasting down a steep hill into a great elm tree. During the ride down the steep hill, Ethan accidentally swerves the sled; a crash occurs, in which the lovers are seriously injured but survive. Mattie becomes a whining invalid, while Zeena, the neurotic wife, takes over the running of the household, and Ethan, who is severely disfigured, feels himself like a handcuffed convict, a prisoner for life.

As Lewis has pointed out, the situation in *Ethan Frome* is very much like the situation in Wharton's own life at the time. If one shifts the sexes, Frome is Wharton trapped in a loveless marriage with the neurasthenic Teddy and passionately in love with a younger man who shared her interests and feelings, Morton Fullerton. The violent ending, of course, may be seen as Wharton's passionate statement about her own desperate situation. The success of *Ethan Frome*, however, does not depend on making such biographical connections; the book is a brilliantly realized work of realistic fiction that owes its power not to some abstractly conceived pessimistic philosophy of life, but to Wharton's successful transposition of her own emotional life into the language of fiction.

Summer was published six years after *Ethan Frome* and was called by Wharton and her friends the "hot Ethan." As in *Ethan Frome*, there is a triangle: Lawyer Royall, elderly guardian of Charity, a pretty young mountain girl, and a visiting architecture student, Lucius Harney. During the idyllic summer months, an intense and passionate affair takes place between Charity and Harney. Harney returns to Boston, and Charity is left to face her guardian, who is also in love with her, and the prospect of an illegal abortion. The novel concludes with a reconciliation between Charity and her guardian and a secure if passionless marriage with him. While it would be a mistake to overemphasize biographical parallels, they are unmistakable. The affair of Charity and Harney suggests Wharton's earlier affair with Fullerton, while the intrusive presence of the fatherly Lawyer Royall suggests Teddy's irksome claims on Wharton's loyalties. An interesting alteration of chronology is in making the marriage with the older man follow the affair rather than precede it, as it had in Wharton's own life. *Summer* was written four years after the Whartons were divorced, and by then, she may have had time to view her marriage to Teddy more dispassionately, as the practical solution it must originally have been. Like Lily's death, the surrender to marriage is a defeat as well as a moral triumph.

Summer is one of Wharton's finest novels, written according to her own testimony, in a state of "creative joy" and reflecting in its characters, scenes, and symbolic structures, the deep well of the unconscious that seems to nourish the most powerful works of American fiction.

The Reef, published the year before the Whartons' divorce, and commonly acknowledged to be Wharton's most Jamesian novel, again deals with conflicts between the individual and society and the problems of marriage. In this novel, however, the society is remote; the inheritor of the society's standards, Anna Leath, an American widow of a French nobleman, is reunited with an old friend, George Darrow, also an American, a lawyer, living in Europe. Anna and Darrow become engaged and are about to be married when Anna discovers that Darrow has had an affair with Sophy Viner, her daughter's governess, a girl of a lower class, and that Sophy, who is also her stepson's fiancée, is still in love with Darrow. For Darrow, the situation is a matter of diplomatic maneuvering, of steering his way between the two women and the stepson, but for Anna, it presents a moral dilemma involving, on the one hand, an inherited code of conduct, which tells her that Darrow must be abandoned, and a personal one, which tells her not to give him up. The moral complexities of the novel are a good deal more complicated than summary can indicate—indeed, are so ambiguous that one is hard pressed to decide where the author stands. It is possible, however, to see in this novel situations parallel to Wharton's earlier involvement with Fullerton, and a possible moral dilemma over her own infidelity. In a sense, Wharton is Sophy Viner, but Sophy (and Wharton's affair with Fullerton) seen in the light of a later moral judgment; Wharton is also Anna, attempting to accept the break with conventional morality that led to Darrow's affair with Sophy. The trap in which Anna finds herself is doubly baited, and no matter which way she turns, she must fall, either morally or emotionally. The fact that Anna chooses Darrow after all suggests the same kind of compromise other Wharton protagonists have made, Justine of *The Fruit of the Tree* and Charity Royall of *Summer* especially, both of whom were betrayed by the weakness of the men they loved but settled for what was finally available.

The Custom of the Country is a different sort of work, influenced by the French realist Honoré de Balzac rather than by Henry James; it attempts to deal, as did Balzac, with the destruction of an aristocracy by the invasion of uncivilized materialists. The protagonist of the novel, Undine Spragg, is a handsome young woman from Apex, a city in the American Middle West. Undine's father made a great deal of money in Apex and now has come East to try his hand in New York City. The Spraggs move into an expensive, vulgar hotel, and the parents would be content to exist on the fringes of New York society, but Undine, who is as ambitious as she is vulgar, manages to meet and then marry Ralph Marvel, an ineffectual member of old New York society. When life with Marvel grows boring, Undine becomes the mistress of a richer and more aggressive New York aristocrat, Peter Van Degen; when Van Degen drops her, she manages to snare the son of an old aristocratic French family, the Marquis de Chelles. Undine marries de Chelles, but she has learned nothing, being without taste, manners, or ideas; her sole interest is in amusing and gratifying herself. As soon as she gets what she thinks she wants, she becomes dissatisfied with it and wants something she decides is better. She grows tired of having to fit herself into the demands of the feudal aristocracy into which she has married; when she attempts to sell family heirlooms, whose value she does not understand, her husband divorces her. Her third husband is a perfect match, a hard-driving vulgar materialist from Apex, Elmer Moffat, whose chief interest is in buying up European art. Moffat also aspires to an ambassadorial post, but is barred because he is married to Undine, a divorced woman.

The Custom of the Country is regarded by some critics as among Wharton's best fiction, but, as Blake Nevius has observed, during the course of the novel, Undine ceases to be a credible character and becomes an "inhuman abstraction." Clearly, she came to represent everything that Wharton detested in the America of 1912, and, at a deeper and vaguer level, perhaps also expressed Wharton's fear and resentment at the displacement of her own class by more energetic and less cultivated outsiders. The fact that such fears were real enough and the implicit social criticisms valid, does nothing to alter the fact that, measured against books such as *The House of Mirth, Ethan Frome, Summer,* and *The Reef, The Custom of the Country* is crude and unconvincing. James had been right years earlier in advising Wharton to write about that part of the world she knew best, for in attempting to deal with the Middle West in *The Custom of the Country,* and later, in *Hudson River Bracketed* and *The Gods Arrive,* with bohemian circles about which she knew very little, she condemned herself to superficiality and caricature. It is difficult to take seriously Undine Spragg of *The Custom of the Country* or Advance Weston, the protagonist of *Hudson River Bracketed* and *The Gods Arrive*, who is said to be from Pruneville, Nebraska, and later Hallelujah, Missouri, and Euphoria, Illinois. Caricature is an expression of outrage, not understanding.

Fortunately, the last of Wharton's novels, *The Buccaneers*, published the year after her death, was a return to the territory of her earlier fiction, old New York of the 1870's. The novel was unfinished at her death and lacks the coherence of her best early work, but she could still write with the sharpness and scenic fullness that had characterized *The House of Mirth* and *The Age of Innocence*.

Wharton was a novelist of manners, then, not a chronicler of large social movements, and her real subject was the entrapment of superior individuals who keenly feel the pull of moral responsibility. Her talents for social observation, for noting subtleties of dress and decoration, for nuance of voice and phrase, and for language—precise and yet expressive—were essential instruments in the creation of her novels. Wharton has been unduly charged with pessimism; her characteristic tone is ironic, the product of a sensibility able to see and feel the claims on both sides of a human dilemma. If her voice faltered in her later years and she conceded too much to the popular taste for which she increasingly wrote, she nevertheless produced some of the finest American fiction published in the first two decades of the century, and her name deserves to stand with those of James and F. Scott Fitzgerald, who outrank her only at their best.

W. J. Stuckey

Other major works

SHORT FICTION: *The Greater Inclination*, 1899; *Crucial Instances*, 1901; *The Descent of Man*, 1904; *The Hermit and the Wild Woman*, 1908; *Tales of Men and Ghosts*, 1910; *Xingu and Other Stories*, 1916; *Here and Beyond*, 1926; *Certain People*, 1930; *Human Nature*, 1933; *The World Over*, 1936; *Ghosts*, 1937; *The Collected Short Stories of Edith Wharton*, 1968.

POETRY: *Verses*, 1878; *Artemis to Actæon*, 1909; *Twelve Poems*, 1926.

NONFICTION: *The Decoration of Houses*, 1897 (with Ogden Codman, Jr.); *Italian Villas and Their Gardens*, 1904; *Italian Backgrounds*, 1905; *A Motor-Flight Through France*, 1908; *Fighting France from Dunkerque to Belfort*, 1915; *French Ways and Their Meaning*, 1919; *In Morocco*, 1920; *The Writing of Fiction*, 1925; *A Backward Glance*, 1934; *The Letters of Edith Wharton*, 1988.

Bibliography

Ammons, Elizabeth. *Edith Wharton's Argument with America*. Athens: University of Georgia Press, 1980. Ammons proposes that Wharton's "argument with America" concerns the freedom of women, an argument in which she had a key role during three decades of significant upheaval and change. This engaging book examines the evolution of Wharton's point of view in her novels and discusses the effect of World War I on Wharton. Contains a notes section.

Auchincloss, Louis. *Pioneers and Caretakers: A Study of Nine American Novelists.* Minneapolis: University of Minnesota Press, 1965. In his chapter on Edith Wharton, Auchincloss strips away what he calls the "glowing hyperbole" that critics bestowed upon her and reveals some of the limitations that are apparent in her novels. Nevertheless, he claims that Wharton succeeded as a writer because she had a "firm grasp" on the society of her day. Cites that, apart from *Ethan Frome*, Wharton will be remembered for her two great novels of manners, *The House of Mirth* and *The Age of Innocence*. A brief but informative look at Wharton, particularly useful in comparing her with the other eight novelists covered in this volume.

Fryer, Judith. *Felicitous Space: The Imaginative Structures of Edith Wharton and Willa Cather.* Chapel Hill: University of North Carolina Press, 1986. This study heralds two women writers in America who, according to Fryer, "depart from the canon" to explore their own experiences. The five chapters on Wharton examine the "meticulously conceived interiors" of her fiction, referring to her major works including her autobiography, *A Backward Glance*. Recommended reading for its feminist perspective.

Gimbel, Wendy. *Edith Wharton: Orphancy and Survival.* New York: Praeger, 1984. Drawing upon psychoanalytic theories and feminist perspectives, Gimbel analyzes the four works that she sees as key to understanding Wharton: *The House of Mirth, Ethan Frome, Summer,* and *The Age of Innocence*. The analyses of these works, with their deeply psychological overtones, are well worth reading.

Lewis, R. W. B. *Edith Wharton: A Biography.* 2 vols. New York: Harper & Row, 1975. An extensive study on Wharton, who Lewis calls "the most renowned writer of fiction in America." Notes that Wharton thoughtfully left extensive records, made available through the Beinecke Library at Yale, on which this biography is based. Essential reading for serious scholars of Wharton or for those interested in her life and how it shaped her writing.

Lindberg, Gary H. *Edith Wharton and the Novel of Manners.* Charlottesville: University Press of Virginia, 1975. Presents Wharton's style with a keen understanding of the ritualism of the social scenes in her work. Strong analytical criticism with a good grasp of Wharton's use of irony.

Lyde, Marilyn Jones. *Edith Wharton: Convention and Morality in the Work of a Novelist.* Norman: University of Oklahoma Press, 1959. Argues that there cannot be a complete understanding of Wharton and her work without examining her theories of morality and social convention. This study discusses her morality in its various aspects, including a chapter on the tragic element in her work. Also analyzes the artistic merit of morality and its relation to social convention. Includes a bibliography.

Wertshoven, Carol. *The Female Intruder in the Novels of Edith Wharton.* Rutherford, N.J.: Fairleigh Dickinson University Press, 1982. Somewhat limited in its view, this study nevertheless investigates an important aspect of Wharton's writings.

PATRICK WHITE

Born: London, England; May 28, 1912
Died: Sydney, Australia; September 30, 1990

Principal long fiction

Happy Valley, 1939; *The Living and the Dead,* 1941; *The Aunt's Story,* 1948; *The Tree of Man,* 1955; *Voss,* 1957; *Riders in the Chariot,* 1961; *The Solid Mandala,* 1966; *The Vivisector,* 1970; *The Eye of the Storm,* 1973; *A Fringe of Leaves,* 1976; *The Twyborn Affair,* 1979; *Memoirs of Many in One,* 1986.

Other literary forms

Patrick White first attempted to achieve literary success as a playwright in London in the 1930's. His work was largely rejected, partly, he implied in his autobiographical memoir, *Flaws in the Glass: A Self-Portrait* (1981), because of lack of connections in the theatrical world (although he did not deny that his talent was immature at that time). In particular, he noted that an effort to dramatize *The Aspern Papers* (1888), Henry James's famous novella based on an incident in the life of Lord Byron's mistress, might have succeeded had it found a sponsor, thanks to James's dialogue. Later, however, White successfully published a number of plays, mostly in the 1960's and 1980's; one play, *The Ham Funeral* (1961), has received much attention.

White's short-story collections, *The Burnt Ones* (1964) and *The Cockatoos: Shorter Novels and Stories* (1974), bring together the best of his shorter fiction published originally in Australian literary journals (for the most part); White also published in *The London Magazine,* where, among others, the fine stories "Clay" and "A Cheery Soul" appeared. White experimented with writing film scripts; one was filmed and received some mildly favorable reviews. His autobiographical memoir, already mentioned, mixes poetic impressionism with trenchant satire.

Achievements

White's stature as a novelist was already considerable, among discerning critics and discriminating readers in the English-speaking world, before it was confirmed by his reception of the Nobel Prize in 1973. The books which established White's reputation after World War II were *The Aunt's Story,* which has been widely recognized as a masterpiece, *The Tree of Man,* and the virtually unforgettable *Voss.* At the same time, White's fiction, though accessible to the general reader, unlike the work of such modernist masters as James Joyce and William Faulkner (or contemporary "experimental" fiction), has never achieved a wide readership. It is uncompromisingly addressed to the same discerning public which respects Joyce, D. H. Lawrence, Thomas Mann, and Marcel Proust.

If rather philistine criticism from intellectual readers as well as from the general public in Australia and elsewhere began in the 1960's, after *Riders in the Chariot*, *The Aunt's Story* is almost universally admired, and *The Tree of Man*, *Voss*, *Riders in the Chariot*, *The Vivisector*, *The Eye of the Storm*, and *A Fringe of Leaves* all have admirers who regard them as virtual classics. White's transformation of Australian history into epic and tragic vision in *The Tree of Man*, *Voss*, and *A Fringe of Leaves* is brilliant, and his vision of the fragmented world of the twentieth century is equally impressive, especially in *The Vivisector* and *The Eye of the Storm*. White's major successes ultimately assure their author a place beside the masters of prose fiction in English, including Joyce, Lawrence, and Graham Greene.

Biography

Patrick Martindale White was born in Wellington Court, London, on May 28, 1912, of parents whose affluence allowed them the opportunity to travel and enjoy the social pretensions available to prosperous Australians able to play the role of landed gentry. White's father, Victor (Dick) White, was one of several brothers who enjoyed prosperity in the family grazier business. Although the Whites could trace their lineage to respectable yeoman stock in Somerset, it was only in Australia that they achieved such success. Ironically, their social aspirations so far as the mother country was concerned were forever tainted by their status as "colonials" and Australians, the former penal colony being one of the least prestigious of the British dominions. White's mother was a Withycombe, and it is to the maternal connection that White attributed most of his imaginative and poetic gifts. At the same time, White disliked and despised his strong-willed and socially ambitious mother, Ruth. Toward his father, White was more ambivalent: he pitied Victor White for his weakness but found him impossible because he hid his emotions behind his social role as a landed gentleman.

Resenting and distrusting his parents as he did, and contemptuous of their social ambitions and their inclination to conceal their humanity behind public personae, White felt as much an outsider and rebel against the class to which he was born as is his painter hero, Hurtle Duffield, in *The Vivisector*, a working-class child adopted by a prosperous Sydney family.

White tended as a child to identify with his working-class nanny and her husband, a circumstance that helps to account for the persistent scorn and irony in his fiction directed toward the assumptions and manners of the Australian upper class. Not only was White an "outsider" in relationship to the Australian affluent class, but also he found that his status in English boarding schools, and later at Cambridge, was that of an outsider, by virtue of his Australian citizenship and accent. Hence, throughout his career, White as artist played the role of an outsider in a double sense, a condition intensified by his frequent alternation of residences between Australia and England in childhood and youth. White's major concentration at Cambridge was modern languages, primarily German, an interest augmented by time spent on the Continent, in the Germany of the Weimar Republic in its waning days, and in the early years of Adolf Hitler's rule, during summer vacations from 1932 to 1935. One German city, Hanover, is depicted in White's fiction as the archetypal German cathedral town from which White's characters Voss and Himmelfarb both originate.

After coming down from Cambridge, White spent a bohemian period in London in the middle and late 1930's, lodging mainly in Ebury Street, where he wrote three unsatisfactory novels and attempted without success to begin a career in the theater as a playwright. During this time, White fell under the influence of various intellectual friends and apprentice artists, the most important being the Australian expatriate Roy de Maistre, who was, like White, homosexual. (White seems to have accepted his homosexuality in his boarding school adolescence, and to have had little difficulty over it at the Cambridge and London of the 1930's.) In 1939, White's unsatisfactory first novel, *Happy Valley*, was published, and soon White voyaged to America to try his hand in New York literary circles and to begin a period of dissipation that lasted for several months. During this New York period, he completed his strong second novel, *The Living and the Dead*, a book that shows him mastering and exorcising some of the literary and cultural influences of his youth. The decision of White's working-class hero, Joe, to go to Spain to fight on the Loyalist side, is a symbol of commitment; it reflects White's own decision, reached after much guilt and self-analysis, to return to England (unlike some other English expatriates, such as W. H. Auden) and to offer himself to the campaign against Hitler.

Receiving a commission in the Royal Air Force's intelligence division, White spent the majority of his war years in North Africa, Alexandria, the Middle East, and Greece. It is clear that his years in the war were a significant rite of passage for him. He gained decisiveness and self-reliance as well as maturity; equally important, he met Manoly Lascaris, a Greek whose mother had been British; Lascaris was to become White's lover and homosexual spouse. Eventually, White and Lascaris decided on permanent residence in Australia, and White arrived there in 1947 with the manuscript of *The Aunt's Story* as a kind of "talisman." Hence, White was an Australian by a conscious choice, however reluctant the choice may have been. At the same time, his country was not always overwhelmed by White's decision, for although White used the Australian heroic past extensively in his fiction, he continued to be an outsider whose work did not always display clear relationships with Australian literary traditions.

White's long career in Australia flourished primarily at two residences: the small "farm" called "Dogwoods," really only a house, some outbuildings, and a few acres at Castle Hill, just outside Sydney and later incorporated into it. In 1963, however, White moved to Martin's Road in Sydney. In the Castle Hill period, White and Lascaris kept some cattle and tried to support themselves, at least partially, by some gardening. In later years, White's writing provided some support.

After five novels and a book of short stories, White was awarded the Nobel Prize in Literature for 1973. He used the money to establish a fund for struggling Australian writers of some talent and literary ambition. His later life was marked by increasing fame and some travel and by considerable attention from the media and from academic critics and scholars. He died in Sydney on September 30, 1990.

Analysis

Patrick White's fiction is concerned with the psychological depth and the emotional density of experience, and with the perceptions of the solitary self. This obsession with the isolated self in its search for fulfillment, its quest for an experience of unity and the divine, and its attempts to resolve the contradictions of its social heritage and its sexual nature, provides the central drama in White's fiction. On the one hand, White's fiction is rich in its command of the nuances of dialogue and social intercourse; it is possible to discuss his work in terms primarily of the novel of manners and social comedy. On the other hand, White's fiction is the work of an author obsessed with tragic vision and a religious quest. After *The Aunt's Story*, White's novels contain characters who struggle and overcome obstacles to understanding and vision, and whose lives culminate in a visionary or mystical affirmation. Stan Parker in *The Tree of Man* testifies to the unity of holiness of being; Elizabeth Hunter finds the eye of God in the center of her storm; Rod Gravenor in his final letter to Eddie Twyborn asserts the reality of love and faith in God. Such affirmations, though they represent White's own beliefs, if his autobiographical statements are to be accepted, are nevertheless to be seen as dramatic statements, paradoxical assertions aimed at overcoming doubts and confusion, and ultimately as aesthetically correct as the statements of faith in the poetry of the seventeenth century metaphysical poets. Despite all the parallels with Victorian novelists who write family novels with complicated plots, White was essentially a religious visionary akin to poets such as T. S. Eliot and W. H. Auden, and one very much at odds with the dominant spirit of his age.

White's first published novel, *Happy Valley*, is regarded by most critics as a failure, and the judgment is accurate. The novel deals with the passions and defeats of a group of characters in an Australian rural setting, but White is not entirely in control of his characters and plot, nor of his own style. The characters are mostly flawed romantics, somewhat obsessed by sex and erotic entanglements, and their emotions are often operatic and even Wagnerian in scope. The novel lacks the saving grace of White's magisterial and sophisticated irony, which tends to control the style in the later books and prevent both author and characters from lapsing into the excesses of emotion. White, however, does use the Australian landscape effectively as a dramatic backdrop for human drama played out under the eye of an inscrutable cosmos.

The Living and the Dead, the second published novel of White's prewar apprenticeship, shows considerable improvement. The novel, set in England, primarily London, casts a critical and retrospective look at the 1930's, but like many novels of the period by English and American writers, it displays a movement from empty intellectualism and social snobbery to political and ideological commitment on the part of some characters. The central figures in the book are Elyot and Eden Standish and their feckless and snobbish mother. Elyot and Eden provide an ironic contrast: Eloyt is a skeptical rationalist who wants to withdraw from experience, while Eden is a romantic who accepts life with its attendant suffering. Each finds a suitably ironic reward: Eden gains love with a working-class hero, only to lose him when he departs to join the Loyalist cause in the Spanish Civil War. Elyot, fearing involvement with others, is doomed to a life of loneliness until he finds himself exposed to the suffering he has tried to avoid by the death of his mother and the departure of his sister for Spain. Ironically, the experience of tragedy helps to heal Elyot's loneliness and alienation; at the end of the novel, he finds a satisfying release from the prison of himself.

Brian Kiernan in *Patrick White* (1980) has pointed out that there are many influences of T. S. Eliot's early poetry evident in the novel: London is Eliot's "Unreal City" of *The Waste Land* (1922), for example. It might be added that Elyot Standish is White's most Prufrockian character; he represents the same kind of paralyzed and life-evading intellectual that Eliot satirized in his early poetry, and White's portrayal indicates his own aversion to such a figure.

If Elyot is skillfully drawn, his mother, with all her vulgarities and superficialities, is equally effective, and her final spasmodic affair with an English jazz musician is poignant, as is the description of her final illness. Less effectively depicted, but still successful, are Eden, Elyot's romantic sister, and Wally Collins, the itinerant jazz musician just back from America, who is presented as representative of the rootless and uncommitted modern urban man. The weakest figure of all is Joe Barnett, the working-class hero, who is too obviously inspired by the abstraction of the virtuous proletarian which afflicted much of the fiction of the 1930's.

The emphasis on commitment and release from alienation with which the novel concludes is handled with much aesthetic tact and restraint. The adoption of the Loyalist cause in Spain is portrayed as more of a humanist commitment than an acceptance of an ideological or religious imperative, although no doubt White's sympathies were leftist. While White's characters find an exit from the modern wasteland through tragic self-sacrifice, the novel does not provide any assurance that the solution found is an enduring one, either for the characters who accept it or for the author.

With his next novel, *The Aunt's Story*, White established himself as a novelist of stature with a mature tragic vision. One of the most difficult things for a novelist to do, White believed, is to make a "virtuous woman" an interesting character. White accomplished this feat with Theodora Goodman, the aunt, who to all outward appearances lives an uneventful life, save for its tragic denouement. The real "story" of the spinster aunt is rendered through White's depiction of her inner life: despite Theodora's apparently barren existence, her experience is rich indeed.

Theodora's tale is told in three economically narrated sections: an Australian sequence called "Meroe"; a European interlude, "Jardin Exotique"; and a climactic American adventure, "Holstius." In these sections, Theodora's childhood, youth, and maturity are portrayed. She has a strong, rather masculine sensibility, and an imaginative nature with deep psychological insight, in an unprepossessing feminine body.

In Part 1, Theodora's journey from innocence to the experience of young adulthood is chronicled. The contrast between the heroine's strong desire for individuality and the conventional femininity and conformity of her sister is strongly marked. At boarding school in adolescence, Theodora develops one of her strongest relationships, a friendship with the sensitive Violet Adams, who, like Theodora, is fascinated by art and poetry. Theodora here reveals her intense and rather hard inner nature: she would like to be a poet, but her chosen subject would be landscapes and studies of rocks.

In her childhood and youth, too, Theodora shows more love for her father's country estate than for the city: Meroe is the "Abyssinia" or happy valley of innocence which provides a romantic metaphor for her years of growth and maturation. Later, following World War I, when Australia, after a brief emergence from its provincial slumber, relapses into a comfortable vacuous middle-class existence, Theodora lives in Sydney and cares for her mean-spirited and snobbish mother in the latter's failing years. In this period, the mysterious murderer Jack Frost provides some excitement and titillation for a bored middle-class population, and serves as a symbol of the mysterious Jungian shadow she longs to encounter. Her major chance for the conventional felicity of marriage and children occurs when she is courted by the apparently strong and manly Huntly Clarkson. Yet in a role reversal typical of many later White novels, Huntly soon is revealed as weak and somewhat feminine in his relationship with the resolute Theodora. Her skillfulness and strength strike a deathblow to their courtship.

Released from an unrewarding life by the death of her mother, Theodora finds herself free to seek her destiny abroad, and her journey of initiation to Europe constitutes the central action in Part 2, "Jardin Exotique," where she encounters a group of European eccentrics in a "grand hotel" setting on the French Riviera. Here Theodora exercises her talent for living, which had been suppressed and frustrated in Australia. She enters imaginatively into the lives of her companions, identifying with them and living their exotic histories vicariously. Her friends, a seedy group of expatriates, all have built up myths of romantic pasts. Theodora not only is a responsive and sympathetic consciousness for them but also is able to enrich their illusions by her own imagination. Ironically, however, each fantasy life proves to have been an artful lie near the end of Part 2, leaving Theodora with the sense of having been cheated when the pathetic reality of a character's past is revealed. The final irony occurs when the Hotel du Midi is destroyed by fire, probably a symbol of the coming war.

This section, rich in fine characterizations and virtuoso stylistic divertissements, is White's portrait of the Europe of the 1930's and his moral evaluation of it. Theodora, at first seduced by Europe and its illusions of a glamorous past and then disillusioned by the emptiness of its reality, emerges from the experience morally tested and unscathed, but still an unfulfilled and psychologically incomplete personality. It is not until Part 3, "Holstius," that Theodora confronts her own tragic destiny.

Part 3 takes place in America, where Theodora is overwhelmed by a sense of the vastness of the American continent and her own sense of isolation. A chance encounter with a traveling salesman on a train near Chicago results in a conversation that is symbolic: the salesman boasts of America's size and population in the best Babbitt or booster style, while Theodora is impressed with the abstractness of the individual self in a country where enormous numbers—of square miles, people, and sums of money—seem to dominate.

Leaving the train in the mountains of Colorado, Theodora wanders into a lonely canyon, driven by an urge to confront the unknown side of her inner self at last. Alone, at night, she hallucinates an experience of mythic force: a meeting with a stunted little man, almost like a folklore dwarf, who informs her that his name is "Holstius" (a name that perhaps both combines and caricatures the Jungian "animus" or male self in a woman, and the idea of "wholeness"). In Theodora's encounter with the imaginary Holstius, the masculine side of her nature emerges and speaks to her at last, and her inner conflicts appear to be resolved. The confrontation is traumatic, however, and the cost of it is the loss of Theodora's sanity, for the next day a nearby farmer and his family are forced to take charge of her, regarding her as mad.

The Aunt's Story is an expression of mature tragic vision, a novel which explores the possibilities and anguish of the solitary self in search of wholeness and fulfillment in a more assured manner than White's first two published novels. Unlike *The Living and the Dead*, it envisons self-discovery and self-fulfillment as a private quest, to which the changing political and social winds are incidental, almost irrelevant. In this respect, and in its hints of a symbolism drawn partly from Jungian psychology, as well as in its masterful weaving of a subtle texture of imagery, *The Aunt's Story* marks the beginning of White's maturity as an artist.

White's next three novels were much larger in scope and intention, epic in length at least. They also project a vision of the Australian past and of the middle twentieth century present influenced by that past. The first, *The Tree of Man*, tells the saga of Australia's pioneer past, as seen through three generations, but mainly through the experience of Stan and Amy Parker, homesteaders who wrest a farm from the wilderness. Stan and Amy are attractive characters, although rather conventional, and their lives are given a depth not found in most novels of pioneer life. Moreover, White provides splendid comic relief through their foils, the irresponsible O'Dowds, so that despite its length, the novel has considerable popular appeal, unlike much of White's fiction. Yet while Stan and Amy's life as lonely settlers in the outback often possesses a beauty and quiet dignity, their later lives are frustrating, and their sense of progress and achievement is dissipated in the disappointing lives of their children, and in Amy's later estrangement from her husband.

A brilliant reversal of perspective occurs in the closing pages. Here, the aged Stan Parker, apparently a neglected and forgotten failure living in a suburb of Sydney, rises to heights of tragic dignity. Accosted by an annoying fundamentalist evangelist, Parker rejects the easy formula for salvation the latter offers and asserts his own faith: he identifies God with a gob of spittle. To the evangelist, this is a blasphemous comment, and some have tended to treat it as a defiant and rebellious one, but, as William Walsh and some other critics have claimed, Parker's statement is a confession of faith in the ultimate goodness of life and of the holiness of being. This event marks the beginning of the paradoxical but assured religious affirmation that surfaces at crucial moments in most of White's subsequent novels.

The sense of an impressive tragic vision is heightened and intensified in White's next novel, *Voss*, which is, like *The Aunt's Story*, one of his better-known works. It describes its hero's Faustian ambition to be the first to conquer the Australian continent by leading an exploratory expedition across it. Voss's noble failure (based on an actual expedition led by the explorer Ludwig Leichardt) is counterbalanced by his mystical love for Laura Trevelyan, which transforms him from an exponent of the heroic and resolute will (like that celebrated by Friedrich Nietzsche in the late nineteenth century) to a more chastened and forgiving spirit. At the end, Voss is ready to accept his failure and death with a sense of Christian (or at any rate, religious) resignation.

Although a humorless and often exasperating character, Voss is a dynamic force who entices stolid Australian businessmen into financing his enterprise. Yet his nature is more complex than most of the unimaginative bourgeois Australians realize; only Laura, a complicated young woman who privately rebels against conventional Christianity and the age's worship of material progress, perceives the hidden sensitivities and beauty of Voss's character.

In the early stages of the novel, Laura and Voss seem to be in conflict, as their opposed but complementary natures seem to strike sparks from each other. Once Voss and his companions embark on their heroic journey in the Australian desert, however, Laura and Voss appear to communicate by a mystical or telepathic bond. Jungian psychology would consider each a person who has partially suppressed his hidden self: Voss has repressed his latent feminine qualities by devotion to the ideals of the masculine will; Laura has suppressed her masculine alter ego in the service of femininity. Their mystic communication enlarges and fulfills both their natures.

Defeated by the Australian climate and landscape, the treachery of his companions, and his own miscalculations, Voss's expedition culminates in his tragic death. Yet the heroic grandeur of Voss's failure is impressive: White's hero has a strength and ambition beyond that of the protagonists of many modern novels, and in his defeat he gains some of the humanity that he had so obviously lacked.

Voss's acceptance of the Southern cross as a symbol of his transformation from Nietzschean ideals to a more humane and forgiving outlook prompted some to assume that White himself was espousing doctrinal and institutional Christianity in *Voss*. This is not so, but White does affirm his personal religious vision, a synthesis of Jungian thought, Christian and Jewish mysticism, and poetic vision. His next novel, *Riders in the Chariot*, is perhaps White's most ambitious attempt to present the religious vision that undergirds all the fiction after *The Tree of Man*. *Riders in the Chariot* draws its title from Ezekiel's biblical vision of the chariot, but its prophetic and at times apocalyptic tone comes partially from William Blake, whose visionary conversation with Isaiah and Ezekiel in *The Marriage of Heaven and Hell* (1790) provides an epigraph. The four main protagonists, two men and two women (one black or "abo" painter, one Jewish mystic, one evangelical Christian, and one nature mystic) are all outcast visionaries, who combine to make a gigantic and impressive human mandala.

Himmelfarb is a scholar who turns from enlightened rationalism to the dense but powerful mystical images of the Cabala, including the "blue fire" of some Cabalist treatises. White's other seekers in the novel are religious questers who follow different and perhaps equally valid paths to their epiphanies and revelations. Miss Hare's nature mysticism is a naïve affirmation of being that resembles the kind of mysticism preached and celebrated by Ralph Waldo Emerson and Walt Whitman. By contrast, Mrs. Godbold's way is that of orthodox Christian piety, and Alf Dubbo's path is that of the romantic transcendentalist vision, as proclaimed by Blake and others.

Riders in the Chariot asserts the primacy of mystical search over conventional life, and it is also Blakean in its harsh indictment of evil in the modern world and in modern history. Evil is seen in various forms in this novel: it is the anti-Semitism and later the Nazism that Himmelfarb encounters; it is the smug self-righteousness of decaying puritanism in Miss Hare's tormentor, Mrs. Jolley; it is the narcissistic upper-class arrogance and contempt for the less fortunate shown by Mrs. Chalmers-Robinson; it is the feeble and thwarted religiosity of the Reverend Pask and his sister. Above all, it is the working-class bigotry and mule-headed chauvinism with its suspicion of outsiders shown by the Australian workmen, who reenact the crucifixion as a blasphemous joke on Himmelfarb on Good Friday. Primarily, White is inclined in this novel to see evil as a kind of spiritual blindness or lack of vision "of the infinite" as Blake's epigraph says, although the malice demonstrated by Mrs. Jolley and White's laborers is hard to explain in such simple terms. Nevertheless, White's sense of the overwhelming presence of evil in the modern world, especially "moral evil," or evil for which humans are responsible, is one of the most convincing features of the book. Equally strong is the sense of moral goodness or innocence in his four central characters, however much they may occasionally surrender to their flaws. Whether one is interested in White's attempt to portray the different paths of mysticism, it is hard to forget the strength of his portraits of four characters who remain admirable while enduring great suffering.

White devoted the early and middle years of the 1960's to works that were smaller in scale. In *The Solid Mandala*, which White considered one of his three best novels, his idiosyncrasies emerge more noticeably than in earlier works. This novel affirms White's Jungian religious vision more strongly than ever, and to underscore the theme for the obtuse reader, the noble example of Fyodor Dostoevski is invoked by Arthur Brown, the inarticulate visionary who is in part a spokesman for White. Arthur is set in contrast with his tragic brother, Waldo, a minor fiction-writer and critic hampered by excessive rationalism and rendered creatively impotent by fear of his emotions and imagination. Ironically, after failing as a writer and ruining his life by aloofness from humanity, Waldo is ambushed by his repressed sexuality near the end: he becomes a pathetic transvestite wearing his late mother's discarded dresses, and thus expressing the thwarted feminine side of his nature.

Arthur Brown's life also ends pathetically in a lonely old age, yet Arthur, one of White's holy simpletons or divine fools, lives a spiritually fulfilled, if obscure and misunderstood, existence. Arthur has a mystical sympathy with animals and nature and with some of the other less articulate characters, especially Dulcie Feinstein, a rich young woman to whom both brothers are attracted. A close communion also exists between Arthur and Mrs. Poulter, a working-class woman who is a kind of surrogate mother and wife to him. Arthur finds meaning in existence through his apprehension of mandalas, the Jungian symbol for the unity and holiness of all being, and of all innocent and life-enhancing forms of existence. Two major mandala symbols dominate Arthur's experience: a large green marble, or "solid mandala," which appears to him to be symbolic of the holiness toward which humanity should strive;

and a mystic dance in the shape of a mandala he performs with Mrs. Poulter.

Arthur and Waldo both lead tragic lives, if judged by conventional human standards, and each is an incomplete person: Arthur, the mystic and visionary, lacks a well-developed rational mind; while Waldo, the rationalist, is dead to all spiritual and transcendental existence. The story is thus a fable about the tragic split in humanity between the rational and the mystical faculties of the mind, between—if some psychologists, such as Robert Ornstein, are to be believed—the left and the right sides of the human brain. Yet despite the tragic nature of his novel, White makes Arthur much the more attractive of the two brothers, and reaffirms once more one of the themes of *Riders in the Chariot* and other novels: if a choice must be made between reason and mysticism, the path of the mystic, however despised in a rationalistic and technological age, is the more rewarding and redemptive road.

Although beneath the rough and grainy surface of *The Solid Mandala* there are surprising riches and pleasures, its sometimes crabbed and eccentric nature might have suggested to some that White had fallen into a creative decline in the 1960's. The three remarkable novels that followed, however, proved that the converse was true: *The Vivisector*, *The Eye of the Storm*, and *A Fringe of Leaves* not only testify to an impressive sustained surge of creative power but also show White in more masterful control of his material and of his artistic form than ever before.

The Vivisector describes the life of a rebellious and obsessed painter, Hurtle Duffield, who triumphs over enormous obstacles—an obscure background, a stultifying upper-class education, the cultural sterility of the Australian environment, numerous unhappy love affairs—to achieve triumph as a modern artist, a master of the techniques of impressionism, surrealism, and abstract impressionism, who successfully shapes Australian material into a solid series of enduring works.

In terms of form, *The Vivisector* is one of White's more daring gambles, for it ostensibly follows the shapeless biographical narrative mode of some of the most primitive works of fiction, tracing Duffield's development from his childhood to his death through a series of selected incidents and periods. Yet close inspection of *The Vivisector* shows that White has made a sophisticated use of a naïve narrative form in his treatment of Duffield's struggle. For example, Duffield's experience is rendered in terms of his relationship to a series of Jungian anima figures who serve as lovers, supports, and muses. These range from his crippled foster sister, Rhoda Courtney, a childhood rival but a supporter of his old age, through Ponce Nan, a vital but tragic prostitute, and Hero Pavloussi, the wife of a Greek businessman with whom he enjoys a brief, passionate, but unsatisfying romance.

As a painter, Duffield is a tireless worker and committed visionary whose paintings recapitulate many motifs familiar to White's readers. At one point, Duffield perfects his craft by painting rocks; the action suggests the need to come to terms with the intractable and substantial nature of the visible and phenomenal world. In his early stages, Duffield is a rebellious and defiantly blasphemous painter who charges God with being the great "vivisector," an unfeeling and cruel being who experiments with human suffering as a scientist dismembers animals—or as Duffield and other artists approach human life, seeing it as raw material for art. Guilt over the suicide of Nan, however, for which he feels partially responsible, and compassion for the frustrated homosexual grocer Cutbush, whom he paints as a surrealist figure machine-gunning lovers, work in Duffield a more tolerant and forgiving nature, and his work at last becomes more a kind of worship than blasphemy. In his last period, weakened by strokes, he becomes obsessed with painting in indigo and is characterized by a wry humility and kindness. Duffield thinks of his final, fatal stroke as a moment when he is "indiggodd," or departing "into God."

If *The Vivisector* is rich in vital characterizations and frequently possesses the exuberance of Duffield's raw energy, *The Eye of the Storm* is a splendidly controlled performance which demonstrates once more that when he chose, White could display a sure mastery of the techniques of the English novel of manners as practiced by such writers as E. M. Forster. *The Eye of the Storm* is constructed around the social comedy of the last days of Elizabeth Hunter, a regal but selfish matriarch of Sydney society who at eighty-six is slowly dying in her home on Moreton Drive while her son and daughter scheme to have her removed from the care of her nurses and placed in a nursing home. As is usual with White, however, the social comedy of the novel's surface masks tragedy and religious vision: in this case, the Learesque tragedy of Mrs. Hunter and her two children, and the crisis of faith suffered by her remarkable nurse, Sister Mary de Santis. Although the present time of the novel amounts to only a few days, White's narration re-creates, through the memories of the characters, the spiritual and psychological histories of their entire lives. Elizabeth Hunter, like White himself the talented offspring of a grazier, has during her life grown from a grazier's wife with social aspirations into a lady of poise and charm. At the same time, this majestic woman is portrayed as a dominating and selfish mother whose poise and beauty have given her untalented and unattractive daughter, Dorothy, an inferiority complex and driven her talented but narcissistic son to become both a successful London actor and a pathetic womanizing failure in private life.

Mrs. Hunter in later life, however, has been transformed during a hurricane on Brumby Island, when, abandoned and alone, she experienced a numinous epiphany in the still of the eye of the storm. As a result, she has become a compassionate, understanding, and deeply religious woman, although her piety is of the unchurched kind. This transformation lends a Learlike poignancy to her last days, when the poorly concealed malice of Basil and Dorothy is embodied in their effort to move her to a nursing home. The irony in this situation is heightened by the fact that Basil Hunter longs to play Lear himself, as the capstone of his career. Another tragic irony is Dorothy's idolizing of the Duchess of Sanseverina in Stendhal's *The Charterhouse of Parma* (1839): longing to be masterful woman like the Sanseverina, Dorothy resents her mother, whose social poise and personality recall that Stendhal heroine. The tragic irony in the actions of the children comes to a climax in their sentimental journey to their home ranch, where they finally surrender to their loneliness and huddle together in an act of incest during the night.

In contrast to the bleak and loveless lives of Basil and Dorothy, Mrs. Hunter finds solace in the loving care of Mary de Santis, her nurse and a reluctant believer in Greek Orthodox Christianity. Sister de Santis' care aids Mrs. Hunter in her final days, and in turn, Sister de Santis finds her own provisional faith reaffirmed by an epiphany of numinous divine immanence at the end of the novel in a mystic moment of water, birds' wings, and morning light, recalling biblical images of revelation.

An interesting and partially comic minor plot in *The Eye of the Storm* involves another of Elizabeth Hunter's nurses, the youthful Flora Manhood, who finds herself caught between resentment of her male lover and a temptation to join her cousin in a lesbian affair. Yet, despite White's obvious sympathy for Flora and her lesbian inclinations, the matter is resolved by her decision to remain heterosexual, while lesbianism is treated with a touch of comic irony. It is curious that White, himself a practicing homosexual, was able to treat homosexuality with enormous sympathy, yet finally imply the desirability of a traditional heterosexual identity.

Without a doubt, *The Eye of the Storm* is one of White's most carefully crafted and formally satisfying novels, and the one that most closely approximates the Jamesian ideal of complete mastery of novelistic form. This novel, which might have been considered the crowning work of a lesser career, was followed by other equally challenging works.

There are many impressive strengths of *A Fringe of Leaves*. Like *Voss*, this epic tale is inspired by the Australian past, specifically the experience of Eliza Fraser, a heroic woman who survived shipwreck, the loss of husband and companions, and captivity by aborigines, to return to civilization and become a legendary heroine. White's heroine, Ellen Gluyas Roxborough, is a woman of enormous appetite for living, who undergoes numerous metamorphoses on her road to destiny. At first an imaginative Cornish farm girl who longs to journey to some mystical or fabled sacred place such as Tintagel, Ellen marries a dry country squire, Austin Roxborough, and is made over, on the surface at least, into a polished eighteenth century lady and a dutiful adornment to her husband's estate near Winchester. On a sentimental journey to Australia (or "Van Diemen's Land") to visit her husband's rakish brother, Garnet, Ellen's inner self emerges, first in a brief affair with Garnet, then in the ordeal of survival of shipwreck and capture by "savages."

The shipwreck and the captivity sections form the heart of the narrative.

In the shipwreck, Ellen gradually has her civilized self stripped from her, along with her clothing, which is removed layer by layer. Later, after losing her husband and becoming a captive of the Australian natives, Ellen is obliged to confront her own authentic humanity. Her will to survive is indomitable; to cling to her sense of being human, she weaves a "fringe of leaves" as a kind of primitive clothing and an assertion of her belonging to a human realm above the world of nature. Yet a central question for her is the question of her relationship to her captors. Is she of the same order as the dark-skinned aborigines? The question is answered when she participates in a ritual feast at the center of the novel: it is a rite of cannibalism which not only provides physical nourishment but also, ironically, a sense of religious fulfillment. At the center of her "heart of darkness," Ellen finds her essential humanity.

The captivity section—which one critic has compared to the captivity narratives of prisoners of the American Indians—is followed by an idyllic interlude which represents a return to innocence for Ellen. In this episode, Ellen meets an escaped convict, a cockney murderer Jack Chance, who in London had brutally murdered his wife, but atones for that by falling in love with Ellen. With Jack, Ellen enjoys her most satisfying sexual relationship, but this Edenic experience, like all others, must end when Ellen crosses the Brisband River (likened to a snake) that separates the Australian wilderness from the settled country.

In the resolution of the novel, Ellen is both a heroine to other pioneers, especially the women, and a penitent. In her own eyes, her guilt over her participation in the cannibal rite and the betrayal of Jack is great, but her will to live triumphs over her sense of unworthiness and self-immmolation. At the close of the novel, it is clear she will return to routine and ordered life by marrying a pleasant, but somewhat inarticulate, Australian settler.

In its depiction of the indestructible will to survive, *A Fringe of Leaves* is a masterpiece, perhaps White's finest novel. Its central character, Ellen Roxborough, may well become one of the unforgettable heroines of literature.

Although *A Fringe of Leaves* has received much favorable comment, White's subsequent novel, *The Twyborn Affair*, was the object of a different reception, especially in America. This work is one of White's most controversial, for it attempts to deal with homosexual experience more candidly than ever before in White's fiction. Moreover, the novel is an interesting experiment in technique, because it is constructed of three sections which are essentially self-contained units, yet which also attempt to form a greater unity of a lengthy novel covering several decades.

Eddie Twyborn, the hero (and sometimes heroine) of the novel, is presented as a feminine personality in the body of a handsome male: an unusual "prisoner of sex" whose incarceration is indeed tragic. In Part 1, Eddie Twyborn appears as the transvestite lover of a likable older man, a somewhat decadent Greek living in France in the pre-World War I period. The couple are spied upon by Joanie Golson, a friend of Eddie's upper-class, overbearing Australian mother, and there is a certain amount of rather strained social comedy here until the affair ends with the death of Twyborn's Greek lover. In Part 2, Twyborn returns to Australia after the war as a decorated hero and tries living as a working man in the outback on a sheep ranch. There, he becomes emotionally entangled with the brutal foreman, Don Prowse, who finally rapes him, and with the owner's wife, who falls in love with him, misunderstanding his sexual nature while beguiled by his charm and sensitivity.

The failure to live peacefully as a man in Part 2 is followed by Twyborn's life in London in Part 3, where he surfaces in the late 1930's in female dress. This time, he is the madam of a brothel patronized by the rich and fashionable, and he becomes something of a celebrity. During this period, he suffers from a thwarted love for his patron, Lord Gravenor, who is finally revealed as homosexual also. A touching reconciliation with his selfish mother, now humbled by age and living in London alone, provides a kind of tragic recognition scene at the novel's end. This is followed by Twyborn's death in the London blitz.

Undoubtedly, Eddie Twyborn—the name is an obvious pun on "twice-born"—is one of the most interesting homosexual heroes in literature, and perhaps White's theme, the irony of a feminine nature in a male body, has never been treated with such insight. The novel's eccentricities, however, are pronounced, and the social comedy in Parts 1 and 3 often becomes tiresome. Like White's other major novels, the work achieves a kind of tragic dignity, despite its flaws, yet it appears vastly inferior to his other novels published in the 1970's.

White's strengths as a writer are many. He is a masterful stylist, and his characterizations are psychologically complex and memorable. His skill at social comedy is complemented by contempt for the arrogance of wealth and power. Beyond these gifts, however, White sought to create tragic fictional works on the Greek or Shakespearean scale in an age of irony and a diminished or disappearing tragic vision. White's fiction also, in the works following *The Aunt's Story*, articulates the author's own prodigious mythology and majestic religious vision. It is a vision drawing on numerous disparate sources—Blake and the Cabala, Carl Jung, Dostoevski, and the Bible—but it forms a synthesis which affirms the importance of a search for transcendence and the significance of mystical experience. Both his vision and his novels are likely to stand the test of time.

Edgar L. Chapman

Other major works

SHORT FICTION: *The Burnt Ones*, 1964; *The Cockatoos: Shorter Novels and Stories*, 1974.

PLAYS: *The Ham Funeral*, 1961; *Four Plays*, 1965; *Big Toys*, 1977; *Signal Driver: A Morality Play for the Times*, 1982; *Netherwood*, 1983.
POETRY: *The Ploughman and Other Poems*, 1935.
NONFICTION: *Flaws in the Glass: A Self-Portrait*, 1981.

Bibliography

Beatson, Peter. *The Eye in the Mandala, Patrick White: A Vision of Man and God*. London: P. Elek, 1976. One of the early books on White that, unlike other early studies, does more than survey his life and fiction. Bases the analysis of the novels on a cosmology derived from eclectic psychological theories and the teachings of world religions. The discussion is divided into the three worlds White's fiction represents: the world of being, the human world, and the natural world.

Bliss, Carolyn. *Patrick White's Fiction: The Paradox of Fortunate Failure*. New York: St. Martin's Press, 1986. This original study treats the fiction as a paradox, arguing that the individual failure so often expressed in the characters' lives does at times lead to their redemption. The theme of redemption through failure is then linked to the writing itself, on which White, according to Bliss's examination of the stylistic elements, imposes failure and at the same time creates a distinctive style. An extensive secondary bibliography is included.

Edgecombe, Rodney Stenning. *Vision and Style in Patrick White: A Study of Five Novels*. Tuscaloosa: University of Alabama Press, 1989. The five novels addressed in this study are *Voss*, *Riders in the Chariot*, *The Solid Mandala*, *The Vivisector*, and *The Eye of the Storm*, considered by Edgecombe to be White's greatest. Links these books by exploring the metaphysical thoughts they share and examines White's distinctive style. This style affirms his novels' thematic emphasis on alienation, isolation, and the subsequent search for a vision to free the individual from spiritual imprisonment.

Morley, Patricia. *The Mystery of Unity: Theme and Technique in the Novels of Patrick White*. Montreal: McGill-Queen's University Press, 1972. This early study is the only one that places White's work in the mainstream of European writing. Also shows how his fiction makes use of the international tradition along with the archetypes of Western literature. Morley argues that, through his intertextuality, White gives a unified view of a world beset by pain and suffering, but one that will offer salvation for those who seek it.

Texas Studies in Language and Literature 21 (1979). This special issue contains nine articles by international scholars on White's work, including one on his Australian and international receptions. Others take up White's style, his use of European literary tradition, his Australianness, his debt to the conventions of Romanticism and the teachings of Jungian psychology, and his theme of rebirth. One article discusses White's plays. A secondary bibliography is also included.

Weigel, John A. *Patrick White*. Boston: Twayne, 1983. Introduces White and his work by tracing his life and discussing each of his novels, as well as his plays. Although introductory and general, the book serves well the beginning reader of White's fiction. Includes a secondary bibliography and a chronology.

Wolfe, Peter. *Laden Choirs: The Fiction of Patrick White*. Lexington: University Press of Kentucky, 1983. While not taking any particular thematic stand, this book offers a substantial analysis of each of White's novels. Focuses in part on White's style, demonstrating how it affects narrative tension, philosophical structure, and the development of character.

JOHN EDGAR WIDEMAN

Born: Washington, D.C.; June 14, 1941

Principal long fiction

A Glance Away, 1967; *Hurry Home*, 1970; *The Lynchers*, 1973; *Hiding Place*, 1981; *Sent for You Yesterday*, 1983; *The Homewood Trilogy*, 1985 (includes *Damballah*, *Hiding Place*, and *Sent for You Yesterday*); *Reuben*, 1987; *Philadelphia Fire*, 1990.

Other literary forms

An intensely lyrical novelist, John Edgar Wideman has also published numerous short stories based upon family members, friends, and neighbors from his childhood community of Homewood, a long-standing all-black subdivision of Pittsburgh, Pennsylvania. Twelve of these pieces are presented as letters in his critically acclaimed collection *Damballah* (1981), which has also been published with two of his novels as *The Homewood Trilogy*. Wideman's autobiographical *Brothers and Keepers* (1984) blends facts with fictionalized characters and incidents as the author scrutinizes his own relationship to his brother, Robert Wideman, imprisoned for life in Pennsylvania's Western State Penitentiary. *Fever* (1989), a collection of twelve stories, combines themes of family and community with those of displacement, estrangement, and cultural loss. Uncollected poetry, reviews, and essays on black American literature by Wideman abound in the foremost scholarly journals and literary digests.

Achievements

When he emerged upon the literary scene in the late 1960's, Wideman stood out from his peers as a black American writer who did not address exclusively themes of racial conflict and militant nationalism. He concentrated instead on individual psychological struggles that transcend color lines. His earliest novels having been enthusiastically received, he was lauded as a successor to William Faulkner. Nevertheless, it can be argued that he really did not tap the depths of his talent until, influenced in part by slave narratives and African folklore, he initiated his Homewood series. Expressing the black American experience epitomized by Homewood's extensive French family and their fictive kin, *Sent for You Yesterday* received the 1984 Faulkner Award for Fiction from PEN, the International Association of Poets, Playwrights, Editors, Essayists, and Novelists. In spite of favorable reviews of his fiction, many people have accused Wideman of indulging in an unconventional style at the expense of theme. More often than not, though, his experimentation extends meaning by illustrating the impact of the past in addition to the inextricable bonds among generations. In fact, his autobiographical *Brothers and Keepers*, which displays some of his innovative techniques, earned a National Book Critics Circle Award nomination. Hailed as "the most authentic black blues voice since Billie Holliday," Wideman certainly merits consideration as one of the best American writers of his generation.

Biography

Born in Washington, D.C., on June 14, 1941, John Edgar Wideman initially aspired to be a professional basketball player. Consequently, he served as both a Benjamin Franklin Scholar at the University of Pennsylvania and captain of the school's championship basketball team. A member of Phi Beta Kappa, he was graduated from the University of Pennsylvania in 1963 with a B.A. in English. Promptly selected as only the second black Rhodes Scholar in history, he received his B.Ph. degree from Oxford University in 1966, specializing as a Thouron Fellow in the eighteenth century novel. He then spent one year as a Kent Fellow at the University of Iowa Writers' Workshop, subsequently returning to lecture at his alma mater, Pennsylvania. While writing and teaching literature at the University of Wyoming, he endured the conviction of his oldest son, Jacob, on charges of fatally stabbing another youth during a camping trip in Arizona. This tragedy recalls the imprisonment of his brother Robert for involvement in a robbery and killing. Wideman is Professor of English at the University of Massachusetts, Amherst, and he frequently contributes articles and review essays to *The New York Times Book Review* and to popular magazines such as *TV Guide*, *Life*, and *Esquire*. He lives in western Massachusetts.

Analysis

The recurring thematic emphasis in John Edgar Wideman's novels is placed upon history, both collective and personal. From homosexual college professors to ghetto junkies, Wideman's characters are often uncomfortable with their places in history and unsure that they even understand those few traditions that they do observe. Therefore, they shuttle between the imaginary and the real in order to rediscover the past, revive it, or at least preserve whatever parts they do recall. Despite Wideman's literary beginnings in the racially turbulent 1960's, when blacks in America articulated their estrangement from Africa, his white as well as black characters crave the rootedness that distinguishes those who have come to terms with their backgrounds. Shifting from the anonymous Northern cities of his first three novels to the clearly delineated Homewood of *Hiding Place* and *Sent for You Yesterday*, Wideman nevertheless consistently indicates that ignorance of heritage results in isolation and psychological turmoil.

Wideman forgoes strictly chronological plot development, adopting instead an intricate experimental style consisting of stream-of-consciousness narrative, long interior monologues, dream sequences, surrealistic descriptions, and abrupt shifts in time, diction, and points of view. Beginning each novel almost exclusively *in medias res*, he employs a technique influenced by the works of T. S. Eliot, James Joyce, and Jean Toomer, yet indisputably original. In *The Lynchers*, for example, he illustrates the traditionally victimized status of black Americans with a preface that cites more than one hundred documented lynchings. Reeling between their own ravaged communities and impenetrable white ones, the black protagonists of his first two novels, *A Glance Away* and *Hurry Home*, occupy a jumbled landscape where blues clubs coexist with biblical icons. Similarly, in *Hiding Place* and *Sent for You Yesterday*, Wideman retells the stories of his ancestors until a shack or a cape acquires the same expressive quality as a cross. As the author himself explains, "You can call it experimentation, or you can call it ringing the changes. . . . I value spontaneity, flexibility, a unique response to a given situation. . . . Getting too close to the edge but then recovering like the heroes of the Saturday matinee serials. That's excitement."

Dedicated to "Homes," Wideman's first novel, *A Glance Away*, creates thematic excitement with its treatment of two drifting men coming to terms with their pasts. After a year spent at a rehabilitation center for drug addicts, Eddie Lawson, a disillusioned young black man, returns to his listless, decaying urban neighborhood. Rather than celebrating, however, he spends his gloomy homecoming confronting the goblins that drove him to the brink in the first place: his mother Martha Lawson's idealization of his dead older brother, his girlfriend Alice Smalls's rejection of him for sleeping with a white woman, and his own self-disgust over abandoning a secure postal job for menial, marginal employment. Dejected and defeated by nightfall, he drags himself to grimy Harry's Place in order to cloak his memories in a narcotic haze. There, he is reconciled by his albino friend Brother Smalls with another outcast named Robert Thurley, a white college professor struggling with his own record of divorce, alcoholism, and homosexuality. Though discrepancies between wealth and power divide the two homeless men, each manages to urge the other to maintain his faith in people despite his guilt-ridden history.

A Glance Away generated much favorable critical response in particular for Wideman's depiction of the alienated Thurley. In trying to disavow his personal past, this connoisseur of food and art embraces a surfeit of creeds and cultures. "In religion an aesthetic Catholic, in politics a passive Communist, in sex a resigned anarchist," he surrounds himself with treasures from both East and West and indulges in a smorgasbord of the globe's delicacies. Yet as a real measure of the displacement that these extravagances so futilely conceal, he quotes lines from T. S. Eliot's "The Love Song of J. Alfred Prufrock," in which a similarly solitary speaker searches for intimacy in a world bereft of its cultural moorings.

Emphasizing his protagonists' self-absorption and the estrangement of their family members and friends, Wideman abandons strictly chronological plot development in favor of lengthy interior monologues. Conversations tend to be short; more likely than not they are interrupted by unspoken flashbacks and asides. Using speech to measure isolation, the author portrays both Eddie and Thurley as incapable of communicating adequately. Eddie, for example, becomes tongue-tied around a group of Southern travelers, shuddering in his bus seat instead of warning them as he wishes of the reality of the Northern mecca that they seek. Similarly, despite the empowering qualities of a gulp of Southern Comfort, Thurley delivers a lecture on Sophocles' *Oedipus Tyrannus* (c. 429 B.C.) fraught with "futility and detachment, . . . introspection and blindness." In one brilliant play on this speechlessness, both men suddenly converse as if they were actors on a stage. This abrupt emphasis on what is spoken—to the exclusion of private thoughts—stresses each man's imprisonment within himself. Flowing from a weaker artist's pen, *A Glance Away* would have become a mere exercise in allusive technique and stream-of-consciousness style. On the contrary, it reads with the effortless ease of a masterfully crafted lyrical poem. Key to its success is Wideman's careful alliance of form and content, not to mention his insightful treatment of a rootlessness that transcends the barriers of race.

The same compact length as the novel which precedes it, *Hurry Home* similarly focuses upon the theme of rootlessness. Its ambitious protagonist, the honors graduate Cecil Otis Braithwaite, is in many ways an upscale Eddie Lawson with a wife and an advanced degree. After slaving through law school, supporting himself with a meager scholarship and his earnings as a janitor, Cecil has lost his aspirations and his love for his girlfriend, Esther Brown. In search of something more, he escapes from his wedding bed to Europe, where he roams indiscriminately for three years among its brothels as well as its art galleries. In the tradition of Robert Thurley of *A Glance Away*, two white men as displaced as Cecil attempt to guide him: Charles Webb, belatedly in search of an illegitimate son, and Albert, a mercenary in Webb's employ who has also abandoned a wife. Too lost to save themselves, however, this pair can offer no enduring words of solace to Cecil.

Hurry Home is more sophisticated than *A Glance Away* in its treatment of the isolation theme. It suggests, for example, that the upwardly mobile Cecil is not merely disturbed by his personal past; he is estranged as well from his African and European cultures of origin. On the other hand, nowhere does *Hurry Home* convey the hope that pervades its predecessor. Cecil travels more extensively than does Eddie to reclaim his past, yet he gains no key to it to speak of. Confronting his European heritage merely confirms his status as "a stranger in all . . . tongues." He flees to the African continent by boat, "satisfied to be forever possessed," only to be forever rebuffed from a past that "melts like a wax casing as I am nearer . . . the flame." When he returns at last to his Washington, D.C., tenement, the fruitlessness of his journey is underscored. There, he finds all the same as when he first entered following his miserable nuptials. Symbolically limning his rootlessness, he switches vocations, abandoning the tradition-steeped protocol of the bar for the faddish repertoire of a hairdresser. Thus, "hurry home," the catchphrase for his odyssey, is an ironic one. Cecil really can claim no place where a heritage nurtures and sustains him, no history that he can truly call his own.

Hurry Home displays a masterful style commensurate with that of the later Homewood novels. In addition to a more controlled stream-of-consciousness technique, recurring Christian symbols, icons of Renaissance art, and fragments from Moorish legend powerfully indicate Cecil's fractured lineage. This second novel being a more refined paradigm than the first, Wideman seemed next inclined to break new ground, to address intently the racial polarization that had unsettled American society by the early 1970's, producing that period's most influential published works.

Distinguished from the previous two novels by its bawdy humor and portrayal of a professional black woman, *The Lynchers* is set in the generic northeastern slum, pockmarked by the self-inflicted wounds of the 1960's, that has become a Wideman trademark. Central to the action are four frustrated black men: Willie "Littleman" Hall, an unemployed dwarf; Leonard Saunders, a ruthless hustler turned repressed postal clerk; Thomas Wilkerson, a plodding fifth-grade schoolteacher; and Graham Rice, an introspective janitor with a persecution complex. Disenchanted with the superficial changes that the Civil Rights movement has wrought—the "job here or a public office there, . . . one or two black faces floating to the top"—these four conclude that violence is the only means to effect a lasting alteration of the white power structure. With Littleman as the ringleader and mastermind, they plan to flex the latent power of the black community and turn the tables on their oppressors by kidnaping and lynching a white policeman.

The plot falls apart, however, once Littleman is badly beaten by the authorities for delivering a militant speech at Woodrow Wilson Junior High School. Suspicion, distrust, and doubt override the remaining conspirators so that they foil themselves instead of their "white butcher pig" enemy. Thus, in a perverse way the weapons of the executioner do revert to black hands. Lynching becomes a symbol of frustration turned inward, of despairing hearts made so taut in their efforts to beat more freely that they burst.

Unlike *A Glance Away* and *Hurry Home*, *The Lynchers* is a total immersion into blackness. Perhaps the critics wanted another black-white character dichotomy, for their assessments of this novel were at best mixed. Nevertheless, Wideman again displays strong gifts of characterization without diminishing the theme's universal appeal. A continuation of his pet preoccupation, rootlessness, *The Lynchers* showcases men who feel acutely that they belong nowhere. Wilkerson, for example, is the Cecil type, the black professional who is alienated from his working-class roots, condescended to by whites possessing similar educational backgrounds and unwelcome in the clubs and restaurants that they patronize. Saunders, like Eddie, is a marginally good citizen, at once attracted to and repelled by "the life" of conning and thieving. In an intricate new twist to this scenario, Wideman depicts the older generation as a group as anchorless as the young. For example, Wilkerson's father, a drunk and a philanderer, stabs a longtime friend to death.

In its familiar inner-city setting and cast of alienated men (a passing reference is even made to Cecil Braithwaite as Littleman's lawyer), *The Lynchers* recalls Wideman's preceding works. In its use of a symbol generated exclusively from the black experience, it acts as a transition between these two novels and Wideman's fourth and fifth endeavors. No longer primarily gleaning symbols from Christianity and the European classics, here Wideman unifies his montage of dialogues with "the hawk," a symbol indigenous to the men's own harsh environment. This frigid, anthropomorphic wind that lashes the streets indicates the blacks' powerlessness and the hollow bravado of their ill-fated intrigue. They cannot even abduct the police officer without using one of their own people, his black girlfriend, Sissie, as a pawn.

After an eight-year interval during which he researched black American literature and culture, Wideman applied folk sources more fully than ever before in *Hiding Place*, one of the three works of fiction which make up *The Homewood Trilogy*. Challenged to enlarge his black readership without limiting the universal relevance of his themes, he chose to emphasize one black family based largely on his own Homewood clan. In this novel's swift, uncomplicated plot, Tommy Lawson, a tough, wisecracking youth from the black neighborhood of Homewood, is running from the police for his involvement in a robbery and killing. He seeks refuge among the weedy plots and garbage piles of desolate Bruston Hill, a once-fertile area to which his ancestor Sybela Owens fled from the South and slavery with Charlie Bell, her white owner's recalcitrant son. In the lone residence at the crest of the Hill, a rotting wooden shack sardonically known as "that doghouse," the reclusive "Mother" Bess Owens reluctantly offers her sister's great-grandson a temporary haven. After Tommy regains the courage to elude the authorities eager to convict him for a murder that he did not commit, Bess reaffirms her ties to her kin and ends her self-imposed isolation. Not knowing whether Tommy is dead, has escaped, or has been captured, she burns her shack and prepares to reenter Homewood to retell Tommy's tragic story so that another like it might never happen again.

Though Bess does not leave her longtime home until the novel's final chapter, *Hiding Place* is as much the story of her isolation from family as it is one of Tommy's. Just as Tommy has shirked his responsibilities as a husband, father, and son, Bess has turned her back upon the younger generations of kin whose ways are alien to her. Widowed and childless, she has retreated into an archaic life-style, shunning the twentieth century amenities of electricity and phones, in order to avoid intimacy with others. Physically rooting herself among Bruston Hill's ruins, she has been running from the present in her mind by focusing her thoughts on the past, especially the deaths of loved ones that have occurred. Only when she becomes involved in Tommy's affairs does she rekindle her active commitment to the family.

In *Hiding Place*, Wideman's style dramatically differs from those of the canonized white writers who were his early models. With a method many reviewers have compared to jazz, his characters unfold the histories of five generations of Lawsons and Frenches. Bess herself repeats certain key events in the family history several times; one of her favorites is the one in which Mary Hollinger revives her cousin Freeda French's stillborn baby by plunging it into the snow. Yet like a jazz improvisation, where instruments alternately play solo and play together, she retells the tale each time in a different way, varying her approach to it with different bits of superstition, mysticism, and folklore. Even Wideman's Clement, an inarticulate orphan similar to Benjy Compson in William Faulkner's *The Sound and the Fury* (1929), bears the unique stamp of the black American experience. As the author himself avows, Clement's assimilation into Homewood reflects the nature of the black community as a tolerant extended family.

Its legacy of songs, tales, and superstitions notwithstanding, the Homewood that finally draws Bess back is a model of urban blight, a "bombed out" no-man's-land of "pieces of buildings standing here and there and fire scars and places ripped and kicked down and cars stripped and dead at the curb." This dying landscape, and in a similar way Bess's ramshackle Bruston Hill homestead, proclaims the present descendants' dissociation from their ancestors and one another. In *Sent for You Yesterday*, the final installment of *The Homewood Trilogy* and the 1984 PEN Faulkner Award winner for outstanding fiction, this undercurrent becomes the novel's predominant theme. Carl French and his lover Lucy Tate relate the stories of a Homewood gone by to the latest generation of listeners, as if the recovery of the past is integral for the entire community's survival and solidarity.

Sent for You Yesterday cannot be divided easily into main story and subplots. All the episodes in it are major in scope and significance. The most memorable ones include the saga of the piano player Albert Wilkes, who slept with a white woman and murdered a white policeman; the tragedy of Samantha, whose college education could not shield her from grief and madness; and the bittersweet adventures of the resilient Brother Tate, an albino and best friend of Carl who communicates only with gestures and scat sounds. Retold by Carl's nephew Doot, a former Homewood resident modeled largely after Wideman himself, each tale conveys a lesson to a younger generation. More than mere exempla, however, the stories emphasize the cyclic nature of the human condition: each generation rises to further, alter, and often reenact the accomplishments of its predecessors. Thus, Uncle Carl's street in Homewood becomes to Doot "a narrow, cobbled alley *teeming* with life. Like a wooden-walled ship in the middle of the city, like the ark on which Noah packed two of everything and prayed for land." This determination to survive that the ark imagery calls to mind impels Carl and Lucy to share Homewood's history. By remembering past lives, by preserving traditions, they ensure their own enduring places in the memories of their heirs.

Traditions preserved and memories presented from black America's African past form the backbeat of *Reuben*, Wideman's next novel of community and interracial struggle. From a rusting trailer that his clients describe as part office, part altar to the gods, the dwarf Reuben serves the poor of Homewood in need of a lawyer, a psychologist, a warrior, or a priest. Like West African *griots* or oral scribes, who commit to unerring memory genealogies, triumphs, faults, and names, Reuben relies upon a mix of law and bureaucratic legerdemain that he has heard from his own employers and remembered. Like an obliging ancestral spirit shuttling prayers from this world to the next, Reuben negotiates pacts between the ghetto's bombed-out streets and the oak, plush, and marble interiors of City Hall. As he prescribes legal strategies and bestows grandfatherly advice, he also steers his clients to confront and abandon the views that have overturned their lives. When words and contracts alone will not do, Reuben rustles deep within collective memory and knots a charm: "A rag, a bone, a hank of hair. Ancient grains of rice. . . ." Reuben transforms garbage into power, excrement into nourishment, gristle into life. He preaches reincarnation and the nature of things dead to rise again, and he catalyzes his clients to seek similar transformations in themselves.

Infused with magic and spiritualism, *Reuben* also is illustrated by the ravaged images of the inner city. Wideman likens ghetto buildings to the rat-infested slave ships' holds, and the people in those buildings to roles of both predator and prey. Much of the Homewood population resembles a coffle of freshly branded slaves, slaves who are bound by laws instead of chains, by the welfare system or underworld crime instead of a plantation economy. Others are human versions of rats: snitching, beating, starving, stealing, and otherwise pestering their neighbors with an eat-or-be-eaten mentality. "There were historical precedents, parallels," Reuben understands. "Indian scouts leading long-hairs to the hiding places of their red brethren. FBI informers, double agents, infiltrators of the sixties. An unsubtle variation of divide and conquer." In this bleak landscape, the game of divide and conquer has changed little since enslavement.

From the beginning of his extensive literary career, critics have often compared Wideman's prose to the experimental fictions of the eighteenth century English writer Laurence Sterne. The sociable Sterne had befriended Ignatius Sancho, a gregarious former slave, a prodigious correspondent, and host of one of London's most popular salons. Sancho admired Sterne's mock humility and imitated his wit and playful style. In turn, Sterne admired the double entendre, self-scrutiny, and flair for detail in the letters of his African friend.

In Wideman's novels, the voices of the African Sancho and the Englishman Sterne converge. These works present black America from the perspectives of the enslaved and the descendants of the enslaved, as well as from the vantage of those whites who served as either tormentors and oppressors or benefactors and friends. These works warn of the potholes where our elders slipped before, and they expose the reader to the vistas that one often fails to notice and enjoy. They achieve Wideman's goal of ever "expanding our notions of reality, creating hard, crisp edges you can't swallow without a gulp."

Barbara A. McCaskill

Other major works
SHORT FICTION: *Damballah*, 1981; *Fever*, 1989.
NONFICTION: *Brothers and Keepers*, 1984.

Bibliography
Berben, Jacqueline. "Beyond Discourse: The Unspoken Versus Words in the Fiction of John Edgar Wideman." *Callaloo* 8 (Fall, 1985): 525-534. This essay centers upon the symbolic significance of Bruston Hill in *Hiding Place*. Security, fertility, kinship, rebirth—these are the qualities that Bruston Hill inspires, in contrast to the uncertainty and unfulfilled hopes that characterize the ghetto below. The ghetto residents often escape from the brutal realities of their lives by spinning lies, fabricating dreams, and creating private fantasy worlds.
Coleman, James W. *Blackness and Modernism: The Literary Career of John Edgar Wideman*. Jackson: University Press of Mississippi, 1989. The book contends that Wideman's fiction has evolved from a modernist emphasis on alienation and despair to a postmodernist portrayal of black communities that are strong and sustaining. Coleman evaluates the fiction for its fantasy, surrealism, magic, ritual, folklore, and mainstream influences. He appends an interview with Wideman on changes in the fiction.
_____. "Going Back Home: The Literary Development of John Edgar Wideman." *CLA Journal* 27 (March, 1985): 326-343. Coleman considers how Wideman transforms his childhood neighborhood into myth that unifies and directs *The Homewood Trilogy*. Once they can connect to their ancestors' lives, alienated and isolated characters in the books can revitalize themselves and rejoin their communities. Important is Wideman's use of gospel music, scat songs, dreams, oral stories, blues, the numbers game, street vernacular, and other aspects of black American folk culture.
Frazier, Kermit. "The Novels of John Wideman: An Analysis." *Black World* 24 (June, 1975): 18-38. This essay determines the relationship between

memory and imagination in Wideman's first three novels. Frazier connects Wideman's fiction to the works of William Faulkner, T. S. Eliot, James Joyce, and Laurence Sterne, and he examines Wideman's style of combining realistic and expressionistic techniques. All the novels have accounted for the damaging toll of enslavement and de facto segregation on black American families and communities.

O'Brien, John. *Interviews with Black Writers*. New York: Liveright, 1973. When questioned about his initial three novels, Wideman identifies literary influences and remarks upon his experimental style. Imagination, memory, culture, and history have inspired his narrative structures.

Putnam, Linda. "Home Again at Last." *Rocky Mountain Magazine* (April 4, 1982): 74-76. Here is a discussion of how the writer changed both style and language midway in his career. Wideman has set out to reestablish connections with his family, to transmit West African culture and myth, and to attract more readers in black communities.

Samuels, Wilfred D. "Going Home: A Conversation with John Edgar Wideman." *Callaloo* 6 (February, 1983): 40-59. This interview investigates how Wideman has found creative inspiration in his family history, African heritage, and black American folk culture. He discusses his concern for reaching black American readers and his transition from mainstream academic pursuits to the study of black American literature.

Wideman, John Edgar. "The Black Writer and the Magic of the Word." *The New York Times Book Review* 113 (January 24, 1988): 1, 27-28. Wideman explains his commitment to preserving black American patterns of speech and signifying. He shows that the double entendre and sound variation in the English of black American speakers are conscious attempts to establish self-esteem and respond to the manipulations of whites. He contends that black writers have been frustrated by publishers and critics who measure their worth according to fluctuating standards of literate speech.

_____. "Fear in the Streets." *The American Scholar* 40 (Autumn, 1971): 611-622. The author reflects upon many themes that pervade his novels and stories. Topics include the violence and anonymity of urban life, racism, and spiritual decay.

Wilson, Matthew. "The Circles of History in John Edgar Wideman's *The Homewood Trilogy*." *CLA Journal* 33 (March, 1990): 239-259. Wilson argues the Homewood sequence as a nontraditional family chronicle. The essay examines interconnections among individual family histories, events from American enslavement, and the histories of the Fon and Kongo cultures. A central theme of the trilogy is that black Americans resist annihilation and vanquish the oppressive acts of whites by telling their own stories and exposing their authentic histories.

THORNTON WILDER

Born: Madison, Wisconsin; April 17, 1897
Died: Hamden, Connecticut; December 7, 1975

Principal long fiction

The Cabala, 1926; *The Bridge of San Luis Rey*, 1927; *The Woman of Andros*, 1930; *Heaven's My Destination*, 1934; *The Ides of March*, 1948; *The Eighth Day*, 1967; *Theophilus North*, 1973.

Other literary forms

Thornton Wilder is as well known for his plays as for his fiction. *Our Town* (1938), *The Merchant of Yonkers* (1939, revised as *The Matchmaker*, 1955), and *The Skin of Our Teeth* (1942) were published with Wilder's own preface as *Three Plays* (1957). Collections of his short plays were published in *The Angel That Troubled the Waters and Other Plays* (1928) and *The Long Christmas Dinner and Other Plays in One Act* (1931). *The Alcestiad: Or, A Life in the Sun* was published posthumously (1977), as were a collection of his essays, *American Characteristics and Other Essays* (1979), and a set of cullings from his diaries, *The Journals of Thornton Wilder, 1939-1961* (1985).

Achievements

Wilder began his career as a teacher and in a sense never gave up the practice of that profession. He attempted to persuade generations of readers of the power of love, the need for individual integrity, the importance of maintaining faith in man's essential goodness. His clear style and straightforward narrative earned for him a broad readership, transcending categories of age, class, or education. Though detractors have labeled him middle class and middlebrow, he received enthusiastic praise throughout his career from such critics as Edmund Wilson, Malcolm Cowley, Edmund Fuller, Henry Seidel Canby, and John Updike. Wilder has been less a subject of scholarly research than some of his contemporaries—F. Scott Fitzgerald and Ernest Hemingway, for example—yet he has remained widely read since his first novel was published in 1926, and his versatility as a writer—of two Pulitzer-Prize-winning full-length plays and dozens of short plays—has brought him worldwide recognition.

Wilder won a Pulitzer Prize for fiction in 1928, a National Book Award in 1967, and the first National Medal for Literature in 1964, besides being the recipient of several honorary doctorates.

Biography

Thornton Niven Wilder was born in Madison, Wisconsin, on April 17, 1897, the son of Amos Parker Wilder and Isabella Thornton Niven Wilder. His father, a newspaper editor, moved the family to Hong Kong in 1906 when he was assigned a diplomatic post there. The young Wilder attended the Kaiser Wilhelm School, then the China Inland Mission Boys' School, where he harbored a brief desire to become a missionary himself. When his family returned to the United States, settling in California, he continued his education at the Thacher School in Ojai, then Berkeley High School, where he first began to write plays and act in class productions. In 1915, he entered Oberlin, a school his father chose because it was less socially elite than his own alma mater, Yale. At Oberlin, Wilder continued his involvement in theatrical productions and contributed prolifically to the college's literary magazine. After two years there, Wilder was allowed by his father to enroll at Yale, where, after a period of homesickness for Oberlin, he again proved himself, in the words of professor and literary critic William Lyon Phelps, to be "a star of the first magnitude . . . unusually versatile, original, and clever." Wilder was graduated with no specific career goals in mind. His father, believing a European experience would be broadening, sent him to study at the American Academy in Rome for a summer. Meanwhile, he searched for a suitable job for his son and found one at Lawrenceville, a preparatory school in New Jersey. There, when his French classes were over, Wilder began a novel with the working title *Memoirs of a Roman Student*, to be published as *The Cabala* in 1926. In the same year, Wilder took advantage of Lawrenceville's proximity to Princeton to earn his master of arts degree. He took a year's leave of absence from teaching and began work on a new novel, *The Bridge of San Luis Rey*, published to enormous acclaim in 1927, and earning Wilder his first Pulitzer Prize.

In 1929, Wilder was invited to teach at the University of Chicago by an Oberlin classmate, Robert Hutchins, who had just been named president of the prestigious Illinois university. Wilder was writing intensely: *The Woman of Andros* was published in 1930, a collection of short plays in 1931, and *Heaven's My Destination* in 1934. He remained at the University of Chicago until the mid-1930's, teaching one semester and writing during the next. More and more, he was drawn to the theater. He completed *The Merchant of Yonkers*, later revised as *The Matchmaker* (and still later transformed into the Broadway musical *Hello, Dolly!*) in 1937 and then turned to a more serious play, *Our Village*, soon retitled *Our Town*. This play was met with great enthusiasm when it opened in New York in 1938 and earned Wilder his second Pulitzer Prize.

The political upheaval in Europe, soon to involve America, found its way into Wilder's next play, *The Skin of Our Teeth*, which evoked a deep response in audiences both in the United States and abroad; the play was awarded a Pulitzer Prize in 1942. Wilder served in the army during World War II, and emerged with his optimism intact and his faith in humanity unshaken.

In the late 1940's, Wilder again turned to fiction, dealing with the problem of authority and dictatorship in *The Ides of March*. This novel reflected his talks with Gertrude Stein, whom Wilder had met in 1934 when Stein was lecturing at the University of Chicago. They shared ideas on the problem of identity and the creation of a believable reality for readers. Stein attempted to deal with these problems in her own novel, *Ida* (1941); Wilder took as his subject Julius Caesar.

In 1950, Wilder delivered the Charles Eliot Norton lectures at Harvard, then traveled—always a stimulation and joy for him—and worked on *The Alcestiad*, his retelling of the Greek legend of Alcestis. In the early 1960's, he retreated to Arizona to write *The Eighth Day*. By the end of the decade, his pace had slowed. He worked on short plays and completed his quasi-autobiographical *Theophilus North*. He died in his sleep on December 7, 1975.

Analysis

Thornton Wilder's seven novels, written over nearly fifty years, show a remarkable consistency in theme and tone. His early books, contemporaneous with Theodore Dreiser's *An American Tragedy* (1925) and Sinclair Lewis' *Arrowsmith* (1925), are far from the realism and naturalism which dominated American literature in the 1920's and 1930's. Though he joined groups active in civil rights and social justice, these themes did not find their way into his works in the manner of John Dos Passos or John Steinbeck. His later works, similarly, show none of the interest in psychoanalysis which may be found in the works of Sherwood Anderson, for example, none of the angry intensity of a Norman Mailer.

Wilder chose not to comment on contemporary politics, social problems, psychological *Angst*, or cultural changes, preferring instead to mine those themes he considered of utmost importance: love, brotherhood, tolerance, and faith. His faith was expressed not in strictly Judeo-Christian terms, but in humanistic convictions which incorporated diverse religious beliefs. Without being didactic, Wilder wished to educate, to inspire, to allow his readers to move beyond an obsession with the individual case to a consideration of humankind and its history. His second novel, *The Bridge of San Luis Rey*, is representative of the themes which recur throughout his works, and his final statement in that book well expresses his one abiding conviction: "There is a land of the living and a land of the dead and the bridge is love, the only survival, the only meaning."

Though Wilder drew on his memories of Rome for his first novel, *The Cabala*, the book is a fantasy, only incidentally autobiographical. The "Cabala" is an aristocratic social circle in which two Americans find themselves involved. These two, Samuele and James Blair, represent Wilder's interest in duality of personality which recurs in later works and results in part from his having been born a twin (his sibling was stillborn). Samuele is a typical Wilder character: innocent, sensitive, stable, with a deep strain of common sense. Blair is the dry intellectual so obsessed by books that he fears real life.

Samuele is the vehicle by which a number of episodes are linked, since he is asked by various members of the Cabala to intervene in the lives of others. First, he is called in to restrain the impetuous and licentious Marcantonio, but fails: the young man engages in incest and then kills himself. Then, Samuele must console the lovely young Alix, unfortunate enough to fall in love with James Blair. Finally, he must deal with the royalist Astrée-Luce in her plot to "prop up" and empower cynical Cardinal Vaini. Samuele is baffled by these obsessed and decadent characters, and is hardly satisfied by an explanation offered to him that the group is possessed by ancient gods who have passed on their power to unsuspecting mortals. Finally, on advice from Vergil's ghost, Samuele returns to America. For Wilder, Europe, for all its richness of culture, was too deeply mired in the past to allow the spirit to grow. Samuele could thrive only in America, a country of youth and intellectual freedom.

In his second novel, *The Bridge of San Luis Rey*, Wilder again uses a structure of separate episodes linked by one thread, this time the collapse of an ancient bridge over a chasm in Peru. Again, he offers a religious figure, but instead of the jaded Cardinal, there is the sympathetic brother Juniper, who searches for meaning in the deaths of those who perished: the Marquesa de Montemayor; Pepita, her maid; Esteban, a young Indian; Uncle Pio, an aging actor, and his ward Jaime. Brother Juniper finds that the five were victims of love, and those who survive are forced to a change of consciousness by the deaths of those they spurned or misjudged.

As in *The Cabala*, Wilder explores twinness in the tale of Esteban and his twin brother Manuel. The two are extraordinarily close, and when Manuel falls in love with a woman, Esteban becomes despondent. Yet he nurses his brother faithfully after Manuel is injured, suffering his delirious ravings until Manuel dies. Nearly mad with grief, Esteban first assumes his dead brother's identity, then attempts suicide, only to die when the bridge collapses. A sea captain, Alvarado, had offered to sign him on his crew, and tried to console him by reminding him, "We do what we can. We push on, Esteban, as best we can. It isn't for long, you know. Time keeps going by. You'll be surprised at the way time passes." Wilder was always conscious of the brevity of life and the need, therefore, to cling to love where one finds it. In *The Bridge of San Luis Rey*, he urges the celebration and fulfillment of love as the only meaning in the world.

From eighteenth century Peru, Wilder moved to pre-Christian Greece in his third novel, *The Woman of Andros*, again dealing with love; its theme, as in *The Bridge of San Luis Rey*, is "How does one live? . . . What does one do first?" Society on the island of Brynos was not essentially different, according to Wilder, from that of his own America. When Chrysis, the central character, says "Lift every roof, and you will find seven puzzled hearts," she speaks of man's bewilderment in the face of the unknown, his search for communion, his need for love—basic human struggles which are not rooted in any particular time or place.

In 1930, however, a number of critics were disappointed with this message. In a time of economic and social crisis, Wilder seemed to retreat into yet another esoteric setting, far removed from the urgencies of the day. One critic writing in *The New Republic* dubbed Wilder a "Prophet of the Genteel Christ" who wrote for a wealthy elite not interested in social problems. The article touched off a month of debate, with letters supporting or attacking Wilder appearing in each issue of the journal. At the end of December, Wilder finally received his greatest support when Sinclair Lewis, accepting the Nobel Prize for Literature, praised his fellow writer "who in an age of realism dreams the old and lovely dreams of the eternal romantic."

Throughout the controversy, Wilder remained silent. He was sensitive to the criticism, however, and in his next novel attempted to find a setting and characters which would appear relevant to his own time. *Heaven's My Destination* concerns the misadventures of George Marvin Brush, a salesman of religious textbooks, who travels across Depression-ridden America preaching, moralizing, and interfering in the lives of ordinary citizens. Converted to Bible Belt Christianity by a woman evangelist at Shiloh Baptist College, he has proceeded to spread his own fundamentalist version of the Gospel wherever he goes. Wilder returned to the episodic structure of his first two novels in presenting George's adventures in picaresque form. Unlike Don Quixote, however, with whom George has been compared, Wilder's protagonist is rarely endearing, more often exasperating.

George is different from the "normal" Americans with whom he interacts, yet Wilder is satirizing not only his earnest hero, but also those who spurn him. George, after a while, becomes depressed by his society and exclaims, "It's the world that's crazy. Everybody's crazy except me; that's what's the matter. The whole world's nuts." Why, asks this ardent believer, is God "so slow" in changing things?

For all his misconceptions, George does act upon truly humanistic beliefs. He takes a vow of poverty and occasionally of silence, refuses his interest from the bank and dislikes raises in pay. "I think everybody ought to be hit by the depression equally," he says, as he gives away his money. Like Samuele, George maintains his integrity in an environment which threatens to corrupt him and is selfless in his efforts to aid those who need him—even if they protest against his interference.

George Brush was Wilder's answer to the critics who dismissed his previous works, and in a sense, he gave them what he thought they deserved—a priggish, monomaniacal American overreacting to mundane occurrences. Even with such a cartoon-strip character, however, Wilder could not help but imbue him with gentleness and humility, and for Edmund Wilson, George

Brush emerged as a "type of saint . . . and therefore a universal character."

In part, it was George's earnestness, his reluctance to see evil and his determination to do good, that caused Wilder to exclaim, "I'm George Brush." Certainly his persistent faith in humanity unites him with his character, but there is further correspondence in Brush's essential isolation, the loneliness which causes him to reach out for companionship. For Wilder, such isolation was characteristically American: solitude was to be treasured, but loneliness was threatening. He once noted an adage which he thought well expressed the American spirit: "If you can see the smoke from your neighbor's chimney, you're too near." In his next novel, thirteen years later, he created yet another lonely, questing character, but this time Wilder eschewed satire and humor to deal seriously with man powerful before the world, yet powerless before death.

The Ides of March, written just after World War II, deals with an archetypal dictator, Julius Caesar. Here, Wilder aimed to revive the spirit of the man from a palimpsest of historical and fictional treatments. The novel, therefore, becomes a study in identity and a technical challenge in creating for readers a believable reality. In structure, *The Ides of March* differs sharply from Wilder's previous work. He assembles fictionalized letters, diary entries, messages, and documents in an effort to offer a vibrant picture of Roman life. Caesar himself is a man obsessed not only with power but also with death, and he must learn how to celebrate life faced with a dark world and an uncaring universe.

Wilder contrasts Caesar with his friend and counselor Lucius Turrinus, who offers a philosophy which was by then familiar to Wilder's readers: "The universe is not aware that we are here," Lucius tells Caesar. "Hope has never changed tomorrow's weather." Yet love could change the world, and Caesar comes to exclaim, "I wish to cry out to all the living and all the dead that there is not part of the universe that is untouched by bliss."

Caesar's urge to seize life and live it to the fullest causes his companions to label him rash and irreverent; but he feels himself to be above them because he has clearly envisioned his own death, and in so doing believes himself "capable of praising the sunlight." Wilder transfers to the Roman dictator much of the sentiment expressed in his play *Our Town*, where Emily Webb dies and is allowed to return to Earth for one day. Only then does she realize how wonderful life is, how desperately she wants to live, and how foolish most people are in squandering their brief existence. Caesar refuses to be foolish; perhaps he will be ruthless, impetuous, temperamental, passionate— but he will live each moment.

The Ides of March had two major inspirations: the war itself, with its focus on the use and misuse of power, the character of a dictator, and the death of innocents; and a personal confrontation with death—first that of Wilder's friend and mentor Edward Sheldon, a playwright whose character informs

Lucius Turrinus, and upon whose wisdom Wilder often relied; then, and most important, the death of his mother, his most ardent supporter and admirer.

After *The Ides of March* was published, Wilder devoted nearly two decades to his plays; not until 1967 would he write another novel. In *The Eighth Day*, Wilder returned to an American setting, the turn-of-the-century Midwest, and to traditional narrative. He carefully unfolds the tale of John Barrington Ashley, tried for the murder of his neighbor, Breckenridge Lansing, and found guilty. Five days after being sentenced to death, he escapes with the help of an unknown accomplice. Five years later, Ashley is found innocent on the basis of new evidence. Ashley's flight, which takes him to Chile, is contrasted with the life of his wife and children in a small town which barely tolerates the outlaw's family.

Wilder's concern, however, is not with one family's history, but with the archetypal family, and Ashley represents not one wronged citizen, but the man of the Eighth Day, a new man with faith in humanity and a strong commitment to working toward a better future. Wilder tells his readers that faith and action can bring about a better life. Throughout the novel, he assigns several characters to speak for him, most notably Dr. Gillies, a country physician, who observes,

> Nature never sleeps. The process of life never stands still. The creation has not come to an end. The Bible says that God created man on the sixth day and rested, but each of those days was many millions of years long. That day of rest must have been a short one. Man is not an end but a beginning. We are at the beginning of the second week. We are children of the eighth day.

On the eighth day, man must begin to forge his own future, and though Dr. Gillies knows that there will be "no Golden Ages and no Dark Ages," still he believes in the power of each individual to work toward the collective fate of humankind.

Because the novel is concerned essentially with imparting a message, the characters—as in *The Cabala* and *Heaven's My Destination*—are not fully realized individuals, but instead are one-dimensional representations of predictable types. The Ashley family, ignored and rebuffed by their neighbors, never lose their aristocratic elegance. They persist in their nightly reading of William Shakespeare even when economic problems would seem severe enough to lower their morale. Here, Wilder pleads for art as the true salvation of mankind, its highest achievement, "the only satisfactory products of civilization."

Through Dr. Gillies, who echoes the sentiments of Chrysis in *The Woman of Andros* and Lucius in *The Ides of March*, Wilder reminds his readers that they occupy only a brief span of time when contrasted with eternity and so must exhibit proper humility. They are small specks in a vast universe, and their duty is not to enhance their own egos, but to work together toward a higher good. "We keep saying that 'we live our lives,'" Dr. Gillies exclaims. "Shucks! Life lives us." Wilder had sent this message for forty years; he insisted again, in the turbulent, self-conscious, self-indulgent late 1960's, on attempting to awaken his readers to his own values.

Wilder was seventy when *The Eighth Day* was published, the time of a writer's life when he might consider writing his autobiography or memoirs. Wilder, however, chose not to reveal his memories or bare his soul: instead, he wrote a last novel, *Theophilus North*, with a protagonist, he once told an interviewer, who was what his twin brother might have been if he had lived.

Theophilus may be Wilder's imaginary brother, but his life bears striking similarities to that of Wilder himself. He has lived in China, attended Yale, and spent a summer in Rome; after teaching at a boys' preparatory school in New Jersey, he leaves his job to explore life and goes to Newport, Rhode Island—a town where Wilder often vacationed—to set his new course. Like Samuele, Theophilus is gentle, well-mannered, polite, helpful. These traits endear him to the Newport natives, and he is asked to intervene in several lives. The structure here, as in many previous Wilder novels, is one of loosely linked episodes.

Theophilus succeeds in such tasks as separating mismatched lovers, liberating an aging man from the manipulation of his daughter, allowing a shrewish wife to mend her ways, extricating one man from his unwitting involvement with criminals, bringing home a wayward husband, finding a lover for a maimed young man, and impregnating a woman whose husband is sterile. Throughout, Theophilus is a typical Wilder hero—a man of good will, of faith, of sincerity.

Theophilus North is Wilder's only novel in which sexuality is of central importance. The sexual episodes are conducted offstage and seem unbelievable and strained. Theophilus, in his seductions and in his everyday relationships with his neighbors, is curiously unaffected and uninvolved. Though he displays emotion, he seems to lack passion.

Wilder's characters, from Samuele to John Ashley, from the circle of Roman aristocrats to Newport society, remain thin and superficial, emblems rather than specific, rounded human beings. Such characterization was in keeping with Wilder's conviction that each individual was, in the long history of the human race, of but little importance. His trials, anguish, suffering, and joy were not significant when placed in the context of all human suffering and all human joy. Rather than writing about individual human beings, Wilder chose to write about humanity; rather than dealing with the intricacies of individual lives, he chose to compress those lives into brief episodes to demonstrate the multiplicity of life.

Wilder, deeply philosophical and reflective, was always the teacher, the educator, with an abiding concern for the future of humanity. "Hope," he wrote in *Theophilus North*, "is a projection of the imagination; so is despair.

Despair all too readily embraces the ills it foresees; hope is an energy and arouses the mind to explore every possibility to combat them." In all his works, he exuded hope and, even in dark times, urged his readers to work together in faith and in love.

Linda Simon

Other major works
   PLAYS: *The Trumpet Shall Sound*, 1920; *The Angel That Troubled the Waters and Other Plays*, 1928 (includes sixteen plays); *The Happy Journey to Trenton and Camden*, 1931 (one act); *The Long Christmas Dinner*, 1931 (one act: as libretto in German, 1961, translation and music by Paul Hindemith); *The Long Christmas Dinner and Other Plays in One Act*, 1931 (includes *Queens of France, Pullman Car Hiawatha, Love and How to Cure It, Such Things Only Happen in Books, The Happy Journey to Trenton and Camden*); *Lucrece*, 1932 (adaptation of André Obey's *Le Viol de Lucrèce*); *A Doll's House*, 1937 (adaptation of Henrik Ibsen's play); *The Merchant of Yonkers*, 1938 (adaptation of Johann Nestroy's *Einen Jux will er sich machen*); *Our Town*, 1938; *The Skin of Our Teeth*, 1942; *The Matchmaker*, 1954 (revision of *The Merchant of Yonkers*); *A Life in the Sun*, 1955 (in German), 1977 (in English; commonly known as *The Alcestiad*; one act as *The Drunken Sisters*, 1952); *Plays for Bleecker Street*, 1962 (three one-acts: *Someone from Assisi, Infancy*, and *Childhood*).
   SCREENPLAYS: *Our Town*, 1940 (with Frank Craven and Harry Chantlee); *Shadow of a Doubt*, 1943 (with Sally Benson and Alma Revelle).
   NONFICTION: *The Intent of the Artist*, 1941; *American Characteristics and Other Essays*, 1979; *The Journals of Thornton Wilder, 1939-1961*, 1985.
   TRANSLATION: *The Victors*, 1948 (of Jean-Paul Sartre's play *Morts sans sépulture*).

Bibliography
Goldstein, Malcolm. *The Art of Thornton Wilder*. Lincoln: University of Nebraska Press, 1965. An early and still useful introduction to Wilder's novels and plays. A short biographical sketch is followed by an in-depth look at his work through the one-act play *Childhood* (1962). Includes bibliographical notes and an index.
Goldstone, Richard H. *Thornton Wilder: An Intimate Portrait*. New York: Saturday Review Press, 1975. An intimate portrait of Wilder by a close friend who had written previous studies on the subject, had access to personal documents, and interviewed family and friends. Includes notes, a selected bibliography, and an index.
Harrison, Gilbert A. *The Enthusiast: A Life of Thornton Wilder*. New York: Ticknor & Fields, 1983. A chatty biographical study of Wilder by a biogra-

pher who was provided access to Wilder's notes, letters, and photographs. Harrison successfully re-creates Wilder's life and the influences, both good and bad, that shaped him.

Simon, Linda. *Thornton Wilder: His World.* Garden City, N.Y.: Doubleday, 1979. A solid biographical study of Wilder that includes examinations of his published works and photographs, notes, a bibliography, and an index.

Wilder, Amos Niven. *Thornton Wilder and His Public.* Philadelphia: Fortress Press, 1980. A short critical study of Wilder by his older brother, who offers an inside family look at the writer. A supplement includes Wilder's "Culture in a Democracy" address and a selected German bibliography.

A. N. WILSON

Born: Stone, England; October 27, 1950

Principal long fiction

The Sweets of Pimlico, 1977; *Unguarded Hours*, 1978; *Kindly Light*, 1979; *The Healing Art*, 1980; *Who Was Oswald Fish?*, 1981; *Wise Virgin*, 1982; *Scandal*, 1983; *Gentlemen in England*, 1985; *Love Unknown*, 1986; *Incline Our Hearts*, 1988; *A Bottle in the Smoke*, 1990.

Other literary forms

Despite the regularity with which A. N. Wilson produces novels, he has never been limited to that form alone. He is one of the best-known journalists in Great Britain, with particularly close connections to *The Spectator*, the prestigious weekly journal of conservative social and political opinion. He has served as the literary editor of that periodical, but his own writing has not been confined to reviewing books, and he is often a commentator on social and political subjects. Wilson has a special interest in religion, and aside from his occasional essays on that subject, he has published a study of the layman's dilemma in matters of Christian belief, *How Can We Know?* (1985). He teaches at the University of Oxford and has written biographies of Sir Walter Scott, John Milton, Hilaire Belloc, Leo Tolstoy, and C. S. Lewis. He has also published volumes of essays and reviews, *Pen Friends from Porlock* (1987) and *Eminent Victorians* (1990).

Achievements

The Sweets of Pimlico gained for Wilson the John Llewelyn Rhys Memorial Prize in 1978, and *The Healing Art* won three prizes, including the Somerset Maugham Award for 1980 and the Arts Council National Book Award for 1981. *Wise Virgin* brought him the W. H. Smith Annual Literary Award in 1983, and his study of Scott, *The Laird of Abbotsford: A View of Sir Walter Scott* (1980), won the Rhys prize for him once again.

There are several formidable writers in Wilson's generation, but it is possible to distinguish Wilson as the best of the new satirists and, as such, one of the most perceptive commentators on Great Britain in the last quarter of the twentieth century. Given his talent, and his capacity to comment attractively (if sometimes improperly) on the excesses of his society, it is not surprising that he has become something of a public personality, the literary figure most often identified with the "Young Fogeys," that amorphous group of literary, social, and political figures who espouse the principles of landowning Toryism and look with nostalgia back to the old Empire and to the days when High Anglicanism was a spiritual power in the land. Part of their conservatism is sheer mischief-making, part of it a matter of temperament and class, but in Wilson's case, it is a love for the aesthetic detail of what he sees as a richer and more caring society (which does not stop him from making wicked fun of it).

Biography

Andrew Norman Wilson, born in Stone, Staffordshire, England, in 1950, was educated at Rugby, one of the great English public schools, and at New College, Oxford. He won the Chancellor's Essay Prize in 1971 and the Ellerton Theological Prize in 1975. He has been a lecturer in English at New College, and at St. Hugh's College, Oxford. Aside from his work in *The Spectator*, he has published in *The Times Literary Supplement* and *The Sunday Telegraph*. Wilson is a Fellow of the Royal Society of Literature. He is married and has two daughters.

Analysis

A. N. Wilson's novels are part of the tradition of sophisticated wittiness, sometimes comic, sometimes satiric, which explores the English caste system (with particular emphasis upon the middle and upper-middle classes), long a subject for English letters, particularly in the 1930's. The promise that World War II would not only stop international tyranny but also destroy the British social hierarchy has not, in fact, come true. Great Britain may have fallen on hard times economically, and may be of less importance politically, but the class structure, though shaken, still prevails.

Evelyn Waugh was the foremost social satirist prior to the war and until his death in 1966, commenting on the dottier aspects of life among the wellborn, the titled, the talented, and the downright vulgar climbers and thrusters, determined to ascend the greasy pole of social, political, and economic success. Wilson's first novel, *The Sweets of Pimlico*, might well have been written by a young Waugh. Thinly plotted, but written with astringent grace and wide-ranging peripheral insights into the fastidious improprieties of the privileged, it tells of the queer love life of Evelyn Tradescant (whose surname alone is appropriately bizarre, but whose credentials are established by the fact that her father is a retired diplomat, Sir Derek Tradescant, of some minor political reputation).

By chance, Evelyn tumbles (literally) into an association with a much older man, Theo Gormann, wealthy, pleased by the attentions of a young woman, and mysteriously ambiguous about his past, which seems to have involved close association with the Nazis before the war. While Theo urges his peculiar attentions on Evelyn, so does his closest friend, John "Pimlico" Price, and Evelyn learns that everybody seems to know one another in varyingly confusing ways. Her father and mother remember the Gormann of Fascist persuasion, and her brother, Jeremy, is also known to Theo through his

Critical Survey of Long Fiction

connection with Pimlico, who proves to be an occasional male lover of Jeremy, who in his last year at Oxford is doing little work but considerable loving, including a sudden excursion into incest with Evelyn. Wilson is teasingly and sometimes feelingly successful in exploring the sexual brink upon which Evelyn and Theo hover in their relationship and which convinces Theo to give part of his estate to Evelyn. Pimlico, the present heir, knows that someone is being considered as a joint recipient of the estate, but he never suspects Evelyn, and Theo dies before the will is changed. All is well, however, since Evelyn and Pimlico decide to marry. It is farce of high order in which coincidence, arbitrary behavior, and sophisticated silliness are mixed with moments of genuine tenderness (but not so tender as to overcome the sly mockery of money and influence in the smart set of south London).

In his next two novels, *Unguarded Hours* and *Kindly Light*, Wilson eschews the underplayed wit of *The Sweets of Pimlico* for comic excess, reminiscent of P. G. Wodehouse in its extravagant playfulness. These theological comedies are strongly cinematic in their incident and character and they display, if ridiculously, Wilson's strong interest in, and deep knowledge of, English Anglicanism and its constant flirtation with Roman Catholicism as well as his affectionate enthusiasm for the detail, the knickknackery of religious ceremony and trapping. The two novels ought to be read in the proper chronological order, since the hero escapes at the end of *Unguarded Hours* in a balloon and begins in the next one, having floated some distance away, once again trying to make his way into the clerical life.

The Healing Art, Wilson's most admired work, reveals how wide his range can be, not only tonally but also thematically. The novel is a "black comedy" in the sense that acts which normally offend are portrayed in such a way that readers enjoy the improprieties without worrying about the moral consequences. Two women, one a university don, one a working-class housewife, meet while having surgery for breast cancer and comfort each other, despite the fact that they otherwise have nothing in common. Their doctor, overworked but peremptory, unfeeling, and vain, may have misread the women's X rays and deems one of them cured and the other in need of chemotherapy. The gifted, handsome, successful younger woman, informed of her possibly fatal condition, refuses treatment, energetically determined to live out her life quickly and to explore her personal relations with some fervor. In the process, she learns much about herself and her male friends and becomes involved in a love affair with the cast-off, occasional mistress of the man whom she presumed was, in fact, her lover (even if such love had not, to the moment, been consummated).

Wilson juxtaposes the range of experience open to a woman of the upper-middle class, searching for some meaning for the last days of her life, surrounded by the many pleasures and alternatives of her world, to the life of a working-class woman, supposedly healthy, but obviously wasting away and ignored by family and by the medical profession as something of a nuisance. The cruelty of it all is subtly explored by Wilson, and the final ironies for both women are unnervingly sad and comic. Wilson proves with this novel that he is serious, and sensitive, particularly in dealing with the emotional lives of the two women.

In *Who Was Oswald Fish?*, which might be called a contemporary black fairy tale, coincidence simply struts through the novel. The mysterious Oswald Fish, a turn-of-the-century architect and designer whose one church, a Gothic ruin in the working-class district of Birmingham, is to be the center of life and death for the parties drawn together to decide its fate, proves to be related to everyone who matters (and some who do not). In the retrieval of Fish's reputation from the neglect and indifference of twentieth century tastelessness and vulgarity, one suicide, one manslaughter, and two accidental deaths occur, the latter two in the rubble of his lovely old church. No one means any harm (although there are two children in this novel who could put the St. Trinian's gang to flight). Fanny Williams, former pop star and model, and survivor of the English rock revolution of the early 1960's, is, in the late 1970's, famous again, as the owner of a chain of trash-and-trend novelty shops dealing in Victorian nostalgia, and she is determined to protect the ruined church from demolition at the hands of soulless civic planners. Sexy, generous, and often charmingly silly, her life is an extravagant mess, a whirlpool of sensual, slapstick nonsense in which some survive and some, quite as arbitrarily, drown. Behind the farcical escapades lies Wilson's deep affection for the rich clutter of Victoriana juxtaposed to the new efficiency.

After the comic excesses of *Who Was Oswald Fish?*, Wilson pulled back into the narrower range of his early work in *Wise Virgin*. There has always been a sense that not only Waugh but also Iris Murdoch influenced him (*The Sweets of Pimlico* had been dedicated to her and to her husband, the literary critic John Bayley), particularly in the way in which she uses love as an unguided flying object, which can strike any character in the heart at any moment. Love tends to strike arbitrarily in Wilson's fiction, for he, like Murdoch, enjoys tracing the madness of fools in love. Also reminiscent of Murdoch, Wilson works interesting technical detail into his novels, often, as has been stated, of the religious world, but in *Who Was Oswald Fish?*, his interest in Victorian architecture and objets d'art predominates and adds amusingly to the texture of the novel. In *Wise Virgin*, Wilson utilizes his own special knowledge as a literary scholar, since his protagonist, Giles Fox, is a medievalist, working on a definitive edition of an obscure text, *A Treatise of Heavenly Love*, on the relation of virginity and the holy life. Fox, irascible, snobbish, and sometimes vicious, has two virgins on his hands, his daughter, whom he has sought to educate without benefit of twentieth century influence, and his assistant, Miss Agar, who is determined to marry him.

Wilson has been accused of gratuitous cruelty in the way in which he allows his characters to comment upon the gracelessness of contemporary British society, and it is true that Fox is a master of the unfair comment and is insensitive to the possibility that some kinds of stupidities, particularly in the less privileged classes, are only innocent gaucheries. Certainly Fox is Wilson's least attractive protagonist, but he is also a man who has suffered much, having lost one wife in childbirth and another in a motor accident, and having himself, in midcareer, gone blind. He is something of a twentieth century Job (although more deserving of punishment), and the tone and plot of the novel suggest black comedy bordering on tragedy. On the lighter side, Wilson satirizes Fox's sister and brother-in-law, who, suffering from that peculiar kind of arrested development which strikes some people as cute, indulge interminably in the baby talk of the schoolboys whom the husband teaches in a public school, clearly based upon Wilson's own school, Rugby.

Gentlemen in England takes place in the late Victorian period of which Wilson is so fond. With this work, Wilson has written a trick novel, partly in the tradition of Thomas Keneally and E. L. Doctorow, in which actual historical events and characters intrude on, and affect, the action. Wilson, however, refuses to use obvious historical allusions carefully chosen to satisfy the vanities of intelligent, well-informed readers. Much of the historical structure requires a deep knowledge of Victorian England. For example, although the novel definitely takes place in 1880, the exact date is never stated but must be gathered from certain facts mentioned by the characters. Allusions to George Eliot and Henry James might be easy to pick up, but those to public figures of the time, such as Charles Bradlaugh, E. B. Pusey, and Sir Charles Wentworth Dilke, require a formidable cultural memory.

The story centers on a father who has lost his Christian faith in the face of Darwinism; a son who is flirting with the late stages of the Oxford movement in religion, with the more theatrical experiments of High Anglicanism, and with the revival of the Roman Catholic Benedictine movement; and a daughter pursued by a disciple of Alma-Tadema, the popular painter of the time. Wilson recounts their family drama in a Victorian style, most reminiscent of the works of Anthony Trollope—slightly arch, witty, but restrainedly so, and inclined to overripe ironies. Like Victorian furniture and design, it is rich and heavy to the point of ponderousness.

Inside this lovingly detailed, historically accurate structure, Wilson plays out pure farce: A mother, still beautiful in early middle age, falls in love with a young painter, who falls in love with the daughter, who is half in love with her mother's old lover, who is half in love with both of them, and who is Wilson's way into the real world of London life. Called, with obvious intent, Chatterway, the former lover is intimately associated with the major figures of London life in that particularly lively year, 1880. *Gentlemen in England* is, in many ways, a work which illustrates Wilson's manipulative curiosity about the ways in which novels can be pushed and pulled about. Kingsley Amis has similar ideas, and his *Riverside Villa's Murder* (1973) anticipated Wilson in its careful re-creation of a 1930's-style English murder mystery in which content, structure, and language were scrupulous imitations of the real thing.

This awareness of the novel as a form which could be used in many ways allows Wilson many humorous moments. In *Who Was Oswald Fish?*, he introduces, in a minor role, Jeremy Tradescant, who was the sexually confused brother of Evelyn, the heroine of *The Sweets of Pimlico*. He goes even further in making a comment on the fate of Evelyn's marriage to Pimlico Price, incomprehensible to all but those who have read the earlier novel. Wilson introduces into *Gentlemen in England* a genuinely thoughtful discussion of the problem of Christian faith, which is tonally at odds with the clutter of Victorian sexual high jinks. He has, in short, no sense of decorum, not because he does not know, but because he knows so well. Sometimes, as in *Scandal* and *Love Unknown*, he seems to have returned to social satire; the latter novel is puzzling until one recognizes that it is based upon the most pathetic kind of popular romance. Wilson is off again, manipulating the genre, enriching junk literature by imposing first-class literary technique on banality and turning it into something it hardly deserves.

Even though Kingsley Amis stills holds sway as the linchpin satirist (though less committed to the class theme), A. N. Wilson may succeed him. His range of interests, however, suggests considerable suppleness, and he may yet produce a novel of genuinely tender feeling. He may also simply continue to reinforce his reputation as the cruelest, and sometimes the most amusing, of the new British novelists of the last quarter of the twentieth century.

Charles H. Pullen

Other major works

NONFICTION: *The Laird of Abbotsford: A View of Sir Walter Scott*, 1980; *The Life of John Milton*, 1983; *Hilaire Belloc*, 1984; *How Can We Know?*, 1985; *Pen Friends from Porlock*, 1987; *Tolstoy*, 1988; *C. S. Lewis*, 1990; *Eminent Victorians*, 1990.

CHILDREN'S LITERATURE: *Stray*, 1987.

Bibliography

Furbank, P. N. *Unholy Pleasure: Or, The Idea of Social Class*. London: Oxford University Press, 1985. Furbank draws on history, sociology, and literature for examples to support his theory about the notion of class in Great Britain. Though the book is an indictment of the British class system, it does serve to provide readers with a scholarly critique to supplement the literary social satire Wilson presents with his fictional characters.
Sutherland, Douglas. *The English Gentleman*. New York: Viking Press, 1978.

Critical Survey of Long Fiction

A lighthearted look at the "gentleman" in his various habitats (school, club, church) and diversions (car, money, wardrobe), providing a point of reference for the world of Wilson's characters. Amusingly illustrated and contains many printed anecdotes about a "gentleman"'s behavior.

Weinberg, Jacob. "A. N. Wilson: Prolific to a Fault." *Newsweek* 112 (September 13, 1988): 75. A short but well-written essay, interspersed with comments by Wilson, on his novels and biographies. Also concerns Wilson as a "Young Fogey," a term used to describe young members of the Conservative party in England.

Wilson, A. N. "PW Interviews A. N. Wilson." Interview by Michele Field. *Publishers Weekly* 231 (May 15, 1987): 262-263. In the course of this interview, Wilson discusses his Anglo-Catholicism, the inevitable comparison of his works with those of Evelyn Waugh, the "cruel" nature of his novels, and his views on the writing of biography. Also contains much valuable biographical information.

Wolfe, Gregory. "Off Center, on Target." *Chronicles* 10, no. 10 (1986): 35-36. Wolfe's essay concerns Wilson's affinities with Evelyn Waugh, particularly in terms of their style and in their perspectives on Western Christianity. Also sees Wilson as in the tradition of P. G. Wodehouse, who epitomized the light comic novel, but in Wilson's hands that novel becomes a vehicle for satire and social criticism.

ANGUS WILSON

Born: Bexhill, England; August 11, 1913
Died: Bury St. Edmunds, England; June 1, 1991

Principal long fiction

Hemlock and After, 1952; *Anglo-Saxon Attitudes,* 1956; *The Middle Age of Mrs. Eliot,* 1958; *The Old Men at the Zoo,* 1961; *Late Call,* 1964; *No Laughing Matter,* 1967; *As If by Magic,* 1973; *Setting the World on Fire,* 1980.

Other literary forms

Angus Wilson started his literary career in 1946, at the age of thirty-three, by writing short stories. The earliest stories were published in *Horizon.* The *Wrong Set and Other Stories* (1949), *Such Darling Dodos and Other Stories* (1950), and *A Bit off the Map, and Other Stories* (1957) deal with the same problems and use the same imagery as his novels. Wilson also wrote drama, and in the 1970's, he became a leading reviewer of fiction. His literary journalism and criticism for *The Spectator, The Observer,* and *London Magazine* center mainly on the problem of the English novel. The range of writers he has discussed in articles, introductions, or lectures is extremely wide and includes, among others, the Victorians, the Bloomsbury Group, Aldous Huxley, D. H. Lawrence, John Cowper Powys, Leo Tolstoy, Fyodor Dostoevski, Irving Shaw, Robert Penn Warren, and William Golding. He also has published three full-length literary monographs: *Emile Zola: An Introductory Study of His Novels* (1952), *The World of Charles Dickens* (1970), and *The Strange Ride of Rudyard Kipling* (1977). Wilson's many lectures and articles display his concern with a wide range of problems relevant to the second half of the century. Most important for the study and understanding of his art is the volume *The Wild Garden: Or, Speaking of Writing* (1963), which contains lectures given in California in 1960. Some of his criticism was collected in *Diversity and Depth in Fiction: Selected Critical Writings of Angus Wilson* (1983). Travel pieces written over several decades are collected in *Reflections in a Writer's Eye* (1986).

Achievements

Most critics agree that by the 1980's, Wilson had secured a place among the most distinguished contemporary British novelists. He is even recognized outside the English-speaking world, particulary France. In the 1960's and 1970's, the number of interviews with the artist increased, signifying his growing recognition among critics. Whether the critics use Stephen Spender's terminology of "modern" and "contemporary," or speak of experimental, psychological, aesthetic, or modern versus the traditional, sociological English novel, they all try to assess Wilson in relation to these categories. Some contend that Wilson's main concern rests with the sociological aspects of human life, but almost all critics concede that his interest goes beyond social issues. Without abandoning his commitment to depicting reality, Wilson had always been committed to probe deeper into the dark depths of the human self. This concern with the inner self separates him sharply from the "angry" writers who also wrote in the 1950's: Kingsley Amis, John Wain, and Alan Sillitoe. Wilson, however, is dedicated to experimenting both in content and method. In his novels and critical writings, he emerges as a champion for a new type of novel, standing between the traditional and the experimental.

Biography

Angus Wilson was born in Bexhill, Sussex, on August 11, 1913, to a middle-class family as the sixth son. His father was of Scottish extraction; his mother came from South Africa, and he spent some time there as a child. In constant financial troubles, his parents tried to maintain pretense and appearance, which left a deep impression on Wilson: at a very early age, he became aware of the chasm separating the real world and the world of fantasy into which many people escape to avoid the unpleasant facts of their lives. Frequently lonely (he was thirteen years younger than his next older brother), he realized that his clowning ability made him popular with the schoolchildren. He attended prep school in Seaford; from there he went to Westminster School and then to Merton College, Oxford. At the University of Oxford, his history training was on the Marxist line; that fact and his left-wing political activities in the 1930's account for his Labour sympathies.

In 1937, he started work at the British Museum, and, with an interruption during World War II, he stayed there until 1955. During the war, he was associated with an interservice organization attached to the Foreign Office, and for a while he lived in the country in a home with a Methodist widow and her daughter. During this time, he had a serious nervous breakdown; his psychotherapist suggested creative writing as therapy. In 1946, Wilson rejoined the staff at the British Museum and, at the same time, started writing seriously. His first published writing, the short story "Raspberry Jam" (1946), reflects his personal crisis and foreshadows the dark atmosphere of most of his work to come. The whole experience at the British Museum, situated in London's sophisticated Bloomsbury district and especially his job as Deputy Superintendent at the Reading Room, provided him with an understanding and knowledge of the cultural establishment and of the management of cultural institutions, which he used later in *The Old Men at the Zoo*. Also, observing scholars, book addicts, and eccentric visitors to the Reading Room gave him material for creating some of his fictional characters, such as Gerald Middleton in *Anglo-Saxon Attitudes*.

In 1952, he published his first novel, *Hemlock and After*, and a critical monograph, *Emile Zola*. He gave talks on the novel for the British Broad-casting Corporation that were later published in *The Listener*. In 1955, a contract with Secker and Warburg as well as his ongoing reviewing activity for *The Spectator* and *Encounter* made it possible for him to resign his post at the British Museum. He then retired to the Sussex countryside, thus reviving his childhood garden-dream. As a result of his freedom from job-related responsibilities, he published four novels in a rapid sequence: *Anglo-Saxon Attitudes*, *The Middle Age of Mrs. Eliot*, *The Old Men at the Zoo*, and *Late Call*. Furthermore, his participation in the cultural and literary life of England as a journalist, critic, and lecturer became more extensive. In 1963, he started his association with the University of East Anglia as a part-time lecturer, becoming professor in 1966. Also in 1966, he became Chairman of the Literary Panel of the Arts Council of Great Britain. In 1967, he lectured at Berkeley, California, as a Beckerman Professor, and in the same year *No Laughing Matter* appeared.

In 1968, he was made Commander of the British Empire and Honorary Fellow of Cowell College of the University of California at Santa Cruz. He honored the Dickens Centennial in 1970 with *The World of Charles Dickens*. Between 1971 and 1974, he served as Chairman of the National Book League while receiving two more distinctions in 1972, becoming a Companion of Literature and a Chevalier de l'Ordre des Arts et des Lettres, the latter a sign of his growing reputation in France. A sixth novel, *As If by Magic*, appeared in 1973; in it he made use of his teaching experience and involvement with young intellectuals. He continued to live in the country, his many activities including travel. His Asian journey resulted in his book *The Strange Ride of Rudyard Kipling*. He was John Hinkley Visiting Professor at The Johns Hopkins University in 1974, and, in 1977, Distinguished Visiting Professor at the University of Delaware; he also lectured at many other American universities. In 1980, he published another novel, *Setting the World on Fire*. His manuscripts, deposited at the Library of the University of Iowa, provide ample material for future researchers.

After suffering a stroke, Wilson died on June 1, 1991, in a nursing home in the southeast of England. He was seventy-seven years old.

Analysis

"Self-realization was to become the theme of all my novels," declared Angus Wilson in *The Wild Garden*. Self-realization does not take place in a vacuum; the process is closely linked with a person's efforts to face and to cope with the world. Wilson's childhood experience, among déclassé middle-class people living in a fantasy world, initiated the novelist's interest in the conflict between two worlds and in the possibility or impossibility of resolving the conflict. The rapidly changing scene in England as the Edwardian Age gave way to the postwar 1920's, with the cultural dominance of Bloomsbury, and then to the radical leftist 1930's, impressed on him the urgency of such a search. His encounter with Marxism at Oxford intensified Wilson's tendency to see the world as one of opposing forces. The dichotomy of town and country, of the classes, and of old and new forms the background of Wilson's fiction as the remnants of Edwardian England disappeared and the dissolution of the British Empire left the island nation searching for its place in the modern world.

In *The Wild Garden*, Wilson describes his creative-writing process in terms of a dialectic; he reveals that he "never felt called upon to declare allegiance to either fantasy or realism," but then he adds that "without their fusion I could not produce a novel." Wilson is desperately looking for syntheses to all kinds of conflicts and insists that self-realization is an absolute necessity to achieve them. His own breakdown as well as Sigmund Freud's impact on his generation pushed Wilson in the direction of psychoanalysis and the search for identity. In an age of tension, violence, and suffering, he insists on the necessity of self-realization in order to overcome despair.

Wilson's heroes all have crippled, wasted lives and broken families, and the novelist explores their "cherished evasions." Bernard Sand in *Hemlock and After* has to be shocked into self-knowledge by facing sadism in his own nature; Gerald Middleton, in *Anglo-Saxon Attitudes*, gets a new chance for a satisfactory, if not happy, life in old age when he is ready to resume responsibility as a scholar and to reveal a shameful hoax. Both of these heroes are presented in their private and public lives because, in Wilson's view, both of these aspects of life are equally important to modern man. This view of human life in the dialectic of the private and the public is even more important for Meg Eliot, the heroine of *The Middle Age of Mrs. Eliot*; after many frustrations she emerges at the end of the novel as a career woman. Similarly, Sylvia Calvert in *Late Call* discovers a meaningful [retirement] life of her own, independent of her family.

Wilson was a very "British" writer with a subtle sense for the typical English understatement, while his Hegelian drive for reconciliation of conflicts agrees with the spirit of the traditional English compromise. He was constantly searching for ways to save the remnants of the liberal, humanistic values that have remained dear to him in a world that did not seem to have any use for them. His heroes and heroines, saved from final disintegration, are restored to some kind of meaningful life through self-knowledge and are brought closer to other people in defiance of loneliness and despair.

In his first novel, *Hemlock and After*, Wilson extends the exploration of the theme of self-knowledge to both the private and public life of his hero. The novel is about Bernard Sand's troubled conscience, a most private matter; but Bernard is an important public figure, described as "the country's own ambassador to the world outside," and a successful, self-confident novelist who organizes a subsidized writers' colony, Valden Hall, in order to support young talent. Overtly successful, his family life is in shambles. His wife, Ella, lives in "neurotic misery"; his son is a staunch conservative in strong disagreement with Bernard's liberal views; his unmarried daughter, a journalist, feels lonely and unhappy. As an indication of the overhanging disaster, Bernard's first novel is entitled *Nightmare's Image*.

In the title, "Hemlock" suggests poisonous wrong, evil, and even violence. Poisoning and violence occur in a "massacre of innocence," as related to Eric, Bernard's young homosexual partner, and to the little girl Elzie, whom the disreputable Mrs. Curry wants to make available to Hugh Rose. Wilson deliberately links the fate of the two young people by calling them both "rabbits." Rose and Mrs. Curry strike their deal at the "Lamb" inn.

The word "After" in the title refers to the aftermath of knowledge: self-knowledge. A crucial scene occurs at the end of Book One when a still complacent and self-confident Bernard watches the arrest of young homosexuals at Leicester Square and is shocked suddenly by the discovery that he experienced sadistic enjoyment in watching the terror in the eyes of those youths. This discovery has a devastating effect on Bernard's life and destroys not only him but also Valden Hall. The long-awaited opening of the young artists' colony becomes a total disaster, as its erupting violence grows into a symbol of the modern predicament. Wilson describes the scene as one of chaos, disorder, disappointment, strain, and hostility.

After this startling event, Bernard's life goes downhill very rapidly; self-knowledge paralyzes his will, and he is entirely unable to act. The discovery of sadistic tendencies makes him suspect of his own motives. He realizes with frightening clarity the abyss of the human soul and is driven to utter despair about the motivation behind any action. He has a horrifying vision of the subtle difference between intention and action, and as a consequence, Bernard loses his determination to deal with Mrs. Curry. At the same time, Ella almost miraculously recovers from her nervous breakdown and, after Bernard dies, acts on his behalf in arranging efficient management at Valden Hall and a prison sentence for Rose and Mrs. Curry. Rose commits suicide in prison, while Mrs. Curry earns an early release with her good behavior. It is briefly indicated that she might continue her former activity; thus the Epilogue ends the novel on an ambiguous note of qualified optimism.

The title *Anglo-Saxon Attitudes*, derived from *Alice's Adventures in Wonderland* (1865), suggests a typically English atmosphere; it is Wilson's most Victorian novel, a broad social comedy. At the same time, it displays experimental technique in the use of the flashback, which provides all the background to Gerald Middleton's crisis in his private and public life. The hero, a sixty-year-old failure, is a historian. In the beginning of the novel, sitting by himself at a Christmas party given by his estranged wife, Inge, Gerald overhears broken sentences of conversation that remind him of the most significant episodes of his life. Wilson makes it very clear that self-knowledge is important for Gerald; it is both a psychological need to him and a matter of "intellectual honesty," a duty to the professional community of historians.

Gerald's crisis of conscience concerns a cruel hoax that occurred back in 1912 when he participated with a team in an excavation. Young Gilbert Stokeway, a disciple of T. H. Hulme and Wyndham Lewis and the son of the leader of the team, put a fake idol in the tomb under research at Melpham. His hoax was successful, and the fake came to be hailed as a pagan idol. At that time, Gerald was a Prufrock-like antihero: disabled physically by a sprained ankle, and disabled emotionally by his love for Gilbert's wife, Dollie. His affair with her played an important role in his silence about the fake idol. Gerald's feelings of guilt center on "the two forbidden subjects of his thoughts," his marriage and the hoax. His life, "rooted in evasion," appears to him empty, meaningless, and futile. His professional career fell victim to his decision not to reveal the hoax. Because of his affair with Dollie, he evaded dealing with Inge's inadequacies as a mother.

In fact, none of the minor characters has a happy, self-fulfilling life. While Gerald still believes in the liberal tradition, neither of his sons adheres to his beliefs. His elder son, Robert, a businessman, stands rather to the right and the younger son, John, is a radical; and they have violent clashes whenever they meet. Both sons are unhappy in their personal relationships as well. Robert is married to the conventional Marie-Hélène but loves the more modern Elvira Portway. John has a short-lived homosexual relationship with an unruly young Irishman, Larry, who is killed in a wild drive in which John loses a leg. Gerald's daughter, Kay, has a serious crisis in her marriage to the smart right-wing young sociologist, Donald. Wilson employs specific imagery to drive home to the reader the overwhelming atmosphere of frustration of all these people. Expressions such as "flat and dead" and "deadly heaviness" abound, referring to the behavior of people at parties when communication is impossible. Gerald's house is "noiseless as a tomb," and during the Christmas party at the home of the "Norse Goddess" Inge, all those present "shivered" in spite of the central heating.

Realizing the failure of his family, Gerald has to admit that he is to take the blame; when he selected Inge to be his wife, he decided for second-best. Yet, at the end, Gerald manages to pull himself out of his dead life. By revealing the hoax, he succeeds in restoring his professional status, and after a long silence, he becomes active again in research. The novel, however, like *Hemlock and After*, ends on a note of qualified optimism as Gerald remains estranged from his family. The picture of Gerald's life, combined with the divergent subplots, reveals a world in which relationships do not last, where options are limited.

Critics believe that they can recognize Wilson in most of his central characters; the novelist, however, admits the connection only in the case of Meg Eliot, the heroine of his third novel, *The Middle Age of Mrs. Eliot*. "Meg," he says, "is in large part modelled on myself," while David Parker's nursery recalled to Wilson childhood memories of a garden of a friendly family.

Meg Eliot, a well-to-do barrister's childless, worldly, spoiled wife, experiences sudden tragedy when her husband dies from a gunshot wound as he tries to protect a local minister. The novel depicts Meg's nervous breakdown and painful recovery: her journey to self-knowledge. She is first revealed to be holding desperately to her old friends; yet, their lives are no more secure than hers. Lady Pirie in her "decaying genteel jail" is preoccupied with her son only; bohemian Polly Robinson lives a kind of "animated death"; and Jill Stokes is obsessed with the memory of her dead husband. These "lame ducks" cannot help Meg, nor can drugs. Meg's brother, David Parker, who runs the nursery with his homosexual partner, is sheltered in the pleasant quiet atmosphere, which suggests a return to lost innocence. Yet, Wilson is ambiguous about the validity of the garden image, since David's nursery is commercial, an irony in itself. Meg cannot share her brother's life-style, his abnegation of action and the human world. Wilson does not censure David for his contemplative life-style, but it is evident that he prefers Meg's choice "to be with people!"

Meg is determined to find meaning in life, in a life with people. Her story is strikingly reminiscent of George Eliot's heroines; similar to them, she used to live in self-delusion and is shocked into consciousness by the "remorse of not having made life count enough" for her husband. Moreover, again like the Victorian woman, she returns to a fuller life. Two factors are important in her recovery. First, she refuses any kind of opium, a George Eliot ideal; second, she is determined to build herself a meaningful, useful life. While she admits that she "used to be Maggie Tulliver," she also resembles Gwendolen Harleth from *Daniel Deronda* (1876). She shares with her an unhappy childhood and the horrors of remorse, but she shares also in Gwendolen's way of redemption. Like the Victorian heroine, Meg too had to learn in a painful way that the outside world could intrude into her life at any time and destroy it if she is taken unaware. As she takes a paying secretarial job, Meg is full of confidence in her farewell letter to David: "At any rate in a few years at least, the modern world won't be able to take me by surprise so easily again."

From the omniscient narrator of his early works, Wilson shifts to a more modern device in *The Old Men at the Zoo* by creating a first-person narrator in Simon Carter. In the beginning of the novel, Simon is a gifted, dedicated yet disabled naturalist, very much like Gerald Middleton at the time of the excavation. He is prevented from continuing research in Africa because of amoebal dysenteria. He joins the London Zoo as an administrator at a crucial time when the zoo itself becomes a battleground of conflicting ideas, reflecting a conflict of values in British politics. Wilson creates an armed conflict between England and Allied Europe, followed by a Fascist invasion of England when all standards of civilized behavior collapse and give way to brutality. When the war breaks out, the Fascists want to put on a spectacle with prisoners of war fighting the zoo animals. Simon is horrified, but as he later tries to drive the animals to safety, he finds himself killing his favorite badgers to feed a boy and his mother.

Almost an antihero, trying to avoid any kind of involvement with people, an administrator following orders, Simon emerges at the end of the novel ready to face the world, to be involved with people, even running for director. Because of his loyalty to the zoo under three different administrations, representing three different political ideologies, some are inclined to view him as a Vicar of Bray. In the twentieth century, however, many people had to face Simon's fundamental dilemma: whether to follow orders or to take up independent responsibility. Simon's American-born wife, Martha, disapproves of his behavior; she would like him to give up his job. Simon refuses, saying, "What do you think I am, a weathercock?" There is cruel irony in this remark; however, Wilson's irony is not pointed at Simon but rather at the general human predicament of a rapidly changing world in which choices are limited and people are continuously bombarded with dilemmas.

Simon's only independent action is his attempt to save the animals, which ends in disaster. In him, Wilson presents modern man struggling with despair in a desperate race to catch up with challenges. Simon's painful adjustment commands respect; he almost achieves heroic status when, after all the horrors and violence, he describes this modern world as "a demie-paradise." In this sense, *The Old Men at the Zoo* is Wilson's least pessimistic novel.

No Laughing Matter is one of Wilson's most complex novels and requires close reading. The narrative is interwoven with dramas, enacted by the characters and reflecting various dramatic styles, including the absurd. Pastiches and parody of writers are important features of the novel, and literary references abound. A *Forsyte Saga*-like family chronicle of the Matthews family, the novel is also a historical document covering the twentieth century to 1967. The father, Billy Pop, a Micawber of the twentieth century, is a failure in his writing profession and ineffectual in his family life, letting his selfish wife dominate the children. All six of them have a crippled childhood and are deprived of privacy. By the end of the novel, they all achieve some kind of success in their professional lives; some even attain fame, such as Rupert, the actor, and Quentin, the political journalist, later a celebrated television commentator. Success does not make him lovable, and his cynicism, enjoyed by a million common viewers, questions the role of the media.

The final scene, in 1967, brings the whole clan together. While Margaret and her brother Marcus, a homosexual art dealer, are discussing and quarreling about Margaret's art, Hassan, who will inherit Marcus's cooperatively run scent factory, makes a final statement: the last words of the novel. He considers Marcus's ideas of a cooperative absurd. Hassan admires "ambition, high profit and determined management." His coldly calculating thoughts cast a dark shadow on the future; they underline once again Wilson's skepticism about the survival of liberal humanistic ideals in the modern world.

A strong moral sense links Wilson to George Eliot, and his sense of the caricature and the grotesque shows affinities with his favorite author, Charles Dickens. At the same time, his fiction is full of experiments into new literary methods. With almost each novel, Wilson made an important step forward in his search for new techniques. Tragedy and laughter coexist in his novels; there is tragedy in the private lives of the characters, but Wilson has a grotesque view of man's behavior, and his ability to create atmosphere through concentrating on speech habits promotes laughter.

In his commitment to duty, in his moral seriousness, Wilson is definitely akin to George Eliot, but he differs from the Victorian in that he cannot believe in "meliorism." George Eliot firmly maintained that self-awareness would lead to self-improvement and in consequence, to the individual's improved performance in the human community. Wilson is much more skeptical. Like E. M. Forster, he, too, is painfully aware of the decline of liberal hopes. In *The Middle Age of Mrs. Eliot*, he came to the sad conclusion that "self-knowledge had no magic power to alter," and in his sixth novel, he killed magic with finality.

In *As If by Magic*, magic, the ultimate evasion, is destroyed forever for the two central characters. Moreover, this time they are not middle-aged or elderly intellectuals paralyzed by frustration; they are young people. Wilson's teaching experience in Britain and America caused him to concentrate on the young, the future generation. Hamo Langmuir is a dedicated young scientist on a worldwide fact-finding tour to study the benevolent affects of his "magic" rice, destined to solve the problem of starvation in underdeveloped countries. His goddaughter, Alexandra Grant, in the company of her fellow hippies, is also on a world tour in search of an occult answer to all human problems. A bewildered Hamo must find out that his magic rice solution has introduced a farming method for which natives are not yet prepared and, consequently, it is causing more damage than good. Hamo falls victim to the anger of a crowd at a moment when he is ready to get involved in the human aspects of research. He, like Alexandra, who gets to Goa at the same time, had to learn through experience that the intrusion of Western ways into radically different cultures can cause disruption and many unnecessary tragedies. At the end of the novel, a sober Alexandra, cured of her hippie ways, resumes the responsibility of building a normal life for her son, a legacy of the hippie venture. A millionaire through an inheritance, she is ready to support and subsidize food research, but she knows by now that the possibilities are limited and that no easy answers are available; magic of any kind is only for the neurotics who are unable to face reality or for the power-hungry who use it to dominate others.

Wilson's concern with human nature and with what it means for the future of the world dominates *Setting the World on Fire*. This novel is a family chronicle like *No Laughing Matter* but more condensed, more limited in time (1948-1969) and in the number of characters. Indeed, the writer concentrates on two brothers, Piers and Tom, the last generation of an old aristocratic family. Literary references are replaced by other arts: theater, music, architecture, and painting. Piers hopes to dedicate his life to the theater, and as a promising student, he earns the admiration of family, friends, and teachers with his stage-managing and directing abilities. The final part of the novel is about the preparations for the first performance of a new play, with the younger brother Tom supporting Piers as best he can in the hectic work. Everything is set for success when, unexpectedly, Scotland Yard intervenes and orders the premises emptied because of a bomb threat. The author of the play, an old employee of the family, masterminded the plot, simultaneously aimed at the family and at the government.

Tom saves Piers's life by knocking him down, but he himself gets killed. On his way home from the hospital where Tom died, Piers is on the verge of a breakdown and about to give up hope as well as artistic ambitions, because what good are the wonders of art in "a chaotic universe"? He calms down, however, and decides to stage the play anyway; he must not "lose the power to ascend the towers of imagination," he says. The tragedy brought Piers to a fuller realization of his duty as an artist, which means doing the only thing left to him: to create in, and for, a world threatened by chaos, violence, and destruction.

Wilson, a mixture of a twentieth century Charles Dickens, George Eliot, and E. M. Forster, and with his increasingly dark vision of the modern predicament, rededicated himself, the artist, to his moral obligation. He continued writing in a desperate attempt to impose some kind of order on chaos and, by making men aware, to try to save mankind from itself.

Anna B. Katona

Other major works
SHORT FICTION: *The Wrong Set and Other Stories*, 1949; *Such Darling Dodos and Other Stories*, 1950; *A Bit off the Map and Other Stories*, 1957; *Death Dance: 25 Stories*, 1969.

PLAY: *The Mulberry Bush*, 1956.

NONFICTION: *Emile Zola: An Introductory Study of His Novels*, 1952; *For Whom the Cloche Tolls: A Scrapbook of the Twenties*, 1953 (with Philippe Jullian); *The Wild Garden: Or, Speaking of Writing*, 1963; *Tempo: The Impact of Television on the Arts*, 1964; *The World of Charles Dickens*, 1970; *The Strange Ride of Rudyard Kipling*, 1977; *Diversity and Depth in Fiction: Selected Critical Writings of Angus Wilson*, 1983; *Reflections in a Writer's Eye*, 1986.

Bibliography

Faulkner, Peter. *Angus Wilson: Mimic and Moralist*. New York: Viking Press, 1980. Follows a chronological approach to Wilson's writings, including pertinent biographical background and evaluations of one or two main works each chapter in order to illustrate the evolution of Wilson's art. Also contains a bibliography of Wilson's major publications and selected secondary sources.

Gardner, Averil. *Angus Wilson*. Boston: Twayne, 1985. The first full-length study of Wilson published in the United States, representing a well-rounded introduction to Wilson's fiction. Includes a biographical sketch and analyses of Wilson's stories and novels through 1980. Contains a useful annotated bibliography of secondary sources.

Halio, Jay L. *Angus Wilson*. Edinburgh: Oliver & Boyd, 1964. The first full-length study of Wilson, this slender volume covers Wilson's writing through *The Wild Garden*. After a biographical sketch, Halio examines Wilson's fiction in chronological order. Concludes with a chapter on Wilson's literary criticism.

_____. ed. *Critical Essays on Angus Wilson*. Boston: G. K. Hall, 1985. Includes an overview of Wilson's writings, several reviews of his work, three interviews with the author, and fourteen essays that offer a diverse study of Wilson's individual works as well as his career as a whole. The selected bibliography draws readers' attention to further resources.

Kissane, Joseph, ed. *Twentieth Century Literature* 29 (Summer, 1983). This special issue on Wilson, commemorating his seventieth birthday, incorporates a variety of approaches to his art: two biographical essays, reminiscences, an interview with the author, and eight critical articles. Includes a comprehensive selected bibliography of works by and about Wilson from 1976 to 1981.

Stape, J. H., and Anne N. Thomas. *Angus Wilson: A Bibliography, 1947-1987*. London: Mansell, 1988. This thorough and indispensable resource includes a foreword by Wilson and a useful chronology of his life. Part 1 is a bibliography of works by Wilson, including books, articles, translations of his works, and interviews. Part 2 is a bibliography of works about Wilson.

ETHEL WILSON

Born: Port Elizabeth, South Africa; January 20, 1888
Died: Vancouver, Canada; December 22, 1980

Principal long fiction

Hetty Dorval, 1947; *The Innocent Traveller*, 1949; *The Equations of Love*, 1952; *Lilly's Story*, 1953; *Swamp Angel*, 1954; *Love and Salt Water*, 1956.

Other literary forms

Eleven short stories and eight essays by Ethel Wilson were published in magazines between 1937 and 1964. Two of the stories, "Hurry, Hurry!" and "Mrs. Golightly and the First Convention," were later anthologized, and two others, "I Just Love Dogs" and "The Window," were selected for *Best British Short Stories of 1938* and *Best American Short Stories: 1959*, respectively. These four stories, three of the others, and one of the essays, along with nine stories and an essay not previously published, were collected in *Mrs. Golightly and Other Stories* (1961). Besides the stories and essays, seven excerpts from novels also appeared separately as short stories in magazines. One of these, "Miss Tritt," from *The Equations of Love*, was anthologized as a short story.

Achievements

Wilson was among the Canadian authors of the 1930's who broke away from the frontier tradition of provincial and didactic romances. She adapted to Canadian backgrounds the universal themes and methods of the realistic and psychological novel. She was one of the first Canadians to achieve a critical reputation abroad, not indeed as a major novelist, but certainly as an important minor one. Her novels are in the main current of the British and French realistic tradition, especially that of the early twentieth century, showing affinities with the works of E. M. Forster, Virginia Woolf, Arnold Bennett, Ivy Compton-Burnett, and Marcel Proust. Nevertheless, she maintained strong individuality in both theme and form. She wrote that authors can be "endangered by the mould or formula becoming apparent, and then the story has no life." Without being innovative, therefore, her novels have a great deal of variety of theme and approach, so that they are difficult to classify.

Perhaps because Wilson did not attempt to follow literary trends, and perhaps also because she began publishing relatively late in her life, when she was nearly fifty, her works did not have a dramatic impact on Canadian letters. She was publishing out of her generation, and her realism and understatement seemed somewhat old-fashioned to those authors of the 1930's who were following naturalistic trends. Still, she was influential in raising the quality of the art in Canada and in quietly introducing the theme of women "finding themselves" in some sense, well before the theme became popular among feminists. Her heroines are not necessarily strong or aggressive but they mature, meet the vicissitudes of their lives with determination and ingenuity, and for the most part succeed in small but important ways. Wilson's treatment of this theme and her impeccable craftsmanship contributed significantly to the maturing of the novel in Canada.

Biography

Ethel Davis Wilson was born in Port Elizabeth, South Africa, on January 20, 1888, to Robert William Bryant and Lila (Malkin) Bryant. Her mother died when she was only two, and her father took her to Staffordshire, England, to be reared by her maternal grandmother and successive aunts and uncles. Her family members were involved in a number of literary activities, including reading, journalism, and translation, and were acquainted with Matthew Arnold and Arnold Bennett. This literary atmosphere no doubt stimulated her interest in letters, and the literary allusions and quotations in her works demonstrate a comprehensive familiarity with the English tradition. Her father died when she was ten, and she went to Vancouver, British Columbia, to join her grandmother, who had moved there. Many of these family and early personal experiences are recounted in *The Innocent Traveller*, the semi-biographical novel based on the life of her aunt.

In Vancouver, Wilson attended Miss Gordon's School, but she was sent to Trinity Hall School in Southport, England, for her secondary education. In 1907, she was graduated from Vancouver Normal School with a Second Class Teacher's Certificate. Between 1907 and 1920, she taught in Vancouver elementary schools.

On January 4, 1921, Wilson married Dr. Wallace Wilson. Their marriage was a happy one, marked by a good deal of traveling in Canada, Europe, and around the Mediterranean, and the successful development of both their careers. Dr. Wilson became a respected physician; he studied internal medicine in Vienna in 1930, represented Canada at the British Medical Association's convention in 1938 and at the World Health Organization in Paris in 1947, and was president of the Canadian Medical Association in 1946 and 1947. The relationship between the Wilsons may have provided details for the happy marriages and the deepening love relationships in *Hetty Dorval*, *Lilly's Story*, and *Love and Salt Water*. The love of travel is also obvious in her work; travel is healing, broadening, and sensitizing to her characters, and Wilson's ability to describe the essential atmosphere of various locales is one of her strongest attributes.

Wilson published her first short story in 1937, and another in 1939 before her career was interrupted by World War II. Although Dr. Wilson was in the Canadian Army and Wilson herself served by editing a Red Cross magazine between 1940 and 1945, she made little use of wartime experiences in her novels, except tangentially in *The Innocent Traveller* and *Love and Salt Water*.

Only the short story "We Have to Sit Opposite" deals specifically with wartime problems.

It is likely that Wilson's career in writing was encouraged by ill-health. She was a victim of arthritis, which by 1956 had become so severe that she could not walk around in London, as she described in her essay "To Keep the Memory of So Worthy a Friend." She wrote, "One of the advantages of being lame is that one can sit and think. . . . And so I often think and think." In her last three novels, several major characters suffer handicaps, either physical or psychological, which affect their relationships with others in various ways and which must be transcended. No doubt her own disability enabled her to interpret this theme sympathetically.

The late 1940's and the 1950's were Wilson's most productive years, all of her novels and most of her short stories and essays being written or published during that period. At the peak of her success, after the publication of *Swamp Angel*, she received three awards: an honorary doctorate from the University of British Columbia in 1955, a special medal from the Canada Council in 1961 for contributions to Canadian Literature, and the Lorne Pierce Gold Medal from the Royal Society of Canada in 1964.

Dr. Wilson died in 1966, and Ethel Wilson lived in retirement in Vancouver until her death in 1980.

Analysis

Although Ethel Wilson's canon is small, it is of high quality. The writing style is direct, simple, and expressive. Only occasionally, in the early books, does the diction or syntax call attention to itself as excellent. In general, only if one should try to paraphrase a passage or change a word would he become aware of that rightness of style that is typical of an artist. Passages describing the beauty of nature are most immediately impressive. Wilson's account of the train journey of the Edgeworths across Canada to Vancouver, in *The Innocent Traveller*, offers a vivid impression of the countryside and evokes the haunting vastness of the plains and forests stretching northward from the train track to the arctic circle. Magnificent descriptions of the Northern Lights occur in more than one book, and the mist-shrouded or sun-brightened mountains of the Vancouver area are sketched with a sensitive pen. Less frequent but equally impressive are descriptions of unsightly scenes, such as the interior of the slovenly Johnson apartment in *Tuesday and Wednesday* (published in *The Equations of Love*). It is not only in description, however, that Wilson excels; her humor is deft, ironic, and humane in passages such as the chapter "Nuts and Figs," from *The Innocent Traveller*, in which Great-Grandfather Edgeworth, in his declining days, proposes to two worthy lady friends in one afternoon and is refused, to the gratification of all three. Thoughtful and philosophical passages are also subtly presented, so that except for a few intrusive statements in the early, less integrated books, the concepts are suggested through economical language and apt symbols.

For Wilson, nature is not only a major inspiration for description, but also a method of characterization. Most of her protagonists are close to nature. Their ability to love and the essential civilization of their emotions are measured by their appreciation of the beauties and dangers of the Canadian mountains, forests, and waters. One notable exception is the garrulous Topaz Edgeworth, who exists in her human relationships rather than in nature, and the other is Hetty Dorval, an antagonist, whose appreciation of nature is one of the deceptive charms of her evil. Wilson's characters are firmly rooted in their environments and grow out of them. Her attitude toward them is dispassionately empathetic; they are clearly and humorously drawn, with subtle complexities. All are believable, and the best of them are memorable. She develops understanding of even her most unsympathetic characters, to the extent that plot is often weakened because she is drawn into digressions about the characters, about whom she cares more than she cares about careful plot structure. Topaz Edgeworth, Nell Severance, Lilly Hughes, and Maggie Lloyd are her most convincing creations, and it is the success of their characterization which causes *The Innocent Traveller*, Lilly's Story, and *Swamp Angel* to be her best novels.

If style and characterization are what make Wilson's novels outstanding, the plots are what keep them from being great. Plotting appears always to have been difficult for Wilson. Her admirers defend the inconsequentiality of her plots as true to life, expressing a philosophy about the fortuitous connections, or lack of connections, between the events in a person's history. Wilson minimizes suspense as a plot device; in fact, she often uses a technique of revealing future events, since causality interests her more than suspense. Still, the novels that are most effectively plotted, *Lilly's Story* and *Swamp Angel*, are recognized to be her best.

The title of Wilson's third book, *The Equations of Love*, suggests her recurring themes as a novelist. The typical protagonist of a Wilson novel is orphaned or otherwise separated from her family, as Wilson herself was as a child. Deprived of parental love, she becomes independent but lonely. This typical protagonist usually takes a journey, which is both a literal "trip"— aboard ship or into the Canadian wilderness—and an interior voyage of self-discovery. She is both soothed and awed by her insignificance in the natural world, which is beautiful but indifferent. Out of her new self-awareness, she learns to give of herself and to build a relationship, usually but not necessarily marriage, that brings new meaning to her life, either happiness or philosophical maturity. Love is the solution to this symbolic orphanhood, yet love, too, is imperfect. Orphanhood leaves its mark, and people make do with various "equations of love." This sense of irrevocable loss, of necessary compromise, saves Wilson's love-stories from sentimentality without veering toward cynicism. There is nobility in the aspiration toward love and self-subordination, triumph in even the flawed achievement of those graces. Wilson is impressed by the human ability to transcend egotism through whatever equation of love is possible to each individual.

For a first novel, *Hetty Dorval* is exceptionally good, although a melodramatic climax undercuts the subtleties of its characterization. It introduces Wilson's recurring themes: orphanhood, egotism, and love; the tempering of the ego by nature or travel; the lasting impact of momentary impressions or casual coincidences; the emotional maturation of a young woman. It is the story of Frances Burnaby, and the influence of Hetty Dorval on her maturation. Hetty crosses Frankie's path only a half-dozen times, but the temptation that she represents is very strong. The two are parallel in certain important respects: both are only children, and both are reared with considerable protection and privilege. Both are attracted by elements of wildness, such as the turbulent Thompson River and the flight of wild geese. Frankie, however, has been reared by her parents with friends and loving discipline. By contrast, Hetty's illegitimate mother, Mrs. Broom, has hidden her maternal role, and with it her model of a loving relationship, to give Hetty a superior social standing: she has pretended to be Hetty's nurse and later her lady's maid, so that Hetty has learned tyranny and self-indulgence. Hetty is seraphically beautiful, with selfish charm, concerned only with her own pleasures. Frankie's mother calls her "The Menace" even before she knows Hetty's full story. Hetty's beauty and charm and her elemental wildness attract Frankie as a child. Even though the younger girl gives up the older woman's friendship, in obedience to her parents' orders, she does not understand the evil in Hetty's character. As she grows up and gains experience, however, in each subsequent contact with Hetty she learns more and comprehends more fully the destructiveness of Hetty's egotism. Frankie's full comprehension of what is morally wrong with Hetty's way of life comes when Richard Tretheway, the man she loves, falls in love with Hetty, and she has to decide what action she should take.

Three of the major characters in the story are orphaned: Frankie loses her father during the course of the story; Richard has lost his mother before Frankie meets him; and Hetty is a psychological orphan, having no publicly acknowledged father or mother. Each has dealt with the problems of isolation in a different way. Frankie grows to love the Tretheway family and builds new familial relationships with them; Richard has tried to substitute as a mother to his younger sister Molly; and Hetty has turned to self-indulgence and the collection and abandonment of men. Each of these compensatory behaviors is one possible equation of love, but Hetty's is not honest or giving. The traits in Frankie's character that are similar to Hetty's are finally subordinated in Frankie as she learns to love. Although Hetty comments near the end of the book about their kinship, Frankie has moved beyond Hetty in self-control and compassion, and has thus ended her egocentric solitude.

Wilson's second novel, *The Innocent Traveller*, is a radical departure from her archetypal plot line. Topaz Edgeworth is not a solitary orphan, but a beloved child in a large and close family. Family is an all-pervasive concept throughout the book; characters are designated according to their role in the family, which changes as they age. Father becomes Grandfather and finally Great-Grandfather Edgeworth. Topaz herself is defined successively in terms of child, daughter, sister, aunt, and great-aunt. Topaz does lose her mother when she is young, but Father marries Mother's sister, and the family continues with virtually imperceptible interruption. Topaz continues to live with her father until she is middle-aged, and after his death, she lives with her older sister in much the same role of dependent daughter. Even with the death of the sister, she lives with her niece in virtually the same role, as if she were daughter to her niece. Although she moves to Canada, the wilderness does not impress her, nor does the new environment broaden her sympathies. *The Innocent Traveller* is a happy book, Topaz a happy woman, with a sense of warmth and security very different from the solitary mood of the other novels. Complementing this happy mood are glowing descriptions of the English and Canadian landscapes and sensitive expressions of a generous, witty, and perceptive philosophy.

What this book contributes to analysis of Wilson's thematic development is the contrast it provides with her recurring story of orphanhood and reconciliation. Topaz is never orphaned; she also never matures. Topaz is characterized as a delightfully irrepressible child, a lovable nonconformist, but gradually (and only between the lines), an irresponsible eccentric, and finally an irritating, futile burden on her family. She is loved, but she does not love deeply in return; she is an affectionate family member, but she does not feel the needs and tragedies of others. She remains childishly egocentric to the last of her life. After her death, "there is no mark of her that I know, no more than the dimpling of the water caused by the wind . . . and when we met together . . . perhaps no one remembers, until afterwards, to mention her name." The contrast between Topaz and Wilson's typical orphaned protagonists is striking. Topaz is never independent and never feels solitary; therefore, she never comes to value loving relationships. She never goes off alone to come to terms with herself and her universe; therefore, she never comes to terms with society. She never feels insignificant in nature; therefore, she never feels the need to establish significance through commitment and love. Having realized these themes from the converse and happy side, Wilson was prepared to use them more powerfully in *The Equations of Love* and *Swamp Angel*.

Tuesday and Wednesday, a novella, the first part of *The Equations of Love*, deals with grotesque and pitiable "equations" in a mood of dark humor or satire. It is the story of the marital reelationship of Myrt and Mort Johnson, no longer a marriage of love, but an equation of shared resentment and frustration, lightened by moments of sensuality and a habitual tender impulse. Mort is shiftless, envious, self-deceived, but good-natured and capable of friendship. Myrt is self-pitying, domineering, lazy, sporadically sensual, often spiteful, but kind when it is no trouble to be kind. They live apart from most human contacts; Mort is too feckless and Myrt too lazy to entertain. They have no family except one aunt and one orphaned cousin, Victoria May Tritt, to whom they are indifferently kind because she is even more lonely and repressed than they are. This kindness passes in her mind as beneficence, and her gratitude constitutes a kind of love for them. Mort has a friend, Eddie, whom Myrt dislikes because of his drinking and brawling, but the two men share a bond of camaraderie and wishful thinking. These are the relationships which pass for love in the seedy near-slums of the city.

One evening, Mort meets Eddie, drunk; during a search in the dark for Eddie's lost suitcase, the inebriated Eddie falls off a pier and drowns. Mort, in his efforts to save his friend, falls into the water and is dragged under by Eddie to his death. Witnesses testify to Eddie's drunkenness, and the police conclude that both men were drunk, reporting the accident to Myrt in those terms. In her typical spite and self-pity, Myrt is not grieved, but affronted by Mort's drinking, abandoning her, and damaging her reputation by his association with the brawling Eddie. To salvage her self-esteem, she bitterly adopts the role of martyr. Victoria May has seen the meeting of Eddie and Mort, however, and knows that Mort was not drunk. In her love for both Myrt and Mort, she tells not only that part of the story but also the fiction that Mort dived after Eddie in a heroic attempt to save his friend. Thus, in her love for this unlikely pair, she both redeems Mort and comforts his wife by recalling Myrt's love for Mort, restoring her self-esteem, and establishing her right to grieve.

Even though *Tuesday and Wednesday* is darkly satirical, the story is in some ways the clearest of Wilson's statements about the success, however flawed, of the human drive for love as a solution to loneliness. Antagonistic though they may be, Myrt and Mort nevertheless love each other in their own way and cling together against their isolation. Mort's love for Myrt, with so little to thrive on, is sad and admirable. Myrt's need for Mort to pierce the shell of her egotism is believable and moving. Victoria May is almost heroic in her lie for Mort. Such unsatisfactory substitutes for love are pitiable, but they transcend the dingy and uninspiring atmosphere in which these characters live.

Lilly's Story, the second half of *The Equations of Love*, approaches the equations in a more positive way, although the heroine begins even more unpromisingly than Myrt and Mort. Lilly is an abandoned child, growing up like an alley cat. Never having experienced love, she expects none, and her first equation of love is the lust she excites to acquire food and stockings from men. Running away from the police, she gets a job as a waitress in a small town some distance from Vancouver and finds another equation of love, a man who provides her some temporary security, like "a kennel into which a bitch crawls." When this man leaves, and she finds she is pregnant, she goes to another small town farther into the wilderness and gets a job as a maid.

In this new environment, Lilly knows love for the first time, her love for her baby; and for her baby's sake, she invents a dead husband and behaves with such circumspection that she earns the respect of the couple whom she serves. Respect is a new equation of love. In this wilderness location, she also learns a new identification with nature which she could not have known in the slums of Vancouver. She lets Eleanor grow up in touch with this natural environment. Lilly also admires the pretty home and gentle manners of her employers, and she allows Eleanor, her child, to receive training from Mrs. Butler, determined that Eleanor will have a better life than her own. Eventually, Lilly leaves the Butlers and finds employment as housekeeper in a hospital. She and the Matron become close friends, and Lilly begins to build relationships that are overcoming her circle of self-protection. Eleanor grows into a lady and goes to nursing school, where she meets and marries a young lawyer. It is from this marriage that Lilly learns what love can be and what she has missed, when she sees Eleanor "come up to her husband with her face raised, and on her face a revealed look that Lilly had never seen on Eleanor's face nor on any face. . . . She had lived for nearly fifty years, and she had never seen this thing before. So this was love, each for each, and she had never known it." Soon after this, a threat from Lilly's past drives her to Toronto, where she meets a widower and marries him, not with the passion that she has observed in Eleanor, but at least with "the perfect satisfaction which is one equation of love."

Lilly could be another Mrs. Broom (*Hetty Dorval*), but instead of hiding her motherhood and spoiling her child, Lilly drags herself out of that egocentric circle in order to prevent egocentrism in Eleanor, and in so doing, she finds loving relationships which almost transform her. Lilly starts off too badly and is too warped by her orphanhood ever to be totally transformed by love, but at least her story is a triumph of the power of love over egocentrism.

Maggie Lloyd, is triply solitary: the protagonist of *Swamp Angel*, her mother died when she was a baby, her young husband in the war, and her baby and her father shortly thereafter. Maggie, unlike Wilson's other orphaned heroines, is never trapped in egocentrism by her loneliness. She has too much giving in her nature, and makes a second marriage out of compassion. Her story opens when she leaves that mistaken equation of marriage and goes into the wilderness, not to find but to reestablish herself. She finds a job as cook and assistant manager to a fishing lodge owner who has been lamed and can no longer manage alone. His wife, Vera, is the orphan in this story who has been warped and damaged by her loneliness.

Vera finds no comfort in the beauty of the wilderness that restores Maggie after her separation. Vera, to the contrary, longs to return to the city from which she came, and instead of building new relationships that might redeem her, she nags at her husband and grows jealous of his admiration for Maggie. She eventually tries to commit suicide but cannot, and the story ends with Maggie trying to think how to break through Vera's egocentrism to help her. Another pair of "orphans" in this story are Maggie's friends Nell Severance and her daughter Hilda. Although their story constitutes a subplot, in some ways they are more important to the theme than is Vera. Nell is a widow who has had more than her share of excitement and romance. She used to be a juggler on the stage, and she met and married a man she loved deeply. Because of her career and eventful marriage, however, she neglected Hilda to the extent that Hilda has always felt a degree of isolation and alienation from her mother. Nell's loved memento from her past life is a small revolver, the Swamp Angel, which was part of her juggling act. Hilda has always resented the revolver, as it reminds her of her neglect as a child, but she has never told her mother of her feelings: this is her gift of love to her mother. Nell is aware of Hilda's aversion to the gun, although she does not know the reason; one day she boxes it and sends it to Maggie: this is her gift of love to her daughter. Hilda goes away on a vacation, and comes back with new self-knowledge and recognition of her love for Albert Cousins, whom she marries not long before Nell dies. Thus, she builds new relationships to end her sense of solitude. These are very loving relationships, successful resolutions to the problems of isolation.

Swamp Angel makes use of two important symbols which specify more clearly than any of Wilson's earlier books the meanings of wilderness/egotism and orphanhood/love. While in the wilderness, Maggie goes swimming. She feels happy, strong, elemental, and in control of her movements. She can swim wherever she wishes; she is alone and completely independent. She also realizes, however, that this feeling is an illusion: she is not a god. The water is sensual and comforting, but it could drown her as impartially as it now buoys her. She swims back to her boat and returns to the lodge, to the things of civilization and the friends she serves in her job. The other key symbol is the Swamp Angel itself. It is a symbol of Nell's past, and she clings to it until she realizes that it makes Hilda uncomfortable. She gives it to Maggie to discard, reflecting that the symbol is less important than the reality, which cannot be taken away, but which grows less important as she grows nearer to death. Like the water in which Maggie swims, the gun symbolizes independence and control, but it also symbolizes egotism. In giving it away, Nell severs herself from the past in order to build a better relationship with her daughter. Unlike Maggie and Nell, Vera clings to her past, cannot find herself in nature, and so cannot build loving relationships with her husband and son. She tries to drown herself in the same lake where Maggie swims and where she throws Nell's gun.

Ethel Wilson's books can be summed up as minor masterpieces of style, insightful, witty, believable, and intelligent. They are prevented from being major works by faults in plotting, and they have not had a great influence upon literary trends. Nevertheless, they are all readable and entertaining, and the best are compelling. They deserve renewed attention in this age of increased receptivity to literature by and about women.

Carol I. Croxton

Other major work
SHORT FICTION: *Mrs. Golightly and Other Stories*, 1961.

Bibliography
McPherson, Hugo. "Fiction: 1940-1960." In *Literary History of Canada: Canadian Literature in English*, edited by Carl Frederick Klinck. 2d ed. Vol. 2. Toronto: University of Toronto Press, 1976. Wilson's fiction is discussed in the context of a supposed "search for identity" thought to infuse Canadian literature's development in the mid-twentieth century. Mc-Pherson notes a contrary individuality in Wilson's writing that transcends her failure at times to reconcile her creative impulses as both "artist and sibyl."
Mitchell, Beverley. "Ethel Wilson." In *Canadian Writers and Their Works: Fiction Series*, edited by Robert Lecker, Jack David, and Ellen Quigley. Vol. 6. Toronto: ECW PRESS, 1985. Wilson's life and complete works are thoroughly examined. An exhaustive bibliography follows Mitchell's straightforward, readable analysis, making this study a must for Wilson readers.
Pacey, Desmond. *Ethel Wilson*. New York: Twayne, 1967. This thorough, readable overview of Wilson's long and short fiction is not deeply analyti-cal, but it does consider Wilson's lightly ironic vision and her valuable contribution to Canadian literature despite her relatively short publishing history. Despite its age, the book still contains some useful insights. A selected bibliography and an index are included.
Woodcock, George. "Innocence and Solitude: The Fictions of Ethel Wilson." In *Modern Times*. Vol. 3. in *The Canadian Novel*, edited by John Moss. Toronto: NC Press, 1982. Woodcock discusses Wilson's originality and vision as they are expressed in her novels and novellas.
_____. "On Ethel Wilson." In *The World of Canadian Writing: Cri-tiques and Recollections*. Vancouver, British Columbia: Douglas and McIn-tyre, 1980. Slightly revised since its 1974 publication, this reflective per-sonal essay enumerates the strengths of both Wilson's personality and her unique works. This volume contains an index of the names of authors mentioned or treated in the book.

P. G. WODEHOUSE

Born: Guildford, Surrey, England; October 15, 1881
Died: Long Island, New York; February 14, 1975

Principal long fiction

The Pothunters, 1902; *A Prefect's Uncle*, 1903; *The Gold Bat*, 1904; *The Head of Kay's*, 1905; *Love Among the Chickens*, 1906; *Not George Washington*, 1907 (with Herbert Westbrook); *The White Feather*, 1907; *Mike: A Public School Story*, 1909 (also known as *Enter Psmith, Mike at Wrykyn, Mike and Psmith*); *The Swoop: How Clarence Saved England*, 1909; *Psmith in the City: A Sequel to "Mike,"* 1910; *A Gentleman of Leisure*, 1910 (also known as *The Intrusion of Jimmy*); *The Prince and Betty*, 1912; *The Little Nugget*, 1913; *Something Fresh*, 1915 (also known as *Something New*); *Psmith Journalist*, 1915 (revision of *The Prince and Betty*); *Uneasy Money*, 1916; *Piccadilly Jim*, 1917; *Their Mutual Child*, 1919 (also known as *The Coming of Bill*); *A Damsel in Distress*, 1919; *The Little Warrior*, 1920 (also known as *Jill the Reckless*); *Indiscretions of Archie*, 1921; *The Girl on the Boat*, 1922 (also known as *Three Men and a Maid*); *The Adventures of Sally*, 1922 (also known as *Mostly Sally*); *The Inimitable Jeeves*, 1923 (also known as *Jeeves*); *Leave It to Psmith*, 1923; *Bill the Conqueror: His Invasion of England in the Springtime*, 1924; *Sam the Sudden*, 1925 (also known as *Sam in the Suburbs*); *The Small Bachelor*, 1927; *Money for Nothing*, 1928; *Summer Lightning*, 1929 (also known as *Fish Preferred and Fish Deferred*); *Very Good, Jeeves*, 1930; *Big Money*, 1931; *If I Were You*, 1931; *Doctor Sally*, 1932; *Hot Water*, 1932; *Heavy Weather*, 1933; *Thank You, Jeeves*, 1934; *Right Ho, Jeeves*, 1934 (also known as *Brinkley Manor: A Novel About Jeeves*); *Trouble Down at Tudsleigh*, 1935; *The Luck of the Bodkins*, 1935; *Laughing Gas*, 1936; *Summer Moonshine*, 1937; *The Code of the Woosters*, 1938; *Uncle Fred in the Springtime*, 1939; *Quick Service*, 1940; *Money in the Bank*, 1942; *Joy in the Morning*, 1946; *Full Moon*, 1947; *Spring Fever*, 1948; *Uncle Dynamite*, 1948; *The Mating Season*, 1949; *The Old Reliable*, 1951; *Barmy in Wonderland*, 1952 (published in the United States as *Angle Cake*); *Pigs Have Wings*, 1952; *Ring for Jeeves*, 1953 (also known as *The Return of Jeeves*); *Jeeves and the Feudal Spirit*, 1954 (also known as *Bertie Wooster Sees It Through*); *French Leave*, 1956; *Something Fishy*, 1957 (also known as *The Butler Did It*); *Cocktail Time*, 1958; *Jeeves in the Offing*, 1960 (also known as *How Right You Are, Jeeves*); *Ice in the Bedroom*, 1961; *Service with a Smile*, 1961; *Stiff Upper Lip, Jeeves*, 1963; *Biffen's Millions*, 1964 (also known as *Frozen Assets*); *Galahad at Blandings*, 1965 (also known as *The Brinkmanship of Galahad Threepwood: A Blandings Castle Novel*); *Company for Henry*, 1967 (also known as *The Purloined Paperweight*); *Do Butlers Burgle Banks?*, 1968; *A Pelican at Blandings*, 1969 (also known as *No Nudes Is Good Nudes*); *The*

Girl in Blue, 1970; *Jeeves and the Tie That Binds*, 1971 (also known as *Much Obliged, Jeeves*); *Pearls, Girls and Monty Bodkin*, 1972 (also known as *The Plot That Thickened*); *Bachelors Anonymous*, 1973; *The Cat-Nappers: A Jeeves and Bertie Story*, 1974 (also known as *Aunts Aren't Gentlemen*); *Sunset at Blandings*, 1977.

Other literary forms

In addition to writing more than ninety novels, P. G. Wodehouse wrote hundreds of short stories, some eighteen plays (of which ten were published), the lyrics for thirty-three musicals, and a vast, uncollected body of essays, reviews, poems, and sketches. So much of Wodehouse's early work has been lost that it is impossible to measure his total literary output, and collections of his stories published under the title "Uncollected Wodehouse" are likely to appear with some frequency for the next twenty years. He also wrote two comic autobiographies, *Performing Flea: A Self Portrait in Letters* (1953) and *America, I Like You* (1956).

Achievements

Wodehouse has always been regarded as a "popular" writer. The designation is just. "Every schoolboy," wrote Ogden Nash, "knows that no one can hold a candle to P. G. Wodehouse." His novels and short stories were among the best-selling works of their generation, but it should be remembered that Wodehouse's appeal transcended his popular audience. Many of the major writers of the twentieth century have professed a deep admiration for the art of "Plum," as Wodehouse was known to his friends and family. T. S. Eliot, W. H. Auden, Bertrand Russell—all were fanatic enthusiasts of Wodehouse. Hilaire Belloc said that he was the greatest writer of the twentieth century, and Evelyn Waugh offered the following tribute to his genius: "Mr. Wodehouse's idyllic world can never stale. He will continue to release future generations from captivity that may be more irksome than our own." It is unfortunately true that critics and readers who expect high seriousness from their literary pleasures will never quite approve of one who makes a light-hearted mockery of most of England's and America's most sacred cows. F. R. Leavis, the celebrated English scholar, pointed to the awarding of an honorary doctorate to Wodehouse as proof of declining literary standards. Other critics have been even more emphatic in their deprecation of Wodehouse's lack of seriousness. For sheer enjoyment, however, or what Dr. Johnson called "innocent recreation," no one can touch P. G. Wodehouse.

Biography

Pelham Grenville Wodehouse was born in Guildford, Surrey, on October 15, 1881, the third of four sons born to Henry Ernest and Eleanor Deane Wodehouse. Wodehouse's father was a member of the English Civil Service and spent most of his working years in Hong Kong; indeed, it was a mere chance that Wodehouse was not born in Hong Kong. Whether it was miscalculation or the event was premature, his birth occurred during one of his mother's rare and rather brief visits to England.

Wodehouse was reared away from his parents; they were, he often remarked, like distant aunts and uncles rather than parents. Wodehouse entered Dulwich College at the age of twelve and remained there for the next six years. The school was not prominent in the sense that Harrow and Eton were prominent; it was simply a good middle-class school. The headmaster was the most impressive figure, and may have served as the model for Wooster's nemesis, the Reverend Aubrey Upjohn; the headmaster was not impressed with his student. He once wrote to Wodehouse's parents: "He has the most distorted ideas about wit and humour. . . . One is obliged to like him in spite of his vagaries." The vagaries, apart from the student's drawing match figures in his classical texts, are unrecorded. In those final years at Dulwich, Wodehouse had found his vocation. He was appointed editor of the school paper and sold his first story to a boy's weekly, *The Public School Magazine*. The story won first prize for fiction in that year.

Following graduation in 1900, Wodehouse went to work for the London branch of the Hong Kong and Shanghai Bank. His work there was not a complete disaster for the banking industry, but very nearly so. Wodehouse was no good at checks and balances and served only as an unpleasant distraction for those who were. At night, he continued to write fiction and reviews or plays and was given a position on the *Globe* in 1902, the year the first of his many novels was published. *Punch* accepted an article from him the next year, and a second novel was also published in 1903. From that time, Wodehouse averaged more than a novel, several short stories, and either a play or musical a year. In 1914, Wodehouse married Ethel Rowley, a widow with one child. The marriage was a happy one, and the author frequently expressed his gratitude to his wife for the support she had given to his work. For the Wodehouse reader, however, the following year had a much greater significance: *Something New*, the first of the Blandings novels, was published. A few years later, *My Man Jeeves* (1919) appeared, the first of the Jeeves and Wooster saga.

Novels and stories appeared with an unfailing regularity, and in the next two decades, Wodehouse became an acknowledged master. In 1939, Oxford paid tribute to his greatness by conferring on him the honorary Doctorate of Letters (D.Litt.). The doctorate meant that Jeeves, Wooster, Emsworth, and the rest were accepted as part of the heritage of English literature. The London *Times* supported the Oxford gesture, noting that the praise given to Wodehouse the stylist was especially apt: "Style goes a long way in Oxford; indeed the purity of Mr. Wodehouse's style was singled out for particular praise in the Public Orator's happy Horatian summing up of Mr. Wodehouse's qualities and achievements."

Wodehouse and his wife had lived in France throughout much of the 1930's, and though war with Germany was believed imminent, he returned to France after he received the doctorate at Oxford. In 1940, he was taken prisoner by the Germans. In various prison camps, he made a series of broadcasts over German radio which were interpreted as a form of collaboration with the enemy. Wodehouse was innocent of all the charges, but it was perhaps his innocence, the vital ingredient in most of his heroes, that almost undid him. The closest Wodehouse came to collaboration was his remark to the effect that he was not unhappy in prison, for he was able to continue his work. One scholar has called that broadcast "clearly indiscreet," but those who have read the Wodehouse letters know that he scarcely thought about anything else beside his work.

After his release, Wodehouse eventually returned to America, where he took permanent residence; he was naturalized in 1955. In 1973 he was knighted, and he died in 1975 at the age of ninety-four.

Analysis

Few of P. G. Wodehouse's novels are ever far from the school environment, for the plots of the later Jeeves and Blandings series of novels frequently derive from the desire of one schoolmate, usually Bertie Wooster, to help another. Yet the early school novels represent a distinct type within the body of Wodehouse's fiction. Perhaps, as one scholar has observed, these eight school novels are no more than "bibliographical curiosities," in that only the most ardent fan of Wodehouse would be led to read them after the later work had been written. Still, the works are different in tone and theme. The novels are set at Wrykyn College, which seems to closely resemble Dulwich, the author's alma mater. The emphasis is on sports, and this emphasis gives a serious tone to the work. Boys are measured largely by their athletic skills. One might suggest that the ever-present sports motif was a symbol of the particular virtues of youth: comaradeship, loyalty, and perseverance. Enlarging upon these virtues, Wodehouse was following what was almost a cliché in the boy's fiction of the time. The cliché, however, was one particularly congenial to the author, who once noted that he would never be able to write his autobiography, for he had not had one of the essentials in the background of an autobiographer—"a hell of a time at his public school."

Wodehouse loved Dulwich College, and the eight school novels are a record of his affection. The schoolmasters are a decent group, the boys with few exceptions are generous and loyal, and the setting of the college is one of great beauty. The distinctive element in the novels is the happiness which pervades them, and the reader need only remember George Orwell's, Graham Greene's, and Evelyn Waugh's accounts of their own school days to notice the sharp difference between Wodehouse and many of his contemporaries. The only curiosity about the novels is not the absence of horror and malice, but that no one in the school novels seems to have learned anything at Wrykyn. It should also be remembered that many of Wodehouse's most celebrated idiots are graduates of Oxford and Cambridge.

Wodehouse once said of his work: "I believe there are two ways of writing novels. One is mine, making a sort of musical comedy without music and ignoring life altogether." The Blandings series of novels is perhaps the best example of the author's determined resistance to "real life." These twenty-odd novels are centered on the beautiful estate of Lord Emsworth, who serves as unwilling host to almost everyone who goes in and out of his ancestral home. Lord Emsworth is old and absentminded, and his affections are limited to his younger brother Galahad, his roses, and his pig, the Empress of Blandings. This pig, as Emsworth remarks several times in each of the novels, has won the silver prize for being the fattest in Shropshire County. Only Galahad can really appreciate the high distinction that has been conferred on the Empress, and one feels that even he is not very serious about the pig. Yet the Empress is very nearly the catalyst for all of the actions that take place in the novels. She is stolen, which makes it imperative to effect a rescue; she is painted an outrageous color and introduced into strange bedrooms to make the recipients of such favors "more spiritual" in their outlook; and on one occasion, her portrait is done at the behest of Lord Emsworth.

This last episode in the life of the Empress occurs in one of the best of the Blandings novels, and is a fair measure of the formula used by Wodehouse in the series. *Full Moon*, in which the portrait is commissioned, has all of the characteristics of the Blandings novels. Emsworth has the insane idea that the pig's portrait should be done by an eminent painter, but they have all turned down his request. While this action is debated, Lady Constance, Emsworth's sister, has come to the castle with a young lady in tow. Her intent is to keep the young woman away from the man to whom she has become foolishly engaged, foolishly because the fellow does not have any money, which is the essential requisite for a good marriage in the mind of Lady Constance. Galahad arranges to have the young man invited to the castle on the pretext that he is Edwin Landseer, celebrated painter of animal pictures, including "Pig at Bey." Galahad's ruse works for a while, but the young man's painting is rejected by Emsworth, who complains that the painting makes the Empress look as if she had a hangover. The young man is ejected from Blandings but soon returns, wearing a beard resembling an Assyrian monarch. He makes a tragic mistake when he gives a love note to one of Emsworth's other sisters, thinking that she is a cook. He is again thrown out. By the novel's end, however, he has successfully won the hand of his beloved, and the sisters are all leaving the estate. Galahad has once more succeeded in spreading "sweetness and light" in all directions, except that of his usually irate sisters.

There are few variations in the Blandings series. At least one and sometimes as many as three courtships are repaired; the pig is safe from whatever threatens it; the sisters have been thwarted in usually about five ways by Galahad; and Lord Emsworth has the prospect of peace and quiet in front of him at the novel's end. Yet Emsworth, Galahad, the sisters, and a host of only slightly less important or interesting characters are among the most brilliant comic figures in the whole of English literature. In writing the Blandings novels, Wodehouse followed his own precept: "The absolute cast-iron rule, I'm sure, in writing a story is to introduce *all* your characters as early as possible—especially if they are going to play important parts later." Yet his other favorite maxim that a novel should contain no more than one "big" character—is seldom observed in the Blanding's series. Each of the characters has his own element of fascination, and each is slightly crazy in one way or another. As absurd and funny as is Lord Emsworth's vanity about his pig, it is only a little more so than his sisters' vanity about their social position and wealth. If the formula for this series does not vary, neither does the uniform excellence of each novel in the series.

There are more than a dozen novels which use Jeeves and Bertie Wooster as the main characters. These novels have commonly been regarded as Wodehouse's "crowning achievement," but the author once noted that the idea of the latent greatness of Jeeves came to him very slowly. In his first appearance in a short story, he barely says more than "Very good, Sir." Jeeves is the manservant to Bertie Wooster, who is preyed upon by aunts, friends, and women who wish to help him improve his mind as a prerequisite to marriage with him. Wooster has been dismissed as silly and very stupid. Compared to Jeeves, perhaps he is both, but he is also extremely generous with both his money and time, and it is his unfailing willingness to help others which invariably places him in the precarious situation which is the main plot. Wooster is an Oxford graduate, but detective novels are most demanding reading. He never uses a word of more than two syllables without wondering whether he is using the word properly. Wooster is the "big" character in the Jeeves series, and such a character, according to Wodehouse, is worth "two of any other kind."

The marriage motif is very much a part of the Wooster and Jeeves saga, but frequently the central issue of this series is helping Bertie keep away from the wrong woman. It is not quite accurate to describe him as one of "nature's bachelors," for he has been engaged to nearly a score of females and is threatened with marriage in nearly every one of the novels in the series. Some of these women are insipid and poetic, others are coarse and athletic; the worst are intellectual women who want to improve his mind. He is assigned books to read which he finds boring and incomprehensible, told never to laugh aloud, and threatened, after marriage, to have his membership in the Drones Club revoked. Bertie is quite content with the state of his mind and soul. At the threat of marriage and all the other threats that the novels present,

Jeeves comes to the rescue. In spite of Bertie's chronic need of Jeeves' aid, he is ostensibly the main character in the novels and one of Wodehouse's most brilliant creations. It is through the eyes of Bertie that the reader observes and passes judgment on what is taking place in the novel. Such a process was an enormous technical difficulty for his creator: Wooster must be stupid and generous in order for the plot to develop, but not so stupid that the reader casts him off.

The character of Jeeves, perfect as it is, is one of the most traditional aspects of Wodehouse's craft, for the wise servant of a stupid master is a hoary cliché. Jeeves has never been to Oxford, and he has no aristocratic blood flowing in his veins to spur him into action. His central motive for rescuing Bertie and the legions of others who come to him for counsel is a manifestation of what is called in this series of novels "the feudal spirit." Though not a university man, Jeeves knows French, Latin, and the whole of English literature. He quotes freely from the Shakespearean tragedies, and even has at his disposal a host of obscure lines from obscure poets in Latin and English. He is not a gloomy person, but Benedictus de Spinoza is his favorite author. He is well acquainted with psychology, and his rescue of Bertie or others in trouble frequently derives from his knowledge of the "psychology" of the individuals in question. He is moved by the feudal spirit, but he is tipped in a handsome way by his employer for services rendered, and he accepts the just praises of all whom he serves.

The series is also distinguished by a host of lesser figures who threaten to jostle Bertie out of his role as the main character. Gussie Fink-Nottle is an old schoolmate of Bertie, and he is engaged to a particularly insipid woman, Madelaine Basset, a romantic intellectual. She has a poetic phrase for everything, and drives Bertie and all who know her crazy merely by opening her mouth. Madelaine is one of Bertie's ex-girl friends, and she imagines that Bertie is still in love with her. The hero's duty is to see that the pending nuptials between Gussie and Madelaine take place, but Gussie, who is even less intelligent than Bertie, keeps fouling things up. Bertie goes at once to his aid, but nothing works until Jeeves puts his brain to the trial.

Jeeves never fails in his destined role as guardian angel to Wooster, but the plots frequently have an additional twist. Jeeves, though not omniscient as a character, has recourse to a body of information that none of the others shares. As a butler and member of a London club for butlers, he has access to a private collection of anecdotes supplied by other butlers about their masters. It is a point of honor for a manservant to supply all vital information about his employer—tastes, eccentricities, and even weaknesses—so that others will be well advised before taking employment with the same person. The collection has something about almost every rich male in England, and when affairs take on a desperate note, Jeeves is dispatched to London to find out something about the adversary that might serve as blackmail. Thus, one of the silliest of Wodehouse's creations, a proto-Fascist named Spode who is inclined to bully everyone and especially Wooster, is disarmed when it is discovered that he designs ladies' underwear. As Wooster is being threatened with decapitation by Spode, he mentions the name of Spode's company, *Eulalie Soeurs*, and the man is silent and servile, though it is only at the very end and with the bribe of a trip around the world that Jeeves tells Wooster the meaning of that magic phrase.

The Jeeves novels, then, have at least three plots running through them, and it is in his scrupulous concern for the development of the plot that the author exhibits one of his greatest talents. The key to Wodehouse's concerns for the logic and probability of his plots derives, perhaps, from his lifelong interest in detective novels; Wodehouse frequently avowed that they were his favorite kind of reading. The plots of the great Wodehouse comedies develop like that of a superb mystery: there is not an extraneous word or action in them.

For most Wodehouse readers, the Blandings and Jeeves series of novels represent the highest level of Wodehouse's art, but there are many other novels that do not fit into either category. In 1906, Wodehouse published *Love Among the Chickens*, which has in it the first of Wodehouse's several "nonheroes," Ukridge. Ukridge has almost no attractive qualities. He does not work; rather, he lives by his wits and is able to sponge off his friends and from many who scarcely know him. Another character who figures prominently in several novels is Psmith. The name is pronounced "Smith," and its owner freely admits that he added the *P* to distinguish himself from the vast number of Smiths. The name is one mark of the young man's condescending arrogance, but he is helpful toward all who seek his assistance. A Psmith novel usually ends with the marriage of a friend or simply a bit of adventure for the central figure. Psmith does not hold a regular job, and like many of the other young male protagonists in a Wodehouse novel, he seems to be a textbook study in the antiwork ethic. The heroes in the Psmith series, like the central figure himself, are not ignorant or stupid men, but the novelist's emphasis is on their old school ties and on physical excellence. They are, as one critic noted, "strong, healthy animals." They are good at sports and they triumph over poets and other intellectual types. On occasion, they may drink heavily, but they make up for an infrequent binge by an excess of exercise.

Evelyn Waugh once suggested that the clue to Wodehouse's great success was the fact that he was unaware of the doctrine of original sin. In the Wodehouse novel, virtue is inevitably triumphant, and even vice is seldom punished with anything that might be called severity. In Wodehouse's catalog of bad sorts, one group alone stands out: intellectual snobs. In his frequent descriptions of such types, Wodehouse may have consciously been responding to the disdain with which intellectuals have usually treated his work; in turn, the author had almost no sympathy for the group that he often described as "eggheads." Whatever may have been his motivation, the athletes and the innocents invariably triumph over those who carry on about their own minds or some esoteric art form. It is therefore hard to agree with critics such as George Orwell who find elements of snobbery in the Wodehouse novels. It is true that the creator of Blandings Castle loved big houses and grand vistas, but the aristocrats are too obviously flawed in intellect or temper for any to assume Wodehouse was on their side. It may be, however, that Wodehouse was an inverse snob in his treatment of intellectuals, both male and female. None of them succeeds in his fiction.

There is nothing like a consensus over the source or qualities of Wodehouse's greatness as a writer. Scholars have traced Wooster and Jeeves back through English literature to authors such as Ben Jonson, but source studies do not account for Wodehouse's genius. He has been called the laureate of the Edwardian age, but there is little resemblance between the Edwardian world and that of P. G. Wodehouse. For most readers, the triumph of a Wodehouse novel is in its artistry of presentation. All the aspects of fiction—good story, effective characters, and dialogue which is often brilliant—are present. Wodehouse once summed up his career as well as anyone ever has: "When in due course Charon ferries me across the Styx and everyone is telling everyone else what a rotten writer I was, I hope at least one voice will be heard piping up: 'But he did take trouble.'" Wodehouse did indeed take trouble with his work, but given the rich abundance of that work and the incredible smoothness of each volume, the reader would never know.

John R. Griffin

Other major works

SHORT FICTION: *Tales of St. Austin's*, 1903; *The Man Upstairs, and Other Stories*, 1914; *The Man with Two Left Feet, and Other Stories*, 1917; *My Man Jeeves*, 1919; *The Clicking of Cuthbert*, 1922 (also known as *Golf Without Tears*); *Ukridge*, 1924 (also known as *He Rather Enjoyed It*); *Carry on, Jeeves!*, 1925; *The Heart of a Goof*, 1926 (also known as *Divots*); *Meet Mr. Mulliner*, 1927; *Mr. Mulliner Speaking*, 1929; *Jeeves Omnibus*, 1931 (revised as *The World of Jeeves*, 1967); *Mulliner Nights*, 1933; *Blandings Castle and Elsewhere*, 1935 (also known as *Blandings Castle*); *Mulliner Omnibus*, 1935 (revised as *The World of Mr. Mulliner*, 1972); *Young Men in Spats*, 1936; *Lord Emsworth and Others*, 1937 (also known as *The Crime Wave at Blandings*); *Dudley Is Back to Normal*, 1940; *Eggs, Beans, and Crumpets*, 1940; *Nothing Serious*, 1950; *Selected Stories*, 1958; *A Few Quick Ones*, 1959; *Plum Pie*, 1966; *The Golf Omnibus: Thirty-One Golfing Short Stories*, 1973; *The World of Psmith*, 1974.

PLAYS: *Gentleman of Leisure*, 1910 (with John Stapleton); *The Play's the Thing*, 1926 (adaptation); *Good Morning, Bill*, 1927 (adaptation); *A Damsel in Distress*, 1928 (adaptation with Ian Hay); *Baa, Baa Black Sheep*, 1929 (with Ian Hay); *Candlelight*, 1929 (adaptation); *Leave It to Psmith*, 1930 (adaptation with Ian Hay); *Anything Goes*, 1936 (with others); *Carry On, Jeeves*, 1956 (adaptation with Guy Bolton).

NONFICTION: *William Tell Told Again*, 1904 (with additional fictional material); *Louder and Funnier*, 1932; *Bring on the Girls: The Improbable Story of Our Life in Musical Comedy, with Pictures to Prove It*, 1953 (with Guy Bolton); *Performing Flea: A Self-Portrait in Letters*, 1953 (revised as *Author! Author!*, 1962, W. Townend, editor); *America, I Like You*, 1956 (revised as *Over Seventy: An Autobiography with Digressions*, 1957).

EDITED TEXTS: *A Century of Humour*, 1934; *The Best of Modern Humor*, 1952 (edited with Scott Meredith); *The Week-End Book of Humor*, 1952 (edited with Meredith); *A Carnival of Modern Humor*, 1967 (edited with Meredith).

Bibliography
Cazalet-Keir, Thelma, ed. *Homage to P. G. Wodehouse*. London: Barrie & Jenkins, 1973. Though not strictly a scholarly or critical work, this collection of essays by various admirers provides insight into Wodehouse's appeal to readers. Also contains pieces by co-workers such as Guy Bolton, who worked with Wodehouse on musicals.

Green, Benny. *P. G. Wodehouse: A Literary Biography*. New York: Rutledge Press, 1981. This very useful study, arranged chronologically, traces the connections between Wodehouse's personal experiences and his fictional creations. Illustrations, a chronology, notes, a bibliography and an index are included.

Hall, Robert A., Jr. *The Comic Style of P. G. Wodehouse*. Hamden, Conn.: Archon Books, 1974. Provides a discussion of three types of Wodehouse's stories, including school tales and juvenilia, romances and farces, and the various sagas. The fascinating, detailed analysis of Wodehouse's narrative techniques and linguistic characteristics is indispensable for anyone interested in understanding his style. Contains an index and a bibliography.

Sproat, Iain. *Wodehouse at War*. New Haven, Conn.: Ticknor & Fields, 1981. This volume is necessary to those studying the sad war events that clouded Wodehouse's life and to those interested in exploring the individual psychology that produced such comic delight. Sproat, a politician as well as a fan, vindicates Wodehouse's innocence in the infamous Nazi broadcasts, which are reprinted here. Includes appendices of documents in the case.

Usborne, Richard. *Wodehouse at Work to the End*. 1961. Rev. Ed. London: Barrie & Jenkins, 1976. Includes individual chapters on Wodehouse's major series characters, very helpful appendices of lists of his books, plays, and films, and an index. For the diehard fan, each chapter is followed by a brief section called "Images," with humorous quotations from the works.

The introduction refers to other secondary sources.

Voorhees, Richard J. *P. G. Wodehouse*. New York: Twayne, 1966. An excellent introductory volume on Wodehouse, with chapters on his life, his public school stories, his early novels, the development of his romantic and comic novels, a description of the Wodehouse world, and a discussion of the place of that world in British literature. A chronology, notes and references, and a bibliography of primary and secondary sources are provided.

LARRY WOIWODE

Born: Carrington, North Dakota; October 30, 1941

Principal long fiction

What I'm Going to Do, I Think, 1969; *Beyond the Bedroom Wall: A Family Album*, 1975; *Poppa John*, 1981; *Born Brothers*, 1988; *Indian Affairs*, 1991.

Other literary forms

Larry Woiwode is known primarily for his longer fiction, but he has frequently published short stories in such prominent literary periodicals as *The Atlantic* and *The New Yorker*; several of his stories have been chosen for anthologies of the year's best. *The Neumiller Stories* (1989), a collection of thirteen previously uncollected stories, including three new ones penned in the 1980's, expands the "family album" of narratives about the Neumiller clan that Woiwode began in his novels *Beyond the Bedroom Wall* and *Born Brothers*. He has also published a well-received book of poetry, *Even Tide* (1977).

Achievements

Woiwode's first novel, *What I'm Going to Do, I Think*, won for him the prestigious William Faulkner Foundation Award for the "most notable first novel" of 1969 and brought him immediate critical attention. It reached the best-seller list and has been translated into several foreign languages. His second novel, *Beyond the Bedroom Wall*, actually begun before *What I'm Going to Do, I Think*, was nominated for both the National Book Award and the National Book Critics Circle Award. It became an even bigger commercial and critical success than his first novel. Woiwode's third novel, *Poppa John*, however, was much less successful commercially and critically. The novel's premise and protagonist indeed represented a departure from the regional narrative Woiwode had successfully employed in his previous fiction, but subsequent criticism may yet redeem it from its detractors.

Poppa John notwithstanding, critics are quick to credit Woiwode's idiosyncratic, family-centered narratives with helping indirectly to rehabilitate the family chronicle, a genre long considered out of fashion. After a decade of relative publishing silence, Woiwode returned to this narrative genre in *Born Brothers* and *The Neumiller Stories*. Woiwode's evolving canon of Neumiller narratives depicts prodigal sons and daughters who, no matter where they tread, fulfill their destiny in rediscovering their roots and the family relationships which nurtured them early in their lives. Woiwode unabashedly admires the traditional nuclear family, and his fiction underscores the value of finding one's way by retracing one's steps. His narrative strength is thus seen in the fact that, even among readers accustomed to despondent, "lost" protagonists preoccupied with discovering the mysteries of life in the squalor of the city or some illicit relationship, Woiwode can make such old-fashioned premises seem startlingly fresh and appealing.

In the ebb and flow of many a writer's career, an acclaimed "first novel" often permanently overshadows subsequent efforts, and the disappointment with—and apparent dearth of fresh ideas that followed after—the publication of *Poppa John* provoked many critics and readers to wonder if Woiwode had lost his narrative vision. Such a concern seems to have been effectively answered with the publication of *Born Brothers* and *The Neumiller Stories*.

Biography

Larry Alfred Woiwode (pronounced "why-wood-ee") was born in Carrington, North Dakota, October 30, 1941, and spent his early years in nearby Sykeston, a predominantly German settlement amid the rugged, often forbidding north-midwestern terrain. No doubt the beauty as well as the stark loneliness of this landscape heightened the author's appreciation for the effect of nature upon individual character. At the age of ten, he moved with his family to Manito, Illinois, another evocatively Midwestern environment capable of nurturing the descriptive powers of a budding fiction writer.

He attended the University of Illinois for five years but failed to complete a bachelor's degree, leaving the university in 1964 with an associate of arts in rhetoric. He met his future wife, Carol Ann Patterson, during this period and married her on May 21, 1965. After leaving Illinois, Woiwode moved to New York City and supported his family with free-lance writing, publishing in *The New Yorker* and other prestigious periodicals while working on two novels.

He has been a writer-in-residence at the University of Wisconsin, Madison, and has had extended teaching posts at Wheaton College (Illinois) and at the State University of New York at Binghamton, where he has served as a faculty member intermittently since 1983. In 1977, he was awarded the Doctor of Letters degree from North Dakota State University.

Analysis

As a novelist, Larry Woiwode stands apart from most of his contemporaries in refusing to drown his characters in the angst-ridden excesses that have become so conventional in the modern American novel. His characters are not helpless victims of their times but participants in them; they are accountable not so much for what has happened to them but for what they do in response to their circumstances. Their conflicts, from Chris Van Eenanam's enigmatic search for manhood in *What I'm Going to Do, I Think* to Poppa John's drive to recover his self-identity, are not merely contrived psychological dramas played out inside their own consciousness, but compelling confrontations with the very concrete world of everyday life. This is a world which registers as authentic to the reader precisely because of Woiwode's gift for realism.

Woiwode's characters eventually recognize that the answer to their dilemmas is only partly in themselves. In the reestablishment of personal trust in friendships and the nostalgia of forgotten familial relationships, they recover a sense of balance and worth in themselves. However obliquely, each major Woiwode character finds himself in a quest for a transcendent moral order, a renewed trust in God and man that would give him a reference point for his life. This quest animates their rejection of narcissism and a search for a love and security that only marital and familial relationships can foster.

Woiwode's willingness to affirm that these relationships are central to self-fulfillment and to the stability of American culture makes him unique among a generation of writers whose thematic concerns tend to focus on their characters' dehumanization in society and alienation from family life and marital fidelity. Woiwode thus belongs in the company of self-consciously moralistic writers such as Walker Percy and Saul Bellow, who are more interested in the ways human beings survive and thrive in a fallen world than in the ways they capitulate to it.

Nevertheless, when compared with other writers of his caliber, Woiwode has not been a particularly prolific author. In the two decades immediately after he had ended an abortive college career to pursue free-lance writing, he produced only four major works: one long, rather complex family chronicle, one medium-length novel, one short novel, and a book of poems. Yet two of his three novels were critically acclaimed, national best-sellers, and are among the best American novels written since 1960. The publication in consecutive years of *Born Brothers* and *The Neumiller Stories* seems to have redeemed Woiwode from the ambivalent response to *Poppa John*, and Woiwode's reputation as an important American writer in the second half of the twentieth century seems secure.

Woiwode's first novel, *What I'm Going to Do, I Think*, is an absorbing character study of two newlyweds, each of whom is originally drawn to the other as opposites proverbially attract. Chris Van Eenanam, the protagonist, is a listless mathematics graduate student, an unhappy agnostic unsure of his calling in life. The novel's title accentuates his self-doubt and indecision, echoing something Chris's father once said in observing his accident-prone son, "What I'm going to do, I think, is get a new kid." Ellen Strohe, his pregnant bride, is a tortured young woman, dominated by the overbearing grandparents who reared her after her parents' accidental death. Neither she nor Chris can abide their interference and meddling.

Despite the fact that little action takes place "live" before the reader, the psychological realism in Woiwode's use of compacted action and flashbacks and the patterned repetition of certain incidents carry the reader along as effortlessly as might a conventionally chronological narrative. The reader learns "what happens" primarily as events filter through the conversations and consciousness of Chris and Ellen Van Eenanam during their extended honeymoon at her grandparents' cabin near the northwestern shore of Lake Michigan.

In this retreat from the decisions Chris elects not to face, the couple, now intimate, now isolated, confront a grim modern world, which has lost its faith in a supreme being fully in control of his created universe. This loss is exemplified most dramatically in the lives of Chris and Ellen as they try to sort out the meaning of affection and fidelity in their new relationship as husband and wife and as potential parents. Ellen's pregnancy is at first a sign of a beneficent nature's approval of their union, but later, as each has a premonition of their unborn child's death, it becomes a symbol of an ambivalent world's indifference to their marriage and its apparent fruitlessness.

In the absence of a compensatory faith even in mankind itself, a secondary faith arguably derived from faith in God, Chris and Ellen come to realize that they have lost their ability to navigate a hostile world with lasting, meaningful relationships. Neither mathematics nor nature can fill the vacuum left by an impotent faith whose incessant call is to fidelity and perseverance without passion or understanding. In a suspenseful epilogue which closes the novel with an explanation of what has happened to them in the seven years following their marriage, Chris and Ellen return to their honeymoon cabin. Chris retrieves the rifle he has not touched in many years, and, as the action builds toward what will apparently be his suicide, he repeats to himself the beginning of a letter (suicide note?) that he could not complete: *"Dear El, my wife. You're the only person I've ever been able to talk to and this is something I can't say. . . ."*

As he makes his way to the lake, he fires a round of ammunition into a plastic bleach container half-buried in the sand. In the novel's enigmatic final lines, Chris fires "the last round from his waist, sending the bullet out over the open lake." This curious ending seems intended by Woiwode to announce Chris's end of indecision—a recognition that his life can have transcendent meaning only in embracing fully his marriage commitment to Ellen.

The expansiveness and comic vitality of Woiwode's second novel, *Beyond the Bedroom Wall*, offer a marked contrast to *What I'm Going to Do, I Think*. In *Beyond the Bedroom Wall*, Woiwode parades sixty-three characters before the reader by the beginning of chapter 3. True to its subtitle, "A Family Album," *Beyond the Bedroom Wall* is a sprawling, gangly work of loosely connected snapshots of the Neumiller family. An engaging homage to the seemingly evaporating family unit at the end of the twentieth century, the novel's "plot" is nearly impossible to paraphrase, consisting as it does of some narrative, some diary entries, and even its protagonist Martin Neumiller's job application for a teaching position. Since Woiwode published nearly a third of the forty-four chapters of *Beyond the Bedroom Wall* as self-contained short stories in *The New Yorker*, it is no surprise that the book reads as a discontinuous montage of events, images, and personalities.

The novel opens in part 1 with the funeral of Charles Neumiller, a German immigrant farmer who had brought his family to America before the war, and it continues, to part 5, closing with stories of the third generation of Neumillers in 1970, bringing the Neumiller family full circle from birth to life to death. Yet it is Martin Neumiller, Charles's son, a god-fearing, devoutly Catholic man and proud son of North Dakota, whose adventures and misadventures give the novel any unity it possesses. "My life is like a book," he says at one point. "There is one chapter, there is one story after another." The eccentric folks he encounters in and out of his extended family form a burlesque troupe of characters who boisterously sample both the joys and the sorrows of life on Earth. In the Neumiller "family album," Woiwode lends concreteness to his notion that reality is a fragile construction, one that sometimes cannot bear scrutiny "beyond the bedroom wall," that is, beyond the dreamy world of sleep, of its visions of what might be. Woiwode intimates that whatever hope there may be for fulfilling one's dreams, it is anchored in "walking by faith, and not by sight," by trusting in and actively nurturing family intimacy.

The rather sentimental, "old-fashioned" quality Woiwode achieves in this family chronicle, his evocation of once-embraced, now-lamented values, prompted critic and novelist John Gardner to place Woiwode in the company of literature's greatest epic novelists: "When self-doubt, alienation, and fashionable pessimism become a bore and, what's worse, a patent delusion, how does one get back to the big emotions, the large and fairly confident life affirmations of an Arnold Bennett, a Dickens, a Dostoevsky? *Beyond the Bedroom Wall* is a brilliant solution."

Woiwode's eye for the rich details of daily life enables him to move through vast stretches of time and space in executing the episodic structure in this novel. His appreciation for the cadences of Midwestern speech and his understanding of the distinctiveness of prairie life and landscape and its impact on the worldviews of its inhabitants recall other regional writers such as Rudy Wiebe and Garrison Keillor at their best.

Poppa John is shockingly short when compared with the massive *Beyond the Bedroom Wall*, and is more a novella than a novel. The book takes its title from the character Ned Daley played for many years on a popular television soap opera. His immense popularity beginning to overshadow the show itself, he is abruptly written out of the show in a dramatic "death." Ned thus finds himself suddenly unable to recover a sense of purpose, so long has he lived within the disguise of Poppa John, the fiery father figure, who often quoted Scripture to his television family. Now close to seventy, outspoken and Falstaffian in appearance and behavior, he seeks his deeply lost identity.

Ned to his wife, but Poppa John to everyone else, he is lost in the malevolent nostalgia of growing old without self, or self-respect.

The novel opens two days before Christmas, a few months after Poppa John's television "death." Facing the Christmas season with wife, Celia, broke, broken, and without prospects for the future, the couple wander New York City, squandering their savings on gifts they had always wanted to buy for each other. Forced to "be himself," he finds he has leaned too heavily on the preacherlike Poppa John character, and his life begins to unravel. He is finally forced to face his own inconsistencies, his doubts, and even his sins, as Ned, an "elderly boy," is incapable of trusting in a life beyond the present. Speeding to a climax in its closing pages, the novel depicts Poppa John "coming to himself" on Christmas Day, realizing that he, after all these years, does believe in God, and therefore can come to believe in himself.

Poppa John perhaps deserved a better critical reception than it received; as a more than interesting attempt to portray an elderly actor's disintegrating life, it contains some of Woiwode's most lyrical scenes. In the end, however, it remains an unsatisfying chronicle—in part because the complexity apparent in Poppa John's character is never fully realized, presented as it is in a very compressed time frame. While Poppa John emerges as a potentially authentic character in the early parts of the novella, Woiwode gives the reader little insight into the motivations which would prompt his sudden conversion experience at the climax of the story.

In *Born Brothers*, Woiwode has returned to the characters, setting, and moral center that brought him his greatest and most uniformly favorable critical attention. Woiwode begins what he calls not a sequel but a "companion volume" to *Beyond the Bedroom Wall* in the middle of the twentieth century, the narration filtered through the consciousness of Charles Neumiller, a lost soul searching his memories for a meaning to life and a purpose for living it. He finds both in exploring his relationship with his brother Jerome. Charles's fragmentary childhood memories in fact become the narrative building blocks for the often elliptical and multiperspectived chronicle that unravels before the reader in an even more challenging sequence than that of *Beyond the Bedroom Wall*. *Born Brothers* contains less a plot than a chain of remembrances; as family members and their ahistorical interactions with Charles are paraded before the reader in a kind of visual patchwork, one is compelled to enter Charles's consciousness and see the world through his convoluted epistemology.

Despite his outward sophistication and sense of being, Charles is obsessed with suicide; he seems incapable of conceiving of a meaningful order outside the family structure that had shaped his life and has now dissipated with the death of his mother and the collapse of his marriage. In part, it is Woiwode's intent to explain American society's apparent moral disintegration—rampant promiscuity, unwanted pregnancy, and divorce—by reference to the absence of strong family ties. Charles longs for the bond of brotherhood he once shared—or thinks he shared—with elder brother Jerome. That idyllic childhood in North Dakota, free from the cares and stresses modern, industrial life, impinges without provocation upon Charles's consciousness. Charles's strange career as a "radio personality" who is both the interviewer and the interviewee is somehow emblematic of his need for conversion, for freedom from self. He needs an "outside," a reference point, which, Woiwode hints, will come only from faith in the transcendent God whose eternal family Charles is invited to join.

Woiwode makes few compromises for the reader unwilling to attend to— or, perhaps eavesdrop upon—Charles Neumiller's open-ended musings. To refer to his ramblings as stream-of-consciousness narration is to give too precise a labeling, for not merely a consciousness is under consideration here but the history of a mind and a life as well. The journey to and through that history is not one that the casual reader will be inclined to take, which underscores the main criticism of Woiwode's prose shared even by critics sympathetic to his family chronicle: his apparent inattention to the toll his often exhaustive detail takes on both his characters and his readers. Jonathan Yardley's judgment seems most apt: "It's a pity to see a writer of Woiwode's talent and humanity stuck, at mid-career, in the endless exploration and reexploration of material that has yielded its last fresh insight if not its last lovely sentence."

To understand Woiwode's craft and achievement, one must finally recognize the essentially religious character of his narratives and their thematic structure. While believing that the most important human questions are, in fact, religious ones, Woiwode rejects the notion that there can be legitimate, compelling "novels of ideas"; for him, such fiction connotes mere propagandizing. Woiwode handles such questions not by placing philosophical soliloquies in the mouths of sophisticated, worldly protagonists, but by creating authentically ordinary characters, and settling them comfortably into the concrete and utterly mundane world of daily life.

In achieving this effective depiction of what might be called heightened normality, Woiwode's prose is consistently active, alive, and unassuming, approaching at times the crisp clarity of Ernest Hemingway but touched with a finely tuned lyricism. While Woiwode has sometimes been criticized for lapsing too easily into didacticism or marring an otherwise evocative scene with excessive detail, his keen eye for the extraordinary ordinariness of life makes his narrative vision compelling and believable.

Woiwode thus stands out as a moderating influence among contemporary novelists, an advocate for restoring a moral, even religious voice to modern letters. Woiwode promises to become one of North America's more studied and imitated writers of regional narrative.

Bruce L. Edwards, Jr.

Other major works
SHORT FICTION: *The Neumiller Stories*, 1989.
POETRY: *Even Tide*, 1977.

Bibliography

Connaughton, Michael E. "Larry Woiwode." In *American Novelists Since World War II*, edited by James E. Kibler, Jr. 2d ser. Detroit: Gale Research, 1980. An early assessment of Woiwode's gift for regional fiction, which explores the themes and narrative style of his first two novels.

Gardner, John. Review of *Beyond the Bedroom Wall*, by Larry Woiwode. *The New York Times Book Review* 125 (September 28, 1975): 1-2. An enthusiastic review of what most critics believe is Woiwode's best novel; Gardner's plaudits won a wide audience for Woiwode beyond the small circle of intellectuals who had hailed his first novel.

Pesetsky, Bette. Review of *Born Brothers* by Larry Woiwode. *The New York Times Book Review* 93 (August 4, 1988): 13-14. An affirmative evaluation of Woiwode's narrative mode and a defense of its difficult thematic structure.

Woiwode, Larry. "An Interview with Larry Woiwode." *Christianity and Literature* 29 (1979): 11-18. An early, revealing interview in which Woiwode discusses those influences which shaped his narrative vision. Notable is his discussion of the centrality of family to his characterization.

THOMAS WOLFE

Born: Asheville, North Carolina; October 3, 1900
Died: Baltimore, Maryland; September 15, 1938

Principal long fiction
Look Homeward, Angel, 1929; *Of Time and the River*, 1935; *The Web and the Rock*, 1939; *You Can't Go Home Again*, 1940; *The Short Novels of Thomas Wolfe*, 1961.

Other literary forms
During his lifetime Thomas Wolfe published four major works: two novels, *Look Homeward, Angel* and *Of Time and the River*; a collection of short stories, *From Death to Morning* (1935); and his description of his life as a creative artist, *The Story of a Novel* (1936). In addition to his major works, he also sold a few lengthy stories to magazines; *Scribner's Magazine* published "A Portrait of Bascom Hawke" (April, 1932) and "The Web of Earth" (July, 1939). Both of these have since been republished as short novels in *The Short Novels of Thomas Wolfe* (1961), a collection edited by C. Hugh Holman. Because Wolfe viewed each piece of his writing as only a part of some larger design, he frequently adapted past material to meet a present need. For example, he modified "A Portrait of Bascom Hawke" for later inclusion in *Of Time and the River*, and "The Child by Tiger" (1937), a short story he published in the *Saturday Evening Post*, appeared two years later with changes in point of view in *The Web and the Rock*. After his death, Wolfe's editor at Harper's, Edward Aswell, put together three posthumous books from two large packing cases of unfinished manuscript that Wolfe left behind. Two of these books—*The Web and the Rock* and *You Can't Go Home Again*—are novels; the third is a volume of stories, entitled *The Hills Beyond* (1941). Wolfe began his career (unsuccessfully) as a playwright with *The Mountains*, which he wrote in 1920 but which was not published until 1940 by the University of North Carolina at Chapel Hill, Wolfe's alma mater. *Thomas Wolfe's Purdue Speech* (1964), delivered by Wolfe in 1938, is a statement of his development as an artist. Wolfe's letters and notebooks have also been published, allowing for firsthand insight into his personal and creative life.

Achievements
Wolfe captured the essence of what it meant to be young in his time with the publication of *Look Homeward, Angel*. He further influenced readers of the Depression-plagued 1930's with stories he published in magazines such as *The New Yorker*, *Harper's Bazaar*, *Redbook*, *Scribner's Magazine*, and the *Saturday Evening Post*. Widely read in America and abroad, Wolfe was a well-respected author during his lifetime, a man who in a very real sense lived

the part of the driven artist. Wolfe is still read, even if not to the extent of his more significant contemporaries, Ernest Hemingway, William Faulkner, and F. Scott Fitzgerald. In retrospect, Wolfe's achievement is especially remarkable when one considers that his literary life spanned little more than a decade. In 1957, Faulkner ranked Wolfe above all of his contemporaries: "My admiration for Wolfe is that he tried the best to get it all said; he was willing to throw away style, coherence, all the rules of preciseness to try to put all the experience of the human heart on the head of a pin." Wolfe's weaknesses are now recognized, but he is still praised for his strengths. A balanced view of his work has emerged, and his reputation as an important figure in twentieth century American literature is secure.

Biography

Born on October 3, 1900, in Asheville, North Carolina, Thomas Wolfe was the youngest of the seven surviving children of Julia Elizabeth Westall and William Oliver Wolfe. Of Pennsylvania Dutch-German stock, Wolfe's father was a man of intense vitality, a stonecutter who instilled in Wolfe a love of language, whether it be the high rhetoric of Elizabethan poetry or the low vernacular of the mountain people surrounding Asheville. Wolfe's mother was more attuned to the values of commerce than her husband (she was forever speculating in real estate). In fact, one biographer has termed the match an "epic misalliance." Domestic relations in the Wolfe household were often strained; young Wolfe grew up a witness to his father's drunken rampages and his mother's ensuing resentment. From this family cauldron came much of the autobiographical material Wolfe poured forth in *Look Homeward, Angel*.

In September of 1912, Wolfe entered the North State Fitting School, where he came under the influence of his teacher, Margaret Roberts (Margaret Leonard in *Look Homeward, Angel*). Roberts encouranged Wolfe's voracious appetite for reading by introducing him to the best of English literature. In 1916, at the precocious age of fifteen, Wolfe entered the University of North Carolina at Chapel Hill. Six feet tall and still growing (he would eventually reach six feet six inches), Wolfe was a skinny, long-legged youth, sensitive to the criticism of his older classmates. Wolfe's first year at Chapel Hill was unremarkable, but he eventually made a name for himself as an excellent student and a campus literary figure. In March of 1919, *The Return of Buck Garvin*, a play Wolfe had written in a dramatic writing course, was performed by the Carolina Playmakers, with Wolfe performing in the title role.

After graduating in 1920, Wolfe entered Harvard University to pursue his interests as a playwright. He was especially attracted by the famous workshop given by playwright George Pierce Baker (whom he would later depict as Professor Hatcher in *Of Time and the River*). Wolfe hoped to make a literary name for himself, but after a series of setbacks, he accepted an appointment as an Instructor in English at the Washington Square College of New York University and began teaching in February of 1924, continuing to do so intermittently until 1930.

In October of 1924, Wolfe made his first trip to Europe. Many of his experiences there he later incorporated into *Of Time and the River*. Returning to New York in August of 1925, Wolfe met Aline Bernstein, a wealthy married woman who was involved in the theater world of New York. For the next seven years, Wolfe participated in a stormy on-and-off again affair with Bernstein, who was seventeen years his elder. She was the mother-mistress Wolfe seemed to need; certainly, she inspired *Look Homeward, Angel*, which he commenced while abroad with Bernstein in July of 1926.

The popular image of Wolfe as a literary lion is in part caused by the critical success he achieved with *Look Homeward, Angel*, but mostly owing to his personal appearance and habits. Often dressed in shabby clothes, he was known to prowl the streets of Brooklyn, where he had settled after another trip abroad in 1931. One night while wandering the streets he was overheard to say, "I wrote ten thousand words today! I wrote ten thousand words today!" Although Wolfe resented efforts to publicize his eccentricities, it was inevitable that his behavior and fame would make him a legendary figure.

In December of 1933, Wolfe began work on what was to become *Of Time and the River*. It was also during this period that Maxwell Perkins, Wolfe's editor at Scribner's, worked closely with the author on the formation of the novel. Wolfe incorporated his experiences at Harvard, in Europe, and with Bernstein into *Of Time and the River*, which picks up the Eugene Gant story where *Look Homeward, Angel* concludes. In 1937, after critics had raised questions concerning Perkins' influence on his work, Wolfe left Scribner's for Harper and Brothers. His editor at Harper's was Edward C. Aswell, and Wolfe left two large crates containing nearly a million words of manuscript with him before leaving on a tour of the West in May of 1938. In July, Wolfe fell ill with pneumonia and was hospitalized near Seattle. In September, having been transferred to The Johns Hopkins Hospital in Baltimore, he underwent brain surgery for complications he suffered from tuberculosis. He died on September 15, 1938.

Analysis

Throughout Thomas Wolfe's fiction there is evidence of a powerful but sometimes uncontrolled mind at work. Few would argue Wolfe's genius, but many have questioned how well he directed it. Part of the difficulty may have come from his self-professed intention to create an American mythology. The result would be the record of an individual, lonely and lost in the flux of time, forever exploring the diversity of American life. Partly because of his early death and partly because of his own difficulties in giving form to ideas, Wolfe never managed to unify the vast body of his work. Add to this the considerable amount of influence his editors exerted upon his manuscripts, and there still remain some intriguing questions about the interrelationship of segments in the writings and the final form of his novels.

Wolfe wrote with passionate intensity, producing vast quantities of manuscript. His central themes focus on a lonely individual, the isolated artist, in search of self-discovery and the true meaning of the American experience. In *Look Homeward, Angel*, the first of these themes is most pronounced, for this is autobiography very thinly veiled. The story of Eugene Gant is in many ways the story of Thomas Wolfe. After the publication of *Look Homeward, Angel*, which was generally well-received, some critics began to raise questions concerning the novel's weaknesses, especially the obvious attempt by Wolfe to capture experience at the expense of artistic control. It was not until 1936, however, that the landmark case against Wolfe would be launched with the publication in the *Saturday Review* of "Genius Is Not Enough," Bernard DeVoto's indictment of Wolfe and his fiction.

DeVoto was responding to *The Story of a Novel*, Wolfe's extremely frank account of his own life as a writer and the work that went into *Of Time and the River*. For Wolfe, writing was a chaotic experience, something done with great pain and toil. DeVoto acknowledged that Wolfe was a genius "of the good old-fashioned, romantic kind, possessed by a demon, driven by the gales of his own fury, helpless before the lava-flood of his own passion"; he further argued, however, that such genius was in and of itself not enough. Today the legacy of DeVoto's remarks remains manifest in a series of stereotypes: by some readers (especially academics), Wolfe is still thought of as one who never controlled his rhetoric, as one who was unable to organize his work, and as one who sometimes pushed autobiography to the limits of reporting.

To illustrate Wolfe's lack of rhetorical restraint, DeVoto pointed to *Of Time and the River*, commenting that Wolfe invested each experience he described with so much raw emotion that a midnight snack took on the same importance as the death of Oliver Gant. As DeVoto stated, "If the death of one's father comes out emotionally even with ham-on-rye, then the art of fiction is cockeyed." As for the charge that Wolfe was a writer who never exerted sufficient control over his material, DeVoto and others have cited the sprawling sections of his mammoth novels where there is supportive evidence that episodes stand by themselves rather than in relation to others. The extent of Wolfe's involvement with his editors (Maxwell Perkins at Scribners from 1928 to 1937; Edward Aswell at Harper's from 1937 to 1938) also raises questions about his own ability to revise and organize his novels.

Perhaps the most revealing example of editorial influence on Wolfe's fiction concerns *Of Time and the River*. While Wolfe was working on the novel, Perkins met with him day and night for more than a year in an attempt to help him gain control over the voluminous amount of material he had written. Often Perkins would ask Wolfe to go home and cut a section, only to find that he would return with an episode thousands of words longer. In one of the most dramatic decisions any editor has made with a figure as significant as Wolfe, Perkins, without Wolfe's final approval, sent the manuscript of *Of Time and the River* to the printer in September of 1934. Perkins made the decision because he felt the novel was as complete as Wolfe could make it and that Wolfe needed to get on with other work. Whatever the reasons, the ultimate responsibility for the publication of any book rests squarely upon the writer. Because Wolfe was so deferential to his editor and because he was unable or unwilling to see his novel through to the end, he opened himself to questions concerning his craftsmanship, questions which are still being asked today.

Finally, there remains the issue of autobiography in Wolfe's novels. Wolfe himself claimed that autobiography was a part of any serious creative work, but there are in his novels, especially *Look Homeward, Angel*, sections that read like a mere diary. There is also a great deal of artistic invention in his novels, and certainly almost all writers use material based on their own experiences; nevertheless, many of Wolfe's depictions were so thinly fictionalized that individuals were easily recognized, and many were hurt and embarrassed by what they thought were the unflattering portraits Wolfe rendered of them. Wolfe's use of autobiography pushed to journalistic limits raises more questions about his fictional method.

Although Wolfe's rhetoric, his conception of structure, and the autobiographical element within his work have been discussed as weaknesses, these three elements can also be cited as the strengths of his writing. For example, it is true there is ample evidence to support DeVoto's claim that Wolfe's rhetoric is often artificially heightened, but at the same time, one of his most compelling attributes is his ability to depict something as insignificant as a "ham-on-rye" so clearly that readers may suddenly find themselves hungry. More to the point, however, are passages such as the Laura James sections of *Look Homeward, Angel*, where Wolfe manages to capture as well as any writer what it means to be young and in love. There are also numerous passages within his other novels that stand as some of the most poetic set pieces to be found in prose. In large measure, Wolfe is still read today because of the magnificence of his style, however extravagant it may be at times.

Wolfe held to an organic theory of art, one in which content dictates form. He was constantly searching for new ways to communicate experience; in this sense, the criticism directed at him for being a "formless" writer may in some ways be unfair. Certainly there is no doubt that in his attempts to depart from traditional formats he sometimes lost control of his material—*Of Time and the River*, for example, is marred by this flaw. On the other hand, he did manage to find an effective structure in "The Web of Earth," his lengthy story written under the influence of James Joyce. The entire work is filtered through the consciousness of an old woman engaged in reminiscence, and it is the finest example of artistic unity in Wolfe's work. In *Look Homeward, Angel*, Wolfe modified a traditional novelistic form, the *Bildungsroman* (the story of a youth initiated by experience into maturity), organizing the novel not around a unified sequence of events but instead around a series of sense impressions. In this way, the loose structure serves to complement the rhapsodic style. The result is a powerful rendering of the book's central theme—that of an artistic youth lost and in search of self-knowledge and self-definition.

As for the contention that Wolfe is too highly autobiographical, that his writing too often approaches mere reportage, there can be no denying that on occasion, he is guilty as charged. In most instances, however, he was by no means a mere reporter of events. His fiction is memorable because he was such an apt interpreter of human beings and everyday experiences. He was able to synthesize experience into art; he himself claimed that everything in a work of art is changed, that nothing is a literal representation of actual experience. Whether he always achieved this transmutation, it can safely be said that Wolfe is still read today because his novels stand as a testimony to human experience artistically rendered from a unique and personal vision.

Look Homeward, Angel, Wolfe's first and most significant novel, made use of extensive autobiographical material. In many ways, it is the story of his own life, the life of his family, his neighbors, and the region in which he lived. For those who know something of Wolfe's background, there are unmistakable connections between the fictional characters in *Look Homeward, Angel* and the real people among whom Wolfe grew up in Asheville, North Carolina. After the novel's publication, many from his hometown—and indeed many in his own family—were angered by what they took to be unflattering depictions of themselves in the novel. Wolfe's own account of the reaction to his novel can be found in *The Story of a Novel*, wherein he describes the uproar in Asheville and provides his own defense of his fictional method. Essentially, Wolfe believed that the people he described, whatever their faults, were magnificent. As magnificent as he thought his characters were, however, he often described them (no doubt truthfully) with all their faults made highly visible.

The ethics of his method can be questioned when one considers how it must have been to have lived in Asheville at the time the novel was published, to have opened its pages and to have found the characters so thinly fictionalized that their real counterparts could be easily identified. The ethical issue is not so much whether Wolfe was accurate in his depictions of the whole range of humanity he described, but rather how one would feel if he were identified as the model for the town drunk or as the counterpart of the unscrupulous businessman. It did not take long for the people of Asheville to start pointing fingers at one another after figuring out who was who in the novel. Perhaps with some justification, all fingers eventually pointed toward Wolfe himself; the controversy over what he had done to his town and the people in it was so pronounced that he was unable to return to Asheville until seven years after the publication of *Look Homeward, Angel*.

Wolfe departed from the development of a traditional plot in *Look Homeward, Angel* and instead made use of impressionistic realism to tie events and characters together. The narrator moves in and out of the consciousness of the principal characters, giving readers impressions of their inner feelings and motivations. As much as anything else, *Look Homeward, Angel* is the story of a quest, a search for self-knowledge and for lasting human interaction. The subtitle of the novel is *A Story of the Buried Life*, and much of what Wolfe depicts concerns itself with the inner lives of the characters in the novel—what they really think and feel as well as how isolated and alienated they are from one another. In this sense, the novel explores the relationship of time, change, and death as elements which will always frustrate man's desire for happiness and fulfillment.

Look Homeward, Angel was initially entitled *O Lost* and then *Alone, Alone*. The title on which Wolfe finally settled comes from "Lycidas," John Milton's poem in which the archangel Michael is asked to look back toward England to mourn a young man's death and all the unfulfilled potential it signifies. Eugene Gant, is, like most of Wolfe's protagonists, the isolated and sensitive artist in search of meaning and companionship in a hostile world. Given this theme, it is ironic that some of Wolfe's least effective passages are the results of his attempts to describe Eugene's feelings of loneliness and despair. In such segments (which recur in almost all of Wolfe's works), he often lapses into contrived language; rather than arising from natural consequences or from the interplay between one character and another, feelings seem forced by authorial intervention. On the other hand, the novel does contain some of his finest writing, especially when he describes people, places, and things with visionary intensity.

Look Homeward, Angel covers the first twenty years of Eugene Gant's life—his adolescence, his four years at the private school of Margaret Leonard, and his four years at the university. A pattern of potential fulfillment destroyed by frustration is personified in Eugene's parents, Eliza and Oliver, who are modeled after Wolfe's own mother and father. Oliver Gant is a stonecutter who passionately desires to create something beautiful, to carve an angel's head. He is an unfulfilled artist, a man of intense vitality who desires a full and sensuous life. His intensity, his capacity for life, is checked by his wife, Eliza, who is his antithesis; parsimonious, cold, and materialistic. This pattern of frustrated potential recurs throughout the novel. In one example, after spending his first year at the university and losing his innocence in a brothel, Eugene returns home to spend the summer at Dixieland, his mother's boardinghouse. There he meets and falls in love with Laura James (based on his own first love, Clara Paul). In his descriptions of the young, passionate love that develops between them, Wolfe's prose becomes a lyrical celebration that turns to tragic frustration as Eugene learns that Laura is engaged to marry another young man back home, that she will never be a part of his life again. Thus, potential (in this example, physical and spiritual union between Eugene and Laura) is checked by reality (separation and isolation). This pattern manifests itself in varying ways throughout the novel. The story of a youth coming of age by initiation into experience, *Look Homeward, Angel* is a comprehensive account of the inner life of a sensitive and artistic youth.

With the publication of *Look Homeward, Angel*, Wolfe was thrust (not unwillingly) into the limelight as a legend, a novelist who demonstrated enormous potential. His success was spectacular, but because he was a driven artist (much like his fictional counterpart, Eugene Gant), his initial success created a good many subsequent problems. He immediately felt the burden to surpass his first effort with an even better second novel. At the same time, he ran into difficulty giving form to his expansive ideas (a problem with which he would grapple for the remainder of his life). During this same period, he also began leading a turbulent private life. He was involved with Aline Bernstein (the "A. B." to whom *Look Homeward, Angel* is dedicated), and their relationship—as tempestuous as any could conceivably be—would figure heavily in the remainder of his life and work.

Composed of eight sections, each of which is named after some epic or mythic figure, *Of Time and the River* exceeds nine hundred pages in length and spans two continents, continuing the story of Thomas Wolfe as personified in the character of Eugene Gant. Wolfe continues the story with Eugene's departure from Altamont for study at Harvard. He stated his ambitious theme for *Of Time and the River* in *The Story of a Novel*; his central idea was to depict the search for a father, not only in a literal but also in a figurative sense. While trying to exemplify his theme, Wolfe also struggled to form *Of Time and the River* out of the vast amount of manuscript he had written (a detailed discussion of that struggle is related in *The Story of a Novel*). The struggle reached its peak when his editor, Maxwell Perkins, sent the novel to press without Wolfe's knowledge. In one of his letters to Perkins, Wolfe claimed that another six months' work would have allowed him to complete the necessary revisions that would have made the book less episodic. There can be no doubt that had Wolfe written *Of Time and the River* without Perkins' influence, it would have been a very different novel—perhaps a better one than it is. As it stands, it is, as Wolfe himself noted, episodic; its parts are not always aligned to form a unified plot. Even so, there are fine passages throughout that more than compensate for its ponderous pace and meandering plot. In *The Story of a Novel*, Wolfe describes how he wrote one scene that ran to eighty thousand words (about two hundred pages). He was attempting to capture "the full flood and fabric" of four people simply talking to one another for four continuous hours. This scene, as good as he thought it was, eventually was cut, but it illustrates the massive amount of writing he did for the novel as well as the extensive amount of cutting he did to get it into publishable form.

Perhaps the novel's most magnificent scene is that which describes the death of Eugene's father, who has been slowly dying of cancer. Gant, the paternal figure whose presence was so unforgettable in *Look Homeward, Angel*, is now old and enfeebled. His death, which comes in a final moment of tranquillity, stands in stark contrast to his life, which was lived with violent gestures and howling protests. Often drunk, sometimes violent, he was a hard man to live with, but his death comes as a reminder that life lived intensely— however excessively—is life worth living. The death of his wife, Eliza, would not begin to elicit the intensity of emotion aroused by his final moments, for she stands as a testimony to all that opposes the force and fury of his life.

Other memorable scenes in the novel include those that take place in Boston with Eugene's uncle, Bascom Pentland. Uncle Bascom and his demented wife are two of the more finely drawn eccentrics in the novel. These segments as well as others involving Eugene's dreams to become a playwright, his time spent as an English instructor at a city university in New York, and his eventual travel to Europe, all contribute to Wolfe's attempt to describe the vast array of people, places, and things unique to the American experience.

While working out his central theme of a search for a father, Wolfe developed a three-part vision of time: time present, time past, and time eternal. The first, time present, is the time in which the actual events in the novel take place, the time of reality. The second, time past, represents all of the accumulated experience that affects time present. The third, time eternal, stands for the lasting time of oceans, forests, and rivers, of things that form the permanent backdrop for man's experiences. These three levels of time allow Wolfe to contrast, in a vast and symbolic scale, the relationship of past, present, and eternal experience with the experience of Eugene Gant. The result is an intensely personal search for meaning, an attempt to reconcile opposites, to find something lasting and meaningful.

Throughout the novel, a scene that takes place in the present may be linked with past scenes and eternal scenes. In this way, all three levels of time are united. For example, a train ride taking place in present time provides Eugene with the opportunity to recall the travelers of earlier days, their epic searching, their longing for discovery, for movement. During the same segment, Eugene speculates that other men in the future (eternal time) will also travel the earth in search of one another. The novel frequently develops itself in this way, and it is these segments which give the novel its mysterious, almost haunting, quality. At the same time, however, these same passages become repetitious (if not tedious), and illustrate once again the lack of restraint so evident throughout Wolfe's work. In contrast to these overwritten segments are a good many specific characterizations as well as a variety of satiric passages aimed at mediocre people, middle-class values, and intellectual pretenders.

This is a vast and comprehensive book that ends when Eugene sets sail back to America. Aboard ship he meets Esther Jack (Aline Bernstein), who, although certainly not the father for whom he is searching, is nevertheless someone who can help him transcend the tormented youth he has endured to this point in his life.

Both *The Web and the Rock* and *You Can't Go Home Again* were put together by Edward Aswell, Wolfe's editor at Harper's, and published posthumously as novels. It was not until 1962, when Richard S. Kennedy published *The Window of Memory: The Literary Career of Thomas Wolfe*, that the extent of Aswell's influence on the two novels became fully known. Just before his death, Wolfe left a large packing crate of manuscript with Aswell. From that collection of manuscript, it was generally assumed that Aswell found two separate narratives, which he then published as the two posthumous novels. Surprisingly, however, Professor Kennedy discovered, after an extensive study of Wolfe's papers and manuscripts at Harvard University, that Aswell constructed *The Web and the Rock* and *You Can't Go Home Again* from what was a massive—but fragmentary—amount of manuscript that Wolfe apparently intended to condense into a single narrative. Had Wolfe lived, he most certainly would not have published the two novels as Aswell published them. In a very real way, they are as much the product of Aswell's editorializing as they are a product of Wolfe's imagination. Even so, the two novels represent a significant part of Wolfe's creative output, and analysis of them can help put his entire achievement into a clearer perspective.

Wolfe claimed that he was turning away from the books he had previously written, that *The Web and the Rock* would be his most "objective" work to date. It should be noted that at that time, Wolfe had become particularly sensitive about the criticism he had received from DeVoto and others concerning his alleged inability to exert artistic control over his material. As a result, not only did he claim his new novel to be objective, but also he abandoned his previous protagonist, Eugene Gant, in favor of a new one, George "Monk" Webber. The change was more in name than in substance, however, for Webber, like Eugene Gant, bears a close resemblance to Wolfe himself. Indeed, *The Web and the Rock* is quite similar to Wolfe's earlier works: its first half parallels *Look Homeward, Angel*, while its second half stands as a sequel to *Of Time and the River*.

One of the strongest chapters in the novel is enlightening insofar as it illustrates how Wolfe continually reshaped past material. "The Child by Tiger" was first published in 1937 as a short story, but in the eighth chapter of *The Web and the Rock*, Wolfe reworks the story with changes in character and point of view. It is a moving story about the nature of good and evil, innocence and experience. Dick Prosser, a black man of ability and potential, is the object of the racial prejudice that was so pronounced in the South during the early part of the twentieth century. He is a man who befriends several young white boys; he teaches them how to throw a football, how to box, and how to make a fire. In short, he becomes a kindly father-figure who initiates them into experience. There is, however, another side to Prosser. Driven to the point of madness by prejudicial treatment, by his own apocalyptic brand of religion, and by his involvement with a woman, he goes on a shooting spree one night, killing blacks and whites alike. Eventually shot by the mob formed to hunt him down, his bullet-riddled body is hung up for display in the window of the undertaker's parlor. In the course of these events, the young men who were Prosser's friends are initiated into a world full of violence and death. For the first time in their lives, they experience profound loss, and they witness evil as it is personified in the bloodthirsty mob. Woven within the story are stanzas from William Blake's poem "The Tiger," from which the chapter title is derived.

In what makes up the second half of the novel, Wolfe deals with his own experiences in New York City. He explores his relationship with Bernstein, depicting her as a sophisticated mistress and himself as a brilliant but ego-centric genius. Their relationship is described in detail—from their love-making and eating to their quarrels and reconciliations. These segments are remarkable for their candor and intriguing because of the insight they provide into the tempestuous relationship between the two. Webber's past experiences, the environment in which he was reared, and his ancestry symbolically form the web in which he is snared, and, as Esther Jack becomes a part of that web, he escapes to Germany. His search for the rock, the strength and beauty of vision that is represented by the father-figure for whom he longs, is interrupted by his realization at the end of the novel that "you can't go home agin." In short, he knows that he must look to the future to escape the past.

Continuing the chronicle of George Webber's life and artistic development, *You Can't Go Home Again* metaphorically develops the theme that Webber cannot go "home," cannot return to past places, old ideas, and former experiences because time and change have corrupted them. In this sense, "home" is an idealized vision of America as it appeared to George in his youth. These youthful visions come into abrupt contact with reality, and the resulting clash allows Wolfe to explore the very fabric of American society.

The novel begins approximately six months after *The Web and the Rock* ends. Webber has returned home to America, and, against his better judgment, he decides to resume his relationship with Esther Jack. He also resumes work on his novel *Home to Our Mountains* (*Look Homeward, Angel*) and finds a publisher, James Rodney & Co. (Scribner's), as well as a sympathetic editor and father-figure, Foxhall Edwards (Maxwell Perkins). Before his book is published, however, he returns home for the first time in years to attend the funeral of his Aunt Maw. Home in this novel is Libya Hill (like the Altamont of *Look Homeward, Angel*, the locale still represents Asheville, North Carolina). On the train trip home, he meets his childhood friend Nebraska Crane, a one-time big-league baseball star. Crane, a Cherokee Indian, is now satisfied to lead the simple life of a family man and part-time tobacco farmer, standing in contrast to Webber, whose intellectual drive and literary ambition make him a driven "city" man.

Also on the train is Judge Rumford Bland, a blind syphilitic whose corruption serves to symbolize the corruption in Libya Hill toward which Webber is traveling. Upon his arrival, Webber finds that his quiet boyhood town has become crazed from a land-boom mentality that has everyone making huge paper fortunes in real estate (these events parallel those immediately preceding the Depression). Thus, his idealized expectations of home are shattered by the corruption and madness running rampant throughout Libya Hill.

After the publication of his novel, Webber receives abusive letters from the residents of Libya Hill. Typically, Wolfe incorporated his own experiences into his fiction. In this instance, he drew upon his unpleasant memories of what happened after he published *Look Homeward, Angel*. An entire book in the novel ("The World That Jack Built") is devoted to the wealthy lives of Esther and Frederick Jack (the Bernsteins). Writing about his own breakup with Aline Bernstein, Wolfe describes Webber's move to Brooklyn and the end of his relationship with Esther Jack. In Brooklyn, Webber learns to love the low-life characters who inhabit the streets—the prostitutes, the derelicts, and the petty criminals—for they are very much a part of the American experience. To ignore them—or worse yet, to explain them away somehow—would be to deny the underbelly of America that Webber (and Wolfe) found so compelling.

After his years in Brooklyn (with scenes devoted to his relationship with Foxhall Edwards, his editor), Webber tires of New York and sails for Europe. In Germany, he is welcomed with the fame and notoriety he has sought for so long, but he also witnesses the darker side of Nazi Germany. The novel is the story of one man's pilgrimage, a search for a faith that will endure within a society so corrupt that each individual is destroyed by it. *You Can't Go Home Again* is not an entirely cynical book, however, for it concludes with a sense of hope and faith in the future.

Throughout his novels, Wolfe explored isolation, death, and the changes wrought by time—themes that exemplify his interest in the darker elements of life. In his attempts to capture the essence of a moment, he often overlooked the artistic demands that the novel imposes upon any writer. He was not a craftsman of the novel because he often sacrificed form, unity, and coherence to capture experience. His reputation is linked directly to his ambitious attempts to say it all, and *Look Homeward, Angel*, although only the beginning of the story Wolfe desired to tell, stands as his most satisfying and fully realized work.

Philip A. Luther

Other major works

SHORT FICTION: *From Death to Morning*, 1935; *The Hills Beyond*, 1941; *The Complete Short Stories of Thomas Wolfe*, 1987.

PLAYS: *Mannerhouse*, 1948; *Welcome to Our City*, 1962 (published only in Germany as *Willkommen in Altamont*); *The Mountains*, 1970.

POETRY: *The Face of a Nation: Poetical Passages from the Writings of Thomas Wolfe*, 1939; *A Stone, a Leaf, a Door: Poems by Thomas Wolfe*, 1945.

NONFICTION: *The Story of a Novel*, 1936; *Thomas Wolfe's Letters to His Mother*, 1943; *The Portable Thomas Wolfe*, 1946; *The Letters of Thomas Wolfe*, 1956; *The Notebooks of Thomas Wolfe*, 1970; *The Thomas Wolfe Reader*, 1982; *Beyond Love and Loyalty: The Letters of Thomas Wolfe and Elizabeth Nowell*, 1983; *My Other Loneliness: Letters of Thomas Wolfe and Aline Bernstein*, 1983.

Bibliography

Donald, David Herbert. *Look Homeward*. Boston: Little, Brown, 1987. Donald's fine late biography stresses Wolfe's accomplishment as a social historian and his novels as "a barometer of American culture." Like others, Donald admits the presence of much bad writing but confesses to responding enthusiastically to the good. Makes full use of Wolfe's letters to his mistress, Aline Bernstein.

Evans, Elizabeth. *Thomas Wolfe*. New York: Frederick Ungar, 1984. This quarto volume provides an excellent shorter introduction to Wolfe for both the beginning and the advanced student. Economical and accurate, it is keyed clearly to Wolfe scholarship and is rich in unpretentious literary allusion. Though Evans is cautious in her admiration of Wolfe's fiction, she is appreciative of it as well. Contains a chronology and a good short bibliography.

Field, Leslie A., ed. *Thomas Wolfe: Three Decades of Criticism*. New York: New York University Press, 1968. This collection of essays and excerpts is still valuable for its discussions of Wolfe's themes and style as well as its criticism of specific novels and short stories, including a critical commentary on his best-known story, "Only the Dead Know Brooklyn."

Holman, C. Hugh. *The World of Thomas Wolfe*. New York: Charles Scribner's Sons, 1962. An older text, an example of the "controlled research" concept popular in the 1960's, this book is specifically designed for high school and college students. A good cross section of Wolfe criticism is offered, with practical information for further study. Topics for library research and term papers are suggested.

Kennedy, Richard S. *The Window of Memory*. Chapel Hill: University of North Carolina Press, 1962. Remains indispensable to the study of Wolfe; objective, scholarly, and analytic, it melds the work and the man into an artistic synthesis. Particularly valuable as a study of the creative process.

Nowell, Elizabeth, ed. *The Letters of Thomas Wolfe.* New York: Charles Scribner's Sons, 1956. Indispensable to any student of Wolfe, beginning or advanced, because—as Nowell states—he wrote his letters "for himself" as much as for his correspondents, and as such they are as revealing of his mind as his books. The collection lacks most of Wolfe's letters to Aline Bernstein and contains a limited index.

Rubin, Louis D., Jr., ed. *Thomas Wolfe: A Collection of Critical Essays.* Englewood Cliffs, N.J.: Prentice-Hall, 1973. A collection, with an introduction by Rubin, of a dozen stimulating essays by a variety of critics, scholars, and writers ranging from the impressionistic—a mode Wolfe inevitably inspires—to the scholarly. Contains the notorious Bernard De Voto review (1936) of *The Story of a Novel* entitled "Genius Is Not Enough."

VIRGINIA WOOLF

Born: London, England; January 25, 1882
Died: Rodmell, Sussex, England; March 28, 1941

Principal long fiction

The Voyage Out, 1915; *Night and Day*, 1919; *Jacob's Room*, 1922; *Mrs. Dalloway*, 1925; *To the Lighthouse*, 1927; *Orlando: A Biography*, 1928; *The Waves*, 1931; *Flush: A Biography*, 1933; *The Years*, 1937; *Between the Acts*, 1941.

Other literary forms

To say that Virginia Woolf lived to write is no exaggeration. Her output was both prodigious and varied; counting her posthumously published works, it fills more than forty volumes. Beyond her novels her fiction encompasses several short-story collections. As a writer of nonfiction, Woolf was similarly prolific, her book-length works including *Roger Fry: A Biography* (1940) and two influential feminist statements, *A Room of One's Own* (1929) and *Three Guineas* (1938). Throughout her life, Woolf also produced criticism and reviews; the best-known collections are *The Common Reader: First Series* (1925) and *The Common Reader: Second Series* (1932). In 1967, the four-volume *Collected Essays* was published. Additional books of essays, reviews, and sketches continue to appear, most notably the illuminating selection of autobiographical materials, *Moments of Being* (1976). Her letters—3,800 of them survive—are available in six volumes; when publication was completed, her diaries stood at five. Another collection, of Woolf's essays, also proved a massive, multivolume undertaking.

Achievements

From the appearance of her first novel in 1915, Virginia Woolf's work was received with respect—an important point, since she was extremely sensitive to criticism. Descendant of a distinguished literary family, member of the avant-garde Bloomsbury Group, herself an experienced critic and reviewer, she was taken seriously as an artist. Nevertheless, her early works were not financially successful; she was forty before she earned a living from her writing. From the start, the rather narrow territory of her novels precluded broad popularity, peopled as they were with sophisticated, sexually reserved, upper-middle-class characters, finely attuned to their sensibilities and relatively insulated from the demands of mundane existence. When in *Jacob's Room* she first abandoned the conventional novel to experiment with the interior monologues and lyrical poetic devices which characterize her mature method, she also began to develop a reputation as a "difficult" or "high-brow" writer, though undeniably an important one. Not until the brilliant fantasy *Orlando* was published did she enjoy a definite commercial success. Thereafter, she received both critical and popular acclaim; *The Years* was even a bona fide best-seller.

During the 1930's, Woolf became the subject of critical essays and two book-length studies; some of her works were translated into French. At the same time, however, her novels began to be judged as irrelevant to a world beset by growing economic and political chaos. At her death in 1941, she was widely regarded as a pioneer of modernism but also reviewed by many as the effete, melancholic "invalid priestess of Bloomsbury," a stereotype her friend and fellow novelist E. M. Forster dismissed at the time as wholly inaccurate; she was, he insisted, "tough, sensitive but tough."

Over the next twenty-five years, respectful attention to Woolf's work continued, but in the late 1960's, critical interest accelerated dramatically and has remained strong. Two reasons for this renewed notice seem particularly apparent. First, Woolf's feminist essays *A Room of One's Own* and *Three Guineas* became rallying documents in the growing women's movement; readers who might not otherwise have discovered her novels were drawn to them via her nonfiction and tended to read them primarily as validations of her feminist thinking. Second, with the appearance of her husband Leonard Woolf's five-volume autobiography from 1965-1969, her nephew Quentin Bell's definitive two-volume biography of her in 1972, and the full-scale editions of her own diaries and letters commencing in the mid-1970's, Woolf's life has become one of the most thoroughly documented of any modern author. Marked by intellectual and sexual unconventionality, madness, and suicide, it is for today's readers also one of the most fascinating; the steady demand for memoirs, reminiscences, and photograph collections relating to her has generated what is sometimes disparagingly labeled "the Virginia Woolf industry." At its worst, such insatiable curiosity is morbidly voyeuristic, distracting from and trivializing Woolf's achievement; on a more responsible level, it has led to serious, provocative revaluations of the political and especially the feminist elements in her work, as well as to redefinitions of her role as an artist.

Biography

Daughter of the eminent editor and critic Sir Leslie Stephen and Julia Jackson Duckworth, both of whom had been previously widowed, Virginia Woolf was born in 1882 into a solidly late Victorian intellectual and social milieu. Her father's first wife had been W. M. Thackeray's daughter; James Russell Lowell was her godfather; visitors to the Stephens' London household included Henry James, George Meredith, and Thomas Hardy. From childhood on, she had access to her father's superb library, benefiting from his guidance and commentary on her rigorous, precocious reading. Nevertheless, unlike her brothers, she did not receive a formal university education, a lack she always regretted and that partly explains the anger in *Three Guineas*, where she proposes a "university of outsiders." (Throughout her life she declined all academic honors.)

In 1895, when Woolf was thirteen, her mother, just past fifty, suddenly died. Altruistic, self-sacrificing, totally devoted to her demanding husband and large family, the beautiful Julia Stephen fulfilled the Victorian ideal of womanhood and exhausted herself doing so; her daughter would movingly eulogize her as Mrs. Ramsay in *To the Lighthouse*. The loss devastated Woolf, who experienced at that time the first of four major mental breakdowns in her life, the last of which would end in death.

Leslie Stephen, twenty years his wife's senior and thus sanguinely expecting her to pilot him comfortably through old age, was devastated in another way. Retreating histrionically into self-pitying but deeply felt grief, like that of his fictional counterpart, Mr. Ramsay, he transferred his intense demands for sympathetic attention to a succession of what could only seem to him achingly inadequate substitutes for his dead wife: first, his stepdaughter Stella Duckworth, who herself died suddenly in 1897, then, Virginia's older sister Vanessa. The traditional feminine role would eventually have befallen Virginia had Leslie Stephen not died in 1904. Writing in her 1928 diary on what would have been her father's ninety-sixth birthday, Woolf reflects that, had he lived, "His life would have entirely ended mine. . . . No writing, no books;— inconceivable."

On her father's death, Woolf sustained her second incapacitating breakdown. Yet she also gained, as her diary suggests, something crucial: freedom, which took an immediate and, to her parents' staid friends and relatives, shocking form. Virginia, Vanessa, and their brothers Thoby and Adrian abandoned the Stephen house in respectable Kensington to set up a home in the seedy bohemian district of London known as Bloomsbury. There, on Thursday evenings, a coterie of Thoby Stephen's Cambridge University friends regularly gathered to talk in an atmosphere of free thought, avant-garde art, and sexual tolerance, forming the nucleus of what came to be called the Bloomsbury Group. At various stages in its evolution over the next decade, the group included such luminaries as biographer Lytton Strachey, novelist E. M. Forster, art critic Roger Fry, and economist John Maynard Keynes. In 1911, they were joined by another of Thoby's Cambridge friends, a colonial official just returned from seven years in Ceylon, Leonard Woolf; Virginia Stephen married him the following year. Scarcely twelve months after the wedding, Virginia Woolf's third severe breakdown began, marked by a suicide attempt; her recovery took almost two years.

The causes of Woolf's madness have been much debated and the treatment she was prescribed—bed rest, milk, withdrawal of intellectual stimulation— much disputed, especially since she apparently never received psychoanalytic help, even though the Hogarth Press, founded by the Woolfs in 1917, was one of Sigmund Freud's earliest English publishers. A history of insanity ran in the Stephen family; if Virginia were afflicted with a hereditary nervous condition, it was thought, then that must be accepted as unalterable. On the other hand, the timing of these three breakdowns prompts speculation about more subtle causes. About her parents' deaths she evidently felt strong guilt; of *To the Lighthouse*, the fictionalized account of her parents' relationship, she would later say, "I was obsessed by them both, unhealthily; and writing of them was a necessary act." Marriage was for her a deliberately sought yet disturbing commitment, representing a potential loss of autonomy and a retreat into what her would-be novelist Terence Hewet envisions in *The Voyage Out* as a walled-up, firelit room. She found her own marriage sexually disappointing, perhaps in part because she had been molested as both a child and a young woman by her two Duckworth stepbrothers.

More recently, feminist scholars especially have argued as a cause of Woolf's madness the burden of being a greatly talented woman in a world hostile to feminine achievement, a situation Woolf strikingly depicts in *A Room of One's Own* as the plight of William Shakespeare's hypothetical sister. Indeed, the young Virginia Stephen might plunder her father's library all day, but by teatime she was expected to don the role of deferential Victorian female in a rigidly patriarchal household. Yet once she settled in Bloomsbury, she enjoyed unconventional independence and received much sympathetic encouragement of her gifts, most of all from her husband.

Leonard Woolf, himself a professional writer and literary editor, connected her madness directly with her genius, saying that she concentrated more intensely on her work than any writer he had ever known. Her books passed through long, difficult gestations; her sanity was always most vulnerable immediately after a novel was finished. Expanding on his belief that the imagination in his wife's books and the delusions of her breakdowns "all came from the same place in her mind," some critics go so far as to claim her madness as the very source of her art, permitting her to make mystical descents into inner space from which she returned with sharpened perception.

It is significant, certainly, that although Woolf's first publication, an unsigned article for *The Guardian*, appeared just two months after her 1904 move to Bloomsbury, her first novel, over which she labored for seven years, was only completed shortly after her marriage; her breakdown occurred three months after its acceptance for publication. Very early, therefore, Leonard Woolf learned to keep a daily record of his wife's health; throughout their life together, he would be alert for those signs of fatigue or erratic behavior that signaled approaching danger and the need for her customary rest cure. Rational, efficient, uncomplaining, Leonard Woolf has been condemned by some disaffected scholars as a pseudosaintly nurse who benignly badgered his patient into crippling dependency. The compelling argument against this extreme interpretation is Virginia Woolf's astonishing productivity after she recovered from her third illness. Although there were certainly periods of instability and near disaster, the following twenty-five years were immensely fruitful as she discarded traditional fiction to move toward realizing her unique vision, all the while functioning actively and diversely as a fine critic, too.

After Woolf's seventh novel, *The Years*, was finished in 1936, however, she came closer to mental collapse than she had been at any time since 1913. Meanwhile, a larger pattern of breakdown was developing in the world around her as World War II became inevitable. Working at her Sussex home on her last book, *Between the Acts*, she could hear the Battle of Britain being fought over her head; her London house was severely damaged in the Blitz. Yet strangely, that novel was her easiest to write; Leonard Woolf, ever watchful, was struck by her tranquility during this period. The gradual symptoms of warning were absent this time; when her depression began, he would recall, it struck her "like a sudden blow." She began to hear voices and knew what was coming. On February 26, 1941, she finished *Between the Acts*. Four weeks later, she went out for one of her usual walks across the Sussex downs, placed a heavy stone in her pocket, and stepped into the River Ouse. Within minutes Leonard Woolf arrived at its banks to find her walking stick and hat lying there. Her body was recovered three weeks later.

Analysis

In one of her most famous pronouncements on the nature of fiction—as a practicing critic, she had much to say on the subject—Virginia Woolf insists that "life is not a series of gig lamps symmetrically arranged; but a luminous halo, a semi-transparent envelope surrounding us from the beginning of consciousness to the end." In an ordinary day, she argues, "thousands of ideas" course through the human brain; "thousands of emotions" meet, collide, and disappear "in astonishing disorder." Amid this hectic interior flux, the trivial and the vital, the past and the present, are constantly interacting; there is endless tension between the multitude of ideas and emotions rushing through one's consciousness and the numerous impressions scoring on it from the external world. Thus, even personal identity becomes evanescent, continually reordering itself as "the atoms of experience . . . fall upon the mind." It follows, then, that human beings must have great difficulty communicating with one another, for of this welter of perceptions that define individual personality, only a tiny fraction can ever be externalized in word or gesture. Yet, despite—in fact, because of—their frightening isolation as unknowable entities, people yearn to unite both with one another and with some larger pattern of order hidden behind the flux, to experience time standing still momentarily, to see matches struck that briefly illuminate the darkness.

Given the complex phenomenon of human subjectivity, Woolf asks, "Is it not the task of the novelist to convey this varying, this unknown and uncircumscribed spirit . . . with as little mixture of the alien and external as possible?" The conventional novel form is plainly inadequate for such a purpose,

Critical Survey of Long Fiction

she maintains. Dealing sequentially with a logical set of completed past actions that occur in a coherent, densely detailed physical and social environment, presided over by an omniscient narrator interpreting the significance of it all, the traditional novel trims and shapes experience into a rational but falsified pattern. "Is life like this?" Woolf demands rhetorically. "Must novels be like this?"

In Woolf's first two books, nevertheless, she attempted to work within conventional modes, discovering empirically that they could not convey her vision. Although in recent years some critics have defended *The Voyage Out* and *Night and Day* as artistically satisfying in their own right, both novels have generally been considered interesting mainly for what they foreshadow of Woolf's later preoccupations and techniques.

The Voyage Out is the story of twenty-four-year-old Rachel Vinrace, a naïve and talented amateur pianist who sails from England to a small resort on the South American coast, where she vacations with relatives. There, she meets a fledgling novelist, Terence Hewet; on a pleasure expedition up a jungle river, they declare their love. Shortly thereafter, Rachel falls ill with a fever and dies. The novel's exotic local, large cast of minor characters, elaborate scenes of social comedy, and excessive length are all atypical of Woolf's mature work. Already, however, many of her later concerns are largely emerging. The resonance of the title itself anticipates Woolf's poetic symbolism; the "voyage out" can be the literal trip across the Atlantic or up the South American river, but it also suggests the progression from innocence to experience, from life to death, which she later depicts using similar water imagery. Her concern with premature death and how survivors come to terms with it prefigures *Jacob's Room*, *Mrs. Dalloway*, *To the Lighthouse*, and *The Waves*. Most significant is her portrayal of a world in which characters are forever striving to overcome their isolation from one another. The ship on which Rachel "voyages out" is labeled by Woolf an "emblem of the loneliness of human life." Terence, Rachel's lover, might be describing his creator's own frustration when he says he is trying "to write a novel about Silence, the things people don't say. But the difficulty is immense."

Yet moments of unity amid seemingly unconquerable disorder do occur. On a communal level, one such transformation happens at a ball being held to celebrate the engagement of two English guests at the resort's small hotel. When the musicians go home, Rachel appropriates the piano and plays Mozart, hunting songs, and hymn tunes as the guests gradually resume dancing, each in a newly expressive, uninhibited way, eventually to join hands in a gigantic round dance. When the circle breaks and each member spins away to become individual once more, Rachel modulates to Bach; her weary yet exhilarated listeners sit quietly and allow themselves to be soothed by the serene complexity of the music. As dawn breaks outside and Rachel plays on, they envision "themselves and their lives, and the whole of human life advancing nobly under the direction of the music." They have transcended their single identities temporarily to gain a privileged glimpse of some larger pattern beyond themselves.

If Rachel transforms briefly through her art the lives of a small community, she herself privately discerns fleeting stability through her growing love for Terence. Yet even love is insufficient; although in the couple's newfound sense of union "divisions disappeared," Terence feels that Rachel seems able "to pass away to unknown places where she had no need of him." In the elegiac closing scenes of illness (which Woolf reworked many times and which are the most original as well as moving part of the novel), Rachel "descends into another world"; she is "curled up at the bottom of the sea." Terence, sitting by her bedside, senses that "they seemed to be thinking together; he seemed to be Rachel as well as himself." When she ceases breathing, he experiences "an immense feeling of peace," a "complete union" with her that shatters when he notices an ordinary table covered with crockery and realizes in horror that in this world he will never see Rachel again. For her, stability has been achieved; for him, the isolating flux has resumed.

Looking back on *The Voyage Out*, Woolf could see, she said, why readers found it "a more gallant and inspiring spectacle" than her next and least-known book *Night and Day*. This second novel is usually regarded as her most traditional in form and subject—in its social satire, her obeisance to Jane Austen. Its dancelike plot, however, in which mismatched young couples eventually find their true loves, suggests the magical atmosphere of William Shakespeare's romantic comedies as well. References to Shakespeare abound in the book; for example, the delightfully eccentric Mrs. Hilbery characterizes herself as one of his wise fools, and when at the end she presides over the repatterning of the couples in London, she has just arrived from a pilgrimage to Stratford-upon-Avon. Coincidentally, *Night and Day* is the most conventionally dramatic of Woolf's novels, full of dialogue, exits and entrances; characters are constantly taking omnibuses and taxis across London from one contrived scene to the next.

Like *The Voyage Out*, *Night and Day* does point to Woolf's enduring preoccupations. It is too a novel depicting movement from innocence to maturity and escape from the conventional world through the liberating influence of love. Ralph Denham, a London solicitor from a large, vulgar, middle-class family living in suburban Highgate, would prefer to move to a Norfolk cottage and write. Katharine Hilbery measures out her days serving tea in her wealthy family's beautiful Chelsea home and helping her disorganized mother produce a biography of their forebear, a great nineteenth century poet. Her secret passions, however, are mathematics and astronomy. These seeming opposites, Ralph and Katharine, are alike in that both retreat at night to their rooms to pursue their private visions. The entire novel is concerned with such dualities—public selves and private selves, activity and contemplation, fact and imagination; but Woolf also depicts the unity that Ralph and Katharine can achieve, notwithstanding the social and intellectual barriers separating them. At the end, as the couple leaves Katharine's elegant but constraining home to walk in the open night air, "they lapsed gently into silence, travelling the dark paths side by side towards something discerned in the distance which gradually possessed them both."

The sustained passages of subtle interior analysis by which Woolf charts the couple's growing realization of their need for each other define her real area of fictional interest, but they are hemmed in by a tediously constrictive traditional structure. Except for her late novel, *The Years*, also comparatively orthodox in form, her first two books took the longest to finish and underwent the most extensive revisions, undoubtedly because she was writing against her grain. Nevertheless, they represented a necessary apprenticeship; as she would later remark of *Night and Day*, "You must put it all in before you can leave out."

Woolf dared to leave out a great deal in the short experimental novel she wrote next. Described in conventional terms, *Jacob's Room* is a *Bildungsroman* or "novel of formation" tracing its hero's development from childhood to maturity: Jacob Flanders is first portrayed as a small boy studying a tide pool on a Cornish beach; at twenty-six, he dies fighting in World War I. In structure, style, and tone, however, *Jacob's Room* defies such labeling. It does not move in steady chronological fashion but in irregular leaps. Of the fourteen chapters, two cover Jacob's childhood; two, his college years at Cambridge; the remainder, his life as a young adult working in London and traveling abroad. In length, and hence in the complexity with which various periods of Jacob's existence are treated, the chapters range from one to twenty-eight pages. They vary, that is, as the process of growth itself does.

Individual chapters are likewise discontinuous in structure, broken into irregular segments that convey multiple, often simultaneous perspectives. The ten-page Chapter 8, for example, opens with Jacob's slamming the door of his London room as he starts for work in the morning; he is then glimpsed at his office desk. Meanwhile, on a table back in his room lies his mother's unopened letter to him, placed there the previous night by his lover, Florinda; its contents and Mrs. Flanders herself are evoked. The narrator then discourses on the significance of letter-writing. Jacob is next seen leaving work for the day; in Greek Street, he spies Florinda on another man's arm. At eight o'clock, Rose Shaw, a guest at a party Jacob attended several nights earlier, walks through Holburn, meditating bitterly on the ironies of love and death. The narrator sketches London by lamplight. Then, Jacob is back in his room reading by the fire a newspaper account of the Prime Minister's speech on Home Rule; the night is very cold. The narrator abruptly shifts perspective from congested London to the open countryside, describing the snow that has been accumulating since mid-afternoon; an old shepherd crossing a field hears a distant clock strike. Back in London, Jacob also hears the hour chiming, rakes out his fire, and goes to bed. There is no story here in any conventional sense, no action being furthered; in the entire ten pages, only one sentence is direct dialogue. What Woolf delineates is the *texture* of an ordinary day in the life of Jacob and the world in which he exists. Clock time moves the chapter forward, while spatially the chapter radiates outward from the small area Jacob occupies. Simultaneously, in the brief reference to the Prime Minister, Woolf suggests the larger procession of modern history that will inexorably sweep Jacob to premature death.

Such indirection and understatement characterize the whole novel: "It is no use trying to sum people up," the narrator laments. "One must follow hints." Thus, Jacob is described mainly from the outside, defined through the impressions he makes on others, from a hotel chambermaid to a Cambridge don, and by his surroundings and possessions. Even his death is conveyed obliquely: Mrs. Flanders, half asleep in her Yorkshire house, hears "dull sounds"; it cannot be guns, she thinks, it must be the sea. On the next page, she stands in her dead son's London room, holding a pair of Jacob's old shoes and asking his friend pathetically, "What am I to do with these, Mr. Bonamy?" The novel ends.

To construct Jacob's ultimately unknowable biography out of such fragments, Woolf evolves not only a new structure but a new style. Long, fluid sentences contain precise physical details juxtaposed with metaphysical speculations on the evanescence of life and the impossibility of understanding another person. Lyrical descriptions of nature—waves, moths, falling snow, birds rising and settling—are interspersed to suggest life's beauty and fragility. Images and phrases recur as unifying motifs: Jacob is repeatedly associated with Greek literature and myth and spends his last fulfilling days visiting the Parthenon. Most important, Woolf begins to move freely in and out of her characters' minds to capture the flow of sense impressions mingling with memory, emotion, and random association, experimenting with that narrative method conveniently if imprecisely labeled "stream of consciousness."

Jacob's Room is not a mature work, especially with its intrusive narrator, who can be excessively chatty, archly pedantic, and sententious. Woolf protests the difficulties of her task ("In short, the observer is choked with observations") and cannot quite follow the logic of her new method; after an essay-like passage on the necessity of illusion, for example, she awkwardly concludes, "Jacob, no doubt, thought something in this fashion. . . ." Even the lovely passages of poetic description at times seem self-indulgent. The book definitely shows its seams. Woolf's rejection of traditional novel structure, however, and her efforts to eliminate "the alien and the external" make *Jacob's Room* a dazzling advance in her ability to embody her philosophic vision: "Life is but a procession of shadows, and God knows why it is that we embrace them so eagerly, and see them depart with such anguish, being shadows."

Within three years, Woolf had resolved her technical problems superbly in *Mrs. Dalloway*. The intruding narrator vanishes; though the freedom with which point of view shifts among characters and settings clearly posits an omniscient intelligence, the narrator's observations are now subtly integrated with the thoughts of her characters, and the transitions between scenes flow organically. Woolf's subject is also better suited to her method: whereas *Jacob's Room* is a story of youthful potential tragically cut off, *Mrs. Dalloway* is a novel of middle age, about what people have become as the result of choices made, opportunities seized or refused. Jacob Flanders had but a brief past; the characters in *Mrs. Dalloway* must come to terms with theirs, sifting and valuing the memories that course through their minds.

The book covers one June day in the life of Clarissa Dalloway, fifty-two years old, an accomplished London political hostess and wife of a Member of Parliament. A recent serious illness from which she is still recovering has made her freshly appreciate the wonder of life as she prepares for the party she will give that evening. Peter Walsh, once desperately in love with her, arrives from India, where he has had an undistinguished career; he calls on her and is invited to the party, at which another friend from the past, Sally Seton, formerly a romantic and now the conventional wife of a Manchester industrialist, will also unexpectedly appear. Running parallel with Clarissa's day is that of the mad Septimus Warren Smith, a surviving Jacob Flanders, shell-shocked in the war; his suicide in the late afternoon delays the arrival of another of Clarissa's guests, the eminent nerve specialist Sir William Bradshaw. Learning of this stranger's death, Clarissa must confront the inevitability of her own.

Mrs. Dalloway is also, then, a novel about time itself (its working title at one point was *The Hours*). Instead of using chapters or other formal sectioning, Woolf structures the book by counterpointing clock time, signaled by the obtrusive hourly tolling of Big Ben, against the subjective flow of time in her characters' minds as they recover the past and envision the future. Not only does she move backward and forward in time, however; she also creates an effect of simultaneity that is especially crucial in linking Septimus' story with Clarissa's. Thus, when Mrs. Dalloway, buying flowers that morning in a Bond Street shop, hears "a pistol shot" outside and emerges to see a large, official automobile that has backfired, Septimus is standing in the crowd blocked by the car and likewise reacting to this "violent explosion" ("The world has raised its whip; where will it descend?"). Later, when Septimus' frightened young Italian wife Rezia guides him to Regents Park to calm him before their appointment with Bradshaw, he has a terrifying hallucination of his dead friend Evans, killed just before the Armistice; Peter Walsh, passing their bench, wonders, "What awful fix had they got themselves in to look so desperate as that on a fine summer morning?" This atmosphere of intensely populated time and space, of many anonymous lives intersecting briefly, of the world resonating with unwritten novels, comic and tragic, accounts in part for the richly poignant texture of nearly all Woolf's mature work.

In her early thinking about *Mrs. Dalloway*, Virginia Woolf wanted to show a "world seen by the sane and the insane, side by side." Although the novel definitely focuses on Clarissa, Septimus functions as a kind of double, representing her own responses to life carried to an untenable extreme. Both find great terror in life and also great joy; both want to withdraw from life into blissful isolation, yet both want to reach out to merge with others. Clarissa's friends, and indeed she herself, sense a "coldness" about her, "an impenetrability"; both Peter and Sally believe she chose safety rather than adventure by marrying the unimaginative, responsible Richard Dalloway. The quiet attic room where she now convalesces is described as a tower into which she retreats nunlike to a virginal narrow bed. Yet Clarissa also loves "life; London; this moment of June"—and her parties. Though some critics condemn her party-giving as shallow, trivial, even corrupt (Peter Walsh could make her wince as a girl by predicting that she would become "the perfect hostess"), Clarissa considers her parties a form of creativity, "an offering," "her gift" of bringing people together. For Septimus, the war has destroyed his capacity to feel; in his aloneness and withdrawal, he finds "an isolation full of sublimity; a freedom which the attached can never know"—he can elude "human nature," "the repulsive brute, with the blood-red nostrils." Yet just watching leaves quivering is for him "an exquisite joy"; he feels them "connected by millions of fibres with his own body" and wants to reveal this unity to the world because "communication is health; communication is happiness."

Desperate because of his suicide threats, Septimus' wife takes him to see Sir William Bradshaw. At the center of the novel, in one of the most bitter scenes in all of Woolf's writing (certainly one with strong autobiographical overtones), is Septimus' confrontation with this "priest of science," this man of "lightning skill" and "almost infallible accuracy" who "never spoke of 'madness'; he called it not having a sense of proportion." Within three minutes, he has discreetly recorded his diagnosis on a pink card ("a case of complete breakdown . . . with every symptom in an advanced stage"); Septimus will be sent to a beautiful house in the country where he will be taught to rest, to regain proportion. Rezia, agonized, understands that she has been failed by this obtuse, complacently cruel man whom Woolf symbolically connects with a larger system that prospers on intolerance and sends its best young men to fight futile wars. Septimus' suicide at this point becomes inevitable.

The two stories fuse when Bradshaw appears at the party. Learning of the reason for his lateness, Clarissa, deeply shaken, withdraws to a small side room, not unlike her attic tower, where she accurately imagines Septimus' suicide: "He had thrown himself from a window. Up had flashed the ground;

through him, blundering, bruising, went the rusty spikes. . . . So she saw it." She also intuits the immediate cause: Bradshaw is "capable of some indiscriminate outrage—forcing your soul, that was it"; seeing him, this young man must have said to himself, "they make life intolerable, men like that." Thus, she sees, "death was defiance," a means to preserve one's center from being violated, but "death was also an attempt to comunicate," and in death, Septimus' message that all life is connected is heard by one unlikely person, Clarissa Dalloway. Reviewing her own past as she has reconstructed it this day, and forced anew to acknowledge her own mortality, she realizes that "he had made her feel the beauty." Spiritually regenerated, she returns to her party "to kindle and illuminate" life.

In her most moving, complexly affirmative novel, *To the Lighthouse*, Woolf portrays another woman whose creativity lies in uniting people, Mrs. Ramsay. For this luminous evocation of her own parents' marriage, Woolf drew on memories of her girlhood summers at St. Ives, Cornwall (here transposed to an island in the Hebrides), to focus on her perennial themes, the difficulties and joys of human communication, especially as frustrated by time and death.

The plot is absurdly simple: an expedition to a lighthouse is postponed, then completed a decade later. Woolf's mastery, however, of the interior monologue in this novel makes such a fragile plot line quite sufficient; the real "story" of *To the Lighthouse* is the reader's gradually increasing intimacy with its characters' richly depicted inner lives; the reader's understanding expands in concert with the characters' own growing insights.

Woolf again devises an experimental structure for her work, this time of three unequal parts. Approximately the first half of the novel, entitled "The Window," occurs during a single day at the seaside home occupied by an eminent philosopher, Mr. Ramsay, his wife, and a melange of children, guests, and servants, including Lily Briscoe, an amateur painter in her thirties, unmarried. Mrs. Ramsay is the dominant consciousness in this section. A short, exquisitely beautiful center section, "Time Passes," pictures the house succumbing to time during the family's ten-year absence and then being rescued from decay by two old women for the Ramsays' repossession. Periodically interrupting this natural flow of time are terse, bracketed, clock-time announcements like news bulletins, telling of the deaths of Mrs. Ramsay, the eldest son Andrew (in World War I), and the eldest daughter Prue (of childbirth complications). The final third, "The Lighthouse," also covers one day; the diminished family and several former guests having returned, the lighthouse expedition can now be completed. This section is centered almost entirely in Lily Briscoe's consciousness.

Because Mr. and Mrs. Ramsay are both strong personalities, they are sometimes interpreted too simply. Particularly in some readings by feminist critics, Mr. Ramsay is seen as an insufferable patriarch, arrogantly rational in his work but almost infantile emotionally, while Mrs. Ramsay is a Victorian

Earth Mother, not only submitting unquestioningly to her husband's and children's excessive demands but actively trying to impose on all the other female characters her unliberated way of life. Such readings are sound to some extent, but they undervalue the vivid way that Woolf captures in the couple's monologues the conflicting mixture of motives and needs that characterize human beings of either sex. For example, Mrs. Ramsay is infuriated that her husband blights their youngest son James's anticipation of the lighthouse visit by announcing that it will storm tomorrow, yet his unflinching pursuit of truth is also something she most admires in him. Mr. Ramsay finds his wife's irrational habit of exaggeration maddening, but as she sits alone in a reverie, he respects her integrity and will not interrupt, "though it hurt him that she should look so distant, and he could not reach her, he could do nothing to help her." Lily, a shrewd observer who simultaneously adores and resists Mrs. Ramsay, perceives that "it would be a mistake . . . to simplify their relationship."

Amid these typical contradictions and mundane demands, however, "little daily miracles" may be achieved. One of Woolf's finest scenes, Mrs. Ramsay's dinner, provides a paradigm (though a summary can scarcely convey the richness of these forty pages). As she mechanically seats her guests at the huge table, Mrs. Ramsay glimpses her husband at the other end, "all in a heap, frowning": "She could not understand how she had ever felt any emotion of affection for him." Gloomily, she perceives that not just the two of them but everyone is separate and out of sorts. For example, Charles Tansley, Mr. Ramsay's disciple, who feels the whole family despises him, fidgets angrily; Lily, annoyed that Tansley is always telling her "women can't paint," purposely tries to irritate him; William Bankes would rather be home dining alone and fears that Mrs. Ramsay will read his mind. They all sense that "something [is] lacking"—they are divided from one another, sunk in their "treacherous" thoughts. Mrs. Ramsay wearily recognizes that "the whole of the effort of merging and flowing and creating rested on her."

She instructs two of her children to light the candles and set them around a beautiful fruit centerpiece that her daughter Rose has arranged for the table. This is Mrs. Ramsay's first stroke of artistry; the candles and fruit compose the table and the faces around it into an island, a sheltering haven: "Here, inside the room, seemed to be order and dry land; there, outside, a reflection in which things wavered and vanished, waterily." All the guests feel this change and have a sudden sense of making "common cause against that fluidity out there." Then the maid brings in a great steaming dish of *boeuf en daube* that even the finicky widower Bankes considers "a triumph." As the guests relish the succulent food and their camaraderie grows, Mrs. Ramsay, serving the last helpings from the depths of the pot, experiences a moment of perfect insight: "There it was, all around them. It partook . . . of eternity." She affirms to herself that "there is a coherence in things, a stability; something, she meant, that is immune from change, and shines out . . . in the face of the flowing, the fleeting." As is true of so much of Woolf's sparse dialogue, the ordinary words Mrs. Ramsay then speaks aloud can be read both literally and symbolically: "Yes, there is plenty for everybody." As the dinner ends and she passes out of the room triumphantly—the inscrutable poet Augustus Carmichael, who usually resists her magic, actually bows in homage—she looks back on the scene and sees that "it had become, she knew . . . already the past."

The burden of the past and the coming to terms with it are the focus of Part III. Just as "a sort of disintegration" sets in as soon as Mrs. Ramsay sweeps out of the dining room, so her death has left a larger kind of wreckage. Without her unifying artistry, all is disorder, as it was at the beginning of the dinner. In a gesture of belated atonement for quarreling with his wife over the original lighthouse trip, the melodramatically despairing Mr. Ramsay insists on making the expedition now with his children James and Cam, although both hate his tyranny and neither wants to go. As they set out, Lily remains behind to paint. Surely mirroring the creative anxiety of Woolf herself, she feels "a painful but exciting ecstasy" before her blank canvas, knowing how ideas that seem simple become "in practice immediately complex." As she starts making rhythmic strokes across the canvas, she loses "consciousness of outer things" and begins to meditate on the past, from which she gradually retrieves a vision of Mrs. Ramsay that will permit her to reconstruct and complete the painting she left unfinished a decade ago, one in which Mrs. Ramsay would have been, and will become again, a triangular shadow on a step (symbolically echoing the invisible "wedge-shaped core of darkness" to which Mrs. Ramsay feels herself shrinking during her moments of reverie). Through the unexpectedly intense pain of recalling her, Lily also comprehends Mrs. Ramsay's significance, her ability "to make the moment something permanent," as art does, to strike "this eternal passing and flowing . . . into stability." Mrs. Ramsay is able to make "life stand still here."

Meanwhile, Mr. Ramsay and his children are also voyaging into the past; Cam, dreamily drifting her hand in the water, begins, as her mother did, to see her father as bravely pursuing truth like a tragic hero. James bitterly relives the childhood scene when his father thoughtlessly dashed his hopes for the lighthouse visit, but as they near the lighthouse in the present and Mr. Ramsay offers his son rare praise, James too is reconciled. When they land, Mr. Ramsay himself, standing in the bow "very straight and tall," springs "lightly like a young man . . . on to the rock," renewed. Simultaneously, though the boat has long since disappeared from her sight and even the lighthouse itself seems blurred, Lily intuits that they have reached their goal and she completes her painting. All of them have reclaimed Mrs. Ramsay from death, and she has unified them; memory can defeat time. "Yes," Lily thinks, "I have had my vision." Clearly, Woolf had achieved hers too and transmuted the materials of a painful past into this radiant novel.

Although Woolf denied intending any specific symbolism for the lighthouse, it resonates with almost infinite possibilities, both within the book and in a larger way as an emblem of her work. Like the candles at the dinner party, it can be a symbol of safety and stability amid darkness and watery flux, its beams those rhythmically occurring moments of illumination that sustain Mrs. Ramsay and by extension everyone. Perhaps, however, it can also serve as a metaphor for human beings themselves as Woolf portrays them. The light-house signifies what can be objectively perceived of an individual—in Mrs. Ramsay's words, "our apparitions, the things you know us by"; but it also signals invisible, possibly tragic depths, for, as Mrs. Ramsay knew, "beneath it is all dark, it is all spreading, it is unfathomably deep."

In *The Waves*, widely considered her masterpiece, Woolf most resolutely overcomes the limits of the traditional novel. Entirely unique in form, *The Waves* cannot perhaps be called a novel at all; Woolf herself first projected a work of "prose yet poetry; a novel and a play." The book is a series of grouped soliloquies in varying combinations spoken by six friends, three men and three women, at successive stages in their lives from childhood to late middle age. Each grouping is preceded by a brief, lyrical "interlude" (Woolf's own term), set off in italic type, that describes an empty house by the sea as the sun moves across the sky in a single day.

The texture of these soliloquies is extremely difficult to convey; the term "soliloquy," in fact, is merely a critical convenience. Although each is intro-duced in the same straightforward way ("Neville said," "Jinny said"), they obviously are unspoken, representing each character's private vision. Their style is also unvarying—solemn, formal, almost stilted, like that of choral figures. The author has deliberately translated into a rigorously neutral, dig-nified idiom the conscious and subconscious reality her characters perceive but cannot articulate on their own. This method represents Woolf's most ambitious attempt to capture the unfathomable depths of separate human personalities which defy communication in ordinary life—and in ordinary novels. The abstraction of the device, however, especially in combination with the flow of cosmic time in the interludes, shows that she is also concerned with depicting a universal pattern which transcends mere individuals. Thus, once more Woolf treats her theme of human beings' attempts to overcome their isolation and to become part of a larger stabilizing pattern; this time, however, the theme is embodied in the very form of her work.

It would be inaccurate, though, to say that the characters exist only as symbols. Each has definable qualities and unique imagery; Susan, as an exam-ple, farm-bred and almost belligerently maternal, speaks in elemental images of wood smoke, grassy paths, flowers thick with pollen. Further, the characters often evoke one another's imagery; the other figures, for example, even in maturity picture the fearful, solitary Rhoda as a child rocking white petals in a brown basin of water. They are linked by intricately woven threads of common experience, above all by their shared admiration for a shadowy seventh character, Percival. Their gathering with him at a farewell dinner before he embarks on a career in India is one of the few actual events recorded in the soliloquies and also becomes one of those miraculous moments of unity comparable to that achieved by Mrs. Ramsay for her dinner guests; as they rise to leave the restaurant, all the characters are thinking as Louis does: "We pray, holding in our hands this common feeling, 'Do not move, do not let the swing-door cut to pieces this thing that we have made, that globes itself here. . . .'" Such union, however, is cruelly impermanent; two pages later, a telegram announces Percival's death in a riding accident. Bernard, trying to make sense of this absurdity, echoes the imagery of encircling unity that characterized their thoughts at the dinner: "Ideas break a thousand times for once that they globe themselves entire."

It is Bernard—identified, significantly, throughout the book as a story-teller—who is given the long final section of *The Waves* in which "to sum up," becoming perhaps a surrogate for the author herself. (As a young man at school, worrying out "my novel," he discovers how "stories that follow people into their private rooms are difficult.") It is he who recognizes that "I am not one person; I am many people," part of his friends as they are part of him, all of them incomplete in themselves; he is "a man without a self." Yet it is also he who on the novel's final page, using the wave imagery of the universalizing interludes, passionately asserts his individuality: "Against you I will fling myself, unvanquished and unyielding, O Death!" Life, however obdurate and fragmented, must be affirmed.

The Waves is without doubt Woolf's most demanding and original novel, her most daring experiment in eliminating the alien and the external. When she vowed to cast out "all waste, deadness, and superfluity," however, she also ascetically renounced some of her greatest strengths as a novelist: her wit and humor, her delight in the daily beauty, variety, and muddle of material existence. This "abstract mystical eyeless book," as she at one point envisioned it, is a work to admire greatly, but not to love.

The six years following *The Waves* were a difficult period for Woolf both personally and artistically. Deeply depressed by the deaths of Lytton Strachey and Roger Fry, two of her oldest, most respected friends, she was at work on an "essay-novel," as she first conceived of it, which despite her initial enthusiasm became her most painfully frustrating effort—even though it proved, ironically, to be her greatest commercial success.

In *The Years*, Woolf returned to the conventional novel that she had rejected after *Night and Day*; she planned "to take in everything" and found herself "infinitely delighting in facts for a change." Whereas *The Waves* had represented the extreme of leaving out, *The Years* suggests the opposite one of almost indiscriminate putting in. Its very subject, a history of the Pargiter clan spanning fifty years and three generations, links it with the diffuse family sagas of John Galsworthy and Arnold Bennett, whose books Woolf was expressly deriding when she demanded, "Must novels be like this?"

Nevertheless, *The Years* is more original than it may appear; Woolf made fresh use of her experimental methods in her effort to reanimate traditional form. The novel contains eleven unequal segments, each standing for a year; the longest ones, the opening "1880" section and the closing "Present Day" (the 1930's), anchor the book; the nine intermediate sections cover the years between 1891 and 1918. Echoing *The Waves*, Woolf begins each chapter with a short panoramic passage describing both London and the countryside. Within the chapters, instead of continuous narrative, there are collections of vignettes, somewhat reminiscent of *Jacob's Room*, depicting various Pargiters going about their daily lives. Running parallel with the family's history are larger historical events, including Edward VII's death, the suffrage movement, the Irish troubles, and especially World War I. These events are usually treated indirectly, however; for example, the "1917" section takes place mainly in a cellar to which the characters have retreated, dinner plates in hand, during an air raid. It is here that Eleanor Pargiter asks, setting a theme that suffuses the rest of the novel, "When shall we live adventurously, wholly, not like cripples in a cave?"

The most pervasive effect of the war is felt in the lengthy "Present Day" segment, which culminates in a family reunion, where the youngest generation of Pargiters, Peggy and North, are lonely, cynical, and misanthropic, and their faltering elders are compromised either by complacency or failed hopes. Symbolically, Delia Pargiter gives the party in a rented office, not a home, underscoring the uprooting caused by the war. Yet the balancing "1880" section is almost equally dreary: the Pargiters' solid Victorian house shelters a chronically ailing mother whose children wish she would die, a father whose vulgar mistress greets him in hair curlers and frets over her dog's eczema, and a young daughter traumatized by an exhibitionist in the street outside. One oppressive way of life seems only to have been superseded by another, albeit a more universally menacing one.

The overall imagery of the novel is likewise unlovely: children recall being scrubbed with slimy washcloths; a revolting dinner of underdone mutton served by Sara Pargiter includes a bowl of rotting, flyblown fruit, grotesquely parodying Mrs. Ramsay's *boeuf en daube* and Rose's centerpiece; London is populated with deformed violet-sellers and old men eating cold sausages on buses. Communication in such a world is even more difficult than in Woolf's earlier books; the dialogue throughout is full of incomplete sentences, and a central vignette in the "Present Day" section turns on one guest's abortive efforts to deliver a speech toasting the human race.

Despite these circumstances, the characters still grope toward some kind of transforming unity; Eleanor, the eldest surviving Pargiter and the most sympathetic character in the novel, comes closest to achieving such vision on the scale that Lily Briscoe and Clarissa Dalloway do. At the reunion, looking back over her life, she wonders if there is "a pattern; a theme recurring like music . . . momentarily perceptible?" Casting about her, trying to connect with her relatives and friends but dozing in the process, she suddenly wakes, proclaiming that "it's been a perpetual discovery, my life. A miracle." Answering by implication her question posed fifteen years earlier during the air raid, she perceives that "we're only just beginning . . . to understand, here and there." That prospect is enough, however; she wants "to enclose the present moment . . . to fill it fuller and fuller, with the past, the present and the future, until it shone, whole, bright, deep with understanding."

Even this glowing dream of eventual unity is muted, though, when one recalls how Eleanor's embittered niece Peggy half pities, half admires her as a person who "still believed with passion . . . in the things man had destroyed," and how her nephew North, a captain in the trenches of World War I, thinks, "We cannot help each other, we are all deformed." It is difficult not to read the final lines of this profoundly somber novel ironically: "The sun had risen, and the sky above the houses wore an air of extraordinary beauty, simplicity and peace."

Woolf's final work, *Between the Acts*, also deals with individual lives unfolding against the screen of history, but her vision and the methods by which she conveys it are more inventive, complex, and successful than in *The Years*. Covering the space of a single day in June, 1939, as world war threatens on the Continent, *Between the Acts* depicts the events surrounding a village pageant about the history of England, performed on the grounds of Pointz Hall, a country house occupied by the unhappily married Giles and Isa Oliver. The Olivers' story frames the presentation of the pageant, scenes of which are directly reproduced in the novel and alternate with glimpses of the audience's lives during the intervals between the acts. The novel's title is hence richly metaphorical: the acts of the drama itself are bracketed by the scenes of real life, which in turn can be viewed as brief episodes in the long pageant of human history. Equally ambiguous, then, is the meaning of "parts," connoting clearly defined roles within a drama but also the fragmentation and incompleteness of the individuals who play them, that pervasive theme in Woolf's work.

In *The Years*, Woolf had focused on the personal histories of her characters; history in the larger sense made itself felt as it impinged on private lives. This emphasis is reversed in *Between the Acts*. Though the novel has interesting characters, Woolf provides scant information about their backgrounds, nor does she plumb individual memory in her usual manner. Instead, the characters possess a national, cultural, *communal* past—finally that of the whole human race from the Stone Age to the present. That Woolf intends her characters to be seen as part of this universal progression is clear from myriad references in the early pages to historical time. For example, from the air, the "scars" made by the Britons and the Romans can be seen around the village as can the Elizabethan manor house; graves in the churchyard attest that Mrs. Haines' family has lived in the area "for many centuries," whereas the Oliver family has inhabited Pointz Hall for "only something over a hundred and twenty years"; Lucy Swithin, Giles's endearing aunt, enjoys reading about history and imagining Piccadilly when it was a rhododendron forest populated by mastodons, "from whom, presumably, she thought . . . we descend."

The pageant itself, therefore, functions in the novel as more than simply a church fund-raising ritual, the product of well-meaning but hapless amateurs (though it exists amusingly on that level too). It is a heroic attempt by its author-director, the formidable Miss La Trobe, to make people see themselves playing parts in the continuum of British history. Thus, the audience has an integral role that blurs the lines "between the acts"; "Our part," says Giles's father, Bartholomew, "is to be the audience. And a very important part too." Their increasing interest in the pageant as they return from the successive intermissions signals their growing sense of a shared past and hence of an identity that both binds and transcends them as individuals.

The scenes of the pageant proceed from bathos to unnerving profundity. The first player, a small girl in pink, announces, "England am I," then promptly forgets her lines, while the wind blows away half the words of the singers behind her. Queen Elizabeth, splendidly decorated with six-penny brooches and a cape made of silvery scouring pads, turns out to be Mrs. Clark, the village tobacconist; the combined applause and laughter of delighted recognition muffle her opening speech. As the pageant progresses from a wicked though overlong parody of Restoration comedy to a satiric scene at a Victorian picnic, however, the audience becomes more reflective; the past is now close enough to be familiar, triggering their own memories and priming them for the last scene, Miss La Trobe's inspired experiment in expressionism, "The Present Time. Ourselves." The uncomprehending audience fidgets as the stage remains empty, refusing to understand that they are supposed to contemplate their own significance. "Reality too strong," Miss La Trobe mutters angrily from behind the bushes, "Curse 'em!" Then, "sudden and universal," a summer shower fortuitously begins. "Down it rained like all the people in the world weeping." Nature has provided the bridge of meaning Miss La Trobe required. As the rain ends, all the players from all the periods reappear, still in costume and declaiming fragments of their parts while flashing mirrors in the faces of the discomfited audience. An offstage voice asks how civilization is "to be built by orts, scraps and fragments like ourselves," then dies away.

The Reverend Streatfield, disconcerted like the rest of the audience, is assigned the embarrassing role of summing up the play's meaning. Tentatively, self-consciously, he ventures, "To me at least it was indicated that we are members of one another. . . . We act different parts; but are the same. . . . Surely, we should unite?" Then he abruptly shifts into a fund-raising appeal that is drowned out by a formation of war planes passing overhead. As the audience departs, a gramophone plays a valedictory: "Dispersed are we; we who have come together. But let us retain whatever made that harmony." The audience responds, thinking "There is joy, sweet joy, in company."

The qualified optimism of the pageant's close, however, is darkened by the bleak, perhaps apocalyptic postscript of the framing story. After the group disperses, the characters resume their usual roles. Lucy Swithin, identified earlier as a "unifier," experiences a typically Woolfian epiphany as she gazes on a fishpond, glimpsing the silver of the great carp below the surface and "seeing in that vision beauty, power and glory in ourselves." Her staunchly rational brother Bartholomew, a "separatist," goes into the house. Miss La Trobe, convinced that she has failed again, heads for the local pub to drink alone and plan her next play; it will be set at midnight with two figures half hidden by a rock as the curtain rises. "What would the first words be?"

It is the disaffected Giles and Isa, loving and hating each other, who begin the new play. In a remarkable ending, Woolf portrays the couple sitting silently in the dark before going to bed: "Before they slept, they must fight; after they had fought they would embrace." From that embrace, they may create another life, but "first they must fight, as the dog fox fights the vixen, in the heart of darkness, in the fields of night." The "great hooded chairs" in which they sit grow enormous, like Miss La Trobe's rock. The house fades, no longer sheltering them; they are like "dwellers in caves," watching "from some high place." The last lines of the novel are, "Then the curtain rose. They spoke."

This indeterminate conclusion implies that love and hate are elemental and reciprocal, and that such oppositions on a personal level are also the polarities that drive human history. Does Woolf read, then, in the gathering European storm, a cataclysm that will bring the pageant of history full circle, back to the primitive stage of prehistory? Or, like W. B. Yeats in "The Second Coming," does she envision a new cycle even more terrifying than the old? Or, as the faithful Lucy Swithin does, perhaps she hopes that "*all* is harmony could we hear it. And we shall."

Eight years earlier, Virginia Woolf wrote in her diary, "I think the effort to live in two spheres: the novel; and life; is a strain." Miss La Trobe, a crude alter ego for the author, is obsessed by failure but always driven to create anew because "a vision imparted was relief from agony . . . for one moment." In her brilliant experimental attempts to impart her own view of fragmented human beings achieving momentary harmony, discovering unity and stability behind the flux of daily life, Woolf repeatedly endured such anguish, but after *Between the Acts* was done, the strain of beginning again was too great.

Perhaps the questions Virginia Woolf posed in this final haunting novel, published posthumously and unrevised, were answered for her in death.

Kristine Ottesen Garrigan

Other major works

SHORT FICTION: *Monday or Tuesday*, 1921; *A Haunted House and Other Short Stories*, 1943; *Mrs. Dalloway's Party*, 1973 (Stella McNichol, editor); *The Complete Shorter Fiction of Virginia Woolf*, 1985.

NONFICTION: *The Common Reader: First Series*, 1925; *A Room of One's Own*, 1929; *The Common Reader: Second Series*, 1932; *Three Guineas*, 1938; *Roger Fry: A Biography*, 1940; *The Death of the Moth and Other Essays*, 1942; *The Moment and Other Essays*, 1947; *The Captain's Death Bed and Other Essays*, 1950; *A Writer's Diary*, 1953; *Granite and Rainbow*, 1958; *Contemporary Writers*, 1965; *Collected Essays, Volumes 1-2*, 1966; *Collected Essays, Volumes 3-4*, 1967; *The London Scene: Five Essays*, 1975; *The Flight of the Mind: The Letters of Virginia Woolf, Vol I, 1888-1912*, 1975 (published in the United States as *The Letters of Virginia Woolf, Vol. I: 1888-1912*, 1975; Nigel Nicolson, editor); *The Question of Things Happening: The Letters of Virginia Woolf, Vol. II, 1912-1922*, 1976 (published in the United States as *The Letters of Virginia Woolf, Vol. II: 1912-1922*, 1976; Nigel Nicolson, editor); *Moments of Being*, 1976 (Jeanne Schulkind, editor); *Books and Portraits*, 1977; *The Diary of Virginia Woolf*, 1977-1984 (Anne Olivier Bell, editor, 5 volumes); *A Change of Perspective: The Letters of Virginia Woolf, Vol. III, 1923-1928*, 1977 (published in the United States as *The Letters of Virginia Woolf, Vol. III: 1923-1928*, 1978; Nigel Nicolson, editor); *A Reflection of the Other Person: The Letters of Virginia Woolf, Vol. IV, 1929-1931*, 1978 (published in the United States as *The Letters of Virginia Woolf, Vol. IV: 1929-1931*, 1979; Nigel Nicolson, editor); *The Sickle Side of the Moon: The Letters of Virginia Woolf, Vol. V, 1932-1935*, 1979 (published in the United States as *The Letters of Virginia Woolf, Vol. V: 1932-1935*, 1979; Nigel Nicolson, editor); *Leave the Letters Till We're Dead: The Letters of Virginia Woolf, Vol. VI, 1936-1941*, 1980 (Nigel Nicolson, editor); *The Essays of Virginia Woolf*, 1987-1989 (3 volumes).

Bibliography

Abel, Elizabeth. *Virginia Woolf and the Fictions of Psychoanalysis*. Chicago: University of Chicago Press, 1989. With a focus upon symbolism and stylistic devices, this book comprehensively delineates the psychoanalytic connections between Woolf's fiction and Sigmund Freud's and Melanie Klein's theories. Sometimes difficult to follow, however, given Abel's reliance on excellent but extensive endnotes.

Baldwin, Dean R. *Virginia Woolf: A Study of the Short Fiction*. Boston:

Twayne, 1989. Baldwin's lucid parallels between Woolf's life experiences and her innovative short-story techniques contribute significantly to an understanding of both the author and her creative process. Also presents the opportunity for a comparative critical study by furnishing a collection of additional points of view in the final section. A chronology, a bibliography, and an index supplement the work.

Beja, Morris. *Critical Essays on Virginia Woolf.* Boston: G. K. Hall, 1985. In an excellent composite of literary analyses, Beja directs attention to both reviews and critical essays on Woolf's writings in order to demonstrate her universal and ageless appeal. Several critical disciplines are represented. Includes essay endnotes and an index.

Ginsberg, Elaine K., and L. M. Gottlieb, eds. *Virginia Woolf: Centennial Essays.* Troy, N.Y.: Whitston, 1983. Sixteen papers cover, among other topics, Woolf's style, gender consciousness, and feminist inclinations. Style, approach, and interpretation vary widely by presenter, and the text as a whole requires some familiarity with Woolf's writings. Notes on contributors, endnotes following each paper, and an index are provided.

Guiguet, Jean. *Virginia Woolf and Her Works.* Translated by Jean Stewart. London: Hogarth Press, 1965. Through an examination of Woolf's writings, Guiget concentrates upon the author's creative processes and her pursuit of a self-identity. A brief historical orientation, an analysis of Woolf's diaries for personality traits and beliefs, and a discussion of earlier literary criticism precede a primary emphasis on Woolf's body of literature. Although strenuous reading, this text accomplishes its purpose and concludes with a bibliography, an index of Woolf's work, and a general index.

Warner, Eric, ed. *Virginia Woolf: A Centenary Perspective.* New York: St. Martin's Press, 1984. With a non-partisan approach, this text offers seven papers and two panel discussions from Fitzwilliam College's Virginia Woolf Centenary Conference in Cambridge, England. Notes at the end of each presentation, notes on the contributors, and an index are provided.

HERMAN WOUK

Born: New York, New York; May 27, 1915

Principal long fiction

Aurora Dawn, 1947; *The City Boy*, 1948; *The Caine Mutiny*, 1951; *Marjorie Morningstar*, 1955; *Slattery's Hurricane*, 1956; *Youngblood Hawke*, 1962; *Don't Stop the Carnival*, 1965; *The Lomokome Papers*, 1968; *The Winds of War*, 1971; *War and Remembrance*, 1978; *Inside, Outside*, 1985.

Other literary forms

Herman Wouk has written three plays; the first, *The Traitor*, was produced on Broadway in 1949 and was published by Samuel French the same year. His most successful theatrical work, *The Caine Mutiny Court-Martial* (based upon the novel published in 1951), appeared on Broadway in 1954 and was published by Doubleday the same year. *Nature's Way* was produced on Broadway in 1957, and was published by Doubleday the following year. Eric Bentley, speaking of *The Caine Mutiny Court-Martial*, said that Wouk showed a gift for crisp dialogue that no other regular writer for the American theater could rival. Wouk collaborated with Richard Murphy in writing the screenplay for *Slattery's Hurricane* (1949). *This Is My God*, which Wouk first published in 1959 and followed with a revised edition in 1973, is a description and explanation of the Jewish way of life. The volume was a Reader's Digest Condensed Book Club selection, and an alternate selection for the Book-of-the-Month Club in 1959.

Achievements

It is a peculiarity of American criticism to denigrate popular success in literature. Almost from the outset of his career, Wouk has been a very popular writer; putting aside prejudicial presuppositions, this can be acknowledged as a genuine achievement, for Wouk has not attained his popular status by catering to the baser tastes of his readers. Beginning with *The Caine Mutiny* (1951), his books have appeared regularly on the best-seller list. Several of his titles have been selections of the country's major book clubs. Wouk was awarded the Pulitzer Prize for Fiction in 1952 for *The Caine Mutiny*. That same year, Columbia University presented him the Medal of Excellence, an honor extended to distinguished alumni. Three universities have awarded him honorary doctoral degrees.

Wouk might be described as a traditional novelist, in that his writing does not reflect the experimental qualities that are to be found in so much twentieth century American fiction. Like John Updike, he has chosen to give primacy of place to the narrative element in fiction; he has brought to the novel his own peculiar brand of rough-hewn vigor. At a time when the conventional wisdom judges it bad form for a novelist to take a clear stand on moral issues—as if ambiguity itself were a virtue—Wouk has consistently declared his moral position in his writings. This has not always been to the benefit of his fiction, but by and large, his novels are stronger for his conviction that literary art does not subsist in a vacuum but is part of a larger moral universe.

Biography

Herman Wouk was born in New York City on May 27, 1915. He is the son of Abraham Isaac and Esther (Levine) Wouk. Wouk's father, an industrialist in the power laundry field, started out as an immigrant laundry worker earning three dollars a week. Wouk was educated at Townsend Harris Hall and at Columbia University, where he was graduated with honors in 1934. While at Columbia, he studied philosophy and was editor of the *Columbia Jester*. From 1934 to 1935 he worked as a gag writer for radio comedians, and from 1936 to 1941, he was a scriptwriter for Fred Allen. In 1941, Wouk moved to Washington, D.C., following his appointment to the United States Treasury Department as a dollar-a-year man; his job was to write and produce radio shows to sell war bonds. He left this work to join the navy. After completing Officer Candidate School, he was commissioned an ensign and assigned to mine sweeper duty in the Pacific fleet. He served in the navy from 1942 to 1946. Three of those years were spent aboard the destroyer-minesweeper *U.S.S. Southard*, and eventually he was to be promoted to the position of Executive Officer of that ship. He was decorated with four campaign stars during the war, and received a Unit Citation as well. When Wouk was processed out of the navy in 1946, he held the rank of lieutenant.

Wouk married Betty Sarah Brown in December, 1945. They have had three sons, Abraham Isaac (who died before reaching his fifth birthday), Nathaniel, and Joseph.

Wouk began his career as a serious writer while he was in the navy; before his release from the service, he had completed a good portion of his first novel. That novel, *Aurora Dawn*, was published by Simon and Schuster in 1947. The following year, his second novel, *The City Boy*, was published. Neither of these works gained a great deal of attention for Wouk, but with the publication of *The Caine Mutiny* in 1951 (awarded the Pulitzer Prize the following year), he was quickly established as a writer of consequence. His play, *The Caine Mutiny Court-Martial*, began its successful run on Broadway in 1953. *Marjorie Morningstar* appeared in 1955, and his nonfiction work on Jewish culture and religion, *This Is My God*, in 1959. The 1960's saw the publication of *Youngblood Hawke* and *Don't Stop the Carnival*. His sprawling two-volume fictional account of World War II, which he began writing in 1962, was published in the 1970's; the first volume, *The Winds of War*, appeared in 1971, and the second, *War and Remembrance*, in 1978. Wouk wrote the teleplay for the eighteen-hour television movie based on *The Winds of War*, which was broadcast during the week of February 6-13, 1983. He was coauthor of the teleplay for the television adaptation of *War and Remembrance*, which appeared in 1988.

Wouk's great popular success has enabled him to devote his full time to his craft, but he has on occasion taken academic or semiacademic positions. From 1953 to 1957, he was a visiting professor of English at Yeshiva University, and during 1973-1974, he was scholar-in-residence at the Aspen Institute for Humanistic Studies. He has served on the board of directors for institutions and organizations such as the College of the Virgin Islands, the Washington National Symphony, and Kennedy Center Productions. He is a member of the Authors Guild and the Dramatists Guild.

Analysis

Herman Wouk is a novelist in the tradition of the great English novelists of the nineteenth century; he is also a spiritual descendant of such American writers as James Fenimore Cooper, William Dean Howells, Theodore Dreiser, and James T. Farrell. What he has in common with these writers is narrative prowess, a commitment to realism, and a lively moral consciousness. Furthermore, like these writers, Wouk addresses himself to the population at large. Since World War II, there has been detectable in American fiction a distinction between writers who seem to be inclined to write primarily for other writers or for academic critics, and those inclined to write for a general audience. That Wouk is numbered among the latter would appear to be traceable to a definite decision on his part. His first novel, *Aurora Dawn*, has the flavor of the experimental fiction that began to proliferate in the postwar period. If one were to have speculated in 1946 upon the course that Wouk's literary career was going to take, it would have been a safe guess to say that he would probably continue down the road of experimentation, that he would become more and more concerned with language as an end in itself, and that eventually, he would be writing books destined to be read only in upper-division English courses in universities. This was not what happened, however; in his second novel, *The City Boy*, Wouk followed a conventional narrative pattern and told his story in language which was not constantly calling attention to itself.

In *Aurora Dawn* and *The City Boy*, Wouk was still stretching his muscles and attempting to find his proper level as a writer. He came into his own with *The Caine Mutiny*. In that novel, and in every novel that has followed it, there can be recognized the presence of a central theme, treated in various ways and from varying perspectives. The theme is the conflict between traditional values and a modern consciousness which is either indifferent to those values or flatly antipathetic toward them. The conflict is not treated in abstract terms, but in terms of individuals who are caught up in it, and how the individual fares is in great part determined by the side with which he chooses to ally himself.

Wouk's first novel, *Aurora Dawn*, which he began while serving as an officer in the navy, is an effort at satire. The butt of the satire is the advertising industry and, more generally, the foolishness of anyone in business whose ethical consciousness is dimmed by avarice. The moral of the story is explicit: greed is the root of all evil. Andrew Reale, the novel's young protagonist, is bright, energetic, and imaginative, but until he undergoes a conversion at novel's end, his primary concern is getting ahead. He wants to be successful above all else, and to him, success means money. In his scramble to get to the top as quickly as possible, his myopia becomes acute and his values are severely twisted. He is willing to make compromises where compromises should not be made. A connection is intimated between Reale's moral weakness and his failure to continue to adhere to the religious principles according to which he was reared, a recurring theme in Wouk's fiction.

Reale's obsessive pursuit of success leads him to jilt his fiancée, the beautiful and innocent Laura Beaton, so that he can take up with the beautiful but frivolous Carol Marquis, daughter of the despicable but very rich Talmadge Marquis. It leads him to be crassly manipulative in his dealings with the Reverend Calvin Stanfield, who is simple, straightforward, and a good man. Finally, it leads him, in a move of pure expediency, to quit an employer who has been generous with him so that he can join forces with Talmadge Marquis. All Reale's machinations, however, are to no avail. The hastily courted Carol Marquis runs off with an eccentric painter, and Laura Beaton, brokenhearted at Reale's rejection of her, marries an older man. In the end, Reale gets better than he deserves. His thwarted attempt to blackmail Father Stanfield proves to be the occasion of a conversion experience for him. He suddenly sees the wickedness of his ways and decides to alter his course. Laura Beaton is miraculously released from her unconsummated marriage, so that Reale is able to get the woman of his dreams after all. Fleeing the wicked city, the bride and groom go off to live together in New Mexico.

The novel is not realistic and cannot be judged according to the criterion of verisimilitude. It is a light, playful work in which humor plays an important part. Despite several brilliant passages, however, the novel does not come across as successful satire, and that would seem to be attributable to the fact that Wouk is vacillating and hesitant in what he wants to say. What he takes with one hand, he gives back with the other. The novel is clever, in both good and bad senses. While its language is often lively, it can as well be pretentious and self-conscious at times. The anachronistic devices of addressing the reader directly, inserting explicit authorial commentary on the action, and interspersing the narrative with short philosophical asides do not always work to maximize the effect. The humor of the novel is capable of being right on the mark, but for the most part it is a bit forced; Wouk, the radio gagman, is too much in evidence. The flaws to be found in *Aurora Dawn* are flaws which are not uncommon in a first novel. Despite its weaknesses, however, already in evidence in this work are the two traits that have subsequently become the chief strengths of Wouk's fiction: a vigorous talent for narrative and a lively sensitivity to moral issues.

Perhaps the most striking thing about Wouk's second novel, *The City Boy*, is that, stylistically, it represents a marked departure from the standards he had established in his first novel. The language of the work does not call attention to itself; it is clear, straightforward, and unpretentious. The novel is humorous in tone, and its plot structure is loose. It revolves around the adventures—most of which take place in an upstate summer camp—of a New York City boy, Herbie Bookbinder. John P. Marquand's comparison of this novel with Mark Twain's *The Adventures of Tom Sawyer* (1876) is well-founded. In many respects, Herbie is an urban version of the scamp from the Midwestern frontier. He is a bright and enterprising lad, and if he is mischievous at times, it is seldom with malice of forethought. Much of what he does is calculated to impress Lucille Glass, the object of his single-minded puppy love. Herbie is unlike Tom Sawyer in that he is an outsider as far as other boys are concerned, this because of his poor athletic skills and his penchant for things intellectual. A goodly amount of Herbie's efforts in the novel are given over to his attempts to gain the status of a regular guy. He succeeds, finally, and as a result is welcomed into the full fellowship of his peers. *The City Boy* is a light novel—in some respects a boy's book—but in it, Wouk's moral consciousness is manifested by his underscoring the difference between good and evil in the actions of the characters.

The Caine Mutiny is Wouk's best novel, the work on which his reputation rests. The novel takes place against the backdrop of war, but it cannot be regarded as a "war story" in any simplistic sense. It is a story about the subtle and complicated relationships that exist among men who are part of the enclosed world that constitutes the military establishment. One of its central themes concerns the matter of authority—how it is exercised within a military context, and how it is abused. The novel explores the manner in which various personality types act and react within a hierarchical, authoritarian structure. In addition, it examines the ways in which the lives of those caught up in the trauma of war are altered, sometimes profoundly. Other themes which the novel treats are loyalty and disloyalty, patriotism, doers versus sayers, personal integrity, and the process by which young men are tested in stressful situations.

The Caine Mutiny can easily be misread. One might conclude that its chief concern is the everlasting battle between despotism and democracy, that Captain Queeg therefore is clearly the villain of the piece, and that its heroes are Lieutenant Maryk, Willie Keith, Tom Keefer, and the others who were involved in the mutiny. It is not that simple. If it were, *The Caine Mutiny* would be little more than a melodrama. Captain Queeg is not a hero, but neither is he a diabolical type. He is a sorry human being; he has serious personal problems (his eccentricity is not amusing—he is, in fact, a sick man); and, perhaps most serious, given his status as a commanding officer, he is incompetent professionally. For all that, he is consistent in trying to do his job to the best of his ability. Queeg's problem is that he is a man who is in over his head; he can at times scarcely cope with situations which are his duty to control. The circumstances surrounding the event which led to the mutiny are sufficiently ambiguous as to render doubtful the claim of the mutineers that, had they not relieved Queeg of command when they did, the ship would have been lost.

Wouk's assessment of the situation seems to be communicated most directly through the character of Lieutenant Greenwald, the young aviator-lawyer who defends Maryk at the court-martial. Greenwald is a dedicated navy man, and he is not sympathetic with the mutineers, but he decides to defend Maryk because he respects the Executive Officer's personal integrity and because he is convinced that Maryk, in assuming command of the *Caine* during the typhoon, was acting in good faith. Greenwald succeeds in having Maryk acquitted of the charge of mutiny, mainly by drawing out of Queeg in the courtroom telltale signs of his emotional instability, but he takes no joy in his victory. After the trial, he puts the damper on the victory celebration being staged by the *Caine*'s officers when he gives them a stinging tongue-lashing. His ire is directed particularly at Tom Keefer, whom he perceives correctly as being the chief instigator of the mutiny, but one who refused, when the matter came to a head, to put himself on the line. Greenwald's position seems to be that, while the *Caine*'s officers are legally innocent, they are morally guilty. However sophisticated a rationale they might provide for their actions, what was at the bottom of those actions, in his view, was disloyalty, and disloyalty, for a military officer, is an unforgivable sin. One might say that the trial does not prove either clear-cut guilt or innocence. If anything, it demonstrates the complexity and ambiguity of all human situations. Greenwald's position is that, given the ambiguity, it is always better not to second-guess legitimately constituted authority. It is the chief responsibility of the naval officer to do his duty through thick and thin.

If there is a clear villain in *The Caine Mutiny*, Tom Keefer would appear to be the most likely candidate for the role. Keefer is, in many respects, the preeminently modern man. He is committed to what he presumably regards as the absolute truths of Freudian psychology, which he employs in a reductionist way, as weapons against those who do not share his world view. He is in the navy, but not of it, and, in fact, he rather enjoys and exploits his position as an iconoclastic outsider. He maintains an attitude of supercilious superiority toward people such as Queeg, and toward everything that the navy represents. His view is narrow, restricted by the dictates of his overriding egotism. Keefer is a carping critic of the navy, but he does not hesitate to take selfish advantage of what the navy can offer him at every turn. His hypocrisy allows him to talk a big game, but when the pressure is on and when circumstances call for words to be translated into action, he invariably backs off. Perhaps the most damning thing that could be said of Keefer is that he is a coward, as he demonstrates when he is captain of the *Caine* and precipitously abandons ship. By the novel's end, however, Keefer seem to have arrived at a degree of self-awareness which hitherto had eluded him; he confesses to Willie Keith, succeeding him as commanding officer, that Keith is a better man than he. He is right.

Willie Keith is the central character of the novel; his moral education is the real subject of *The Caine Mutiny*. Willie is an aristocratic rich kid from New York who comes to learn, among other things, the value of democracy. His relationship with Maria Minotti, alias May Wynn, can be interpreted in this way. The bulk of Keith's education, however, takes place in the navy. When he first comes aboard the *Caine*, he is very much under the influence of Tom Keefer, and he accepts Keefer's cynical interpretation of things as the correct one. Eventually, Keith realizes that the navy, though imperfect, is not a bad organization. What is more, given the realities of the modern world, it is a necessary organization. Unlike Keefer, Keith is prepared to acknowledge that the navy in World War II is contributing toward the preservation of the way of life into which both men have been born and to which they are devoted, and that, excepting a total transformation of human nature, navies will probably always be needed to insure the protection of men's freedom. Keith is not changed into a mindless patriot and militarist, but his criticism of the navy and its personnel becomes more discriminate, more intelligent, more responsible. He learns to judge matters according to criteria which are not self-centered, and develops an appreciation for the larger scheme of things. He takes pride in his work, and as he rises in rank, his conscientiousness increases; he tries to be the best officer he can.

The world of the navy, in *The Caine Mutiny*, is in certain respects a microcosm of the world at large. It is beset by all sorts of problems, but there is no perfect alternative somewhere to which one might flee. A man's maturity is measured by his ability to establish standards of excellence and to work assiduously to achieve them in spite of various limitations, sometimes severe— limitations in himself, in others, and in the situation.

On the surface, Wouk's fourth novel, *Marjorie Morningstar*, would seem to lead nowhere. It is the story of a young Jewish woman, the daughter of immigrants established comfortably in the middle class of New York, who has been sufficiently Americanized as to have for her chief ambition the desire to become a famous actress, a star. Marjorie Morningstar (née Morgenstern) is a beautiful woman whose theatrical talent, while not scintillating, is probably sufficient to underwrite the realization of her dream, given a lucky break here and there. She is willing to make the sacrifices, within certain bounds, and to invest the hard work which the ascent to stardom inevitably entails. If Marjorie is determined about anything, it is that she is not going to allow herself to lapse into the staid, conventional life that is the destiny of the vast majority of nice, middle-class Jewish girls. She is going to be different; she is going to break out of the mold. After several fruitless efforts to break into the theater and to make it big, after a sequence of adventures with an assortment of men, chiefly with Noel Airman, she ends up doing what she vowed she would never do. She marries a Jew, a successful lawyer by the name of Milton Schwartz, and she retires to a plush suburb to live the most conventional of conventional lives. The novel, then, would seem to end on an almost laughably anticlimactic note, but only if one fails to perceive the kind of statement that it is attempting to make.

If *The Caine Mutiny* delineates the education of Willie Keith, the education of Marjorie Morningstar is the primary concern of the novel that bears her name. If Marjorie comes full circle, as it were, and ends by embracing the conventional, it is because she discovers that the conventional is worthy of being embraced, the conventional not only as representing middle-class morality, but also, and much more important, as embodying traditional cultural and religious values. The glamorous life to which Marjorie aspired, whether or not she was always fully conscious of the fact, was a life that repudiated traditional values. As a teenager and young woman, she fought her own tradition, particularly as manifested in the Jewish religion; she looked upon it as crude and superstitious, a carry-over from humankind's primitive past. This tradition, however, was more deeply embedded in her, was more integral a part of her identity than she was willing to admit, and throughout her various experiences it guided her actions more than she knew.

Marjorie's failure to realize her dream of becoming a star actually represents the triumph of her better, truer self. Her concern shifts from thin, superficial values to those with substance and depth. The drama of her quest for self-realization is played out principally around her long and erratic affair with Noel Airman. When she first meets Airman, who is some ten years her senior, she is scarcely more than a girl, and she is completely enamored of him. He is handsome, intelligent, urbane, and witty, a talented composer of popular songs who shows promise of becoming a success in the theater. Noel represents much of what she wants to become, and all of what she has decided is most valuable in life, which is emphasized by the fact that she throws decorum to the winds and pursues him actively. When she finally catches him, however, she realizes that she does not really want him. The man who was once her ideal, her hero, the man whom she wanted to marry more than anyone else, is at last perceived, albeit faintly, as a god with clay feet.

Who is this Noel Airman? He is Saul Ehrmann, a man who has actively repudiated his Jewish identity and its associated traditions, but who has failed to come up with a viable substitute for either. He is a rootless vagabond, a shameless Casanova, a man who eschews commitment as a matter of principle, and who tries hard to make a profession of cynicism. It would be wrong, however, to think of him entirely in negative terms. He is not a character lacking in complexity, and he is not devoid of critical self-knowledge, which at times can be acute and penetrating. Still, this self-awareness serves only to accentuate the pathetic quality of the man, for in the final analysis, he is impotent to act upon his better impulses. He does not have the moral stamina to follow through, and this is so, Wouk implies, precisely because he has cut himself off from his tradition.

The fact that Marjorie arrives at a new state of consciousness which allows her to see Airman for what he is, and accordingly to reject him, is attributable in part to her brief but fateful acquaintance with Michael Eden. Eden, like Airman, is a Jew, but, unlike Airman, he is not in flight from the fact. He is a strong, taciturn man whose personal sufferings have led him to dedicate himself to a melancholy but determined altruism. He is involved in the very risky business of rescuing Jews from Nazi Germany. Here is a man who is every bit as bright and talented as Airman but who has what Airman lacks— integrity and a sense of purpose in life. Although it is not Marjorie's destiny to marry Eden, meeting him has the effect of altering her perception of Airman. Milton Schwartz, the man she marries, has in common with Eden a fundamental decency.

Wouk's sixth novel, *Youngblood Hawke*, based to some extent on the life of Thomas Wolfe, could be the story of many a young American writer of this century, and for that reason, the novel, besides its intrinsic worth as a work of fiction, has considerable value as a historical document. The story of Arthur Youngblood Hawke is a success story, but it is a story of failure as well. Indeed, Hawke's case is in many respects a tragic one. Hawke is a lanky, down-home Kentuckian who, after being released from the navy at the end of World War II, moves to New York to conquer the city and the country, by his pen. He comes to his task with a spotty education, with an explosive imagination, and with a seemingly boundless store of energy. Writing is his life, and his engagement in it is passionate. There is much about Hawke which smacks of the all-American boy. He is crude and unpolished, but straightforward and gentle in his dealings with people—except with those who deserve otherwise. He is an honest man, in his way, and an assiduous worker. He wants to be a success as a writer. He wants to become a millionaire, not so that he can give up writing but so that, freed from financial worries, he can devote himself to it without distractions. Hawke is in the mold of the rustic innocent who has long played a part in American literature.

His early success works against him in the long run. His first novel, though receiving rough treatment at the hands of the critics, gains a large popular audience; his second novel wins the Pulitzer Prize and increasing respect from the critics. He is associated with a solid, respectable publishing house whose head values his work, has faith in his future, and is willing to be very generous in making contractual arrangements with him. Hawke's obsessional longing for financial independence, however, prompts him to break ties with his publisher and begin publishing his own books; he also makes some risky investments. His luck turns, and in a matter of months he finds himself on the threshold of bankruptcy. He determines that he is going to write his way out of his debts; leaving behind the plush life that he enjoyed only too briefly in New York, he returns to Kentucky, and there, living in a cabin in the woods, he works furiously to complete what proves to be his final novel. In fact, he overworks, devoting himself not only to the novel but also, earlier, to a theatrical production which he hopes will strike it rich. The strain brought about by his frenetic activities exacerbates an old head injury, and, after a wild chase to South America made in a state of delirium, he ends up back in New York. He is hospitalized there and dies at the age of thirty-three.

As Youngblood Hawke lies dying, his vaguely addressed prayer is that he might be given more time so that he can work. Everything that he has done he considers as only preparatory exercises to his great multivolume *Comedy*. That *Comedy* was never written is not simply attributable to the fact that Hawke showed poor business sense or that he was careless of his health. There is evidence in the novel to warrant the conclusion that Hawke's failure to fulfill his chief artistic ambition amounts to an exacting payment he has had to make for his sins. There have been two principal women in his life, but, by his own admission, there should have been only one. In the beginning of the novel, before he bursts upon the American literary scene, he meets a young editor, Jeanne Green, who subsequently becomes for him what Maxwell Perkins was for Thomas Wolfe. Jeanne, besides being a very talented editor, is, like Hawke, essentially a small-town person. She is simple, unpretentious, genuine. Hawke falls in love with Jeanne almost immediately—his better self tells him that this is the woman in his life, the woman he should marry—but he becomes involved in a torrid affair with a wealthy, sophisticated, fundamentally selfish New Yorker, Frieda Winters. Frieda is older than he; she is married, has three children, and is no stranger to adulterous affairs. Hawke is honest enough with himself to admit that he is involved in adultery; the reader is told that he hates both the word and the fact. He does not have the moral courage, however, to extricate himself from the affair—not until, as it turns out, it is too late. His relationship with Frieda proves to be an enervating experience; if it does not exactly destroy him, it contributes substantially toward his destruction.

What allowed Hawke to become involved in an affair which he knew to be wrong? One explanation is that he failed to be true to the basic religious principles which he had been taught as a boy but which in his impetuous youth he attempted to reject. Unlike Marjorie Morningstar, whose roots in a religious tradition were sufficiently deep and tenacious to carry her through the hard times, Hawke succumbs to the facile moral standards of a secularized society.

Wouk's next novel, *Don't Stop the Carnival*, is the weakest of his entire corpus. It is a comic novel and it would seem to have some kind of satiric intent, but the humor, instead of carrying the moral import of the tale, more often than not obstructs it. The work's humor is hampered by obtrusive, heavy-handed moralizing, and its seriousness is trivialized by a humor which too often degenerates into tedious slapstick. Most damaging for the novel is the fact that Wouk's narrative talent, which is his forte, serves him poorly here. The plot is too often based upon contrivance, and in some instances blatant authorial manipulation is very much in evidence. Add to this fact that characterization is unconvincing, and the sum total is a generally undistinguished piece of fiction that holds the reader's attention only by an adamant act of will. It is not that the novel is completely lacking in substance, but the detectably substantive elements are not allowed to emerge fully. There is, for example, a statement being made about the haplessness of "liberal" types who are awash in a world that in many respects is the result of their own brand of thinking, but the message is befuddled by static of various kinds and one must strain to detect it.

Wouk's impressive companion novels, *The Winds of War* and *War and Remembrance*, published in 1971 and 1978, respectively, are in effect a single, sustained work of fiction, and therefore can be discussed together. Wouk spent sixteen years in completing the work, and it seems likely that he regards it as his *magnum opus*. *The Winds of War* is focused primarily on the European theater, beginning with the German invasion of Czechoslovakia and Poland, putting special emphasis upon the latter. The Battle of Britain is also treated at close range. The book ends with the bombing of Pearl Harbor, the point at which *War and Remembrance* takes up the story. This book, while continuing to trace the course of events in Europe, especially those events having to do with the systematic extermination of the Jews by the Nazis, shifts attention to the Pacific theater and provides poignant descriptions of the major naval battles fought there. The book ends with the dropping of the atomic bombs and the Japanese acceptance of unconditional surrender. In these two massive volumes which constitute a single work, an ambitious fictional history of World War II, Wouk once again shows himself to be a master of narrative. This is not a mere chronicle of events; rather, major events of the war are given dramatic immediacy by the tactic of having one of the many key characters in the narrative involved in those events. One is even provided access to the Axis point of view through excerpts from the analytic histories of the German General Armin von Roon, interspersed throughout the work.

The key character in the work is Victor "Pug" Henry, a naval officer who has given thirty years of his life to military service. He is a staid, conservative man, a patriot but not a jingoist, dedicated to professional excellence and quietly guided by deeply embedded religious principles. Following his various adventures in Europe and in the Pacific, one is not only brought into direct contact with important historical personages but treated to his thoughtful reactions to them as well. Wouk is the type of artist who likes to paint on a large canvas, but the canvas he is covering in this work is of mammoth proportions. All the more remarkable, then, is the control he exercises here; nothing gets away from him. There is about this wide-ranging tour de force a satisfying unity and completeness. It is thickly peopled with a vast array of characters, and their attitudes toward the war run the full gamut from self-sacrificing heroism to cold-blooded murderousness.

One of the most interesting characters in the work is Aaron Jastrow, a Jewish-American, world-renowned scholar and former Yale professor who at the outbreak of the war is living in active retirement in Italy. In tracing the story of Aaron Jastrow, and that of his Polish cousin Berel, Wouk recounts in moving fashion the sickening circumstances of the infamous "final solution." Aaron himself was born in Poland and reared in a strict Orthodox tradition. As he reached young manhood, he put aside his religion and settled into a benevolent agnosticism. Accompanied by his niece Natalie, he is hounded by the Nazis throughout Europe for years, until he finally ends up in the land of his birth, in a death camp. His life is choked out in the gas chambers. He speaks to the reader directly through *A Jew's Journey*. What one learns from this document is that the most significant journey in the waning months of Jastrow's life is a spiritual one. His personal confrontation with the horrors of Nazism has the effect of returning him to the religion of his birth. When he comes to die, he is possessed of an inner peace his murderers could never know, and he represents a basic human dignity which they have chosen to abandon for themselves and to attempt to destroy in others.

The Winds of War and *War and Remembrance* are about a specific war, but they are about war in general as well. Wouk does not romanticize World War II, but he suggests that it was absolutely essential that the Allied forces emerged as victorious. It was an unspeakably grim yet nevertheless necessary struggle. The bombs that ended the war, however, changed the nature of war forever. If mankind were capable before Hiroshima and Nagasaki of arguing that all-out war, however cruel and crude, was a workable solution to human problems, that argument proved no longer tenable. World War II was perhaps the most gruesome war that human beings have ever inflicted upon themselves. Wouk's thesis is that wars in the future will not be avoided simply by proclaiming them to be unthinkable. One must think about them; one must think especially about the most gruesome of wars. Through memory, perhaps a pathway to peace can be found.

Herman Wouk's *Inside, Outside* appeared in 1985. *The Caine Mutiny* is by consensus Wouk's single best work of fiction, but *Inside, Outside* could arguably be offered as a legitimate contender for that honor. Here one finds all Wouk's considerable skill in operation: his commanding ability to create characters that live and breathe and convince, telling their interesting and interlocking stories within the context of a fictional world which, while complex, never degenerates into incoherence. Wouk's characters move and make their marks in a world that can be as confused and disorienting as that created by any other modern fictionist, but the core, the center, of Wouk's world, although subjected to great strain, always manages to hold; that is, although Wouk's characters live in an extremely difficult and demanding world, that world preserves its essential meaningfulness. Wouk does not burden himself with the absurd task of attempting to populate an absurd universe.

It is difficult to specify what makes for the peculiar success of this novel, but certainly at work is Wouk's uncanny ability—which is singularly devoid of self-advertising and therefore easy to overlook—to create what one might call fictional immediacy. Wouk can effect the magic of bringing into being a fictional world which more than half persuades the reader that it is not fictional at all. In other words, he is a maker of art.

Inside, Outside revolves around the life and times of one Israel David Goodkind. It is principally his story, and he tells it with verve. The novel is interestingly structured. The time frame of the narration is 1973. In that year, Goodkind, a successful New York lawyer, finds himself in the rather unusual position—given the fact that he has been a lifelong Democrat—of serving in Washington as a special assistant to President Richard M. Nixon. The job, though flattering in its way, is anything but exacting, and Goodkind begins to expend his considerable free time in writing; however, this activity is not simply an idle exercise with which to fill the gaps in his undemanding day. He takes his writing quite seriously, and he intends to produce something of real literary worth. He endeavors to fulfill an ambition he has harbored since his youth, but which thus far he has not managed to accomplish. He writes about his own life, which takes him back to the turn of the century and the stories of his parents, two Jewish immigrants from Russia. They both arrive in New York; there they meet and marry, and there their children, Israel and Lee, are born. The reader follows the entire course of Goodkind's life as he recounts its developments, its delays, its assorted dramatic and melodramatic reversals, with meticulous and loving detail. The reader is brought into the very center of Goodkind's world and discovers it to be a world which is at once intensely provincial and intensely cosmopolitan—the kind of combination which is possible perhaps only in New York City. It is a wide world, thickly populated with a rich variety of relatives and friends. The reader is given the opportunity to meet them all, and, with differing degrees of completeness, to come to know their stories, too.

Such is the main strand of the novel's narrative. Its secondary strand is no less compelling. Goodkind is interrupted periodically in his recounting of his past by the pressing events that take place around him in 1973 as he continues his writing project. Two significant historical events mark that time period. One is the Israeli-Egyptian War; the other is the resignation of President Nixon in the wake of the Watergate scandal. The first event takes place within the time frame of the novel, and Goodkind reports on it as he writes. The second event draws closer and closer, but the novel ends without the president's resignation having yet taken place. The Israeli-Egyptian War plays an important symbolic role in the narrative because one of the central themes of the novel is the situation of the Jew in the modern world.

The "inside" of the novel's title refers to the somewhat self-enclosed, clearly identifiable, but far from homogeneous world of Jewish religion and culture, whereas the "outside" refers to the world at large. Herman Wouk is something of an oddity among contemporary American novelists because of his undisguised and unapologized-for religious convictions. This fact largely explains the decided and persistent moral tone of his fiction. One can find expressions, more or less strong, more or less developed, of his commitment to Judaism throughout his fiction, but in no other novel, it seems, does his religious faith play so central and integral a part than in *Inside, Outside*.

What Wouk gives the reader in this novel, along with much else besides, is a dynamic and dramatic picture of the manifold consciousness that constitutes late twentieth century Judaism. The picture he presents is intricate, complicated, and in some respects even contradictory. Wouk deals with the rich reality that is Judaism in a manner which is—variously—intensely objective and intensely subjective. He seems to leave nothing out of the picture; negative elements are treated with as much thoroughness as are positive elements. Nevertheless, Wouk does not treat the heart of his subject matter, the essential identity of Judaism, with anything but respect and reverence.

If by novel's end one cannot identify its protagonist as a typical modern Jew, that is only because one has come to understand that there is no such thing. I. David Goodkind is a representative modern Jew, but so are many who are quite different from him, and Goodkind himself is far from simple. On the one hand, Goodkind reflects the "inside" component of his world, but a distinct "outside" dimension to his personality exists as well. Both together, "inside" and "outside," make up who he is. Goodkind is a religious Jew who faithfully practices his religion. He is also a political Jew who sympathizes with the Zionist tradition and takes great patriotic pride in the state of Israel. At the same time, Goodkind is a thorough American. In a larger sense, he is an eminently modern man, one who, even in spite of himself at times, reflects the consciousness of the contemporary Western intellectual, with all the limitations peculiar to it. His judgments on the major issues that impinge upon his life have to them a ring of confident cosmopolitanism, which disguises their lack of substantial metaphysical foundations. For example, although he is in many respects exemplary for his perspicacity and sensitivity, he is obtuse in response to some of the clear signs of decadence in modern culture.

Mention might be made of the unorthodox manner in which the novel deals with the character of President Nixon. Wouk goes beyond the crude journalistic stereotypes to discover in Nixon not merely a caricature but a real human being. Finally, *Inside, Outside* is simultaneously a serious and a humorous work, and both of these faces complement each other, helping to bring each into greater relief. In some of his other novels, Wouk has demonstrated his facility in handling humor, but that skill is especially in evidence in *Inside, Outside*.

Despite his broad popular appeal, Wouk has generally not found favor with the critics, especially academic critics. The common response of the latter has been simply to ignore him. It is difficult to explain precisely why this is so. Perhaps Wouk's very popularity militates against him, as if there existed a necessary relationship between popularity and artistic worth: the more popular a writer, the poorer the quality of what he writes. Perhaps Wouk's traditionalist world view and forthright advocacy of Judeo-Christian moral principles, to which many critics today are hostile, account in part for the critical neglect of his work. In any case, Wouk deserves more critical attention than he has received. He is not the greatest among the many fine novelists to appear in the United States since World War II, but neither is he an inconsequential figure. His prose is solid and vigorous, eschewing precosity and self-indulgence. Writing with intelligence and sensitivity, he appeals neither to a small clique of literary aesthetes nor to the lowest common denominator of a general audience. His attitude toward fiction is that shared by all the major novelists of literary history; his fiction is not concerned with itself but with the world at large. His fiction does not attempt the irrelevant task of creating a moral universe from scratch, but accepts and responds to the moral universe which is already in place.

Dennis Q. McInerny

Other major works

PLAYS: *The Traitor*, 1949; *The Caine Mutiny Court-Martial*, 1953; *Nature's Way*, 1957.

SCREENPLAY: *Slattery's Hurricane*, 1949 (with Richard Murphy).

TELEPLAYS: *The Winds of War*, 1983; *War and Remembrance*, 1988.

NONFICTION: *This Is My God*, 1959, 1973.

Bibliography

Browne, James R. "Distortion in *The Caine Mutiny*." *College English* 17 (January, 1956): 216-218. Focuses on the problem created in *The Caine*

Mutiny by what appears to be a reversal of authorial attitude toward one of the novel's central characters, Captain Queeg. Browne makes a reasonable case for this reversal being the cause of a major flaw in the novel.

Carpenter, Frederick I. "Herman Wouk." *College English* 17 (January, 1956): 211-215. Although his article was written fairly early in Wouk's career, and the treatment of his work ends with a discussion of *Marjorie Morningstar*, it nevertheless represents one of the more thoughtful and even-handed accounts of the novelist and his books. Carpenter regards Wouk as a serious writer and examines his worth against the background of modern American fiction with considerable perception.

Frankel, Theodore. "The Anatomy of a Bestseller: Second Thoughts on *The Caine Mutiny*." *The Western Humanities Review* 9 (Autumn, 1955): 333-339. "Mr. Wouk has a great talent. It is tragic that he has seen fit to put it into the service of political obscurantism." With those two sentences, Frankel ends this article. Their tone suggests the negative stance he takes with respect to *The Caine Mutiny*. While several of Frankel's criticisms are well-founded, some of the presuppositions of his analysis raise their own set of problems.

Geismar, Maxwell. "The Age of Wouk." *Nation* 181 (November 5, 1955): 399-400. A reaction not so much to Wouk as to the praise and status afforded the novelist by *Time* in its cover-story treatment of him. Geismar argues that *Time* wants to make Wouk the Representative Writer of most of what is bad in American culture. It is not clear whether Geismar considers Wouk to be worthy of *Time*'s coverage of the novelist.

McElderry, B. R., Jr. "The Conservative as Novelist: Herman Wouk." *Arizona Quarterly* 15 (Summer, 1959): 128-136. McElderry contends that both *The Caine Mutiny* and *Marjorie Morningstar* are structurally defective because of the lack of logic that characterizes the narratives. Although acknowledging that both novels display considerable literary talent, McElderry concludes that Wouk's conservatism is to blame for his faulty artistry.

Rosenfeld, Isaac. "For God and the Suburbs." Review of *Marjorie Morningstar*, by Herman Wouk. *Partisan Review* 22 (Fall, 1955): 565-569. On the basis of data gleaned from fictional, sociological, and ideological categories, Rosenfeld judges the novel to be seriously flawed. Wouk's problem is not that he defends conservative values but that he does so in ways that are artistically below par.

RICHARD WRIGHT

Born: Natchez, Mississippi; September 4, 1908
Died: Paris, France; November 28, 1960

Principal long fiction
Native Son, 1940; *The Outsider*, 1953; *Savage Holiday*, 1954; *The Long Dream*, 1958; *Lawd Today*, 1963.

Other literary forms

In addition to his five novels, Richard Wright published collections of essays and short stories and two autobiographical volumes. Two collections of short stories, the early *Uncle Tom's Children* (1938) and the posthumously collected *Eight Men* (1961), represent some of Wright's finest fiction. Wright himself felt that the characters in *Uncle Tom's Children* were too easily pitied and that they elicited from readers a sympathy that was unlike the tough intellectual judgment he desired. Wright later wrote that his creation of Bigger Thomas in *Native Son* was an attempt to stiffen that portrayal so that readers could not leniently dismiss his characters with simple compassion, but would have to accept them as free, fully human adults, whose actions required assessment. Nevertheless, the stories of *Uncle Tom's Children* are carefully written, and the characters, though sometimes defeated, embody the kind of independence and intractability that Wright valued in his fiction.

Two stories from *Eight Men* reveal the themes to which Wright gave sustained development in his novels. In "The Man Who Was Almos' a Man," the main character learns that power means freedom, and although he first bungles his attempt to shoot a gun, his symbol of power, he lies to his family, keeps the gun, and at the conclusion of the story leaves home to grow into manhood elsewhere. In "The Man Who Lived Underground," the main character, nameless at first, is accused of a crime he did not commit. Fleeing underground to the sewers of the city, he becomes a voyeur of life, seen now from a new perspective. The values that served him badly above ground do not serve him at all below. By the end of the story, he has come to understand that all men are guilty; his name is revealed, and with his new values, he ascends once more to accept responsibility for the crime. Since all men are guilty, it is less important to him that the crime is not his own than that he acknowledges freely that he shares in human guilt.

Even more important than these two collections is the first volume of Wright's autobiography, *Black Boy* (1945), which opens up a world of experience to the reader. It traces the first seventeen years of Wright's life—from his birth in Mississippi and the desertion of the family by his father, through years of displacement as he travels from one relative to another with his ill mother and religious grandmother. The early years find Wright, like his later protagonists, an outsider, cut off from family, from friends, from culture. He is as out of place among blacks as among whites, baffled by those blacks who play the roles whites expect of them, himself unable to dissimulate his feelings and thoughts.

Although the work is nonfiction, it is united by powerful metaphors: fire, hunger, and blindness. Wright's inner fire is mirrored throughout the work by actual fires; indeed, his first act is to set afire the curtains in his home. His physical hunger, a constant companion, is an image of his hunger for knowledge and connection, and his two jobs in optical factories suggest the blindness of society, a blindness given further representation in *Native Son*.

What Wright learns in *Black Boy* is the power of words. His early life is marked by physical violence: he witnesses murders and beatings, but it is the violence of words which offers liberation from his suffocating environment. Whether it is the profanity with which he shocks his grandmother, the literalness with which he takes his father's words, or the crude expressions with which he taunts Jewish shopkeepers, he discovers that words have a power which make him an equal to those around him. When he feels unequal, as in his early school experiences, he is speechless. The culmination of this theme occurs when Wright acquires a library card and discovers through his readings in the American social critics of the early part of this century, men such as H. L. Mencken and Sinclair Lewis, that he is not alone in his feelings and that there are others who share his alienation and discontent.

When Wright finally sees his father many years after his desertion, his hatred dissolves: he realizes that his father, trapped by his surroundings, with neither a cultural past nor an individual future, speaks a different language from his own, holds different thoughts, and is truly a victim and therefore not worthy even of his hatred. Wright's characters must never be victims, for as such they hold no interest. At the end of the book, he goes north, first to Memphis and, when that fails, north again to Chicago, pursuing the dream, having now the power of words to articulate it and to define himself.

The record of his years in Chicago is found in the posthumously published second autobiographical volume, *American Hunger* (written in 1944, published in 1977). Largely a record of his involvement and later disillusionment with the Communist party, this book is interesting for its view of a later, mature Wright who is still struggling with institutions which would limit his freedom.

Achievements

In his best work, Wright gives American literature its strongest statement of the existential theme of alienated man defining himself. Wright's use of the black American as archetypal outsider gives his work a double edge. On the one hand, no American writer so carefully illuminates the black experience in America: the ambivalence of black feeling, the hypocrisies of the dominant culture, and the tension between them find concrete and original manifestation in Wright's work, a manifestation at once revealing and terrifying.

It is not only in his revelation of black life, however, that Wright's power lies, for as much as his writing is social and political, it is also personal and philosophical. The story of alienated man is a universal one; because the concrete experiences of the outsider are so vividly rendered in Wright's fiction, his books have an immediate accessibility. Because they also reveal deeper patterns, they have further claims to attention. Much of Wright's later fiction seems self-conscious and studied, but it cannot diminish the greatness of his finest work.

Biography

Born in Mississippi of sharecropper parents, Richard Wright had a lonely and troubled childhood. His father deserted the family early, and after his mother suffered a stroke, Wright was forced at a young age to work to help support the family, which moved frequently from one relative to another. His portrayal of his mother is of a stern but loving parent, unable to contend with the stronger personality of his extremely religious grandmother. Wright's grandmother believed that all fiction was "the devil's lies"; her chief goal was to force Wright into a religious conversion, a goal in which she was singularly unsuccessful.

Wright moved from school to school, attempting to make friends and make his talents known. Though both tasks were difficult, he became valedictorian of his class. Even this accomplishment was spoiled when the principal insisted that Wright read a speech which the principal himself had written, and Wright refused. An uncle told Richard, "They're going to break you," and society, both black and white, seemed intent on doing so. Wright was determined to resist, not to be claimed by his environment as he felt so many blacks around him were.

Wright left Mississippi for Memphis, Tennessee, had little luck there, and—with money stolen from the movie theater where he worked—moved to Chicago. When others stole, Wright disapproved—not for moral reasons, but because he felt stealing did not change the fundamental relationship of a person to his environment. When it offered a chance to change that environment, Wright accepted it.

In Chicago, Wright became involved with others who viewed the country as he did, first in a federal theater project and then with the Communist John Reed Club, which supported his writing until Wright's goals differed from their own. In 1937, he moved to New York City to become the editor of the *Daily Worker*. A year later, he published his first important work, *Uncle Tom's Children*, after which he won a Guggenheim Fellowship, which provided him with the time and funds to write *Native Son*. The novel was published to great acclaim and was followed by a second major work, *Black Boy*.

Although his writing career was a success, Wright was arguing more frequently with the Communist party, with which he finally broke in 1944, and was becoming less optimistic about the hope of racial progress in America.

In 1946, Wright moved to France, where he spent the rest of his life. Although he wrote a great deal there, nothing in his later work, with the possible exception of *The Outsider*, approaches the strength of *Native Son* and *Black Boy*. The existentialism which was always implicit in his work became the dominant theme, but—displaced from his native environment—Wright never again found a convincing dramatic situation in which to work out his preoccupations.

Wright died in France of a heart attack on November 28, 1960. Since his death, three of his works, *Eight Men*, *Lawd Today*, and *American Hunger*, have been published.

Analysis

Richard Wright's best work is always the story of one man's struggle to define himself and by so doing make himself free and responsible, fully human, a character worthy not of pity but of admiration and horror simultaneously. Typically, the character is an outsider, and Wright uses blackness as a representation of that alienation, though his characters are never as interested in defining their blackness as in defining their humanity. Although many characters in Wright's works are outsiders without being aware of their condition, Wright is never interested in them except as foils. Many of them avoid confronting themselves by fleeing to dreams; religion and liquor are two avoidance-mechanisms for Wright's characters, narcotics that blind them to their surrounding world, to what they are and what they might be.

Even Wright's main characters must not think about that world too often: to let it touch them is to risk insanity or violence, and so his characters strive to keep the fire within in check, to keep the physical hunger satisfied. Thus, all of Wright's protagonists are initially trapped by desire and by fear—fear of what might happen to them, what they may do, if they risk venturing outside the confines of black life in America, and the desire to do so. The life outside may be glimpsed in movies; Bigger Thomas, for example, goes to a film and watches contrasting and artificial views of black and white society. Yet as untruthful as both views are, they remind Bigger of a reality beyond his present situation. Desire is often symbolized by flight; Bigger, like other Wright characters, dreams of flying above the world, unchained from its limitations.

Most of Wright's stories and novels examine what happens when the protagonist's fear is mastered for a moment when desires are met. The manifestation of desire in Wright is almost always through violence (and it is here, perhaps, that he is most pessimistic, for other, more positive manifestations of desire, such as love, can come only later, after the protagonists have violently acted out their longings). Violence is central to Wright's fiction, for as important as sex may be to his characters, power is much more so, and power is often achieved through violence; in Wright's world, beatings and murders are frequent acts—central and occasionally creative.

Once the character has acted, he finds himself trapped again in a new set of oppositions, for in acting, he has left the old sureties behind, has made himself free, and has begun to define and create himself. With that new freedom comes a new awareness of responsibility. He is without excuses, and that awareness is as terrifying as—though more liberating than—the fears he has previously known. Although Wright does not always elaborate on what may follow, the characters open up new possibilities for themselves. If one may create one's self by violence, perhaps, Wright sometimes suggests, there are other, less destructive ways as well.

Some of Wright's novels end on this note of optimism, the characters tragically happy: tragic because they have committed violent and repulsive acts, but happy because for the first time they have *chosen* to commit them; they have freed themselves from their constraints, and the future, however short it may be, lies open. Others end simply with tragedy, the destruction achieving no purpose, the characters attaining no illumination.

Lawd Today, written before *Native Son*, but not published until after Wright's death, tells the story of Jake Jackson from his awakening on the morning of February 12, 1936, to that day's violent conclusion. Jackson is Wright's most inarticulate protagonist: he has a banal life, undefined dreams, and a vague sense of discontent which he is unable to explain. Violent and prejudiced, he speaks in clichés, a language as meaningless as his life.

Technically, the book incorporates a montage of radio broadcasts, newspaper articles, and religious and political pamphlets into the narration of Jake's day. Divided into three sections, *Lawd Today* opens with Jake's dream of running up an endless staircase after a disappearing voice. That dream gives way to the reality of his life: hunger, anger, and recrimination. Tricked by Jake into an abortion for which Jake still owes five hundred dollars and now claiming to have a tumor which will cost another five hundred dollars to remove, Jake's wife represents his entrapment. In the first section, "Commonplace," Jake reveals his brutish and trivial character: his anger at his wife, a jealousy and resentment that lead him to bait her so he can hit her, a mock-battle straightening his hair, and a meeting with friends who work with him at the post office. As they play bridge to pass the time until work, Wright presents without comment their stupid, cliché-ridden conversation.

Section two, "Squirrel Cage," shows the men at work. They are all alienated in meaningless, routine jobs, but Jake's position is the most desperate, for his wife has been to see his boss, and he is now threatened with the loss of his job. Falling deeper into debt by borrowing more money and making mistakes on the job, Jake is trapped by his work—despite his own protestations, as a self-proclaimed Republican and capitalist, that work is liberating. This section, too, ends with a long, rambling, and banal conversation among the men at work.

In the concluding section, "Rat's Alley," the men go to a brothel for a good time on some of Jake's borrowed money. There, Jake is robbed and then beaten for his threats of revenge. Finally, Jake stumbles homeward, his day nearing an end. The February weather, pleasant when the book began, has turned bad. All of Jake's frustration and anger finally erupt; he beats his wife, whom he finds kneeling asleep by the bed in an attitude of prayer. As they struggle, he throws objects through the window. She grabs a shard of broken glass and slashes him three times. The book ends with Jake lying in a drunken stupor, bleeding, while his wife is on her knees, also bleeding, praying for death. Outside, the wind blows mercilessly.

Although some of the experimentalism of *Lawd Today* seems artificial, and although the protagonist is too limited to sustain the reader's interest, this early work is powerful and economical. The situation, if not the character, is typical of Wright's work, and the reader understands Jake's violent frustration. *Lawd Today* has its flaws, but it foreshadows the strengths of Wright's best work and in its own right is a daring and fascinating novel.

Along with *Black Boy*, *Native Son* is one of Wright's finest achievements: a brilliant portrayal of, as Wright put it, the way the environment provides the instrumentalities through which one expresses himself and the way that self becomes whole despite the environment's conspiring to keep it divided.

The book parallels Theordore Dreiser's *An American Tragedy* (1925): both are three-part novels in which there is a murder, in part accidental, in part willed; an attempted flight; and a long concluding trial, in both cases somewhat anticlimactic. Both novels are concerned with the interplay of environment and heredity, of fate and accident, and both have protagonists who rebel against the world which would hold them back.

In the first part of *Native Son*, Bigger Thomas is a black man cut off from family and peers. Superficially like his friends, he is in fact possessed of a different consciousness. To think about that consciousness is for him to risk insanity or violence, so Bigger endeavors to keep his fears and uncertainty at a preconscious level. On the day of the first section, however, he is required by welfare to apply for a job as a menial at the home of the rich Dalton family. Mr. Dalton is a ghetto landlord who soothes his conscience by donating sums of money for recreational purposes. That it is a miniscule part of the money he is deriving from blacks is an irony he overlooks. Mrs. Dalton is blind, a fact that is necessary to the plot as well as being symbolic. Their daughter, Mary, is a member of the Communist party, and from the moment she sees Bigger, who wants nothing more than to be left alone, she begins to enlist his support.

The first evening, Bigger is to drive Mary to a university class. In reality, she is going with Jan Erlone, her Communist boyfriend, to a party meeting. Afterward, they insist that Bigger take them to a bar in the black part of town. Jan and Mary are at this point satirized, for their attitudes toward blacks are as limited and stereotyped as any in the novel. Bigger does not want to be seen by his friends with whites, but that fact does not occur to Mary. After much drinking, Bigger must carry the drunken Mary to her bedroom. He puts her to bed, stands over her, attracted to the woman he sees. The door opens and Mrs. Dalton enters. When Mary makes drunken noises, Bigger becomes frightened that Mrs. Dalton will come close enough to discover him, so he puts a pillow over Mary's face to quiet her. By the time Mrs. Dalton leaves, Mary is dead.

Wright wanted to make Bigger a character it would be impossible to pity, and what follows is extremely grisly. Bigger tries to put Mary's body in the furnace and saws off her head to make her fit. However accidental Mary's death may appear to the reader, Bigger himself does not regard it as such. He has, he thinks, many times wanted to kill whites without ever having the opportunity to do so. This time there was the act without the desire, but rather than seeing himself as the victim of a chance occurrence, Bigger prefers to unite the earlier desire with the present act, to make himself whole by accepting responsibility for the killing. Indeed, not only will he accept the act, but also Bigger determines to capitalize on it by sending a ransom note. Later, accused of raping Mary as well, an act he considered but did not commit, he reverses the process, accepting responsibility for this, too, even though here there was desire but no act. His only sign of conscience is that he cannot bring himself to shake the ashes in the furnace; this guilt is not redemptive, but his undoing, for, in an implausible scene in the Dalton basement, the room fills with smoke, the murder is revealed to newspaper reporters gathered there, and Bigger is forced to flee.

He runs with his girl friend, Bessie Mears. She, like Bigger, has a hunger for sensation, which has initially attracted him to her. Now, however, as they flee together, she becomes a threat and a burden; huddled with her in an abandoned tenement, Bigger wants only to be rid of her. He picks up a brick and smashes her face, dumping her body down an airshaft. His only regret is not that he has killed her, but that he has forgotten to remove their money from her body.

The rest of the plot moves quickly: Bigger is soon arrested, the trial is turned into a political farce, and Bigger is convicted and sentenced to death. In the last part of the novel, after Bigger's arrest, the implications of the action are developed, largely through Bigger's relations to other characters. Some of the characters are worthy only of contempt, particularly the district attorney, who, in an attempt at reelection, is turning the trial into political capital. Bigger's mother relies on religion. In a scene in the jail cell, she falls on her knees in apology before Mrs. Dalton and urges Bigger to pray, but toughness is Bigger's code. He is embarrassed by his mother's self-abasement, and although he agrees to pray simply to end his discomfort, his attitude toward religion is shown when he throws away a cross a minister has given him and throws a cup of coffee in a priest's face. In his view, they want only to avoid the world and to force him to accept guilt without responsibility.

Bigger learns from two characters. The first is Boris Max, the lawyer the Communist party provides. Max listens to Bigger, and for the first time in his life, Bigger exposes his ideas and feelings to another human. Max's plea to the court is that, just as Bigger must accept responsibility for what he has done, so must the society around him understand its responsibility for what Bigger has become and, if the court chooses to execute Bigger, understand the consequences that must flow from that action. He does not argue—nor does Wright believe—that Bigger is a victim of injustice. There is no injustice, because that would presume a world in which Bigger could hope for justice, and such a world does not exist; more important, Bigger is not a victim, for he has chosen his own fate. Max argues rather that all men are entitled to happiness. Like all of Wright's protagonists, Bigger has earlier been torn between the poles of dread and ecstasy. His ecstasy, his happiness comes from the meaningfulness he creates in his existence, a product of self-realization. Unhappily for Bigger, he realizes himself through murder: it was, he feels, his highest creative act.

If Max articulates the intellectual presentation of Wright's beliefs about Bigger, it is Jan, Mary's lover, who is its dramatic representation. He visits Bigger in his cell and, having at last understood the futility and paucity of his own stereotypes, admits to Bigger that he too shares in the responsibility for what has happend. He, too, addresses Bigger as a human being, but from the unique position of being the one who is alive to remind Bigger of the consequences of his actions, for Bigger learns that Jan has suffered loss through what he has done and that, while Bigger has created himself, he has also destroyed another.

Native Son ends with the failure of Max's appeals on Bigger's behalf. He comes to the cell to confront Bigger before his execution, and the novel closes with Bigger Thomas smiling at Max as the prison door clangs shut. He will die happy because he will die fulfilled, having, however terribly, created a self. *Native Son* is Wright's most powerful work, because his theme, universal in nature, is given its fullest and most evocative embodiment. In the characterization of Bigger, alienated man at his least abstract and most genuine, of Bigger's exactly rendered mind and milieu, and of Bigger's working out of his destiny, *Native Son* is Wright's masterpiece.

Wright's next novel, *The Outsider*, written in France and published thirteen years after *Native Son*, suffers from a surplus of internal explanation and a failure to provide a setting as rich as that of *Native Son*. Still, its portrayal of Cross Damon and his struggle to define himself, while too self-conscious, adds new dimensions to Wright's myth.

As the novel opens, Damon is trapped by his life. His post-office job is unfulfilling, his wife is threatening, and his underage mistress is pregnant. He "desires desire," but there is no way for that desire to be completed. "A man creates himself," he has told his wife, but the self Damon has created is a nightmare. He broods, his brooding as close as he comes to religion. Another underground man, Damon gets his chance for new life on the subway. Thought dead after his identification papers are found near the mangled body of another, Damon gets a chance to create himself anew. He must invent, he thinks, not only his future, but also a past to fit with his present; this new opportunity brings with it a different and more potent sense of dread.

From the beginning of this new life, Damon is remarkably successful at the mechanics of creating a past. He easily obtains a birth certificate and a draft card. At a deeper level, however, he traps himself as surely as he has been trapped in his old life, so that his new one becomes a continuous act of bad faith. Even before he leaves Chicago, he hides in a brothel where he encounters a co-worker who recognizes him. Damon murders the man and throws his body out a window. The pattern of violence, so typical of Wright's characters, begins in earnest for Damon

Taking a train to New York, Cross meets two people who will influence his new life, a black waiter who introduces him to the world of Communist politics in New York City, and Ely Houston, the district attorney, who is the most articulate person in the novel and the only one fully to understand Damon. Houston asks Damon why, when all blacks are outsiders, so few seem conscious of this fact. Wright suggests that being man is too much to be borne by man, that the struggle to define oneself is too difficult; the novel is a testament to that suggestion.

The Communist party members, too, are outsiders, and there is nothing unified about their company. Each one that Damon meets is playing god, hoping to protect and extend his personal power. Their awareness of their motives varies, but they are a threat to Damon, and the action of the book is propelled by a series of murders: Damon himself wants to act like a god. Near the end of the book, Houston comes to understand that Damon is the killer, but—rather than indicting and punishing him legally—Houston allows him to go free, alone with his knowledge of what he is. Damon is horrified by his fate, but he is robbed of even that when he is killed by two Communist party members who fear him.

The Outsider is both an extension and a modification of Wright's earlier views; it is far more pessimistic than *Native Son*, and the influence of the French existentialists is more pervasive. Like earlier Wright heroes, Damon is engaged in defining the world and himself. "The moment we act 'as if' it's true, then it's true," he thinks, because each man, in the absence of a god, it able to create the world and its truth. From Fyodor Dostoevski, Wright again borrows the notion of underground man and the idea that without a god, all is permitted. Yet as each man plays god, as each becomes criminal, policemen, judge, and executioner, there are no longer limits. Man desires everything, and desire is described as a floating demon. Men are jealous gods here—the worlds they create are petty, their jealousy destructive. Cross Damon is loved in the novel, but that love, unlike the love in *Native Son* which is held up as potentially meaningful, is here without promise. Although he creates himself and his world in *The Outsider*, all that is made is violent and brutal, a world without redemption even in the act of self-realization.

At the end of the novel, Cross Damon dies, not with Bigger Thomas' smile, but with the knowledge that alone, man is nothing. Searching in his last moments of freedom for a clean, well-lighted place in which to rest before he confronts the world again, Cross finds only death. Before he dies, he admits his final act of bad faith: he has thought that he could create a world and be different from other men, that he could remain innocent. Like Joseph Conrad's Kurtz in *Heart of Darkness* (1902), Damon dies realizing the futility of that hope; having looked into his own heart of darkness, he dies with the word *horror* on his lips.

It is Wright's bleakest conclusion, the book his most relentless examination of the consequences of his own philosophy. If *The Outsider* lacks the narrative drive of *Native Son*, it remains a strongly conceived and troubling piece of fiction.

Wright's last novel, *The Long Dream*, despite some effective scenes, is one of his weakest. The story of Rex "Fishbelly" Tucker's growing up and coming to terms with his environment is a pale repetition of earlier themes. The first section describes Tucker's youth. His father, an undertaker, is the richest black man in town, but his money comes also from a brothel he runs on the side. Tucker admires his father's success while detesting his obsequiousness with whites. When, however, Fishbelly is arrested, he twice faints at the white world's threats. Having presented himself as a victim, he becomes one. Walking home after his father has arranged his freedom, Fishbelly sees an injured dog, which he puts out of its misery. Fishbelly then comes upon a white man, pinned to the ground with a car door in his body. When the white man calls out to Fishbelly, using the term "nigger," Fishbelly walks on, leaving the man to die.

In the second section, Fishbelly finds a woman, but she and forty-one others are burned to death in a fire at the bar. The rest of the novel is an unconvincing story of the police who want the return of the cancelled checks that Fishbelly's father has used to pay them off, the police's arranged murder of the father, the subsequent framing and imprisoning of Fishbelly for rape, and Fishbelly's keeping the checks for his future use. All of this is badly contrived. At the end, Fishbelly is on a plane leaving for France, where his childhood friends are stationed in the army which they describe as exciting. He is talking to an

Italian whose father has come to America and found a dream, where Fishbelly himself has known only a nightmare. France, he dreams, will offer him what America has not.

In Fishbelly's attempt to understand himself and his environment, he is a typical Wright protagonist. He is weaker than Wright's usual characters, however, and that shallowness, coupled with an implausible plot, prevents Wright's last work of long fiction from succeeding.

Unlike many highly acclaimed books of the 1940's, *Native Son* and *Black Boy* have not dated. They are a lacerating challenge to contemporary readers and writers—a challenge to share the relentless integrity of Richard Wright's vision.

Howard Faulkner

Other major works

SHORT FICTION: *Uncle Tom's Children*, 1938, 1940; *Eight Men*, 1961.

PLAY: *Native Son: The Biography of a Young American*, pr. 1941 (with Paul Green).

NONFICTION: *Twelve Million Black Voices*, 1941; *Black Boy*, 1945; *Black Power*, 1954; *The Color Curtain*, 1956; *Pagan Spain*, 1957; *White Man, Listen!*, 1957; *American Hunger*, 1977.

Bibliography

Baldwin, James. *The Price of the Ticket: Collected Nonfiction, 1948-1985*. New York: St. Martin's Press/Marek, 1985. The essays "Everybody's Protest Novel" and "Alas, Poor Richard" provide important and provocative insights into Wright and his art.

Bloom, Harold, ed. *Richard Wright*. New York: Chelsea House, 1987. Essays on various aspects of Wright's work and career, with an introduction by Bloom.

Fabre, Michel. *The Unfinished Quest of Richard Wright*. Translated by Isabel Barzun. New York: William Morrow, 1973. The most important and authoritative biography of Wright available.

_____. *The World of Richard Wright*. Jackson: University Press of Mississippi, 1985. A collection of Fabre's essays on Wright. A valuable but not sustained full-length study.

Kinnamon, Keneth. *The Emergence of Richard Wright*. Urbana: University of Illinois Press, 1972. A study of Wright's background and development as a writer, up to the publication of *Native Son* (1940).

Walker, Ian. "Black Nightmare: The Fiction of Richard Wright." In *Black Fiction*, edited by A. Robert Lee. New York: Barnes & Noble Books, 1980. Replying to critics who read Wright as a social realist, Walker looks at the unreal and the nightmarish in Wright's fiction.

Walker, Margaret. *Richard Wright: Daemonic Genius*. New York: Warner Books, 1988. A critically acclaimed study of Wright's life and work written by a respected novelist.

Webb, Constance. *Richard Wright: A Biography*. New York: Putnam, 1968. A well-written biography which remains useful.

FRANK YERBY

Born: Augusta, Georgia; September 5, 1916
Died: Madrid, Spain; November 29, 1991

Principal long fiction

The Foxes of Harrow, 1946; *The Vixens*, 1947; *The Golden Hawk*, 1948; *Pride's Castle*, 1949; *Floodtide*, 1950; *A Woman Called Fancy*, 1951; *The Saracen Blade*, 1952; *The Devil's Laughter*, 1953; *Bride of Liberty*, 1954; *Benton's Row*, 1954; *The Treasure of Pleasant Valley*; 1955; *Captain Rebel*, 1956; *Fairoaks*, 1957; *The Serpent and the Staff*, 1958; *Jarrett's Jade*, 1959; *Gillian*, 1960; *The Garfield Honor*, 1961; *Griffin's Way*, 1962; *The Old Gods Laugh: A Modern Romance*, 1964; *An Odor of Sanctity*, 1965; *Goat Song*, 1968; *Judas, My Brother*, 1968; *Speak Now: A Modern Novel*, 1969; *The Dahomean*, 1971; *The Girl from Storyville*, 1972; *The Voyage Unplanned*, 1974; *Tobias and the Angel*, 1975; *A Rose for Ana Maria*, 1976; *Hail the Conquering Hero*, 1977; *A Darkness at Ingraham's Crest*, 1979; *Western*, 1982; *Devilseed*, 1984; *McKenzie's Hundred*, 1985.

Other literary forms

In addition to his novels, Frank Yerby wrote poetry and short stories that are often found in anthologies of black literature. One story, "Health Card," first published in *Harper's Magazine*, won a special O. Henry Memorial Award in 1944.

Achievements

Yerby wrote many best-selling historical novels over a long career beginning in the 1940's. Most of his best work, however, dates from the 1960's, after he had established himself as a prolific popular novelist. Yerby excelled at creating complicated, fast-moving plots that give vivid impressions of historical eras and periods. Often the novels contradict myths and stereotypes of the periods in question. Almost every novel, too, suggests the futility of finding real truth in the universal confusion of the human condition. While Yerby's protagonists are flawed, often by ruthlessness and infidelity, they are also characterized by a fierce sense of dignity of the worth of a human life.

Biography

Frank Garvin Yerby, a black American novelist, was born in Augusta, Georgia, on September 5, 1916. He received an A.B. at Paine College in 1937 and an M.A. at Fisk College in 1938. Subsequently, he did graduate work in education at the University of Chicago.

From 1939 to 1941, Yerby taught English, first at Florida A. & M. and then at Southern University and Agricultural and Mechanical College. Married in 1941, he worked from 1941 to 1944 at the Ford Motor Company in

Dearborn, Michigan, as a technician and then as an inspector at Fairchild Aircraft from 1944 to 1945. In 1944, he won an O. Henry Memorial Award for the short story "Health Card," a story that dealt sensitively with black issues. In 1945, he started work on a novel, *The Foxes of Harrow*, which he aimed to make a commercial success. Thereafter, Yerby wrote many similar melodramatic best-sellers. His books have sold millions of copies and have been translated into at least fourteen languages.

Divorced in the 1950's, Yerby moved to France and then to Spain, where he died in 1991. He had four children from his first marriage. His second wife was his researcher and general manager; some of his later novels give evidence of considerable research. He traveled widely, and sometimes his travels involved investigating locales of works in progress.

Analysis

Frank Yerby is a best-selling author, and much of what he has done has clear commercial appeal, a point on which Yerby has made inconsistent remarks. His plots are intricate and involved, but in many of his novels, the characterizations are basically flat. His most-used era is that of the nineteenth century South, yet he has written about many other places and times in his more than thirty novels. Occasionally, he has set a novel in modern times. The superficial reader of best-sellers will find in Yerby's novels fast-paced narrative with appropriate amounts of violence and sex.

Yerby is more, however, than a mere best-selling writer. His short stories written early in his career show promise and develop radically different themes from those of his costume novels. In the 1960's, secure after many commercial successes, Yerby began to do his best work, dealing with larger issues of race and religion which figure less prominently in his earlier novels. The characters in these later novels are no longer cardboard figures, while the backgrounds are as richly detailed and vividly re-created as ever. Yerby's historical novels must be evaluated within the context of that often unappreciated genre. His novels almost always show the conflict between two worlds or orders, as great historical novels do. Yerby rarely deals with actual historical figures but rather creates characters who have to deal with the essential conflicts of their eras. Often his novels, even the early ones, destroy widely held myths and stereotypes; Darwin Turner suggests that this revisionism might be Yerby's most significant contribution as a novelist. While extensive research is not evident in his early work, many of Yerby's later novels have been thoroughly researched. Yerby is at his best in creating the color and movement of a particular era.

Yerby's typical protagonist is, in the words of his main character in *The Serpent and the Staff*, an *auslander* or outsider, excluded from the ruling social order. The protagonist experientially develops a philosophy that often approaches modern existentialism, an attitude that life has no answer but that man still must cope with the bleakness of human existence with both dignity and humanity. This pattern emerges in Yerby's first novel, *The Foxes of Harrow*, and is developed in three of his best novels: *Griffin's Way*, *An Odor of Sanctity*, and *The Dahomean*.

The Foxes of Harrow, Yerby's first novel, is set in the South and covers the years from 1825 to just after the end of the Civil War. Superficially, it is a novel about a clever schemer who rises to own a plantation with a neo-classical mansion, Harrow, and who has marriages to beautiful white women and a liaison with a stunning mulatto. Much of the novel is composed of stock devices of pulp fiction, and Yerby himself recently said of *The Foxes of Harrow* that he set out to write a popular novel that would make him a lot of money, regardless of literary merit. Yerby added, however, that he became strangely involved with the writing of the novel and, despite himself, exceeded the ambitions of the pulp genre. Stephen Fox, the protagonist, is an outsider, originally shanty Irish. He is not merely the rogue that early reviewers took him for, whose success and eventual fall conform to a predictable pulp outline. Fox sees all values and ideals slip from him, so that at the end, he is a failure despite his humanity and perception. He is superior to the Southerners with whom he sympathetically deals. More than merely a novel of stock devices, *The Foxes of Harrow* is a story about the failure of a culture.

In the opening of the novel, Yerby's authorial voice establishes a pensive tone as he describes a visit to Harrow, now in ruins, in the twentieth century. Harrow is the symbol of a lost cause. Thus, for symbolic purposes, Harrow is cut off from the modern world. Bathed in moonlight, the ruins of Harrow have a decadent grandeur. The visitor feels driven from room to room and finally away from the house, never wanting to look back. The shortness of the opening, six brief paragraphs, makes the tone all the more striking, and the mood shifts quickly into the dialogue and description of the arrival of Stephen Fox in New Orleans in 1825.

Yerby is at his best in the novel in creating vivid images and scenes of the region during the forty or so years the novel spans. New Orleans appears as a lush feudalistic world where color is measured by degrees, given the novel's constant references to mulattos, quadroons, and octaroons, references which are historically true to the setting. New Orleans emerges as a backward society that refuses to drain the marshes where the mosquitoes carrying yellow fever breed and instead fires cannon to disperse the plague. The society also destroys the creativity of freed blacks. In one case, a thoroughly educated black returns from France and is killed for acting as if he were equal to whites. The most poignant scene occurs at the end of the novel, when the young heir to Harrow returns after the war to New Orleans to be confronted by a former slave of Harrow now in control. This former slave presents the heir's unknown half brother (by a beautiful mulatto) to his former master, who sees the image of his father as a young man—but the half brother is mentally retarded. As the scene concludes, Yerby deftly shows the social history of the next one hundred years of the South. The former slave, now the ruler, knows that power will again return to the whites but suggests that blacks and whites can live together and respect one another. The heir, a combination of the worst of his father's roguish tendencies and the excesses of New Orleans, emphatically denies that such equality and reconciliation between the races is possible.

Yerby is weakest in his creation of character in *The Foxes of Harrow*, for the characters are one-dimensional and move woodenly through a convoluted, overheated plot. Stephen Fox is the fox, the rogue set off from Southern society by his birth, whose goals are riches and the most beautiful woman in New Orleans, Odalie Arceneaux, a cold, haughty belle. Her sister Aurore is a foil to her, for she is warm and beautiful and in love with Stephen, who is too blind at first to see her love. As pulps have it, Odalie dies in childbirth, and Stephen then marries gentle Aurore, but only after having fathered a child by a beautiful mulatto when Odalie had spurned his strong sexual drives.

Underneath this claptrap, though, is an author working with social issues not to be found in the typical 1946 pulp novel. In one scene, a black woman recently inducted into slavery throws herself into the Mississippi rather than live in bondage. Old Calleen, a trusted slave at Harrow, later tells her grandson Inch (the son of the drowned slave) that someday, the rightness of their freedom will be made apparent. More significantly, in understated dialogue Stephen talks to his son Etienne about freeing slaves and says that the country must treat all people equally, including the blacks and the poorest whites. When his son dismisses the poor, white or black, Stephen uses history as a defense, mentioning the French Revolution, Haiti, and Nat Turner. It is in his sympathy and balance in treating social matters that Yerby's "moral mobility" appears, a phrase that a London *Times* writer used in reviewing a later Yerby novel.

Griffin's Way was published in 1962, sixteen years after *The Foxes of Harrow*, and is a departure in some respects from Yerby's work up to that time. It treats the Mississippi of the 1870's unglamorously, highlighting squalor, inbreeding among whites, and the violence of the Klan in a manner more characteristic of William Faulkner than of the standard best-selling author. The novel shows the paralysis of humane white society after the war, a paralysis symbolized by the central hero's amnesia and invalid status.

Much of the novel debunks the grandeur and opulence of the old South which Yerby himself had occasionally exploited in earlier novels. The ruined South appears first through the eyes of a Northerner, Candace Trevor, a New England minister's daughter married to a paralyzed Southerner and hired as a nurse for Paris Griffin as the novel opens. She despises the Southern "courtesy" to which women are subjected, dismisses the neoclassical architecture in the poorly constructed homes, and comments on how most planters lived in squalor even before the war. Unlike her father, she believes in a Darwinian theory of evolution and sees the darker forces in herself as part of the ape still remaining in man. Candace knows that to cure Paris of his amnesia she must find the key to it from Paris' oversexed wife Laurel. Ferreting out answers with the right leading questions, she discovers the tawdry, twisted story that led to Paris' amnesia and emotional paralysis. It is only her austere moral upbringing that allows her to control her love for Paris to use her knowledge to help him.

When Candace does cure him, Paris tries to return to his home, Griffin's Way, and to his wife Laurel, but while his cure is a rebirth, it does not allow a return. To begin with, he has returned to a world changed by the war, a world of political corruption and violence, a world that has regressed, so that even a sixty-mile trip, once possible in three hours, now involves an arduous three-day journey because the railroads remain unrepaired even five years after the war. Three years later, with the railroad rebuilt, Paris and Laurel visit Vicksburg, where Paris, despite his humanity, appears troubled by the apparent ascendancy of blacks. Yerby balances the situation by having Paris also see the obvious corruption of the black superintendent of schools, who lives in the grand style of the old South on money intended for the schools. Paris is thus caught between two worlds: he rejects the Klan as apes but resents a black man wearing a suit as if he is accustomed to it. Even renewed, Paris still represents the paralysis of the humane white during the Reconstruction.

Yerby entitled the last third of the novel "Apocalypse," and this part has unresolved elements, unresolved on account of Yerby's honesty in dealing with his material. Paris watches the new world tumble around him, powerless to do anything. Black militants and white Klansmen fight all over the South, but Paris can only catalog the battles; he cannot change events. His moment of action does allow him to rescue Samson, a former slave, and Samson's wife by helping them escape to the North. He can do nothing to help his brother, his mulatto wife, and their children, who are burned in their house except for one daughter, who dies after being repeatedly raped, all of them victims of the Klan. He also helps a black minister escape, but only after the dynamiting of the minister's house, which killed a daughter. At his daughter's funeral, the minister delivers a stern sermon to the Klan members, who then threaten his life so that Paris must again help him. The Klan members finally back off from Paris' house when one accidentally shoots Laurel, still very much a symbol of Southern womanhood. The novel ends with dawn imagery, the night having been endured and the humane whites now waiting for the light of morning. Whether the whites threatened by the Klan can start anew is unclear. Given the implied parallel to modern events, Yerby seems to be saying that it is too soon to tell if the twentieth century can rise above racial violence; nevertheless, the concluding imagery does suggest hope.

In *An Odor of Sanctity*, Yerby is at his best as a historical novelist. It is a long, deftly paced novel which, while using many of the stock elements of Yerby's novels of the 1940's and 1950's, also deals intelligently with a religious theme. Once again, Yerby creates an outsider, Alaric Teudisson, as hero; he is set off by his odor of sanctity, a saintly force in him of which he is not fully aware for most of his life. Teudisson must deal with the complex culture of medieval Spain, a battleground for Christians, Moors, and numerous bands of marauding barbarians.

Like earlier Yerby protagonists, Teudisson is involved in many liaisons and several marriages. Teudisson is a striking blond of Visigoth extraction who, before the male hormones take effect, is so "beautiful" that at one point he is almost made a catamite. Thereafter, Teudisson has numerous sexual encounters, one unconsummated marriage, and finally a marriage to a woman who has been repeatedly raped by bandits, a marriage which shows Teudisson's magnanimity and one which also brings Teudisson genuine happiness and a family.

The religious motif of *An Odor of Sanctity* adds depth to what would otherwise be an entertaining but rather shallow melodrama. Despite himself, Alaric Teudisson becomes a saint by the end of the novel. As a man, Teudisson is handsome but scarred by battle, but as a boy, his beauty, so unlike the usual rough Goth face, led his mother and others to think he was marked for the priesthood. He turns from his religious impulses to lead a secular life, however, and while doing so, he finds his saintliness. In dealing with women, he shows a compassion and love that is the basis of his profound sexual appeal; at one point of seeming dissolution, he has numerous prostitutes loving him because he has talked to them and treated them as human beings and not merely as sex objects. Misused by a woman, he always responds with kindness. By the end of the novel, Teudisson becomes the arbiter between Moor and Christian factions when a certain group of fanatic Christians want to destroy all tolerance for the predominant Moors. Throughout the novel, Teudisson has been a genuine ecumenist. At the end, Teudisson, doubting his saintly powers because he is unable to save his wife, willingly seeks crucifixion and thus enters sainthood and legend. In losing himself, he gains sainthood.

As in most of his novels, Yerby's greatest strength in *An Odor of Sanctity* is his re-creation of a time, a re-creation imbued with color and action. Again, a humane authorial voice speaks throughout the novel. The book shows that the diversity of medieval Spain is indeed its glory. While the Moorish culture encourages learning and recognizes Christ as a prophet, the contrasting Christian culture (except for Teudisson and a few Church fathers) is dark and intolerant. In showing the clash between these cultures, *An Odor of Sanctity* is first-rate historical fiction.

If one of Yerby's novels is destined to last, it is *The Dahomean*, a novel unlike any of his others. It is a simple, moving tale of the life of a black man in his African culture before he was sold into slavery. Yerby neither idealizes nor sensationalizes his material but presents a story composed of love, envy, and hatred that reads as a legend, a story of characters and events drawn larger than life. The protagonist, Nyasanu, is like other Yerby protagonists because he is an alien or outsider: he is far less violent and far more handsome than most men of his society. Caught in the ugliness of the American slave-system, he has the tragic quality of some of the great existentialist heroes.

Yerby begins the chronological narrative of Nyasanu as he is about to enter manhood, a passage marked by the painful ritual of circumcision. The early parts of the novel present such rituals in convincing detail. Yerby moves the reader from Nyasanu's initiation to an enemy's attempt to destroy his guardian tree to his wedding and the deflowering of his bride. In "A Note to the Reader," Yerby explains that the novel is based on research into the customs of the Dahomeans of the nineteenth century, but Yerby adds to his research his own respect of this African culture.

As Nyasanu moves through his period of manhood, Yerby depicts the society of the Dahomeans as a stage for the great primal emotions and forces of life. Nyasanu has encounters with numerous women, but his sexual expe-riences are never merely sensational, the stuff of popular fiction: Nyasanu has a reality which sets him apart from Yerby's typical protagonists. In addition to his sexual encounters, Nyasanu has the experience of real brotherhood, for his society expects each male to have his three closest friends identified in order. Battles with warring tribes give Nyasanu the chance to show bravery and also to distinguish himself as more sensitive to violence than the average Dahomean. In addition, Yerby shows the diversity of Dahomean society, which includes both male homosexuals and Amazonian warriors.

In a moving discussion with his number one friend, Kpadunu, Nyasanu learns that the generations are all of one fabric. Each generation faces the same problems of love, the family, and death. The old priests, therefore, give answers based on the past to the young and the unsure, and—given the coherence of their society—the answers generally hold. Facing the problem of belief in the gods which these old priests try to inculcate in the young, Nyasanu realizes that their wisdom is not divine but experiential, that the past of his society answers the present needs. Ironically, his friend Kpadunu is trying to help Nyasanu rise above the control of priests by showing where their wisdom resides, yet he actually makes the skeptical Nyasanu believe more than he did, so that he must face the priestly prediction that his life will end in Dahomey but will begin again in another place.

Nyasanu does learn that he can count on the inexorability of fate and not the protection of the gods. In quick succession, he loses his friend Kpadunu, his wife in childbirth, and his father. He comes to see his heroism as mere foolishness in taking risks. Rather than listening to the gods, he simply faces life as chieftain and husband of Kpadunu's widow. Far more than the ritual of circumcision, his acceptance of life and his rejection of the illusion of divine protection marks Nyasanu's adulthood. When Nyasanu next appears in the novel, he is chieftain and has four wives. His life is successful until he is sold into slavery with the aid of his homosexual brother and rival.

The betrayal of Nyasanu has the archetypal pattern of tragedy, the hero fallen from great heights, undone by his own blindness in not facing the evil of his brother and his incestuous brother-in-law and by his pride in not following the past and living with his extended family in the same compound. He faces the guns of his attackers with his sword, only to be told to put his sword down, for in the modern era, swords are powerless against guns. First, he must watch the murder of his mother (the slavers see that she is too old to have children), the subsequent murder of all his children (the slavers know that they would die on the voyage across the Atlantic), and the subjugation of his wives, the rape of some and the suicide of one. His response is disassociation, a silence which lasts the rest of his life.

Like a classical tragedy, *The Dahomean* treats terrible despair in its conclusion but leads to an illumination, Nyasanu's enlightenment. He recognizes the evil of blacks selling blacks into American slavery, although they have no conception of the degradation of this foreign slavery, their domestic slavery being gentle and indulgent. Philosophically, Nyasanu faces the bleakness of life with the realization that there are no answers. Truth is only that there is no truth. Nyasanu acquits himself with honor; like a great tragic hero, he has his dignity, the dignity of silence in the face of the emptiness of the human condition.

Dennis Goldsberry

Bibliography

Bone, Robert A. *The Negro Novel in America.* Rev. ed. New Haven, Conn.: Yale University Press, 1965. A general survey of black novels. Bone dismisses Yerby as the "prince of pulpsters."

Hemenway, Robert, ed. *The Black Novelist.* Columbus, Ohio: Merrill, 1970. Darwin Turner comments on Yerby's "painful groping for meaning" behind a "soap-opera façade."

Klotman, Phyllis. "A Harrowing Experience: Frank Yerby's First Novel to Film." *College Language Association Journal* 31 (December, 1987): 210-222. Focuses on the changes made to Yerby's story when *The Foxes of Harrow* was adapted to the screen.

Mendelson, Phyllis Carmel, and Dedria Bryfonski, eds. *Contemporary Literary Criticism.* Vol 7. Detroit: Gale Research, 1977. Contains excerpts of positive criticism about Yerby's use of racial themes.

Metzger, Linda, and Deborah A. Straub, eds. *Contemporary Authors.* New Revision Series 16. Detroit: Gale Research, 1986. A sympathetic look at Yerby's work. Also contains an interview with the novelist.

JOSÉ YGLESIAS

Born: Tampa, Florida; November 29, 1919

Principal long fiction

A Wake in Ybor City, 1963; *An Orderly Life*, 1967; *The Truth About Them*, 1971; *Double Double*, 1974; *The Kill Price*, 1976; *Home Again*, 1985.

Other literary forms

In addition to his novels, José Yglesias has contributed many articles and short stories to such respected journals as *The New Yorker*, *The Nation*, *Esquire*, *The Atlantic*, and *The Sunday Times Magazine*. He has also translated novels by Juan Goytisolo and Xavier Domingo from Spanish into English. His four major nonfictional works have been praised for their clear narrative prose. Focusing on Spain and Latin America, these works provide the American reader with the all too rare opportunity to meet individual Spaniards and Latin Americans, to see their socioeconomic and political situation from their own perspective. In *The Goodbye Land* (1967), which first appeared in serial form in *The New Yorker* in the spring of 1967, Yglesias recounts his 1965 trip to Galicia, Spain, where his father, a native Galician, returned home to die. Some forty years after his father's death, Yglesias visits his father's birthplace in search of the many unanswered questions concerning his last years. In uncovering the truth about his father, Yglesias also discovers the captivating beauty of the Galician people. His second book of nonfiction, *In the Fist of the Revolution* (1968), describes the everyday life of a small town, Mayarí, in post revolutionary Cuba, while *Down There* (1970) is a broader analysis of Latin-American reality. Based on interviews he conducted in 1969 with various groups of politically involved Latin Americans (in Cuba, Brazil, Chile, and Peru), the book captures many of the hopes and frustrations experienced by Latin America's militantly anti-American youth. In *The Franco Years* (1977), Yglesias presents a candid analysis of the controversial Spanish dictator, Generalísimo Francisco Franco, and the alternatives facing post-Franco Spain.

Achievements

José Yglesias' many contributions to magazines such as *The New Yorker* have made his name both known and respected throughout the American literary establishment. Several of his stories have appeared in *Best American Stories* (1972 and 1975). His books on Spain and Latin America have been recognized not only for their documentary value but also for their literary merit. Yglesias' fluid narrative style and seemingly effortless ability to describe the complex and diverse realities of the Spanish-speaking world, have brought him several prestigious academic awards. He was the recipient of a John Simon Guggenheim Memorial Foundation Fellowship both in 1970 and 1976. As a result of these grants, he produced a penetrating analysis of Francisco Franco's waning influence in contemporary Spain, *The Franco Years*. In 1974, he was awarded a grant from the National Endowment for the Arts. Because of his bilingual upbringing (his father was Spanish and his mother Cuban), he was the ideal writer to visit postrevolutionary Cuba. He spent three months there in the spring of 1967 with the people of Mayarí. On the basis of this unique experience, he wrote *In the Fist of the Revolution*, a rare glimpse of the Cuban people as they truly are, and not as Americans prefer to imagine them. Curiously, it is Yglesias' nonfiction that has received the greatest praise from reviewers and critics. His novels, for the most part, have not enjoyed such acclaim. Possibly, since each novel deals with a Cuban-American or Mexican-American protagonist, a better understanding and appreciation of Hispanic-American reality would allow the American critic to view these works with a broader perspective, opening areas of literary investigation.

Biography

José Yglesias was born in Tampa, Florida, on November 29, 1919. Reared in a Spanish-speaking home in the Cuban sector of Tampa known as Ybor City, his mixed Hispanic heritage was to play a major role in his development as a writer. Perhaps it was the fact that his father left home to return to his beloved Galicia when Yglesias was only a child, or perhaps it was the schizo-phrenic experience of growing up in America as a Cuban-American that planted the first seeds of interest in his Hispanic-American heritage. Whatever the cause, Yglesias' enthusiastic quest to learn all he could about his back-ground is evident throughout his fiction. His novels generally center around the fragmented psyche of a Hispanic-American protagonist who is searching for his spiritual center. Two days after he was graduated from high school in Tampa, Yglesias left for New York City, where he experienced the freedom that always accompanies the abandonment of one's hometown environment; on the other hand, mistaken frequently for a Puerto Rican, he became even more conscious of his identity as a Hispanic American. During World War II, he served in the United States Naval Reserve for three years, where he received the Naval Merit Citation. After the war, he decided to go back to school. He attended Black Mountain College for one year (1946-1947) before returning to New York City, where he met his wife-to-be, Helen Bassine. They were married on August 19, 1950. Before devoting himself full-time to writing, he worked in New York City for a pharmaceutical company, rising from an entry-level job to an executive position. His initial attempts at writing consisted almost entirely of reviews or articles for literary magazines; he also translated several books from Spanish into English. It was not until 1963, with the publication of his first novel, *A Wake in Ybor City*, that he began to utilize fully the rich material that his Tampa/Manhattan connection provided him. Presently living in North Brooklin, Maine, he continues to be active both in the world of fiction and nonfiction. His wife, Helen, and his son, Rafael, are both accomplished novelists.

Analysis

There is a special quality to each of José Yglesias' novels, a kind of aura that seems to tell the reader that he or she is entering a fictional world radically different from the Anglo-American tradition. Although each novel is unique unto itself, there is in all of his novels a definite tension underlying the seemingly natural flow of events, a kind of double vision that stems from Yglesias' diverse and at times conflicting heritage. Brought up in a Cuban-American environment that was more Latin than American, he moved to New York City while still young. There, he encountered head-on the rather old and impersonal but nonetheless captivating charm of mainstream America. Having experienced the tenuous acceptance that is given to all those who succeed in Anglo-America's melting pot, Yglesias has never rejected his Latin roots. The result is a unique mestizo portrayal of American reality. The vision presented in *A Wake in Ybor City*, *An Orderly Life*, *The Truth About Them*, *Double Double*, *The Kill Price*, and *Home Again*, is at once reminiscent of the seventeenth century Spanish *picaro* and the twentieth century New York intellectual. Like the Peruvian novelist José Maria Arguedas, who committed suicide in 1969, Yglesias presents the world through the eyes of one who belongs simultaneously to two distinct realities. Thus, the reader is treated to a rare opportunity: an inside view of the world as seen from the perspective of a semi-outsider.

Yglesias returns to the place of his youth, Ybor City, for the setting of his first novel, *A Wake in Ybor City*. An omniscient third-person narrator recounts three days in the life of a Cuban-American family in 1958. The novel's simple structure and fluid style pose no problem to the reader, who quickly finds himself more and more involved in a moving depiction of a family's struggle to face several crises that threaten to destroy their uncommonly close ties with one another.

The story is simple. An aging widow, Dolores, anxiously awaits the arrival of her children, who will be visiting her from Havana, Cuba. Elena, the eldest daughter, is married to a wealthy and influential Cuban aristocrat, Jaime. They are scheduled to arrive the next day with Dolores' other daughter, Clara, and her son, Jimmy. During the two days following their arrival, several unforeseen events occur that rock the very foundation of Dolores' family, perhaps foreshadowing the political upheaval that was to undo Batista's Cuba the following year.

Almost immediately, the reader is introduced to Dolores' extended family. First, there are her two widowed sisters, Mina and Clemencia. Then come the children and their families. Mina's son Feliz is a weak man, totally dominated by his mother and equally unsuccessful with other women. He has been married four times. Clemencia's son Roberto is visiting for the summer from New York City with his Jewish-American (non-Cuban) wife, Shirley, and their two children. Roberto is a struggling artist who, in his idealistic youth (he is now thirty-seven) was involved with the political left. Of all the characters, Roberto comes closest to being Yglesias' alter ego. Dolores, besides her two daughters who are visiting from Cuba, has two sons, one in Miami (Mario) and another one, her youngest, Armando. Although Armando is living at home, he previously had served in the Army, during which time he was married to and later divorced from an American (non-Cuban) girl named Katie. Of all the children, Armando seems the most lost. His association with a local gangster, Wally Chase, distresses his mother. One of the two reasons for Elena's visit to Ybor City is to offer Armando a lucrative position in Cuba. Armando initially refuses this offer but later is forced to accept it when his boss is mysteriously killed. Armando is suspected of involvement in the slaying and flees, with the help of his family, to Cuba. The other reason for Elena's return is to obtain permission from her sister's ex-husband, Esteban, to adopt Jimmy. Jimmy's sudden and unexpected death, a result of complications that arise after an emergency appendectomy, shocks the reader as well as Dolores' entire family.

What might, at first reading, appear to be a typically melodramatic story, whose unexpected and tragic ending leaves the reader stunned and therefore properly entertained, takes on a somewhat deeper significance upon further reflection. What Yglesias has done in fabricating his tale about a wake in Ybor City is to introduce the Anglo-American reader to some of the characteristic elements of Cuban-American life that ordinarily are not accessible to mainstream Americans. In particular, *A Wake in Ybor City* focuses on two important aspects of Cuban-American life: the family, and the male's ambivalent role in the family structure.

From the outset, it is clear that Dolores, Mina, and Clemencia are the spiritual as well as the political authorities of this Cuban-American family. The fact that the reader never learns their surnames suggests that the matriarchal structure portrayed here is representative of the Cuban-American family in general. Moreover, their given names reveal some of the qualities of the typical matriarch. Of the three, Mina (a mine of hidden wealth) is the realist. She is a practical woman whose earthy wisdom constantly returns the family to everyday reality where difficult decisions must be made and their consequences accepted. Clemencia ("Mercy") is a compassionate and understanding woman. Dolores ("Sorrows") is the dominant one among the three and embodies the role of the suffering mother. She is a romantic, a writer of heroic dramas and pastoral poems that reflect her subjective and distorted vision of her family. Together, these three women are the heart, head, and loving arms that control and sustain the life of this Cuban-American family. Living as an isolated island within the American mainstream, their primary mission is to protect the family at all costs. As the novel progresses, it becomes clear that the new matriarch who is to succeed the three aging women is Elena. It is her responsibility to take the reins of authority so that the family structure can continue to exist in relative peace and security. Elena has already helped set up her brother Mario in Miami. It is she who arranges Armando's escape to Cuba, and it is she who is organizing the legal adoption of her nephew Jimmy before his untimely death. Perhaps Elena's failure to save Jimmy, the family's youngest, from death is a foreshadowing of the eventual breakdown of the matriarchal family structure. To the extent that the younger members, such as Roberto, decide to leave the security of Ybor City and enter into the mainstream of American (non-Cuban) society, the inhibiting influence of the dominant mother figure will diminish.

The undisputed primacy of women in the Cuban-American family gives rise to a particular problem concerning the men, commonly referred to as machismo. Since the male's role in the family is ambivalent at best, he feels pressured to prove his manhood outside the family structure. This machismo is expressed by extramarital sexual conquests or by even more violent manifestations of strength and superiority. Except for Roberto, who has abandoned the matriarchal environment of Ybor City, the other male characters fail miserably in their quest for manliness within the family structure. Feliz, who has been married four times, is still an adolescent psychologically. For him, it is baseball which allows a man to prove his worth. Esteban, although a highly committed revolutionary, can only relate to women as sex-objects. Armando, whose marriage to Katie failed shortly after he brought her back home to live with his mother, fears any form of adult responsibility. Even Roberto, who is the strongest of the male characters, has difficulty looking directly at women. Jimmy, the youngest grandson, is virtually smothered by the attention given to him by all the women of the family. Perhaps the best indication of female superiority is Dolores' criticism of God for having allowed her grandson to die. According to Dolores, her status as one of the family's matriarchs has given her the right to scold God. In such a female-dominated environment, there is little place for the man to feel useful, let alone important. With these insightful vignettes of Cuban-American life, *A Wake in Ybor City* introduces the American (non-Cuban) reader to a part of America normally outside his experience.

Unlike Yglesias' first novel, which described an entire family's struggle to maintain its Cuban-American identity in the threatening ambience of a changing Tampa, Florida, *An Orderly Life* focuses on one individual. His name is Rafael Sabas. In many ways, Rafe resembles Roberto of *A Wake in Ybor City*. If Jimmy's death prefigured the family's eventual loss of Latin-American identity by allowing itself to be absorbed into America's amorphous mass of humanity, Rafe represents the extreme to which one may fall prey to the great American dream while still carrying within him the seeds of his Latin heritage. Narrated in the first person, *An Orderly Life* allows the reader an intimacy with its protagonist that is absent in Yglesias' first novel. The year is 1963, and Rafe has just been offered the vice-presidency of a prestigious New York pharmaceutical house; Yglesias employs repeated flashbacks so that the reader can come to know Rafe as he climbs the social ladder of success.

In a sense, the novel presents Rafael Sabas' definition of a happy man. In the final sentence of the book, Rafe defines himself in just those terms. When the reader considers that this "happy man" has spent the last twenty years of his life using and abusing friends and business partners alike so that he might continue to climb the corporate ladder, it is clear that *An Orderly Life* is meant to be a stinging indictment of the American way of life.

Rafe is the epitome of the cold and calculating executive who will not rest until he has made it to the top. There was a time, however, when his zeal to get ahead in life was relatively uncontaminated by the lust for wealth and power. In the 1930's, while attending City College in New York he joined the Young Communist League, where he came to know and later to develop a deep friendship with two politically active students, Jerry and Gloria. During World War II, he served in the Navy, where he spent much of his free time trying to improve himself by reading grammar books and college composition texts. While still in the service, he married a lovely young woman named Betty Evans, whom he first met while at City college. After leaving the service, he joined his father-in-law's pharmaceutical firm, Smith-Jonas, where he gradually worked his way to the vice-presidency. Blessed with two children, a loving wife, and a beautiful home in Scotch Plains, Rafe at age forty-two seems to be what he claims—a happy man. The reader, however, is aware of the numerous betrayals, compromises, and lies that Rafe was pressured into making in order to protect his professional career. At one point, the reader hears him say that he would never let sex or friendship get in the way of his professional advancement. When given the opportunity to help his poverty-stricken cousin Abel in Cuba, he calmly rationalizes that his cousin was anti-Castro, and therefore deserving of his plight. The list of betrayals is long, to the point of seeming contrived. What would be merely another saga concerning a ruthless executive's struggle in the corporate jungle of New York City takes on a deeper significarce, however, when one remembers that Rafael Sabas comes out of the Cuban-American community of Tampa, Florida. As such, *An Orderly Life* is not only a powerful statement against the inherent evils of the corporate milieu, but also a sensitive portrayal of a Cuban-American male's struggle for manhood (machismo).

Rafe's inordinate need to "win," be it in friendship, love, or business, is less difficult to understand if the reader looks upon these affairs and betrayals as the adventures of one who is struggling to prove his worth as a man. Yglesias provides many subtle reminders that Rafe is basically an insecure man whose search for self-affirmation is hidden by his many seemingly "manly" acts of conquest. For example, Rafe's constant need to demonstrate his sexual prowess outside marriage is but a mask concealing his true feelings of inferiority in his relationship with women. Although quick to "enjoy" a woman, any woman, he is unable to look directly into her eyes. Moreover, in choosing the woman he wants as his wife, he selects a virgin whose purity and innocence inhibits him when expressing his love sexually. From the traditional Latin male's perspective, Rafael Sabas is truly a happy man, for he has proven himself to be *macho*—on the one hand, a loving father who provides his family with a comfortable and secure environment, on the other hand, a successful business executive who has managed to play at the game of life and win.

Yglesias' third novel, *The Truth About Them* focuses once again on the family history of a Cuban-American clan, whose American experience dates from 1890, when the narrator's aristocratic grandmother first arrived in Tampa, Florida. Although much of their life in America is associated with the up-and-down fortunes of Florida's cigar industry, this working-class family displays a pride and cohesiveness that defies all obstacles. During the lean years of the 1930's, some members of the clan are forced to go north to New York City in search of jobs. Before long, however, they find themselves drifting back to Ybor City, owned and controlled by the cigar company. The narrator, much like Roberto of *A Wake in Ybor City*, is truly a Cuban-American. Brought up in the very Latin atmosphere of Ybor City, he eventually becomes a left-wing journalist and learns to swim freely in America's traditionless mainstream. Eager to learn more about his Latin roots, however, he visits postrevolutionary Cuba, an experience that engenders a newfound pride in his Cuban background.

In a sense, *The Truth About Them* is a very straightforward reconstruction of a family's history. It is neither more nor less than what is proclaims itself to be—an attempt at uncovering and relating the truth about one's heritage. Since this novel covers a greater time-span than that of *A Wake in Ybor City*, it serves to fill in the historical background lacking in Yglesias' first novel. Written in an episodic style (several adventures were first published separately in *The New Yorker*), this fictionalized family portrait with its rich and varied characters, its fast-moving plot, and its free-flowing style, offers a panoramic vision of a part of America generally unknown to non-Cuban Americans. Its detailed and loving depiction of a specific ethnic group seems to say that America is that much greater for having accepted as its own such resolute and distinctive communities.

As the years separate the 1960's from the present, the value of *Double Double*, Yglesias' tongue-in-cheek depiction of this turbulent decade, continues to increase. The focus, once again, is on one main character, Seth Evergood. Through Yglesias' skillful use of interior monologues, the reader comes to know Seth very well and, more important, comes to experience the excitement, the energy, the confusion, the hypocrisy, and above all, the naïve innocence that characterized the 1960's.

The reader follows Seth Evergood, a politically avant-garde author-lecturer, through a series of adventures that recall many of the so-called movements of the 1960's: student rights, draft resistance, the Black Panthers, Third World involvement, the Puerto Rican Liberation movement, Flower Power, and so on. What makes *Double Double* a truly valuable re-creation of the 1960's, however, is not merely its many references to specific historial events or people, but rather its double perspective on an age that has come to be looked upon both as the best of times and the worst of times.

The reader first encounters Seth as he is completing a lecture at a small Pennsylvania college to a group of intensely idealistic young students. They respond to his call for more student involvement and possible draft resistance by enthusiastically accompanying him to the town bus depot, where he supposedly must catch the next bus to New York City in order to arrive on time for an important meeting concerning the political upheaval in Bolivia.

On the surface, Seth Evergood seems to be what his name indicates—a man standing for all that is good and wholesome in life. Once the reader is permitted to enter into Seth's heart and head, however, it becomes obvious that he is an extremely insecure man. Although attracted by the chaotic social ferment of the 1960's and capable at times of believing his own revolutionary rhetoric, Seth is fundamentally a confused and disillusioned individual. Wanting desperately to stand above his fellow men and to lead them in their quest for freedom, Seth has difficulty accepting his own reality. Dependent on amphetamines and aspirin to help him through each day, undergoing psychoanalysis regarding his marriage, he nevertheless allows himself to become involved in a dangerous adventure. His friend Gary asks Seth to accompany him on a trip to Vermont to pick up contraband for the Black Panther organization. In the meantime, Seth is offered a contract to write a book about his father, James Evergood, who led the International Brigade in the Spanish Civil War. The trip to Vermont brings Seth and Gary to a commune, where they spend an unforgettable night replete with drugs, sex, and heavy "existential rapping." On the following day, when Seth turns the ignition of his car to begin their trip back to New York, there is an explosion, and *Double Double* comes to a sudden end, much like the era of the 1960's—with a roar, but with little evidence that such a reality or unreality ever existed.

For the most part, reviewers have failed to see Yglesias' deliberate attempt to capture the Camelot atmosphere that pervaded this decade. Resembling a bubble that floats effortlessly through the air enchanting all who see its delicate, transparent beauty, the 1960's captured the imagination and aspirations of many people. Like all bubbles, however, this euphoric time in American history was destined to come to an abrupt and violent end. *Double Double* has been criticized as a "cliché-ridden" depiction of the 1960's. If one focuses, however, on the schizophrenic world of the protagonist, Seth Evergood, it becomes clear that what appears to be a superficial portrayal of the 1960's is actually a highly original re-creation of an era that was both defined and destroyed by the unbalanced interplay between idealism and realism— with Seth Evergood as the embodiment of this conflict.

In his fifth novel, *The Kill Price*, which focuses on a theme that is too frequently avoided—death and dying—Yglesias displays a growing mastery over the narrative form. The few but well developed characters (a dying man named Wolf, his wife, and three friends) and the concentration of place and time (Wolf's apartment on the night of his death) permit the reader to share in the fear, the frustration, and ultimately the personal revelation that one inevitably experiences on witnessing the death of a loved one. The feeling of immediacy that is created by such an intense convergence of time and place is counterbalanced by Yglesias' timely retreats into the thoughts and feelings of the protagonist, Jack Moreno, Wolf's closest friend. Besides the intimacy that Jack's interior monologues allow the reader, the necessary distance for reflection is also established. It is Yglesias' skillful juxtaposition of cinematiclike close-ups and fade-outs that make *The Kill Price* a superbly written novel. Whereas the close-ups capture the magnitude of the moment, subsequent fade-outs transport the reader away from the immediate situation and allow for internalization of events.

The first third of the novel recounts Jack's memories as he walks over to Wolf's West Side apartment. Jack is a successful New York journalist whose cosmopolitan, jet set life-style is in conflict with the values of his Chicano upbringing in El Paso, Texas. He reflects about his past, how he abandoned his story on César Chávez and the Farm Worker's movement in Los Angeles to be with T. D., Wolf's wife, when Wolf was forced to return a second time to the hospital, and how his efforts to comfort T. D. eventually led to their having an affair. Further reflections inform the reader about Wolf's past, how he was previously married to Mary Anne, had a son by her, and eventually went through a painful divorce which he later used as material for his novel, *Breaking Away*.

When Jack arrives at Wolf's apartment, he is greeted by Carol, a New York actress who was Wolf's girl friend before he and T. D. were married. Although Wolf is suffering from an advanced case of lung cancer and is near death, the three closest people in his life (Jack, T. D., and Carol) act as if there is nothing terribly wrong, for Wolf has been told that he is recuperating from an attack of pleurisy. Although it is obvious that Wolf is aware of the seriousness of his condition, he, too, plays along in the charade. Wolf's former brother-in-law, Perry, arrives shortly after Jack. A long-time acquaintance of both Wolf and Jack, Perry has never managed to penetrate into their inner circle of friendship. He joins in the tacit deception concerning Wolf's illness, directing Wolf's attention from his present condition by requesting the film rights to his novel. He further distracts Wolf by offering to arrange to have his son, whom Wolf has not seen in more than a decade, come and stay with him and T. D. The charade comes to a sudden end, however, when Wolf dies, leaving his friends behind to deal with death's seemingly unchallenged dominion over life.

Although the actions seems to center around Wolf's untimely death, the novel's true focus is on Jack. His friend's death is but the catalyst that awakens him to his own inner emptiness. Wolf's terminal illness is the most dramatic reminder of death to appear in the novel. There is the death of a neighborhood, depicted by the West Side's deterioration; there is the death by drugs of the black celebrity Tiny Dick, whom Jack had once encountered while flying back to New York; there is the death of a lost love, as experienced by Wolf in his painful divorce from Mary Anne; moreover, the nation itself, presently embroiled in the Watergate fiasco, is in a state of moral decay.

Of all the forms of death present in *The Kill Price*, none is more devastating than the death one experiences on rejecting the truth about oneself. In leaving El Paso, first to go to Iowa for his college education and then on to New York for his career as a journalist, Jack was not going *to* some place as much as he was fleeing *from* some reality—his Chicano heritage. It takes the harrowing experience of seeing his best friend unable to express openly the truth of his imminent death, to force Jack to acknowledge that the life he has been living in New York is no life at all, but a lie. As his surname indicates (*Moreno* means "dark"), he is Chicano, and it is by embracing his Mexican-American heritage that he will truly begin to live, and therefore know how to die—in dignity and peace.

The vision presented in *A Wake in Ybor City, An Orderly Life, The Truth About Them, Double Double, The Kill Price*, and *Home Again* allows the reader a rare glimpse into the schizophrenic existence of the Cuban-American as he attempts to enter the mainstream of American society. Yglesias draws deeply from the well of his dual heritage and shares a refreshingly different perspective on American reality. American society may be likened to a finely woven tapestry whose cultural threads weave in and out, creating an endless array of patterns. Yglesias' novels, by focusing on one particular thread, the Cuban-American reality, help the reader to appreciate the unfathomable richness of America's multicultural heritage.

Richard Keenan

Other major works

NONFICTION: *The Goodbye Land*, 1967; *In the Fist of the Revolution*, 1968;

Down There, 1970; *The Franco Years*, 1977.

TRANSLATIONS: *Island of Women*, 1962 (published in England as *Sands of Torremolinos*); *Villa Milo*, 1962; *The Party's Over*, 1966.

Bibliography

Ivory, Ann, ed. "Jose Yglesias." In *Contemporary Authors*. Vols. 41-44, first revision series. Detroit: Gale Research, 1974. Lists a chronology on Yglesias and his Cuban American background. Mentions Yglesias' interest in recording the lives of Hispanic people and his travels to Spain, the first of which resulted in *The Goodbye Land*, described here as a work of "warmth and kindness." This study includes some extracts of reviews on his work, such as *Publishers Weekly*'s appraisal of *The Kill Price* (a "splendidly written . . . deeply probing story"). There are scant critical resources on Yglesias; this is the most comprehensive available, and a sympathetic one too.

Nelson, Milo G. Review of *Double Double*." *Library Journal* 99 (May 15, 1974): 1410. Not a favorable look at Yglesias, the reviewer taking exception to what he terms "the clichés that abound by trendy conversations of political movements, such as Black Panthers." The book, he asserts, is nevertheless "greatly uplifted by the surprise ending." There is no mention made, unfortunately, of the sensational times to which this book is faithful.

Review of *The Kill Price*. *Booklist* 72 (May 1, 1976); 1244. Calls this work, in which the main character is a terminal cancer patient, a "painful, honest, rather talky novel of discovery." Offers insight into the author's essential dilemma that the only healing will come through death. Applauds Yglesias for including sexual content without being sensational.

AL YOUNG

Born: Ocean Springs, Mississippi: May 31, 1939

Principal long fiction
Snakes, 1970; *Who Is Angelina?*, 1975; *Sitting Pretty*, 1976; *Ask Me Now*, 1980; *Seduction by Light*, 1988.

Other literary forms
In addition to his fiction, Al Young has produced several volumes of poetry, the first being *Dancing: Poems* in 1969. His twin themes are the American family and individual maturation. Early in this century, Ezra Pound warned modern poets that music separated from dance will atrophy, as will poetry separated from music; accordingly, Young's love of the rhythms of life places music between poetry and dance. His second volume of poems is entitled *The Song Turning Back into Itself* (1971). Here, the singer of life confronts images of a Whitmanesque America less musical, choral perhaps, certainly panoramic: the singer's song becomes the poet's vision. In *Geography of the Near Past* (1976) and *The Blues Don't Change: New and Selected Poems* (1982), the music and the dancing continue along Young's thematic lines of loving and growing.

In 1981, Young published his autobiographical *Bodies and Soul: Musical Memoirs*, which makes use of specific pieces of music to provide continuity and to set the tone for related essays, each based on personal recollection. *The Blues Don't Change* incorporates musical rhythms and quotations of Chinese poets into a collection of poems designed to dance with "laughter in the blood." In 1989 he published a tribute to the jazz musician Charles Mingus, *Mingus/Mingus: Two Memoirs*, written with Janet Coleman.

Besides work represented in major anthologies such as the *Heath Introduction to Poetry* (1975) and *How Does a Poem Mean?* (1976), edited by John Ciardi and Miller Williams, Young has written articles and stories for *New Times, Rolling Stone, Evergreen Review, Journal of Black Poetry, Essence, Massachusetts Review*, and other national publications. He has also written screenplays and scenarios for Laser Film Corporation and Stigwood Corporation in New York and Verdon Productions, First Artists Ltd., and Universal Pictures in California.

Achievements
During the mid-1960's, Young founded and edited *Loveletter*, an avant-garde review which has received awards from the National Arts Council. He is the West Coast editor of *Changes*, and in 1975 was guest fiction editor of the *Iowa Review*. With Ishmael Reed, he edits the biennial anthology *Yardbird*

Reader, and was coeditor of *Yardbird Lives*, published in 1979.

A selection of Young's poems and an introductory essay are included in the 1979 anthology *Calafía: The California Poetry*. *Calafía* is a widely recognized project that examines the poetry of the West Coast, with recognition of a regional tradition extending back through the nineteenth century.

Young was a Wallace E. Stegner fellow in 1966, and in 1969, he was the recipient of the Joseph Henry Jackson Award for his first collection of poetry, *Dancing*. The California Association of Teachers of English selected Young to receive a special award in 1973. He was a Guggenheim fellow in 1974 and received grants from the National Endowment for the Arts in 1968, 1969, and 1974. In 1980 he received the Pushcart Prize for poetry and in 1982 the Before Columbus Foundation award.

Biography

Albert James Young, the son of Mary (Campbell) and Albert James Young, attended the University of Michigan from 1957 to 1961 and received his A.B. in Spanish from the University of California at Berkeley in 1969. He and his wife Arline June (Belch) were married in 1963 and have a son, Michael James.

Young taught writing at the San Francisco Museum of Art during the late 1960's and was linguistic consultant for the Berkeley Neighborhood Youth Corps. From 1969 to 1973, he held the Stanford University Edward H. Jones lectureship in creative writing. He was the 1979 director of Associated Writing Programs, an organization of graduate university administrators, teachers, and students of creative writing, was writer-in-residence at the University of Washington in Seattle from 1981 to 1982, and served as consultant to the New York writer's organization Poets & Writers from 1974 to 1975.

Having lectured at numerous universities in the United States, and having traveled extensively in Canada, Mexico, Portugal, Spain, and France, Young has also had presentations of his work produced and broadcast by KQED-TV, San Francisco, and the Pacifica Radio Network—appropriately, since, among various other jobs, his early career included an acting role in a television documentary about Archie Moore, a year as a disc jockey, and, prior to that, eight years as a professional jazz musician.

Analysis

Al Young's concern for language, a concern that embraces mistrust and love, is clearly evinced in his prose. Unfortunately, his second novel, *Who Is Angelina?*, and his fourth, *Ask Me Now*, have third-person narrative personae who stand distractingly close to their author; they appear hesitant to act freely for want of purpose. Readers of the first and third novels, however, will quickly recognize Young's ability to render in his first-person narrative personae a vibrant male voice of new adulthood (*Snakes*), or sagacious middle-age (*Sitting Pretty*).

The author's background as a professional musician enables him to use music descriptively as well as metaphorically; the reader shares the experience of making music and feeling music make life known. The music of language also affects Young's style. Sparingly, he alters standard syntax and diction, sometimes punctuation, in order to set the speech closer to its natural human tone. His objective is not merely to create contemporary dialect, but also to create an enduring contemporaneity, to offer rhythmically, as the poet-musician should, the nonverbal meanings that language can carry in its sounds. Young accomplishes this quality of speech through narrative personae who speak softly or stridently, sometimes too literally, yet with voices constant and sincere.

Love, like a curse or a whimper, extends most intensely from the individual to those nearby. The contemporary American social dilemma is thereby represented in Young's prose just as it appears in his poetry: each person must somehow maintain the unity, fidelity, and consistency love requires while grappling for the freedom and oneness that American mythology promises. Although *Snakes* and *Sitting Pretty* are more successful, all of Young's novels contain graphic portrayals of mainstream urban America—middle-class people who try to be good at being themselves. They emote, they dream, and they reason. At worst, they stand too large on the page; at best, they find purpose to complement the dignity they feel. Whether he narrates with commentary from a third-person point of view, or with the immediacy of first-person sensory experience, Young confronts the problems of individuals growing into their individuality, and the qualities of life central to the congregate American family.

The narrative persona of Young's first novel, *Snakes*, is M. C. Moore, who recollects his youth and adolescence in the mature, seasoned voice of the novel's *master-of-ceremonies*. A novel of formation, *Snakes* is in the *Bildungsroman* tradition and is rendered in a tone of voice at once nostalgic and fatherly. Although he has only snapshots of his true parents by which to remember them, M. C. gradually finds their love implanted in his own initialed name, "so it sound[s] like you had some status, his first lover explains, "whether you did or not." For M. C., the process of learning who he is becomes the composition of his own music.

M. C. discovers music in his soul and he makes music the core of his world. He finds music everywhere, "in the streets, in the country, in people's voices" . . . and "in the way they lead their lives." Providing counterpoint, M. C.'s grandmother Claude offers guidance and family history, and M. C. is her captive audience: "I could listen to Claude talk all day long, and did, many a time. Her voice was like music." The association expands as his views of love and music merge, and women ultimately become "lovable fields of musical energy."

While living with relatives in the South, M. C. learns at the age of ten that music will be his life. His Uncle Donald, a "night rambler" with a "talent for getting hold of a dollar," turns their impoverished household into a "blind pig," or a Meridian, Mississippi, version of a speakeasy. During his first exposure to the amoral world of adults, M. C. meets Tull, an itinerant jazz pianist who in effect provides the novel's premise: "You'll get it if you keep at it. Listen, just take your time, one note a time over here with your right hand. Just take your time, that's all it is to playin' the piano or anything else. Take your time and work it on out." The impression lasts; M. C. goes on to structure his life around his love of music and his faith that music will help him grow.

Literature also has a formative effect on him. It is not literature as found in the classroom or in books—M. C. attends high school in body only, and barely earns his diploma—rather, literature personified in Shakes, his closest friend, whose name is short for Shakespeare. Shakes has a "greedy memory and a razor tongue." He is bright, musical, and funny: "You hip to Cyrano de Bergerac? Talk about a joker could talk some trash! Cyrano got everybody told! Didn't nobody be messin with Cyrano, ugly as he was."

Yet there is more to know about life than its music and its literature; such knowledge appears in the person of Champ, who exposes M. C. to contemporary jazz and the business hemisphere of that musical world. In his bemusing, self-sacrificial way, Champ also demonstrates his worsening drug addiction and the consequential brutalization of his sensibilities. "Poor Champ," M. C. soon observes while he learns to jam, to feel his music come alive inside himself and issue forth, "who wanted to play an instrument so badly, would stand around working his arms and fingers for hours sometimes, shaping the smoky air in the room into some imaginary saxophone. . . . We all wanted to get good."

The evil to which Champ submits himself opposes the good that he gives M. C.—music as growth and expression. "Up until Champ, I was pretty lame. . . ." M. C.'s band, "The Masters of Ceremony," discovers in their art a meaning that transcends the music they produce, and although the group separates after one demo and some local gigs, M. C.'s early success provides him with a clearer view of the possibilities of his life and a deep sense of wonder. He emerges from his plain, ordinary background complete, communicative, and capable of more, having also achieved his own narrative voice, that husky, now masculine voice the reader has heard maturing since the story's outset. He boards the New York bus a musician, grown: "I don't feel free . . . but I don't feel trapped." Awkwardly, painfully, naturally, M. C. has learned to look for the subtle ironies that enrich both life and art. Ready at last for the rest of what he will be, the young adult takes with him his guitar, his music, and precious recordings of his song "Snakes," which throughout the novel parallels his experience of youth: "The tune sounded simple the first time you heard it, but it wasn't all that simple to play."

While the narrative voice of *Snakes* provides contrast and consistency—a gradual merging of the maturing young man with his adult consciousness—the narrative voice of *Who Is Angelina?* accomplishes neither. Angelina is already grown, but her adult life has entered a phase of meaningless triviality. This she blames on the shifting cultural milieu of Berkeley, California. Life in Berkeley seems different now—dangerous—and the people's sense of freedom and fun, that community spirit of festivity, is gone. She uses the burglary of her apartment as the justification, and a friend's convenient cash as the means, to skip town—an act she considers the prerequisite for introspection. She flees not only her fictional problems but also her reader as well; a character with both brains and beauty who struggles with mere communal ennui is less than sympathetic. Moreover, even the reader who can overlook her escapist behavior needs to know more about her, and most of her background is provided through recollection and reminiscence. The novel's principal events—travel in Mexico, some romantic sex, an emergency trip home to Detroit, an encounter with a street thief—facilitate reflection by the viewpoint character, and the reader must simply accept her gradual appraisals. Dramatically, little takes place. Most of this novel is exposition; what little action there is consists of Angelina's consideration of an adaptation to what goes on around her.

The unifying thematic metaphor of *Who Is Angelina?* is the act of taking away: Angelina is robbed (her reaction is passive); her lover's mysterious occupation suggests more of the same; her father is robbed and nearly killed; a friend's purse is stolen (her reaction this time is spontaneous and violent). Eventually, Angelina's searching appears to reach some sort of resolution that makes her worthy of new self-esteem. Yet the reader can only observe, not participate in this search, because—unlike *Snakes*'s composer-narrator—Angelina does not experience within the narrative a process of growth.

Plainly, Angelina is a woman experiencing a crisis of self-identity during a series of events that propel her toward introspection. What she ultimately discovers within herself is a typical American complex of contradictions, such as the one she describes to a fellow traveler early in her journey, the contradiction Americans create by equating individuality with isolation: "Angelina explained that in America it's the individual who matters most and that she and her family, such as it was, lived at separate ends of what's called reality. She too was lonely and fed up with a kind of life she'd been leading."

Whether the narrator addresses the reader directly or through the medium of a letter to a former lover, the exposition continues: "Everyone nowadays is busy digging for roots. Well, I know them well and it doesn't make a damn bit of difference when it comes to making sense of who I am and why I make the kinds of mistakes I do. In the end, I've discovered, it all comes down to being in competition with yourself." At moments, Angelina's concern waxes angry and the culturally contemplative author intrudes: "I'm not so sure that all those chitlins, hamhocks, hog maws, pigsfeet, spareribs and cooking with lard—soulfood so-called—isn't contributing more toward bringing about black genocide, as the phrasemongers would have it, than Sickle Cell Anemia." An important discovery about herself does take place, however, and this is what her wandering is all about. The exploration has been a contemporary one that many young, single Americans never complete: "The truth was that, most of all, she loved open-hearted vulnerable strangers for whom she wasn't strictly obliged to feel anything."

In the end, Angelina also learns that she has been changing at the same time that her surroundings have been changing. Because she has confused one process with another, separation followed by a reassertion of self followed by a return to her point of departure appears to be cathartic. If so, the reader hopes that she also learns that life is and continues to be a process of change, some small part of which is subject to each individual's conscious control. Angelina's recognition of this consciousness is both the special story and the ordinariness of Young's second novel.

Sidney J. Prettymon, the narrative persona of *Sitting Pretty*, is streetwise, sardonic, and ironically self-conscious. He establishes early a mock superstitious mentality—astronauts may mess up the moon so that it can no longer be full—and verbalizes "the integral aspects of [his] personal philosophy to be cool." Prettymon is dangerously learned: "I cut this article out of the National Inquirer that maintain how you can succeed and develop yourself and transformate your whole personality by the buildin' up your vocabulary." His inborn sense of linguistic sound combines comically with his interest in discovering associative meanings (*radical chic* connotes to him the concubine of a politically motivated Arab husband of many wives), but the best humor to be found in *Sitting Pretty* is derived from Prettymon's command of the text. The reader is at all times close to Prettymon, and he exploits the closeness. Having pondered his plot-situation at the story's outset, he describes himself to himself as being "on the threshold of destiny, temptation, and fate." Turning aside, he speaks directly to the reader: "Now, that's bad! [good] Let me run through that one again so yall can savor it. . . ."

The narrative opens below the closing sentence of Mark Twain's *The Adventures of Huckleberry Finn* (1884); in many ways, Sidney J. Prettymon is a contemporary, self-possessed Jim. As Twain's narrative control allowed him to elevate linguistic puns through burlesque to high satirical levels, Young's narrative is successful here by virtue of its consistently controlled authorial distance: "All I mean by imagination," Prettymon says, "is the way stuff look when you pull back from it and give it some reflection room." Prettymon as first-person narrative persona allows the author to work most effectively; because his imagination provides Prettymon with overview, it allows him to construct connotative ironies.

The incongruous coexistence of common insight and aesthetic misinterpretation (Huck does not misinterpret aesthetic qualities; he misses them entirely) works through sarcastic understatement: "Carpe Diem, like they say in Latin. Save the day." The author's hand moves subtly, characterizing by misquotation.

Like M. C.'s unknown parents, Prettymon has given his son an inspirational name with which to command respect—Aristotle: "He is a lawyer." Professionally successful, Aristotle is a son ungrateful for his name, and working-class Prettymon must struggle to disguise his pride as resentment: "He go around callin hisself A. Winfred Prettymon. I'm the one give him his first name and that's his way of gettin back at me. I wanted him to stand out and be distinguished and be the bearer of a name that smack of dignity." Telephoning his daughter, Prettymon again creates linguistic pandemonium, quoting Ralph Waldo Emerson in order to reinforce some fatherly advice, then addressing the reader as the individualistic, pro-consumer Henry David Thoreau: "I hung up fast, then taken the receiver back off the hook again so the operator couldn't ring me back for that extra ten cent. I ain't go nothing but the vastest contempt for the Phone Company. Leeches and rascals! Need to be investigated."

Sitting Pretty is Young's best novel in three ways: consistency of viewpoint, ingenuity of the narrative-persona, and control of the language. The last must be perfect for an author to choose suggestive, convincing variations consistent with popular speech. Young's rendering of black dialect for artistic purpose is found throughout his fiction, and it works effectively here. The novel's language is an unconcealed treasure:

> What with all that racket and commotion and the drink I'd just taken, I was startin to feel randy—a term the Professor use, British word for horney—randy for my own private bottle of sweet wine. Got a job lines up and just *know* Aristotle gon spring my Plymouth loose. Clebratin time! Time to do that quiet furlough down to Adamo's again.

Surprised, uniquely joyful, Sidney J. Prettymon rediscovers his treasure again and again.

Whereas Young's first and third novels may be paired according to their points of view and the consistency of their narrative voices, *Ask Me Now*, Young's fourth novel, contains narrative weaknesses similar to those found in *Who Is Angelina?* Like Angelina, Woody Knight also finds himself in a world changing at a pace inconsistent with his own ability to change, a major source of frustration for this retired pro-basketball player who has always depended upon the musical, built-in rhythms of his game. In life on the outside, it seems to Woody, the court lines keep shifting.

The sequence of events that brings crisis and reunion to Woody's middle-class family is, like the catalytic changes Angelina experiences, rather improbable. As the narrative opens, Woody is not trying to control the ball and the players in motion, but a double arm-load of groceries, rain, a raucous crowd in a shopping mall, the theft of his car. and his wife's winning of a sweepstakes raffle, all in the time it takes to report his loss to a security man who mistakes him for someone he is not. This complexity of absurd events may be American, middle-class normality, but the mid-life, change-related distance Woody discovers growing between himself and his wife (the prize she wins is a trip to Reno, America's emblematic city of the free and the damned), his children, and society becomes less believable as the plot progresses.

The kidnaping of his daughter by the street gang who stole his car and hid cocaine in one of its tires provides crisis and denouement, but at the cost of increasing the distance between Woody and the reader. Secondary characters quickly become contemporary types that provide color, not credibility, and a final chase scene produces climactic anger, not release. On Woody's mind as the final seconds tick away—the police and the mobsters in the mysterious limousine move aside—is the "elbow room" he valued so highly on the court, the kind of elbow room Angelina sought in her flight to Mexico City. Although this moment contains a great burst of energy—Woody charging in to rescue his daughter, his family, and himself—the climax rings false: he finds and then abandons his daughter in order to pursue the criminal, whom the police ultimately must rescue from a murderous Woody. Despite rather than because of his heroics, all ends well. New insights are gained by all, including that minority of readers for whom the fiction maintains its illusion of reality.

The unbelievable crime and the stock family crisis notwithstanding, Young's control of language is complemented by the twin metaphors of basketball as dance and music as movement. Woody works the ball along the novel's narrative line with eloquence and style. If what he does and what others do to him is too pat, too contrived, his responses are genuine. Woody is a man both worthy of respect and capable of love. He proves himself. The crisis past, he finds himself renewed, as did Angelina, yet, for the reader, there remains at best an evanescent certainty that Woody's reaction to events, not himself, and his reaction to selected alternatives, not decisions, have brought resolution. Unlike the courageous M. C. and the umbrageous Prettymon, Woody is yet incompletely his own. His story ends, but his score remains tied with time remaining on the clock.

Young's main characters experience their passages with a fortitude that affects their worldviews. M. C. copes with the pressures of adolescence and street danger while Angelina seeks alternatives to her past; Prettymon nurtures his self-concept and Woody deals clumsily with his mid-life crisis: their stories inform their thoughts and expression. The music and love in their living is heard and felt; the reader wants to dance with them, to celebrate. "Celebratory" is a good word to describe Young's style. His major characters are able to seek and find better versions of themselves when they become able and willing to celebrate what they already are.

For his fifth novel, Young again employs a first-person narrative persona, female and clairvoyant. Mamie Franklin is a woman in her forties, rich in impressions and experience. Having grown up in Mississippi an admirer of her namesake and imaginary tutor/yogi Benjamin Franklin, having made those feelings real through writing, having left home early to perform in the style of Dinah Washington with her husband's group, the Inklings, and having married and begot her son Benjie out of wedlock, she lives now in Santa Monica with Burley, the man she loves and whose love is returned until—cataclysmically—Mamie's past and future upheave into the narrative present.

As in *Snakes* and the adventures of Sidney J. Prettymon, there is a running commentary on situation and circumstance along with a steady stream of verbal ironies and satiric asides. Mamie works part-time in Beverly Hills as a domestic for one Mr. Chrysler and his French wife Danielle, who live in "a big stockbroker Tudor" graced with eucalyptus, or "Noxema trees." Mamie has the confidence of her employers, in fact their favor, as she drives her Honda Civic (nicknamed Sweepea) up the front driveway and strolls into the house. There she discovers a strange, unclothed woman with toes and fingernails painted black who looks like "a bleached-out, fuzzy-headed raccoon," and a Monopoly board, which compromises Mr. Chrysler ("that man loves to play Monopoly . . . with real money").

This kind of fun—the world according to Mamie Franklin—enlivens the novel's complication. Regarding the 1970's, that too-short period when black consciousness merged with African-American professional development and economic opportunity, Mamie says, "[I]t mighta looked to the public like anything black was gonna make money . . . but that wasn't nothin but an illusion."

More than witty, these quips come from a woman who made her living as a performer during the 1950's, when the business of entertainment reinstituted racial segregation, and who now sees further deterioration in the filmmaking business: "This old brotherhood junk, funny stuff and jive everybody use to be talkin—all that went out the minute the money started gettin shaky. . . ." With a tonal admonition for more education, she observes that the film industry is being run by young white men who "started readin *Variety* and *Billboard* when they were nine." For Mamie, age enables one to "ripen into know-how, or better yet, know-when." After all, she says, "The smarter you are, the harder you smart when you fall."

Throughout the novel, light and light imagery brighten the reader's way like the sunlit flowers of Alice Walker's *The Color Purple* or the moonlit landscapes of Nathaniel Hawthorne's tales. Mamie's vision captures both the brilliance and the business of the California landscape while nuances of Eastern philosophy energize her sensibility and evoke a mood of resolution. Such evocations occur in dreams or dreamlike experiences, such as the surreal state of shock following the reality of an eathquake or the emotional upheaval of sexual renewal. "It was all done with light," Mamie says of cinematic production and marketing. Like the girl she "use to be" watching a film at the Grand Lux Theatre, Mamie learns that "pretty much every last one of us out here [in California] gettin seduced." As girl and as mother, as woman and as lover, Mamie looks over her shoulder to see "nothin but light, not a thing but light quiverin and makin patterns on a screen."

Throughout her life, Mamie has had enlightening experiences. She recalls a vision of sunlight playing over a leaf, how the light "shimmered all around it; then the leaf sends out this invisible feeler [and] suck up the light around it, drink it up, sip on it like you would a glassa buttermilk." Similarly, when Mamie's housemate Burley returns in spirit, he describes his passage from life: "It was like this hole opened up in the middle of my forehead and the light started pourin into it. . . ."

Moreover, Mamie contemplates the textuality of her life by the light of her contemplations, suggesting that such affects the storyteller, too:

> Where do you begin when you start tellin your story and rememberin as you go along? Do you start with the source of light itself, the sun? Or do you start with what the sun touches, the moon? Or do you only deal with what the moonlight touches?

We must consider the light by which we live our lives, Mamie suggests, as we rewrite the texts of our lives:

> It's actually possible in one lifetime to do so much and to get caught up in so many of your own illusions and lies and half lies until it can finally come down to sun versus moon versus moonlight.

Celebratory and down-to-earth, Young's novels glow with human warmth. In the mode of vernacular speech, *Seduction by Light* rings true with contemporary experience while transmuting everyday life into the light of love.

J. Battaglia

Other major works

POETRY: *Dancing: Poems*, 1969; *The Song Turning Back into Itself*, 1971; *Geography of the Near Past*, 1976; *The Blues Don't Change: New and Selected Poems*, 1982; *Heaven: Collected Poems, 1958-1988*, 1989.

NONFICTION: *Bodies and Soul: Musical Memoirs*, 1981; *Kinds of Blue: Musical Memoirs*, 1984; *Things Ain't What They Used to Be: Musical Memoirs*, 1987; *Mingus/Mingus: Two Memoirs*, 1989 (with Janet Coleman).

Bibliography

Bell, Bernard W. *The Afro-American Novel and Its Tradition*. Amherst: University of Massachusetts Press, 1987. Bell compares African-American writers and their works. Especially useful is his comparison of Young's *Snakes* to 1960's novels by Gordon Parks, Kristin Hunter, Rosa Gunn, Barry Beckham, and Louise Meriwether. Because Bell classifies these works as

Bildungsromane in the European literary tradition, his analysis helps establish Young as a viable black-experience author in the United States and abroad.

Davis, Thadious M., and Trudier Harris, eds. *Dictionary of Literary Biography.* Vol. 33. In *Afro-American Fiction Writers After 1955.* Detroit: Gale Research, 1984. This reference provides a cursory glance at Young's career as a postmodernist writer on the American scene. The citation itself is brief yet helpful to place the author in the mainstream of contemporary writers of various ethnic backgrounds.

Johnson, Charles. *Being and Race: Black Writers Since 1970.* Bloomington: Indiana University Press, 1988. Contains a thorough discussion of the common background of black American writers plus lengthy discussions of female and male viewpoint-writing, with philosophical references and a preface which establishes the text's postmodernist critical approach.

Kirkpatrick, D. L., ed. *Contemporary Novelists.* 4th ed. New York: St. Martin's Press, 1986. This compilation features a condensed biography of Young plus an extensive listing of the author's works through 1982. A useful guide to Young as an emerging American artist, this reference profiles him among novelists of various ethnic backgrounds.

Matney, William C., ed. *Who's Who Among Black Americans.* 5th ed. Lake Forest, Ill.: Educational Communications, 1988. A collection of interviews and personal profiles, this presentation of the author considers his manifold interests as a young African-American writer. Those who know Young as poet, musician, screenwriter, editor, or teacher will find useful material regarding the manifold interests of the novelist.

Ostendorf, Berndt. *Black Literature in White America.* Totowa, N.J.: Barnes & Noble Books, 1982. Considers black writers' roots and the influence of music on their lives and art as both expression and performance. While the references to Young are brief and pertain to his poetry, the musical context of this presentation will be useful for those researching Young's concern for music in American culture and literature.

Shockley, Ann Allen, and Sue P. Chandler. *Living Black American Authors: A Bibliographical Directory.* New York: R. R. Bowker, 1973. Recognition of black writers was new during the early 1970's, especially in the overall context of American letters. This article contains extensive interpretive detail regarding Young's early works, his achievements other than fiction-writing, and his personal values and insights.

ORIGINS AND DEVELOPMENT
OF THE NOVEL BEFORE 1740

The English-speaking world has long considered 1740, the year in which Samuel Richardson's *Pamela* was published, pivotal in the development of the novel, a broad term which for several centuries has been applied to many different forms of long fiction. Richardson's first novel remains a convenient landmark in the history of the form because, at least in England, it went further than any previous work in exploring an individual character's "sensibility," that wonderful mix of perception, culture, logic, sentiment, passion, and myriad other traits that define one's individuality. *Pamela* has been called the first intellectual novel, that subgenre in which most of the greatest novelists of the nineteenth and twentieth centuries have worked.

Nevertheless, while 1740 is an important date in the development of one type of novel, to see all earlier novels as primitive ancestors of *Pamela* would distort the history of this multifarious form. The novel followed substantially different lines of development in Spain, France, and England, three countries notable for their contributions to the early growth of this form in Europe. Moreover, different types of novels exist side by side in every period, each type appealing to a different taste, much as different types of the novel flourish today. Finally, certain earlier works have exerted as profound and lasting an influence on the novel in Europe as that attributed to *Pamela*.

The Novel in England, 1580-1740

Whereas the French novel underwent constant refinement during the century and a half preceding 1740, with French writers producing masterpieces at intervals throughout the period, the English novel flowered briefly before 1600, then lay dormant for more than a century until it was revitalized by Daniel Defoe. The seventeenth century in England produced but one work of genius in the form, John Bunyan's *The Pilgrim's Progress* (1678, 1684), a novel ignored by contemporary literary society because of its style and theme.

Though overshadowed by the unsurpassed drama of the Elizabethans, the 1580's and 1590's saw an outpouring of original fictional narratives, including one voluminous work and a host of shorter works in the pastoral and satiric modes. Like the French a decade later, English writers were heavily influenced by translations of the late Greek romances, as well as by the satires of the humanists, the pastorals of Sannizaro and Montemayor, and the tragic love *novelle* of Bandello. Other influential sources were the manuals of courtly behavior and noble ethics written by the Italians Baldassare Castiglione, *Il Cortegiano* (1528, *The Courtier*), and Stefano Guazzo, *La civile conversazione* (1547, *The Civil Conversation*). These inspired similar guides in England and provided a format of learned discourse imitated by writers of fiction.

The most distinctive feature of the English novels of that time is their commitment to moral improvement by the individual and by the state as a whole. Since, with the exception of Sir Philip Sidney, the principal novelists of that time were sons of the middle class, much of their writing was suffused with middle-class values: hard work, thrift, cautious ambition. As the period advanced, fictional works became more overtly addressed to the middle class, with more middle-class characters taking principal roles. In the 1580's, this bourgeois appeal typically took the form of the romance, intended to instruct the upwardly mobile reader in courtly ways; later, satire held sway, a satire moved by the spirit of reform rather than the resigned contempt of the Spanish picaresques.

The most influential fiction early in this period was John Lyly's *Euphues, the Anatomy of Wit* (1579), actually less a novel than a moral handbook for wealthy budding scholars. In it, bright young Euphues exchanges academic arguments with wise old Eubolus on the issue of worldly experience versus the codified wisdom of the ages. Euphues fails to heed Eubolus' sage advice and decides to taste the world, only to become the emotional captive of Lucilla, a courtesan who strips him of his money and his dignity. A chastened Euphues vows to spend the rest of his life contemplating philosophy and warning the young. *Euphues, the Anatomy of Wit* was a continuing hit with a wide audience, and Lyly's peculiar style established a fashion that persisted for a decade. Called *euphuism*, this style features the culling of exotic lore from the pseudohistories of the ancients, primarily the Roman Pliny. In euphuistic argumentation, these strange bits are used as evidence for or against certain courses of action. That euphuism succeeded where other linguistic experiments such as *marivaudage* failed, shows the hunger of Lyly's audience for a mode of discourse that would make them appear learned.

Lyly's most enthusiastic follower was Robert Greene, a highly original novelist in his own right, who composed an amazing variety of euphuistic romances between 1580 and 1587. In such Greene works as *Mamillia* (1583), *The Myrrour of Modestie* (1584), *Morando, The Tritameron of Love* (1587), and *Euphues His Censure to Philautus* (1587), one can see most clearly the amalgamation of sources—Italian *novelle*, the Bible, Castiglione, Greek epic—in Elizabethan fiction. Unlike Lyly, however, Greene brings to these romances a spirit of comic realism that invests his characters with greater fullness and sympathy than Lyly's does. Greene's later romances (such as *Menaphon*, 1589, and *Greene's Never Too Late*, 1590) reject euphuism in favor of a somewhat colloquial conversational style better suited to his more realistic characters.

When Greene turned away from Lyly in 1588, he was responding to the new fashion for pastoral love stories established by Sidney's huge romance, *Arcadia*, which had been circulating in manuscript since 1580, but which was not published until 1590 (revised in 1593). *Arcadia*, an aristocratic work similar to Honoré d'Urfé's *L'Astree* (1610), shows the blending of the Greek romances, with their pastoral and heroic elements, and the intensely emotional love pastorals of Sannizaro and the Elizabethan sonneteers, including Sidney himself. There is a good deal of the chivalric spirit present here, too, as knightly combats, with armor and emblems vividly described, are the primary means of settling disputes. Amid the shipwrecks, the kidnapings, the heroic rescues, and the seemingly endless love laments of the sexually frustrated heroes, Musidorus and Pyrocles, two genuinely sympathetic characters emerge, Amphialus and his wife, Parthenia. Theirs is a tragic tale, the Homeric conflict between a soldier's sense of duty and his regard for his wife, whose desire for his safety leads her to endanger herself and ultimately lose her life. The power of this story within the *Arcadia* derives from Sidney's almost Shakespearean refusal to take sides—his willingness to let the story unfold and allow the reader to judge. Had the novel's main plot, his heroes' often silly attempts to win the favor of a pair of princesses, been exchanged for a serious investigation of ethical issues, Sidney might have produced a work of the stature of Miguel de Cervantes' *Don Quixote de la Mancha* (1605, 1615).

Among the traits that limited Sidney as a novelist was his contempt for the common people, as shown in *Arcadia* in several episodes that caricature plebeians as stupid, greedy, and bestial. Since the future of publishing in England meant appealing to the powerful London middle class, it was inevitable that novels would emerge with middle-class heroes and heroines. Greene's later romances are of this category, as are the works of Thomas Deloney, a silk weaver, whose *Jack of Newbery* (c. 1596) and *Thomas of Reading* (c. 1597) feature romanticized artisan heroes within vividly authentic backgrounds of English town and rural life.

Deloney's contribution to English literary history has been much disputed by scholars of the twentieth century. Although some have considered him "an astonishing genius" and others have disregarded him entirely, most current critics and historians take a middle view of Deloney's significance as a prose writer. While not a genius, Deloney was one of the first English authors to write for and about the rising middle class. His perceptiveness of the prevailing literary climate, whether educated or merely fortuitous, was accurate, for his popularity among the middle class was unsurpassed. His works, within only a few years of their publication, were literally read out of existence. The twentieth century's debt to Deloney is substantial, for his portrayal of middle-class values, concerns, and language are the roots of the modern novel.

That Deloney became a spokesman for the middle class was only a portion of his accomplishment. Another reason for the popularity of his works was that they were written in prose. Prior to Deloney's time, written works were composed in verse or dramatic form, making the exploration of rising social issues a laborious chore. Less artificial, prose fiction better addressed such subject matter, and Deloney proved himself a more talented master of the form than most prose fiction writers of his time.

What makes Deloney's fiction outstanding are his skillful use of dialogue and his excellent characterizations. Presenting three-dimensional middle-class characters drawn from his hard-working colleagues, Deloney engages them in dialogue fit for the stage. Instead of the lofty language familiar only to kings and nobles, however, he captures the idiomatic speech and straightforwardness of the common people of his day.

Deloney's plot development is less remarkable, although it should not be dismissed lightly. *Jack of Newbury*, considered his most unified prose work, is a tale about a young man who works for a wealthy clothier and eventually becomes the master of the business when the owner dies, leaving the conscientious young Jack (known as John) to marry the widow. The majority of the work centers on John's adventures after his wife has died and he has become a wealthy man. *Thomas of Reading* is a less unified work, yet reaches a level of plot sophistication higher than that of *Jack of Newbury*. In it, King Henry I is made aware of the value of the clothing industry in England, and by deliberately supporting the clothiers, he enables them to raise their social positions. Such a change in social status was finally an attainable goal for the working class, and thus a tale of this type appealed to a wide audience.

While many of Deloney's characters typically grasp the beneficent hand of capitalism, Deloney does, however, ensure that they do not succumb to the snobbishness common to those who already enjoy aristocratic freedoms. After diligently earning their wealth, these protagonists liberally distribute it, thus allowing the entire community to prosper from their good fortune. Despite such indirect moralizing, Deloney was accepted as the militant spokesman for the middle class, and the political disjunction between his views and those of Sidney gives evidence of the social rift that would lead to civil war in the next century.

Already, class and religious tensions, the fires fanned by economic decline, were sparking sharp satires, some obviously political, others less partisan in their scourge of social abuse. In the latter group are Greene's tales of "connycatching" (1591-1592), which purport to expose the methods of actual thieves and con artists so that decent citizens may beware. These contribute to the development of fiction in England, because Greene's reproving tone is a thin veil for his real interest in exploring the romantic, sympathetic side of the criminal stereotype. Such characters as Ned Browne, Nan the whore, Laurence the cutpurse, and Cuthbert Connycatcher blend the *picaros* with the courageous imps of the medieval jestbooks. The candor and colloquial discourse of these stories created a fashion for rogue books that persisted through the seventeenth century and influenced Defoe.

Brilliantly capitalizing on the connycatching fad was Greene's boon companion, Thomas Nashe, one of literature's sharpest tongues and quickest wits. After achieving notoriety through vicious anti-Puritan pamphlets and personal attacks on literary foes, Nashe penned the age's premier satiric novel, *The Unfortunate Traveller: Or, The Life of Jack Wilton* (1594). Lacking the fellow feeling of a Lazaro, a Gil Blas, or even one of Greene's connycatchers, Nashe's Jack Wilton astounds the reader with the range of his amoral exploits and the depth of his depravity. He satirizes through deeds, not only words: he outcheats the greatest cheats, plots the deaths of murderers, tortures the heartlessly cruel. Though he makes a perfunctory repentance at the end of the novel, Jack is a thorough villain, who satirizes not from a sense of moral outrage but because his clever foes are so gullible or have the audacity to be as villainous as he. His attacks on Italy, for example, are inspired by the Italians' allegedly unquenchable thirst for vengeance, a trait which Jack has much reason to fear.

Just as outrageous as Jack's character is Nashe's cast of minor figures: King Henry VIII, Thomas More, Erasmus, and most other notables of the early sixteenth century. Jack spends a good deal of the novel as the servant of Henry Howard, the earl of Surrey, and together they romp through dangerous escapades. History as rewritten by Thomas Nashe is a pageant composed for Jack Wilton, poor in birth but inexhaustibly rich in wit. The plot and the person are incredible, but Nashe so deftly appeals to the cynical reader that it is easy to see this book as a realistic fiction rather than what might more accurately be described as a fantasy of revenge. The dark tragedies of Cyril Tourneur, John Webster, George Chapman, and Thomas Middleton in the Jacobean years partake of this same spirit and were surely influenced by *The Unfortunate Traveller*.

Because satiric fiction of the next decades returned to the pattern and subject matter of the connycatching works, prose writers who followed Nashe perhaps found his brilliance inimitable. The best of these writers, Thomas Dekker, presented collections of jests and stories carefully describing the shifts of London thieves and beggars in his *The Bellman of London* (1608) and *Lanthorn and Candlelight* (1608), both heavy-handed condemnations of the outlaws from the perspective of the outraged citizen demanding protection. Dekker affects neither Greene's sympathy nor Nashes's worldly-wise cynicism. Because his works create no real characters, they cannot really be said to be novels.

Just as the French religious wars of the sixteenth century precluded the growth of the novel in that country, so the strides in English fiction taken during the Elizabethan years were halted in the seventeenth century as the economy worsened and religious tensions increased. Though novel readers continued to demand reprints of Elizabethan fictions, no significant works in this genre were produced in the country until well after the Restoration of the monarchy in 1660. The appetite for novels during the first two-thirds of the century was satisfied by translations of contemporary French works, with *L'Astrée* and the heroic novels of Madame de Scudéry enjoying great popularity. Ironically, when the century did produce a great English novelist, John Bunyan, he was ignored by the readers of French novels because of his allegorical method and his Puritan views.

Bunyan's masterpiece, *The Pilgrim's Progress*, was partly written during his second imprisonment for unauthorized preaching, some six years after his first imprisonment (1660-1672), during which he had written his spiritual autobiography, *Grace Abounding to the Chief of Sinners* (1666), an intensely moving study reminiscent of Augustine's *Confessions*. It would be misleading to say that *The Pilgrim's Progress* was influenced by any literary source except the Bible, since the uneducated Bunyan is not known to have been familiar with any other of the seminal works noted earlier. This partly explains why Bunyan's style avoids affectations that make most fiction of this period undigestible for modern readers. Also, Bunyan wrote for an audience as simple as himself, one not demanding the veneer of learning applied by aristocratic writers.

If the Bible did influence Bunyan's masterpiece, one can find in Revelation the source for his use of the dream-vision framework, as well as such features as the castlelike heaven, the goal of Christian's journey. The allegorical hindrances the pilgrim encounters on his trek, such as the Castle of Despair and the Hill of Difficulty, seem original with Bunyan, though certainly the mode of the allegorical journey is familiar from Edmund Spenser's *The Faerie Queene* (1590, 1596), a work probably known to Bunyan. Undeniably original are Bunyan's characters, such as Timorous, Mistrust, and Talkative, who not only embody the vices for which they are named but who also talk as authentically as actual people in whom one recognizes these dominant traits. The arguments of these characters are so plausible that the reader sympathizes with Christian's frequent doubts about how to proceed and whom to believe. Moreover, Bunyan's characterizations are so concise, his observations so exact, that a character's presence for one or two pages is sufficient to keep him or her sharply defined in the reader's memory. Though Christian is accompanied by Faithful, for example, through only a small portion of Part I of *The Pilgrim's Progress*, one builds up enough sympathy for this character to feel shocked when he is murdered by the citizens of Vanity Fair.

Bunyan as a novelist works so economically, so un-self-consciously, that the reader quickly loses the sense of artifice, even though the work is in an unorthodox form. In other words, *The Pilgrim's Progress* is one of those rare works of fiction that readers usually do not regard as fiction because they apprehend it as truth. Passing directly into the cultural mainstream of the people without having been authorized, as it were, by literary society, Bunyan's allegory can be said to have influenced most English writers since the mid-eighteenth century, although its traces are often hard to mark because it has been so well assimilated.

Beginning just after the appearance of *The Pilgrim's Progress*, though in no way inspired by Bunyan's work, the novelistic career of Aphra Behn appealed to the aristocratic and city audience to which Bunyan gave no thought. Predictably, her novels and stories follow the French heroic pattern, with its idealized, beautiful characters and exotic settings. In her best work, *Three Histories* (1688), a collection which includes the notable *Oroonoko: Or, The History of the Royal Slave*, Behn adds a wrinkle which makes her heroic works irresistible: the stories purport to be true, and she includes sufficient London names and places to make the assertion believable. At a time when London society craved gossip about the fashionable, and saw the *roman à clef* as a way to satisfy that craving, readers preferred to accept the illusion of allegedly actual people performing impossibly heroic acts rather than explicit fiction attempting the accurate portrayal of reality. In *Oroonoko*, for example, a pair of African lovers (with ideal European aristocratic manners) are swept across continents and oceans from one harrowing scrape to another, until both are murdered. Despite the implausibility of the events, readers accepted Behn's claim that the incidents actually occurred.

Behn's popularity occasioned many imitators. In competition with them were the writers of sensational accounts of authentic voyages to exotic places. Both forms appealed to the taste, present in every age, for examples of individual survival or death in the midst of calamitous events. It was to suit this taste that the most famous adventure novel of modern times, *Robinson Crusoe*, was written. Drawing on numerous accounts of travelers' shipwrecks, isolation, and survival, Daniel Defoe created a study of the individual in collision with environment that surpassed in realism any previous English fiction, except perhaps *The Pilgrim's Progress*. *Robinson Crusoe* and Defoe's novel of the following year, *Moll Flanders*, created a fashion for realistic characterization that made possible the character studies of Richardson, Fielding, and their successors.

Firmly established as a journalist, political propagandist, and editor of popular periodicals, Defoe brought to the writing of *Robinson Crusoe* an unerring sense of public taste and a sure knack for the detail or turn of phrase that would convince the reader of the authenticity of a story. Though the central fact of the book, an Englishman's survival on an uninhabited island for twenty-eight years, is as improbable as many of Behn's turns of plot, Defoe makes the entire story plausible by his scrupulous attention to even the tiniest fact of Crusoe's existence. Where Behn or one of her imitators would have focused on the emotional trauma of shipwreck and isolation, Defoe, eminently practical in all his endeavors, focuses on the mundane *how* of existence: how to ensure a supply of meat when all the powder and bullets are gone, how to make a shovel without iron, how to bake bread without an oven. Nevertheless, Defoe does not slight Crusoe the moral and emotional creature: perhaps the greatest masterstroke of the novel is Defoe's first making the reader confront and gradually accept the narrator's aloneness, then presenting the fearsome truth that Crusoe is not alone. Though Defoe's sincerity as an ethical writer has often been questioned, there is nothing feigned about Crusoe's confused response to his savage visitors. Behn's *Oroonoko* has been called the first novel to make equality of the races an issue, but Crusoe's profound dilemma over his proper reaction to the Indians' cannibalism is a more authentic grappling with the issue than is Behn's portrait of the dark-skinned slaves as noble innocents.

Following the immediate success of *Robinson Crusoe*, Defoe wrote two sequels in the same year, one a series of further adventures and the other Crusoe's reflections on his miraculous life. Meanwhile, Defoe's prolific imagination was at work on a new project, the "private history" of a London woman, who, originally a poor orphan, grows up to lead an exciting, inevitably scandalous life before finally achieving security and station. *Moll Flanders* differs in plot and setting from *Robinson Crusoe*, but the psychological authenticity of this purportedly true memoir is brought about by standard Defoe methods. Where Crusoe lovingly recounts his ingenious solutions to minute logistical problems, Moll recalls verbatim the coolly calculated speeches, the nuances of dress and gesture, that had been either her making or undoing in romantic affairs. These are Moll's tools of survival just as surely as Crusoe's odds and ends are his, and Defoe, through his everlastingly coy narrator, convinces the reader that her predicament within society is perhaps more precarious than Crusoe's without. Moreover, one accepts the extremity of her situation because she, like Robinson, wastes few words bewailing it, instead moving immediately from the recognition of disaster to the search for means to survive. One does not pity Moll; rather, one sees oneself in her plight and soon comes unconsciously to share her values.

The reader accepts Moll's authenticity as an autobiographer because she is neither more nor less conscious of her motives than one would expect her to be. She is intuitively ethical, knowing that her need for money does not justify her thievery, especially from people no better off than she is; nevertheless, she is not so aware of herself as to realize that her panic-stricken repentance in Newgate is not real. Neither she nor Defoe is hiding tongue in cheek when she vows to live honestly, then immediately lies. When, at the end, Moll, rich and secure, says that she and her husband (the fourth of five, but the only one surviving) will spend the rest of their days in penitence, the reader can stand back and chuckle. With the realization that it would be useless to demand that the protagonist be more introspective, the reader understands that Defoe has established Moll's character to be the child of a society where money is everything and only the rich can afford to be morally precise. The greatness of the novel is that Defoe never mentions this point; the closest Moll comes to this is to say that a woman without a dowry is lost, and that a woman without looks or a dowry is truly lost.

The irony of the novel is that Defoe, in his Preface, would have the reader believe that *Moll Flanders* is a story of despicable deeds fervently repented, rather than one of inevitable deeds and a sprinkling of penitent words. With his eye on the prejudices of his audience, he could not bring himself to say that Moll could not repent because society could not forgive, and because it was really society that needed repentance. He, like his flesh-and-blood heroine, dared give the lie to his public time and again, in one "true" history after another, but he, like she, dared not take off the mask.

Christopher J. Thaiss

ORIGINS AND DEVELOPMENT OF THE NOVEL
FROM 1740 TO 1890

No primary genre of literature has been so often defined and redefined as the novel and still, no consensus has been reached. Several scholars have suggested that the only valid definition of the novel is the history of the genre itself. The origins of the modern novel, however—the novel as it appears in bookstores today, encompassing both serious fiction and best-sellers—are more easily traced. The modern novel in the eighteenth century and its rise in the nineteenth coincided with the rise of the middle class. In consequence, as Ian Watt observes in *The Rise of the Novel* (1957), one of the paramount features of the novel has been its focus on a detailed re-creation of the bourgeoise interior: the clothes, the furnishings, the belongings of the middle class. The novel is also distinguished, Watt points out, by its emphasis on individual characterization, an emphasis which can be related to the social and political movements of the eighteenth and nineteenth centuries. These movements recognize the dignity of the individual and the equality of all men. Despite all its transmutations and variations, the novel today performs the same function it has served since the eighteenth century: it offers reports (to borrow a title from Anthony Trollope) on *The Way We Live Now*.

Since American literature was, in its early stages, merely an outgrowth of English literature, this survey will treat the development of the English novel before turning to the history of the form in America. It is well to note at the outset, however, that there are several notable differences between the English and the American novel. While generalizations about "the novel" in a given nation must always be hedged, it is true that, as Richard Chase observes in *The American Novel and Its Tradition* (1957), "The American novel tends to rest in contradictions and among extreme ranges of experience," while "the English novel has followed the middle way." Frederick R. Karl, in *A Reader's Guide to the Nineteenth Century British Novel* (1972), argues that "unlike the American novel, the English novel principally takes place in time, not space." He then maintains that the "temporal" emphasis of the English novel, as opposed to the "spatial" aspect of the American novel, is related to the greater "blandness" of English fiction, since people who live in a restricted space must pay closer attention to time and also must modify their behavior more rigorously than those who occupy large areas, feel no sense of crowding, and need give much less heed to the passage of time and the markings of its flow.

More important than such dissimilarities, though, are the general likenesses, one of the most significant being the tendency traced in Erich Kahler's study, *The Inward Turn of Narrative* (1972). Kahler's thesis is that throughout the eighteenth and nineteenth centuries, the consciousness of Western man turned more toward an inner vision of reality, and that the novel reflects this slow but momentous shift in human attention. As Watt indicates, the "realism of the novel allows a more immediate imitation of individual experience" than do other literary forms, and "this surely explains why the majority of readers in the last two hundred years have found in the novel the literary form which most closely satisfies their wishes for a close correspondence between life and art."

The narrative element of the novel can be traced back to preliterate eras when storytellers recounted long narratives, such as the Sumerian epic of *Gilgamesh*, which dates to about 2000 B.C. Such narratives, however, were in the form of verse, which facilitated memorization; narrative prose fiction was a much later development. Precursors of the modern novel can be found in every literate culture, ranging from Greek romances such as Chariton's *Chaereas and Callirhoe* (c. A.D. second century) to *The Tale of Genji* of Murasaki Shikibu in eleventh century Japan. The novel as it is now known, however, began in the eighteenth century, following related but distinct lines of development in England, Spain, and on the Continent.

The Eighteenth Century Background

Many factors contributed to the birth of the English novel in the eighteenth century. An important social phenomenon was the growing trend of country people gravitating to the cities—especially in London. Although no reliable figures are available, it is certain that the population of London multiplied several times from 1660 to 1740. With the growth of the city came the attendant blessings and curses: a more rapid and wider spread of ideas, an easier dissemination of reading material, the development of a more commercial society (although England's economy remained primarily agrarian until the Industrial Revolution), and the miseries of urban crime (which had been flourishing since the Elizabethan era, but never so widely), unhealthy living conditions, insufficient housing, disease, and what has been called the greatest social curse of the period, the high incidence of drunkenness. As late as 1780, infant and child mortality was still at a shockingly high level; it was rare for a family to have more than half of its children reach adulthood.

Such a lively and perilous time was, in a sense, made for Daniel Defoe (1660-1731), regarded by many critics as the first significant English novelist. As a small businessman (often a failed one), occasional spy, prolific writer under various names in a number of genres, a Dissenter (one who refused to accept the Established Church of England, though still a Protestant), and generally energetic citizen (who was accused of being a Trimmer, a person who switched from Whig to Tory, or vice versa), Defoe seems to represent nearly all the conditions which prepared the way for the appearance and popular acceptance of the English novel. These conditions include an emphasis on the individual, both as a social entity and a being with a soul, and an interest in his daily affairs (Defoe displays this emphasis clearly in *Moll Flan-*

ders, 1722), the treatment of narrative in measured time rather than in eternal time (thus the novel deals with events in a more specific temporal frame than that of the heroic romance—Henry Fielding's *Tom Jones*, 1749, is perhaps the quintessential example of such a careful temporal treatment). Other conditions in Defoe's works that prepared readers for the novel are people seen acting in a real setting, which includes earning a living, eating, drinking, and making love; an interest in improving one's social and economic status, usually by legal means, but not exclusively so (Moll Flanders tries to live honestly but circumstances force her into thievery); a growing independence, of children from parents, of citizens from their government, of parishioners from the Church, and of everyone from traditional ideas and beliefs, especially those received from the past and from authoritative sources; an emphasis on interior scenes and urban experiences (though the countryside was to figure prominently in the English novel for two centuries, much of the most important action takes place indoors, with the most detailed description being saved for interiors—the classic later example of this accent is the work of Charles Dickens, 1812-1870); and finally, an unprecedented attention to the interests and aspirations of women.

As a man of his age, Defoe represents as well as anyone that most significant fact about the English novel: It is the ultimate expression of the middle class. No literary form was written and read by the ever-growing middle class as much as the novel. By the time Samuel Richardson (1689-1761) published *Pamela* in 1740-1741, the reading public was rapidly expanding, though it was still very small by modern standards. Again, no reliable numbers are available, but scholarly estimates indicate a figure of about seventy or eighty thousand, which was only one or two percent of the total population. The figure increased as the century waned, but even by 1800, only a small fraction of the population, perhaps some 100,000 people, were capable of reading a novel.

1740 to 1764

In 1740, potential novel-readers were chiefly interested in family life, the details of everyday living, and the problems of morality on an individual basis. Wide generalizations concerning what constituted ethical conduct, as were found in Alexander Pope's poetry, may have been widely quoted, but, they were not taken much to heart; also, the novel could do what no verse essay by even so skilled a versifier as Pope could do: it could show morality being lived. Richardson's *Pamela: Or, Virtue Rewarded* satisfied these interests, and the book was extremely popular. The fact that Richardson tells most of the story by way of letters is an indication of the particularity of detail and expression and the interest in the individual that engaged the attention of readers near the middle of the century.

As to the economy and the stability of the government, the nation was in reasonably good condition. At this point, England was enjoying a rewarding trade relationship with its colonies in the New World and was in the initial stages of the process of taking over India. The wars in which it engaged took place on foreign soil. George II (1683-1760) was not a skilled ruler, but the country was controlled chiefly by ministers, who were intent on keeping or increasing their power, always with an eye, however, to avoiding open conflict with the people. The most notable civil disorder of the era (not counting the abortive attempts to restore the Stuarts to the throne, which had little effect on the lives of ordinary citizens) were the Gordon Riots, an anti-Catholic outburst, which did not take place until 1780 and were confined to small sections of London, lasting but a few days.

Although called the Age of Reason and the official philosophy was one of rationalism, the actual lives of most people were not at all lived according to such theories, and this fact is more clearly reflected in the novel than in any other form of literature. The best-known heroes of the early novel are either criminals, such as Moll, or rebels against a hostile society, such as Clarissa and Sophia Western from *Tom Jones* (the former running away from home and being drugged and seduced, the latter also escaping from her father and nearly being raped). Tom Jones is turned out of his benefactor's house on very slender evidence of wrongdoing, is beaten, robbed, almost hanged, and takes almost eight hundred pages to establish his innocence. (Typical of the increasingly middle-class morality of the time and one of the chief themes of *Tom Jones*, virtue is what a person owes to others, while prudence is what one owes oneself.) These works deal primarily with the lives of one or two central characters, further evidence of the eighteenth century emphasis on the individual.

Individuality, as a concern and as a thematic focus, is most strikingly advanced in the entertaining but often nearly surrealistic *Tristram Shandy* (1760-1767), by Laurence Sterne (1713-1768). Some critics believe that Sterne's book did more than any other to open the way for the later psychological novel. This concern was also indicated by the spread of Methodism, whose first meetings were held in 1729. In its early stages, before it hardened into an established denomination, it was an emotional movement which went back to the individualistic roots of Protestantism. The focus on the life of the individual is also reflected in the earlier, and continuing, enthusiasm for biography. Defoe augmented this tradition by basing *Robinson Crusoe* (1719) largely on the experience of the Scottish sailor Alexander Selkirk, who was marooned on an island for some four and a half years. Typically, Defoe transforms Crusoe into a resourceful, God-fearing middle-class person who hardly changes at all during more than twenty-five years on the fictional island—unlike Selkirk, who emerged from his experience in a half-bestial state.

Along with an increasing emphasis on the particulars of people's lives, the early novel depended heavily on a flexible, readable prose style that was far from inflated expression of the romances of earlier times. Much of the brevity and liveliness of this "new" style was the product of journalists and "hack" writers, who were compelled to produce considerable quantities of material for an unliterary audience in short periods. Defoe is again a classic example. He did not start writing long fiction until he was sixty, by which time he had produced hundreds of expository works of a very readable nature, most of them published in periodicals. On a more lofty plane, but still of a vigorous composition, were the widely admired informal essays of Joseph Addison (1672-1719) and Richard Steele (1672-1729), published chiefly in the popular periodicals *The Tatler* (1709-1711) and *The Spectator* (1711-1712). The styles of Richardson and Fielding (1707-1754) are also somewhat more elevated, as befits the stories of more socially eminent characters (Fielding was the more "literary," having had a superior education and an admirable career in the law, along with previous experience as a successful dramatist); but Tobias Smollett (1721-1771) wrote in a very plain style, displaying the "common touch" to a high degree and attaining a much enjoyed earthy humor.

One reason that prose fiction sold so well during this era was the Licensing Act of 1737, directed at the theater, which amounted to a form of censorship enforced by a sensitive government under the leadership of Prime Minister Sir Robert Walpole, who had been the butt of several satirical passages in popular plays. In effect, this law forced Fielding to turn from drama to the novel; it also encouraged bland theater, thus winning a greater readership for contentious periodicals, such as the famous *Spectator Papers*, by Addison and Steele, which led a growing list of well-written and topical journals. The emphasis on individualism in this period was further reflected in the new esteem for portraiture, leading to illustrious careers for such great portrait painters as Sir Joshua Reynolds (1723-1792), a popular member of Samuel Johnson's celebrated Club, and Thomas Gainsborough (1727-1788). Johnson's group, who met more or less regularly in the 1760's and 1770's, was a culmination of another eighteenth century tendency that exhibits the desire of people to come to know others on a quasi-individual basis; this was the popularity of the coffeehouses, establishments where upper-middle-class men gathered to discuss events of the day, the latest articles in the current periodicals, and one another. One of Johnson's salient criticisms of men he did not like was that they were "unclubbable."

Since the novel was written chiefly for the middle class and selected most of its characters from the ranks of this group, it reflects the lamentable fact that nearly all the truly charitable work which was done during this mid-century period (and there was an unfortunate paucity of it, by modern standards) was accomplished by the middle class. It was this stratum of society that instituted the parish groups who gave to the poor and who looked after unwed mothers and orphaned offspring (though, as *Moll Flanders* clearly demonstrates, the care was woefully inadequate for many). The two institutions that would be expected to take the lead in such endeavors simply failed to do so in any meaningful fashion until the next century; they were the government and the church, both of which were more determined to promulgate their primacy and power rather than to form any effective organized assistance for the unfortunate members of society. Foreign wars and economic shifts created a large body of such people; indeed, former military people who become idlers appear as minor characters in decades of British fiction.

Perhaps the chief cultural irony of this period is that the novel both protested against the conditions of society and yet depended on them for its existence. The cosmic concerns expressed by earlier writers (John Milton, 1608-1674, is perhaps the most obvious example) did not attract the interest of readers as they had. People were more interested in how to get along, how to live both successfully and morally, and how to come to terms with the rapidly changing times. For such guidance, it was not the philosophers or great poets to whom most readers turned, but the novelists, for these middle-class authors spoke to the real needs and concerns of their readers. Addressing this issue, Johnson's moral strictures against licentious material in the newly popular novels were severe but were based on a genuine concern for the virtue of the readership, many of whom were "the young, the ignorant, and the idle." Apart from the ethical aspect of this influential declaration of concern, Johnson's remarks, in an essay published in *The Rambler* in 1750, also reveal the great effect that fiction was having on a number of its readers, who, Johnson notes, "regulate their own practice" on the models of the leading characters in novels.

One of the few major historical events that captured the imagination of the everyday reader was the voyage around the world in 1740 to 1744 of George Anson (1697-1762) and, later, the Pacific explorations in 1768 to 1779 of James Cook (1728-1779). Thus, the passages in Smollett's *Roderick Random* (1748) dealing with the hero's experience on a naval vessel were of considerable relevance to the novel reader. As the feats of explorers and colonizers became known, a greater sense of empire began to be felt in the populace, as well as the recognition of ever-increasing opportunities for trade. England's navy, strong for centuries, was now the guardian of a lively British maritime commerce around the world, with the colonies providing invaluable raw materials and opening areas for further colonization and economic development for enterprising adventurers.

1764 to 1800

The date 1764 is of special significance in the history of long fiction because it marks clearly the beginning of a distinct change in the direction of English culture, especially as reflected in the novel. The first genuine Gothic novel (the novel of suspense, terror, exotic setting, and effects) was published in that year. *The Castle of Otranto* (1764), by Horace Walpole (1717-1797), enjoyed an enormous success and signaled a shift in public taste toward the exotic, the extraordinary, toward violent passions—toward the Romantic Movement, adumbrations of which can be found this early.

Another early sign of Romanticism is a different sort of novel, also the first of its kind: *The Vicar of Wakefield* (1766), by Oliver Goldsmith (1728-1774), regarded as the harbinger of the novel of sensibility, another signal of the Romantic "temperament." These two impulses, the Gothic and the sentimental, were to gain an even greater hold on the interests and reading habits of the later eighteenth century Englishman. Further evidence of this shift in enthusiasm can be found in a seemingly unrelated art, that of architecture. Whereas the earlier eighteenth century had seen the construction of practically designed and constructed buildings, with symmetrical proportions and even measurements (the double cube was a popular design), a kind of "proper" organization also found in the well-trimmed and geometrically planned formal gardens (the topiary art reached its highest point in this era), the later age preferred wild countrysides spotted with ruined or half-ruined castles, or rude country dwellings, charming in their quaint rusticity. These "wild" settings became increasingly common in novels and were a staple feature of the Romantic novel to come.

Another important stand of Romanticism was anticipated by the publication of Bishop Thomas Percy's *Reliques of Ancient English Poetry* (1765) which brought to its clearest exposure an interest in the medieval past, which had been growing since early in the century. The enormous popularity of the volume by Percy (1729-1811) testified also to the wider interest in ancient and/or exotic poetry (some specimens of Oriental and Scandinavian verse had already appeared in print) that came to characterize Romanticism. Further, nature, which was to play so large a part in later novels (notably those of the Romantic Sir Walter Scott), is secondary to the concern for human welfare, especially in terms of emotional states.

Such pre-Romantic tendencies were not confined to England. One of the most popular novels of sensibility was *The Sorrows of Young Werther* (1774) by Johann Wolfgang von Goethe (1749-1832), a pathetic tale of unrequited love and sad but eloquent protestations of passion and self-pity. It has been claimed that the suicide rate among young readers rose sharply soon after this novel was published. Goethe's novel reveals a typical connection between the novels of sensibility and gothicism in that much of the scenery in his tale is wild and "natural." The pre-Romantic tendencies revealed in these novels can also be discovered in the often socially critical, homespun Scottish poetry of Robert Burns (1759-1796) and in the mystic verses of William Blake (1757-1827).

Probably the most extreme manifestation of sensibility is to be found in Henry Mackenzie's *The Man of Feeling* (1771); in this short novel, the hero falls to weeping more than fifty times. All this sentimentality (which was, in later novels, to be the basis of some extremely humorous satire, as in Jane Austen's *Northanger Abbey*, 1818) was in part an expression of the flowering social consciousness of the age. This sense of an imperative to develop sensitivities to the needs and concerns of others allied itself with the perennial didactic element in the novel (and in the national consciousness). Just as the early novelists often claimed a morally elevating purpose in order to have their works accepted by the public (and not roundly condemned from the pulpit), so the writers of this era genuinely believed that their novels were stimulating readers to loftier sentiments and more generous acts. In Parliament, the moving and eloquent speeches by the liberal Edmund Burke (1729-1797), many of which were devoted to opposing the government's narrow-minded policy of taxation in the American colonies, ratified officially the growing belief that people had a right to be helped by others and that the willingness to do so was a sacred duty for any who were able. A popular phrase in the novel of sensibility asserted that the true gentleman "was never an indifferent spectator of misery in others." This attitude assumed, of course, that human nature was essentially benevolent, a notion that did not take hold in popular fiction until this period.

The notion that human nature is, if uncorrupted by evil forces, naturally good was urged upon the English nation by the influential French philosopher Jean-Jacques Rousseau (1712-1778), whose asseveration that man in his natural state is moral gave rise to a widespread discussion of the doctrine of the "noble savage." This theory relates to the whole atmosphere of primitivism that is found in the ballad revival (intensified by Percy's volume) and associated phenomena, such as the novel of ideas, a genre that usually endorsed liberal educational and social concepts. Typical of the genre was Thomas Day's *Sanford and Merton* (1783-1789), a humorless tract in the form of a novel which tries to prove that a "natural" education is better than an excessively structured one and that morality is always rewarded. Many of the novels of ideas dealt with education in Rousseauistic terms, but the most striking novel of liberal tendencies was William Godwin's *Caleb Williams* (1794), which has the distinction of being one of the earliest novels of propaganda and also perhaps the first novel of crime and detection.

These novels of social concern illustrate an important phenomenon of the period: the novel was beginning to occupy a position which had formerly been held by the drama. While a few excellent satires can be found near the close of the century—such as Goldsmith's *She Stoops to Conquer* (1773) and Richard Brinsley Sheridan's *The Rivals* (1775) and *The School for Scandal* (1777)—generally, the burgeoning concern for human rights and social reform is to be found most fully developed in the novel (though a number of poems also revealed such concerns). Alan D. McKillop's discussion of the role of the novel, in *English Literature from Dryden to Burns* (1948), in which he argues that the novel "entails a critical or analytical attitude toward characters represented under actual or conceivable social conditions" and that the "critical attitude is directed toward both individual character and the social situation," suggests the way in which the novel was coming ever closer to the real lives of its readers as the eighteenth century came to a close. Despite the excesses of the sentimental novel and the novel of terror (the Gothic), the central trend of prose fiction was toward an attempt to grasp and come to terms with the world as it had to be dealt with by individual people every day.

Perhaps the best example of this tendency is the work of Frances "Fanny" Burney (1752-1840), whose moralistic but readable novels of domestic life contain a great deal of sensible advice (either by demonstration or declaration) for their readers, especially young women. The extensive readership attained by her novels illustrates another aspect of the times: more women were beginning to read novels (and to write them—Burney had a great many followers in the field of domestic fiction). This trend helped to prepare the way for the woman who is, in the view of numerous critics, the best female novelist in the language, Jane Austen (1775-1817).

It could be argued that, for the common man, the Industrial Revolution—which might be said to date from 1769, the year of James Watt's first patent for a steam engine—was more important than any political unrest. For intellectuals, however, among them many novelists, the disappointment over the Reign of Terror, which was seen as a betrayal of the worthy liberal sentiments that had inspired the Revolution, was deep and of great duration. The youthful William Wordsworth (1770-1850) was among the most grimly unsettled of the poets to be shocked by the bloody course that the insurrection took; and, the also young Sir Walter Scott (1771-1832), though not as morbidly struck as the poet, was deeply disappointed. The reason for the perhaps greater significance of the industrial advance among the lower and middle classes was that individual lives were more directly affected. This fact is of signal importance in the development of the English novel, because this genre, as no other, concentrates on the inner lives of people. Whether the author achieves a detailed delineation of the thoughts and emotions of a character (as does Richardson) or a clear demonstration of the character's motives by action (as in Fielding), the novel depended on a single person, both in his relationships with others and in his interpretation of the meaning of his own life, for most of its interest and value. This dependency was to increase in the ages following the eighteenth century. That the trend was to be informed by what could be considered a semirevolutionary bent (the single person pitted against society or a tradition) was only the predictable result of the tenor of the times.

1800 to 1832

The first decades of the nineteenth century were the peak of Romanticism in English literature, its chief exemplars being the five great Romantic poets John Keats (1795-1821), Percy Bysshe Shelley (1792-1822), William Wordsworth (1770-1850), George Gordon, Lord Byron (1788-1824), and Samuel Taylor Coleridge (1772-1834). All of these artists wrote verse that emphasized the imaginative intuition of the individual man as the way to achieve truth.

Sir Walter Scott was a powerful force in the popularization of both Romantic poetry and the Romantic novel. His *Minstrelsy of the Scottish Border* (1802) capitalized on the widening interest in old ballads and folk tales, especially of the rural type. Scott turned to the novel as an act of self-defense when Byron became so popular that the verse of the "Wizard of the North" could no longer command an adequate market. At the time, Scott had no idea of what a favor was being accorded him. The publication of *Waverley* (1814), the first of the so-called Waverley novels—all of which are set in the past and many of which provide insightful, if not fully accurate, visions of historical events and persons—marked the commencement of a groundswell of enthusiasm among readers for depictions of wild Scottish scenery and vigorous actions performed by impossibly virtuous and somewhat leaden heroes, in the defense of improbably sweet and chaste heroines. Scott's talent for characterization was never highly praised, except in his portraits of lower-class characters such as thieves, pirates, and gypsies, but his powers of description were unequaled in his day. In his better works, such as *The Heart of Midlothian* (1818) and *The Bride of Lammermoor* (1819), he attained Gothic effects that rival those in any of the novels in the genre, even the works of Mrs. Ann Radcliffe (1764-1823) and Charles Robert Maturin (1780-1824).

While verse was the prevailing form during the Romantic period, the novel was still popular; the growth of the population, especially in cities, and the proliferation of lending libraries permitted a wider dissemination of fiction and thus greater economic rewards for writing and publishing novels. There was, however, still a stigma attached to both the writing and the reading of fiction. Scott published his first several novels anonymously, and Jane Austen took considerable pains to conceal from all but members of her family that she was actually writing novels. A period which can boast the wide sweep and narrative drive of Scott's historical fiction and the elegant but barbed domestic vignettes of Austen is rich indeed.

An additional aspect of the novel in this era was the fairly new emphasis on regional fiction. Maria Edgeworth (1767-1849) dealt with the problems, charms, and complexities of life in Ireland with sensitivity and perception. Relations between Ireland and England had been strained since the time of Elizabeth I. Edgeworth offered some penetrating arguments in favor of the Irish side of the question, most notably on the injustice of the English practice of absentee landlordism. Although satire was not the predominant tone of the fiction of the period, the novels of Thomas Love Peacock (1785-1866) provide an entertaining vision of the romance as seen through more modern eyes, with lively touches of humor. The very titles of some of his most popular works indicate the nature of his approach: *Headlong Hall* (1816), *Nightmare Abbey* (1818), and *Crotchet Castle* (1831).

1832 to 1870: The Early Victorian Age

Although Victoria did not gain the throne until 1837, several events suggest the year 1832 as a suitable date to designate the opening of the era that bears her name. It is well to note, however, that the designation indicates how mixed and complex the cultural and historical period was. It followed epochs that were identified according to their obvious characteristics: the Age of Reason, the Enlightenment, the Age of Pope, the Age of Johnson, the Romantic Age. A seventy-year period named after the reigning monarch is something of an evasion, but the era was so complicated and contradictory that the choice is understandable. As Walter Houghton notes in *The Victorian Frame of Mind* (1957), "Studies in this area have emphasized only a few characteristics, notably moral earnestness and optimism, to the obscuring of others, equally important, like enthusiasm and anxiety." He goes on to explain how difficult it is to capture the spirit of the period, because it is composed of so many divergent and at times contradictory elements.

Indeed, anxiety was underlying a great deal of the surface optimism for which Victorian England is famous. Thus, the celebrated attack by Matthew Arnold (1822-1888) on the ignorant remark about the era's wonderful condition by an English industrialist makes a great deal of sense. Another indication of the anxiety and conflict which pervaded the period can be found in the Oxford, or Tractarian, Movement, which started in 1833 and persevered until 1841. It was an attempt to elevate the position of the Church (in that time, this meant always the Church of England, the Anglican Church) in the lives of the people. There were complicated theological and even political reasons for the zeal of the reformers, but one can perceive in this intense conviction that there was a need for such a radical change, an aura of uncertainty and even anxiety about the cultural substance of the life of the time.

The novelist who, for many readers, epitomizes the Victorian Age, Charles Dickens (1812-1870), published his first major work between 1836 and 1837. *Pickwick Papers* demonstrates an additional aspect of the Victorian "personality": a delightful sense of humor, chiefly based on charming eccentricity of character. It is typical of the age, however, that the tone of Dickens' novels almost steadily darkened throughout his lifetime. Indeed, one can trace an increasing tendency toward grimness as the century passed, in novelists from Dickens through Thomas Hardy (1840-1928).

In part, the increasing pessimism of the Victorian Age reflected a growing awareness of urban blight, of the complex consequences of the Industrial Revolution. There were few novels specifically about industry, but Dickens' impassioned plea for more humanity and less materialism, as found in *Hard*

Times (1854), was echoed in the works of lesser writers who were very popular in their day. Dickens protested against a variety of social abuses, from inhuman schools for poor children, as in *Oliver Twist* (1837-1839), to the corruption and inefficiency of the courts of chancery, as in *Bleak House* (1852-1853); particularly intense was his resistance to the cruel working conditions created by the factory system, presented most sharply in *The Old Curiosity Shop* (1840-1841), a work whose excessive emotional stress causes it to cross the border into bathos, a common failing of the era's novels. Despite these social concerns, the central thrust of the novel in the Victorian period remained toward a revelation of the ways by which more or less common people attempted to meet the challenges of life, generally on an individual basis. The principal tone tended to be comic in the early years of the period, growing more somber as the decades passed, and ending with the cold pessimism of Thomas Hardy.

The spiritual crises (particularly the conflicts with Charles Darwin's evolutionary hypothesis, but also with other challenges to orthodox Christianity, such as Higher Criticism of biblical texts) that afflicted many of the artists and thinkers of the Victorian era lent the later novels of this period a philosophical depth and seriousness unprecedented in English fiction. The most impressive novelist who wrote in this vein was George Eliot (1819-1880), in whose works one of Thomas Carlyle's most iterated principles is demonstrated repeatedly: the assertion that life can only take on its true meaning when the individual is willing to renounce earthly glory and material possessions. The theme of renunciation that resounds through *Adam Bede* (1859), *The Mill on the Floss* (1860), *Silas Marner* (1861), and *Middlemarch* (1871-1872) is an echo of the same stress placed by Carlyle (1795-1881) on this human recognition of limited claims and of the virtue of humility. These two "philosophers" of the period, Carlyle being the earlier, reveal two diverging tendencies in the Victorian attitude toward prominent people. While Carlyle (in his famous essay, *On Heroes, Hero-Worship, and the Heroic in History*, 1841) praises the "hero" in history as the kind of person who makes historical events happen, Eliot presents her leading characters as simple persons who demonstrate the Victorian trend away from the usual vision of the lofty, noble, aristocratic hero of the past (as in Scott's historical novels). As Mario Praz establishes in *The Hero in Eclipse in Victorian Fiction*, 1956, the romantic hero gave way to the middle-class man or woman who exhibited worthy moral traits, some bravery, and a becoming lack of egotism. Such central characters allowed Eliot and a host of lesser writers to explore the intellectual and emotional depths of people who appear common (they certainly occupy common places in society) but who display in the novels profound levels of sensitivity and spiritual resources. Eliot's often noted remark, that she found God inconceivable but duty indispensable, illustrates a typical attitude of many of the respected authors of the middle and later Victorian period.

1870 to 1890: The Late Victorian Age

This era, referred to as the "late Victorian Age," usually includes the last decade of the century; it is also known as the "Realistic Period." The generation opened with the death of Dickens, in 1870, and the publication of Darwin's *The Descent of Man* in 1871, a work which further elucidated the theory of evolution, which by this time was being more generally accepted. In the same year, one of Hardy's early novels, *Desperate Remedies*, appeared. This gloomy title not only indicates the grim philosophy that Hardy revealed in nearly all of his novels but also suggests the plight of many of the inhabitants of Great Britain, who had encountered several political and cultural "realities": the repressive policies of Lord Palmerston, prime minister in 1855-1858 and in 1859-1865; the positivistic interpretation of history in the works of Hippolyte Taine (1828-1893), whose *History of English Literature* was translated in 1873; and the naturalism of Émile Zola (1840-1902). The potato famine that had struck Ireland in 1846 was a harbinger of the hard times to strike the rest of the British Isles. As the previously expanding economy began to slow down and settle into less expansive patterns, the competition from other industrial nations, especially the United States and Germany, began to take a severe toll. The near monopoly in international trade that England had enjoyed for decades was irrevocably broken. For the laboring classes, the results were catastrophic. There were extended periods of unemployment, and the rate of emigration, before but a trickle, rose rapidly. It is estimated that some twenty thousand English citizens emigrated to America in 1886, and that an even greater number left in the following two-year period.

An inevitable result of the ruptures in the previously booming economy was the increased interest in socialistic projects and leaders. In 1880, three Labor party candidates won seats in Parliament; soon afterward, several socialistic organizations were founded, the most remarkable being the Fabian Society, started in 1884, which was later to count H. G. Wells (1866-1946) and George Bernard Shaw (1856-1950) among its members. The disorder in society that this sort of expedient implies was indeed present. Faith in a number of institutions, such as the Church, the Monarchy, Parliament, the economic system, religion, and even science, began to wane.

By an odd but not unique quirk of psychology, the novels of Anthony Trollope (1815-1882) found their popularity largely on the basis of their calm tone, the certitude of a pleasant outcome (now and then, Trollope stops the story to inform the reader that there is no cause for anxiety, since he has arranged it so that all will be well), and the relatively trivial concerns of the characters, many of whom are country parsons with very little of serious import in their actions and conversation. This phenomenon was repeated during the anxious days of World War II, when Trollope was again popular. This impulse to escape was to be expressed in a much different manner in the 1890's by the Decadents, who championed "art for art's sake" (on the theory that art is far above life and therefore should not soil its hands trying to deal with it). The most famous of the Decadents was Oscar Wilde (1856-1900), whose semi-Gothic supernatural novel *The Picture of Dorian Gray* (1891) was a sort of fictional announcement of the bizarre extremes of this movement.

Thus, while the empire was expanding abroad, life at home for the lower classes—the upper-middle class was not harmed much by the unemployment and the emigration—was not prosperous. The resistance among writers to the principles of expansion of the empire and the heartless exploitation of both foreign and domestic laborers was vocal. In the novel, one finds such impassioned propagandistic works as Hardy's *The Mayor of Casterbridge* (1886) and George Gissing's *Workers in the Dawn* (1880).

From a more purely literary standpoint, however, the age was a rich one, as the novel achieved a wider scope and a greater depth than it had yet known. Though George Eliot is best known for her novels of domestic life, such as *Middlemarch: A Study of Provincial Life*, she also took up social causes with an intensity and thoughtfulness not found before in the English novel—the prime example is *Daniel Deronda* (1876), which deals with "the Jewish question." Although England had had a skilled Jewish prime minister, Benjamin Disraeli (1804-1881), in office for several long periods in the nineteenth century, anti-Semitism was still widespread and often institutionally sanctioned. Eliot, along with Hardy and George Meredith (1828-1909) in particular, also helped to create what was to become known as the psychological novel. Certainly, foreign writers of the realistic school—most notably the French realists Honoré de Balzac (1799-1850), Stendhal (Marie Henri Beyle, 1783-1842), and Gustave Flaubert (1821-1880)—had assisted in opening the paths to psychological realism, but the English novelists of the late nineteenth century carried this tendency to a lofty height. British literary historians occasionally enjoy claiming that the American-born Henry James (1843-1916), who could be classified as the most insightful of all psychological realists, was more of an English novelist than an American one, since he lived the last thirty-five years of his life in England and wrote a great deal more about English society than he did about that of his native land. The claim is hotly contested, however, by students of the novel in the United States, and there is much in James's work that proclaims its author as essentially American, wherever he chose to reside.

The period ended with the death of Robert Browning (1812-1889). This most Victorian of writers, whose optimistic poems are so well-known as to mislead casual readers, is a fitting representative of the era which, to a large degree, ended when his life did. The way was already prepared for the more modern writings of later poets such as Rudyard Kipling (1865-1936), a severe critic of the empire-building practices of the government, and William Butler Yeats (1865-1939). The novelists to follow included Robert Louis Stevenson

(1850-1894), Joseph Conrad (1857-1924), Arnold Bennett (1867-1931), and D. H. Lawrence (1885-1930). The works of these authors, and of the other imposing figures who were to carry this magnificent genre down to the present, would not, however, have been possible without the efforts of the countless writers of long fiction who opened the avenues of what F. R. Leavis has aptly called *The Great Tradition* (1964).

Background to the American Novel

By general consent, the first American novel was *The Power of Sympathy*, very probably by William Hill Brown (the matter of authorship is somewhat obscured by the assignment of the book to Sarah Wentworth Morton for a number of years); it was not published until 1789. There had been numerous literary achievements, of varying aesthetic merit, since the founding of the two earliest settlements in what were to be the colonies, one at Jamestown, Virginia, in 1607, and the other at Plymouth, Massachusetts, in 1620. No memorable fiction was produced, however, until late in the next century. Most of the earliest works were practical, semihistorical pieces, such as Captain John Smith's *True Relation* (1608, an account of his experiences in Virginia) and his *A Description of New England* (1616). A substantial body of religious literature began to appear, including the famous *Bay Psalm Book* (1640, which had the distinction of being the first book to be printed in America), Roger Williams' *Bloudy Tenent of Persecution* (1644), the poetry of Edward Taylor (c. 1645-1729), and the fiery sermons and tracts of Increase Mather (one of whose titles, *Case of Conscience Concerning Evil Spirits*, 1693, provides an indication of the force of the Puritan tendency in these writings) and Cotton Mather (1663-1728). These and similar works, well into the eighteenth century, provided information, attitudes, some impressive poetic imagery, and much moralizing; what they almost entirely lacked was any recognizable belletristic quality. This was especially true of the prose. Fiction did not begin to find a general readership until the second half of the eighteenth century, and most of the fiction published at that time in the colonies was either British (because no international copyright law existed, much importing and pirating of novels from the mother country occurred) or closely based on British models, chiefly novels by Daniel Defoe, Samuel Richardson, and Henry Fielding.

The delay in the appearance of native fiction of high quality is usually attributed to a variety of causes, both cultural (a heavy dependence by the colonies on Britain for literary forms and techniques endured until long after the American Revolution, 1776-1781) and natural (the enormous land mass of the "new" continent and the regionality it stimulated). Many scholars believe that the primary reason for the delayed and tentative beginning of American long fiction, apart from the influence of British examples, was simply the absence of an indigenous culture rich in tradition; in Henry James's formulation (*Hawthorne*, 1879), it requires "an accumulation of history and custom . . . to form a suggestion for the novelist."

On the other side of the situation, it has been noted that this paucity of social and historical substance compelled American novelists to discover or create other bases for their themes, founded on more abstract material. The result, claim the scholars who are impressed favorably by this phenomenon, was a fiction rich in symbolism and allegory, a literature abundant in metaphysical significance and elevated by a textual density. Of special interest in this connection is the massive achievement of *Moby Dick* (1851), in which Herman Melville (1819-1891) created a symbol of evil (or, some readers believe, of something far more complex) that may represent the highest attainment in the English language of a thematic expression. Nathaniel Hawthorne's "romances," as he wished his fictions to be designated, are almost by definition apart from the British genre of the realistic novel of social life. It is inviting to speculate about what Mark Twain (1835-1910) would think, given his preliminary instructions to readers to eschew a search for any motive, moral, or plot (with a dire warning of severe punishment for offenders), of the current scholarly attention given to *The Adventures of Huckleberry Finn* (1884), which discovers in the novel archetypal characters (such as Jim, who is intepreted as a surrogate, spiritual father to Huck) and events (such as the journey down the Mississippi River, which has been elucidated as a recapitulation of the quest motif found in primitive myth). In *Form and Fable in American Fiction* (1961), Daniel Hoffman makes a persuasive case for the enormous reliance of American novelists on folklore and the extensive utilization of allegorical and symbolic modes of signification.

Since America comprises such a vast expanse of territory, and since this area includes regions settled by people with diverse backgrounds and ambitions, it has been customary to divide the country into several sections, noting the most imposing characteristics of each. The differences among these regions are striking evidence of the geographical reasons for what is often perceived as the rich variety of American literature. For a considerable time, the cultural life of America was synonymous with the cultural life of New England, and Boston was judged the cultural capital of the country as well its publishing center—the first printing press in America was established in Cambridge in 1639—until well into the nineteenth century, when it relinquished that distinction to New York. More isolated by topographical features than any other major division of the nation, New England was marked by a Puritan fervor (which has often been overstated) and a moralistic emphasis. The middle states—usually regarded as including New York, New Jersey, Pennsylvania, and perhaps Maryland and Delaware—were distinguished by the great diversity of their settlers and the resulting manifold qualities of thought and concerns. By contrast, the South developed a more homogenous culture a sort of feudal society based on the establishment of slavery. From a literary standpoint, the chief cultural benefit of the plantation system was that it allowed the growth of a leisured class of "aristocrats" who had the time and the education to read widely and write articulately.

The last general division in the national consciousness, which was soon to be broken into constituent regions, was the West, an area that was unknown, untraveled, and thus possessed, for the first settlers and many later immigrants, an awesome charm. As the frontier moved West, more and more was learned that removed the mystery from the land, but until late in the nineteenth century, the image of the West held by many Americans (and foreign visitors) was still marked by a sense of romance, unreality, freedom, and unlimited opportunity. A measure of the linguistic importance of this regional aspect of America may be seen in the fact that, at the First Continental Congress, in 1774, many of the delegates were frustrated because they found themselves nearly unable to comprehend the speech of other members.

In establishing the periods of American literature, great variance is found, and there are quarrels regarding most delineations of the periods. The wisest deduction would appear to be that American literature is so complex, despite the evident relative simplicity of the nation's history and culture, that clear separations are just not possible or, perhaps, legitimate. Furthermore, the person who most historians agree was the first American professional author, Charles Brockden Brown (1771-1810), did not publish until near the turn of the century, and then he was only moderately successful. This account denotes the difficulty of the situation in American letters for a serious novelist. As in England, the novel in America was chiefly the product of middle-class authors and the reading material of middle-class citizens. These middle-class writers, however, were not as close to social and political subjects as their British counterparts. The current explanation for this distance is that there existed a severe tension between several pairs of opposing impulses and enthusiasms. Among these, the more obvious are those between the intense desire for freedom and the fact of slavery, the opposing attractions of Romanticism and rationalism, and the antagonism between the desire for economic power and what Leslie Fiedler calls "the need for cultural autonomy." One result of these tensions and the difficulty of obtaining a unified vision of American society was that the most important authors tended to resort to forms of escape, distancing them from the people. James Fenimore Cooper (1789-1851) escaped to the frontier, Hawthorne fled to the past with his insightful studies of the Puritan ethos, Melville found liberation in distant settings and on the sea, Mark Twain escaped to the near past and the West, and Henry James went to Europe in order to find suitable subject matter for his art.

1789 to 1820

Several conditions prevailed prior to that period in England that hindered the development of the novel there. These conditions also existed, but with greater impact, in the Colonies until the time of the Revolution and afterward, lessening as the decades passed; and they are important in understanding why the American novel did not develop as fast as its European (chiefly British) model. Apart from the problem of colonial, later state, loyalties (Alexander Cowie, in *The Rise of the American Novel*, 1948, points out that most citizens, even after a national identity had been established, would declare their "country" as the state from which they came), there was a scattered population, making the dissemination of books difficult and expensive; an uneven and low level of public education, an area in which America lagged sadly behind Europe; and finally, a lack of publishers. Although, in the last decade of the eighteenth century, more than fifty new magazines were published, few had any chance of persisting, and almost all were content either to print fiction from abroad or to focus on practical, expository material. This new-country emphasis on the pragmatic had a further dampening effect on the production of worthy native fiction.

The early American novels which were set in America and dealt with distinctively American concerns were almost entirely of a moralistic nature, since the moral strictures that had militated against lively, imaginative novels in England were felt in America as well—in some regions, mainly New England, with even more force than in Britain. As a consequence, the fiction that was turned out well into the nineteenth century tended to be both didactic and imitative of English forms, such as the novel of domestic life, the sentimental novel (these categories often overlapped), the Gothic romance, and the historical novel.

William Hill Brown's *The Power of Sympathy* (1789) fits into the category of the novel of domestic life with more than a suggestion of the qualities of the sentimental novel, and it has a heavily moralistic dedication; yet, it is replete with sensational elements such as near incest, seduction, abduction, and violence. The influence both of the story of Moll Flanders, the lowborn protagonist of Defoe's tale of suffering, thievery, and intrigue, and of Richardson's account of the grim adventures of the upper-middle class Clarissa Harlowe is seen here. Of an equally lively nature but better written—Brown's style is ponderous and much in the vein of the lesser English authors of the eighteenth century—is Susanna Rowson's popular *Charlotte: A Tale of Truth* (1791, published in the United States as *Charlotte Temple*, 1797), which also displays the effects of the pressure of a Puritan morality and very probably a sympathetic reading by the author of the works of Fanny Burney. Other novels of this type, written chiefly by women, established this subgenre in American literature for decades to come.

The Gothic romance, while it was presented in some impressive early examples, mostly those of Charles Brockden Brown, did not flourish as had the domestic and sentimental novels. The most apparent reason for this weakness was the lack of didactic themes. The Gothic setting and plot did not encourage moralizing on the author's part. There was also often a touch of the picaresque in these productions, which tended to discourage moral lessons. Like the British models, such as William Beckford's *Vathek* (1786) and Matthew Gregory Lewis' *Ambriosio: Or, The Monk* (1796), the American Gothic novel developed a body of Gothic machinery designed to terrify. As in England, the form stimulated a number of parodies of its most extreme features: unlikely plots, bizarre settings, and unwholesome characters whose actions often descend into the lunatic.

As a reaction against these types developed in the form of the early historical novel, marked by the introduction of American Indians as important characters, the level of the quality of fiction in the New World began to rise, but at a slow pace—it is noteworthy that it was not until nearly fifty years after the American Revolution that American novelists dealt significantly and seriously with the event. The delay was once again largely the result of a powerful British cultural influence on the new nation. When that influence was overcome, and as the country commenced to become more unified (improved roads and modes of travel had a great deal to do with this advance), the ground was laid for the important achievements of writers.

1820 to 1865

The unrest which is at the heart of the American novel, especially in the nineteenth century, is particularly evident in the work of James Fenimore Cooper (1784-1851). It is not so evident in a lesser book, such as *Satanstoe* (1845), as in the more famous novels: *The Last of the Mohicans* (1826), *The Prairie* (1827), *The Pathfinder* (1840), and *The Deerslayer* (1841)—the central titles in his famous Leatherstocking Tales, which recount the adventures of one of the most influential characters in early American fiction, the redoubtable Natty Bumppo. Cooper's presentation of this interesting personage's experiences on the frontier could be said to have brought about the development of the Western genre, or at least to have brought it to the highest point to which it aspired (the culmination of the trend may perhaps be found in Owen Wister's *The Virginian*, 1902, which, while a more sophisticated work, still emphasizes the virtues of Western heroes in contrast with the evils and corruption of the East). As Richard Chase, in *The American Novel and Its Tradition* (1957), declares, Cooper is at his best when he can "accept without anxiety or thought the vivid contradictions of Natty Bumppo and his way of life." Chase and many other literary historians point out that the unrest mentioned above was the result of unresolved disunities in a nation that had been formed largely from disparate elements: progressive thinkers and conservative traditions, European influence and American innovation, and what would later be termed the "highbrow" versus the "lowbrow."

Such oppositions might well be expected in a new country whose physical borders were still expanding, with new states being added every several years, and whose population was still being enlarged by immigration at a rapid pace (more than fifty million people came to America during the nineteenth century, from many areas of Europe and Asia). The lack of serenity in American political and economic life was mirrored by its artistic sphere. A sort of inferiority complex in the arts persisted in the United States long after the insulting remark by the British writer Sidney Smith, in 1820: "In the four quarters of the globe, who reads an American book? Or goes to an American play? Or looks at an American picture or statue?" Many Americans were forced to agree that the artistic accomplishments of the new nation were slight. As late as the 1840's, Margaret Fuller (1810-1850), the scholarly author and friend of most of the transcendentalists (whose most illustrious member was Ralph Waldo Emerson, 1803-1882), asserted that, in order for America to produce a literature of its own, "an original idea must animate this nation." Few of these fresh concepts were to be found in a culture that was influenced by Europe and whose chief concerns were advancing its political growth and consolidating its economy.

Into this wasteland of artistic sterility, as many viewed it, there came the imposing figure of Nathaniel Hawthorne, who turned to his Puritan forebears for material to be used in some of the finest short stories and at least two of the most impressive novels (*The Scarlet Letter*, 1850, and *The House of the Seven Gables*, 1851) to be created in the nineteenth century. One of Hawthorne's ancestors had been a judge at the Salem witch trials and had participated in the condemnation to ghastly torture of innocent women. The sensitive descendant of this old, honored, and guilty family could not rid himself of the sense of wrongdoing and, fortunately for his art, developed a haunting penetration into the nature of good and evil. Also of benefit to his writing was a more distinctive and loftier prose style than had been attained previously. Many scholars would concur with Irving Howe's judgment in *The Literature of America: Nineteenth Century* (1970), that Hawthorne is "the first great American novelist."

Howe and others see the Puritan influence elsewhere as well, in the works of writers as diverse as Herman Melville and Mark Twain. These authors were not only producing native American novels of high quality, but they were also helping to legitimize the acceptance of American fiction in the United States. Their success was partially a result of nonartistic phenomena, such as the fact that the population of the nation, in 1840, was roughly four times what it had been at the time of the Revolution and that the territory controlled by the country was enlarged by about the same proportion. Prosperity was causing people to take pride in their accomplishments and also providing more leisure in which to read fiction. While the stress on personal advancement sometimes took the form of immoral self-aggrandizement, there was a countervailing impulse toward endorsement of the leveling effects of democracy. This conflict, like so many others appearing in the United States toward the mid-century, can be discovered as an underlying theme in the better novels of Melville: *Redburn* (1849), *White-Jacket* (1850), *Moby Dick* (1851), and *Billy Budd, Foretopman* (a novella not published until 1924 but now considered as one of his finest works).

The mid-century also saw the growth of "local-color" fiction, which ranged in the following decades from the Western sketches of Bret Harte (1836-1902) to the poetic realism of Sarah Orne Jewett (1849-1909). To some extent, the local colorists were preserving or re-creating a simpler, preindustrial America in the nostalgic mood of Twain's *The Adventures of Tom Sawyer* (1876). Though Twain produced but one generally accepted masterpiece, *The Adventures of Huckleberry Finn*, the influence of nearly all of his stories, especially the early ones, was enormous. It is perhaps not too much to say that this emotionally troubled author (particularly in his later years) assisted America in realizing how much it has lost by the westward spread of civilization.

Harriet Beecher Stowe (1811-1896), a then little-known writer from the civilized East, fond of reading the romances of Sir Walter Scott and deeply impressed by the grim phenomenon of slavery, has been credited with awakening the conscience of the North to the horrors of that institution. *Uncle Tom's Cabin* (1852) is hardly a great book, and its dependence on romantic elements is at times humorous, or would be, were the subject of the novel not so unhappy. No doubt, Abraham Lincoln was exaggerating when he remarked, upon meeting Stowe, that he was pleased to greet the little lady who had started the big war, but there is no question that this novel contributed greatly to the Abolitionist movement. In so doing, it proved that a work of fiction could have a profound social and political effect on the nation, a fact never before so clearly established.

The post-Civil War period, satirically named "The Gilded Age" by Twain and his collaborator, Charles Dudley Warner (1829-1900) in their novel of that title, published in 1873, was also perceived, especially by later historians, as the age of realism. There had been novels with realistic elements before the war, but the forthright recognition by novelists of the harsh realities of the Reconstruction period tends to justify that designation. James, whose emphasis was on psychological realism, while he did live mostly in Europe and often wrote about Europeans, never lost his interest in the American personality; his novels are filled with fascinating American characters, often seen in conflict with, or corrupted by, the older society of Europe, such as the charming Isabel Archer of *The Portrait of a Lady* (1881) and the very American Christopher Newman of *The American* (1877). Even when James was writing chiefly about European characters who visit America, as in *The Europeans* (1878), one might say that the attentive reader gleans more information about the nature of American morals and attitudes, as with the Wentworth family in that story, than about those of the foreign characters. James's psychological realism influenced his good friend and constant admirer, William Dean Howells (1837-1920), most notably in *The Rise of Silas Lapham* (1885). Howells was much more concerned with external reality and much cruder in his treatment of emotional nuances than was James.

Indeed, under the influence of naturalism, Howells went so far as to claim that art should be eliminated altogether and fiction turned into a sort of factual, semiscientific report of life as it is. He never attained this goal, but some of the naturalistic writers came very close to doing so: Howells' influence on Frank Norris (1870-1902), Stephan Crane (1871-1900), and Theodore Dreiser (1871-1945) was considerable. In a larger way, James and Twain affected the course of American long fiction for a longer time. As depth psychology came into vogue, the examinations of characters' motives and states of mind so highly evolved in James's novels (the later ones, such as *The Wings of the Dove*, 1902, and *The Ambassadors*, 1903, are especially impressive for this achievement) became very influential. Although his popularity with readers has never equaled Twain's, James has had a powerful effect on later writers, even on some writing in the late twentieth century.

The spread of literacy, which accelerated sharply after the war, helped to create a market for fiction, and a great number of minor authors emerged. Some of them had superior credentials, such as the historical novelist Francis Marion Crawford (1854-1909), who, during his travels and studies, attained a reasonable fluency in more than fifteen languages. Most of these authors are, unfortunately, little read today. Stylistically, the most prominent influence on the period was Twain, to whom, much later, both William Faulkner and Ernest Hemingway admitted a debt. In another way, Twain encouraged the advance of the naturalist movement, which has been defined as simply realism with predilection for the nasty, by his increasing pessimism. This gloomy outlook, largely the result of business reverses (Twain was a poor businessman, and the expanding economy encouraged unwise investments), can readily be seen in the naturalistic writers.

The dejection in Twain's later work (most sharply revealed in the posthumously published *The Mysterious Stranger*, 1916) was not without valid cause. The Gilded Age had followed what some experts consider the first experience of truly modern warfare, characterized by the participation of large numbers of civilians, the massing and action of large bodies of troops, and the phenomenon of individual battles often being decided on the basis of extensive massacres; also, it has been judged the first war in which victory was primarily the result of an industrial superiority. The epoch was modern in other ways as well, which, though not so bloody, were distressing: the growth of the economy created new industries and sudden fortunes (making possible the power and arrogance of the "Robber Barons"), and it also brought into being a new class of urban poor and the beginnings of extensive slum areas. These grim conditions led inevitably to clashes between corporations and nonorganized workers, thus impelling the rapid expansion of the labor movement. The American Federation of Labor was founded in 1881.

By 1890, America was well on its way to becoming a modern country, with all the blessings and curses that such a development implies. As usual, the novelists tended to fix their attention on the curses; yet, this penchant could be regarded as something of a duty for novelists, especially in the modern era. When the liberal educator and writer Thomas Wentworth Higginson (1823-1911) was asked how one could best learn about "American society in its formative process," he recommended reading the novels of Howells. It might not be too much to say that any American who desires to understand in depth the most significant trends in the early development of his nation and his people would be well advised to peruse the novels produced by one of the most varied and energetic cultures yet to come into existence.

Fred B. McEwen

ORIGINS AND DEVELOPMENT OF
THE NOVEL SINCE 1890

The environment in England during the 1880's and 1890's was an especially fertile one for the development of new trends in literature. As the century came to a close, all the giants of the novel, except George Meredith, had either died or stopped writing. Even Thomas Hardy, who can be justly classified as either "Victorian" or "modern," quit writing prose in 1895 and turned to poetry. The great Victorian poets, too, were disappearing: Matthew Arnold died in 1888, Robert Browning in 1889, and Alfred, Lord Tennyson in 1890. Among the great intellectuals who had influenced the age, only John Ruskin was left to scribble away, and he was writing about society rather than art. The Victorian stage, for decades the province of producers and directors who spared no expense to provide "spectacle" to audiences whose penchant for grand performances demanded ever greater mechanical wonders on the boards, was becoming the province of men such as George Bernard Shaw. His plays, while amusing at times, generally abandoned the grandiose for the middle class, and did so with a striking (and sometimes disturbing) sense of realism. Upstarts such as Oscar Wilde and Walter Pater were turning their backs on "traditional" subjects in art and presenting material that could only be described by the general populace as "decadent." The younger generation of writers had turned away from their English ancestors, seeking inspiration from French novelists whose naturalistic treatment of subjects glorified the commonplace and vulgar while minimizing the good in traditional morality; Honoré de Balzac and Émile Zola became the luminaries whom budding authors copied with dedication and fidelity. Among this generation of writers and readers, the Victorian notion of "high seriousness" was giving way to a concern for subjects only whispered about during the heyday of that glorious queen who gave her name to the period. That aging lady still occupied the throne, but everyone knew that she was to die soon, and with her would pass an "age" in English life.

On the other side of the Atlantic, the novel was also undergoing a transformation. By the close of the nineteenth century, most American novelists had declared their independence from their English forebears. Whether one agrees with Ernest Hemingway that "all American literature springs from one book," Mark Twain's *The Adventures of Huckleberry Finn* (1884), it is nevertheless true that by the 1880's, American writers had turned to their own country for literary inspiration. The heritage of the American past, the attitudes and concerns of the founding fathers and the Puritan heritage they had bequeathed to their heirs, the legends of the original Indian inhabitants of the land, and the particular curiosities associated with the various regions of the country had supplanted earlier tendencies to anglicize American situations and frontier characters. Whereas the Indians in James Fenimore Cooper's

Leatherstocking Tales speak (and often act) like eighteenth century gentle-men, those of late-century novelists exhibit no such artificiality. American writers had become interested in American society, a society that had, in a period of barely more than a century, grown from adolescent imitation of the English culture which had given it birth to an adult life that was in many ways different from that of its parent.

While Britishers such as Matthew Arnold could dismiss America as "unin-teresting," and an expatriate such as Henry James lament the absence of castles, kings, and monuments which in Europe heralded a link to the past of a thousand or more years, most American writers of the last decades of the nineteenth century took a look around them, found what they saw of interest to themselves and to their countrymen, and wrote about it with fidelity not to British literary tradition but to their own growing awareness of the unique qualities of their own country. The absence of a society that dated back a thousand years may have made it difficult for Americans to write "social novels" in the manner of Jane Austen, George Meredith, or George Eliot, for, as Alfred Kazin has observed, the "social novel" most often flour-ishes in a society "deeply settled," one that "knows itself thoroughly" and "takes itself for granted."

What the American writer lacked may have been a handicap in the 1830's, but by the 1880's, he had abandoned his attempts to imitate his British counter-parts; instead, he had turned to the problems and the people around him for inspiration and had found ample material for his work. The American expe-rience had been, for almost three hundred years, one of change and devel-opment, characterized by the ever-present challenge to conquer the frontier. America was not, and had in fact never been, one society, but was rather a collage of many; its various regions—South, Northeast, Midwest, Pacific Coast—developed separate cultures in which political homogeneity was often the only common link to other areas in this vast expanse of yet unsubdued country. The American novelist, turning from romance to realism, found his subject in the various regions about which he chose to write. As a conse-quence, novelists as diverse as William Dean Howells and Mark Twain were both "realists" in depicting the American scene, though they differ signifi-cantly in subject matter and technique. Both treat American life, but life in the Northeast was quite different from that in the Far West or along the Mississippi River. Hence, the modern American novel, born of a drive to portray a country and its people realistically, became for almost half a century a novel of regions and subcultures.

By the end of the 1800's, the novel had gained acceptance in America as a serious literary form, but even then, there was strong sentiment among readers that novels were purely entertainment, unless some explicit moral was woven into the narrative. Beginning in the 1880's, however, a young American, a New Yorker by birth, a Bostonian by upbringing, and an expatriate by choice, began to change that perception, both in his homeland and in England.

Henry James may well be considered the first modern critic of the novel, and since the modern novel is the product of a self-conscious artist who is concerned with his craft as well as his message, it is well to begin a discussion of the development of the modern novel with James. Considering his own works to be art as well as social commentary, James spent four decades explaining, in essays and in prefaces he affixed to the collected edition of his works, how good prose fiction may be identified and judged. James's essay "The Art of Fiction" (1884), written as an answer to Walter Besant's essay of the same title, comes closer than any other document published during the final decades of the century to being a manifesto for the modern novelist. Besant's essay had summarized the Victorian position on the role and limits of the novel: it was to provide wholesome entertainment, treat certain subjects only, avoid others at all costs, attempt verisimilitude but not at the expense of moral education, provide swift and unrelenting justice for moral offenders (especially where sexual transgressions were involved), and support the aims of society at large. In "The Art of Fiction," James struck out against almost all of these notions. The only requirement a novelist has, he says, is that he be "interesting." "We must grant the artist his subject matter," he insists, and judge the value of the work by the artist's success in executing his own design. No subject should be taboo, James argues, no artificial strictures should be placed on the novelist's creativity as long as that talent is put in the service of depicting life as it really is. Where Besant had tried to develop appropriate classifications for novels (similar to those used to describe various forms of poetry), James swept away such prescriptive categories, claiming that a novelist must be free to explore incidents and characters and develop his story in such a way as to be pleasing to the reader.

James fancied himself the consummate realist, interested in portraying life as it is lived by sensitive individuals full of thought and reflection. Much like Jane Austen, he limited his artistic gaze to a narrow segment of society, foregoing the panoramic techniques of the romancer and the historical novelist and avoiding the sweeping pronouncements of the social novelist to explore the nuances of social life among the upper classes. James has been called the first international novelist, and he was undoubtedly the first major figure to explore the clash of American and European cultures; in *The American* (1877), *The Portrait of a Lady* (1881), *The Ambassadors* (1903), *The Golden Bowl* (1904), and numerous other works, he presents American men and women, usually naïve and filled with the optimism characteristic of their countrymen, confronting the wiser but more jaded men and women of England and the Continent.

A late masterpiece, *The Golden Bowl*, may serve as an example of James's method. In that novel, a young American girl, Maggie Verver, falls in love with an Italian nobleman, Prince Amerigo. Amerigo is charmed by her naïveté but apparently prefers the company of her more worldly-wise and well-traveled American friend Charlotte Stant, with whom Amerigo has apparently had an affair some time before. Because Maggie is rich, he agrees to marry her, and only after the two are already married does Maggie discover the true nature of the relationship between her friend and her husband. At the end of this sordid tale of social intrigue and betrayal, Maggie emerges victorious—after a fashion. Her friend marries Maggie's father and returns with him to America, leaving to the heroine a Prince who is apparently reformed enough to recognize where his loyalty should lie. In winning, however, Maggie loses, too; her father, whom she adores, returns to America, never to see her again, and she is at best a sadder and wiser woman for the "victory."

As an allegory of the conflict of cultures, James's novel is largely pessimistic about the modern condition. Such an attitude is clearly characteristic of the realists in general, who, looking scientifically at the contemporary scene, found little to cheer about in the present condition of society. These men and women were willing to express their displeasure openly, despite the threat of censure from a reading public accustomed to having their literary lessons presented either in romantic garb or in stark allegorical narrative, either of which were sufficiently distant to allow them to say with St. Paul, "But for the grace of God, there go I." James and his contemporaries who examined the American or British scene under their figurative microscopes would not allow their readers to achieve such distance.

James's novels and his critical pronouncements signaled a change in the attitude toward the novel shared by several of his contemporaries who were just beginning to regard themselves as artists as well as (or rather than) social reformers or educators, or mere entertainers. From James, it is only a short step to Joseph Conrad, who declared in his Preface to *The Nigger of the "Narcissus"* (1897) that "any work which aspires to the condition of art must carry its justification in every line." Conrad's own works testify to his constant concern for selecting the right word or phrase to characterize the situation he chooses to create. Always the careful observer of men in conditions that tested their fortitude and challenged their values, Conrad wrote of the sea as a constant metaphor for the human condition in general. In his works, events take on a significance beyond the literal, but Conrad is no simple allegorist whose story serves as an excuse for presenting a philosophical proposition. For the most part, his men and women are interesting as people, not as mere representations of abstract principles. In *Heart of Darkness* (1902), for example, the "horror" that Kurtz sees as he lies on his deathbed in the heart of Africa strikes the reader as especially poignant because no one in the story is really larger-than-life; the simple possibility that men could be so corrupted makes the tale a chilling commentary on the tenuousness of civilization as a means of staving off the bestial side of man's nature.

Writers such as James and Conrad concerned themselves with the structure of their works, with choosing incident and detail to give the works a sense of balance and completeness that satisfies the reader's aesthetic sensibilities. Quietly, these novelists were redefining their readership: no longer would they write for the general audience (though they may have claimed to do so), but rather for those discerning few who could detect what James would call in another essay "the figure in the carpet." No longer would plot, action, and moral pronouncement be the glue to bind the parts of the novel to the whole or to solidify the bond between the reader and writer. The artist was becoming aware that he could communicate with his reader—albeit a certain kind of reader—by other means: patterns of images that would themselves suggest larger themes than the story conveyed (symbolism, *leitmotiv*), conscious attempts to balance or juxtapose incidents and characters whose stories are often unrelated on the literal level, and clear links with the great literature or folk culture of the past. The fragmentation of the audience for fiction, which had begun at least a decade before James began writing, became complete by the decade after he died.

While James was abroad writing pronouncements on the status of American and British fiction, his friend and contemporary William Dean Howells remained at home and did the same. Using his position as editor of several popular magazines, Howells influenced the taste of countless readers by promoting the kind of fiction he believed best suited the public's needs. Like James, he was a realist: his own novels display a careful concern for realistic presentation of information, often a meticulous attention to detail and an extraordinary accumulation of facts, and a concern for the contemporary social and political milieu in his own country. Howells, less daring than James, remained faithful to nineteenth century moral ideals and practices; hence, his realistic vision is limited by his moral sensibilities. In *The Rise of Silas Lapham* (1885), for example, Howells combines his penchant for providing realistic detail with his strong sense of moral purpose to create a portrait of American society and American business that shows how the drive for material betterment can often lead to spiritual poverty and, eventually, to ruin both in this world and possibly in the next. As a portrait of American commerce, it is most unflattering, but it is typical both of Howells' own outlook and that of many other realistic novelists who were looking around them and finding little to like in the contemporary scene.

Two novelists, one English, one American, may serve to characterize the naturalistic movement in the English-language novel during this period of transition from Victorian to modern sensibilities. Like other naturalists, both Thomas Hardy and Theodore Dreiser were followers of the school of realism: their works are filled with minute descriptions of ordinary places and events, with scenes and characters from the middle and lower classes, and neither makes any attempt to glorify his heroes and heroines by raising them to epic proportion.

Thomas Hardy's novels, usually set in the Wessex district of England, depict the life of common folks who struggle to eke out an existence against an unforgiving nature. A follower of Charles Darwin and Herbert Spencer, Hardy displays in his novels a world where natural selection and determinism are the primary moving forces, and where chance is ever present to ruin the best design of even the very best men. *The Mayor of Casterbridge* (1886) offers a good example of Hardy's philosophy of determinism and of the role that chance plays in human lives. In this novel, Michael Henchard, a man of strong will but somewhat irrational temperament (in the opening scene, a drunken Henchard sells his wife and daughter), rises by his own industry to become a wealthy farmer and prominent citizen in his local community. As chance would have it, however, he soon falls victim to a series of setbacks: He finds his wife again and, believing he should win her back to make restitution for his earlier behavior, abandons a woman who loves him; he loses all his money to another farmer, largely because the weather favors the other's crops, loses his wife again to this rival, who also supplants him as mayor of the town, and is reduced at the end of the novel to a penniless beggar who wanders off to die alone on the barren countryside.

This note of extreme pessimism characterizes Hardy's other works, and is in fact typical of many naturalistic novelists; the work of Frank Norris in America, especially in a novel such as *McTeague* (1899), bears a striking resemblance to Hardy's fiction. Like most naturalists, Hardy ignored the Victorian conventions prescribing subject matter for fiction, and turned to issues that would eventually cause him to be rejected by the British public of his day. In *Tess of the D'Urbervilles* (1891), his heroine, forced to yield to a young nobleman who abandons her after he has used her, suffers the fate one would expect for prostitutes in Victorian England; Hardy's Tess, however, evokes not horror but pity in the reader, a feeling that apparently made many Victorian readers uncomfortable. In *Jude the Obscure* (1895), Hardy abandoned any pretense of dealing out Victorian justice or shying away from taboo subjects. In this novel, he treats frankly and sympathetically the extramarital, adulterous relationship of Jude Fawley and Sue Bridehead. These two struggle to maintain a life built on genuine love in a society whose conventions work against their ever being happy. As in other Hardy novels, chance intervenes to bring misery to both hero and heroine, destroying them for no apparent reason. *Jude the Obscure* was Hardy's last novel, for he was sternly criticized for his open treatment of adultery, a subject he felt he had only touched on and not fully explored in this work. Disappointed that the public was unwilling to face contemporary issues head-on, Hardy abandoned the novel and turned to poetry.

The kind of restraints that caused Hardy to abandon the novel worked against American novelists as well; Theodore Dreiser's experience is a good example. Dreiser was initially stymied in his attempts to publish *Sister Carrie*, which was finally published in 1900, because that work dealt openly with the problems of an impoverished girl who becomes a man's mistress as a means of preserving her life. The book was derided in numerous literary and religious circles, for it suggested that submission to evil, even in an extremity, did not necessarily lead to a life of ignominy. Unlike Hardy's Tess, Carrie succeeds by using her wits and feminine charm. Without the least hint that he believes his heroine has been wrong in her actions, Dreiser traces Carrie's rise to prominence in society, while simultaneously portraying the decline and eventual suicide of her original benefactor, Hurstwood. There is in this novel, and in most of Dreiser's others, a strong implication that the little man (or woman) in America can succeed only by abandoning the platitudes preached both in the pulpit and the public forum, and that those who succeed do so at the expense of others.

Regardless of the methods one uses, however, there is no guarantee of success. In the greatest of his novels, *An American Tragedy* (1925), Dreiser portrays the sad results of the American dream gone awry. His protagonist, Clyde Griffiths, a shallow young man, self-centered and greedy for the "good things in life," enters the world of business and society to find that success depends much more upon birth and chance than upon honest striving for advancement. Clyde is made to look like a fool in the high society where he seeks membership. By accident, he causes a girl who really loves him to become pregnant, and when he discovers that she is a hindrance to his chances to climb the social ladder, he plots to kill her, only to discover that he is too much the coward to commit the deed. Cruel chance does for him what he cannot do for himself, however, as the girl accidentally falls from a boat and drowns (the kind of death Clyde had planned for her). Ironically, Clyde is accused of committing the crime he had plotted but failed to carry out, and is eventually convicted.

It is impossible not to see an intellectual kinship between Dreiser and Hardy, both of whose characters succeed or fail according to circumstances over which they have no control. The works of these novelists provide some of the finest statements of naturalism, the stepchild of scientific determinism and literary realism.

The death of Queen Victoria in 1901 and the ascension of Edward VII marked the beginning of a new political age in England, but the fiction of the next two decades continued to show strong ties to that which had preceded it. On more than one occasion, the literature of the period has been disparagingly dismissed as mere journalism. That journalistic style, however, was often a façade that covered serious treatments of problems plaguing England as she entered the new century. Novelists in turn-of-the-century England, much more than their fellow artists in America, felt the impact of the intellectual advances that had been made during the preceding century. Living in what has been called "a contracting moral universe, in which the received moral imperatives had lost their urgency" (John Batchelor, *The Edwardian Novelists*, 1982), they attempted to find substitutes for religious imperatives in secular ones. Duty in society replaced obedience to God as the principle of right living for many Edwardians, and novelists reflected that attitude in their works.

Heroes were needed, of course, but heroism seemed impossible in the modern environment. Further, the English countryside that had provided a wholesome counterpart to the squalor of the city for earlier novelists was fast disappearing as suburbs spread out around the metropolitan areas. The spread of the suburbs was paralleled by the retreat of the Empire, as Britain's world-wide system of colonial enterprise was clearly in danger of falling apart. The "glory that was England" under Victoria was fading, and the impending conflict with Germany, foreseen as early as 1900, caused concern among the populace and influenced the works of Edwardian novelists. The period was characterized by a general anxiety about the state of the individual and society. The major figures of the period—John Galsworthy, Arnold Bennett, H. G. Wells, Ford Madox Ford, E. M. Forster—adopted the form of the novel that their Victorian predecessors had bequeathed them, but they were living in a society quite changed both intellectually and politically. It is small wonder that one of the most popular images in Edwardian novels is the abyss.

On the popular front, two voices emerged as the "spokesmen" for the novel in England: Arnold Bennett and John Galsworthy. Bennett's popularity was important to him, and some critics have complained that he prostituted a fine talent in order to satisfy his desire to be regarded as a social lion. A disciple of realism, in his best works, such as *The Old Wives' Tale* (1908), he demonstrates a keen eye for detail and an ability to make interesting, even significant, the lives of commonplace people. He and Galsworthy did much to popularize the chronicle novel, multiple volumes dealing with the same character or group of characters. Others in his works, such as *The Grand Babylon Hotel* (1902), are predecessors of the modern documentary novels that explore life in particular institutions or forms of business. Galsworthy achieved success as both a playwright and novelist, giving Edwardian England a portrait of its Victorian heritage and its contemporary problems in his famous series, *The Forsyte Saga* (1906-1921).

Both Galsworthy and Bennett paid close attention to external detail, but their unwillingness or inability to explore the motivations and inner feelings of characters with the same sensitivity as they gave to outer descriptions made them targets for writers who believed that the job of the artist was not to substitute for the photographer, but to explore the reality of experience that could not be seen on the surface. Virginia Woolf's famous essay "Mr. Bennett and Mrs. Brown" (1924) provided the rationale for certain post-World War I novelists to reject traditional realism.

Ford and Forster bridge the gap between the Edwardian period and the 1920's. Ford had achieved recognition during the early years of the war with the publication of *The Good Soldier* (1915), but in his Tietjens sequence of four novels (1924-1928), he examined in detail the changes that had occurred in society and their effect on the hero, whom he has carefully drawn to represent the traditionally good English gentleman. Forster published four novels before 1910, all of them typical English social novels, at times melo-dramatic. His most significant work, *A Passage to India*, did not appear until 1924, and while the style and method of narration recall his own earlier works and those of the novelists of the turn of the century, the book's theme reflects both the effects that the war had on sensibilitites in England, and a timeless concern for the paradox of human experience that Forster shared with other members of the literary circle to which he belonged, the Bloomsbury Group (which included Virginia Woolf). More than in any of his other novels, Forster depicts in *A Passage to India* a certain tragic quality about human life. One of his characters, Mrs. Moore, reflects at one point in the novel that "Pathos, piety, courage—they exist, but are identical, and so is filth. Everything exists, nothing has value." For anything in life to have value, man must make that thing worthwhile; no values are preordained. That philosophy, the product of modern science strengthened by the experiences of World War I, links Forster to as unlikely a colleague as Ernest Hemingway, whose characters often express the same idea, and act to establish meaning for their own lives in the face of certain defeat.

During this same period in America, the novelists who rose to prominence were often much like their British counterparts. The first two decades of the twentieth century have been called by Walter Allen (*The Modern Novel in Britain and the United States*, 1964) a period of comparative sterility in Amer-ican fiction. If one excludes Henry James and Theodore Dreiser, that descrip-tion may be just, for no giant of American literature emerged until after World War I. The American populace was being swept away by sensation-alism, as the new journalists captured the country's interest with their exposés of business, politics, and life in the cities and the country. Novelists such as Upton Sinclair achieved popular acclaim for fiction that called attention to the rot at the core of American institutions; Sinclair's *The Jungle* (1906), which graphically displayed the horrors of the meatpacking industry, was read for its sociological impact as much as for its literary merit. It became fash-ionable for the novelist to look deeply into the American scene and expose the corruption or absence of value in institutions that had long been considered honorable.

Among American novelists who focused their gaze in this fashion, none was more popular than Sinclair Lewis, whose works consistently drew atten-tion to the inadequacies of the American dream. Like Dreiser and Sherwood Anderson, Lewis was a Midwesterner by birth; a student of the American realists, he concentrated on mid-America, depicting in *Main Street* (1920), *Babbitt* (1922), and other earlier works the pettiness and emptiness of life in what was generally regarded as the bastion of modern American morality. Lewis pointed out to his countrymen, and to readers abroad (where he achieved a certain degree of popularity), that the heartland of America was filled with George Babbitts, whose lives consisted of belonging to clubs that gave members status by telling them what to think, men whose advancement in society was always at the expense of someone less fortunate. Lewis was awarded the Nobel Prize for literature in 1930, the first American so honored.

There were others writing in America during this period whose works were less sensational, but of considerable literary merit. Edith Wharton, a writer of the Jamesian school of social realism, turned to Eastern society for her subject and created novels that rival James's for their penetrating insights into social situations and the impact on character that society can have. The American penchant for local color and regionalism continued unabated, and among novelists who provided this kind of literature were Willa Cather and Ellen Glasgow. In her stories of the Nebraska plains where she was reared, of the Virginia area where she was born, and of other regions, Cather constantly reminded her readers of the plight of the individual in modern society. Her insight into contemporary America rivals, and often surpasses, that of Sinclair Lewis. Glasgow's region was the old South, where she was born and reared. Her stories showed the fixation of the South on its past, and her vision was pessimistic. A fine novelist in her own right, she is also important as a forerunner of the Southern writers who were to form a literary subculture in America during the later decades of the century.

World War I provided a distinct dividing line between the nineteenth century sensibility and the new age in both England and America. Although Americans had had, in their Civil War, a preview of the kind of destruction modern warfare could produce, few people in either country were psychologically prepared for the carnage of World War I. In both countries, the postwar period was characterized by rapid social change and a heightened sense of the tenuousness of modern life in the face of total war. Though it is hard to offer a generalization that can encompass all English and American novelists, it is safe to say that in both countries, the 1920's were characterized by a certain gaiety of spirit that masked a genuine disillusionment with institutions and (in Britain) with the class system. This feverish gaiety gave way to the Great Depression, reflected in British and American novels by a growing sense of concern for the future of a society based on capitalism, a growing trend toward social violence, and an increasing tendency to look for solutions to social problems outside the existing political frameworks that had been functioning in these countries for so long.

There were, as one might expect, a large number of novels written about the war itself, many of them by men who had taken part in the fighting.

Several of these novels have taken their place among the modern classics: John Dos Passos' *Three Soldiers* (1921) and Hemingway's *A Farewell to Arms* (1929) fall into that category. The impact of the war on the literature of the next decades extended far beyond the novelists whose works deal directly with the conflict. Institutions that had stood for a century or more had been shaken by the four-year conflict. The worth of the individual, already called into question by the discoveries and theories of nineteenth century science, had been almost shattered by the wholesale destruction that the machinery of modern warfare had wreaked. Such events left many sensitive young men and women in shock, and those who turned to the novel as a means of expressing their dismay reflected the general disillusionment of the populaces of both countries.

The breakdown of public agreement about what is significant in human life, the new view of the nature of consciousness introduced by the study of psychology, and a desire to discover new ways to reach their audience caused writers of the post-World War I period to experiment with the form of the novel. In fact, the period immediately following the end of hostilities on the Continent can best be described as the Age of Experimentation. The tendency to try new ways of representing reality is most noticeable in novelists who abandoned traditional narrative conventions, adopting instead the method suggested by William James in his discussions on psychology. Determining that reality cannot best be portrayed by a simple recitation of physical detail, these writers attempted to put down on paper the thought processes of characters, to re-create the stream of consciousness. The term "stream of consciousness" was first used by William James as a metaphor to describe the way thoughts pass through the mind just below the surface level, prior to their being formulated into intelligible patterns that men normally express as sentences. The technique of limiting the perspective of the novel to a single character was of course nothing new; Daniel Defoe's *Robinson Crusoe* (1719) makes use of the first-person narrator, as do myriad other eighteenth and nineteenth century works. That one could further limit the perspective, and hence more closely approximate the way in which reality was really apprehended, was first argued explicitly by Henry James, who in the Preface to *The Ambassadors* discussed his method of limiting his descriptions to whatever might impinge on the "center of consciousness" of his hero. James's hero, however, is presented as having already formulated his thoughts, so that what one reads in a James novel is the intellectual reflections of a character who has observed something outside himself, rather than the record of those impressions as they first impinge upon his consciousness. The great experimenters in the modern novel—Dorothy Richardson, Virginia Woolf, and James Joyce in England, William Faulkner in America—attempted to record the stream of consciousness itself.

Virginia Woolf once observed that "human character changed" decisively "on or about December 1910" ("Mr. Bennett and Mrs. Brown"). Despite the whimsical precision of her statement, the sentiment was real; during the decade from 1910 to 1920, a number of literary figures, captivated by the new way of apprehending reality, began experimenting with the form of the novel. Woolf herself provided a key to understanding both the purpose and method of the new movement. In an essay appropriately entitled "Modern Fiction" (1925), she dismissed the efforts of Galsworthy, Bennett, and Wells as materialistic, condemning them for "spend[ing] immense skill and immense industry making the trivial and the transitory appear the true and the enduring," without capturing life as it really exists. Those novelists were hidebound by the tradition of the novel, which had always found in external events and relationships the proper material for fiction; but if one should look within, Woolf says, "life, it seems, is very far from being 'like this.'" Instead, Woolf says, life is the action of the mind in contact with the outside world:

> The mind receives . . . impressions—trivial, fantastic, evanescent, or engraved with the sharpness of steel. From all sides they come, an incessant shower of innumerable atoms. . . . Life is not a series of gig lamps symmetrically arranged; but a luminous halo, a semi-transparent envelope surrounding us from the beginning of consciousness to the end.

The job of the writer is to abandon conventions and seek to display this inner life: "Is it not the task of the novelist," Woolf continues, "to convey this varying, this unknown and uncircumscribed spirit, whatever aberration or complexity it may display, with as little mixture of the alien and external as possible? We are not pleading merely for courage and sincerity; we are suggesting that the proper stuff of fiction is a little other than custom would have us believe it."

In her own novels, Woolf tried repeatedly to capture life as a series of impressions upon the mind of sensitive characters such as Mrs. Ramsay in *To the Lighthouse* (1927) or Bernard in *The Waves* (1931). Abandoning conventional concerns for plot, Woolf tried to reproduce, through asyntactical language, parenthetical digressions, juxtaposed sentences whose meanings appear to have no causal relationship, and other similar techniques, the immediacy of the human mind encountering the world around it.

When Woolf wrote "Modern Fiction," she was not introducing a theory so much as commenting upon the works of novelists who had recently entered the literary scene. Early experimenters included Dorothy Richardson, who attempted to capture *in toto* the workings of a single, ordinary mind. Miriam, the heroine of Richardson's twelve-volume *Pilgrimage* (1915-1938), is revealed to the reader solely through the associative patterns of thoughts that race through her consciousness as she goes about her ordinary tasks. Though Richardson's notions of psychology may be pre-Freudian, and though she may avoid with a curious Victorian reticence certain subjects and actions that no doubt would have been on her heroine's mind at some time, she is nevertheless an important figure in the development of stream-of-consciousness fiction. Another early experimenter, whose novels reflect her awareness of Freudian psychology, was May Sinclair. Better than Richardson, Sinclair seems to have understood the real frustrations of women in late Victorian England, and she captures the psychological turmoil of her characters in narratives that are a curious blend of the Jamesian center of consciousness and Richardson's more free-form technique.

Unquestionably the greatest experimenter in this age of the experimental novel was James Joyce. His *A Portrait of the Artist as a Young Man* (1916), a semiautobiographical work about the upbringing of a young Irish Catholic Dubliner, is told with a degree of objectivity hitherto unknown in novels. Not once does the author intrude to tell the reader how he should respond to the hero's actions; even descriptive adjectives are carefully omitted so that the reader is forced to interpret feeling and motive directly from action and speech. The same penchant for authorial self-effacement characterizes Joyce's later masterpieces, *Ulysses* (1922) and *Finnegans Wake* (1939). In these, Joyce abandons the conventions of plot and narrative to present events in a method best described as collage: incidents are set in parallel, compared and contrasted so that meaning must be inferred, gleaned by the reader in the act of judging the text itself, not from authorial intrusions telling him what to believe or what to make of this strange mixture of dialogue, stream-of-consciousness narrative, soliloquies, dramatic vignettes, and other curious interjections of prose that often mystify all but the most careful, attentive reader.

In *Ulysses*, Joyce resorts to a device typical of many modern authors who aim not at the general reader, but at one who brings to the work a strong background in classical and modern literature. By suggesting correspondences between his work and Homer's *Odyssey* (c. 800 B.C.), Joyce forces the reader to look for parallels between the world of modern Dublin and the mythic world of Homer's poem. The drive to raise the significance of modern events to the level of myth has become commonplace among many novelists who consider themselves serious artists, and the works of writers as diverse as Albert Camus and William Faulkner share this tendency to some degree.

In *Finnegans Wake*, the tendency toward myth is still present, but punning and other forms of wordplay dominate that work and have baffled most readers, leading to the production of numerous handbooks explaining what Joyce "means" in his novel. Some critics have thrown up their hands at *Finnegans Wake*, dismissing it in exasperation as not a novel at all. Its "narrative" is circular (the book begins in mid-sentence, and ends with the first half of that sentence), and even the stream-of-consciousness method seems secondary to Joyce's continual play with the multiple meaning of words. In fact, *Finnegans Wake* is often cited as the primary example of what is wrong with the experimental novel by critics and novelists who adhere to the more traditional methods of narrative and who feel that the novel should not abandon its historical function as a bearer of news about the way people live.

Experimentation with form was not confined to writers in England or on the Continent. A number of American novelists quickly adopted wholly or in part the techniques of stream of consciousness or other methods of nontraditional narration. Dos Passos used a kind of collage of narrative forms to achieve the panoramic effect he sought as a means of capturing the expanse and variety of his native land in his *U.S.A.* trilogy (1930-1936). Faulkner carried on experiments with the form of the novel that included juxtaposing stream of consciousness with traditional narrative techniques (*The Sound and the Fury*, 1929), collecting disparate stories with related themes to form a single work (*Go Down, Moses*, 1942), or relating two seemingly unrelated stories in parallel (*The Wild Palms*, 1939). Adding an elaborate style to these other rhetorical devices, Faulkner moved the novel in the direction of modern poetry, where the reader is often called upon to work actively to discover meaning amid a collection of images. Use of stream of consciousness and other nontraditional techniques has now become commonplace in modern fiction.

The reaction to experimentation with form has been strident, perhaps more vehement in England than in America. Since 1923, when D. H. Lawrence dismissed the efforts of Joyce, Richardson, and Woolf as "childish" and "absorbedly self-conscious" ("Surgery for the Novel—or a Bomb," 1923) many critics and novelists have lashed out strongly against the trend to abandon the intellectual bond between the writer and the general reader. Novelists who believe in the efficacy of fiction as social documentary have been loudest in their protests, and their work has remained close in both form and content to the traditional novel as written by their eighteenth and nineteenth century forebears. C. P. Snow, always a staunch believer in the value of the story in the novel, described the trend to "regard novels, and compose novels, as verbal puzzles to be worked out by persons cleverer than the original writer" as a sign of a "period of decline not only in the art itself, but also in the society from which it derives" (*The Realists*, 1978). It is no wonder that Snow's own novels, especially those in the *Strangers and Brothers* series (1940-1970) are traditionally realistic chronicles of English society that focus on intellectual dilemmas and social quandaries faced by men and women who are immediately recognizable to the reader. The swing back toward more traditional forms of narrative after World War II has been hailed by British critic Paul West, who saw the return to convention as a kind of recovery after sickness: "the English novel has recovered from the flux," he wrote in 1965, "and only Lawrence Durrell makes much use of it" (*The Modern Novel*, 1969).

Though he distrusted the experimental fiction of his time, D. H. Lawrence now is ranked as a great innovator himself. Along with Woolf and Joyce, he stands as a preeminent figure of the period between the wars. Like Joyce, he had already published a work of some distinction before the war, exhibiting distinctly modern sensibilities in his first autobiographical novel *Sons and Lovers* (1913). Though similar in some respects to the traditional *Bildungs-roman*, *Sons and Lovers* clearly shows the influence of Freudian theories of psychology; in it, Lawrence depicts the classical Oedipal conflict. In the 1920's, an age that glorified anti-intellectualism, Lawrence was right at home. He rebelled against the modern industrial society because it had, in his view, cheapened the quality of human experience. Intellectualism was at best a form of escape from the fullness of life's experiences, and at worst it ruined all that was worthwhile in life; not surprisingly, almost all of Lawrence's villains are intellectuals. Only those who felt deeply and acted vigorously (even violently) were worthy of praise.

The theories of Sigmund Freud and other psychologists had made the world aware of the submerged part of man's mind that often drove him to actions that he could not explain, and Lawrence found in these theories fertile ground for his works. In a style often reminiscent of Romantic poetry, Lawrence tried to convey the power that these subliminal urges had to drive men and women to act. Unlike Joyce or Woolf, he did not abandon conventional narrative techniques or traditional forms of organization for his works; in fact, *The Rainbow* (1915), one of his best novels, is in many respects a fine chronicle novel in the fashion of Galsworthy or Bennett. Lawrence was always interested, however, in trying to convey what Eliseo Vivas has called the "felt quality of experience," "the ebb and flow of the affective life, particularly the felt quality of erotic passion and of religious emotion." As much as any novelist of the period, he created in his works powerful symbols that could evoke multiple levels of meaning for discerning readers. A man of strong passions himself, he was ultimately disappointed with the public response to his works, complaining on one occasion that his "psychological" stuff simply did not sell well. What did sell well was *Lady Chatterley's Lover* (1928), but for the wrong reasons; the book developed a reputation as a pornographic masterpiece, a label it still bears among young people today.

The brilliance of Joyce, Woolf, and Lawrence has often overshadowed the accomplishments of other British novelists whose careers were contemporary with theirs. Aldous Huxley, the preeminent exponent of the novel of ideas, published his first novels in the years immediately following the armistice. Through careful selection of character types and careful construction of plots that juxtapose characters in situations where they must talk with one another at length, Huxley managed to satirize the more extreme forms of English character and society while retaining a focus on what he saw as an irrecon-cilable problem: man's actions, however noble, inevitably lead to frustration and evil, and man's highest intellectual and artistic aspirations exist in beings that have inescapable biological urges and needs.

Joining Huxley among the ranks of the social comedians were Evelyn

Waugh and Anthony Powell. Both were skilled craftsmen of the novel, and Waugh especially donned the satirist's mantle to shock his countrymen into recognizing the moral vacuity of modern life. Graham Greene first surfaced as a novelist concerned with the social condition of his country; he quickly turned to popular forms of the day—the thriller, for example—taking them over for his own use, and making them the vehicles for serious discussion of moral and theological questions. While none of these novelists practiced experimentation in forms that matched the works of Joyce or Woolf, they often displayed the marks of influence in their close treatment of the inner psychology of character. A host of minor novelists round out the complement of figures whose works provide an insight into the post-World War I period: David Garnett, T. F. Powys, J. C. Powys, William Gehardi, and others all wrote novels that reflect the impact of contemporary events and ideas. L. H. Myers, whose best work was done in the 1930's, was a product of this period. Richard Hughes's *A High Wind in Jamaica* (1929) provided one of the most original treatments of childhood in any British novel. A bleaker vision of maturation appears in William Golding's *The Lord of the Flies* (1954), in which the author examines the responses of a group of isolated young boys who react to their first encounter with the darkness dormant in the human heart.

The rebellion in the novel that became evident in the new experiments with form extended far beyond technical boundaries. As Irving Howe has observed, "modern novelists," those who began writing after the earlier works of Henry James had been published, "had been committed to a peculiarly anxious and persistent search for values" ("Mass Society and Post-Modern Fiction," in *The American Novel Since World War II*, 1969). The novelist of the 1920's and 1930's tested values by juxtaposing his characters against a set of fixed social norms—the business community, the political hierarchy, the wealthy class. The values of these social groups were clearly identifiable, and often open to question. Certainly, in the period between the two world wars, there was ample reason to challenge the worn-out institutions that had led Europe and America into a frenzy of destruction and had wreaked havoc over a continent. Many of the young novelists of the period, especially those in America, did exactly that.

The prominent American novelists of the 1920's were F. Scott Fitzgerald and Ernest Hemingway. Fitzgerald's novels generally reflect the moral degeneracy of the jazz age; his characters, often *nouveau riche*, often pretenders to social status, usually are defeated because they aspire to false values. Fitzgerald's *The Great Gatsby* (1925) remains the best illustration of the sad decay of the American dream. The hero, Jay Gatsby, is a self-made man from the West, who has come East to reap all the benefits that money can buy. He appears to possess unlimited riches, and he attempts to buy his way into Long Island society through lavish parties and extravagant affairs at his home.

The secret to his success, however, is "dirty money": he has made his fortune as a bootlegger, has changed his name to avoid his Jewish heritage, and has never achieved the one thing he really wanted: the love of his sweetheart from more innocent days, Daisy, who is now the wife of the boorish Tom Buchanan. Gatsby's world comes tumbling down around him when, through a series of misadventures, he is murdered by the husband of Tom Buchanan's mistress. Yet for all his pretentions and foibles, Gatsby himself is drawn quite sympathetically by Fitzgerald; it is hard to dislike him, and in fact, his brand of heroism has a certain charm about it which suggests that the old virtues of the American character, so often derided as both unobtainable and psychologically damaging, are presented here as a tragic alternative to the sterility of life in American high society of the jazz age. For Fitzgerald, there appeared to be no way of winning.

The importance of Hemingway to the literature which followed him in America cannot be overestimated. During the 1920's, Hemingway developed three things that were to ensure his success: a writing style characterized by a simplicity unmatched by any writer of equal stature before or after him; a "code" or philosophy by which men must live and die if they wish to be great; and a life-style, based in part on that code, that was to gain him notoriety for several decades and make him as controversial for his personal life as for his fiction. Like many writers of his generation, he had gone to the war, and its experiences had made an indelible impression on him. Unlike many of them, however, Hemingway found in violent action a certain dignity; it was one way for man to express himself in defiance against a universe that seemed not to care for the individual. His novels, beginning with *The Sun Also Rises* in 1926, develop in fiction the "code" that Hemingway himself lived by publicly: gusto for life, distrust for institutions, commitment to duty. His *A Farewell to Arms* may be the best novel about World War I, and ranks with Stephen Crane's *The Red Badge of Courage* (1895) as one of the finest American war novels ever written. When he turned his attention to the Spanish Civil War in the mid-1930's, Hemingway again produced a literary work that captures at once the futility of war and the opportunities for true heroism that war offers the brave.

Hemingway wrote for four decades, always clinging to his original artistic premise that good art must be simple and suggestive. A late work, *The Old Man and the Sea* (1952), shows Hemingway's method of simplicity at its best: The hero, an old fisherman who has failed to catch anything for eighty-four days, goes out alone into the Gulf Stream off Florida, where he hooks a magnificent fish and finally lands him after a three-day battle, only to have the carcass eaten by sharks on the trip back to his dock. The reader suffers with the hero, feels his triumph at the catch, and experiences his despair when the fish is taken away by the agents of nature. One is left with a curious feeling, however, that the hero has triumphed despite the apparent failure;

this feeling is precisely the one that Hemingway sought to convey in all of his works.

It soon became fashionable for young novelists to imitate the "Hemingway style," that spare prose devoid of complex sentences and elaborate rhetoric. Hundreds of popular adventure stories, filled with toughs and soldiers of fortune, rogues from every walk of life, filled bookstands across the country; some writers and readers even went so far as to try to adopt the Hemingway code as a model for living. Since the virtues he promoted—courage in the face of overwhelming odds, bravery, self-sufficiency—were the ones that had traditionally been associated with the American hero, Hemingway soon developed a large following both among the general public and in academic circles. Always subject to criticism for his aggressively masculine persona, Hemingway has been judged with increasing severity as the values which he incarnated have become increasingly unfashionable. His legacy to American literature, however—and indeed, to world literature—cannot be ignored.

With the Depression, many young novelists turned their attention to social and political issues with renewed interest. Any hope that may have begun to grow during the 1920's was shattered during this decade of mass unemployment and the growing spread of Fascism. In America, novelists concerned with the plight of victims of the Depression used realistic methods to depict graphically the effects of economic privation. James T. Farrell's *Studs Lonigan* trilogy (1932-1935) is one of the best of a number of American works during the period that present "a corrupt and vicious social order that [the novelist believed] must be destroyed" (Allen, *The Modern Novel in Britain and the United States*). Farrell was one of a number of writers on both sides of the Atlantic who for a time adopted Communism as an alternative to the capitalistic society that was apparently responsible for the condition of life in the Western world in the 1930's.

During the same period, another significant American novelist first began to publish. John Steinbeck's *In Dubious Battle* (1936) deals directly with the problems of workers and the possibilities and restrictions Communism offered. From Steinbeck, America received its greatest literary treatment of the effects of the Depression. *The Grapes of Wrath* (1939) is the story of the Joad family, poor farmers who leave the Dust Bowl of Oklahoma for a better life in California, only to find that conditions there are no better, sometimes worse. Because the plight of the Joads and the other families in this novel appeared so typical, and because their stories were presented so poignantly (often melodramatically), *The Grapes of Wrath* became a parable of the American migrant, and, much like early works of Charles Dickens or Harriet Beecher Stowe's *Uncle Tom's Cabin* (1852), the novel provided a rallying point for reformers, a propaganda piece in the hands of those attempting to aid the victims of a decade of hard living and almost inhuman suffering.

While a group of daring young men and women in England were experimenting with the form of the novel and their counterparts in America fulfilling their role as members of the Lost Generation, a large number of writers, less concerned with artistry than with entertainment, continued to provide the public with what is now referred to as "popular literature." Much of the best-seller material of the 1920's and 1930's lasted no more than a season. One form of popular fiction, however, rose to a new level of prominence, and achieved notice for its artistry both from contemporary critics and in succeeding decades. Detective fiction, fathered by Edgar Allan Poe almost a century earlier and brought to fame by Sir Arthur Conan Doyle at the turn of the century, reached a new level of artistic merit during the period between the wars. In England, Dorothy Sayers and Agatha Christie entered the literary scene, creating detective heroes who would rival the legendary Sherlock Holmes in the public eye. In America, Dashiell Hammett led the way for a number of gifted storytellers whose brand of detective thriller differed noticeably from the British version of the genre. The genteel, intellectual pursuit of the criminal, characteristic of Sayers' Lord Peter Wimsey and Christie's Hercule Poirot, was replaced by the tough-guy tactics of hard-boiled characters such as Hammett's Sam Spade. In England, Graham Greene explored in his thrillers, especially *Brighton Rock* (1938), the violent world that had recently received much attention in the newspapers. In the next half-century, bookstores and public libraries would become filled with the novels of these early mystery-writers and their many successors, and the works of the best of them—writers such as Hammett, Raymond Chandler, and Ross Macdonald—would gradually achieve the recognition generally reserved for "mainstream" fiction.

During this period of exceptional literary activity, the publication of a group of novels by a single Mississippi author highlighted the emergence of Southern fiction. William Faulkner had been writing for a decade and had already published three novels and several short stories when *The Sound and the Fury* appeared in 1929. That novel was followed in rapid succession by *As I Lay Dying* (1930), *Sanctuary* (1931), *Light in August* (1932), and *Absalom, Absalom!* (1936), all of which depicted the fate of the South through the lives of generations of men and women in Faulkner's mythical Yoknapatawpha County. Earlier novels and stories had provided some details about these characters, and later ones, notably *Go Down, Moses* (1942), *Requiem for a Nun* (1951), and the trilogy consisting of *The Hamlet* (1940), *The Town* (1957), and *The Mansion* (1959), round out the portrait of a community that is representative of its region in a way that is unlike any other work by an American author.

Faulkner also dealt with philosophical issues that may have been apparent only to one steeped in traditions such as those found in the South; what he had learned, and what he attempted to portray both in his stories and through the texture of his prose, was the inextricable link between past and present.

The evils upon which Southern society had been built, especially the evil of slavery, remain to entrap even those who, living in the "enlightened" twentieth century, try to put the past behind them. Comprehensive in his view of society, Faulkner presents a cast of characters from all walks of life who share the plight of the Southerner, and who are ultimately destroyed by it: the Compsons, the Sutpens, and blacks such as Charles Bon (*Absalom, Absalom!*) and Joe Christmas (*Light in August*). He also presents characters who endure, such as Dilsey the black housekeeper, the poor farm girl Lena (*Light in August*), and the chameleonlike Snopes family, who attain the reader's grudging admiration for their stubbornness and adaptability, despite their overriding amorality.

Faulkner stands at the forefront of a group of Southern writers, many of whom emerged during the period between the wars and were influenced in one way or another by the Fugitives, a coterie of artists and academics founded early in the century at Vanderbilt University in Nashville, Tennessee. Allen Tate and Robert Penn Warren, both members of this group, wrote works that attempted to define and explain the special conditions that set the South apart from the rest of America. Warren's *All the King's Men* (1946), a fiction based on the political career of Louisiana demagogue Huey Long, achieved popular success and has been critically acclaimed for its sensitive portrait of the characters whose lives fall under the spell of the political tyrant. Carson McCullers, like Faulkner, focuses on the rural and small-town South, presenting a kaleidoscope of characters, many of them physically impaired, to suggest the moral condition of the region. Flannery O'Connor fuses the grotesque and the transcendant in a distinctively Southern vision which has exercised a great influence on contemporary fiction-writers, not only in the South but also in the other regions.

The end of the 1930's found the world once again aroused to arms in a conflict that, like its predecessor, would change the shape of both serious and popular fiction. The novelists' reaction to World War II, however, was quite different from what it had been to World War I. Before England's and, later, America's first encounters with the realities of modern warfare, people had shared a tenuous kind of idealism; the novels of the post-World War I period reflected the disillusionment, horror, and cynicism of those who had seen for the first time what such a war was really like. Works about World War I were often crude, but the sentiments they expressed were shocking to their audience. The novels of World War II, by contrast, are more sophisticated, but the serious novelist found himself reacting to a different kind of problem from that which had faced his predecessors after World War I.

During the first two decades after World War II, a great many "war novels" were published, far more than had been generated in the 1920's and 1930's. Many of these works, however, were merely popular potboilers, not serious attempts to investigate the causes or conditions of the conflict. Among novels that did make an attempt to come to grips with the impact of World War II on those who participated in it, Norman Mailer's *The Naked and the Dead* (1948) offered the best portrait of life in battle as it affects men of different geographical and ideological backgrounds. In Mailer's work, one can see the irony that characterizes many of the new war novels. Through a careful juxtaposition of scenes, Mailer depicts the common soldier plodding through the seemingly meaningless tasks that war brings, and the grand strategy of those in charge. The goal of the army in this novel is the capture of an island in the Pacific. That goal is achieved not through brilliant planning or heroic action, but rather through accident and blundering. To make matters worse, the success of the army accomplishes nothing to help the war effort. Mailer's novel is a study in the effects of power in men's lives, and the changes that war may bring into their lives, but it does not appear to be saying something new about the nature of modern warfare.

Mailer's inability to offer something new is characteristic of many writers of this period. The novelists writing about World War II lacked the advantage of "shock value" as a means of gaining their readers' attention and sympathy. Although the machinery of mass destruction was more devastating than in World War I, World War II produced almost no real surprises except for the destructive power of the atomic bomb, which has been one of the most pervasive, if subtle, influences on literature since the 1940's.

The explosion of the atomic bomb provides a new dividing line for fiction, but one must be careful not to insist too strongly that all literature changed immediately and irrevocably after August, 1945. As had happened after World War I, both in England and in America, many novelists who had established their reputations before the conflict continued to publish during the first postwar decade, and much of their work follows themes worked out either completely or partially in earlier novels. Greene continued to explore religious and moral questions under the guise of thrillers. Waugh continued to write satire. Anthony Powell, who had published five novels in the 1930's, began in the postwar years his masterpiece, *A Dance to the Music of Time*, a series of twelve novels published between 1951 and 1975. Hemingway's novels of the late 1940's and 1950's, show little advance in theme over those of the 1930's. Faulkner continued his saga of the Yoknapatawpha County, crystallizing a world within the borders of this Mississippi region.

The "new voices" in literature were different, though; the young novelist now faced the horror that at any time, man could conceivably destroy himself; the ultimate achievement of Western civilization was, sadly, the perfection of destruction. The novels that deal directly with the possibility and the effects of a nuclear holocaust have been surprisingly few. The subject has not lacked treatment in nonfiction, but in fiction, it has been largely the purview of popular novelists whose sensationalistic treatment has titillated the reading public and aroused momentary curiosity or fear without providing serious study of either the problem or its potential solution. With but few exceptions, the modern writer, choosing to avoid direct confrontation with the issue, has opted instead to examine the experience of people who live daily in the shadow of the threat that total destruction poses.

The Cold War and the threat of nuclear holocaust did give rise to a host of thrillers—spy stories, tales of adventures and intrigue, conventional mysteries—which adapted the traditional formulas that had made these kinds of novels popular since the turn of the century. The international spy novel achieved a new level of prominence, and Ian Fleming's slim volumes about a British intelligence agent gave his own country and America a new hero, . James Bond. A combination of bravado, exceptional knowledge and intelligence, charm, and sex appeal made Bond and the dozens of other characters who populate the world of the spy novel immediate successes with the mass reading public that sought escapism rather than serious investigation of modern problems. Not all spy novels, however, are to be dismissed as escapist fare, written in the slapdash manner of the Bond saga. The novels of John le Carré, for example, distinguished works by any standards, capture the ambience of the Cold War years, the "climate of betrayal," with great authority and insight.

Perhaps the primary issue for the artist of this period became the assertion of the self in a society that promoted anonymity. The group of new writers who emerged after World War II in Britain have often been classed with their fellow dramatists as the "Angry Young Men." Writing about a society in which mobility among classes was becoming much easier, novelists such as John Wain, Kingsley Amis, John Braine, and Doris Lessing struck out against institutions that remained to signal the vestiges of class distinction. Some, like Amis, turned to comedy as the medium for social commentary. Others, Lessing among them, composed sociological dramas in which the line between fiction and reportage is often blurred.

Curiously, many of these writers turned away from the experimental methods of the giants of literature in the preceding generation, finding that older forms of narrative better suited their purposes. The British novels of the 1950's and after often appeared to be throwbacks to their predecessors of a century or more: picaresque, farce, even the massive sweep of society that characterized the Victorian novel appeared once again in the hands of men and women whose avowed purpose was to hold the mirror up to contemporary society.

What makes these novelists quite different from their predecessors is the relativism—moral as well as social—that characterizes their fiction. Even the novelists of the 1920's and 1930's wrote with a sense that absolutes may exist, or indeed did exist. That certainty is almost completely absent in the works of the new generation. The hero of post-World War II novels is most likely to be an existential man, given to establishing his own norms and defining his existence by setting himself up against the flux of experience that he encounters around him. Beneath the comedy of Amis' *Lucky Jim* (1954) or the political rantings of Lessing's early novels there is a strain of metaphysical existentialism that links these works to those of Camus and Jean-Paul Sartre as closely as their form or ostensible subject may link them to their British ancestors.

The reason for this is simple. As James Gindin has observed, "Almost all the contemporary novels are searches for identity, efforts on the part of the hero to understand and to define who or what he is" (*Postwar British Fiction*, 1962). The search to find or define the self, to establish an identity that sets one apart from mass society, is often the goal of modern heroes. Unlike his predecessors, however, the modern hero is often self-questioning, a kind of antihero given to failure and sometimes the victim of acute neurosis or even paranoia.

One of the more common methods adopted by postwar novelists to portray the conflict between the individual and society is the use of an outsider as hero or protagonist. A great number of recent American novels have such characters as heroes: Truman Capote's homosexuals, Saul Bellow's and Bernard Malamud's Jews, the black heroes of James Baldwin and Ralph Ellison.

Two novelists who emerged in the 1950's, Saul Bellow and Bernard Malamud, may serve to represent the course that writers in the mainstream of modern fiction have taken. As observers and recorders of modern American society, both Bellow and Malamud captured the essential frustration that the individual feels when facing the leviathan that modern society has become. In the case of Bellow, much of his fiction is influenced by his Jewish background, but that often provides merely a point of departure for works that explore the modern condition in much broader terms. His *The Adventures of Augie March* (1953), for example, a picaresque novel set in the era of the Great Depression, displays the universal struggle of the individual to free himself from the shackles of society. In *Henderson the Rain King* (1959), Bellow's hero abandons modern society in favor of a more primitive mode of living in Africa, in order to be reborn, as it were, into a new life of self-awareness and to develop a deeper appreciation for himself and others.

Bernard Malamud—like Bellow, of Jewish background—introduced his heritage into his novels with great advantage in works such as *The Assistant* (1957). In that novel, the universal problem of man's desire to achieve moral excellence is treated with great irony, as the hero, an assistant in a small store run by a Jewish family, first tries to take advantage of the family members (robbing from the store, seducing the daughter), but later undergoes a change of heart and carries on the business when the father dies. The hero's acceptance of others' burdens gives the story a particularly poignant quality that, though it borders on the melodramatic, never becomes so.

In the case of both writers, the hero is often on the fringe of society (Bellow's

Augie March) or a subgroup of society (the Gentile assistant in Malamud's novel) or he consciously abandons modern, urban society to find personal meaning for his life outside it (Henderson). In almost every case, the individual is tested to establish meaning for his life outside of or against society, not within it—suggesting that to meld with the society is to become faceless, a kind of nonperson who counts for nothing. Because life has meaning only in the here and now (the existentialist view certainly predominates these works), the nonperson who fades into the anonymity of the mass society is lost forever. A rage to assert the self against the forces that foster anonymity burns within the heart of many modern heroes.

As a result, it is not surprising to find social causes that promote individual identity and individual worth being celebrated in novels that treat the question of identity. During the 1950's and 1960's in America, several works of significance about the plight of the American black made a mark on the literary scene. As black Americans became more aware of their heritage, they learned that blacks had been writing literature for as long as they had been living in America, and that works depicting the black experience had been circulating for some time. Only a few, such as Richard Wright's *Native Son* (1940) and Ralph Ellison's *Invisible Man* (1952), had received widespread critical attention. Fine works such as Arna Bontemps' *Black Thunder* (1937), a historical novel about Gabriel Prosser's aborted slave rebellion in the early nineteenth century, had gone largely unnoticed. The interest in black studies generated during the late 1960's and the 1970's, among Americans both black and white, led to the "discovery" of numerous writers whose works have expanded the boundaries of American fiction.

The larger problems of man's search for his identity could be most poignantly displayed by writers who had themselves been the victims of discrimination that caused them to *be* nonpersons, and these authors produced powerful testimonies to the struggle that oppressed people face in preserving their identity and dignity in a world hostile toward them. Ellison's *Invisible Man* has been called "quite simply the most profound novel about American identity since the war" (Tony Tanner, *City of Words*, 1971). Among black writers who began to receive acclaim in the 1950's, James Baldwin emerged as a major literary figure whose writing presented the black experience candidly and forcefully in novels that are artistically excellent. Baldwin's ability to portray the anger and the pathos of his characters without preaching or moralizing makes works such as *Go Tell It on the Mountain* (1953) and *The Fire Next Time* (1963) stand out among the thousands of post-World War II novels that dramatize contemporary American social problems.

While a number of major novelists were exploring contemporary issues in traditional forms, others, employing a method designated as "fabulation" by the critic Robert Scholes (*Fabulation and Metafiction*, 1979), abandoned attempts at verisimilitude and opted instead to create conscious artifices that moved "away from direct representation of the surface of reality," but which approached "actual human life by way of ethically controlled fantasy." Many important novelists, among them William Gass, Robert Coover, Kurt Vonnegut, Donald Barthelme, and John Barth, produced works that clearly share the qualities of fabulation: concern with design and structure, use of the absurd or surreal, a tendency toward allegory, and formal and narrative characteristics of the Romance tradition as opposed to those normally associated with the novel. At the center of the aesthetic of the fabulators is a belief expressed succinctly by one of their exemplars, John Hawkes, that "the true enemies of the novel [are] plot, character, setting, and theme"; for Hawkes, "structure—verbal and psychological coherence" is the primary concern. For such writers, "realism" is no more than one of many formal constructs available to the novelist.

Critical attention in the 1980's shifted from fabulation and metafiction to a related but distinct mode, postmodernism, a style or movement which, many critics argue, is characteristic of the arts at the end of the twentieth century. Definitions of postmodernism in the arts—and in literature in particular— vary in their emphases, but among the qualities said to define postmodern fiction are a fondness for pastiche (the imitation of readily identifiable styles, whether of an individual author or of a genre), a breakdown of the traditional distinction between high art and popular art, and a rejection of any claims to transcendent truth.

The novels of Thomas Pynchon, perhaps the most widely studied American novelist of the generation that began publishing in the 1960's, are often cited as seminal works of postmodern fiction. In novels such as *The Crying of Lot 49* (1966), *Gravity's Rainbow* (1973), and *Vineland* (1990), obscene ditties and references to kitschy television shows go hand in hand with casually displayed esoteric lore and technological expertise. Articulating the fears and hopes of many of his contemporaries, Pynchon's novels evoke both the insidious menace of power-structures of all kinds and the persistent undercurrent of resistance to their imperious demands. The Indian-born British writer Salman Rushdie, whose novel *The Satanic Verses* (1988) became an international *cause célèbre*, is also frequently mentioned as one of the leading postmodern novelists. Drawing on his experience of two cultures, Rushdie's novels are marked by a deliberately jarring stylistic range, outrageous puns and other forms of wordplay, a mixture of the mundane and the fantastic, and a mocking dismissal of established systems of belief.

The "death of the novel" has been regularly predicted for several decades, but as the twentieth century comes to a close the obituary appears to be premature. Many talented writers are producing work across the whole spectrum of fictional styles. Indeed, there seems little chance that the novel will disappear completely, for as Voltaire once observed, "Fiction is truth in disguise." As long as men and women wish to apprehend and understand the truth about themselves and their world, the novel stands a better than even chance of remaining a viable means of communicating that truth.

Laurence W. Mazzeno

THE ENGLISH NOVEL

To a greater extent than any other literary form, the novel is consistently and directly engaged with the society in which the writer lives and feels compelled to explain, extol, or criticize. The English novel, from its disparate origins to its development in the eighteenth century, from its rise in the nineteenth century to its present perilous state, has been strongly influenced by the social, political, economic, scientific, and cultural history of England. As a realistic form, the novel not only reflects but also helps define and focus society's sense of itself, and as the novel reflects the growth of England first into a United Kingdom, then into an empire, and its decline to its present role in the Commonwealth of Nations, it does so predominantly through the eyes of the middle class.

Indeed, the origins and development of the English novel are most profitably examined in relation to the increasing growth and eventual dominance of the middle class in the course of the past two-and-a-half centuries. Typically concerned with middle-class characters in a world largely of their making, the novel sometimes features excursions into the upper reaches of English society; with more frequency, it presents incursions by members of the upper class into the familiar world of the solid middle class. As a form of realistic literature intended primarily for the middle class, often for their instruction and edification (or excoriation), the novel frequently depicts the worlds of the lower orders of society, not only the exotic cultures subjugated by Imperial Britain, but also the familiarly strange domestic worlds of the "criminal classes," a subculture with its own hierarchies, vocabulary, customs, and occupations.

As distinguished from allegory and romance, the English novel has for its primary focus the individual situated in society, his or her emotions, thoughts, actions, choices, and relationships to others in complex and often bewildering environments. Set against backgrounds that realistically reflect all facets of the English experience, the "histories" or "lives" of the novels' protagonists must hold a necessary interest for readers who, in turn, seek to make sense of, master, cope with, escape from, or become fully assimilated into the society in which they, like their heroes and heroines, find themselves. While any attempt to trace with great particularity the multiple relationships between the history of the English novel and the larger patterns of English society must remain necessarily imperfect, the general outlines of those relationships can be sketched.

Although longstanding debates about the origin of the English novel and the first English novel continue, it is both convenient and just to state that it is with the fiction of Daniel Defoe (1660-1731) that the first novel, in the sense that term came to have in the late eighteenth century and continues to have, appeared. Without considerable injustice it may be said that the novel first developed out of a series of false starts in the seventeenth century and a series of accidents in the eighteenth. The reading public, having been exposed to large amounts of novelistic material, fictions of various lengths, epics and prose romances, appears to have been ready to receive a form that went beyond Aphra Behn's *Oroonoko* (1688), John Bunyan's *The Pilgrim's Progress* (1678), and the works of earlier masters such as Thomas Malory, John Mandeville, Robert Greene, Thomas Dekker, and Thomas Nashe. Such a form would emphasize unified action of some plausibility, considerably individualize and articulate characters, and present stories with such verisimilitude that the readers could find in them highly wrought illusions of the realities they knew best.

The literary children of the eighteenth century, the novel and its sibling the short story, created a taste for fiction of all varieties in a middle-class readership whose ranks were swollen by a newly literate mercantile class. This readership appears to have wanted and certainly received a literary medium of their own, filled with practically minded characters who spoke the same middle-class English language and prized the same middle-class English goals (financial and familial success) as they themselves did. In general, the novel helped make the position of the individual in new, expanding, and increasingly urban social contexts more intelligible; frequently addressed directly to the "dear reader," the novel presented unified visions of individuals in society, the cultural and social conditions of that society, and the rationalist psychology fostered by Francis Bacon, Thomas Hobbes, and John Locke and endemic to the age.

The merchant class had, of course, existed for centuries and had steadily grown in the Age of Discovery and during colonization in the seventeenth century. In that century, a number of events conspired to begin the disestablishment of the feudal, medieval world, a disestablishment that would become final in the early nineteenth century. The beginning of the English Revolution (1641) marked the most noteworthy outbreak of religious and class strife England had yet seen. The subsequent regicide of Charles I in 1649 and the abolition of monarchy and the House of Lords by the House of Commons in that year signaled the formation of the Puritan Commonwealth (1649-1660) and the first rise to political power by the middle class, a rise that the Restoration of the monarchy (Charles II, 1660) checked for a time. In the Glorious Revolution of 1688, Parliament invited William of Orange and his wife, Mary, the Protestant daughter of the Catholic James II, to rule England. James II (the "Old Pretender") fled to France with his son Charles (the "Young Pretender" or "Bonnie Prince Charlie"), established himself in exile and began plotting a return to power that would eventuate in the Scottish rebellions of 1715, 1719, and 1745-1746 on behalf of the Stuart monarchy. The Glorious Revolution may, in part, be seen as establishing the principle that the English people, through Parliament, could choose their own ruler; it may also be seen as another phase in the growth of power of the middle class.

A war with France (1689-1697) saw the beginning of the national debt, but the late seventeenth and early eighteenth centuries (especially during the reign of Queen Anne, 1702-1714) were marked by material progress, increased mercantilism, drastically increased population, and the beginning of an irreversible shift of population from the country to the city. Apart from two major trade monopolies (the Hudson Bay Company in Canada and the East India Company in the Indian subcontinent), trade was open to all after 1689. Free enterprise flourished and with it the middle class, as early eighteenth century England became a mercantile society teetering on the brink of the Industrial Revolution and the concurrent scientific revolution that abetted it. While the governance of England still rested with a relatively small number of families, the hereditary landowners of England had to share power with the new merchant princes of the era.

In this milieu the earliest English novels emerged. Rooted both in the picaresque tradition stemming from the anonymous Spanish *Lazarillo de Tormes* (1553) and Miguel de Cervantes' *Don Quixote de la Mancha* (1605, 1615) and in the pseudohistorical tradition, Daniel Defoe's novels present their fictions as fact, as the "histories" or "lives" of Robinson Crusoe, Colonel Newport, and Moll Flanders, for example. Defoe's novels are distinguished by a realism that employs minute and concerted observations, and a morality that—despite lapses, an occasional blind eye to folly, and some ambiguous presentations of vice—fits well with the morality of the middle class, especially when erstwhile sinners repent and exemplify the Protestant virtues of seriousness, usefulness, social responsibility, and thrift. Like their many literary descendants, Defoe's characters evince a cheerful triumph of person over place and situation, an eventual mastery of the world and its too familiar snares in the common and the uncommon adventures that form their educative encounters with the world and with themselves.

Even more obviously in line with middle-class Puritan ethics is the work of Samuel Richardson (1689-1761), whose epistolary novels of personality, sensibility, and moral conflict present the first multidimensional characters in English prose fiction. *Pamela* (1740) began by accident what Walter Allen calls the "first great flowering of the English novel." Commissioned to compose and print *Familiar Letters* as models of correspondence, moral guides, and repositories of advice to "handsome girls," Richardson expanded the project until it became *Pamela: Or, Virtue Rewarded*. The particular virtue rewarded is chastity, in the face of assaults from a member of the Squirearchy, Mr. B., who is, ironically, a Justice of the Peace. One important artistic concern in the novel is the power of the written word to effect the conversion of wayward characters. One could take the view that Pamela's epistles reinforce traditionally Christian, or social, or merely prudential morality and that they also represent the generally desirable triumph of a member of the lower-middle class over representatives of the upper-middle class and the titled upper class. Virtue is, Richardson suggests, its own reward; it is all the better if it brings other rewards prized by the middle class.

Following Defoe, whose fiction offered a journalistic facticity, and Richardson, who wrote transparent moral sermons, Henry Fielding (1707-1754) was the first to write avowed novels and to depict ordinary English life and the panorama of his age. Like Richardson's, Fielding's beginning as a novelist was fortuitous. Sir Robert Walpole served George I and George II as Prime Minister from 1721 to 1742 and for much of that time he was the object of satire at the hands of several playwrights, Fielding among them. With Walpole's successful introduction of the Licensing Act of 1737, Fielding's career as a dramatist ended, and he turned his ironic and satiric vision to the new prose form, the novel, perfecting that form, many argue, in *Tom Jones* (1749). His *Amelia* (1751) is the first novel of social reform and thus was a point of reference for Charles Dickens and the many contributors to the "Newgate novel" in the nineteenth century. In *Amelia*, Fielding clearly exposes social wrongs and provides possible remedies for them. His portrayal of gambling dens, prison life, and the omnipresent Hogarthian gin mills foreshadows the excessive realism (or naturalism) of Honoré de Balzac and Émile Zola in France and George Moore in late Victorian England.

Two other great eighteenth century novelists, Tobias Smollett (1721-1771) and Laurence Sterne (1713-1768), added various dimensions of eighteenth century English life to the novel's inventory. Smollett brought to the novel the first extended account of one fundament of English trade, prosperity, and adventure—seafaring life (*Roderick Random*, 1748); and, like Fielding and Defoe, he used English military history as background material for some of the finest English picaresque novels. Sterne, in *Tristram Shandy* (1759-1767), departed from the norm that his contemporaries had established, introducing a stream-of-consciousness technique to refract society through the prism of an individual mind, a technique that would not be further developed until the early twentieth century in the novels of James Joyce and Virginia Woolf.

By the end of the eighteenth century, both the novel of sentiment and the Gothic novel had appeared in *The Vicar of Wakefield* (1766) by Oliver Goldsmith (1728-1774) and *The Castle of Otranto* (1765) by Horace Walpole (1717-1797). While Goldsmith's work and others like it continue in prose the situations and characteristics of the highly popular sentimental domestic drama of middle-class life, Walpole's novel exists outside of the conventions of eighteenth century thought and fiction. His is the only novel of those mentioned above that does not take as its premise the world as it exists, society in the country or city, and the generally agreed upon concept of the possible as coextensive with the real.

An emphasis upon shared, common experience and consensus unified society and its conception of itself intellectually, philosophically, and psychologically. This society, in many respects the first truly modern society, emerged near the end of the seventeenth century into an era of Enlightenment and took for its tenets common sense, secular reason, science, and gentility. One fundamental emphasis of this era was upon the necessity to treat life and its problems in the spirit of reason and scientific empiricism rather than in the traditional spirit of appeal to authority and dogma. In this era, the landed gentry and not a few of the merchant princes regarded themselves as "Augustans" and sought to imitate the values and beliefs of the Roman patricians of the age of Augustus. In so doing, they set the intellectual tone of their times by asserting rationalism (and skepticism) as the primary focus of thought, by insisting upon symmetry in all phases of life as well as of art, on artificial ornament and the preference of artifice to "nature," on reserved dignity in preference to any form of enthusiasm, on expansive, urbane sophistication instead of narrow, superstitious thought. It comes, then, as an extraordinary incongruity to find not only Walpole's work but also other novels of horror written, avidly read, and widely praised in this neoclassical Age of Reason.

Nevertheless, Walpole's Gothic story was immensely successful, quite probably so in reaction to the restraint of the age, the dominion exercised by the Protestant ethic, and the evangelicalism of the century born in the advent of Wesleyanism and Methodism. In his conscious outlandishness, Walpole set a new course for fiction. His horrific pseudomedieval tale was followed by the Gothic novels of Clara Reeve (1729-1807), Ann (Ward) Radcliffe (1764-1823)—especially her *The Mysteries of Udolpho* (1794)—Matthew Gregory "Monk" Lewis (1775-1818), and numerous novels of the Romantic period.

The last quarter of the eighteenth century, a period that saw the beginnings of Romanticism, featured the remarkable first ministry of William Pitt, the Younger (1759-1806), a ministry that laid the foundation for much of the reform movement in the nineteenth century. The intellectual tenets of the Augustan Age, already called into question by the Gothic novelists and several poets of the age, were about to suffer a sea change in the triumph of individualism that characterized Romanticism. Economically, however, England maintained rather than altered its newfound tradition of progress, legitimatized by the writings of David Ricardo and Adam Smith. The advances of industry and capitalism begun early in the Augustan Age continued and ensured an economic boom that, with very few setbacks, was to characterize the nineteenth century and fuel the expansion of Empire. Culturally, the pre-Romantic period was marked by an extraordinary growth in literacy, helped in great part by the growth of charity schools, the drive to regularize and teach English (if only for commercial purposes), the increasing new opportunities for the education of women, and the establishment and development of circulating libraries.

Two writers of this transitional period—the era, roughly speaking, between the outbreak of unrest in the American colonies in the early 1770's and the accession of Queen Victoria (1837)—stand apart from the mainstream of the rapidly changing world in which they lived. One, Jane Austen (1775-1817), epitomized an age that had already passed; the other, Sir Walter Scott (1771-1832), eschewed his own world except to the extent that he could translate some of its characteristics to other times. Jane Austen's works, unpublished until the second decade of the nineteenth century, are the last novels of the Enlightenment. Unlike those of the other great eighteenth century novels, the characters presented by "the great feminine Augustan" are drawn almost exclusively from the landed gentry. In her novels she presents minute descriptions of the members of that class, their characters, beliefs, aspirations, and hopes in a period marked by a strong desire for stability on the part of the gentry despite the fact that they were surrounded by the armies of change. A supremely accomplished novelist, Jane Austen set the pattern for all subsequent novels of manners and family. Her characters interest themselves in issues of importance only to themselves—social position, socially and financially advantageous marriages, and the orderly passage of property from one generation to the next. The portraits that emerge are absolutely dissimilar to those of Fielding and his fellows and are essentially those of the placid, insulated upper class; as such, they present not only highly wrought pictures of the gentry but also invaluable insights into a social stratum that has utterly vanished in the present century.

Sir Walter Scott's Romantic novels, unlike Jane Austen's works, deal with the world as it might have been rather than as it then was. His novels transplant nineteenth century heroes of sense, sensibility, and virtue to remote places or historically distant times. Moreover, his pioneer work in shaping the historical consciousness and national identity of Scotland while recounting its seventeenth century and eighteenth century history and his novels of Medieval and Renaissance Britain won him a place as a universally respected novelist of his century.

Both Austen and Scott are anomalies. Austen clearly summarizes the Augustan Age and its concerns, and Scott is surely the spokesman of a movement that grew in the last decades of the eighteenth century and took hold as the dominant intellectual mode of subsequent centuries, Romanticism. Though his novels rarely treat of the world in which he lived, Scott's perceptions were conditioned by the growing intellectual and emotional tenets of Romanticism. Although he sought to explore the political and social conditions of earlier times in English and Scottish history, he consistently chose not to recognize the inescapable facts of the Industrial Revolution, the expensive (both in money and in lives) wars England waged in his own time, and the bloodless social revolution that saw the gentry finally replaced by the middle class as the political and economic rulers of England. The largest element of Scott's Romanticism is a studied medievalism which may be viewed as an escapist alternative (of considerable psychological necessity) to the pervasive and turbulent revolutions in every sector of society and as a reassertion of fundamental and traditional values. One benefit Scott gained by focusing upon Romantic medievalism as his chief fictional concern is that he thereby escaped the social censure and ostracism other Romantics experienced. Not only did he achieve personal respectability as a poet-turned-novelist, but also he created such a large and insatiable reading public for his and others' novels that the novel became and remains the most popular form of literature.

The Victorian novelists, and Charles Dickens as the greatest of them, mark a new era in the novel, an era in which the primary middle-class emphasis on its own place in society and the reformation of society in its own image came to the fore. Society itself expanded in the Victorian Age to include not only England and the United Kingdom but also an empire upon which, proverbially, the sun never set. In consequence, novelists, in their characters, backgrounds, and plots, often surveyed an empire that extended geographically to all continents, covering fully one-tenth of the earth's surface, and financially to the entire populated world. Trade and tradesmen literally moved the empire, opened Australia and Canada to colonization, brought India into the fold (first via the East India Company and then, in 1857, under the Crown) and brought about the foundation of the corporate world with the Companies' Act of 1862.

The reform movement, in part attributable to the Romantic rebellion and in larger part to the middle-class redefinition of societal ideals, came to partial fruition in the 1820's and flourished in the 1830's and in subsequent decades. The hated and inflationary measure of 1815 prohibiting grain imports, the Corn Law, was modified in 1828; the Combination Acts of the era illustrate the pronounced middle-class opposition to trade unionism; the repeal of the Test Act (1828) and the passage of the Catholic Emancipation Bill (1829) brought about a liberalization of attitudes toward Roman Catholics and extended political franchise to a large number of men; the Third Reform Bill (1832) abolished slavery in the empire; the Factory Act (1833) regulated working hours and required two hours of schooling daily for children under the age of thirteen; the New Poor Law (1834) represented another phase of regularizing governmental services and social programs. These reforms typify, without nearly exhausting, the great social legislation of this era. Reform was the byword of the early decades of the nineteenth century and the hallmark of the entire Victorian era as English society evolved. Subsequent reforms in suffrage, for example, seem to have moved at a glacial pace and only included women in 1928, but each new enfranchisement under the ministerial guidance of Benjamin Disraeli and William Gladstone added appreciably to the power of the middle class.

Conditions for novelists also improved in nineteenth century England. As the eighteenth century marked the end of patronage as the primary support of artists and writers, so the explosion of periodicals, the multiplication of newspapers, the growth of publishing firms, and the extension of consumerism to literary works in the nineteenth century made it possible for more writers to try to live by and from the pen. "Grub Street" had meant, since the mid-eighteenth century, hard times for writers such as Dr. Samuel Johnson and Oliver Goldsmith, and in the eighteenth century the supply of writers far exceeded the demand. This, too, was the case in the nineteenth century, but less severely so, and it remains the case despite the paperback, magazine, and other media revolutions of the twentieth century. It has often been suggested that Charles Dickens, William Makepeace Thackeray,and most popular novelists of the century whose novels were first serialized in journals and magazines wrote at such length because they were paid by the line of print; while padding is one possible consequence of such a method of publication and payment, the leisurely pace of the novel, its descriptiveness and its length, date from the eighteenth century and grew without regard to such payment schedules.

The Victorian novel as exemplified in the works of Charles Dickens (1812-1870) not only describes life but competes with it as well. Here one finds a verisimilitude so persuasive that the swarming complexities of Victorian life seem fixed in the novels. While carrying on the traditional celebration of middle-class values, Dickens also tried to make sense of the complex variety of choices open to his readers, of the fabric of society (by explaining, exposing, and mythologizing the middle class), of the ills of his society (by exposing them and calling for their reform), and of the patent injustices of capitalist society (by emphasizing their consequences, the plight of the victims of injustice, and the dehumanization of its perpetrators). To all of these concerns Dickens added a sense of comedy that suffused his early and some of his middle work but that changed to ferocity in his last complete novel, arguably his best after *Bleak House* (1852-1853), *Our Mutual Friend* (1864-1866).

Like Scott and many of his own contemporaries, Dickens is not above providing in his fiction a psychological escape from the mechanized world of his readers, as in *Pickwick Papers* (1836-1837), a genteel picaresque work set in the period before the Age of Steam. Little else but artificially contrived escape exists for the reader and the protagonist of *Oliver Twist* (1837-1839), an intense (and in its initial chapters unrelieved) examination of the workhouse system, one of the more depressing phenomena of the reform movement. Similarly, his descriptions of the criminal classes (so severely criticized, especially in regard to his depiction of child criminals and prostitutes, that he felt compelled to document his observations in the Preface to the novel's second edition) illustrate the predatory relationship of this class to all other classes and form an indictment of the society that spawned and neglected them, an indictment that Dickens reiterated in *Bleak House* and elsewhere. Dickens the social reformer achieves some of his most enduring effects by indulging in the sentimentalism inherent in the sort of melodrama popular in the Victorian Age and still popular in some sectors today.

The Chancery Court and the legal system are the objects of Dickens' satiric wrath in *Bleak House*, a novel that amply illustrates that "the Law is a Ass," while in few other novels has the middle-class Gospel of Wealth been so soundly condemned as in *Dombey and Son* (1846-1848). It is significant that the railway appears for the first time in Dickens' works in this novel. Dickens cast a cold eye on another English social institution, debtor's prison, in *Little Dorrit* (1855-1857), in which London's Marshalsea Prison is the primary setting. On a smaller canvas in *Hard Times* (1854), he took on the Gradgrinds of British industrial Coketowns, complete with their belief in the dullest of "facts."

Similar social issues and notions of reform appear in the Newgate novels (picaresque tales of crime and punishment by incarceration in Newgate Prison) and in the important work of the novelist Elizabeth Gaskell (1810-1865). Both Gaskell and Charles Kingsley (*Alton Locke*, 1850) did much to introduce the working class or proletarian figure as a central focus of fiction, a focus Thomas Hardy would further sharpen late in the century.

William Makepeace Thackeray (1811-1863), a contemporary and sometime friend of Dickens, presented the world of the upper-middle class and limited his novels to that sphere. His *Vanity Fair* (1847-1848) eschewed the conventional novel of intrigue and focused on the steady social climb of Becky Sharp from the position of governess to the ranks of the leisured gentry, a new class only possible to the England of empire and Industrial Revolution. Thackeray is at pains to glorify the virtues of the upper-middle class and to bolster them through his fiction: marriage, home, and children constitute the proper society he portrays. Surely it is still possible to see in these ideals the safe harbors they had become for Victorians: it is also possible to view them as indicative of the societal dichotomy present in nearly every aspect of Victorian thought, a dichotomy that, in this case, emphasized an intense desire for security while positing the need for the adventurous life of acquisition. Like many of his predecessors and contemporaries, Thackeray turned his hand to the historical novel to explore from a nineteenth century perspective the social and literary life of the Queen Anne era, the Jacobite plots to return the Stuarts to monarchy, and the campaigns of the Duke of Marlborough.

Anthony Trollope (1815-1882) brought to the novel two new subject areas drawn from Victorian life: in his Barsetshire novels he introduced the first accurate portraits of English clerics; in his political or parliamentary novels he presented accurate descriptions of English politicians and political life rivaled only by those of Benjamin Disraeli (1804-1881), the first Earl of Beaconsfield and twice Prime Minister of England (1867-1868; 1874-1880). In the novels of Trollope and Disraeli the vast and intricate world of ministries and parliaments, political intrigue, and the multifarious activities of empire in relation to the political process achieve a place in the novelistic tradition of England.

The religious controversies of the era, notably the Oxford movement and the Anglo-Catholicism it induced, are present as background to Trollope's Barsetshire novels. The controversies are the concerns of several characters in the works of George Eliot (Mary Ann Evans, 1819-1880), and enter into *Sartor Resartus* (1835) by Thomas Carlyle (1795-1881) as well as into numerous other novels of the era, many of which use the historical convention of setting stories in Roman times to explore the religious question. The scientific basis for certain religious controversies, such as the influx of German higher criticism, the use of evidence from the expanding science of geology, and the introduction of the theory of evolution by Charles Darwin (1809-1882), also find their way into the novels of the period. The religious question and its attendant fideist, agnostic, and atheistic responses find novelistic expression in the works of such writers as Trollope; Charles Kingsley (1819-1875), the exponent of "Muscular Christianity"; Edmund Gosse (1849-1928), especially in *Father and Son* (1907); and Samuel Butler (1835-1902), particularly in *Erewhon* (1872), *Erewhon Revisited* (1901), *The Fair Haven* (1873), and *The Way of All Flesh* (1903).

Both abrupt and gradual changes in the religious climate are reflected in many Victorian novels, particularly in the otherwise quite dissimilar works of George Meredith (1829-1909) and Thomas Hardy (1840-1928). Meredith's championing of "advanced ideas" generally and his particular advocacy of woman suffrage, free thought, political radicalism, and evolutionary theory (optimistically considered) combine to form a vision of the Comic Spirit that suffuses his works. Hardy was differently affected by the multiplicity of Victorian controversies and conflicting claims; in his works one finds not comedy but a tragic vision of human life dominated by an inexorable sense that the evolutionary process has produced in man a kind of alien species against which the permanent forces of nature are constantly arrayed. Nowhere is this more evident than in *Jude the Obscure* (1895), a novel so universally condemned by churchmen and the conservative literary establishment that Hardy turned away from the novel to become a poet of considerable importance.

Another element in the continuing debate which the Victorians carried on with themselves springs from the social reform movements of the era and collides with the positivistic thought of Auguste Comte (1798-1857), who coined the term "sociology." This element surfaced in some of Dickens' work (*Bleak House, Martin Chuzzlewit*, 1843-1844, *Our Mutual Friend, The Mystery of Edwin Drood*, 1870), rose to a different plane in the novels of Wilkie Collins (*The Woman in White*, 1860; *The Moonstone*, 1868), and formed much of the matter of "yellowback" or pulp novels as "shilling shockers" and "penny dreadfuls." It reached its logical Victorian zenith in the accounts of the world's greatest private consulting detective, Sherlock Holmes, by Arthur Conan

Doyle (1859-1930), narratives that range from *A Study in Scarlet* (1887) to *The Case-Book of Sherlock Holmes* (1927).

The phenomenon of detective fiction captured the interest and imagination of the Victorian public at all levels of society. Organized police forces were first created in the nineteenth century, the science of criminology was born, and ingenious threats to life and, especially, property from the criminal classes grew apace with the unremitting urbanization of England. The steady progress of the fictional criminal, from the endearing rogues of sentimental fiction to the personification of social evil created by Conan Doyle in his Napoleon of Crime, Professor Moriarty, is directly related to the growth of the propertied middle class, to the swelling population of the "underserving poor" (in George Bernard Shaw's phrase), to the ample opportunities for anonymity which urban centers and clear class divisions afforded, to the inevitable lure of easy money, and to the multiple examples of corrupt politicians on a national scale. Crime fiction kept pace with developments in crime and in criminal investigation, and in some cases the fiction anticipated developments in criminal science. The crime thriller, mystery story, and detective novel are still staple items of English fiction and have been so for more than a century, thanks to the efforts of Conan Doyle and the prodigious work of such writers as Agatha Christie (1891-1976) and John Creasey (1908-1973).

Still another subgenre linked to the detective novel was born of the armies of empire, international political events, and the information and communication explosions of the nineteenth century—the spy novel. Espionage had run through several Romantic and Victorian novels, but the Secret Service— John le Carré's "Circus" in his novels of the 1960's and 1970's—first came to prominence in *Kim* (1901) by Rudyard Kipling (1865-1936), and revolutionary espionage and anarchy came to the fore in *The Secret Agent* (1907) by Joseph Conrad (1857-1924). The spy novel in the twentieth century has had great impetus from the events of World War I and World War II (in *The Third Man*, 1950, for example, by Graham Greene), but is most closely associated with the post-1945 Cold War.

Both the detective novel of the Victorian Age and the spy novel born in its last days came to emphasize, of necessity, plot and action over character development and so tended to evolve into forms that do not fully coincide with the mainstream novel as the Victorians established it for themselves and their successors. A primary example of this is Ian Fleming's (1908-1964) character James Bond; a notable exception is John le Carré's (b. 1931) George Smiley: both writers and their characters face each other across an abyss. Yet the impulse to both sorts of fiction is historically rooted in the Romantic fiction of Scott and in the Romantic revival of the late nineteenth century, a revival sparked by an ever more urgent necessity to seek in fiction an escape from the complexities and difficulties of the present, and to find in fiction the disordered world set right, a finer or more exotic world, an adventurous world providing a chivalrous alternative to and a definite release from mercantile and corporate life.

In the Romantic revival of the late Victorian era, Robert Louis Stevenson (1850-1894) provided the best and most enduring fictional alternatives to the everyday life of Edinburgh, London, and the great industrial cities of the United Kingdom. Stevenson's novels of Scotland (*Kidnapped*, 1886; *The Master of Ballantrae*, 1888; *David Balfour*, 1893; *Weir of Hermiston*, 1896), his *Treasure Island* (1883) and *The Strange Case of Dr. Jekyll and Mr. Hyde* (1886) set a new fashion for tales of adventure and terror with such prime ingredients as soldiers, rebellions, pirates, and a monstrous transmogrifica-tion. His example was followed by H. Rider Haggard (1856-1925) in *King Solomon's Mines* (1885), Anthony Hope (1863-1933) in *The Prisoner of Zenda* (1894), P. C. Wren (1885-1941) in *Beau Geste* (1924), and by the writers of "best-sellers" in succeeding generations. The novels of Alistair MacLean (b. 1922), Frederick Forsythe (b. 1938), Jack Higgins (Harry Patterson, b. 1929), and the hundreds of novels about World War II continue the Scott-Stevenson tradition, mixing reality with escapism.

The end of Queen Victoria's reign and the accession of Edward VII (1901) truly marked the end of an age and of a century in which the novel rose to literary supremacy. On the eve of the twentieth century, England had passed several relatively peaceful decades since the Napoleonic era. The military excursions of the Crimean War (1854-1856), the Sepoy Rebellion in India (1857), a war with China (1857-1858), and the Boer War in South Africa (1899-1902) in no way prepared the empire for the global struggle that began in 1914 in the reign of George V and lasted as the Great War (now, World War I), until 1918. This and other military conflicts of the twentieth century have left clearly discernible marks upon the development of the English novel. World War II (1939-1945), the most cataclysmic for England, is also the most notable of the conflicts but not the longest. Wars, "police actions," and skir-mishes in the distant corners of the empire, from Suez (1956) or Palestine (1949) to the Falkland Islands (1982), and extending temporally from the Boer War to the Argentinian conflict, may have matched in sporadic intensity but not in overall bitterness the continuing Anglo-Irish struggle, begun many centuries ago and marked in the twentieth century by the Easter Risings (1918), the partition of Ireland (1922), and the move to Commonwealth status (1937) and to Republic (1949) for the South. World War II, however, has justly overshadowed all other military events of the century and has exerted such an influence upon the course of the English novel that the number of fictional works about Britain's "finest hour" has grown astronomically since 1945: World War II has not yet passed into distant cultural memory but remains, for whole generations, a recent event of personal history that also marks the beginning of the "postmodern" world. Since shortly after the war, beginning around 1947, the empire has been virtually dismantled, and more than a billion people throughout the world have gained political independence.

The British economy has been sapped by expensive modern warfare, the rapid dissolution of the empire, and the emigration of large numbers of the middle class; it has been plagued by taxation (marked by the establishment of the first modern social security system, in 1912, and later by the socialistic British welfare state, 1945-1951), devastated by the Great Depression of 1929 and the wholesale destruction of property in the Battle of Britain and the subsequent saturation bombing of London, and eroded by massive unemployment and the steady devaluation of the pound sterling in recent decades. These events and their economic effects form a background for the rise of the proletarian novel and the novel of social criticism of the 1950's and subsequent decades, including works by Kingsley Amis (b. 1922), John Braine (1922-1986), John Wain (b. 1925), Alan Sillitoe (b. 1928), and others of the now aging "Angry Young Men."

Social issues that occasioned the protests of the Victorian novelists were largely resolved during the last decades of Victoria's reign, ceased to have the same importance in the years when Edward VII was monarch (1901-1910), and, except for the extension of the voting franchise to women (1928), became legally moot in the early years of George V's reign. A divergent set of social issues replaced them for twentieth century novelists such as John Galsworthy (1867-1933), H. G. Wells (1866-1946), Arnold Bennett (1867-1931), and George Moore (1857-1933). Galsworthy, for example, captured the decline and disintegration of Victorian/Edwardian pillars of the middle class into the "lost generation" of the 1920's, and in so doing raised lapsarian questions that contribute to a "modernist" sensibility. Wells, apart from his socialist propaganda, also examined the possibilities of dehumanization and the inevitable destructiveness of the retrograde evolution of English class, social, and scientific structures. Bennett and Moore, like Galsworthy, pilloried the bourgeoisie and Victorianism generally, and both imported techniques from the French naturalistic novel to do so. Although French and other Continental writers exerted considerable influence on the cultural development of the English novel from roughly the mid-nineteenth century onward (one finds such influences extending from the novels of George Eliot to those of Henry James), it is noteworthy that the anti-Victorian writers should employ the naturalistic technique of Balzac and Zola in their novelistic experiments.

The form of the novel, as established in the eighteenth century, had evolved but had not drastically changed throughout the nineteenth century. With the influx of the French aesthetic, symbolist and decadent literature in the 1890's, and the experiments of Bennett and Moore, the stage was set for more radical experiments with the English novel, experiments that centered primarily on the traditional focus of the novel, character, and subordinated all else to it. One must look to the Anglicized American, Henry James (1843-1916), as a primary source for the experimental novel, even if James did remain clearly within the confines of the English novelistic tradition. By emphasizing such elements as angle of narration, the capturing of actual experience and the way people are, the primacy of individual psychology, and the disappearance of the traditional hero, James prepared the way for further experiments by Joseph Conrad, James Joyce (1882-1941), Virginia Woolf (1882-1941), D. H. Lawrence (1885-1930), and Lawrence Durrell (b. 1912), among others. In their fiction variations on the "modernist" questions of ultimate meaning, individual responsibility, and elemental issues of guilt, moral alienation and dehumanization, and atonement find enduring expression as each writer searches for individual answers to similar questions. Whether the scope of the search is global, as in Conrad's settings throughout the empire, or intensely local, as in Joyce's Dublin, Lawrence's Nottinghamshire, or the mind of Woolf's Mrs. Dalloway, it is the same inner search. In the light of the experimental novels of the twentieth century, *Tristram Shandy* no longer seems the *hapax legomenon* it once appeared to be.

Differing from the vast quantity of twentieth century English novels written in the authorized veins of bourgeois or antibourgeois traditions, the abundant novels of adventure, detection, mystery, romance (in all senses), espionage and humor—all forms in which society is reflected and sees itself—the experimental novel has provided a different sort of novelistic focus, the novel of social criticism and satire in which the protagonist is no longer concerned with a place in society but is, as his or her American cousins have been since the days of Nathaniel Hawthorne and Herman Melville, most frequently an outsider who seeks to preserve and justify alienation from a disordered and dissolving society and culture. Set adrift from intellectual, social, religious, and cultural stability and identity, the interbellum generation (1918-1939) and the postwar or postmodern generations have consistently emphasized the futility of human community under the social contract. Not only the "Angry Young Men" but also their predecessors, successors, and contemporaries such as Ronald Firbank (1886-1926), Aldous Huxley (1894-1963), Evelyn Waugh (1903-1966), George Orwell (1903-1950), William Golding (b. 1911), Graham Greene (b. 1904), and John le Carré, engage in social criticism and satire that ranges from assailing the societal, mechanistic, technocratic trivializing of human dignity to asserting the necessity of a solitary quest for personal ethics in an era that lacks an ethical superstructure and in which organized religion is one among many residual elements of limited use.

In the last half of the twentieth century, a reinvigorated strain of fiction has come to reflect the growing ethnic diversity of England's people, their multicultural character and global concerns, as many Commonwealth writers and expatriates have chosen England as their residence and principal forum. Three writers of the 1980's amply illustrate this diversity. Kazuo Ishiguro was born in Nagasaki in 1954; his family moved to England in 1960. Ishiguro's first novel, *A Pale View of Hills* (1982), is narrated by a Japanese widow, a survivor of Nagasaki, who is living in England. *An Artist of the Floating World* (1986) is the story of an old Japanese painter oppressed by guilt over the prostitution of his art in the service of Japanese imperialism. With his universally acclaimed third novel, *The Remains of the Day* (1989), Ishiguro made a bold leap; here his first-person narrator is an English butler in the mid-1950's, a figure at once comic and poignant. Timothy Mo was born in Hong Kong in 1950; his first novel, *The Monkey King* (1978), examines familial relationships in his native city in the 1940's and 1950's. *Sour Sweet* (1982) offers a Dickensian portrayal of the Chinese community in London. Mo's most ambitious work, the wonderfully capacious *An Insular Possession* (1986), concerns cultural, political, and economic conflicts between the Occident and the Orient in Macao and Canton before and during the Opium Wars of the nineteenth century. Salman Rushdie, born in Bombay in 1947, was educated in England. His novel *Midnight's Children* (1980) views the partition of India and the creation of the independent Muslim state of Pakistan through the lens of Magical Realism. *Shame* (1983) covers much of the same territory. Rushdie achieved international notoriety with his patently Joycean novel *The Satanic Verses* (1988), a great wheel of a book that has been condemned by Muslim fundamentalists for its handling of religious themes. In *Haroun and the Sea of Stories* (1990), a children's book written for adults as well, Rushdie, threatened with death and forced into hiding, answers his critics with a celebration of storytelling and the unconstrained imagination.

The English novel, then, to paraphrase William Shakespeare's Hamlet, holds the mirror up to society and shows the very age and body of the time its form and pressure. Even a brief sketch of the varied patterns of societal influences on the development of the English novel demonstrates that the novel is of all literary forms the most responsive to the changing emphases of an evolving society. Whether in overt reaction to the values of a society, in praise of them or in criticism of them, the novel consistently presents the society as the individual must confront it, explains that society to itself, and helps society to define itself.

John J. Conlon

THE AMERICAN NOVEL

While there was a considerable output of early Gothic novels in America, they are now of slight interest outside of academic circles. There was little in these early and generally inferior works that was unique to America; the novelist in America did not begin to write with a native voice until the nineteenth century. By then, fiction was no longer subject to condemnation by a Puritan theocracy (although Puritan habits of mind exerted a powerful influence long after the theocracy ceased to exert institutional control). America, independent of England, had begun to think of itself as a separate entity, with a unique past and tradition to explore and had begun to develop a complex and often contradictory ethos which stamped all of its art more profoundly than did any imported influences.

The American experience is composed of a series of dualities: the Calvinist sense of sin, guilt, and predestination opposed to romantic optimism; religious, scientific, economic, and psychological determinism opposed to belief in free will and self-determination; idealism opposed to materialism; European models of culture opposed to belief in native sources and themes; upper-class values opposed to middle-class aspirations, opposed to lower-class needs; the culture of the East Coast and, later, the Midwest opposed to the culture of the South. All of these contrary but occasionally interlocking forces affected and continue to affect the fiction of America.

The Puritan "experiment," while engendering a colonial theocracy that lasted for fewer than one hundred years, nevertheless continued to influence subsequent generations. Thus, the need to reconcile God and Mammon which plagued the Puritans almost from the beginning is still a fundamental theme in American life and art. The diaries of the colonial governors William Bradford (1590-1649) and John Winthrop (1588-1694) reveal harsh dealings with merchandizers and exploiters who invaded the colonies to reap the wealth of the New World. By the third generation of the theocracy, however, represented by the famous diarist Judge Samuel Sewall (1652-1730), wealth and its material rewards were comfortably integrated into Puritan religious doctrine. Both religious and material salvation were to be obtained by faithfully following "programs" for improvement based on the Scriptures. Thus, the Puritan providential histories recorded lists of virtues, habits, traits, beliefs, and desirable goals, and measured as well their authors' daily progress toward the fulfillment of such programs.

As the influence of the eighteenth century Enlightenment spread to the New World, the meddling God of Calvinism became the Deistic "Great Watchmaker," and the study of the world shifted from a fear-driven attempt to understand first causes to a comfortably assured knowledge of second causes and their worldly applications. Ironically in his autobiography, the professed Deist Benjamin Franklin (1706-1790) listed tables of virtues, such as "temperence, silence, order, resolution, frugality, industry, sincerity, justice, moderation"; appended a mnemonic trope derived from sacred or secular literature; and recorded his success or failure in achieving these goals. The virtues Franklin lists are the same as those proposed in the diary of his reactionary contemporary, the great (and last) Puritan philosopher, Jonathan Edwards (1703-1758). Edwards' program's source in revelation, however, is very different from Franklin's common sense and reason.

Franklin's "practical piety," his attempt to integrate things of the spirit with those of the flesh, flavors much American fiction. The whaling ship *Pequod* created by Herman Melville (1819-1891) in *Moby Dick* (1851) is at once an emblem of modern technology—an efficient and profitable factory ship—and a theater for the metaphysical exploration of moral imperatives, a cosmic battleground for the natural and supernatural forces of good and evil.

Material prosperity, fueled by the industrial revolution, ran rampant after the Civil War, and the effect of money on the moral fiber of America became the dominant theme of fiction of the late nineteenth and twentieth centuries. Mark Twain (Samuel Clemens, 1835-1910), himself a victim of the dichotomy between God and Mammon, satirized the greed and hypocrisy of *The Gilded Age* (1873) even as he pursued the windfalls that world might offer him. William Dean Howells (1837-1920), one of the fathers of American realism, reflected on the pitfalls of an acquisitive society in *The Rise of Silas Lapham* (1885). Silas and his wife inherit and exploit a paint mine in New England and attempt to rise from comfortable but unpretentious middle-class life into wealthy Boston society. Silas' moral compass, however, is compromised in the process, as he is corrupted by the forces of the market. His material rewards come not entirely from his own labor, as before, but through investment and speculation—such "ill-got gains" bring about a moral crisis. Only through eventual renunciation of great wealth does Silas regain his moral stature and, concomitantly, his proper status as a member of the middle class.

This theme, with varying outcomes, persisted in hundreds of novels produced in the late nineteenth and early twentieth centuries. The effects of money, speculation, and class aspirations on the moral character of the American businessman and his family were explored fictively again and again.

The result was not always negative. In fact, Horatio Alger (1834-1899), whose name is synonymous with this theme, exploited, in more than one hundred novels, the "rags-to-riches" myth, accompanied by the notion that life is a school of virtue, and, in an unconscious parody of the Puritan view, that material success is both a cause of and reward for moral virtue. Edwards' and Franklin's program, now expunged entirely of sectarian doctrine, became a new "Way to Wealth." More wish-fulfillment than doctrine for most readers, Alger's vastly popular novels were read as a substitution for success. For every *Ragged Dick* (1867, modeled in part on Andrew Carnegie) there were thousands of trapped stock boys, shopgirls, and factory workers for whom the formula was mere fantasy.

The testing of moral formulae for material success can be found in the twentieth century as well. The novel *The Great Gatsby* (1925), by F. Scott Fitzgerald (1896-1946), illustrates the ironic dichotomy between great wealth and moral carelessness. Among the dead Gatsby's belongings is a schoolboy notebook in which the young "Jay Gatz" had inscribed a shallow, pragmatic success plan, which is a parody of the very lists in Edwards' diary and Franklin's autobiography. Moreover, Gatsby, like Silas Lapham, cannot rise in old-money society; his group, the nouveau riche, are corrupt and amoral. The unifying moral framework that informs Franklin's schema is totally absent from Gatsby's world. For Fitzgerald, this lack of morality is an emblem of modern society. Other twentieth century novelists, including Sinclair Lewis (1885-1951), also dealt overtly with this theme, and many others have continued to incorporate it into their work.

The persistent conflict between notions of free will and determinism that informs American fiction can also be traced to the Puritan era. The Puritans saw man as predestined, irresistibly and irreversibly, to either Heaven or Hell. When the harshness of this creed began to erode church membership, the heretofore heretical position of earned salvation became part of the orthodoxy, and good moral acts became a ticket to, as well as a sign of, salvation, softening the original implacable determinism of Calvinist creed.

It is not surprising that Americans began to perceive themselves as above the forces which might tend to limit free will. They set out to dominate a new continent and succeeded in a remarkably short period of time. They fought to free the colonies from England despite seemingly insurmountable odds. They worked to found a republic on Enlightenment principles and succeeded where even Enlightenment France had failed. This sense of self-reliance, celebrated by the transcendentalist Ralph Waldo Emerson (1803-1882), gave rise to the romantic celebration of the self-determining nation and individual; politically, to the Jacksonian upheaval; and economically, to laissez-faire democracy. Indeed, the rags-to-riches theme in American fiction is an example of this hopeful philosophy, paralleled in all sorts of "how-to" schemes in the nonfictive world. The very words "self-determination" imply freedom to define oneself or nation, free from hindering antecedent forces.

While such optimism can be found in a wealth of fiction aimed at popular audiences, much serious fiction questioned this faith in the ability of the individual to triumph over forces larger than himself. Movements in the intellectual history of the Western world tend to militate against this view. The Puritan vision of the all-powerful and retributive God melted in the heat of the New Science; the Enlightenment brought new forces: physics, chemistry, mathematics, biology. The inability of moral sensibility to keep pace with technological advance, and the veritable meaning of that technology have been the general preoccupations of the modern age.

Darwinian evolution, "social Darwinism" as formulated by William Gra-ham Sumner (1840-1910), Marxist or other deterministic economic theories, Freudian psychology, cyclical theories of history such as Oswald Spengler's were all seen as limiting individual free will. All were opposed to the romantic notion of optimistic self-determination and coincided with an expanding indus-trial base, the resultant concentration of capital, the decline of agrarianism and small-entrepreneurship, and the growth of an ever-larger lower class for whom the American dream was but a distant fantasy.

In fiction, these forces could be found in the naturalist movement exem-plified in the works of Stephen Crane (1871-1900), Frank Norris (1870-1902), Hamlin Garland (1860-1940), and Theodore Dreiser (1871-1945). This literary movement depicted contemporary life with great accuracy, continuing the realist reaction against sentimentality. Unlike the realists, who had merely represented the world they knew with no underlying philosophy, the natu-ralists postulated an underlying world view: that the forces at work in nature were those at work in man as well. Transcendence was a myth. The universe was fundamentally amoral, operating by implacable physical laws, unaware and uncaring of the plight of mankind. Novels such as Crane's *Maggie: A Girl of the Streets* (1893), Dreiser's *Sister Carrie* (1900) and *An American Tragedy* (1925), and Norris' *The Octopus* (1901) all directly or indirectly owe their world view to Émile Zola (1840-1902), the great French naturalist, and to the underlying insights of modern psychology, and physical and biological (evolutionary) science. For these writers, self-determination, self-improve-ment, and free will were romantic illusions. Individuals—and, according to emerging economic theories, whole societies—were shaped by forces over which man had but limited control.

It is revealing, however, that this pessimistic outlook was not easily accepted by the optimistic American temperament. Even ostensibly naturalistic works were softened by implied alternatives, suggesting the efficacy of making a "separate peace." The mystic Vanamee, in *The Octopus*, exemplifies an alter-native life-style of hard primitivism in harmony with the more benign forces of nature. The titular character of *The Adventures of Huckleberry Finn* (1884) "lights out for the territory" at the end of his novel, and the code heroes of Ernest Hemingway (1898-1961) frequently do likewise to escape the corrup-tion of injurious forces.

The pessimism of the naturalists, if not their findings, was also repudiated by the so-called "muckrakers," who wrote novels depicting limiting and defeating social conditions so that the society could understand and thereby change them, thus ameliorating their results—an accommodation of the Enlightenment outlook to modern realities. *The Jungle* (1906) by Upton Sinclair (1878-1968), an exposé of the Chicago meat-packing industry, is a famous example of the genre, which in fact helped to bring about the enact-ment of the first pure food and drug laws.

Another sort of repudiation is represented by the proliferation of Utopian novels during this period. The original settlers of America, North and South, had envisioned religious or economic utopias in the New World. Utopian social schemes, often communal in nature, had been widely attempted during the earlier nineteenth century; the transcendentalist commune Brook Farm, of which Hawthorne briefly was a member, was the most famous example. These communities were organized around modes of life ranging from the vaguely biblical to the nutritional (corn flakes were a product of such a vegetarian social experiment in Battle Creek, Michigan), to the sexual.

While most Utopian communities either dissolved or were absorbed into the mainstream of American life, they resurfaced, fictively, as a reaction against the stark contrasts of the Gilded Age, with its robber barons and ever-expanding slums. Stimulated by Marxist and Fabian social thought, Utopian writers produced some forty-six novels between 1889 and 1900. Like Alger's novels, they were eargerly read by thousands of dreamers. The novels proposed social schemes based on Marxism, Judeo-Christian ideals, and rationalist humanism.

It is easy to see why they were so popular. Their alternative proposals, like those actual Utopian experiments of the preceding era, implied the power of self-determination, the power of man to transform himself and his society through the application of logical principles and the ethical framework of justice, love, altruism, solidarity, and equitable distribution of labor and its fruits. The most famous Utopian novel was by Edward Bellamy (1856-1898), whose *Looking Backward* (1888) influenced John Dewey, William Allen White, Eugene V. Debs, and Norman Thomas. Even the great realist, Howells, wrote a Utopian novel: *A Traveler from Altruria* (1894).

Ironically, none of these utopians saw the totalitarianism implicit in their social schemes until European socialism and Fascism brought the lesson chillingly home. Not surprisingly, however, the most famous novels in English which openly challenge the Utopian vision are by Englishmen: *Brave New World* (1932) by Aldous Huxley (1894-1963) and *Animal Farm* (1946) and *1984* (1949) by George Orwell (1903-1950)—all of which have outlived the fame of the American Utopian novels. The only noteworthy American anti-Utopian novel was by Nathaniel Hawthorne (1804-1864). *The Blithedale Romance* (1852), written after his sojourn at Brook Farm, presciently revealed his disillusionment with attempts at systematic Utopian societies, and demonstrated that such schemes, by definition, must limit individual freedom and stifle creativity.

One might trace other distinctive characteristics of American fiction to their roots in the Puritan tradition. Puritan writing was highly symbolic and emblematic; the Puritans believed that the world itself was an emblem of divine will and purpose, which was to be read as a "text" along with the Bible. This led to a habit of close observation, a habit which, ironically, was transferable to the needs of the New Science and the literary forms of realism and naturalism. This theological practice led to the habit of seeing the world symbolically, and symbolism has permeated American fiction ever since. Hawthorne not only shared the Puritan sense of sin and moral responsibility but also the tendency to emblemize the world. Thus, Hester Prynne's scarlet letter, her creator's reflecting pools, shooting stars—indeed, virtually all the details of Hawthorne's works—have multiple layers of symbolic meanings.

Melville, too, used elements of nature in a richly symbolic manner. The white whale in *Moby Dick* takes on an emblematic meaning which differs with each of the novel's observing characters. The river in Twain's *The Adventures of Huckleberry Finn* is archetypal. The motif of the frontier, in the hands of James Fenimore Cooper (1789-1851) becomes an emblem for the conquest of America, and the carrying of the forces of civilization westward as well as of the closing of opportunity for the primal and improving struggle against dark forces of evil and anarchy are paradigms of the uses to which countless novelists employed the motif.

Even naturalists such as Crane and Norris and realists such as Henry James, Howells, Fitzgerald, and Hemingway use symbolism liberally, whether it be the railroad and wheat in *The Octopus*, the light at the end of the dock in *The Great Gatsby*, or war and blood sports in the novels of Hemingway. Southern literature, generated in a region not originally Puritan but ultimately the most enduringly Calvinist sector of the nation, is richly symbolic in the hands of such masters as William Faulkner (1897-1962), Robert Penn Warren (1905-1989), Carson McCullers (1917-1967), and Flannery O'Connor (1925-1967).

The confessional strain in American fiction also reflects the legacy of Puritanism. The Puritan kept track of his state of grace through the practice of candid and prayerful introspection, often in diary or autobiography, and that personal and confessional mode of thought carried on far beyond the seventeenth century. The Puritan habit, reinforced by psychoanalytic theory, has begotten the personal novel. Often recording the protagonist's search for religious or secular salvation, novelists such as Hawthorne, Melville, James, Fitzgerald, Thomas Wolfe (1900-1938), and J. D. Salinger (born 1919) continue to perpetuate the Puritan habit of measuring one's spiritual state against a demanding, if sometimes self-imposed value system.

From the earliest days of derivative sentimental and Gothic novels, the creators of American fiction engaged in a *de facto* debate which affected all aspects of American art: whether America could even have an indigenous art and culture, and if so, whether it could reach the standards set by European and English masters. The debate was an extension of the European and English eighteenth century ancients-moderns controversy, which, in turn, helped spur the romantic counterreaction.

Although Washington Irving (1783-1859) created several masterpieces of

American legend in "Rip Van Winkle" and "The Legend of Sleepy Hollow" (1820), the plots were borrowed from German folk tales. Only the locales were American—a choice that revealed Irving's belief that America's only grist for an author's creative mill was scenery. Irving's synthesis was carried on later by the local-color movement of the post-Civil War nineteenth century, composed of writers who celebrated regionalism—the customs, dress, dialogue, and topography of their areas of America, but who continued to use sentimental, timeworn plots. These regionalists include the West's Bret Harte (1836-1902), Creole Louisiana's George Washington Cable (1844-1925), the South's Joel Chandler Harris (1848-1908), and New England's Sarah Orne Jewett (1849-1906). These, and many others, formed a transition between the romantic fiction of the earlier time, and the realist and naturalist movements of the late nineteenth and twentieth centuries.

Another creator of American legend, James Fenimore Cooper, found ample native material to fuel his Leatherstocking saga of seven novels. His social schema, however, was decidedly British: eighteenth century Tory political and social conservatism engendered by British leanings supplied by his aristocratic father and further amplified by an extended sojourn abroad, where Cooper was lionized by the British literary establishment. Thus, his novels are only superficially Rousseauian celebrations of noble savagery. They demonstrate, in fact, the same conservative notion of man's place in the social order to be found in the work of Howells. For Cooper, each admirable character, red or white, accepts his or her place in the social strata. There is no crossing of color lines. Villains are not distinguished by color; rather, they are those who either wrongly aspire to a social position not legitimately theirs or who belong to no strata at all—the so-called "borderers" (a prototype of the rootless middle class), who exploit both upper and lower classes for amoral personal gain. Cooper superimposed a rigid hierarchical European social system onto the landscape of the American frontier, setting a pattern for much conservative fiction to follow—much of it by Southern or Western writers.

This European theme of class distinctions was raised to its highest form by Henry James, himself an expatriate, who tested American goodwill, innocence, and pluck against European sophistication, jadedness, and amorality in a series of remarkable novels, from *The American* (1877) and *Daisy Miller* (1879) to the late work *The Ambassadors* (1903). James, like those before him, tended to see America as both morally superior and aesthetically inferior to Europe. Nevertheless, he maintained the hope for a synthesis of the better qualities of both worlds.

The 1920's brought further contrast between European and American values in the works of the Lost Generation, a group of expatriate artists, including Hemingway, Fitzgerald, and Henry Miller (1891-1980), all of whom found, in differing ways, that their jaded and antiheroic sensibilities conflicted with the older values they found abroad.

The marriage of European forms with American experience is also illustrated by the development of the Gothic genre in American fiction. Imported from Europe and England near the end of the eighteenth century, the Gothic has been given a peculiarly American flavor in the works of Edgar Allan Poe (1809-1849) and his predecessors. It is not surprising that Gothic fiction has flourished most persistently in the South. The planter aristocracy, patterned on that of eighteenth century England and existing on the backs of chattel slaves, engendered a radical spread between social classes, between high-church Anglicanism and slave-begotten fundamentalism, between Enlightenment rationalism and primitive superstition. A real world that included slavery, lynchings and floggings, the Ku Klux Klan, secession, forced military subjugation, and economic and cultural invasion by the Yankee "conquerer," not to mention Spanish moss and high humidity, could hardly avoid Gothicism in its fiction. Gothic (and grotesque) elements can be found in the world of such Southern writers as Faulkner, Carson McCullers, Flannery O'Connor, Truman Capote (1924-1984), and many others.

The established patterns of American intellectual life fragmented, if not shattered, by a series of traumatic events beginning with the Holocaust and the nuclear explosions that ended World War II, and continued with such events as the cold war; stalemate in Korea and the defeat in Vietnam; the civil rights movement; the upheavals following the assassinations of President John F. Kennedy, Robert F. Kennedy, and Martin Luther King, Jr.; and the Watergate scandal that eventuated in the resignation of President Richard M. Nixon. Cultural, ethnic, and sexual liberation movements and a turning from broad to narrow and personal concerns have been echoed in a parallel diversity of themes and structure in American fiction.

Thus, the Southern writers noted above no longer represent a region distinctive for its cultural discontinuity; the South has become, ironically, an emblem for a nation which has become alienated from its roots and underlying political and cultural assumptions. These writers now reflect the nation's preoccupation with cultural, sexual, and political "otherness" and the reality of diminished expectations.

A second locus of modern fiction is urban Chicago and New York, where writers such as Saul Bellow (b. 1915), Salinger, John Cheever (1912-1982), Philip Roth (b. 1933), John Updike (b. 1932), and Bernard Malamud (1914-1986) have explored the mores and tribulations of the rising (and often Jewish) middle class.

Finally, since the 1950's, the American novel has been marked by experimentation in form, beginning with the Beat generation and the works of Jack Kerouac (1922-1969) and continuing with the explorations of Norman Mailer (b. 1923), Tom Wolfe (b. 1931), John Gardner (1933-1982), Thomas Pynchon (b. 1937), Stanley Elkin (b. 1930), William Gass (b. 1924), John Barth

(b. 1930), Joseph Heller (b. 1923), and many others who have tested the boundaries of fiction and journalism, linear form, and narrative coherence.

David Sadkin

PICARESQUE NOVEL

The words *picaresque* and *picaro* achieved currency in Spain shortly after 1600; today they are current terms in literary criticism, sometimes misused because of the vague meaning attached to them. The revival of the genre in the twentieth century has been accompanied by an increased critical interest in this type of novel, with the result that some critics try to stretch the definition of the picaresque while others attempt to restrict it. Still, some features are generally accepted as distinct characteristics of the picaresque, including a loose, episodic structure; a rogue-hero (the *picaro*) who is on the move and goes through a series of encounters with representatives of a hostile and corrupt world; a first-person narrative; and finally, a satirical approach to the society in which the adventures occur. The typical social background of the picaresque involves a disordered, disintegrating world in which traditional values are breaking down. The instability of the social structure permits the emergence of the *picaro*, a resilient rogue but not a criminal, a person of low birth or uncertain parentage, an outsider whose adventures take him from innocence to experience. In this sense, the picaresque novel has affinities with the *Bildungsroman*, but unlike the protagonist of the latter, the *picaro* is a fixed character. While he learns survival techniques from his adventures, he does not change inwardly; he remains faithful to his healthy instincts without questioning the larger order of things. Pressured by circumstances to choose between integrity and survival, the *picaro* makes the pragmatic choice and learns to adjust to the corrupt values of his environment.

The picaresque genre emerged in sixteenth century Spain, an age of turmoil and upheaval when medieval homogeneity and social stability were giving way to Renaissance mobility and a greater emphasis on the importance of the individual. All Spanish picaresque novels present a low-life character passing from master to master in search of some financial stability, thus providing a splendid occasion for the author to give an overall picture of Spain in an age of disintegrating values. The differences between the two first examples of the genre, however, already indicate its protean nature.

Lazarillo de Tormes, published anonymously in 1553, presents a *picaro*, a victim of tricksters who by necessity becomes a trickster himself. The novel's anonymous author was the first to employ a realistic first-person narrator, creating a countergenre to the fastidious courtly literature of the period. Some critics suggest that both the anonymous author of *Lazarillo de Tormes* and Mateo Alemán, the writer of the second Spanish picaresque, were Jews or converted Jews, outsiders to the mainstream of Spanish society; in any case, the picaresque view of life is an outsider's point of view as far as protagonist and author are concerned.

Fear of starvation and anger are Lazarillo's true masters. The lesson he draws from his experience of privation and exploitation is not one of resistance or revolt; on the contrary, it is one of conformity. His is a kind of success story because, at the end of the novel, he finds a secure job as a town crier, but this is qualified success, since he pays for it with his honor, marrying the Archpriest's mistress. He accepts the Archpriest's advice to concern himself only with his own advantage. The advice, of course, reflects the hypocritical standards of Spanish society. Lazarillo is more than ready to heed the counsel; his bitter adventures have taught him to be content with low expectations. The feeling of being defenseless and unprotected against the wickedness of the world lends a tragic note to the story of his childhood and adolescence. Though most of his adventures make the reader laugh, anguish and despair prevail throughout the novel. The comic and the serious exist side-by-side, adding a note of ambiguity. *Lazarillo de Tormes* is a mixture of childish immaturity, innocence, and bitter cynicism; it excels in a fusion of modes and attitudes. At the end, Lazarillo compares his rising fortunes to Spain's rising political power; consequently, the unknown author puts not only his *picaro*'s story in an ambiguous light but also extends that ambiguity to the whole empire of Charles V.

Charles V was succeeded by Philip II and Philip III; disillusionment followed triumph in the history of the empire. The picaresque novel, from the beginning a protean genre, adjusted to the new demands. Despair and anguish are present already in Lazarillo's story, but the *picaro* protagonist in Mateo Alemán's *Guzmán de Alfarache* (1599, 1604) is first of all a tormented soul. As an investigator of the prison system, Alemán was well acquainted with prison-life. In Guzmán he presents a repentant sinner. The confessions reveal a lower-class character whom a dehumanizing society has forced to adjust to its corrupt values; the emphasis is not on Guzmán's adventures, however, but rather on his tormented soul. He is a kind of psychological *picaro*, one very much concerned with his soul. Guzmán compares the human predicament to warfare: an existence without any certainty or truth; a life full of hypocrisy and instability.

In spite of the many hilarious tricks played by the rogues on their masters, the Spanish picaresque novels were not intended to be amusing. There is a subtle balance of comedy and seriousness in *Lazarillo de Tormes* and *Guzmán de Alfarache*; at the same time, however, through the encounters of the rogue-hero with various masters—all of them representing the hypocritical, materialistic standards of contemporary Spanish society—these picaresque novels give a fragmented but valid and realistic picture of a society in change.

The protean nature of the picaresque novel made it easy for the genre to spread rapidly all over Europe. Adaptations of *Lazarillo de Tormes* appeared early, in 1561 in France, in 1568 in England. *Guzmán de Alfarache* appeared in 1615 in Germany. The Spanish original blended in each country with the native tradition, and the Spanish *picaro* turned into the English rogue, later a foundling; into the German *Schelm*; and in France, into a *gentilhomme*.

Despite differences in each of these countries, the picaresque consistently performed the function of a countergenre, making legitimate the serious attention given to low-life characters. With the advance of capitalism, the middle class grew in number and influence, and its members found pleasure in a genre that centered on the plight of a low-life character seeking upward mobility. At the same time, printing techniques improved, and booksellers, in order to boost their profits, encouraged more and more printings of picaresque fiction because of its appeal to the taste of the bourgeoisie. As a matter of fact, in the following centuries the genre came to be adopted to reflect a bourgeois world view rather than a truly picaresque outlook. With the optimistic attitudes of the Enlightenment, the picaresque novel lost its quality of despair; the former *picaro*, though in different degrees and in different ways, came to be integrated into the mainstream of society.

In Germany, the Spanish picaresque merged with the native tradition of tales about false beggars. The most significant German novel of the picaresque type is H. J. C. von Grimmelshausen's *Simplicissimus the Vagabond* (1669). The background of the book fits the requirements of the picaresque atmosphere: the Thirty Years' War was certainly a period of disorder and disintegration in German history. Simplicius Simplicissimus, as his name implies, is a naïve, simple, ignorant boy; his peasant background emphasizes this feature. He is almost another Parzival, a "pure fool," but the war destroys his pastoral life. His picaresque wanderings eventually lead him to live the life of a hermit. Compared to what is considered normal and sane in the gambling, warring, drinking, whoring society of contemporary Germany, the seemingly foolish idealism of the hermit is perhaps the only truly sane attitude amid universal madness. While society may consider Simplicissimus mad, his madness makes more sense than the reality created by the so-called respectable people. The German *picaro*, by tearing off the masks, shows the real face of society behind the façade.

In France, the Spanish picaresque merged with the tradition of criminal biographies and books on vagabonds; in the seventeenth century the genre came to be exploited by writers such as Charles Sorel and Paul Scarron, whose comic, realistic novels functioned as a countergenre to the improbable romances that flooded the market. The French *picaro*, born into the middle class, uses his tricks to unmask the society to which he belongs by birth; in consequence, the social criticism always implicit in the genre becomes more obvious. By far the most famous French picaresque novel is Alain René Le Sage's *The Adventures of Gil Blas of Santillane* (1715). Though the adventures of this son of humble parents take place in Spain, Gil Blas is different from the original Spanish *picaro*. Influenced by Molière and La Bruyère, satirists of morals and manners, Le Sage turned his Gil Blas into an observer of rogues rather than a participant in roguery. Indeed, Gil Blas is a noble-hearted adventurer who, in view of his virtuous behavior, deserves the success he achieves in the end.

In England, the first translation of *Lazarillo de Tormes* appeared in 1586, the work of David Rowland; the first English *Guzmán de Alfarache* in 1622. Soon thereafter, the Spanish picaresque merged with the native tradition of anatomies of roguery. The best early English picaresque is Thomas Nashe's *The Unfortunate Traveller: Or, The Life of Jack Wilton* (1594). *Guzmán de Alfarache* was very popular with translators; Richard Head's and Frances Kirkman's *The English Rogue* (1665, 1668) is the best among English adaptations of the original *Guzmán de Alfarache*.

In the eighteenth century, a kind of picaresque enjoyed a boom in English literature. Most of Tobias Smollett's fiction is in the picaresque vein. In his outstanding novel, *Roderick Random* (1748), the protagonist, an orphan, foreshadows the English *picaro* as a foundling. He is a decent young person, and his inherent virtures contrast sharply with the cruelty and viciousness of most of the other characters in the novel. They stand for the attitudes of a dehumanized society that subjects the young protagonist to all kinds of hardships and misfortunes on land and on sea. Resilient, in the true picaresque spirit, Roderick Random bounces back after each misadventure. While his personal fortunes are straightened out in the end when he finds his father and is happily married, on the whole, Smollett presents a rather gloomy view of the human condition.

Daniel Defoe's *Moll Flanders* (1722) is an episodic fictional autobiography of a *picara*, a female rogue. She is a true criminal whose crimes are rooted in capitalistic attitudes. Indeed, Moll is a bourgeois *picara*; inspired by the spirit of profit and investment, she acquires the fortune necessary for investment in the New World by the only means available to her: thievery and prostitution. Her behavior and standards reflect on the materialistic values of the society to which she wants to conform.

Henry Fielding's *Tom Jones* (1749) illustrates better than any other novel of the eighteenth century the transformation of the *picaro* from a roguish outsider to a belonger. Tom Jones is a foundling and thus an outsider, as a true *picaro* is expected to be, and in the course of the novel he must take to the road, where he undergoes various adventures. Never for a minute, however, is there any real doubt that by the end of his journey he will be integrated into society. As a matter of fact, Tom Jones is a kind of vanishing *picaro* on his way to becoming the traditional English fictional hero. This hero always ultimately conforms to accepted norms. Tom Jones's place in the world of Allworthy is only being questioned in order to provide adventures for the amusement of the reader. The element of economic necessity is entirely lacking; in consequence, ambiguity and despair vanish and the adventures provoke wholehearted, easy laughter.

The next step on the path of the vanishing English *picaro* falls in the nineteenth century. In Charles Dickens' *Pickwick Papers* (1836-1837), the picaresque structure is nothing more than a form of convenience. The real rogue is Jingle, yet the hero of the adventure-series is the most respectable Mr. Pickwick. He is the *picaro* turned respectable, in an age when respectability, exemplified by Queen Victoria and the Prince Consort, dominated British society. Mr. Pickwick goes through a series of hilariously comic adventures, he gains experience, he even goes to prison, but in the end he returns to society. Integration, so important in British fiction, is achieved at the end of the adventures.

The American development of the picaresque followed a radically different course. American black humor, born on the pioneer frontier, recalls in its mixture of laughter and terror the atmosphere of the early Spanish picaresque. The early American himself, a lonely figure on a vast, unknown, and possibly hostile continent, is a distant cousin of Lazarillo and Guzmán. It is not surprising, then, that the novel from which, according to Ernest Hemingway, all American literature derives, Mark Twain's *The Adventures of Huckleberry Finn* (1884), is an American picaresque story not only in the obvious picaresque pattern of Huck's adventures but also in the elements of loneliness and terror that fill up the frame.

Huck is an outsider, belonging to the lowest rank of whites in his society; he recognizes that society pays only lip service to ideals and decides to stay true to his own conscience. While the adventures of his trip down the Mississippi match Lazarillo's experiences of near starvation, the haunting experience with his own conscience over the case of Jim, the runaway black slave, makes Huck a relative of Guzmán, tortured about his soul. Huck, the American *picaro*, is a rogue with a conscience who chooses to listen to his own heart rather than follow the sham values of society.

Many features of the original Spanish picaresque pattern and of its *picaro*-rogue hero correspond to trends in modern fiction and to the concept of the modern limited hero or antihero. The episodic, open-ended plot is an appropriate device for the modern writer, who knows "only broken images" for presenting the fragmented reality of a disorderly, chaotic universe. The *picaro* is not unlike the modern alienated individual, born into a world turned upside down. Many critics, therefore, consider the picaresque mode to be one of the most characteristic in twentieth century fiction, while others speak of a picaresque renaissance.

James Joyce's *Ulysses* (1922), the archetype of modern fiction, shows striking similarities with the picaresque. Joyce's "joco-serious" recalls the unbalanced Spanish picaresque atmosphere of half-comical and half-serious attitudes. Leopold Bloom, a Jew in Ireland, is an outsider in society; a betrayed husband, he is also an outsider in his family. Both *Ulysses* and the Spanish picaresque present a series of experiences rather than a coherent narrative. They present a roguelike hero, who is no criminal but still less than an example of virtue and whose life is a hard-luck story. Leopold Bloom experiences a despair and anxiety which was alien to the more respectable *picaros* of the eighteenth and nineteenth centuries but which recalls the mood of *Lazarillo de Tormes*.

The picaresque pattern also emerged in the novels of Britain's "Angry Young Men" in the 1950's. The angry picaresque novel of postwar Britain resulted from serious discontent with the Welfare State. The decade found England in unsettled conditions, with the empire falling to pieces and the class system only slowly weakening in its traditional rigidity. Just as the Spanish picaresque novel arose in part as an expression of the social resentment of the underdog against the privileged classes, so Kingsley Amis' *Lucky Jim* (1954), John Wain's *Hurry on Down* (1953), and Alan Sillitoe's *Saturday Night and Sunday Morning* (1958) reject the values of the phony middle class. Yet their protagonists share Lazarillo's dream of belonging; in consequence, the angry picaresque stays within the pattern of integration characteristic of British fiction.

The American picaresque novel of the twentieth century may describe a restless small-town youth, as in John Updike's *Rabbit, Run* (1960), or a wild drive across the continent, as in Jack Kerouac's *On the Road* (1957). The present-day American rogues display an old American attitude; they try to recapture the heroic spirit of the frontier and to confront the nature of man, of the self. The modern American *picaro* is an outsider; he may be a sensitive adolescent shunning the phoney world, like Holden Caulfield in J. D. Salinger's *The Catcher in the Rye* (1951), or a man fighting the military in order to survive, like Yossarian in Joseph Heller's *Catch-22* (1961); he may be a member of a minority group, black, like Ralph Ellison's *Invisible Man* (1952) Irish, like Ken Kesey's McMurphy in *One Flew Over the Cuckoo's Nest* (1962), or Jewish, like Saul Bellows's Augie March in *The Adventures of Augie March* (1953).

Augie March is the product of the Chicago ghetto environment, the son of Jewish immigrants forced by his dehumanizing environment into a *picaro* attitude. A servant to many masters, resilient and ready to adjust, Augie ultimately refuses any attempt to be adopted and preserves his outsider status. Practical and pragmatic, he is able to do almost anything. While he is open to any new experience, he remains faithful to his own self, considering all his adventures as means to find his true identity. The Invisible Man, a black, learns to accept his invisibility in white America; his picaresque experiences take him through a series of rejections at the end of which he emerges as a truly protean individual and even a trickster.

Despite their physical or mental sufferings, all these American rogues share with their Spanish originals an almost unlimited, exuberant love of life. Their cynicism and cynical rebellion result from a bitter resentment over the false loyalties of the world in which they live. Their sometimes shocking adventures and even more shocking reactions are devices by which the author reveals the sad truth about twentieth century reality, just as the Spanish picaresque authors used the weapons of comedy to unmask the society of their age.

The disorder, instability, and chaotic nature of the present age are reminiscent of the transitional character of the sixteenth century. Modern man, dwarfed by an awareness of his lack of control over events in the outside world as well as over his own behavior, cannot hope for heroism; the best he can achieve is a kind of *picaro* status: as an unwilling conformist, a rebel-victim, sometimes a picaresque saint. In the protean genre of the picaresque, sixteenth century Spanish writers created a fictional form appropriate to present the human predicament in an age of turmoil and instability.

Anna B. Katona

EPISTOLARY NOVEL

The epistolary novel, a prominent form among modern fictions, is defined as a novel presented wholly, or nearly so, in familiar letter form. Its history reaches far back into classical literature, taking special inspiration from the separate traditions of the Roman letter writers Cicero and Pliny, and Ovid's *Heroides*, a series of verse letters celebrating famous heroines of myth. Familiar letters, as such, developed slowly in a world where literacy was rare; but the epistle, a classic rhetorical form, defined by the rules of oratory, was a favorite means of expression for many scholars of the European Middle Ages and Renaissance, yielding learned letters in both prose and verse, most common at first in Latin, then in the vernacular.

The sixteenth century saw the first dated translation of Ovid's *Heroides* into French, in 1500. The mid-century welcomed with great enthusiasm the first "pure" epistolary novels with Juan de Segura's *Processo de cartas* (1548) and Alvise Pasqualigo's *Delle Lettere amorose* (1563). Letters had been used as tools in the earliest modern novels or romances, for they answered the frequent problem of communication between separated lovers, as well as giving the opportunity to multiply complications and mischances by having letters discovered by enemies, lost and intercepted, misinterpreted, or received out of time and season. For example, within the five-volume bulk of Honoré d'Urfé's pastoral novel *L'Astrée* (1610), there are 129 letters which are hidden in hats, stolen, found floating down rivers, or recited from memory.

The seventeenth century in France saw the development of a climate in which letters were one of the most popular forms of written material. The first printed edition of the letters of Abélard and Héloïse came in 1616, and the verse translation published in 1678 by Bussy-Rabutin (himself a celebrated social épistolier) was greeted with great enthusiasm. The collected epistles of Guez de Balzac, first published in 1624, had a great vogue, with many reprintings and new collections. His popular successor, Victor Voiture, was praised still more highly for the light tone and grace of his letters. Within the aristocratic salons of the day, the reading of letters within a circle of friends was a frequent social pastime, and many famous people of the day wrote their letters in the certainty of their being read to a group rather than kept private. Madame de Sévigné wrote to such correspondents as her cousin Bussy-Rabutin in the expectation that they would circulate and increase her reputation as a graceful wit.

Within the salons, expertise in letter-writing grew through mutual compliment and criticism, but the appearance of popular letter manuals offered models to a wider circle of literate people. Jean Puget de la Serre published his enormously successful *Secrétaire de la Cour* in 1623 and followed it in 1641 with the *Secrétaire à la Mode*. These manuals were translated and reissued through countless numbers of printings, became very popular in England, inspired a great number of imitations, and had an untold effect on developing popular epistolary style and thematics. The letter-writers, as they offered epistolary models on varied subjects and occasions, often offered responses as well, and built up a series of letters which told the germ of a story. Samuel Richardson wrote a letter handbook, *The Complete Letter-Writer* (1741), in which can be found the prototype for his epistolary novel *Pamela* (1740).

Familiar letters were regarded as direct transcriptions of events seen or experienced by their writers, and although the epistles of writers such as Guez de Balzac were acknowledged to be polished productions, letters in general carried the cachet of truth and spontaneity. Thus, arising out of the ferment of epistolary literature, the early epistolary novelists claimed for their works, as a matter of course, the privilege of historical truth. The most frequent *topos* of epistolary novels is the statement that they are a collection of real letters, not literary fabrications, and that the author is only an editor of material from other hands. The first great French epistolary novel, *Lettres portugaises* (1669, *Portuguese Letters*), now recognized as the work of Gabriel Guilleragues, was long believed to be a translation from the Portuguese of genuine letters written by a nun to her French lover. Letters offered a freedom of style, being rhetorically defined as written transcriptions of oral communication. Letters could deal with a variety of subjects, using a light touch, and were not forced to follow any subject through all its logical ramifications. Charles de Montesquieu, the author of *Les Lettres persanes* (1721, *Persian Letters*), refers to these advantages of epistolary form in his "Réflections" added to the edition of 1754. Letters carried the atmosphere of lived experience which gave credence and popularity to the memoir but had the added fillip of retelling stories whose ends were unknown. A memorialist has safely arrived at a point from which he can reflect on the past. Letters are written within the flow of present experience, looking back to the last letter written, forward to the next.

Love themes are given a special privilege in the epistolary fiction derived from the tradition of Ovid and Abélard and Héloïse, while the tradition descending from Cicero and Pliny to Guez de Balzac encourages the use of letters to treat a variety of topics of more general interest with the familiar touch of friends in social conversation. The seventeenth and eighteenth centuries saw the rise of the epistolary novel to a dominant prose form throughout Europe, first in France and England, then in Germany and Eastern Europe. Three of the most influential novels of the eighteenth century, *Pamela*, *La Nouvelle Héloïse* (1760, *The New Héloïse*) and *Die Leiden des jungen Werthers* (1774, *The Sorrows of Young Werther*), were all in letter form. It was certainly the exploitation by the writers of the epistolary form itself which gave their novels their immense impact.

In *Portuguese Letters*, the epistolary novel is given an emotionally concentrated model, inspiring numerous translations, "completions," and imitations.

The French edition of 1669, for example, was translated into English in 1678, 1681, 1693, 1694, and 1716. With its five letters, Guilleragues' work is extremely brief, especially considered in the context of novels such as the five-volume *L'Astrée*. Presented by the author, in his guise as editor, as "a correct copy of the translation of five Portuguese Letters which were written to a noble gentleman who served in Portugal," the letters are univocal; that is, the reader hears only the voice of one correspondent. Every attempt is made to establish the credibility of the letters, which are said to have been circulating in private hands. Publication is resorted to only to ensure that a "correct copy" rather than a spurious compilation is in public circulation. The nun's voice cries in genuine pain, expressed through a correspondence whose failure destroys the romantic ties with her French lover. The expectation of a response is inherent in the nun's use of the letter and in the I-you couple which defines the alternate composers of a correspondence. Direct address calls for direct response. The nun's letters begin in answer to a letter from the absent lover, and a two-sided exchange is expected. In fact, while requesting frequent letters, the nun also tries to set the tone, and admonishes her lover not to talk of useless things, nor ask her to remember him. The correspondence, and the romance, have run their course by the fifth and final letter, because the Frenchman does not respond within the expectations of the nun. At first he does not write at all; then his letters are inadequate to feed her passion.

Sentimental analysis, so important in this novel, is doubled by the analysis of the specific written form involved, by the problem of maintaining a satisfactory exchange of letters between parted lovers. The wounded heart of the nun is expressed in complaints of the lack of proper response in the letter chain, as well as of the lack of love. The author exploits the value of the letter as a tool for immediate access to his heroine's emotions, setting the tone for many later epistolary novels in the impassioned style of the nun's effusions. Even Mme. de Sévigné joked that if she responded in like tone to a tender note from a gentleman friend, she would have to write a "portugaise."

In 1721, *Persian Letters* was published anonymously by Charles Louis de Secondat, Baron de Montesquieu. The Introduction once again insists that the letters are a collection chosen from a great number written and received by Persians lodging with the author, letters copied and kept sometimes without the knowledge of the foreign travelers. The editor has "translated" the letters and adjusted them to European tastes, leaving out the flowery language, "sublime expressions," and long complimentary formulas of the originals. In choosing Persians for the chief characters of his novel, Montesquieu gave his novel an exotic background; in professing to adapt this exoticism to European tastes, he could add just as much as he liked for seasoning, without worrying about authentic Oriental style. The choice of Persians also greatly emphasizes the theme of absence inherent in epistolary form; it is the chief difficulty facing Usbek in the administration of his distant harem and the reason for his ultimate downfall as a domestic tyrant. This exotic flavor also allows for comic exploitation in the naïve reactions of the Persians as their letters recount the manners and morals of Montesquieu's world.

Persian Letters includes letters attributed to numerous pens, although the chief correspondents are Usbek and his younger companion Rica. Usbek's exchange with the members of his harem and their keepers provides the story without which this would be no true novel, but this story is only one of the two major strains in the novel. There are a great many letters which serve as discussions of current events in France or deal with moral and philosophical questions. In all of the letters, the name of the writer is given, in many of them a definite correspondent. All are dated according to the Persian calendar, covering a span of eight years. There are several complete letter circuits, letters given with their direct response, and subsequent letters to and from that same correspondent. There are also letter exchanges between secondary characters, such as that between the Chief Eunuch of Usbek's harem and a young protégé destined to replace him. The lapse of time indicated in the complete circuit of response is given great weight, especially at the denouement of the harem intrigue, when Usbek helplessly rages at the distances which make his own responses inadequate.

In Letter CLC, Usbek announces his return to Ispahan. His letters have often been received as much as six months late, and it is abundantly clear that he will not return to his harem until well after the horrible events chronicled in subsequent letters. Letter CXLVIII, Usbek's reply to CXLVII, giving the Chief Eunuch universal power over the harem, arrives after the death of the addressee and is kept by his elderly successor as a sealed relic (noted in Letter CXLIX). Letter CL, from Usbek, seeking to "reactivate" the sealed letter is either intercepted by harem rebels (version given in Letter CLI) or lost during a robbery (Letter CLII). The last letter of the novel, CLXI, written by Usbek's favorite, Roxane, is composed after a self-administered dose of poison, noted in the text, and the process of death defines the compass of the letter. In this letter, the writer details the end of the harem world in her own death, and ends the novel's text and her life when the pen falls from her hand and she dies.

The varied stylistic possibilities of letters are explored in the harem series; different writers are given different tones in which to express their characters, and the tones of the correspondents change as they address different people. Usbek does not write in the same manner to two different wives, and his tone and subject matter change again in addressing the Chief Eunuch or his own friend Nessir. The means of transmission of letters across the great distances is noted; Letter CL is to be delivered by some Armenian merchants traveling to Ispahan, but since the harem has moved to Usbek's country house, a servant is sent to fetch it; it disappears during a robbery on the servant's return trip. Letters are objects subject to many strange fates.

Letters serve a different function in the parallel series devoted to the exploration of various themes of French society and thought through the eyes of the Persian visitors. Here the epistolary form is used much as Voltaire later used it in his *Lettres philosophiques* (1734), where no story line is imposed within the letter framework to produce a true epistolary novel. In this use of the letter form, the epistolary license to touch on any subject with a light and familiar tone is the desired feature. The necessary epistolary use of the first person and direct address to the fictional correspondent gives the opportunity for the epistolary writer to build an automatic bridge of sympathy with the reader. In general, the formal fiction of the letter is given less weight as more is given to thematic development of the individual argument. In the Troglodyte series of letters (X through XIV), Usbek writes to his young friend Mirza, with the correspondence acting as a simple frame, an excuse for thematic development. Within the series, there are only the most perfunctory references to the correspondence, none to the letters themselves. Several texts succeed one another with no transition or attempt to explain differing circumstances of composition for different dates. Although written as a "response" to Mirza's letter, this series is a finished whole and requires no answer to complete it.

Persian Letters was followed by many epistolary novels set in exotic locales or using foreign characters for added interest and a pretext for letters. Laurent Versini, in his *Roman épistolaire* (1979), notes that half of the French epistolary novels between Montesquieu's success and 1750 were exotics. The great novels of the eighteenth century, however, concentrate on domestic situations, set within the countries of origin of their authors: *Pamela* in England, *The New Héloïse* in French Switzerland, and *The Sorrows of Young Werther* in Germany. These three works had enormous influence on the European reading public. All were translated into many tongues and inspired many imitators, both in literary terms and within the realm of everyday life. *The Sorrows of Young Werther*, said to have taken inspiration from *The New Héloïse*, in its turn supposed a direct descendant of *Pamela* and *Clarissa* (1747-1748), was not only one of the great propulsive works of German Romanticism, but was said to have inspired a rash of suicides on its publication as well.

Pamela: Or, Virtue Rewarded, appeared in print one year before *The Complete Letter-Writer*, begun earlier, in which Richardson had set down the novel's premise: a series of letters telling a true story of a virtuous servant girl who defends herself from her employer's advances and eventually is rewarded by his hand in marriage. What is a skeleton in the letter manual is fleshed out to great length in the highly detailed development of the novel. Translated by no less a light than the Abbé Prévost, succeeded by Richardson's own *Clarissa* and *Sir Charles Grandison* (1753-1754), *Pamela* was parodied, reportedly, by Henry Fielding in *Apology for the Life of Mrs. Shamela*

Andrews (1741), and definitely by Fielding's *Joseph Andrews* (1742). *Pamela* continues to arouse debate. Critics have often seen prurience in Richardson's theme and hypocrisy in his happy ending. Pamela's letters chronicle successive scenes of attempted seduction and rape in panting detail, while steadfastly defending the strictest principles of female chastity. Were Pamela's sufferings in some way a calculated "come-on" to a dupe due to be seduced into marriage? Although psychological credibility may be strained by the union of so much innocence and vulnerability with such a ferocious determination to resist and to recount every evidence of Mr. B.'s passion, the use of the letter form argues for Richardson's insistence on Pamela's candor. Richardson's first great epistolary novel is predicated on the assumption that the familiar letter is a direct window on the soul. Pamela may be taken at face value, and every letter carries what is supposed to be the free expression of the state of her soul.

Pamela is presented by the author as a collection of genuine letters, and he intrudes in his guise as editor to explain and provide transitions as well as to point out the moral at the end. In the opening pages, one finds complete letter circuits between Pamela Andrews and her aged, impoverished parents. These early letters introduce several of the major characters and establish the family's virtuous character, as well as a critical facet of Pamela's behavior. The favorable notice she had received from the lady whose death occasions the first letter, had led her to take an inordinate interest in reading and writing, though yet very young (Letter IV gives her age as fifteen), and in general had raised her above her station in education and behavior. The first letter speaks explicitly of itself, drawing attention to rather than leaving in the background the epistolary pretext of the fiction: Pamela's tears are blotting her paper. The means by which the letter is to be sent are discussed, and a postscript opens the theme of letters hidden from and discovered by Mr. B.

As the novel progresses, and Pamela passes through a series of harrowing experiences, including lengthy captivity by Mr. B., the letter exchange with her parents cannot continue, and Pamela writes to them in the hope that one day they will read her words and understand the trials through which she has come. Even her early letters are written in the anticipation of preservation and rereading by her entire family. The letters become a sort of journal, although an outward-turning one, in which the destined readers are often mentioned, and their reactions to a particular scene or reflection are imagined. The entries in this letter-journal are dated according to the day of the week, at times even with the time of day. All circumstances of composition are referred to, including the supply source of the paper, pen and ink, and their places of concealment. Some letters from Mr. B. are included in the form of copies, and any communication received by Pamela is closely analyzed in her subsequent writing. First-person narration and direct address are used throughout. Pamela comments constantly on her style, the effect of her circumstances on her composition, and her intention to set down each event as it happens.

The status of the growing body of manuscript is very important indeed, and is given a large place in the consideration of the epistolary text. Pamela's early letters are often intercepted and read by Mr. B. Her later journal is kept hidden from him by various expedients, sewn in Pamela's petticoats or, on threat of physical search, buried in the garden. In an attempt to have letters carried to her parents by the parson Mr. Williams, Pamela compromises that gentleman and brings him into disgrace with his patron. As a consequence, she has the piquant experience of reading a misdirected letter meant for Mrs. Jewkes, her keeper, and may contrast the style with the letter meant for herself and sent mistakenly to Jewkes. The recopying of Jewkes's letter serves a double purpose, to illustrate the severity of Mr. B. and to enter the text into the secret letter-journal. At last, when Pamela is dismissed from Mr. B.'s sight and is en route to her parents in disgrace, it is the story told by her letters, surrendered to him, which persuades him to change his resolution and marry her. The marriage restores epistolary commerce between Pamela and the elder Andrewses, and they learn the course of their daughter's acceptance into noble society, ending in their reunion on Mr. B.'s estates. The collection of Pamela's letters is left circulating among the family and friends of Mr. B. at the close of the novel, reconciling all to his choice of a wife.

While *Pamela* includes occasional letters from Mr. B. and other characters, the text is essentially univocal. *Clarissa*, Richardson's next novel, employs correspondence of several different characters in presenting and maintaining a multivocal epistolary narration. In Jean-Jacques Rousseau's *The New Héloïse*, it is the love duet of Julie and her Saint-Preux which holds the central position. The letters are presented by the author as a collection of genuine letters, as the title itself announces: *Julie: Or, The New Héloïse, Letters from Two Lovers*, inhabitants of a small town at the foot of the Alps, collected and published by Jean-Jacques Rousseau. By linking his novel with the long-standing epistolary tradition of Abélard and Héloïse, Rousseau stresses the importance of letters as letters, as well as their aura of historic truth (since the first Héloïse was real, so is Julie), and the importance of the love intrigue, with its implication of suffering and sacrifice.

Letter form is given special weight in the first half of the novel, where, as the letters introduce the characters and lay the foundations for later narration, individual texts respond point-by-point to their predecessors. It is in answering Saint-Preux's letters, written while the lovers are in close daily contact, that Julie enters into a romantic relationship with him. It is in a letter that she first receives his expression of affection, and through the letters that they are bound together, even over long absences. The letters are written in the first person, directed to a very definite correspondent, and the mode of communication between the lovers is discussed at length. Themes treated within the letters vary widely and include philosophical discussions, in which cases Rousseau uses the prerogative of the epistolary form to digress from his plot much as Montesquieu did. Within the line of the main narration, letters are important as physical testimony of the loved "other," substitutes for the loved one in absence, and as such they are kissed, caressed, preserved, and reread. Saint-Preux's handling of Julie's letters forces him to recopy them, since the originals are wearing out. This recopying in a certain sense establishes a prototext of the final letter collection represented in the novel. The time-lapse between the letters is important, as is their method of transmission.

Letter XXI presents a highly dramatic scene in which Saint-Preux awaits and receives one of Julie's letters from the hand of the mail-carrier. This passage highlights all the details of transmission: the necessity of naming oneself in claiming the letter, the opening of the outer packet in which the letter has traveled with the correspondence of others, the confirmation that there is indeed a letter for the narrator, and finally the confirmation of the letter itself as a physical object carrying the imprint of the loved one's hand in the superscription. Saint-Preux continues to recount in his own letter, in response to this one received with so much ceremony, the emotion he felt when he held the paper in his trembling hand and the conditions under which he finally opened and read it. The emphasis lies not only on the single letter so dramatized, but also on the entire correspondence. In a text such as Voltaire's *Lettres philosophiques*, no attention is given to building or embroidering the fiction of the epistolary text as a physical reality. In *The New Héloïse*, the highly charged, emotional intimacy between Julie and her Saint-Preux is served by the attention lavished on the mechanics of a letter exchange through which the narration may proceed and by which it is colored. The identification of the reader is sought through the attempt to engage belief in the reality of the characters involved. Again, as in *Pamela*, letters serve as a "hot" medium, transparent to the emotions of the individual writers and immediate to the events which affect them.

The Sorrows of Young Werther, the first major work of Johann Wolfgang von Goethe, is brief and concentrated in its impact, in contrast to the voluminous works of Rousseau and Richardson. Again, the book is presented by the editor as a collection of "all I could find" of Werther's letters. Almost all are addressed to Werther's intimate friend, Wilhelm, with a small number written for the beloved Lotte and her husband Albert. The personality of the correspondent is seldom given much weight within the individual texts, although there are very few letters in which Werther does not use direct address or in which the intended reader is not clearly designated. Wilhelm is almost always the intimate "du," infrequently "ihr" when in the company of Werther's mother. Lotte alone is "Sie," until the last letter, while Lotte and Albert together are "ihr," combining formal address for Lotte with familiar form for her husband. Significantly, as in *Persian Letters*, each epistolary text is dated, and the rhythm of the narration speeds or slows with the ebb and flow of the fictional correspondence. When Werther is overcome by the flux of his emotions during time spent with Lotte, the letters to Wilhelm are dated every two or three days, sometimes daily. When bored and depressed by exterior circumstances, such as his position on an ambassador's staff, the letters come only once a week or so. The infrequent letters may be seen as an attempt at verisimilitude, since, although there is no break in the narration during these periods, the editor notes that certain letters of this period have been withheld as indiscreet.

Unlike Rousseau and Richardson, Goethe devotes little attention to the technical aspects of the epistolary commerce. One knows exactly where and how Pamela gets her pen and paper, one knows how Saint-Preux receives and treats Julie's letters, but there is no indication of how Werther's letters are written or exchanged with Wilhelm. The references to epistolary style are few, but there are some direct responses to Wilhelm's letters, with passages cited as they are answered. Beyond the faithful use of dates, which serves a dramatic purpose in emphasizing the speed with which Werther's passion enfolds and destroys him, there are very few uses of set letter forms. The letters vary greatly in length, some quite long and others reduced to the briefest of paragraphs. No opening formulas are used, and the formal closings are sparse, with at most a simple "Leb wohl" inserted at the end. This manner of closing, however, can be effectively dramatized, as in Werther's closing to his suicide letter: "Lotte! Lotte leb wohl! Leb wohl!"

Goethe uses the letter form as a painfully intimate reflection of the state of mind of his suffering hero. The fragmentary sentences which would be out of place in another narrative form, the stringing together of dated paragraphs which gain weight from their status as letters addressed to an outer eye, the license to speak in the first person about all the secret movements of the soul—these are all possibilities inherent in the epistolary form. That Werther makes what amounts to an aberrant use of the form in his emphasis on one pole of the correspondence, his own, is in a way a facet of the characterization of the tragic hero, so locked in on his own suffering that suicide becomes his only escape. The letter form is also open to the many descriptions of Werther's impressions of the people and things around him, yet even his sweeping pictures of the natural beauty he meets are transmuted into personal reflections. This is not the same use that Montesquieu, or even Rousseau, makes of the possibility of including material exterior to the story line within the narrative of a letter. The emotional impact of *The Sorrows of Young Werther* is concentrated and focused through this use of univocal, inward-turning letter form.

The last days of Werther's life are chronicled by the anonymous editor's voice in a curious text formed by the third-person reminiscences of Lotte, Albert, Werther's servant, and other people who met or talked with Werther in that time. These bits of testimony are woven through by fragments of a last, undated letter addressed to Lotte, and shorter bits directed to Wilhelm. This last attempt at writing anticipates the reactions of Werther's loved ones after his death, and frequent reference is made to their reading the text after the writer's burial. In it, Lotte changes from "Sie" to "du," and is addressed in the most intimate and intense tones. The last words, addressed to her, are written immediately before the fatal shot. The impersonal editorial voice informs the reader that "From the blood on the back of the seat, one can determine, that he did the deed sitting before the writing desk." The contrast between Werther's own heated voice and the cold style of the editor is devastating, producing an impression of the "truth" of the fatal events and the finality of Werther's death.

The Sorrows of Young Werther, *The New Héloïse*, and *Pamela* all depend heavily on the convention that personal letters are the vehicles of personal truth, open and immediate to the individuals that write them. This understanding plays a part in the characterization of the fictional protagonists and in the emotional effects elicited by their letters. In contrast to these novels, *Les Liaisons dangereuses* (1782, *Dangerous Acquaintances*) of Pierre Choderlos de Laclos takes much of its impact from the use made by the libertine protagonists, the Marquise de Merteuil and the Vicomte de Valmont, of this same convention to conceal their emotions and intentions and to seduce and destroy their correspondents. The author plays with several correspondences exchanged within a small social circle, changing styles with each writer and according to each addressee. The totality of the letters is revealed, through various stratagems, to Mme. de Merteuil and her sometime ally Valmont, and each letter becomes the object of discussion and analysis between them. If the progress of the seductions by Merteuil and Valmont are one interest of the narrative, the change in their relationship through the course of the novel is another, a chance brought about in part through Valmont's own surrender to love for his victim Mme. de Tourvel. The terms of his letters to Merteuil are held as a contract, forcing him to the destruction of the loved object and himself.

Dangerous Acquaintances is preceded by a double preface, the first by the "editor," the second by the "writer." Together they form an ironic gem. The editor writes a bit of social commentary, saying that in spite of the author's attempts to make his work seem genuine, it must be a novel, because the contemporary age is too moral for such events to take place. The writer produces the image of a pedantic hired hack, who has pieced together the letters of the novel, chosen from a great body of possible correspondence, as the smallest number of texts necessary to tell the story. The writer complains that the third party, who commissioned him, did not allow him to change the grammar or style of the letters or to cut the chosen texts, "of which several deal separately, and almost without transition, with subjects altogether unconnected with one another." His employers maintain that a variety of styles, even errors, and a diversity of themes are expected of personal letters. Such features, the writer thinks, may both attract and repel the public, and since all the sentiments, or nearly so, are pretended, the identification of the public with the characters will be impaired. The reader of both the Prefaces will find himself in a position of ironic suspension, where neither introductory voice can be believed or wholly rejected, and thus he must approach the novel with suspended judgment.

The complexity of *Dangerous Acquaintances* and the literary virtuosity with which it was composed have attracted a great deal of critical attention. One of the most interesting of such studies, both in regard to this individual work and in its general overview of the epistolary genre, is Jean Rousset's "Le Roman par lettres," included in his collected essays, *Forme et Signification* (1962). Rousset discusses the important factors which enlist the reader's identification with the characters of the epistolary novel: the atmosphere of intimacy provided by the familiar letter form; the fact that the action of the novel is contemporary with the life and voice of the characters; the seductiveness of the bipolar I-you structure which almost forces a reader to identify with the voices of the letters. Rousset further points out that, in the case of *Dangerous Acquaintances*, the reader is, like Merteuil and Valmont, in possession of an entire epistolary text, thus knowing the stratagems employed by the libertines in the composition of their letters. In Rousset's view, this knowledge renders the reader an accomplice of the libertines in their work of seduction.

What are the techniques used by Laclos to write these compromising letters that catch the reader in a dangerous liaison? Great importance is given to the individual letter and its ties with other letters. The names of writer and addressee are given, the dates of composition, and often the place. Frequent reference is made to letters received from the correspondent and other letters written or received by the writers. When Cécile de Volanges runs out of writing materials, Valmont smuggles some to her (Letter LXXIII). The mode of transmission of letters and where and how they are kept is a major motif, since so many of the exchanges are clandestine, and the various ruses of delivery and concealment are continuously under discussion.

In addition to the primary series of letters between pairs of correspondents, there is a secondary exchange within the letters of Mme. de Merteuil and Valmont, of copies of letters to and from third parties, with detailed commentary and analysis of motivation and circumstances of character and composition. This commentary often completely changes the interpretation which must be given to individual passages or entire letters. One particularly titillating example is Letter XLVIII, written by Valmont to Mme. de Tourvel. A naïve reader, such as Mme. de Tourvel, sees in it nothing but Valmont's agitated state of mind, owing to his professed passion for his correspondent. In Letter XLVII, however, Valmont sends the letter to Mme. de Merteuil, who will post it for him from Paris, to preserve a pretense of his remaining in that city. Merteuil and the outside reader are informed that the letter was written on the back of a prostitute, the composition interrupted for intercourse, and that it gives an exact accounting of Valmont's situation and conduct in ambiguous terms. Thus when Valmont says, "The very table on which I write to you, consecrated for the first time to this use, becomes for me the sacred altar of love," the meaning is changed beyond recognition by the added information.

The reading and answering of letters are stressed as acts of self-engagement in the relations of the characters. Valmont sees the future success of his seduction in Mme. de Tourvel's first reply to one of his letters; he sees its near accomplishment in the discovery that all his letters have been saved, even while the lady virtuously denies him any other sign of weakening. Several letters are dictated by one character to another, and the final letter with which Valmont must break Mme. de Tourvel's heart, in order to fulfill his agreements with Merteuil, is copied verbatim from a model supplied in Merteuil's Letter CXLI.

The chain of events by which all the letters are united in the hands of Mme. de Rosemonde, thereby creating the novel text, is a chain of catastrophe. The production of the novel is the destruction of its chief characters. Of the victims, Cécile de Volanges enters a convent, the Chevalier Danceny goes into exile, and Mme. de Tourvel dies of humiliation and a broken heart. Valmont is fatally wounded in a duel with Danceny, but as his last act he confides to the young man the packet of letters detailing his own relations with Mme. de Merteuil, thus revealing the character of his beautiful and outwardly virtuous confederate. Danceny, after circulating some of these letters, passes the entire packet on to Valmont's elderly aunt, Mme. de Rosemonde, the close friend of Mme. de Volanges (Cécile's mother) and Mme. de Tourvel. Mme. de Merteuil herself is cast out of polite society, loses a court case which robs her of her entire fortune, suffers a severe case of smallpox which leaves her horribly disfigured, and finally flees the country, ill and utterly alone but carrying her diamonds with her. Laclos leaves no thread untied, as his bundle of letters is bound into a book.

Dangerous Acquaintances opens with a quote drawn from *The New Héloïse*. In its cynical use of letters as instruments of seduction and betrayal, it destroys the premise of emotional immediacy used to such advantage by Rousseau in his novel. For Saint-Preux, letters are a self-generating system by whose intervention he may always be in the presence of his beloved: "I can no longer separate myself from you, the least absence is unbearable to me, and it is necessary that I either see you or write to you in order to occupy myself with you without ceasing" (Letter XI). For Mme. de Merteuil, the letter is a tool to be used for definite ends: "What good would it do you to soften hearts with Letters, since you would not be there to profit from it?" (Letter XXXIII). Yet in the final analysis, it is through the letters united in the novel that Laclos paints compelling portraits of his characters, not in direct revelations but through the reflections and combinations of the continuing chain of correspondence. Valmont's inner truth finally does correspond with the appearance of love in his first letters to Mme. de Tourvel, and it is Mme. de Merteuil's letters which convince society of the evil character she had always before been able to conceal.

A fertile genre throughout the eighteenth century, the epistolary novel has enjoyed a small vogue among contemporary writers of experimental and avant-garde fiction, with John Barth the most prominent American example. Such writers employ the conventions of the genre in a deliberately anachronistic spirit, achieving ironic distance in a form once favored for its sense of immediacy.

Anne Waterman Sienkewicz

GOTHIC NOVEL

The Gothic novel is a living tradition, a form which has enjoyed great popular appeal while provoking harsh critical judgments. It began with Horace Walpole's *The Castle of Otranto* (1764), traveled through Mrs. Ann Radcliffe, Matthew Gregory Lewis, Charles Robert Maturin, Mary Wollstonecraft Shelley, Edgar Allan Poe, the Brontës, Nathaniel Hawthorne, Charles Brockden Brown, Bram Stoker, Charles Dickens, Thomas Hardy, Henry James, and many others into the twentieth century, where it has surfaced, much altered and yet spiritually continuous, in the work of writers such as William Faulkner, D. H. Lawrence, Iris Murdoch, John Gardner, Joyce Carol Oates, and Doris Lessing as well as in a host of ephemeral genre novels.

The Gothic novel's externals are characterized by sublime but terrifying mountain scenery; bandits and outlaws; ruined, ancient seats of power; morbid death imagery; virgins and charismatic villains; as well as hyperbolic physical states of agitation and lurid images of physical degradation. Its spirit is characterized by a tone of high agitation, unresolved or almost-impossible-to-resolve anxiety, fear, unnatural elation, and desperation.

The first Gothic novel is identified by scholars with a precision unusual in genre study. Horace Walpole began writing *The Castle of Otranto* in June, 1764, finished it in August, 1764, and published it in an edition of five hundred copies on Christmas Eve, 1764. Walpole (1717-1797), the Earl of Orford, was a historian and essayist whose vivid and massive personal correspondence remains essential reading for the eighteenth century background. Before writing *The Castle of Otranto*, his only connection with the Gothic was his estate in Twickenham, which he called Strawberry Hill. It was built in the Gothic style and set an architectural trend, as his novel would later set a literary trend.

Walpole did not dream of what he was about to initiate with *The Castle of Otranto*; he published his first edition anonymously, revealing his identity, only after the novel's great success, in his second edition of April, 1765. At that point, he no longer feared mockery of his tale of a statue with a bleeding nose, mammoth, peregrinating armor, and an ancient castle complete with ancient family curse. With his second edition, he was obliged to add a preface explaining why he had hidden behind the guise of a preface proclaiming the book to be a "found manuscript," printed originally "in Naples in the black letter in 1529. . . ." The reader of the first edition was told that *The Castle of Otranto* was the long-lost history of an ancient, Catholic family in the north of England. The greater reading public loved it, and it was reprinted in many editions. By 1796, it had been translated into French and Spanish and had been repeatedly rendered into dramatic form. In 1848, the novel was still active as the basis for successful theatrical presentations, despite the fact that the original Gothic vogue had passed.

Close upon Walpole's heels followed Radcliffe, Lewis, and Maturin. These, of course, were not the only imitators ready to take advantage of the contemporary trend (there were literally hundreds of those), but they are among the few who are still read, for they made their own distinctive contributions to the genre's evolution.

Mrs. Ann Radcliffe (1764-1823) was born just as Walpole's *The Castle of Otranto* was being published. She was reared and continued to live her life in a middle-class milieu, acquainted with merchants and professionals; her husband was the editor of *The English Chronicle* and a Fellow of the Society of Antiquaries. She lived a quiet life, is believed to have been asthmatic, and seems to have stayed close to her hearth. Although she never became a habitué of literary circles, and in her lifetime only published a handful of works, she is considered the grande dame of the Gothic novelists and enjoyed a stunning commercial success in her day; she is the only female novelist of the period whose work is still read.

Radcliffe's works include *The Castles of Athlin and Dunbayne* (1789); *A Sicilian Romance* (1790); *The Romance of the Forest* (1791); *The Mysteries of Udolpho* (1794), her greatest success; *The Italian: Or, The Confessional of the Black Penitents* (1797); *The Poems of Ann Radcliffe* (1816); and, published after her death, *Gaston de Blondeville* (1826). She also wrote an account of a trip she made with her husband, *A Journey Made in the Summer of 1794 Through Holland and the Western Frontiers of Germany* (1795). Her remarkably sedate life contrasts strikingly with the melodramatic flamboyance of her works. Her experiences also fail to account for her dazzling, fictional accounts of the scenery of Southern Europe, which she had never seen.

Matthew Gregory Lewis, called "Monk" Lewis in honor of his major work, conformed in his life more closely to the stereotype of the Gothic masters. Lewis (1775-1818) was a child of the upper classes, the spoiled son of a frivolous beauty, whom he adored. His parents' unhappy marriage broke up when he was at Westminster Preparatory School. There was a continual struggle between his parents to manage his life, his father stern and aloof, his mother extravagant and possessive.

Lewis actually spent his childhood treading the halls of large, old manses belonging both to family and to friends. He paced long, gloomy corridors—a staple of the Gothic—and peered up at ancient portraits in dark galleries, another permanent fixture in Gothic convention. Homosexual, flamboyant, and deeply involved with the literati of his day, Lewis found an equivocal public reception, but *The Monk* (1796), an international sensation, had an enormous effect on the Gothic productions of his day. Lewis died on board ship, a casualty of a yellow-fever epidemic, in the arms of his valet, Baptista, and was buried at sea.

Lewis' bibliography is as frenetic as his biography. His only Gothic novel is the infamous *The Monk*. He spent most of his career writing plays heavily influenced by Gothic conventions; he also translated many Gothic works into English and wrote scandalous poetry. Among his plays are *Village Virtues* (1796), *The Castle Spectre* (1796), *The East Indian* (1800), *Adelmorn, the Outlaw* (1801), and *The Captive* (1803). He was responsible for the translations of Frîedrich Schiller's *The Minister* (1797), August Kotzebue's *Rolla: Or, The Peruvian Hero* (1799), and Johann Zschokke's *Rugantino: Or, The Bravo of Venice* (1805). He was notorious for a satirical poem, *The Pursuits of Literature* (1794), and for an imitation of Juvenal's thirteenth satire, *Love of Gain* (1799).

The Reverend Charles Robert Maturin is the final major Gothic artist of the period. Maturin (1782-1824) was Irish, a Protestant clergyman from Dublin, and a spiritual brother of the Marquis de Sade. He was a protégé of Sir Walter Scott and an admirer of Lord Byron. His major Gothic novel is *Melmoth the Wanderer* (1820), as shocking to its public as was Lewis' *The Monk*. An earlier Gothic was *The Fatal Revenge: Or, The Family of Montorio* (1807), written under the pseudonym of Dennis Jasper Murphy. He also wrote *The Milesian Chief* (1812); a theological treatise, *Women: Or, Pour et Contre* (1818); a tragedy, *Bertram* (1816), produced by Edmund Kean; and *The Albigenses* (1824).

Among the legions of other Gothic novelists, a few writers, no longer generally read, have made a place for themselves in literary history. These include Harriet Lee, known for *The Canterbury Tales* (1797-1805, 5 volumes); her sister Sophia Lee, known for *The Recess* (1785, 3 volumes); Clara Reeve, known for *The Olde English Baron* (1778); Mrs. Regina Maria Roche, known for *The Children of the Abbey* (1796); Mrs. Charlotte Smith, known for *Emmeline, the Orphan of the Castle* (1788); Charlotte Dacre, known for *Zofloya: Or, The Moor* (1806); and Mary-Anne Radcliffe, known for *Manfroné: Or, The One Handed Monk* (1809).

Critics generally agree that the period Gothics, while having much in common, divide into relatively clear subclassifications: the historical Gothic, the school of terror, and the *Schauer-Romantik* school of horror. All Gothics of the period return to the past, are flushed with suggestions of the supernatural, and tend to be set amid ruined architecture, particularly a great estate house gone to ruin or a decaying abbey. All make use of stock characters. These will generally include one or more young and innocent virgins of both sexes, monks and nuns, particularly of sinister aspect, and towering male and female characters of overpowering will whose charismatic egotism knows no bounds. Frequently the novels are set in the rugged mountains of Italy and contain an evil Italian character. Tumultuous weather often accompanies tumultuous passions. The Gothic genre specializes in making external conditions metaphors of human emotions, a convention thought to have been derived in part from the works of William Shakespeare. Brigands are frequently employed in the plot, and most Gothics of the period employ morbid, lurid imagery, such as a body riddled with worms behind a moldy, black veil.

The various subdivisions of the Gothic may feature any or all of the above, being distinguished by relative emphasis. The historical Gothic, for example, revealed the supernatural against a genuinely historical background, best exemplified by the works of the Lee sisters, who, although their own novels are infrequently read today, played a part in the evolution of the historical novel through their influence on Sir Walter Scott. The school of terror provided safe emotional titillation; safe, because the morbidity such novels portrayed never took place in a genuine, historical setting, but in some fantasy of the past, and because the fearful effects tended to be explained away rationally at the end of the work. Mrs. Radcliffe is the major paradigm of this subgroup. The *Schauer-Romantik* school of horror, best represented by Lewis and Maturin, did not offer the reassurance of a moral, rational order. These works tend to evoke history, but from a point of view that stirs anxiety without resolving or relieving it. They are perverse and sadistic, marked by the amoral use of thrill.

There are very few traditional Gothic plots and conventions; a discrete set of such paradigms was recycled and refurbished many times. Walpole's *The Castle of Otranto*, Radcliffe's *The Mysteries of Udolpho*, Lewis' *The Monk*, and Maturin's *Melmoth the Wanderer* represent the basic models of the genre.

Walpole's *The Castle of Otranto*, emphatically not historical Gothic, takes place in a fantasy past. It is not of the school of terror either; although it resolves its dilemmas in a human fashion, it does not rationally explain away the supernatural events it has recounted. This earliest of the Gothics trembles between horror and terror.

The story opens with Manfred, Prince of Otranto, ready to marry his sickly son, Conrad, to the beautiful Isabella. Manfred, the pattern for future Gothic villains of towering egotism and pride, is startled when his son is killed in a bizarre fashion. The gigantic statuary helmet of a marble figure of Alphonse the Good has been mysteriously transported to Manfred's castle, where it has fallen on and crushed Conrad.

Manfred precipitously reveals that he is tired of his virtuous wife, Hippolita, and, disdaining both her and their virtuous daughter, Mathilda, attempts to force himself on the exquisite, virginal Isabella, his erstwhile daughter-in-law elect. At the same time, he attempts to blame his son's death on an individual named Theodore, who appears to be a virtuous peasant lad and bears an uncanny resemblance to the now helmetless statue of Alfonso the Good. Theodore is incarcerated in the palace but manages to escape.

Theodore and Isabella, both traversing the mazelike halls of Otranto to escape Manfred, find each other, and Theodore manages to set Isabella free. She finds asylum in the Church of St. Nicholas, site of the statue of Alfonso the Good, under the protection of Father Jerome, a virtuous friar. In the process of persuading Jerome to bring Isabella to him, Manfred discovers that Theodore is actually Jerome's long-lost son. Manfred threatens Theodore in order to maneuver Jerome into delivering Isabella. The long-lost relative later became a popular feature of the Gothic.

Both Isabella and Theodore are temporarily saved by the appearance of a mysterious Black Knight, who turns out to be Isabella's father and joins the forces against Manfred. A round of comings and goings through tunnels, hallways, and churches ensues. This flight through dark corridors also became almost mandatory in Gothic fiction. In the course of his flight, Theodore falls in love with Mathilda. As the two lovers meet in a church, Manfred, "flushed with love and wine," mistakes Mathilda for Isabella. Wishing to prevent Theodore from possessing the woman he thinks is his own beloved, Manfred mistakenly stabs his daughter. Her dying words prevent Theodore from revenging her: "Stop thy impious hand . . . it is my father!"

Manfred must now forfeit his kingdom for his bloody deed. The final revelation is that Theodore is actually the true Prince of Otranto; he is the direct descendant of Alfonso the Good. The statuary helmet flies back to the statue; Isabella is given to Theodore in marriage, but only after he has completed a period of mourning for Mathilda; order is restored. The flight of the helmet remains beyond the pale of reason, as does the extraordinary, rigid virtue of the sympathetic characters, but Manfred's threat to the kingdom is ended. Here is the master plot for the Gothic of the Kingdom.

Radcliffe's *Mysteries of Udolpho*, presents apparently unnatural behavior and events but ultimately explains them all away. Not only will the sins of the past be nullified, but also human understanding will penetrate all the mysteries. In *The Mysteries of Udolpho*, the obligatory Gothic virgin is Emily St. Aubert; she is complemented by a virginal male named Valancourt, whom Emily meets while still in the bosom of her family. When her parents die, she is left at the mercy of her uncle, the villainous Montoni, dark, compelling, and savage in pursuit of his own interests. Montoni whisks Emily away to Udolpho, his great house in the Apennines, where, desperate for money, he exerts himself on Emily in hopes of taking her patrimony while his more lustful, equally brutal friends scheme against her virtue. Emily resists, fainting and palpitating frequently. Emily's propensity to swoon is very much entrenched in the character of the Gothic heroine.

Emily escapes and, sequestered in a convent, makes the acquaintance of a dying nun, whose past is revealed to contain a murder inspired by lust and greed. Her past also contains Montoni, who acquired Udolpho through her evil deeds. Now repenting, the nun (née Laurentini de Udolpho) reveals all. The innocent victim of Laurentini's stratagems was Emily's long-lost, virtuous aunt, and Udolpho should have been hers. Ultimately, it will belong to Emily and Valancourt.

This novel contains the obligatory Gothic flights up and down dimly lit staircases and halls and into dark turrets; there are also fabulous vistas of soul-elevating charm in the Apennines, which became a hallmark of Gothic, and blood-chilling vistas of banditti by torch and moonlight. There is also mysterious music that seems to issue from some supernatural source and a mysterious disappearance of Emily's bracelet, both later revealed to be the work of Valancourt. A miniature picture of the first Marchioness of Udolpho, who looks unaccountably like Emily, threatens to reveal some irregularity about pure Emily's birth, but in the end reveals only that the poor, victimized Marchioness was Emily's aunt. In Udolpho, in a distant turret, Emily finds a body being devoured by worms. Emily is thrown into a frenzy, fearing that this is the corpse of her deluded aunt, Montoni's wife, but it is revealed to be merely a wax effigy placed there long ago for the contemplation of some sinning cleric, as a penance. The dark night of the soul lifts, and terror yields to the paradise that Emily and Valancourt will engender. This is the master plot for personal Gothic: the Gothic of the family.

Radcliffe was known to distinguish between horror and terror and would have none of the former. Terror was a blood-tingling experience of which she approved because it would ultimately yield to better things. Horror she identified with decadence, a distemper in the blood that could not be discharged, but rendered man inactive with fright. Lewis' *The Monk* demonstrates Radcliffe's distinction.

The Monk concerns a Capuchin friar named Ambrosio, famed for his beauty and virtue throughout Madrid. He is fervent in his devotion to his calling and is wholly enchanted by a picture of the Virgin, to which he prays. A young novice of the order named Rosario becomes Ambrosio's favorite. Rosario is a beautiful, virtuous youth, as Ambrosio thinks, but one night Ambrosio perceives that Rosario has a female breast, and that "he" is in fact "she": Mathilda, a daughter of a noble house, so enthralled by Ambrosio that she has disguised herself to be near him. Mathilda is the very image of the picture of the Virgin to which Ambrosio is so devoted, and, through her virginal beauty, seduces Ambrosio into a degrading sexual entanglement which is fully described. As Mathilda grows more obsessed with Ambrosio, his ardor cools. To secure him to her, she offers help in seducing Antonia, another virginal beauty, Ambrosio's newest passion. Mathilda, the madonna-faced enchantress, now reveals that she is actually a female demon. She puts her supernatural powers at Ambrosio's disposal, and together they successfully abduct Antonia, although only after killing Antonia's mother. Ambrosio then rapes Antonia in the foul, suffocating stench of a charnel house in the cathedral catacombs. In this scene of heavy breathing and sadism, the monk is incited to his deed by the virginal Antonia's softness and her moist pleas for her virtue. Each tear excites him further into a frenzy, which he climaxes by strangling the girl.

Ambrosio's deeds are discovered, and he is tried by an inquisitorial panel. Mathilda reveals his union with Satan through her. The novel ends with Satan's liberation of Ambrosio from the dungeon into which the inquisitors have thrown him. Satan mangles Ambrosio's body by throwing him into an abyss, but does not let him die for seven days (the de-creation of the world?). During this time, Ambrosio must suffer the physical and psychological torments of his situation, and the reader along with him. The devil triumphs at the end of this novel. All means of redressing virtue are abandoned and the reader is left in the abyss with Ambrosio.

The same may be said of Maturin's *Melmoth the Wanderer*, a tale of agony and the failure of redemption. The book may be called a novel only if one employs the concept of the picaresque in its broadest sense. It is a collection of short stories, each centering on Melmoth, a damned, Faust-like character. Each tale concerns Melmoth's attempt to find someone to change places with him, a trade he would gladly make, as he has sold his soul to the devil and now wishes to be released.

The book rubs the reader's nerves raw with obsessive suffering, detailing scenes from the Spanish Inquisition which include the popping of bones and the melting of eyeballs. The book also minutely details the degradation of a beautiful, virginal island maiden named Immalee, who is utterly destroyed by the idolatrous love of Melmoth.

The last scene of the book ticks the seconds of the clock as Melmoth, unable to find a surrogate, waits his fall into Satan's clutches. The denouement is an almost unbearable agony that the reader is forced to endure with the protagonist. Again the horror is eternal. There will never be any quietus for either Ambrosio or Melmoth, or for the reader haunted by them. These are the molds for the Gothic of damnation.

The reading public of the late eighteenth and early nineteenth centuries was avid for both horror and terror, as well as for supernatural history. Such works were gobbled greedily as they rolled off the presses. Indeed, the Gothic reading public may have begun the mass marketing of literature by insuring the fortunes of the private lending libraries that opened in response to the Gothic binge. Although the libraries continued after the Gothic wave had crested, it was this craze that gave the libraries their impetus. Such private lending libraries purchased numerous copies of long lists of Gothic works and furnished each subscriber with a list from which he might choose. Like contemporary book clubs, the libraries vied for the most appetizing authors. Unlike the modern clubs, books circulated back and forth, not to be kept by subscribers.

William Lane's Minerva Public Library was the most famous and most successful of all these libraries. Lane went after the works of independent Gothic authors, but formed the basis of his list by maintaining his own stable of hacks. The names of most of the "stable authors" are gone, and so are their books, but the titles linger on in the library records echoing one another and the titles of the more prominent authors: *The Romance Castle* (1791); *The Black Forest: Or, The Cavern of Horrors* (1802); *The Mysterious Omen:*

Or, Awful Retribution (1812).

The logistics of the lending library subscription are best exemplified by the Minerva model. Minerva had five classes of subscriptions. The first class paid approximately five pounds per year, though half-year subscriptions were also available. The first-class subscriber could choose twenty-four volumes from the list if he lived in the city, thirty-six if he lived in the country. The lower the subscription rate, the fewer choices one had. A fifth-class subscription meant four choices in town, eight in the country, and none could be from the new publication lists.

By the time that *Melmoth the Wanderer* had appeared, most of this had run its course. Only hacks continued to mine the old pits for monks, nuns, fainting innocents, Apennine banditti, and Satanic quests, but critics agree that if the conventions of the Gothic period from Walpole to Maturin have dried out and fossilized, the spirit is very much alive. Many a modern novel which is set miles from an abbey and contains not one shrieking, orphaned virgin or worm-ridden corpse, may be considered Gothic. If the sophisticated cannot repress a snicker at the obvious and well-worn Gothic conventions, they cannot dismiss the power and attraction of its spirit, which lives today in serious literature.

Modern thinking about Gothic literature has gravitated toward the psychological aspects of the Gothic. The castle or ruined abbey has become the interior of the mind, racked with anxiety and unbridled surges of emotion, governed melodramatically by polarities. The traditional Gothic is now identified as the beginning of neurotic literature. In a perceptive new study of the genre, *Love, Misery, and Mystery* (1978), Coral Ann Howells points out that the Gothic literature of the eighteenth century was willing to deal with the syntax of hysteria, which the more prestigious literature, controlled by classical influences, simply denied or avoided. Hysteria is no stranger to all kinds of literature, it is true, but current thinking seeks to discriminate between the literary presentation of hysteria or neuroticism as an aberration from a rational norm and the Gothic presentation of neuroticism as equally normative with rational control, or even as the dominant mode.

The evolution of the modern Gothic began close to the original seedbed, in the works of Edgar Allan Poe. In "The Fall of The House of Usher," for example, the traditional sins of the Gothic past cavort in a mansion of ancient and noble lineage. A young virgin is subjected to the tortures of the charnel house; the tomb and the catacombs descend directly from Lewis. So too do the hyperbolic physical states of pallor and sensory excitement. This tale is also marked, however, by the new relationship it seeks to demonstrate between reason and hysterical anxiety.

Roderick·Usher's boyhood friend, the story's narrator, is a representative of the normative rational world. He is forced to encounter a reality in which anxiety and dread are the norm and in which the passions know no rational bounds. Reason is forced to confront the reality of hysteria, its horror, terror, and power. This new psychological development of the Gothic is stripped of the traditional Gothic appurtenances in Poe's "The Tell-Tale Heart," where there are neither swooning virgins nor charnel houses, nor ruined once-great edifices, save the ruin of the narrator's mind. The narrator's uncontrollable obsessions both to murder and to confess are presented to stun the reader with the overwhelming force of anxiety unconditioned by rational analysis.

Thus, a more modern Gothic focuses on the overturning of rational limits as the source of horror and dread, without necessarily using the conventional apparatus. More examples of what may be considered modern Gothic can be found in the works of Nathaniel Hawthorne. Although Hawthorne was perfectly capable of using the conventional machinery of the Gothic, as in *The House of the Seven Gables* (1851), he was one of the architects of the modern Gothic. In Hawthorne's forward-looking tales, certain combinations of personalities bond, as if they were chemical compounds, to form anxiety systems that cannot be resolved save by the destruction of all or part of the human configuration. In *The Scarlet Letter* (1850), for example, the configuration of Hester, Chillingsworth, and Dimmesdale forms an interlocking system of emotional destruction that is its own Otranto. The needs and social positions of each character in this trio impinge on one another in ways that disintegrate "normal" considerations of loyalty, courage, sympathy, consideration, and judgment. Hester's vivacity is answered in Dimmesdale, whose violently clashing aloofness and responsiveness create for her a vicious cycle of fulfillment and rejection. Chillingsworth introduces further complications through another vicious cycle of confidence and betrayal. These are the catacombs of the modern Gothic.

Another strand of the modern Gothic can be traced to Mary Shelley's *Frankenstein*, published in 1818, just as the Gothic was on the wane. Her story represents an important alternative for the Gothic imagination. The setting in this work shifts from the castle to the laboratory, forming the Gothic tributary of science fiction. Frankenstein reverses the anxiety system of the Gothic from the past to the future. Instead of the sins of the fathers, old actions, old human instincts rising to blight the present, man's creativity is called into question as the blight of the future. Frankenstein's mind and laboratory are the Gothic locus of "future fear," a horror of the dark side of originality and birth, which may, as the story shows, be locked into a vicious cycle with death and sterility. A dread of the whole future of human endeavor pursues the reader in and out of the dark corridors of *Frankenstein*.

Bram Stoker's *Dracula* (1897) may be considered an example of a further evolution of the Gothic. Here one finds a strong resurgence of the traditional Gothic: the ruined castle, bandits ranging over craggy hills, swooning, morbidly detailed accounts of deaths, the sins of the past attacking the life of the present. The attendant supernatural horror and the bloodletting of the vampires, their repulsive stench, and the unearthly attractiveness of Dracula's vampire brides come right out of the original school of *Schauer-Romantik* horror. The utterly debilitating effect of the vampire on human will is, however, strong evidence for those critics who see the Gothic tradition as an exploration of neurosis.

Stoker synthesizes two major Gothic subclassifications in his work and thereby produces an interesting affirmation. Unlike the works of Radcliffe and her terror school, *Dracula* does not ultimately affirm the power of human reason, for it never explains away the supernatural. On the other hand, Stoker does not invoke his vampires as totally overwhelming forces, as in the horror school. *Dracula* does not present a fatalistic course of events through which the truth will not win out. Man is the agency of his salvation, but only through his affirmation of the power of faith. Reason is indeed powerless before Dracula, but Dr. Van Helsing's enormous faith and the faith he inspires in others are ultimately sufficient to resolve Gothic anxiety, without denying its terrifying power and reality.

Significantly, in the contemporary Gothic, reason never achieves the triumph it briefly found through the terror school. Twentieth century Gothic tends toward the *Schauer-Romantik* school of horror. Either it pessimistically portrays an inescapable, mind-forged squirrel cage, or it optimistically envisions an apocalyptic release through faith, instinct, or imagination, the nonrational human faculties. For examples of both twentieth century Gothic trends, it may be instructive to consider briefly William Faulkner, whose works are frequently listed at the head of what is called the Southern Gothic tradition, and Doris Lessing, whose later works have taken a turn that brings them into the fold of the science-fiction branch of Gothic.

Faulkner's fictions have all the characteristic elements of the Southern Gothic: the traditional iconography; decaying mansions and graveyards; morbid, death-oriented actions and images; sins of the past; and virgins. *The Sound and the Fury* (1929) is concerned with the decaying Compson house and family, the implications of past actions, Quentin's morbid preoccupation with death and virginity, and features Benjy's graveyard and important scenes in a cemetery. *As I Lay Dying* (1930) is structured around a long march to the cemetery with a stinking corpse. *Absalom, Absalom!* (1936) is full of decaying houses, lurid death scenes, and features prominently three strange virgins, Rosa Coldfield, Judith Sutpen, and Clytie, five if Quentin and Shreve are to be counted. In this work, the past eats the present up alive and the central figure, Thomas Sutpen, is much in the tradition of the charismatic, but boundlessly appropriating Gothic villain.

These cold Gothic externals are only superficial images that betray the presence of the steaming psychological modern Gothic centers of these works. Like Hawthorne, Faulkner creates interfacing human systems of neurosis whose inextricable coils lock each character into endless anxiety, producing hysteria, obsession, and utter loss of will and freedom. The violence and physical hyperbole in Faulkner reveal the truly Gothic dilemmas of the characters, inaccessible to the mediations of active reason. As in Hawthorne, the combinations of characters form the catacombs of an inescapable though invisible castle or charnel house. Through these catacombs Faulkner's characters run, but they cannot extricate themselves and thus simply revolve in a maze of involuted thought. The Compsons bind one another to tragedy, as do the Sutpens and their spiritual and psychological descendants.

There is, however, an alternative in the modern Gothic impulse. In her insightful, imaginative study of the modern evolution of the Gothic, *Ghosts of the Gothic: Austen, Eliot, and Lawrence* (1980), Judith Wilt assigns Doris Lessing a place as the ultimate inheritor of the tradition. Lessing does portray exotic states of anxiety, variously descending into the netherworld (*Briefing for a Descent into Hell*, 1971) and plunging into outer space (the Canopus in Argos series), but the novel on which Wilt focuses is *The Four-Gated City* (1969). This novel has both the trappings and the spirit of Gothic. The book centers on a doomed old house and an old, traditional family succumbing to the sins of the past. These sins Lessing portrays as no less than the debilitating sins of Western culture, racist, sexist, and exploitative in character. Lessing does indeed bring down this house. Several of the major characters are released from doom, however, by an apocalyptic World War III which wipes away the old sins, freeing some characters for a new, fruitful, nonanxious life. Significantly, this new world will be structured, not on the principles of reason and logic, which Lessing excoriates as the heart of the old sins, but on the basis of something innately nonrational and hard to identify. It is not instinct and not faith, but seems closest to imagination.

Lessing's ultimately hopeful vision, it must be conceded, is not shared by most contemporary practitioners of the genre. While never exhausted, the Gothic enjoyed a resurgence in the 1980's that has been sustained into the 1990's. The enormous popularity of Stephen King and his imitators, the proliferation of films with a strong Gothic element, and the adoption of the genre by a number of avant-garde writers—all have contributed to this resurgence, which critics have identified as a significant literary trend.

Typical of the diversity of writers mentioned under this rubric are those represented in a special section on "The New Gothic," edited by Patrick McGrath in the literary magazine *Conjunctions* 14 (1989). McGrath, himself a writer of much-praised Gothic fictions, assembled work by veteran novelists such as Robert Coover and John Hawkes as well as younger writers such as Jamaica Kincaid and William T. Vollmann; the group includes both the best-selling novelist Peter Straub and the assaultive experimental novelist Kathy Acker. McGrath contributes an essay in which he seeks to outline some of the characteristics of the New Gothic. While resisting any attempt at rigid definition (the Gothic, he says, is "an air, a tone, a tendency"; it is "not a monolith"), McGrath acknowledges that all of the writers whom he places in this group "concern themselves variously with extremes of sexual experience, with disease and social power, with murder and terror and death." That much might be said about most Gothic novelists from the beginnings of the genre. What perhaps differentiates many of the writers whom McGrath discusses from their predecessors—what makes the New Gothic new—is a more self-consciously transgressive stance, evident in McGrath's summation of the vision which he and his fellow writers share: "Common to all is an idea of evil, transgression of natural and social law, and the gothic, in all its suppleness, is the literature that permits that mad dream to be dreamt in a thousand forms."

The Gothic novel, once nothing but a popular phenomenon, has sent its roots into the heart of serious culture. Once the mere equivalent of a simple thrill, it is now the instrument for the questioning of traditional society. The Gothic novel has become a method for exploring and perhaps controlling the interior darkness which haunts modern man.

Martha Nochimson

HISTORICAL NOVEL

Popular legend records that the historical novel was born out of frustration—specifically out of Sir Walter Scott's frustration at having been displaced by Lord Byron as the most popular poetic romancer of his day. Scott's early narrative poems, such as *Marmion: A Tale of Flodden Field* (1808) and *The Lady of the Lake* (1810), had established him as the premier storyteller in verse in the first decade of the nineteenth century, but when Byron began publishing his Oriental tales (*The Giaour*, 1813; *The Bride of Abydos*, 1813; and so on), Scott saw his public turning away. Not one to acquiesce easily, Scott resurrected the manuscript of a prose work he had penned almost ten years earlier. The work told of the climactic struggles of the Scottish barons to restore the House of Stuart to the throne, culminating in their final defeat in 1746, some fifty years before Scott had originally written the tale. Since an additional decade had now passed, Scott altered his subtitle to read "'Tis Sixty Years Since," and sent off to his publishers the manuscript of *Waverley: Or, 'Tis Sixty Years Since* (1814), thus creating what was to become one of the most popular forms of fiction.

The first edition of *Waverley* was published anonymously, presumably so that Scott would not suffer embarrassment if this experiment in prose were a failure. It was not; the reading public made *Waverley* a best-seller, and a similar reception awaited the novels that followed it from Scott's prolific pen. Before he died in 1832, the father of the historical novel had brought to life the stories of Scotland, England, and to a lesser extent France during the Middle Ages, the Renaissance, and the eighteenth century. Historians may well claim that Scott's history is faulty, or that it is told from a slanted point of view; literary critics may fault him for letting his penchant for "adventure" override concerns for character development, coherence of plot, and thematic exposition. Whatever faults scholars may find, though, none can deny the immediate success these novels had, nor belittle the impact of this new literary venture on the development of fiction. The popularity of the historical novel has, in fact, never abated, and for the last 150 years, it has ranked with the detective story and the thriller as one of the forms of literature with the widest audience appeal.

The educated reader may well wonder, however, why certain novels have been singled out under the appellation "historical." The fact that all novels are set in some period links them to history; even novels set in the future share that link, however tenuously. What makes a particular novel "historical?" This problem of definition has plagued critics, and virtually everyone who has written of the historical novel has evolved a standard that allows some novels to be included in this category while others are excluded. Most critics agree, however, that there are certain characteristics that identify the historical novel, and that writers of historical fiction have certain aims and limitations which mark their works as distinct from other forms of prose narratives, and which form a general set of criteria by which their works may be judged.

Since Aristotle, critics have generally contrasted the writings of the historian and the poet (or writer of imaginative literature), seeing their approaches to recording human events as essentially dichotomous. For Aristotle, the historian dealt with the particular, the imaginative writer with the universal; the former wrote of what actually happened, the latter of what was probable in consonance with the verities of human character (*Poetics*, IX). While modern students of classical and medieval history have come to recognize that not all "history" is as factual as Aristotle would have liked to believe, the distinction is still useful. The historian is responsible for representing as accurately as possible past events as they really happened. Because the facts of the past do not of themselves speak to men in the present, the historian must discern the significance of the data he collects. For most historians, however, any interpretation of the significance of those facts is clearly distinguished from the account of the facts themselves.

The notion of interpretation provides the key to understanding the relationship between the historian and the historical novelist. Like the historian, the historical novelist examines the facts of history, but rather than interpreting them analytically, he attempts to bring the past to life and interpret the significance of historical events through the conventions of literature: characterization, plot, and thematic development. He uses the tools of his trade—image, symbol, juxtaposition and parallelism, and a host of other rhetorical devices—to provide his interpretation. His aim is to transport the reader imaginatively to a period removed from the present. The best historical novelists accomplish their aims without violating the spirit of the historical process; they invent only when the chronicles are silent, and they rearrange only sparsely, or more often not at all. Thus, a main characteristic that sets apart the historical novel from other forms of fiction is the novelist's ability to present events of the past without remaining rigidly tied to historical documents (which themselves may be inaccurate). Coupled with the skill to delineate the interaction of human characters in the context of the historical period, his interest in recapturing the past distinguishes the truly successful historical novelist from proponents of mere costume romance.

A large number of novels set in the past are indeed no more than costume romances, attempts to disguise modern situations or fantasies (usually involving sex or violence) in the garb of former times. Often, too, the use of history becomes a means of providing an *apologia* for present conditions, or of producing a lament for times past without a serious attempt to examine the actualities of those times. Southern American fiction (which includes some of the best historical novels) contains numerous examples of this kind of writing, the most notable being Margaret Mitchell's *Gone with the Wind*

(1936). A best-seller in the year of its publication and for years afterward, Mitchell's novel remains the most popular novel ever written by a Southerner. Unfortunately, the characters in the novel are stereotypes of the Old South: the gallant plantation youth (Ashley Wilkes), the demure Southern belle (Melanie), the rebellious vixen (Scarlett O'Hara), the hardened, aristocratic outcast (Rhett Butler)—the list could be extended considerably. For all its popular success, the novel presents only a superficial view of the real conflicts that engulfed the South as it moved through this traumatic period of transition. For the majority of the American public, though, the portrait of the South that Mitchell creates has become the accepted one, largely because the work achieved wide readership among the general public and almost simultaneously provided the script for one of Hollywood's most successful motion pictures.

Generally, regardless of their intent, writers of historical novels have followed one of two approaches toward historical events and characters. By far the larger group has written works in which their major characters are fictional personages who live during periods in which great events occur: the glorious years of the Roman Empire, the age of the Crusades, the time of the English, American, French, or Russian Revolutions, the Hundred Years War, the Napoleonic wars, the American Civil War, or the two world wars. More often than not, the historical novel is set in a time of crisis. The fictional characters often, though not always, interact with real personages in some way. This technique of placing fictional characters on the fringe of great events, used by Scott in his novels and adopted by many others, can provide an effective sense of the period without violating (except, perhaps, for the purist) the sense of history that the reader brings to the work.

In works that attempt to retain a high degree of verisimilitude, the contact between real and fictional characters generally remains slight; in works better termed "historical romances," such contact is often magnified, sometimes to the point of suggesting that the fictional character has had an impact on real-life events. A recent example of this approach can be found in the World War II novels of Herman Wouk, *The Winds of War* (1971) and *War and Remembrance* (1978). Wouk's fictional hero, Victor "Pug" Henry, a Navy Captain, becomes the confidant of President Franklin D. Roosevelt and his emissary to various foreign capitals, where he meets with Winston Churchill, Adolf Hitler, Benito Mussolini, and Joseph Stalin. Henry's influence in shaping Roosevelt's opinion about the war (and his other exploits with foreign leaders) is purely fictional, and accounts in part for Wouk's own admission in the Preface to *War and Remembrance* that he is writing a "historical romance."

Linking history to the narrative tradition of the romance has been a common practice for many writers who have chosen to focus on fictional characters living during a period of crisis. Among the more famous practitioners of this method is the French novelist Alexandre Dumas (père) who, through his loose weaving of historical fact and fancy, provided the worldwide reading public with figures and stories that have become part of the cultural heritage of the West: Porthos, Athos, and Aramis, the "Three Musketeers," and idealistic young D'Artagnan, the real hero of Dumas' novel of the reign of Louis XIV. *The Three Musketeers* (1844) is only one of many, however, that Dumas wrote about that period, and about other episodes in French history, including explorations of the age of Henri IV, the Franco-Spanish War of the sixteenth century, the reign of Louis XV, and the French Revolution.

The methodology employed by artists choosing to focus on fictional characters in real-life time of crisis can be seen most vividly in Charles Dickens' *A Tale of Two Cities* (1859). This chilling look at the impact of the French Revolution has given many generations of readers a feeling for that event that even Thomas Carlyle's history of the Revolution fails to evoke. In this work, Dickens re-creates the horrors of the Revolution by detailing the effects of the Reign of Terror on the lives of fictional characters whose destinies take them between Paris and London. Few major figures of history appear in Dickens' book, and those who do are given subordinate roles. The historicity of the novel lies in Dickens' graphic portrayal of the masses, and of the individuals affected by the actions of the "citizens" of the Revolution. The fictional Madame DeFarge, whose insatiable appetite for the blood of aristocrats is motivated as much by a desire for personal vengeance as by any desire for liberty and equality, reinforces the notion that the exploits of the real-life Robespierre and his real-life henchmen were neither anomalous nor necessarily high-minded.

Similarly, the frustrations of the Manette family, and the heroism of both Sidney Carton and Charles Darnay, become representative of thousands whose stories are unnoted by the historian, whose personal tragedies and triumphs have been reduced to mere statistics. Thus, history is not violated, but rather is vivified by the presentation of characters and incidents that, though unrecorded in chronicles of the period, might have easily occurred. In the best historical novels, the reader senses that, had these events occurred, they would have done so with the same consequences that the novelist has presented.

A second, less common approach to historical fiction is that of choosing as a main character a person who really did live and whose history is recorded in some form. Such an approach is in many ways more difficult; those who choose this method are limited to a great degree by the facts of history in structuring plot, delineating character, providing motivation, and even in developing themes. Usually, the greater the figure chosen, the more restricted the novelist is in exploring the subject through the medium of fiction. Some have done so, and been fairly successful. Howard Fast achieved popular acclaim for his portraits of George Washington (*The Unvanquished*, 1942) and Thomas Paine (*Citizen Tom Paine*, 1943). Robert Graves's *I, Claudius* (1934) is a daring attempt to present the decadent life of the Emperor's court in post-Augustan Rome through the eyes of one of the major figures of that period.

Another highly successful examination of historical forces seen through the eyes of a major historical figure is found in Russian novelist Aleksandr Solzhenitsyn's *Avgust chetyrnadtsatogo* (1971, 1983; *August 1914*, 1972, 1989). Solzhenitsyn offers a view of Russia's disastrous World War I defeat at the Battle of the Tannenburg Forest through the eyes of the Second Army's commander, General Samsonov. Also worthy of note is Gore Vidal's ongoing fictional chronicle of American history. In *Washington, D.C.* (1967), *Burr* (1973), *1876* (1976), *Lincoln* (1984), *Empire* (1987), and *Hollywood* (1990), Vidal skillfully interweaves his fictional characters into the lives of figures such as Presidents Martin Van Buren, Abraham Lincoln, and Theodore Roosevelt, as well as luminaries such as John Hay, Henry Adams, and others easily recognizable by students of American history.

An even greater cast of historical personages come to life in *Freedom* (1987), a novel by American journalist and critic William Safire. This long book (nearly a thousand pages of text and more than two hundred pages of notes and commentary that Safire calls his "Underbook") details life in Washington, D.C., and northern Virginia following the announcement of secession by the Confederate states and the momentous decision by Abraham Lincoln to issue the Emancipation Proclamation. The daily lives—both public and private—of more than two dozen key figures involved on both sides of the Civil War are chronicled in Safire's lively and insightful account. Relying heavily on the historical record, Safire represents his figures with exceptional psychological sensitivity. His decision to steer clear of lengthy analyses of battles and to concentrate instead on the political arena—in which decisions were often affected by personality clashes among men and women with oversized egos—makes this study of the causes and consequences of war particularly distinctive. For the student of historical fiction, Safire offers a perceptive observation about his process of composition: "The reader of any historical novel asks, 'How much of this is true?'" Safire's answer is to provide an "Underbook" citing the many sources from which he has drawn his portraits. This historical dimension "is close to the way it happened," reconstructed from "firsthand sources" such as letters and diaries. The rest, he reminds his readers, "is fiction, a device that overrides the facts to keep the reader awake or—when it works best—to get at the truth." Safire's novel gives the reader a sense of peering over the shoulder of real people whose lives seem a bit more dramatic than one might have imagined they could ever have been.

Writing about real people, however, is not without its dangers. One need only review the controversy surrounding the publication of William Styron's *The Confessions of Nat Turner* (1967). This Pulitzer Prize-winning novel is a fictional account of the leader of a slave revolt in the Tidewater region of

Virginia in 1831. Historical records detailing Turner's revolt are sparse; the primary documentary evidence is contained in a twenty-page pamphlet written by the prosecuting attorney at Turner's trial and ostensibly dictated by Turner himself shortly before he was executed. Contemporary newspaper accounts offer some corroboration, but they are biased. From these slim historical sources, Styron creates what he calls "a meditation on history," a musing, first-person, reflective account of the motivation for Nat's actions.

In addition to taking the daring step of telling his hero's story in the first person, Styron also modifies the available facts to make his character more interesting psychologically. Omitting Nat's wife and father from the story, Styron attributes his hero's education to the efforts of good white masters and emphasizes the thin line between religious fanaticism and repressed sexual desire. Styron's Nat, believing that he is being driven by an Old Testament God who has made him the instrument of vengeance on the white community for their treatment of blacks, puts to use the education he received from whites to incite other slaves to revolt.

Effusive praise from white critics has been far overshadowed by the condemnations issued by blacks. *William Styron's Nat Turner: Ten Black Writers Respond* (1968), a collection of essays by noted black intellectuals, systematically attacks the novel on grounds both literary and historical. These critics assert that Styron's hero's meditations are a white man's thoughts, that his hero's aspirations are those which white men think black men have, and that his hero's rationale for acting is actually a reflection of the white community's rationalization for the institution of slavery. Social historians have criticized the novel for not presenting a portrait of the real Nat Turner; they charge Styron with avoiding the real issues that led to Turner's revolt. In their view, the book simply does not fulfill one of the main criteria for good historical fiction: it is not sufficiently true to the historical record.

Despite these pitfalls, there is clear evidence that the best historical novels can rank with the finest novels of any kind. One need only look to the works of America's foremost novelist of the twentieth century: William Faulkner. In many ways, the entire corpus of Faulkner's work is an extended study of the history of his region, the American South. Faulkner tries to make sense of what happened there in a society that contained, side by side, aspects of feudal or baronial European culture and the individualizing tenets of the American Dream. As one might expect, Faulkner focuses on the great crime of slavery; that dehumanizing institution on which Southern society was based bred racial hatred which continued long after slavery was officially abolished as a result of the Civil War. That catastrophe plays a central role in Faulkner's fiction, either as a subject itself or as an event that looms in the consciousness of those who populate Faulkner's mythical Yoknapatawpha County. Among his novels, *Absalom, Absalom!* (1936) is possibly the best example of a novel intensely concerned with the way man comes to understand the past, and the way he tries to make sense of it so that the present becomes explicable. In the novel, a young Southerner, Quentin Compson, and his Canadian roommate at college, Shreve McCannon, attempt to piece together the family history of Thomas Sutpen, a self-styled Southern aristocrat whose grand design for establishing a dynasty in the wilds of northern Mississippi is ruined when his son kills the fiancé of Sutpen's only daughter, then flees the country. Quentin must piece together Sutpen's story from oral narratives and meager written accounts, none of which reveals the whole truth about the past. *Absalom, Absalom!* has been described as a kind of detective story, in which Quentin and Shreve make a "persistent attempt to understand the past from partially perceived fragments surviving about it" (Hugh Holman, *The Immoderate Past*, 1977). Because he is a son of the South, Quentin sees in the story of Sutpen the tragedy of his heritage. The novel reveals to the reader the impossibility of ever knowing the past completely; it is to humankind's credit, however, that it tries to do so, because in the past, one may find an explanation for the present, and thereby develop some hope for the future.

Absalom, Absalom! is, in the final analysis, a novel about the historical process itself, a story of the way one comes to understand one's own past. Ironically, these discoveries about the tenuousness and fragility of the historical method appear in a novel that contains almost no references to real personages; yet the reader senses that what is being read is as real as any historical account of the South. The saga of life in Faulkner's fictional Jefferson, Mississippi, and surrounding countryside may be far removed from places where great events have occurred, but the impact of history on the lives of men and women in this rural Southern community is transformed by Faulkner into a statement of the way events mold the human race. In Yoknapatawpha County, one finds the engagement with the living past that continues to inspire the best historical novelists.

Laurence W. Mazzeno

DETECTIVE NOVEL

The detective story is a special branch of the crime story that focuses attention on the examination of evidence that will lead to the solution of the mystery. The Oxford English Dictionary records the first printed use of the noun "detective" in the year 1843. The term had become established in the language because of the formation of the first detective bureaus, the original of which was the Bow Street Runners, a group of detective-policemen organized by Henry Fielding and John Fielding in their capacities as magistrates in London. The Runners operated out of the Fielding residence on Bow Street and were the precursors of the detective branch of Scotland Yard. Some time later, in the beginning years of the nineteenth century, the Sûreté Générale, the first modern police force, was formed in Paris with a detective bureau. With the establishment of detective bureaus, the way was open for the detective story to be developed out of existing literary sources.

In the eighteenth century, the chaplain of Newgate Prison in London was authorized to publish the stories of notorious criminals in *The Newgate Calendar*. From this practice sprang the often wholly fictional "Newgate" novels, given over to accounts of sensational crimes. In France, François Vidocq, a criminal himself, became head of the Sûreté and later published his memoirs, recounting his exploits in capturing criminals. It is also likely that some of the ambience of the early detective story was derived from the Gothic novel. William Godwin's *Caleb Williams* (1794), for example, although not a detective novel, is a story of a crime solved in order to free an innocent man.

From these beginnings, it remained for Edgar Allan Poe to devise the detective story in its now familiar form. Poe wrote three short works which are certainly detective stories, as well as others that are sometimes included in the genre. The first of these was "The Murders in the Rue Morgue" (1841), which was followed by "The Mystery of Marie Rogêt" (1842) and "The Purloined Letter" (1845). Poe initiated the device of establishing the character of the detective and then using him for several stories. Poe's detective, M. Dupin, is a recluse, an eccentric, aristocratic young man with a keen analytical mind. He has an unnamed but admiring friend who marvels at Dupin's mental prowess and is willing to be his chronicler. Dupin examines the evidence in a given case and solves the crime after the regular police have exhausted their methods—a circumstance that was to become one of the commonplaces of detective fiction.

Apparently impressed by the *Mémoires* (1828-1829) of François Vidocq, Poe set his stories in Paris and borrowed his policemen from the Sûreté. Meanwhile, in France itself, Émile Gaboriau began to produce detective stories that also owed much to Vidocq. His detective, M. Lecoq, a representative of the official police, became the chief figure in a number of tales of detection. The detective short story was thus established and enjoyed great popularity in the century to follow.

Probably the first full-length novel of detection was *The Notting Hill Mystery* (1865) by Charles Felix, but it was quickly followed by Wilkie Collins' *The Moonstone* (1868), which critics consider to be the first important detective novel. Collins introduced Sergeant Cuff of Scotland Yard, who, with the help of amateurs, was able to solve the mystery. The first detective in English fiction, however, antedated Sergeant Cuff by fifteen years when Inspector Bucket appeared in the pages of Charles Dickens' *Bleak House* (1853). Detective novels were published at a slow, sporadic pace until the advent of Sherlock Holmes, the most famous of all fictional detectives, in Arthur Conan Doyle's *A Study in Scarlet* (1887).

Holmes starred in four novels and fifty-six short stories and eventually came to have a life independent of his creator, Doyle, who even killed him off in one tale only to have to bring him back for further adventures. A house on Baker Street in London has been identified as the place where Holmes occupied a flat and is now a tourist attraction. Clubs honor his memory with birthday parties, and a biography has been written based on incidental remarks and inferences about his "life" in the works in which he appeared. The Sherlock Holmes stories follow the pattern established by Poe's Dupin: Holmes is a bachelor given to esoteric studies, an eccentric who plays the violin and occasionally takes cocaine. A keen observer with amazing talents for analysis and deduction, an amateur boxer who performs astonishing feats of physical strength, Holmes is a virtual superman, while the commonsensical Dr. Watson, the narrator of his exploits, provides a perfect foil.

The success of the Sherlock Holmes stories resulted in an outpouring of detective fiction; many authors adopted the basic technique of establishing the character of the detective and then recounting a series of his "cases." R. Austin Freeman introduced Dr. John Thorndyke, who based his solutions on more strictly scientific evidence rather than the deductions favored by Holmes. An American writer, Jaxque Futrello, introduced Professor Van Dusen, who was called "the thinking machine" and who became one of the early omniscient detectives in the tradition of Sherlock Holmes.

With *Trent's Last Case* (1913), by E. C. Bentley, the modern era of the detective story began. Mary Roberts Rinehart modified the pattern of the detective novel by providing a female amateur as a first-person narrator who worked with the official police and who provided the key to the solution almost by accident. Another prolific writer was Carolyn Wells who wrote seventy-four mystery novels, most of which starred Fleming Stone as the detective. She also made an important contribution to the theory of the detective story with her book *The Technique of the Mystery Story* (1913).

As the detective story moved closer to its "classical" stage, it became more realistic and was written with more literary skill. The detectives became less bizarre and less inclined to become involved in physical danger or in personally grappling with the criminal in the manner of the great Holmes. The adventure-mystery involving a sleuth who was proficient both physically and mentally was given over to thrillers such as the Nick Carter stories, while the strict detective tale became purely analytical. In this form, the detective story featured the detective as its chief character and the solution to an interesting mystery as its chief interest. There was generally a narrator in the Watson tradition, and absence of any love interest, and neither characterization nor the tangential demands of the plot were allowed to interfere with the central business of unraveling the puzzle. With these characteristics established, the detective story moved into its golden age.

The period of 1920 to 1940 represented the golden age of the novel of detection. It included the work of Dorothy L. Sayers, Agatha Christie, Earl Derr Biggers, and S. S. Van Dine (Willard Huntington Wright). Hundreds of novels were written during this period and were enjoyed by persons at all levels of literary sophistication. The expectation of the reader was that a clever detective would be faced with a puzzling crime, almost always a murder or a series of murders, which had not been committed by a professional criminal; the solution of this mystery would come about by the examination of clues presented in the novel. Only a few of the chroniclers of the fine art of murder thus defined can be discussed here.

Dorothy L. Sayers was perhaps the most literary writer of the practitioners of the detective novel; she attempted a combination of the detective story and the "legitimate" novel. Her book *The Nine Tailors* (1934) is a good example of the work of her detective, Lord Peter Wimsey, and of her careful research into background material. She is considered to be one of the finest of the mystery writers of this period. Lord Peter Wimsey is a snobbish man given to airy commentary and a languid manner, but he has the needed analytical skills to solve the mysteries.

Although she may not have had the skill in characterization nor the literary quality of Sayers, Agatha Christie surpassed her rivals in the sheer ingenuity of her plots and her manipulation of the evidence which her detective, Hercule Poirot, had to evaluate. Her most famous book over a long career was *The Murder of Roger Ackroyd* (1926). Christie used such traditional ploys as the somewhat dense associate (in this instance, Captain Hastings), the least likely person as the murderer, the unexpected turn of the plot, and an exotic manner of committing the crime. Poirot became the most fictional detective since Sherlock Holmes and appears in thirty-three of Christie's novels. Christie invented yet another fictional detective who became almost as beloved as Poirot. Miss Jane Marple is a quiet "Victorian" lady who figures in eleven novels and in a collection of short stories. Her methods are based on a shrewd knowledge of human behavior, keen observation, a remarkable memory, and the ability to make startling deductions from the evidence. Despite the popularity of Hercule Poirot and Miss Marple, neither stars in the book that is widely considered to be Christie's best: *Ten Little Indians* (1939).

Rivaling M. Poirot and Miss Marple in the affections of detective-novel fans was the Chinese-Hawaiian-American detective, Charlie Chan, created by Earl Derr Biggers. Charlie Chan's widespread popularity was especially enhanced by the fact that his stories were turned into some forty-five motion pictures. Chan's characterization includes the frequent use of Chinese aphorisms, an extremely polite manner, and his generally human qualities. Chan is especially interesting in that he was the first example, in this kind of fiction, of an Oriental who was a sympathetic character rather than a villain.

S. S. Van Dine is the author of twelve novels starring the detective Philo Vance, who, like Lord Peter Wimsey, is an English aristocrat, although all of his cases have an American urban setting. An extremely erudite man with a world-weary air, Vance was the best-educated and most refined detective of this era. Van Dine, under his real name of Wright, was a literary critic who made the detective story an object of research and study. The result was the publication of the so-called "twenty rules for detective stories," only one of several efforts to define the exact characteristics of the form. Both readers and writers of this period had definite expectations and resented efforts in the field that did not follow certain specifications. The idea of fair play with the reader was essential; that is, the game must be played with all of the evidence needed to solve the crime. There must be no love interest to detract from the business of solving the mystery; the detective could not be the criminal; and the solution could not come about as a result of accident or wild coincidence. During the detective novel's golden age, these rules were taken quite seriously by those who believed that a permanent form of popular fiction had been established.

While the classic detective story was being developed in England and the United States, there was also an American development that was to turn the detective novel in a new direction. Manfred B. Lee and Frederic Dannay collaborated to create a detective who would achieve worldwide fame. Ellery Queen, ostensibly the author of the novels which describe his cases, is an amateur detective and professional writer who works with his father, Inspector Richard Queen of the New York police. Inspector Queen provides the clues and investigative techniques while his son, Ellery, puts the evidence together. They are not supermen, after Sherlock Holmes, nor are they all-knowing in the manner of Philo Vance, but professionals dealing with a more realistic crime scene than that of their predecessors. Ellery Queen was thus a crossover figure leading to the police-procedural story and to the kind of detective fiction that came to reflect the actual criminal class in America as well as the working of the criminal justice system.

In the 1930's, while the classic detective story was thriving, another kind of mystery story was coming into being—the hard-boiled detective novel. The preeminent writers of this school were Dashiell Hammett, Raymond

Chandler, and—in the next generation—Ross Macdonald. Some of these writers began writing for *Black Mask*, a pulp magazine originating in the 1920's. Dashiell Hammett's Sam Spade, who appeared in *The Maltese Falcon* (1930), is characteristic of the new detective: a private eye in a not-very-successful office who solves crimes by following people around in unsavory neighborhoods, having fights in alleys, and dealing with informers. He is cynical regarding the political dealings which go on behind the scenes and is aware of the connections between criminals and the outwardly respectable. He trusts no one, while he himself follows the dictates of a personal code. Hammett's *The Thin Man* (1934), which became the basis for a series of motion pictures, was a return to the more traditional form of detective fiction.

Another of the hard-boiled school was Raymond Chandler, who wrote seven novels about his sleuth Philip Marlowe. Chandler, describing the ideal detective hero, said: "Down these mean streets a man must go who is not himself mean, who is neither tarnished nor afraid." Such a man is aware of the corruption he will find, but he is governed by a code which will include faithfulness to the client and an abhorrence of crime without an avenging or sadistic bent. Chandler specialized in complex plots, realistic settings, and snappy dialogue in novels such as *The Big Sleep* (1939), *Farewell, My Lovely* (1940), and *The Lady in the Lake* (1943). Chandler was also a theoretician of the detective story, and his essay "The Simple Art of Murder" (1944) is an important document in the annals of crime fiction.

After the introduction of the hard-boiled detective and the many stories involving the routine investigations of official law enforcement agencies, the tradition of the superman detective declined. Fictional detectives lost their aristocratic manners and eccentricities, while the crimes being investigated gained interest not because they involved yet another bizarre or ingenious way to commit murder, but because of the influence of the psychological make-up or the social status of the criminal. The criminal was also less likely to be an amateur than a habitual malefactor. Limiting the suspects by setting the story in confined quarters—such as a country house or an ocean liner— gave way to a story that took the reader into the mean streets referred to by Chandler. These stories often involved the brutality of the police, more violence on the part of the detective, frankness in matters of sex, and the use of formerly taboo language. Mickey Spillane's Mike Hammer typified a new breed of private detectives, given to acts of sadistic violence.

This often brutal social realism is also reflected in the work of Erle Stanley Gardner, best known for his creation of the lawyer/detective Perry Mason. The hero of more than eighty novels, Mason was first characterized in the hard-boiled tradition; early novels such as *The Case of the Velvet Claws* (1933) and *The Case of the Curious Bride* (1934) emphasize the fast-paced action and involuted plots that superseded the literary quality typical of Sayers' work. While retaining his early penchant for extra-legal tactics, Mason developed gradually into a courtroom hero, allowing his assistant detective Paul Drake to do his research while Mason excelled in the spectacular oral combat of the cross-examination. Many of Gardner's plots were drawn from his own legal experiences as an attorney; having founded the Court of Last Resort, Gardner demonstrated a concern for the helpless. In keeping with this concern, he modified the detective genre by introducing the state as the villain and attacking the urban evils of capitalistic greed for wealth and power.

In championing the defenseless, Gardner was the voice of a modern Everyman during the decades between 1930 and 1960. Viewing themselves as vulnerable to the dictates of the state (such as the establishment of Prohibition and income tax), readers achieved vicarious satisfaction in seeing the problems of average people solved. The mass popularity of Mason's cases was not only a result of their being victories over the "system" but also of the medium they employed. Gardner was, by his own admission, a "product of the paperback revolution," and he further lowered the literary standards of classical detective fiction by dictating his novels. He was also the script supervisor for the Perry Mason television series (starring Raymond Burr and running from 1957 to 1966), which furthered the personal appeal and accessibility of the detective. Unlike the superhuman Lord Peter Wimsey and Philo Vance, whose intellectual and aristocratic qualities are extraordinary and intimidating, Perry Mason is a successful but common professional, combining in his career the wit of the golden age sleuth with the cynical pertinacity of the hard-boiled detective.

While the hard-boiled mystery developed one element of the classic detective novel—the appeal of a recurring hero with yet another case to solve— in a strikingly new direction, the sheer fascination of deduction which characterized the golden age of the detective novel was developed in a new subgenre: the police procedural, a kind of fictional "documentary" often purporting to be taken from actual police files. These stories detail the routines of investigative agencies, taking the reader into forensic laboratories and describing complex chemical testing of the evidence. Hard-working policemen interview suspects, conduct stake-outs, shadow people, investigate bank accounts. Even if there is a major figure who is in charge of the case, the investigation clearly is a matter of teamwork, with standard areas of expertise and responsibility: in short, a realistic depiction of actual police methods. These stories date from World War II and are typified by the television series "Dragnet" and the Broadway play *Detective Story*. One of the major writers of the police procedural is Ed McBain, who has written more than thirty novels about the "87th precinct" in a fictional urban setting that closely resembles New York City. The police procedural has proved to be a versatile form which can be used as the basis for a symbolic story with intentions far beyond that of the crime-solving, as in Lawrence Sanders' *The First Deadly Sin* (1973). Similarly, Tom Sharpe's *Riotous Assembly* (1971) is a police procedural set in South Africa which uses the form in order to ridicule apartheid, hypocrisy, and racial stereotyping.

Ostensibly, the psychological crime novels of Georges Simenon should also belong in the police procedural category; however, Inspector Jules Maigret of the Paris Police Department uses neither scientific nor rational methods to identify murderers. Similar to Perry Mason in his bourgeois appeal (Maigret is heavy-set, smokes a pipe, and is fond of domesticity) and in his delegation of research responsibilities to subordinates, Maigret solves crimes by absorbing the ambience of the place in which they were committed. By familiarizing himself with social customs, geography, and personalities, Maigret "becomes" the suspect and uses psychology and intuition to discern the criminal's identity. Patience rather than flamboyance characterizes Maigret; he relies on the hunches of his sympathetic imagination instead of on factual clues. While Maigret inhabits the sordid world of the hard-boiled detective, he sees himself as a "repairer of destinies" and acts more like a humble priest eliciting confessions than a vindictive policeman triumphing over evil.

In addition to departing from convention in Maigret's unique style of detection, Simenon also defies genre restrictions in the style of his work. *The Strange Case of Peter the Lett* (1931) was written in 1929, but it has little in common with the analytical works of the golden age. Accused of being too literary in his early psychological novels, Simenon probes the ambiguity of man's behavior, acknowledging his capacity to sin while maintaining a sympathetic understanding of his actions. Readers of the Maigret novels are unable to see evil in terms of black and white, as readers of Gardner's works do, and come away with as much compassion for the murderer as for the victim. Simenon denies both the mental action of the classical period of detective fiction and the physical action of the hard-boiled period, promoting instead the action of the heart. In so doing, he demonstrates the versatility of the detective-fiction genre.

The detective story has developed not only into the police procedural but also into the spy mystery and the adventure thriller. With the decline of the classic detective story featuring the fine-tuned mind of a clever detective who will carefully examine the evidence and solve an intricate puzzle, it appears that the detective story is once again merging into the larger category of the crime story, which has traditionally used a murder as the dramatic focus for a wide variety of human issues.

F. William Nelson

WESTERN NOVEL

The literary genre known as the Western, which is generally considered to have emerged in full-blown form with Owen Wister's *The Virginian: A Horseman of the Plains* (1902), took much of its nourishment from the fertile soil of nineteenth century popular American literature. Among its antecedents were the Leatherstocking Tales of James Fenimore Cooper, a series of five novels of the American frontier featuring a self-sufficient and morally incorruptible backwoods character named Natty Bumppo. Though Cooper was ultimately ambiguous about the meaning of the frontier in American life, he demonstrated not only that frontier materials could sustain serious literary consideration, but also that the frontier's pristine beauty, the savagery of its conflicts, and its colorful inhabitants, both red and white, could have immense popular appeal.

Hard upon Cooper's heels came the House of Beadle and other dime-novel publishers who chose to ignore the serious cultural questions which Cooper could at least identify if not resolve. For the most part, the dime novels were cynically commercial in intention, with scant regard for all but the most lurid themes, episodes, and personalities in frontier history.

Finally, the Western was indebted to the "local-color" movement of the late nineteenth century, of which the works of Bret Harte are familiar examples. Although the local colorists, by definition, failed to find in their materials matters of general cultural importance, they demonstrated the popular appeal and the literary validity of close attention to local and regional folkways, the distinctive personalities, dialect, and daily experience of the common man.

Owen Wister (1860-1938), creator of the first genuine Western, was not the kind of person one would ordinarily think of as the author of cowboy novels. Born into a wealthy Philadelphia family, Wister received the best education his day could offer, culminating in a degree from Harvard. Culturally sophisticated, Wister enjoyed close friendships with Henry James, William Dean Howells, and Theodore Roosevelt, and his abilities as a pianist impressed even the aged Franz Liszt, for whom he played at Bayreuth. Talent and family connections, unfortunately, did not bring happiness: unable to find a satisfying career either in the arts or in the tawdry business world recommended by his father, Wister suffered a nervous breakdown in 1885, and his doctor prescribed a recuperative trip to Wyoming. It was during this vacation on the cattle ranch of a family friend that he became impressed with the fictional potential of the American cowboy and began the literary experimentation that would lead to creation of the Western.

The Virginian was not, by any means, the first appearance of the cowboy in American literature: the local colorist Alfred Henry Lewis, several dime novelists, Wister himself as early as 1891, and others had featured cowboy heroes in novels and stories. It was Wister's nameless Virginian, though, who first provided just the right combination of colorful dress and speech, violent environment, and romantic potential to set the pattern for a new literary genre.

Henry James, perhaps not altogether honestly, expressed admiration for *The Virginian*, and it is true that many readers with simplistic preconceptions regarding Westerns are surprised at the sophistication of the novel. Although somewhat episodic (*The Virginian* grew in part from short stories), the two main plots—the corruption of Trampas from an honest cowhand to a rustler, which results in the lynching of the Virginian's friend Steve and Trampas' death at the Virginian's hands in the famous walkdown; and the Virginian's courtship of the eastern schoolmarm, Molly Wood—are complex and skillfully narrated. Critics have observed that *The Virginian*, a cowboy novel, contains not a single scene in which cowboys actually work with cows, but such facile judgments do scant justice to the social and historical realism of the novel. The cowboy's dress, his language, his customs, his ethics, his humor, and the environmental imperatives within which he operates—all of these are carefully depicted and assessed.

Wister's literary output was not great, for he was not a prolific writer, and the West was only one of his concerns. Moreover, *The Virginian* is marred by much of the same confusion over the meaning of the West that had haunted Cooper: How can one relate the morally innocent—yet savage and violent—tenor of Western life to the culturally sophisticated, yet corrupt, East? The marriage of the Virginian and Molly indicates some sort of cultural accommodation, but in his final collection of Western stories, *When West Was West* (1928), Wister concludes that no such accommodation is possible.

Important as *The Virginian* was in the creation of the Western, no single work can create a genre, and it remained for Wister's many successors and imitators to develop, out of the materials provided by *The Virginian*, the Western formula. By far the most prominent of Wister's early successors was Zane Grey (1872-1939). Grey's family had figured with some significance in the history of the Ohio River frontier, and he was reared on tales of ancestral exploits, partly, no doubt, to compensate for the painful reality of the family's more recent decline from wealth and influence. Like Wister, Grey was unable to adjust idealistic youthful dreams and aspirations to the mundane necessities of earning a living. After completing, with undistinguished marks, a dental course at the University of Pennsylvania, Grey attempted to open a dental practice in New York City. He soon abandoned dentistry in favor of writing, but his early efforts, a trilogy recounting the exploits of his pioneer ancestors, sold poorly.

After a summer in Arizona and Utah in 1906, Grey discovered characters, settings, and themes that he thought he could turn into literature, and his first Western, *The Heritage of the Desert* (1910), a story of Mormons, rustlers, and the rejuvenative, indeed redemptive, qualities of the West, sold well enough to encourage him. Grey's phenomenal literary success began in 1912, with the publication of *Riders of the Purple Sage*, surely the most famous Western ever written. In that novel, Grey introduces a black-clad gunfighter-hero, Lassiter, whose bloody encounters with the Mormons in the dramatic canyonlands of southern Utah established important literary precedents. Grey exhibited, in that and many later novels, a much greater debt to the dime novels than did Wister: there is much less subtlety in Grey's violent scenes, much less complexity in his characters' emotions and motives, and much less restraint in his descriptions of setting.

Nevertheless, Grey shared with Wister an unfeigned love for the West and its history and culture, and took pains to try to portray it realistically. Grey chose a wide variety of western settings for his novels, and an even wider variety of character types, including ethnic minorities that interested few other authors. Furthermore, he invested his books with a philosophical burden often missing in popular writing: the West alone, in his view, offered free scope for development of complete human beings, including those primitive virtues and self-reliant skills that the overcivilization of the East had submerged.

Most of Grey's best work appeared during little more than a decade, between *Riders of the Purple Sage* and *Under the Tonto Rim* (1926). Thereafter (and occasionally during that decade as well), the urgency of his message, the originality of his characters, and the carefulness of his descriptions are much less poignant. Much of Grey's unevenness results, no doubt, from the sheer quantity of his work: During a career of thirty-odd years, Grey wrote nearly one hundred novels and stories and dozens of magazine articles.

Even at that, Grey's output is put into the shade by the production of the mightiest literary engine in Western literature since the dime novelists, a would-be epic poet named Frederick Schiller Faust (1892-1944), who supported both his literary aspirations and his sybaritic life in an Italian villa by writing more than six hundred Western novels and stories under some twenty pseudonyms, the best known of which was "Max Brand." Though Faust, who was reared in California, knew the West well, there is little of the actual West in his books; he preferred instead to borrow his plots from the Greek and Roman classics, garbing Oedipus and Agamemnon in chaps and six-guns and cynically dismissing his Western works as "cowboy junk."

It is tempting to take Faust's cynicism at face value and disdain to consider seriously his Western works. It is a perilous temptation, for in spite of his scornful attitude and rapid composition (during one thirteen-week period in 1920, he turned out 190,000 publishable words), Faust wrote some very fine novels. *The Untamed* (1919), his first Western novel, features a memorable hero, Dan Barry, who lives an isolated, wild life in the desert, tames a wild horse and a wolf, and never finds a way to make an accommodation with civilization. *Destry Rides Again* (1930), later made into a popular motion picture, is a revenge story recounting the way a framed man gets even with the jury members. Unlike Grey's Lassiter, Harry Destry wins more through guile and cleverness than violence.

Faust's work, then, represents a considerable retreat from the realism of Wister and Grey, demonstrating that good novels only have to be believable, not necessarily authentic. The career of Clarence Edward Mulford (1883-1956) followed Faust's in that respect, and called to mind, as well, the dime-novel tradition in his love of violence. Reared in Illinois, Mulford was working in a minor civil service position in Brooklyn when he began to write Westerns, and never visited the West until eighteen years after he had started writing about it. He was unimpressed; western reality interfered with his imaginary conception of the West, and he never again left his eastern home. His first Western, *Bar-20* (1907), and many thereafter featured an actual working cowboy named Hopalong Cassidy, whose proletarian speech and bloodthirsty love for fighting made him a far cry from the character of the same name played on film by William Boyd.

Bertha M. Bower (1871-1940), by contrast, was as deeply rooted as a cottonwood tree in the real West; one of her four husbands, Clayton Bower, was a Montana cattleman, and she spent her entire life in the region about which she wrote. In *Chip, of the Flying U* (1906), which was illustrated by her friend, the cowboy artist Charles M. Russell, Bower established her trademark: the unglamorous cowboy character. Though Chip himself is extraordinary—he occasionally quotes William Shakespeare, and he is a gifted though untutored artist—Bower chose to make literature out of the smaller human dramas that occurred in the cowboy's daily work routine.

Ernest Haycox (1899-1950), whom many critics consider the finest literary craftsman to emerge from the popular Western tradition, was one of a younger generation of writers who became popular during the period between 1930 and 1950. Like many of the older writers, he put in his apprenticeship in the pulp magazines, writing fast-moving Western romances with shallow characters and plenty of action. Like Faust, Haycox had serious literary aspirations, but unlike Faust, he wished to realize those aspirations through the use of Western materials. In several mature novels toward the end of his career, beginning with *Bugles in the Afternoon* (1944) and culminating in his posthumous masterpiece, *The Earthbreakers* (1952), Haycox demonstrated the resilience of the Western formula.

Bugles in the Afternoon, a novel about Custer's Seventh Cavalry and the events leading up to its annihilation at the Battle of the Little Big Horn, is marred for many contemporary readers by its unabashed love for the military life. In spite of that, its main theme, how much the individual owes to the group, is extensively explored, and the depth of its realism, as seen in Haycox's poignant descriptions of bleak North Dakota towns and of the Seventh Cavalry soldiers and their equipment, is memorable.

Haycox was born, reared, and educated in Oregon, and it was of Oregon, with its mouldy, misty forests, its succulent soils, and its salty, windy estuary towns that he wrote most effectively. The three great novels of his maturity, *Long Storm* (1946), *The Adventurers* (1954), and *The Earthbreakers*, are all set in Oregon's lower Willamette Valley. The main theme of each of the novels is the endurance and gradual victory of idealism over forces of savagery and cynicism. The great peril of such a theme is sentimentalism, and one must acknowledge that Haycox is occasionally ensnared by it, particularly in the two earlier novels. Haycox, like Grey, never learned to make sin attractive enough to make victories over it appear genuine; his villains, such as the Southern sympathizer Floyd Ringrose in *Long Storm*, who clumsily tries to subvert Oregon's strong Union commitment during the Civil War, are too often melodramatic caricatures. Ringrose abuses women and children, drinks too much, brags ridiculously, conspires ineptly, and fights poorly.

At his best, though, Haycox deftly sidesteps the perils of sentimentalism. In *The Earthbreakers*, he places his hero, an ex-mountain man named Rice Burnett who has chosen to guide a wagon train to the Willamette Valley where he will stay and settle, in the midst of several characters representing various degrees of commitment to civilization and forces him to make genuine—often painful—choices concerning with whom and to what degree he will ally himself. Burnett has a yearning for civilization, though his love for the wild, free life of a trapper will not die easily or completely, but defining what that civilization is, among the various choices available, is no easy matter. Burnett is an appealing hero, a far cry from the superhuman gunslingers of much popular Western fiction and even from the overly idealistic characters of Haycox's earlier books.

Haycox's craftsmanship had a profound influence on popular Western literature. In 1952, a group of novelists, many of them Haycox disciples, founded the Western Writers of America. The WWA, which has grown steadily in size and sophistication, began publishing *The Roundup*, a monthly magazine with news, reviews, and articles on writing and the publishing business. The association also began making awards at each annual meeting for the best writing the previous year in several categories. The effect of the organization has been to establish higher literary standards and to assist aspiring writers in meeting those standards.

Although Haycox's influence on younger writers was undeniable, none of his direct disciples or imitators climbed to the master's level. One of his leading competitors in sales, if not in literary quality, was Frederick Dilley Glidden (1908-1975), who wrote under the name of the Kansas gunfighter Luke Short. If many newspapermen are frustrated novelists, Glidden the novelist was a frustrated newspaperman. Born in Illinois, he was graduated with a journalism degree from the University of Missouri. Though he worked here and there for brief periods on newspapers, the onset of the Great Depression cost him one job after another. Finally, in 1935, he began writing Westerns to support himself.

Like many writers of Westerns, Glidden was capable of massive production: during the 1940's, he wrote fourteen novels. That degree of success enabled him to move to Aspen, Colorado, where he spent most of the rest of his life. At about that time, he began to lose interest in Western writing; during the 1950's, he wrote only six novels and began trying, with very little success, to break into other fields.

Glidden admired Haycox and competed successfully with him for a time in the high-paying "slick" magazines such as *Collier's*, but in literary quality he was no match for Haycox. In fact, most of his novels could be regarded as throwbacks to the pre-Haycox days, when characterization and setting were not as important as action. Unlike most literary chroniclers of the masculine world of the frontier, Glidden knew how to develop convincing heroines. *Hard Money* (1940) and *Paper Sheriff* (1966), which is perhaps his best novel, both feature at least one female character of believable complexity.

Undoubtedly the best-known Western writer today is Louis L'Amour (1908-1988). Since the age of fifteen, when he left his North Dakota home to ease the financial burden on his family, L'Amour lived a colorful life not unworthy of some of his characters. His travels throughout the country working at a multitude of occupations (he was even a professional boxer) inspired him with a vision of the diversity of American culture and of the sturdy masculine virtues required to settle the American continent. L'Amour began writing for magazines during the 1930's. Soon he conceived a plan for a massive fictional saga of the westward movement based on the stories of three families: the Sacketts, the Talons, and the Chantrys. After 101 books at the time of his death, not all of which were part of the saga, the project remained incomplete.

On the covers of his books and in his frequent television appearances, L'Amour was much more interested in discussing Western history than writing techniques and literary theory. He was convinced that his strongest suit as a writer was the authenticity of his novels, and some of them even contain historical footnotes. Critics have pointed out that L'Amour confused authenticity with believability, and that, like the works of Zane Grey, his novels often suffer from their heavy burden of undigested historical data.

L'Amour's *Hondo* (1953) expresses the opinion, well in advance of the current ecological movement, that man is responsible for the use he makes of his natural environment. Perhaps even more prevalent in L'Amour's fiction is the disillusioned, hard-bitten hero for whom survival is the only goal: *Shalako* (1962) is a notable example. Such novels were only the beginning of vast changes in values in the Western literature of the 1960's and 1970's, which paralleled changes in American culture as a whole. Several publishers widened the chink opened by Doubleday's Double-D Western series, which featured, to the astonishment of readers of traditional Westerns, graphic descriptions of sex and violence and other formerly taboo material. Perhaps it is appropriate that the lead in establishing the subgenre of the "sex Western" was taken by Playboy Press. With its series written by staff writers under the collective name of "Jake Logan," Playboy introduced graphic and lengthy sex scenes alongside more traditional Western elements. The trend caught on; as the Jake Logan series grew, other series, such as the "Longarm" series published by Jove Publications, appeared, and one today can choose among several such series each containing several dozen titles. The assembly-line nature of those series, incidentally, is revealed in their packaging by number as much as by title. During its burgeoning years, the sex Western was a controversial issue: much of *The Roundup* during 1982 was taken up by a heated debate regarding the validity of the sex Western, many writers haughtily disdaining its economic temptations. More recently, though, the debate seems to have receded to the same level of historical curiosity as initial reactions to the miniskirt and rock and roll music. In response to the unprecedented openness of sexual discussion and expression in American life, often to the point of unabashed hedonism, the sex Western seems to have attained a solid place in Western literature.

Equally noteworthy is the rise of the "violence Western," the leading proponent of which is an Englishman named Terry Harknett, who writes the "Edge" series under the name George Gilman. The depiction of extreme violence in Westerns clearly parallels larger cultural developments, yet the Edge series and the novels of another Englishman, J. T. Edson, are often revolting by any standard. Gilman's *The Living, the Dying, and the Dead* (1978), for example, after an assortment of shootings, stabbings, dismemberments, and disfigurements, culminates with a scene in which the rotting corpse of a dead prostitute is dissected.

Fortunately, not all trends in popular Western literature pander to the most ignoble human instincts. Stephen D. Overholser's "Molly" series, for example, attempts to reach those touched by the call for greater freedom and equality for women. The series contains sex, which the author says he tries to make a plausible and integral part of the story, but it also recounts the activities of an independent, resourceful woman on the frontier.

One of the most significant developments in popular Western literature during the 1970's and 1980's was the increasing acceptance of the Western among literary critics and intellectual historians as an object of serious study. Some of this is certainly a result of the general democratization of American life since the 1960's and the rise of New Left historiography, with its emphasis on the life of common people. One may view this trend most graphically, perhaps, by comparing the two editions, ten years apart, of Richard W. Etulain's bibliography of Western literary studies. In *Western American Literature: A Bibliography of Interpretive Books and Articles* (1972), the entries on even such famous popular writers as Zane Grey often included some fairly flawed and fugitive articles and reviews, and even those appeared in limited numbers. By the time his *Bibliographical Guide to the Study of Western American Literature* appeared in 1982, Etulain could choose from a fertile field of books and articles from major presses and journals, and in much greater quantities than the previous decade. Etulain and Fred Erisman's *Fifty Western Writers: A Bio-Bibliographical Sourcebook* (1982) featured essays on Zane Grey, Luke Short, and Louis L'Amour cheek-by-jowl with the likes of Frank Waters, John Steinbeck, and Jack London. And the massive *Literary History of the American West*, sponsored in 1987 by the Western Literature Association, gave ample space to the development of the popular Western. Finally, the Western Writers of America have themselves begun to take a more searching look at their craft through substantive articles in their revamped journal, *The Roundup*. Before 1988 *The Roundup* was little more than a pamphlet which appeared ten times a year with the appearance and substance of a trade journal. Beginning in September of that year, it changed to a much larger and intellectually substantial quarterly format.

The popular Western, then, gives every sign of remaining a living part of American literary legacy. Far from becoming ossified in outworn romantic horse opera clichés, the Western remains largely abreast with ongoing developments in the culture at large, while keeping in touch with important elements in American history and traditional values.

Gary Topping

FANTASY NOVEL

Contemporary publishers use the heading "Fantasy" in a narrow sense which distinguishes the works bearing that label from those billed as "Horror" or "Science Fiction," but this distinction is a matter of marketing strategy which should not be taken too seriously. For the purposes of this essay, the term "fantasy" will be taken to refer to all works of fiction which attempt neither the realism of the realistic novel nor the "conditional realism" of science fiction.

Among modern critics, the primacy of the realistic novel is taken for granted. In their eyes, realistic novels not only describe normality but also constitute the normal kind of fiction; fantasy, in dealing with the supernatural, seems itself to be almost perverse.

Prior to the rise of the novel in the eighteenth century, however, this was far from being the case. Prose forms such as the imaginary voyage, the dialogue, and satire blurred even the basic distinction between fiction and nonfiction, let alone that between "realistic" and "fantastic" subject matter. The separation of realistic and fantastic began not with the casting out of fantastic genres from the literary mainstream, but rather with the withdrawal of a realistic genre—the novel—from a mainstream which had easily accommodated fantastic motifs.

To speak of the "fantasy novel" in the context of the eighteenth century comes close to committing a contradiction in terms: novels were about life as it was lived and had left behind the conventions of allegory and fable along with the decorations of the marvelous and the magical. It is arguable, though, that the withdrawal left behind a connecting spectrum of ambiguous works, and—more important—that it soon led to some important reconnections. Jonathan Swift's use of the techniques of narrative realism in his chronicling of the imaginary voyages of Lemuel Gulliver gave to his work a crucial modernity which is responsible for its still being widely read and enjoyed today.

The rise of the Gothic novel in the last decades of the eighteenth century, in connection with the emergence of the Romantic movement which spread from Germany to France, England, and America, represents a definite reaction against the advancement of literary realism. The Gothic novel, indeed, is almost an "antinovel" of its day, substituting a fascination with the ancient for a preoccupation with the modern, an interest in the outré for an obsession with the everyday, an exaltation of the mysterious for a concern with the intelligible, a celebration of the barbaric for a smug appreciation of the civilized. From the standpoint of today, the Gothic can be seen to have been subversive in several different ways. It was subversive in a literary context because it opposed the dominant trend toward the development of the modern realistic novel. It was subversive in a sociological context because it reflected the fact that the values of the ancien régime were under stress, and that the decadence of that regime was symptomatic of its imminent dissolution. It was subversive in a psychological context because it provided a parable of the impotence of the conscious mind to complete its oppressive victory over the forces of the unconscious, whose imprisonment could never be total.

Gothic novels dealt with strange events in strange environments, organized around the passions of the protagonists. The passions were frequently illicit in a perfectly straightforward sense, often involving incest and the breaking of sacred vows, but the more careful and controlled Gothics—the archetypal example is *The Mysteries of Udolpho* (1794) by Ann Radcliffe—emphasized the extent to which the trend toward a less permissive morality would eventually rule, especially in England.

With the exception of the Gothic novels, very few of the products of the Romantic rebellion were cast in the form of long prose narratives. Short stories were produced in much greater quantity, and the evolution of the short story in Europe and America is closely intertwined with the Romantic reaction against realism and classicism. Poetry, too, was affected very dramatically. Even the Gothic novel underwent a rapid decline—not into nonexistence but into inconsequential crudeness. After the appearance, in 1824, of James Hogg's *The Private Memoirs and Confessions of a Justified Sinner*—a true masterpiece of psychological terror involving paranoid delusions—there followed a long period in which Gothic romance was primarily associated with the lowest stratum of the literary marketplace: with the partworks and "penny dreadfuls" marketed for the newly literate inhabitants of the industrial towns. Such interminable narratives as *Varney the Vampyre* (1847) by James Malcolm Rymer and *Wagner the Wehr-Wolf* (1865?) by G. M. W. Reynolds achieved considerable success in their own time but have nothing to offer modern readers.

Although the Gothic novel was primarily a species of horror story, its supernatural trappings did overflow into moralistic fantasies which might be comic extravaganzas, such as James Dalton's *The Gentleman in Black* (1831) and *The Invisible Gentleman* (1833), or earnest parables, such as John Sterling's *The Onyx Ring* (1839). The themes of these novels—tricky deals with the devil, invisibility, wish-granting rings, and personality exchange—were to become the staples of what Nathan Drake had called "sportive Gothic," while curses, ghosts, vampires, and madness remained the characteristic motifs of "gloomy Gothic."

The writers who produced the most notable works of fantasy in the mid-nineteenth century—including Edgar Allan Poe and Nathaniel Hawthorne in America, George MacDonald and William Gilbert in England, and Théophile Gautier and Charles Nodier in France—worked primarily in the short-story medium. The novels written by these authors often have fantastic embellishments, but for the most part they pay far more heed to the restraints of conventional realism than their short stories.

The revival of the fantasy novel in the last two decades of the nineteenth century was associated with several trends which can be traced through the fiction of the last hundred years to the present day. The partial eclipse of substantial work in fantastic fiction in the mid-century period is clearly related to the repressive morality of that period—it is notable that in France, where the repression was less effective than in Britain, America, and Germany, the Romantic heritage was more effectively conserved. It is possible, in consequence, to see the various threads of the revival in terms of reactions against and attempts to escape from that repression.

During this repressive period, indulgence in fantasy came to be seen as a kind of laxity: it was in the Victorian era that the notion of "escapism" was born. An exception was made in the case of children's literature (though even here there was a period when fantasy was frowned upon), and there eventually arose in Britain a curious convention whereby fantasies were considered suitable reading for Christmas, when a little token indulgence might be overlooked, an idea that led to the emphasis on fantasy in the Christmas annuals to which Dickens and William Makepeace Thackeray contributed. Such writers as Thackeray, George MacDonald, and Lewis Carroll brought to the writing of books nominally aimed at children an artistry and seriousness which commended them to the attention of adults and helped to open a space for the production of fantastic novels within the British literary marketplace.

Another form of fantastic fiction which became to some extent associated with the British Christmas annuals was the ghost story, which became extremely popular in the 1880's and remained so for half a century, during which virtually all the classic British work in that genre was done. There is, however, something intrinsically anecdotal about ghost stories which keeps them more-or-less confined to short fiction. Though there have been some excellent novellas, there have never been more than half a dozen outstanding ghost *novels*. J. Sheridan Le Fanu, who stands at the head of the line of British ghost-story writers, produced several neo-Gothic novels, but almost all of them are so ponderous as to be well-nigh unreadable. M. R. James wrote only short stories, and Algernon Blackwood's novels have not worn nearly as well as his shorter pieces.

The Victorian interest in ghosts, however, went far beyond the traffic in thrilling anecdotes. The influence of such contemporary fads as Spiritualism and Theosophy sparked a new interest in the occult which began to be reflected quite prolifically in literary production. The great majority of the spiritualist fantasies of communication with the dead and accounts of the afterlife supposedly dictated by the dead through mediums are wholly inconsequential in literary terms, despite the eventual involvement in such movements of writers of ability such as Arthur Conan Doyle. They did, however, lay important groundwork for those authors who followed. The fevered

Rosicrucian romances of Edward Bulwer-Lytton, Marie Corelli's exercises in unorthodox theology, and commercially successful accounts of life "on the other side" by such writers as Coulson Kernahan and Elizabeth Stuart Phelps paved the way for much more substantial posthumous fantasies by Wyndham Lewis (*The Childermass*, 1928) and C. S. Lewis (*The Great Divorce*, 1945) and for the theological romances of Charles Williams and David Lindsay. Williams' *All Hallows Eve* (1945) is possibly the best of the ghost novels, while Lindsay's *A Voyage to Arcturus* (1920) is a masterpiece of creative metaphysics.

The 1880's also saw a renaissance of comic fantasy, exemplified in Britain by the novels of F. Anstey and in America by Mark Twain's *A Connecticut Yankee at King Arthur's Court* (1889). The calculated irreverence of these stories reflects a self-confident rationalism which stands in opposition to the mystical movements inspiring most posthumous fantasy. The primary target held up for ridicule in these stories, however, is not the vocabulary of fantastic ideas itself, but rather the moral pretensions of the contemporary middle classes. Anstey's stories use fantastic premises in order to expose the limitations of the attitudes that were rigidified within closed Victoian minds.

In the twentieth century, this tradition of humorous fantasy has thrived more in America than in Britain—the leading American exponent of the species has been Thorne Smith—and this reflects, in part, the fact that as Britain has become somewhat less obsessed with the protocols of middle-class culture, America has become gradually more so. It was in America also that the absurd logical consequences of fantastic premises began to be exploited for pure amusement, largely in connection with the short-lived magazine *Unknown*, whose leading contributors were L. Sprague de Camp and Fletcher Pratt, who produced in collaboration a series of excellent comic fantasies.

A third species of fantastic fiction which first became clearly delineated in the last decades of the nineteenth century is the kind of story which translocates contemporary men into fabulous imaginary worlds. Stories of this kind are among the oldest that are told. The mundane world has always had its fantastic parallels; its earthly paradises, the land of Cokaygne, and the land of Faerie. In the mid-nineteenth century these alternate worlds were retired into juvenile fiction, except for a few desert islands populated in a relatively mundane fashion. Victorian romances of exploration, however, celebrating the journeys of white men into the heart of the dark continent of Africa, reopened imaginative spaces for more exotic traveler's tales.

Numerous "lost race" stories and a few "hollow Earth" romances were published before 1880, but the writer who first made a considerable popular impact with exotic romances of exploration was H. Rider Haggard, first in *King Solomon's Mines* (1885), later in *She* (1887) and *The Ghost Kings* (1908). The example which he set was rapidly taken up by others, and the fantasization of the lands where adventurers went exploring proceeded rapidly. Because this was also the period when interplanetary stories were beginning to appear among early scientific romances, it was perhaps inevitable that writers began to displace their more exotic imaginary worlds to the surfaces of other planets. The example set by Edwin Lester Arnold in *Lieut. Gullivar Jones: His Vacation* (1905) was rapidly followed by Edgar Rice Burroughs and many others. In *The Lost World* (1912), Arthur Conan Doyle revitalized remote Earthly locations with survivals from prehistory, and this too was an example enthusiastically followed. A new vocabulary borrowed from scientific romance allowed later writers to send heroes through "dimensional gateways" of one kind or another into magical fantasy worlds as exotic as could be imagined: the most determined of all writers of this kind of escapist fantasy was the American Abraham Merritt, author of *The Moon Pool* (1919) and *The Face in the Abyss* (1932).

Though the lost-land story set on the Earth's surface was gradually destroyed by news of real explorations—the last classic example was James Hilton's *Lost Horizon* (1933)—the borrowing of conventions from science fiction has allowed the basic story-framework to be retained to the present day. Contemporary humans can still be precipitated into magical imaginary worlds with the aid of a little fake technology, or even a light sprinkling of jargon. The removal of imaginary worlds from darkest Africa to other planets and other dimensions, however, coincided with another and possibly more important innovation in the use of the theme, which was to dispense with the protagonist from the familiar world.

Although traditional fairy tales had, at the time of their origin, been set in the believed-in world, their remote printed descendants could not help but seem to their consumers to be set in an entirely imaginary milieu. The magicalized medieval milieu of such stories became a stereotype useful to modern writers, who began to repopulate it with complex characters whose adventures were filled with allegorical significance. The pioneers of this kind of enterprise were the German Romantic Fouqué, in his novel *The Magic Ring* (1813), and George MacDonald, in *Phantastes* (1958), but their example was followed in far more prolific fashion by William Morris, whose several romances of this kind include *The Wood Beyond the World* (1894) and *The Water of the Wondrous Isles* (1897). The form gathered further momentum in the work of Lord Dunsany, most notably in *The King of Elfland's Daughter* (1924) and *The Charwoman's Shadow* (1926); other contemporary examples include Margaret Irwin in *These Mortals* (1925) and Hope Mirrlees in *Lud-in-the-Mist* (1926). These sophisticated but slightly effete fairy tales then began to give way to a more active brand of heroic fantasy, first featured to extravagant extent in E. R. Eddison's *The Worm Ourobouros* (1922).

Modified fairy-tale fantasy reached new heights of popularity in the fantastic volumes included in James Branch Cabell's "Biography of Manuel," set in the imaginary magical European kingdom of Poictesme. It was also developed in a much more extravagant way by several of the contributors to the magazine *Weird Tales*, who used imaginary lands set in remote eras of prehistory in order to develop the subgenre commonly known as "sword-and-sorcery" fiction. Because it was restricted initially to the pages of a pulp magazine, this subgenre was developed primarily in the short-story form, although it is actually better adapted to novel length. Its most famous progenitor, Robert E. Howard, wrote only one novel featuring his archetypal hero Conan: *Conan the Conqueror* (originally "Hour of the Dragon," 1935). The first important novel of this kind to be published initially in book form was *The Well of the Unicorn* (1948) by "George U. Fletcher" (Fletcher Pratt), but since the advent of the paperback book the species has become established as a successful brand of pulp fiction.

The most notable modern novels set entirely in imaginary worlds tend to give the appearance of being hybrids of sophisticated fairy romance and a variety of heroic fantasy not too far removed from American "sword-and-sorcery" fiction. The masterpieces of the genre are *The Once and Future King* by T. H. White—published in its entirety in 1958 but absorbing three earlier novels—and *The Lord of the Rings* by J. R. R. Tolkien, published in three volumes between 1954 and 1955.

One of the most striking side effects of the development of fantasy novels of this kind for adults has been the revitalization of work done primarily for the juvenile market, which is often remarkably sophisticated in both technical and ideative terms. Tolkien's juvenile novel *The Hobbit* (1937) is an old example; more recent ones include Ursula K. Le Guin's trilogy of novels set in the world of "Earthsea" and various works by Alan Garner, Susan Cooper, and Lloyd Alexander.

The paperback publication of Tolkien's *Lord of the Rings* in the 1960's sparked off countless exercises in imitation, which have proved popular enough to make the trilogy the basic form of modern fantasy fiction. The reborn genre has gone from strength to strength in commercial terms, making bestsellers out of dozens of writers, many of them direly mediocre in terms of the quality of their prose. Nor is it simply oral fairy tales which have been rehabilitated within modern commercial fiction; following the success of Richard Adams' *Watership Down* (1972), animal fables—which were also popular in medieval times—have similarly been produced in some quantity.

This exploitation of imaginary worlds is the most striking aspect of the evolution of fantasy novels during the last hundred years, and it is not entirely surprising that the "Fantasy" label is now retained for such novels by publishers. There has, however, been a parallel evolution of occult and horrific fantasy. The Decadent movements of the *fin de siècle* period saw the emergence of a kind of fiction which reveled in the "unnatural," and though most of the fantastic fiction of this kind was cast in short-story form, there were a few notable novels, including Oscar Wilde's *The Picture of Dorian Gray*

(1891) and Hanns Heinz Ewers' *The Sorcerer's Apprentice* (1907) and its sequels.

In parallel with these works there appeared a new wave of stories which developed the Gothic images of fear into new archetypes, treating them with a determined quasi-scientific seriousness. The great success in this line was Bram Stoker's *Dracula* (1897), which has never been out of print since publication and which surely stands as the most heavily plundered fantasy of all time, being the sourcebook for literally hundreds of vampire stories and films.

This resurgence of fiction which deals with the supernatural in a deadly earnest fashion may seem rather paradoxical. It was possible for nineteenth century rationalists to imagine that their victory over superstitious belief was almost won, and to look forward to a day when the irrational might be banished from human affairs. If anything, the reverse is true: superstition, mysticism, and irrationality thrive now to a greater extent than ever before, and modern fiction reflects that fact.

Fantasy novels intended to evoke horror and unease are more prolifically produced and consumed today than they were in the heyday of the Gothic, and the world's best-selling novelist, Stephen King, is primarily a horror writer. In addition, the role played by occult forces within the neo-Gothic novel is crucially different; in Gothic novels, normality was usually restored, and when the forces of the supernatural *did* break free, they usually did so in order to punish the guilty and liberate the innocent. In later neo-Gothic fantasies, however—whether one looks at the respectable middlebrow tradition which extends from Mervyn Peake's Gormenghast trilogy to the works of Angela Carter or the lowbrow tradition which extends from Dennis Wheatley to James Herbert and Clive Barker—the Gothic elements are superimposed in a wholesale manner upon the mundane world, subjecting it to a surrealization from which there can be no possibility of redemption.

The new flood of horror stories which have carved out an important niche in the popular fiction market seem to some onlookers to be the equivalent of the penny-dreadful Gothics of Victorian England. To some, these stories constitute a pornography of violence which is doubly disturbing in its apparent moral neutrality (mutilation comes to the innocent and guilty alike in multitudinous "slasher novels" about the exploits of serial killers) and in its apparent hopelessness (escape or redemption from a particular menace is conventionally seen as a purely temporary respite).

What the abundant and simultaneous popularity of gross paranoid fantasies, quasi-medieval fairy tales, and quaint tales of talking animals can reveal about the present state of the world in which we live is difficult to judge. There is no doubt, however, that the motifs of these stories (and of science fiction) are also making considerable inroads upon the hallowed turf of the "mainstream" novel, loosening the constraints of its "normal" realism quite considerably. Modern readers, in striking contrast to their mid-nineteenth century counterparts, have been liberated from the straitjacket of true belief, not merely for one day a year but for 365, so that they can once again indulge at will the hypothetical extremes of hope and anxiety.

Brian Stableford

SCIENCE-FICTION NOVEL

The emergence of the "modern" novel in the eighteenth century, with its emphasis on narrative realism and its intimate involvement with the affairs of everyday life, is correlated with a gradual separation between mundane and imaginative fiction, a crucial breaking of categories that was later to be represented by such distinctions as that between "Realism" and "Romance." There have always been problems in defining the boundary which marks this categorical break, as there have always been problems in defining exactly what is meant by the term "novel," but from the end of the eighteenth century onward writers and critics have been aware of some such fundamental distinction and convinced of its propriety.

Many individual works lie within the borderland between mundane and imaginative fiction, but there is one entire genre which occupies a curiously ambiguous position, a genre which depends on the use of the imagination to a considerable degree but which tries to make its imaginative products responsible in some way to a realistic outlook. The names given to this genre all have in common a somewhat oxymoronic flavor: "scientific romance," "realistic romance," "science fiction."

There are, as might be expected, two conflicting traditions in science-fiction criticism. One of these traditions stresses the close alliance between science fiction and other kinds of fantasy, and values the genre for its venturesome qualities. The other tradition emphasizes the responsibilities of the conscientious science-fiction writer in maintaining a firm base within scientific possibility and in the avoidance of any traffic with the occult. Brian Aldiss, in *Billion Year Spree* (1973; revised as *Trillion Year Spree*, 1986), suggests that science fiction is "characteristically cast in the Gothic or post-Gothic mode" and traces its ancestry from Mary Shelley's *Frankenstein* (1818). Robert Heinlein, by contrast, contributes to a symposium on *The Science Fiction Novel* (1959), introduced by Basil Davenport, a spirited defense of science fiction as a species of realistic fiction, likening the method of science-fiction writers to the scientific method itself. In this view, science fiction becomes an assembly of literary *Gedanken-experimenten*.

Not unnaturally, adherents of these two views differ very markedly on the issue of which texts should be labeled "science fiction" and which ought to be cast out as pretenders. Everyone agrees, though, that publishers and critics tend to use the label irresponsibly—on the one hand, extending it promiscuously to cover stories which are "really" fantasy, and on the other hand, refraining from its use in respect of many prestigious works which, though "really" science fiction, might somehow be stigmatized or devalued if they were so named in open court.

Despite the fact that several different histories of science fiction have been compiled by adherents of different definitions, it is to the history and development of the genre that one is inclined to turn in the hope of discovering a reasonable analysis of the genre's characteristics and relationships with other literary traditions.

There is, in fact, no evidence whatever of a coherent tradition of literary endeavor extending from *Frankenstein* to more recent science fiction. Although there are echoes of Gothic freneticism in a few of the works produced in the last decades of the nineteenth century, when fiction recognizably akin to that which today bears the label began to proliferate, most of it is very different in character.

One can recognize four main stimuli which encouraged writers in the late nineteenth century to produce more-or-less careful and conscientious works about imaginary inventions, future societies, and alien worlds. The first was the revolution in transportation, which brought the products of the Industrial Revolution into the everyday world of the middle classes in the shape of steam locomotives and steamships. This stimulated the growth of the novel of imaginary tourism, the greatest and most popular exponent of which was Jules Verne, author of *Journey to the Centre of the Earth* (1864), *From the Earth to the Moon* (1865), and *Twenty Thousand Leagues Under the Sea* (1870). Most of the early novels of space travel have a distinctively Vernian flavor and represent the more ambitious extreme of this particular subspecies. Examples include *Across the Zodiac* (1880) by Percy Greg and *A Columbus of Space* (1909) by Garrett P. Serviss.

A second important stimulus was the discussion provoked by the publication of Charles Darwin's *On the Origin of Species* (1859) and *The Descent of Man* (1871). Literary reconstructions of the prehistoric past became common, and so did speculations regarding the possible evolutionary future of mankind. The most famous examples are *The Time Machine* (1895) by H. G. Wells and *The Hampdenshire Wonder* (1911) by John D. Beresford.

The same period saw a revitalization of speculation about the possibilities of social and political reform by virtue of increasing awareness of the extent that technology might encourage—and perhaps even compel—dramatic changes in the social and political order. Edward Bellamy's *Looking Backward: 2000-1887* (1888) became a runaway best-seller in America and provoked numerous replies in kind, including *News from Nowhere* (1891) by William Morris and *Caesar's Column* (1890) by Ignatius Donnelly. Whereas Morris' novel was one of many offering an alternative manifesto for the future Utopia, Donnelly's was the first in what was later to become a thriving tradition of "dystopian" works developing the hypothesis that the world was getting worse and not better, and that technology would help to secure its damnation.

The last important stimulus which proved prolific in this period was the anticipation of war in Europe and the fascination of exploring the potential of new weapons. George Griffith, in *The Angel of the Revolution* (1893), presented a dramatic image of war fought with aircraft and submarines, and this too became a continual preoccupation in the work of H. G. Wells, the most eclectic imaginative writer of the period, reflected in such works as *The War in the Air* (1908) and *The World Set Free* (1914).

The perception by readers and writers that these disparate literary subspecies had something fundamental in common, sent critics and publishers in search of a category label. The one most widely used at the time was "Scientific Romance."

The supposedly realistic quality of these stories was prejudiced in several different ways. For one thing, the writers were primarily interested in the more melodramatic implications of the premises on which they worked, and this led them toward the production of highly colored thrillers rather than sober speculations about the role of science and technology in future human affairs. This was largely a matter of the markets for which the authors worked: the advent of scientific romance coincided with an expansion of literacy and a corollary expansion of the kinds of reading-matter that were available. It became possible for the first time for a fairly large number of writers to make a living from their work, provided that they appealed to a wide audience, and most of the successful science-fiction writers belonged to this cadre of new professionals.

Second, and perhaps more important, a realistic approach had to be compromised by the use of literary devices. It was not possible for Jules Verne to describe the operation of a genuinely sophisticated submarine, or for George Griffith to describe a workable airship. Both writers had to guess what kind of physical principles such craft would depend on. Both, not surprisingly, guessed incorrectly. A more serious problem was faced by Wells in *The Time Machine* when he wished to expose for contemplation the long-term future of the human race and the planet Earth. No matter how well-based in evolutionary theory his images of the future might be, in order to embed them in a literary work he needed a means of transporting an observer to report back news of them, and that means could only be a pure invention. Spaceships, too, are used in much science fiction simply as a literary device for opening up the immense imaginative territories provided by an infinite range of alien worlds. Whereas Verne, in *From the Earth to the Moon*, was concerned with the spaceship as a vehicle, an artifact in its own right, Wells in *The First Men in the Moon* (1901) simply wanted a way to get his characters to the moon so that they could investigate the mysteries of Selenite society and provide an eyepiece for a serious exercise in speculative sociology.

Science fiction has no option but to rely upon such literary devices; there is no other way to avoid the logical trap pointed out by Karl Popper in the Introduction to *The Poverty of Historicism* (1957)—that it is by definition impossible to know today what new knowledge will materialize tomorrow. Writers attempt to conceal the arbitrariness of these devices by the use of scientific or pseudoscientific jargon, which creates an illusion of plausibility, but this is merely laying a carpet over a hole in the floor.

The imaginative realms to which the writers of scientific romance built literary highways were soon "invaded" by writers who were not in the least concerned with fidelity to scientific possibility, but who merely wanted new playgrounds to incorporate into their dreams. There grew up, especially in America, a tradition of exotic interplanetary romance founded in the works of Edgar Rice Burroughs, author of *A Princess of Mars* (1917). Burroughs was the first of many to exploit a rich new vocabulary of ideas in the service of a purely romantic fiction. He set his fantasies in an imaginary world inside the Earth and in a variety of undiscovered islands on its surface, as well as on other planets. The closest British parallel is to be found in Arthur Conan Doyle's novel *The Lost World* (1912), though the tradition has many affinities with the work of H. Rider Haggard.

When, in the 1920's, Hugo Gernsback began publishing pulp magazines in the United States specializing in science fiction, he issued a prospectus which put the emphasis very strongly on fidelity to scientific fact and the careful exploration of technological possibility, but in his own and rival magazines exotic interplanetary romance quickly took over. The audience which supported the pulp magazines demanded thrillers, the more highly colored the better. Gernsback's pretentions could not be maintained if the label "science fiction" was to be viable as a brand-name for pulp fiction, and they were very soon abandoned in fact, although editorial propaganda continued to maintain a hollow pretense.

In Britain the situation was rather different. The literary marketplace was organized differently, and following World War I, cheap books displaced popular magazines to a very large extent. The category label "science fiction" was not imported until 1945, and even "scientific romance" was not used freely or consistently. World War I had a tremendous impact on the attitudes of the nation, and postwar works of futuristic speculation were often desperately embittered. Their seriousness was rarely in doubt—many are grim stories of alarmism which try hard to impress the reader with the realistic nature of their forebodings.

There appeared a series of future war stories looking forward to the possible self-destruction of civilization, the best of which are *The People of the Ruins* (1920) by Edward Shanks, *Theodore Savage* (1922) by Cicely Hamilton, and *Tomorrow's Yesterday* (1932) by John Gloag. Anxiety about the fruits of "progress" also ran high, with many European writers producing bitter parables in which the lot of mankind is made worse by unwise meddling with the secrets of nature or by the appropriation by power groups of sophisticated technological means of maintaining their power. Key examples include *The Absolute at Large* (1922) by Karel Čapek and *Brave New World* (1932) by Aldous Huxley.

There is a certain irony in the fact that throughout the 1920's and 1930's, the works produced in the United States labeled "science fiction" actually bear far less resemblance to commonly held notions of the nature of the genre than the unlabeled speculative fiction produced in Europe. This situation began to change, however, in the 1940's. The dominant trend in American pulp science fiction from 1938 on—closely associated with the magazine *Astounding Science Fiction* and its editor John W. Campbell, Jr.—was toward a more sensible and more scrupulous development of hypotheses, while from approximately the same date the British literary community became gradually more aware of American science fiction. By the end of the 1940's, the label was used very widely in Britain both by publishers and by commentators. One of the effects of World War II was that the United States and Britain were brought much more closely together in cultural as well as in political terms. American science fiction began to be imported into Europe on a large scale, bringing with it a diffuse cultural context which affected the attitude of literary critics toward futuristic and speculative works.

Although virtually all the science fiction produced in Britain between the wars was in the novel form—cheap books being the main form of mass-produced fiction in Britain—this was not true of American science fiction of that period. American science fiction very rarely achieved book publication before 1950, so that longer works were produced mainly as magazine serials. Several pulp magazines boasted that they presented a full-length novel in every issue, but "full-length" in this context could mean anything between twenty thousand and fifty thousand words—almost never anything longer. For some thirty years after Gernsback's founding of the first science-fiction magazine in 1926, science fiction's specialist writers devoted themselves first and foremost to the production of short stories, novelettes, and novellas. The long science-fiction novel was virtually nonexistent in America until the 1960's, though British writers regularly turned out works well over 100,000 words in length, including such epics as Olaf Stapledon's *Last and First Men* (1930) and Wells's *The Shape of Things to Come* (1933).

This situation changed dramatically in the 1960's, mainly because of the spectacular market success of the paperback book. Paperbacks surpassed magazines as the chief medium of popular fiction in America and achieved the same degree of success in Britain. Once this had happened, it became inevitable that writers would switch their main effort into the writing of novels. The old pulp writers adapted—the most important among them being Campbell's star protegés, Isaac Asimov and Robert A. Heinlein. The postwar generation of magazine writers adapted too, prominent among them being Arthur C. Clarke, Frederik Pohl, Frank Herbert, John Brunner, Robert Silverberg, and Philip K. Dick. In addition, there emerged in the 1960's many new writers who made their first impact upon the literary scene as writers of science-fiction novels including J. G. Ballard, Samuel R. Delany, Ursula K.

Le Guin, and Norman Spinrad.

There are some novelists who always have tried to avoid the science-fiction label because they consider it to carry a definite stigma by virtue of its longtime association with pulp fiction. These writers include Kurt Vonnegut, Jr., in America and John Wyndham in Britain, both of whom have written abundant work which would be covered by any conceivable definition of science fiction. The recent willingness of American "mainstream" writers to borrow from the imagery of science fiction, however, and the increasing interest in the genre taken by American academics have helped to overcome this stigma to some extent. Science fiction is no longer written exclusively by specialist writers or read almost exclusively by specialist readers, and the situation of the genre within American culture is now much more similar to the situation which it had in British culture between the wars. Militating against the possibility that the most serious science-fiction novels will be taken as seriously as they deserve, however, is that fact that the invasion of the publishing category by exotic romances of various kinds never has been repelled. The category therefore continues to shelter a great deal of rather crude blood-and-thunder dream-fantasy, which, by dint of sheer weight of numbers, is frequently far more evident to onlookers than that fraction of the labeled "science fiction" which still endeavors to offer the fruits of responsible and realistic speculation.

Arguably, the main achievement of the science-fiction novel in its hundred-year history has been in helping people to become more aware of the dangers posed by new technological developments. Science fiction has always been most effective in its more alarmist and pessimistic moods, and its literary quality has been at its highest when its anxieties have run similarly high. Two science-fiction novels—Huxley's *Brave New World* and George Orwell's *Nineteen Eighty-Four* (1949)—may arguably be said to have had a greater impact on the popular imagination than any other literary works of this century. In its anticipations of social and environmental catastrophe, science fiction has been at its strongest: examples include *A Canticle for Leibowitz* (1960) by Walter M. Miller, Jr., *The Drowned World* (1962) by J. G. Ballard, *Cat's Cradle* (1963) by Kurt Vonnegut, Jr., *Stand on Zanzibar* (1968) by John Brunner, *Do Androids Dream of Electric Sheep?* (1968) by Philip K. Dick, and James Morrow's *This Is the Way the World Ends* (1986).

Science fiction has had more positive achievements, too, in emphasizing and popularizing hopeful possibilities. It is impossible to measure the contribution made by the imaginative stimulus of science fiction to the realized dream of putting men on the moon, but there can be no doubt that the inspiration of many rocket scientists originated from their reading of science fiction.

In recent times the use of science-fictional ideas as metaphors representing facets of the human condition has increased in scope. These developments, first seen in such novels as Ursula K. Le Guin's *The Left Hand of Darkness*

(1969) and Robert Silverberg's *Dying Inside* (1972), have helped to open up new common ground between science fiction and the "mainstream" novel so that a profitable cross-fertilization of images and methods can take place. This influence can be seen particularly clearly in such works as Margaret Atwood's *The Handmaid's Tale* (1985) and Fay Weldon's *The Cloning of Joanna May* (1989), two of the many novels which use science-fictional methods to explore the politics of feminism.

Science fiction is a uniquely changeable kind of fiction because it continually absorbs, with an alacrity which compensates for its lack of any authentic powers of foresight, the implications of contemporary advancements in technology. The rapid elaboration and microminiaturization of information technology, in parallel with the development for medical purposes of partially mechanized human "cyborgs," inspired in the 1980's a "cyberpunk" movement spearheaded by such writers as William Gibson, Bruce Sterling, and Michael Swanwick. This movement combined dystopian ideas of the disintegration of civilization with images of superhumanly enhanced individuals equipped with exotic weaponry and the ability to enter the hypothetical "cyberspace" where computer programs operate. Cyberpunk proved briefly controversial because more traditionally inclined writers of "hard" (or technophilic) science fiction such as Gregory Benford and David Brin found the movement's apparent moral nihilism (more reasonably regarded as moral skepticism) hard to swallow. The emerging technologies of genetic engineering, and hypothetical "nanotechnologies" involving machinery whose microminiaturization has advanced by a further order of magnitude, subsequently began to feed into this kind of high-tech picaresque science fiction and soon began to make dramatic changes to the conceptual horizons of hard science fiction as imagined in such works as Greg Bear's *Eon* (1985) and Gregory Benford's *Tides of Light* (1989).

In the meantime, however, the increasing popularity of horror and heroic fantasy fiction encouraged many writers to straddle genre boundaries in search of wider audiences. The vocabulary of ideas built up over the years by science-fiction writers became a key resource of horror writers such as Stephen King and Dean R. Koontz, while an increasing number of modern science-fiction stories were set in hypothetical "alternative pasts" rather than foreseeable futures—examples include James Blaylock's *Homunculus* (1986) and Brian Stableford's *The Empire of Fear* (1988). Hybrid works skillfully mixing science fiction and fantasy motifs, such as Tim Powers' *The Anubis Gates* (1983), also became increasingly common. Given that science fiction is also the label under which earnest religious fantasies such as James Morrow's *Only Begotten Daughter* (1990) are marketed, it has become more difficult than ever before to see where the boundaries of the genre lie, or to dictate where they ought to lie. As long as contemporary scientific discoveries continue to transform the spectrum of possible futures at a rapid pace, though, it will be sensible to argue that the science-fiction novel can serve as an essential tool of psychological adaptation for those who find reasons for hope, as well as reasons for anxiety, in the advancement of science and technology.

Brian Stableford

THE NOVELLA

The word "novella" comes from the Latin word *novellus*, a diminutive of the word *novus*, which means "new." It first became associated with the telling of stories in the thirteenth century with collections of "new" versions of old saints' tales, exempla, chivalric tales, and ribald stories. Eventually, the term became associated with tales that were fresh, strange, unusual—stories, in short, that were worth the telling. The most decisive historical event to establish the term "novella" as a designation for a "new" kind of fiction was Giovanni Boccaccio's decision to give the name "novella" to the tales included in *Il Decamerone* (1348-1353; *The Decameron*) in the fourteenth century.

What made Boccaccio's stories "new" was the fact that they marked a shift from the sacred world of Dante's "divine" comedy to the profane world of Boccaccio's "human" comedy. The resulting realism of the *Decamerone* should not be confused, however, with the realism developed by the eighteenth century novel. The focus in Boccaccio's tales is not on a character presented in a similitude of everyday life, but on the traditional world of story, in which characters serve primarily as "functions" of the tale.

With Miguel de Cervantes, in the sixteenth century, as with Boccaccio before him, something "new" also characterizes the novella. First, Cervantes in his *Novelas ejemplares* (1613; *Exemplary Novels*, 1846) does not present himself as a collector of traditional tales but as an inventor of original stories. As a result, he becomes an observer and recorder of concrete details in the external world and a student of the psychology of individual characters. Although plot is still important, character becomes more developed than it was in *The Decameron*, and thus psychological motivation rather than story motivation is emphasized. Characters exist not solely for the roles they play in the stories but also for their own sake, as if they were real.

In Germany, in the first quarter of the nineteenth century, the novella began to detach itself from the notion of the form inspired by Boccaccio and Cervantes and to be supported by a theory of its own. Friedrich von Schlegel agreed with the Renaissance idea that a novella was an anecdote that must be capable of arousing interest, but he noted that the modern retelling of already-known traditional stories necessarily focuses the reader's attention away from mythic authority and toward the authority of the subjective point of view of the narrator. Johann Wolfgang von Goethe added an important new element to the definition of the novella form by arguing that it depicted an unheard-of event that actually took place; thus, although the event can be accounted for by the laws of nature, it must be strange and unusual.

In addition to this theorizing about the novella during the nineteenth century in Germany, numerous examples of the form contributed to its development. The first such example is Goethe's story entitled simply *Novelle* (1826), an exemplary story that dramatically changes the nature of the genre by shifting the focus from simple events to events that take on a symbolic meaning and form. After Goethe, the novella develops as a most self-conscious genre, a sophisticated literary narrative that deals with the most basic metaphysical and aesthetic issues.

Whereas the logic of Goethe's *Novelle* is governed by the narrative demands of the story and by aesthetic artifice, the logic of the most famous novella of Ludwig Tieck, *Der Blonde Eckbert* (in *Volksmärchen*, 1797), follows the convention of the fairy tale as an externalization of unconscious processes. This act of grounding the supernatural in the psychological is taken to further extremes in the novellas of E. T. A. Hoffmann, whose stories also are often self-conscious manipulations of the relationship previously developed in the fairy tale form between fantasy and the everyday. In Hoffmann's best-known novella, *Der Sandman* (1816; *The Sandman*, 1844), the protagonist is caught between fantasy and reality, a dichotomy that Hoffmann makes more explicit than does Goethe or Tieck. The advance of Hoffmann's tale over those of his predecessors lies in its ironic tone, which parodies the romantic view of reality. Hoffmann has the ironic sensibility of Franz Kafka in perceiving that the supernatural world is serious and sardonic at the same time.

Although the term "novella" is used to refer both to the short pieces of fourteenth century fiction best exemplified by *The Decameron* and the highly developed nineteenth century German form, it is more often used in the twentieth century to refer to a number of works of mid-range length, somewhat longer than the short story and somewhat shorter than the novel. The modern novella derives from various preexisting types. It began in the nineteenth century with a quasi-realistic normalizing of the old romance and parable forms and has maintained these romance conventions in such gothic novellas as Horace Walpole's *The Castle of Otranto* (1764) and Henry James's *The Turn of the Screw* (1898) and in such parabolic novellas as Gustave Flaubert's *La Légende de Saint Julien l'Hospitalier* (in *Trois Contes*, 1877) and Flannery O'Connor's *Wise Blood* (1952).

It is not simply the Gothic trappings and decorations that constitute the Gothic novel, but rather the placing of characters into traditional romance tales and the resulting transformation of those characters into archetypes of the mythic story. The transformation of "real" people into parabolic figures by the latent thrust of the traditional romance story is characteristic of the novella form and can be seen in an explicit way in *The Castle of Otranto*, in which, even as characters act out their desires on the surface of the plot, desire becomes objectified and totally embodied in the latent and underlying plot.

In *The Turn of the Screw*, this basic combination is focused in a particularly explicit way, becoming the crux and central theme of the story. The issue of whether the ghosts in the story are real or whether they are projections of the governess' imagination is reflective of the basic problem of the novella form—that is, whether a given story features characters who are presented as if they are real or whether they are presented as embodiments of psychological archetypes. This ambiguity is so thorough in James's novella that every detail can be read as evidence for both interpretations of reality at once.

Just as Walpole returned to the medieval romance for a model for his gothic tale, Flaubert returned to the medieval saint's legend or folktale for the exemplar for *La Légende de Saint Julien l'Hospitalier*. Furthermore, just as Walpole's romance differs from the medieval form by combining traditional story with psychologically real characters, so does Flaubert's moral fable differ from its medieval source by self-consciously foregrounding the static and frozen nature of the medieval story itself. The subject matter of Flaubert's story, although it has a moral issue at its center, is more particularly the generic means by which the medieval tale is moral and representative. The movement from the parable of Flaubert to the modern parables of the American writer Flannery O'Connor is a movement from a relatively simple story to a more complex and ironic form. Just as the narrative and symbolic aim of Flaubert's story is the spiritual transformation of its central characters, so also is the central aim of O'Connor's *Wise Blood* to lead its central character to a vision of his own fragmentation so he can be reborn.

Perhaps the two best-known modern parable forms of the novella are William Faulkner's *The Bear* (1942) and Ernest Hemingway's *The Old Man and the Sea* (1952). These two stories differ from the parables of Flaubert and O'Connor in that they both seem to be less illustrations of moral issues than reenactments of primitive rituals that enforce the moral issue. Although they are quite different in their individual syntactical rhythms, both stories are characterized by a highly formal structure and style in which moral values evolve ritually from the hero's encounter with the natural world. Of the two stories, *The Old Man and the Sea* seems closer to the parable form than does *The Bear*, primarily because of the conventional expectation that the parable is a relatively clean structural form, functional and bare in style and point of view.

One of the most common narrative devices of the novella is the convention of the double or *Doppelgänger*. There are both historical and aesthetic reasons for the predominance of this motif in the form. Because the novella is a combination of the old romance form, in which characters are projections of psychic states, and the new realistic novel form, in which characters are presented as if they were real people with their own psychological life, novellas often present both types of characters, especially in such works as Herman Melville's "Bartleby the Scrivener" (1853) and Joseph Conrad's *Heart of Darkness* (1902), in which the narrators seem to be realistic characters with individual psyches, while the central characters Bartleby and Kurtz seem to be manifested as psychological archetypes.

Perceiving reality to be a function more of mind than of external reality, the nineteenth century fiction writer could present inner life by means of dreamlike romance projections. If, however, he wished to reveal the inner life in a realistic manner, yet to avoid getting lost in a quagmire of introspection, the only answer was to present that subjective and often-forbidden side of the self in terms of an external projection—as a character who, although the reader could respond to him as if he were a separate external figure, was really a projection of the mind of the protagonist. The most obvious means by which such an inner state could be projected as if it were outer reality was to present the projection as a figure somehow very much like the protagonist, not an identical double, but rather an embodiment of some hidden or neglected aspect of the self that had to be confronted and dealt with.

Robert Louis Stevenson's *The Strange Case of Dr. Jekyll and Mr. Hyde* (1886) is perhaps the purest example of this use of the convention; that Dr. Jekyll represents the conventional and socially acceptable personality and Mr. Hyde the uninhibited and criminal self is the most obvious aspect of Stevenson's novella. A more accomplished and subtle treatment of the convention can be seen in Conrad's *The Secret Sharer* (1912), for here the double is not merely a manifested hidden self or a figure imagined to be outside the protagonist, but rather an actual self whose crime is at the core of the moral issue facing the protagonist. Although it can be said that the double in *The Secret Sharer* represents some aspect of the captain's personality that he must integrate, it is more probable that he is brought on board to make explicit and dramatically concrete the dual workings of the captain's mind: he is distracted and split between his external responsibilities and his concealed secret.

Because of its moderate length, its highly formalized structure, and its focus on the ultimate metaphysical limitations of humanity, the novella has often been compared to classical tragedy. The central character of the novella often seems to be caught in the inevitability of fate or the story, being doomed at the same time as a victim of some limitation within the self. The essential issue is that the "tragic novella" creates the illusion that the character is responsible for his own defeat, even though the reader realizes that he is witnessing the fatality demanded by the fable itself. The two most emphatic examples of this tragic form are Stephen Crane's *The Blue Hotel* (1898) and Katherine Anne Porter's *Noon Wine* (1936).

The three basic devices in *The Blue Hotel* that give it a sense of classical tragedy are its formalized structure, which suggests a classical five-act tragedy; a central character neither eminently good nor evil, whose misfortune results not from vice or depravity but from some error, frailty, or limitation; and the creation through metaphor and allusion of the sense that the events and characters are not contemporary and real but archetypal and ritualistic. The most essential requirement is that the protagonist is made to seem responsible for his own downfall, even though his downfall is governed by the rules of the ritual or fable itself.

Whereas the tragedy in *The Blue Hotel* is brought on by the protagonist's mistake about the nature of the world around him, in Porter's *Noon Wine* the downfall is brought on by a limitation in the protagonist's ability to perceive himself. The tragic figure is Royal Earl Thompson; the other two figures, Helton and Hatch, are projections of two aspects of Thompson's personality and situation. Helton makes it possible for him to live a lie about himself, and Hatch forces him to confront that lie.

One of the narrative forms that serve as important antecedents to the modern novella is the fairy tale, for fairy-tale devices appear in the novella in various self-conscious ways: as a dreamlike state of being that is laid bare; as a structural device to develop a parabolic story; as the means to create the sense of metaphysical mystery in external reality; and as a way to suggest traditional character types and story situations. The fairy-tale conventions in the modern novella are never allowed to lapse into the marvelous and the supernatural; rather, they reflect the extraordinary nature of ordinary life, in which extreme situations seem to transform the world into a kind of reality akin to that found in fairy tales. Carson McCullers' *The Ballad of the Sad Café* (1951) and Franz Kafka's *Die Verwandlung* (1915; *The Metamorphosis*, 1936) are two typical examples. McCullers' story seems to take place in the realm of dreams rather than in external reality, for it is a story turned inward on itself, narcissistic and grotesque just as the central figure Miss Amelia's eyes are crossed, peering inward—sealed off from the ordinary world by the obsessions of the story itself. The effect of the work depends primarily on the poetic voice of the storyteller, which lyrically transforms the grotesque external reality into the inner story of the lover; the details of the story are thus transmuted by the teller until they bear no connection to the external world.

Perhaps the most successful example of this combination of fantasy and reality in the modern novella is Kafka's *The Metamorphosis*. The extreme step Kafka takes is to make the transformation of the psychic into the physical the precipitating premise from which the rest of the story follows. The only suspension of disbelief required in the story is that the reader accept the premise that Gregor Samsa awakes one morning from uneasy dreams to find himself transformed into a giant dung beetle. Once the reader accepts this event, the rest of the story is quite prosaic and detailed, fully externalized in a realistic fashion. *The Metamorphosis* is an exemplar of the typical novella effort to present an inner state of reality as a fantastic but real outer event.

The most common theme and technique in the contemporary novella is metafictional self-reflexivity, embodied in stories that have to do with the nature of storytelling itself. Philip Roth's *The Ghost Writer* (1979), in which external reality and fictional reality become inextricably blurred as the central character tells a story about the almost mythical figure Anne Frank, is an obvious example. Perhaps the most commercially successful attempt at this kind of self-reflexive fiction, however, is Kurt Vonnegut, Jr.'s *Slaughterhouse-Five: Or, The Children's Crusade, a Duty-Dance with Death* (1969), which uses the popular science-fiction genre as a vehicle to explore methods of storytelling.

More sophisticated than *Slaughterhouse-Five* are the metafictional works of John Barth, Robert Coover, and William H. Gass. *Dunyazadiad* (in *Chimera*, 1972) reflects Barth's fascination with the notion of characters in fiction becoming readers or authors of the very fiction they inhabit. *Dunyazadiad* takes its premise and its situation from the Scheherazade story, as told by her younger sister Dunyazade on the final night of the famous 1,001 nights. Barth transports a modern storyteller (himself) back to "Sherry's" aid to supply her with the stories from the future that she has told in the fictional past.

Just as Barth takes his inspiration from the origins of storytelling in *The Arabian Nights' Entertainments*, Coover traces his debts back to Cervantes, who created a synthesis between poetic analogy and literal history and thus gave birth to the modern novel. Coover's most popular novella, *The Babysitter* (in *Pricksongs & Descants*, 1969), is his most forthright example of this mixture of fantasy and reality. The story is a confused combination of the two realms in which, as is usual in the novella, unreality predominates over external reality. The story presents the fantasy reality in the same mode as external reality, so that in trying to unravel the two, the reader gets hopelessly lost in the mix. Gass carries the self-reflexive mode to even further extremes. The primary premise of his novella *Willie Masters' Lonesome Wife* (1968) is that the book the reader holds in his hands is the wife herself. This trope is carried out by such devices as varying the typography and the texture of the book pages and by using graphics and other purely physical devices to give the reader the sense that he or she is not simply seeing through the medium of the book but is dealing with the medium itself.

The main trend of irrealism in the contemporary novella is the story's complete forsaking of its illusion of reality to expose the reality of its illusion. Although the story's presenting itself as a self-admitted fiction rather than "as if" it were real seems more obvious in the contemporary novella than ever before, the novella as a genre has always been more likely to lay bare its fictionality than has the novel, which has traditionally tried to cover it up.

One basic difference between the characters in early novellas by Cervantes and Goethe and the characters in completely function-bound folktales and romances that existed before them is that figures in the novella seem to exist both as if they were real people in an existentially real world and as representative figures manipulated for the purposes of the story. In contemporary novellas such as those by Barth, Coover, and Gass, this background aesthetic tension is foregrounded so that the conflict between fiction and reality becomes the self-conscious conflict of the characters themselves. Contemporary novella characters become inextricably enmeshed in their own dual fiction/reality status; the two realms entangle to suggest that all existential dilemmas are fictional, just as all fictional dilemmas are existential. Thus the study of the fictionality of the novella becomes a study of the only reality there is.

Charles E. May

TERMS AND TECHNIQUES

Allegory: A literary mode in which a second level of meaning, wherein characters, events, and settings represent abstractions, is encoded within the surface narrative. The allegorical mode may dominate the entire work, in which case the encoded message is the work's primary excuse for being, or it may be an element in a work otherwise interesting and meaningful for its surface story alone. Elements of allegory may be found in Jonathan Swift's *Gulliver's Travels* (1726) and Thomas Mann's *The Magic Mountain* (1924).

Anatomy: Literally the term means the "cutting up" or "dissection" of a subject into its constituent parts for closer examination. Northrop Frye, in his *Anatomy of Criticism* (1957), uses the term to refer to a narrative that deals with mental attitudes rather than people. As opposed to the novel, the anatomy features stylized figures who are mouthpieces for the ideas they represent.

Antagonist: The character in fiction who stands as a rival or opponent to the *protagonist*.

Antihero: Defined by Seán O'Faoláin as a fictional figure who, deprived of social sanctions and definitions, is always trying to define himself and to establish his own codes. Ahab may be seen as the antihero of Herman Melville's *Moby Dick* (1851).

Archetype: The term "archetype" entered literary criticism from the psychology of Carl G. Jung, who defined archetypes as "primordial images" from the "collective unconscious" of mankind. Jung believed that works of art derived much of their power from the unconscious appeal of these images to ancestral memories. In his extremely influential *Anatomy of Criticism* (1957), Northrop Frye gave another sense of the term wide currency, defining the archetype as "a symbol, usually an image, which recurs often enough in literature to be recognizable as an element of one's literary experience as a whole."

Atmosphere: The general mood or tone of a work; it is often associated with setting, but can also be established by action or dialogue. A classic example of atmosphere is the primitive, fatalistic tone created in the opening description of Egdon Heath in Thomas Hardy's *The Return of the Native* (1878).

Bildungsroman: Sometimes called the "novel of education," the *Bildungsroman* focuses on the growth of a young *protagonist* who is learning about the world and finding his place in life; typical examples are James Joyce's *A*

Portrait of the Artist as a Young Man (1916) and Thomas Wolfe's *Look Homeward, Angel* (1929).

Biographical criticism: Criticism that attempts to determine how the events and experiences of an author's life influence his work.

Bourgeois novel: A novel in which the values, the preoccupations, and the accoutrements of middle-class or bourgeois life are given particular prominence. The heyday of the bourgeois novel was the nineteenth century, when novelists as varied as Jane Austen, Honoré de Balzac, and Anthony Trollope both criticized and unreflectingly transmitted the assumptions of the rising middle class.

Character: Characters in fiction can be presented as if they were real people or as stylized functions of the plot. Usually characters are a combination of both factors.

Classicism: A literary stance or value-system consciously based on the example of classical Greek and Roman literature. While the term is applied to an enormous diversity of artists in many different periods and in many different national literatures, "classicism" generally denotes a cluster of values including formal discipline, restrained expression, reverence for tradition, and an objective rather than a subjective orientation. As a literary tendency, classicism is often opposed to *Romanticism*, although many writers combine classical and romantic elements.

Climax/Crisis: Whereas climax refers to the moment of the reader's highest emotional response, crisis refers to a structural element of plot. Crisis refers to a turning point in fiction, a point when a resolution must take place.

Complication: The point in a novel when the conflict is developed or when the already existing conflict is further intensified.

Conflict: The struggle that develops as a result of the opposition between the *protagonist* and another person, the natural world, society, or some force within the self.

Contextualist criticism: A further extension of formalist criticism, which assumes that the language of art is constitutive. Rather than referring to preexistent values, the art work creates values only inchoately realized before. The most important advocates of this position are Eliseo Vivas, *The Artistic Transaction* (1963), and Murray Krieger, *The Play and Place of Criticism* (1967).

Conventions: All those devices of stylization, compression, and selection that constitute the necessary differences between art and life. According to the Russian formalists, these conventions constitute the "literariness" of literature and are the only proper concern of the literary critic.

Deconstruction: An extremely influential contemporary school of criticism based on the works of the French philosopher Jacques Derrida. Deconstruction treats literary works as unconscious reflections of the reigning myths of Western culture. The primary myth is that there is a meaningful world which language signifies or represents. The Deconstructionist critic is most often concerned with showing how a literary text tacitly subverts the very assumptions or myths on which it ostensibly rests.

Defamiliarization: Coined by Viktor Shklovsky in 1917, the term denotes a basic principle of Russian formalism. Poetic language (by which the formalists meant artful language, in prose as well as in poetry) defamiliarizes or "makes strange" familiar experiences. The technique of art, says Shklovsky, is to "make objects unfamiliar, to make forms difficult, to increase the difficulty and length of perception. . . . Art is a way of experiencing the artfulness of an object; the object is not important."

Detective story: The so-called "classic" detective story (or "mystery") is a highly formalized and logically structured mode of fiction in which the focus is on a crime solved by a detective through interpretation of evidence and ratiocination; the most famous detective in this mode is Arthur Conan Doyle's Sherlock Holmes. Many modern practitioners of the genre, however, such as Dashiell Hammett, Raymond Chandler, and Ross Macdonald, have deemphasized the puzzlelike qualities of the detective story, stressing instead characterization, theme, and other elements of mainstream fiction.

Determinism: The belief that a man's actions are essentially determined by biological and environmental factors, with free will playing a negligible role. (See *Naturalism*.)

Dialogue: The similitude of conversation in fiction, dialogue serves to characterize, to further the plot, to establish conflict, and to express thematic ideas.

Displacement: Popularized in criticism by Northrop Frye, the term refers to the author's attempt to make his story psychologically motivated and realistic, even as the latent structure of the mythical motivation moves relentlessly forward.

Dominant: A term coined by Roman Jakobson to refer to that which "rules, determines, and transforms the remaining components in the work of a single artist, in a poetic canon, or in the work of an epoch." The shifting of the dominant in a *genre* accounts for the creation of new generic forms and new poetic epochs. For example, the rise of realism in the mid-nineteenth century indicates realistic conventions becoming dominant and romance or fantasy conventions becoming secondary.

Doppelgänger: A double or counterpart of a person, sometimes endowed with ghostly qualities. A fictional character's *Doppelgänger* often reflects a suppressed side of his personality. One of the classic examples of the *Doppelgänger* motif is found in Fyodor Dostoevski's novella *The Double* (1846); Isaac Bashevis Singer and Jorge Luis Borges, among others, offer striking modern treatments of the *Doppelgänger*.

Epic: Although this term usually refers to a long narrative poem which presents the exploits of a central figure of high position, the term is also used to designate a long novel that has the style or structure usually associated with an epic. In this sense, for example, Herman Melville's *Moby Dick* (1851) and James Joyce's *Ulysses* (1922) may be called epic.

Episodic narrative: A work that is held together primarily by a loose connection of self-sufficient episodes. *Picaresque novels* often have an episodic structure.

Epistolary novel: A novel made up of letters by one or more fictional characters. Samuel Richardson's *Pamela* (1740-1741) is a well-known eighteenth century example. In the nineteenth century, Bram Stoker's *Dracula* (1897) is largely epistolary. The technique allows for several different points of view to be presented.

Euphuism: A style of writing characterized by ornate language that is highly contrived, alliterative, and repetitious. Euphuism was developed by John Lyly in his *Euphues, an Anatomy of Wit* (1578) and was emulated frequently by writers of the Elizabethan Age.

Exposition: The part or parts of a fiction which provide necessary background information. Exposition not only provides the time and place of the action, but also introduces the reader to the fictive world of the story, acquainting him with the ground rules of the work.

Fantastic: In his study *The Fantastic* (1970), Tzvetan Todorov defines the fantastic as a *genre* that lies between the "uncanny" and the "marvelous."

All three *genres* embody the familiar world, but present an event that cannot be explained by the laws of the familiar world. Todorov says that the fantastic occupies a twilight zone between the uncanny—when the reader knows that the peculiar event is merely the result of an illusion—and the marvelous—when the reader understands that the event is supposed to take place in a realm controlled by laws unknown to man. Thus, the fantastic is essentially unsettling, provocative, even subversive.

Flashback: A scene in a fiction that depicts an earlier event; it can be presented as a reminiscence by a character in the story or it can simply be inserted into the narrative.

Foreshadowing: A device to create suspense or dramatic irony by indicating through suggestion what will take place in the future.

Formalist criticism: There have been two particularly influential formalist schools of criticism in the twentieth century: the Russian formalists and the American New Critics. The Russian formalists were concerned with the conventional devices used in literature to defamiliarize that which habit has made familiar. The New Critics believed that literary criticism is a description and evaluation of its object and that the primary concern of the critic is with the work's unity. Both schools of criticism, at their most extreme, treated literary works as artifacts or constructs divorced from their biographical and social contexts.

Genre: In its most general sense, the term "genre" refers to a group of literary works defined by a common form, style, or purpose. In practice, the term is used in a wide variety of overlapping and, to a degree, contradictory senses. Thus, tragedy and comedy are described as distinct genres; the novel (a form which includes both tragic and comic works) is a genre; and various subspecies of the novel, such as the *Gothic* and the *picaresque*, are themselves frequently treated as distinct genres. Finally, the term *genre fiction* refers to forms of popular fiction in which the writer is bound by more or less rigid conventions. Indeed, all these diverse usages have in common an emphasis on the manner in which individual literary works are shaped by the expectations and conventions of a particular genre: this is the subject of genre criticism.

Genre fiction: Categories of popular fiction such as the mystery, the romance, and the Western. Although the term can be used in a neutral sense, "genre fiction" is often pejorative, used dismissively to refer to fiction in which the writer is bound by more or less rigid conventions.

Gothic novel: A form of fiction developed in the eighteenth century which focuses on horror and the supernatural. In his Preface to *The Castle of Otranto* (1764), the first Gothic novel in English, Horace Walpole claimed that he was trying to combine two kinds of fiction, with events and story typical of the medieval romance and character delineation typical of the realistic novel. Other examples of the form are Matthew Lewis' *The Monk* (1796) and Mary Shelley's *Frankenstein* (1818).

Grotesque: According to Wolfgang Kayser (*The Grotesque in Art and Literature*, 1963), the grotesque is an embodiment in literature of the estranged world. Characterized by a breakup of the everyday world by mysterious forces, the form differs from fantasy in that the reader is not sure whether to react with humor or with horror and in that the exaggeration manifested exists in the familiar world rather than in a purely imaginative world.

Hebraic/Homeric styles: Terms coined by Erich Auerbach in *Mimesis: The Representation of Reality in Western Literature* (1953), to designate two basic fictional styles: the Hebraic, which focuses only on the decisive points of narrative and leaves all else obscure, mysterious, and "fraught with background," and the Homeric, which places the narrative in a definite time and place and externalizes everything in a perpetual foreground.

Historical criticism: In contrast to *formalist criticism*, which treats literary works to a great extent as self-contained artifacts, historical criticism emphasizes the historical context of literature; these approaches, however, need not be mutually exclusive. Ernst Robert Curtius' *European Literature and the Latin Middle Ages* (1940) is a prominent example of historical criticism.

Historical novel: A novel that depicts past historical events, usually public in nature, and that features real as well as fictional people. Sir Walter Scott's Waverley novels established the basic type, but the relationship between fiction and history in the form varies greatly depending on the practitioner.

Implied author: According to Wayne Booth (*The Rhetoric of Fiction*, 1961), the novel often creates a kind of second self who tells the story—a self who is wiser, more sensitive, and more perceptive than any real person could be.

Interior monologue: Defined by Édouard Dujardin as the speech of a character designed to introduce the reader directly to the character's internal life, the form differs from other monologues in that it attempts to reproduce thought before any logical organization is imposed upon it. See, for example, Molly Bloom's long interior monologue at the conclusion of James Joyce's *Ulysses* (1922).

Irrealism: A term often used to refer to modern or postmodern fiction that is presented self-consciously as a fiction or a fabulation rather than a mimesis of external reality. The best-known practitioners of irrealism are John Barth, Robert Coover, and Donald Barthelme.

Local colorists: A loose movement of late-nineteenth century American writers whose fiction emphasized the distinctive folkways, landscapes, and dialects of various regions. Important local colorists included Bret Harte, Mark Twain, George Washington Cable, Kate Chopin, and Sarah Orne Jewett. (See *Regional novel*.)

Metafiction: The term refers to fiction that manifests a reflexive tendency, such as Vladimir Nabokov's *Pale Fire* (1962) and John Fowles's *The French Lieutenant's Woman* (1969). The emphasis is on the loosening of the work's illusion of reality to expose the reality of its illusion. Such terms as *irrealism*, *postmodernist fiction*, "antifiction," and "surfiction" are also used to refer to this type of fiction.

Modernism: An international movement in the arts which began in the early years of the twentieth century. Although the term is used to describe artists of widely varying persuasions, modernism in general was characterized by its international idiom, by its interest in cultures distant in space or time, by its emphasis on formal experimentation, and by its sense of dislocation and radical change.

Motif: A conventional incident or situation in a fiction which may serve as the basis for the structure of the narrative itself. The Russian formalist critic Boris Tomashevsky uses the term to refer to the smallest particle of thematic material in a work.

Motivation: Although this term is usually used in reference to the convention of justifying the action of a character from his or her psychological makeup, the Russian formalists use the term to refer to the network of devices that justify the introduction of individual *motifs* or groups of *motifs* in a work. For example, compositional motivation refers to the principle that every single property in a work contributes to its overall effect; realistic motivation refers to the realistic devices used to make the work plausible and lifelike.

Myth: Anonymous traditional stories dealing with basic human concepts and antinomies. Claude Lévi-Strauss says that myth is that part of language where the "formula *tradutore, tradittore* reaches its lowest truth value. . . . Its substance does not lie in its style, its original music, or its syntax, but in the story which it tells."

Myth criticism: Northrop Frye says that in myth, "we see the structural principles of literature isolated." Myth criticism is concerned with these basic principles of literature; it is not to be confused with mythological criticism, which is primarily concerned with finding mythological parallels in the surface action of the *narrative*.

Narrative: Robert Scholes and Robert Kellogg, in *The Nature of Narrative* (1966), say that by narrative they mean literary works which include both a story and a storyteller. Narrative usually implies a contrast to "enacted" fiction such as drama.

Narratology: The study of the form and functioning of narratives; it attempts to examine what all *narratives* have in common and what makes individual *narratives* different from one another.

Narrator: The character who recounts the *narrative*. Wayne Booth describes various dramatized narrators in *The Rhetoric of Fiction* (1961): unacknowledged centers of consciousness, observers, narrator-agents, and self-conscious narrators. Booth suggests that the important element to consider in narration is the relationship between the narrator, the author, the characters, and the reader.

Naturalism: As developed by Émile Zola in the late nineteenth century, naturalism is the application of the principles of scientific *determinism* to fiction. Although it usually refers more to the choice of subject matter than to technical conventions, those conventions associated with the movement center on the author's attempt to be precise and scientifically objective in description and detail, regardless of whether the events described are sordid or shocking.

New Criticism. See *Formalist criticism*.

Novel: Perhaps the most difficult of all fictional forms to define because of its multiplicity of modes. Edouard, in André Gide's *The Counterfeiters* (1926), says the novel is the freest and most lawless of all *genres*; he wonders if fear of that liberty is not the reason the novel has so timidly clung to reality. Most critics seem to agree that the novel's primary area of concern is the social world. Ian Watt (*The Rise of the Novel*, 1957) says that the novel can be distinguished from other fictional forms by the attention it pays to individual characterization and detailed presentation of the environment. Moreover, says Watt, the novel, more than any other fictional form, is interested in the "development of its characters in the course of time."

Novel of manners: The classic example of the form might be the novels of Jane Austen, wherein the customs and conventions of a social group of a particular time and place are realistically, and often satirically, portrayed.

Novella, novelle, nouvelle, novelette, novela: Although these terms often refer to the short European tale, especially the Renaissance form employed by Giovanni Boccaccio, the terms often refer to that form of fiction which is said to be longer than a short story and shorter than a novel. "Novelette" is the term usually preferred by the British, whereas "novella" is the term usually used to refer to American works in this *genre*. Henry James claimed that the main merit of the form was the "effort to do the complicated thing with a strong brevity and lucidity."

Phenomenological criticism: Although best-known as a European school of criticism practiced by Georges Poulet and others, this so-called "criticism of consciousness" is also propounded in America by such critics as J. Hillis Miller. The focus is less on individual works and *genres* than it is on literature as an act; the work is not seen as an object, but rather as part of a strand of latent impulses in the work of a single author or an epoch.

Picaresque novel: A form of fiction that centers around a central rogue figure or picaro who usually tells his own story. The plot structure is normally *episodic*, and the episodes usually focus on how the picaro lives by his wits. Classic examples of the mode are Henry Fielding's *Tom Jones* (1749) and Mark Twain's *The Adventures of Huckleberry Finn* (1884).

Plot/Story: Story is a term referring to the full narrative of character and action, whereas plot generally refers to action with little reference to character. A more precise and helpful distinction is made by the Russian formalists, who suggest that plot refers to the events of a *narrative* as they have been artfully arranged in the literary work, subject to chronological displacement, ellipses, and other devices, while story refers to the sum of the same events arranged in simple, causal-chronological order. Thus, story is the raw material for plot. By comparing the two in a given work, the reader is encouraged to see the *narrative* as an artifact.

Point of view: The means by which the story is presented to the reader, or, as Percy Lubbock says in *The Craft of Fiction* (1921), "the relation in which the narrator stands to the story"—a relation which Lubbock claims governs the craft of fiction. Some of the questions the critical reader should ask concerning point of view are: Who talks to the reader? From what position does the narrator tell the story? At what distance does he place the reader from the story? What kind of person is he? How fully is he characterized?

How reliable is he? For further discussion, see Wayne Booth, *The Rhetoric of Fiction* (1961).

Postmodernism: A ubiquitous but elusive term in contempory criticism, "post-modernism" is loosely applied to the various artistic movements which have followed the era of so-called "high modernism," represented by such giants as James Joyce and Pablo Picasso. In critical discussions of contemporary fiction, the term "postmodernism" is frequently applied to the works of writers such as Thomas Pynchon, John Barth, and Donald Barthelme, who exhibit a self-conscious awareness of their modernist predecessors as well as a reflex-ive treatment of fictional form.

Protagonist: The central character in a fiction, the character whose fortunes most concern the reader.

Psychological criticism: While much modern literary criticism reflects to some degree the impact of Sigmund Freud, Carl Jung, Jacques Lacan, and other psychological theorists, the term "psychological criticism" suggests a strong emphasis on a causal relation between the writer's psychological state, var-iously interpreted, and his works. A notable example of psychological criticism is Norman Fruman's *Coleridge, the Damaged Archangel* (1971).

Psychological novel: A form of fiction in which character, especially the inner life of characters, is the primary focus. The form has been of primary impor-tance, at least since Henry James, and it characterizes much of the work of James Joyce, Virginia Woolf, and William Faulkner. For a detailed discussion, see *The Modern Psychological Novel* (1955) by Leon Edel.

Realism: A literary technique in which the primary convention is to render an illusion of fidelity to external reality. Realism is often identified as the primary method of the novel form: it focuses on surface details, maintains a fidelity to the everyday experiences of middle-class society, and strives for a one-to-one relationship between the fiction and the action imitated. The realist movement in the late nineteenth century coincides with the full development of the novel form.

Reception aesthetics: The best-known American practitioner of reception aes-thetics is Stanley Fish. For the reception critic, meaning is an event or process; rather than being embedded in the work, it is created through particular acts of reading. The best-known European practitioner of this criticism, Wolfgang Iser, says indeterminacy is the basic characteristic of literary texts; the reader must "normalize" the text either by projecting his or her standards into it or by revising his or her standards to "fit" the text.

Regional novel: Any novel in which the character of a given geographical region plays a decisive role. Although regional differences persist in America, there has been a considerable leveling in speech and in other ways as well, so that the sharp regional distinctions evident in nineteenth century American fiction no longer obtain. Only in the South has a strong regional tradition persisted to the present. (See *Local colorists*.)

Rhetorical criticism: The rhetorical critic is concerned with the literary work as a means of the communication of ideas, the means by which the work affects or controls the reader. Such criticism seems best suited to didactic works such as satire.

Roman à clef: A fiction wherein actual persons, often celebrities of some sort, are thinly disguised.

Romance: The romance usually differs from the novel form in that the focus is on symbolic events and representational characters rather than on "as-if-real" characters and events. Richard Chase says that in the romance, character is depicted as highly stylized, a function of the plot rather than as someone complexly related to society. The romancer is more likely to be concerned with dreamworlds than with the familiar world, believing that reality cannot be grasped by the traditional novel.

Romanticism: A widespread cultural movement in the late-eighteenth and early-nineteenth centuries, the influence of which is still felt. As a general literary tendency, Romanticism is frequently contrasted with *classicism*. Although there were many varieties of Romanticism indigenous to various national literatures, the term generally suggests an assertion of the preeminence of the imagination. Other values associated with various schools of Romanticism include primitivism, an interest in folklore, a reverence for nature, and a fascination with the demoniac and the macabre.

Scene: The central element of narration; specific actions are narrated or depicted that make the reader feel he or she is participating directly in the action.

Science fiction: Fiction in which certain givens (physical laws, psychological principles, social conditions: any one or all of these) form the basis of an imaginative projection into the future or, less commonly, an extrapolation in the present or even into the past.

Semiotics: The science of signs and sign systems in communication. Roman Jakobson says that semiotics deals with the principles which underlie the structure of signs, their use in language of all kinds, and the specific nature of various sign systems.

Sentimental novel: A form of fiction popular in the eighteenth century in which emotionalism and optimism are the primary characteristics. The best-known examples are Samuel Richardson's *Pamela* (1740-1741) and Oliver Goldsmith's *The Vicar of Wakefield* (1766).

Setting: Setting refers to the circumstances and environment, both temporal and spatial, of a *narrative*.

Spatial form: An author's attempt to make the reader apprehend the work spatially in a moment of time rather than sequentially. To achieve this effect, the author breaks up the *narrative* into interspersed fragments. Beginning with James Joyce, Marcel Proust, and Djuna Barnes, the movement toward spatial form is concomitant with the modernist effort to supplant historical time in fiction with mythic time. For the seminal discussion of this technique, see Joseph Frank, *The Widening Gyre* (1963).

Stream of consciousness: The depiction of the thought-processes of a character, insofar as this is possible, without any mediating structures. The metaphor of consciousness as a "stream" suggests a rush of thoughts and images governed by free association rather than by strictly rational development. The term "stream of consciousness" is often used loosely as a synonym for *interior monologue*. The most celebrated example of stream of consciousness in fiction is the monologue of Molly Bloom in James Joyce's *Ulysses* (1922); other notable practitioners of the stream-of-consciousness technique include Dorothy Richardson, Virginia Woolf, and William Faulkner.

Structuralism: As a movement of thought, structuralism is based on the idea of intrinsic, self-sufficient structures which do not require reference to external elements. A structure is a system of transformations which involves the interplay of laws inherent in the system itself. The study of language is the primary model for contemporary structuralism. The structuralist literary critic attempts to define structural principles that operate intertextually throughout the whole of literature as well as principles that operate in *genres* and in individual works. The most accessible survey of structuralism and literature is Jonathan Culler, *Structuralist Poetics* (1975).

Summary: Those parts of a fiction which do not need to be detailed. In *Tom Jones* (1749), Henry Fielding says "If whole years should pass without producing anything worthy of . . . notice . . . we shall hasten on to matters of consequence."

Thematics: Northrup Frye says that when a work of fiction is written or interpreted thematically, it becomes an illustrative fable. Murray Krieger defines thematics as "the study of the experiential tensions which, dramatically entangled in the literary work, become an existential reflection of that work's aesthetic complexity." See Krieger's *The Tragic Vision* (1960).

Tone: Tone usually refers to the dominant mood of the work. (See *Atmosphere*.)

Unreliable narrator: A narrator whose account of the events of the story cannot be trusted, obliging the reader to reconstruct—if possible—the true state of affairs himself. Once an innovative technique, the use of the unreliable narrator has become commonplace among contemporary writers who wish to suggest the impossibility of a truly "reliable" account of any event. Notable examples of the unreliable narrator can be found in Ford Madox Ford's *The Good Soldier* (1915) and Vladimir Nabokov's *Lolita* (1958).

Victorian novel: Although the Victorian period extended from 1837 to 1901, the term "Victorian novel" does not include the later decades of Queen Victoria's reign. The term loosely refers to the sprawling works of novelists such as Charles Dickens and William Makepeace Thackeray—works which frequently appeared first in serial form and which are characterized by a broad social canvas.

Vraisemblance/Verisimilitude: Tzvetan Todorov defines vraisemblance as "the mask which conceals the text's own laws, but which we are supposed to take for a relation to reality." When one speaks of vraisemblance, one refers to the work's attempts to make the reader believe that it conforms to reality rather than to its own laws.

Western novel: Like all varieties of *genre fiction*, the Western novel—generally known simply as the "Western"—is defined by a relatively predictable combination of conventions, *motifs*, and recurring themes. These predictable elements, familiar from the many Western series on television and in film, differentiate the Western from *historical novels* and idiosyncratic works such as Thomas Berger's *Little Big Man* (1964) which are also set in the Old West. Conversely, some novels set in the contemporary West are regarded as Westerns because they deal with modern cowboys and with the land itself in the manner characteristic of the *genre*.

Charles E. May

INDEX

Abortion, The (Brautigan), 375-376.

Absalom, Absalom! (Faulkner), 1102-1106, 3772, 3832, 3840-3841.

Absentee, The (Edgeworth), 1022, 1026-1028.

Acceptance World, The (Powell, A.), 2677.

Accidental Man, An (Murdoch), 2441, 2448-2452.

Accidental Tourist, The (Tyler), 3343-3344.

Achebe, Chinua, 1-19; *Anthills of the Savannah*, 6, 14-17; *Arrow of God*, 6, 10-12; *A Man of the People*, 6, 12-14; *No Longer at Ease*, 6, 8-10; *Things Fall Apart*, 6, 7-8.

Acrobats, The (Richler), 2848.

Active Service (Crane), 777-778.

Adam Bede (Eliot), 1035-1038.

Adams, Richard, 3862.

Adulthood Rites (Butler, O.), 498-499.

Adventures of Augie March, The (Bellow), 278, 3775, 3808.

Adventures of Ferdinand, Count Fathom, The. See *Ferdinand, Count Fathom*.

Adventures of Gil Blas of Santillane, The (Le Sage), 3805-3806.

Adventures of Huckleberry Finn, The (Twain), 3318-3319, 3323-3325, 3745, 3750, 3807.

Adventures of Peregrine Pickle, The. See *Peregrine Pickle*.

Adventures of Roderick Random, The. See *Roderick Random*.

Adventures of Sir Launcelot Greaves, The. See *Sir Launcelot Greaves*.

Adventures of Tom Sawyer, The (Twain), 3318-3319, 3321-3323.

Adventures of Wesley Jackson, The (Saroyan), 2946, 2952.

African Witch, The (Cary), 574, 576.

After Many a Summer Dies the Swan (Huxley), 1683-1684.

Afternoon Men (Powell, A.), 2675-2676.

Agatha Christie (Christie), 651.

Age of Innocence, The (Wharton), 3536-3537.

Age of Longing, The (Koestler), 1914-1915.

Age of Thunder (Prokosch), 2740.

Agee, James, 20-27; *A Death in the Family*, 26; *The Morning Watch*, 22-26.

Agents and Patients (Powell, A.), 2676.

Agnes de Castro (Behn), 270, 271-272.

Aiken, Conrad, 28-38; *Blue Voyage*, 13-32; *Conversation*, 31, 35-36; *Great Circle*, 30-31, 32-33; *A Heart for the Gods of Mexico*, 31, 34-35; *King Coffin*, 30-31, 33-34.

Ainsworth, William Harrison, 39-48; *Old Saint Paul's*, 45-46; *Rookwood*, 43-44; *The Tower of London*, 44-45.

Aissa Saved (Cary), 574, 575.

Albany Cycle, The (Kennedy), 1852-1856.

Albigenses, The (Maturin), 2328. ·

Aldington, Richard, 49-62; *All Men Are Enemies*, 56-57; *The Colonel's Daughter*, 55-56; *Death of a Hero*, 54-55; *Lawrence L'Imposteur*, 53; *Rejected Guest*, 59-60; *The Romance of Casanova*, 60; *Seven Against Reeves*, 59; *Very Heaven*, 58-59; *Women Must Work*, 57-58.

Aldrich, Thomas Bailey, 63-73; *Daisy's Necklace and What Came of It*, 65; *Prudence Palfrey*, 68-70; *The Stillwater Tragedy*, 70-71; *The Story of a Bad Boy*, 66-68.

Aleck Maury, Sportsman (Gordon), 1398.

Alemán, Mateo, 3803, 3804.

Alexandria Quartet, The (Durrell), 1011-1014.

Alger, Horatio, 3795.

Algren, Nelson, 74-82; *The Devil's Stocking*, 81; *The Man with the Golden Arm*, 76-80; *Never Come Morning*, 76-78; *A Walk on the Wild Side*, 80-81.

All Hallows Eve (Williams), 3860.

All Men Are Enemies (Aldington), 56-57.

All My Friends Are Going to Be Strangers (McMurtry), 2223-2224.

All the King's Men (Warren), 3440-3441, 3772.

Allegory, 454-455, 458, **3880.**

Alley Jaggers (West, P.), 3523.

I

Alnilam (Dickey), 917-919.
Ambassadors, The (James, H.), 1715, 1727-1728.
Ambrosio. See *Monk, The*.
Amelia (Fielding, H.), 3782.
American Civil War, 3038-3039.
American Democrat, The (Cooper), 732.
American Dream, An (Mailer), 2252-2254.
American Scene, The (James, H.), 1714.
American Tragedy, An (Dreiser), 1002-1004, 3759.
American Visitor, An (Cary), 574, 576.
Americana (DeLillo), 863-864.
Amis, Kingsley, 83-100, 3774, 3775, 3808; *The Anti-Death League*, 93-94; *The Green Man*, 94-95; *Lucky Jim*, 89-91, 3775, 3808; *The Old Devils*, 90, 95-98; *Take a Girl Like You*, 89, 91-92, 97-98.
Amis, Martin, 101-107; *Dead Babies*, 102-103; *London Fields*, 104-106; *Money*, 104; *Other People*, 103-104; *The Rachel Papers*, 102; *Success*, 103.
Amrita (Jhabvala), 1753-1754.
Anatomy, **3880**.
Anatomy Lesson, The (Roth), 2903.
Ancient Evenings (Mailer), 2260-2261.
. . . And the Wife Ran Away (Weldon), 3475.
Anderson, Sherwood, 108-118; *Beyond Desire*, 116; *Dark Laughter*, 116; *Kit Brandon*, 116; *Many Marriages*, 116; *Marching Men*, 112-113; *Poor White*, 109, 115-116; *Windy McPherson's Son*, 110, 112; *Winesburg, Ohio*, 113-115, 116.
Angel at the Gate, The (Harris, W.), 1531.
Angel of the Revolution, (Griffith), 3866-3867.
Angel Pavement (Priestley), 2715.
Angels on Toast (Powell, D.), 2685-2686.
Angle of Repose (Stegner), 3130, 3131-3133.
Anglo-Saxon Attitudes (Wilson, Angus), 3591-3592.
Angry Young Men, 84, 366, 3391.
Animal Farm (Orwell), 2595-2597, 3789, 3798.
Ann Veronica (Wells), 3484.
Anna of the Five Towns (Bennett), 295-296.
Another Country (Baldwin), 181-183.
Anpao (Highwater), 1619-1620.

Answer from Limbo, An (Moore, B.), 2395-2396.
Answered Prayers (Capote), 555.
Antagonist, **3880**.
Anthills of the Savannah (Achebe), 6, 14-17.
Antic Hay (Huxley), 1677-1678.
Anti-Death League, The (Amis, K.), 93-94.
"*Antigua, Penny, Puce*." See *Antigua Stamp, The*.
Antigua Stamp, The (Graves), 1419.
Antihero, **3880**.
Anything for Billy (McMurtry), 2220.
Apartment in Athens (Wescott), 3509.
Ape and Essence (Huxley), 1684-1685.
Apes of God, The (Lewis, W.), 2082-2083.
Aphrodite in Aulis (Moore, G.), 2409-2410.
Apology for the Life of Mrs. Shamela Andrews. See *Shamela*.
Apple of the Eye, The (Wescott), 3503-3505.
Appointment in Samarra (O'Hara), 2581-2583.
Apprenticeship of Duddy Kravitz, The (Richler), 2849-2851.
Arcadia (Sidney), 3722-3723.
Archetype, **3880**.
Aristos, The (Fowles), 1199.
Armah, Ayi Kwei, 119-131; *The Beautyful Ones Are Not Yet Born*, 122-124; *Fragments*, 124-126; *The Healers*, 129-130; *Two Thousand Seasons*, 128-129; *Why Are We So Blest?*, 126-128.
Armies of the Night, The (Mailer), 2256-2258.
Arrival and Departure (Koestler), 1913-1914.
Arrow of God (Achebe), 6, 10-12.
Arrow of Gold, The (Conrad), 716.
Arrowsmith (Lewis, S.), 2073-2074.
Arthur Mervyn (Brown), 411.
Arthur Rex (Berger), 311-312.
Artist of the Floating World, An (Ishiguro), 1708-1709, 3793.
As for Me and My House (Ross), 2882, 2883-2884, 2885-2887.
As I Lay Dying (Faulkner), 1096-1097, 3832.
As if by Magic (Wilson, Angus), 3595.
Ascent to Omai (Harris, W.), 1531.

Asiatics, The (Prokosch), 2737.
Ask Me Now (Young), 3716-3717.
Ask Me Tomorrow (Cozzens), 763,
766-767.
Aspidistra in Babylon, An (Bates), 246.
Assassins, The (Prokosch), 2734.
Assistant, The (Malamud), 2266,
2271-2273, 3775.
At Fault (Chopin), 643-645.
At Heaven's Gate (Warren), 3443.
At Lady Molly's (Powell, A.), 2678.
At Play in the Fields of the Lord
(Matthiessen), 2308-2309, 2311,
2312-2316.
At Swim-Two-Birds (O'Brien, F.), 2553,
2554-2555.
Atmosphere, **3880.**
Atwood, Margaret, 132-143, 3871;
Bodily Harm, 138-140; *Cat's Eye*, 141;
The Handmaid's Tale, 140-141; *Life
Before Man*, 136-138; *Surfacing*,
135-136.
Auchincloss, Louis, 144-156; *The
Embezzler*, 152-153; *The House of Five
Talents*, 147-148; *The House of the
Prophet*, 153-154; *Portrait in
Brownstone*, 149-150; *The Rector of
Justin*, 150-152.
August Is a Wicked Month (O'Brien, E.),
2545.
August 1914 (Solzhenitsyn), 3839.
Aunt's Story, The (White), 3548-3549.
Aurora Dawn (Wouk), 3666-3667.
Austen, Jane, 157-171, 3784; *Emma*,
164-166; *Mansfield Park*, 162-164;
Northanger Abbey, 166-167; *Persuasion*,
167-168; *Pride and Prejudice*, 161-162;
Sense and Sensibility, 160-161.
Autobiography of Miss Jane Pittman, The
(Gaines), 1243-1244.
Autocracy of Mr. Parham, The (Wells),
3485.
Avgust chetyrnadtsatogo. See *August 1914*.
Avignon Quintet, The (Durrell), 1014-1015.
Awakening, The (Chopin), 645-648.

Babbitt (Lewis, S.), 2071-2073.
Babbittry, 2071.
Babel-17 (Delany), 853-854.
"Baby Is Three" (Sturgeon), 3236.
"Babysitter, The" (Coover), 3879.
Bachelor of Arts, The (Narayan), 2483.

Backward Place, A (Jhabvala), 1756.
Bad Man, A (Elkin), 1048.
Bad Man from Bodie. See *Welcome to
Hard Times*.
Baldwin, James, 172-189, 3776; *Another
Country*, 181-183; *Go Tell It on the
Mountain*, 178-181, 3776; *Just Above My
Head*, 183-188.
Ballad and the Source, The (Lehmann),
2020-2023.
Ballad of Love, A (Prokosch), 2739.
Ballad of the Sad Café, The (McCullers),
2165-2167, 3877.
Ballard, J. G., 190-199; *Concrete Island*,
195; *Crash*, 194-195; *The Crystal World*,
194; *The Drought*, 193; *The Drowned
World*, 192-193; *Empire of the Sun*, 197;
Hello, America, 196; *High Rise*, 195;
The Unlimited Dream Company, 196;
The Wind from Nowhere, 192.
Balthazar. See *Alexandria Quartet, The*.
Bamboo Dancers, The (Gonzalez),
1363-1364.
Banville, John, 200-209; *Birchwood*,
202-203; *The Book of Evidence*,
207-208; *Doctor Copernicus*, 203-204;
Kepler, 204-205; *Mefisto*, 206-207; *The
Newton Letter*, 205-206; *Nightspawn*,
201-202.
Bar-20 (Mulford), 3852.
Barbary Shore (Mailer), 2250-2251.
Barchester Towers (Trollope), 3309-3310.
Barnes, Julian, 210-216; *Before She Met
Me*, 211-212; *Flaubert's Parrot*, 212-213;
A History of the World in 10½ Chapters,
215; *Metroland*, 211; *Staring at the Sun*,
213-215.
Barometer Rising (MacLennan),
2213-2214.
Barr, Robert, and Stephen Crane; *The
O'Ruddy*, 779.
Barren Ground (Glasgow), 1332-1333.
Barth, John, 217-232, 3878-3879;
Dunyazadiad, 3878; *The End of the
Road*, 223-224; *The Floating Opera*,
221-223; *Giles Goat-Boy*, 227-229;
LETTERS, 229-231; "The Literature of
Exhaustion," 217; "The Literature of
Replenishment," 217; *The Sot-Weed
Factor*, 225-227.
Barthelme, Donald, 233-238; *The Dead
Father*, 235-236; *The King*, 236-237;

Paradise, 236; *Snow White*, 235.
"Bartleby the Scrivener" (Melville), 3875-3876.
Bates, H. E., 239-248; *An Aspidistra in Babylon*, 246; *The Cruise of the Breadwinner*, 246; *The Distant Horns of Summer*, 245-246; "Dulcima," 246; *Love for Lydia*, 244-245; *The Poacher*, 243; *Spella Ho*, 243-244; *The Triple Echo*, 246.
Baumgartner's Bombay (Desai), 878-879.
"Bear, The" (Faulkner), 3874, 3875.
Beastly Beatitudes of Balthazar B., The (Donleavy), 948-979.
Beat movement, 484, 1859-1860.
Beattie, Ann, 249-253; *Chilly Scenes of Winter*, 250-251; *Falling in Place*, 251-252; *Love Always*, 252.
Beauchampe (Simms), 3043.
Beauchamp's Career (Meredith), 2363-2365.
Beautiful and the Damned, The (Fitzgerald), 1141-1144.
Beautiful Greed, The (Madden), 2233-2235.
Beautyful Ones Are Not Yet Born, The (Armah), 122-124.
Bech (Updike), 3357.
Bech Is Back (Updike), 3357.
Beckett, Samuel, 254-266; *Company*, 263; *How It Is*, 262-264; *Ill Seen Ill Said*, 263; *The Lost Ones*, 262-263; *Malone Dies*, 260-261; *Mercier and Camier*, 259-260; *Molloy*, 260; *Murphy*, 258; *The Unnamable*, 261; *Watt*, 258-259.
Beet Queen, The (Erdrich), 1068-1070.
Before She Met Me (Barnes), 211-212.
Behn, Aphra, 267-274, 3727; *Agnes de Castro*, 270, 271-272; *The Fair Jilt*, 272; *The History of the Nun*, 271; *The Nun*, 271; *Oroonoko*, 270, 272, 3727.
Being There (Kosinski), 1925-1926.
Bela Lugosi's White Christmas (West, P.), 3524.
Bell for Adano, A (Hersey), 1610, 1613-1614.
Bellamy, Edward, 3866.
Bellarosa Connection, The (Bellow), 287-288.
Bellefleur (Oates), 2538.
Bellow, Saul, 275-290, 3775-3776, 3808;
The Adventures of Augie March, 278, 3775, 3808; *The Bellarosa Connection*, 287-288; *Dangling Man*, 277; *The Dean's December*, 286-287; *Henderson the Rain King*, 280-282, 3775; *Herzog*, 282-283; *Humboldt's Gift*, 285-286; *Mr. Sammler's Planet*, 283-285; *More Die of Heartbreak*, 287; *Seize the Day*, 278-280; *A Theft*, 287; *The Victim*, 277-278.
Beloved (Morrison), 2433.
Bend in the River, A (Naipaul), 2476-2477.
Bend Sinister (Nabokov), 2464-2465.
Bendigo Shafter (L'Amour), 1936.
Benford, Gregory, 3871.
Bennett, Arnold, 291-302, 3760; *Anna of the Five Towns*, 295-296; *Clayhanger*, 298-299; *Hilda Lessways*, 299; *A Man from the North*, 295; *The Old Wives' Tale*, 296-297; *Riceyman Steps*, 300; *These Twain*, 299-300.
Bentley, E. C., 3843
Berger, Thomas, 303-317; *Arthur Rex*, 311-312; *Crazy in Berlin*, 307; *The Feud*, 315; *Killing Time*, 308-309; *Little Big Man*, 307-308; *Neighbors*, 312-313; *Orrie's Story*, 315; *Regiment of Women*, 309-310; *Reinhart in Love*, 307, 314; *Reinhart's Women*, 313-314; *Sneaky People*, 310-311; *Vital Parts*, 309; *Who Is Teddy Villanova?*, 311.
Bernard Carr trilogy, The (Farrell, James), 1079.
Bertram (Maturin), 2321.
Between the Acts (Woolf), 3658-3661.
Beulah Land (Davis), 809-810.
Beulah Quintet. See *Killing Ground, The*, *Know Nothing*, *O Beulah Land*, *Prisons*, and *Scapegoat, The*.
Beyond Desire (Anderson), 116.
Beyond the Bedroom Wall (Woiwode), 3622-3623.
B. F.'s Daughter (Marquand), 2303.
Big as Life (Doctorow), 935.
Big Money, The (Dos Passos), 961-962.
Big Rock Candy Mountain, The (Stegner), 3130-3131.
Big Sleep, The (Chandler), 605, 606-607, 3846.
"Big Two-Hearted River" (Hemingway), 1597-1598, 3763, 3769.

Biggers, Earl Derr, 3845.
Bijou (Madden), 2237-2238.
Bildungsroman, 1140, **3880.**
Bill of Rites, a Bill of Wrongs, a Bill of Goods, A (Morris), 2413.
Billy Bathgate (Doctorow), 939-942.
Billy Budd, Foretopman (Melville), 2354-2356.
Billy Phelan's Greatest Game (Kennedy), 1854.
Biographical criticism, **3881.**
Biography of the Life of Manuel, The (Cabell), 515-516.
Birchwood (Banville), 202-203.
Birds of America (McCarthy, M.), 2154-2155.
Birth of a Grandfather, The (Sarton), 2963-2965.
Birthday King, The (Fielding, G.), 1113, 1114-1115.
Black Arrow, The (Stevenson), 3192.
Black Book, The (Durrell), 1011.
Black Boy (Wright), 3679-3680.
Black Is My Truelove's Hair (Roberts), 2874, 2875-2876.
Black Marble, The (Wambaugh), 3430.
Black Marsden (Harris, W.), 1531.
Black Prince, The (Murdoch), 2452.
Black Thunder (Bontemps), 3776.
Blair, Eric Arthur. *See* **Orwell, George.**
Blake, William, 3551.
Blandings novels, The (Wodehouse), 3612-3613.
Bleak House (Dickens), 3786-3787, 3843.
Blind Date (Kosinski), 1926-1928.
Blindness (Green), 1433-1434.
Blithedale Romance, The (Hawthorne), 1579-1580, 3798.
Blood Meridian (McCarthy, C.), 2146-2147.
Blood of the Lamb, The (De Vries), 887-888.
Blood Oranges, The (Hawkes), 1562-1564.
Blood Red, Sister Rose (Keneally), 1843-1844, 1846.
Blood Tie (Settle), 3004, 3008-3009, 3010.
Blue Hammer, The (Macdonald), 2177-2178.
"Blue Hotel, The" (Crane), 3876-3877.
Blue Knight, The (Wambaugh), 3428-3429.
Blue Voyage (Aiken), 13-32.
Bluest Eye, The (Morrison), 2425-2426.

Boat, The (Hartley), 1554-1555.
Boccaccio, Giovanni, 3873.
Bodily Harm (Atwood), 138-140.
Body in the Library, The (Christie), 657.
Bogmail (McGinley), 2190-2191.
Bontemps, Arna, 3776.
Book of Bebb, The (Buechner), 449-451.
Book of Common Prayer, A (Didion), 928-931.
Book of Daniel, The (Doctorow), 935-937.
Book of Evidence, The (Banville), 207-208.
Book of Lights, The (Potok), 2660, 2664-2665.
Book of the Hopi (Waters), 3447.
Books Do Furnish a Room (Powell, A.), 2680.
Boomerang (Hannah), 1487.
Born Brothers (Woiwode), 3624-3625.
Boston (Sinclair), 3054-3055.
Bostonians, The (James, H.), 1725-1727.
Boswell (Elkin), 1047-1048.
Bourgeois novel, **3881.**
Bow Bells, 47.
Bowen, Elizabeth, 318-325; *The Death of the Heart*, 322-323; *Eva Trout*, 324; *The Heat of the Day*, 323-324; *The Hotel*, 320; *The House in Paris*, 321-322; *The Last September*, 320-321; *To the North*, 321.
Bower, Bertha May, 3852.
Bowles, Paul, 326-334; *Let It Come Down*, 329-330; *The Sheltering Sky*, 328-329; *The Spider's House*, 330-331; *Up Above the World*, 331-332.
Boy (Hanley), 1474-1475.
Boyle, Kay, 335-347; *The Bridegroom's Body*, 342-343; *Crazy Hunter*, 342; *Decision*, 343; *Generation Without Farewell*, 344; *Gentlemen, I Address You Privately*, 341-342; *Monday Night*, 343; *My Next Bride*, 341; *1939*, 344; *Plagued by the Nightingale*, 340; *Primer for Combat*, 349; *The Underground Woman*, 345-346; *Year Before Last*, 340-341.
Boyle, T. Coraghessan, 348-353; *Budding Prospects*, 350; *East Is East*, 352-353; *Water Music*, 349-350; *World's End*, 351-352.
Boys and Girls Together (Saroyan), 2954-2955.
Bradbury, Ray, 354-364; *Dandelion Wine*, 360-361; *Dark Carnival*, 357-358;

Death Is a Lonely Business, 361-362; *Fahrenheit 451*, 360; *The Golden Apples of the Sun*, 359; *A Graveyard for Lunatics*, 361-362; *The Illustrated Man*, 359; *The Martian Chronicles*, 358-359; *Something Wicked This Way Comes*, 361; *The Toynbee Convector*, 362.

Braine, John, 365-372; *The Crying Game*, 366-367; *The Jealous God*, 369, 370-371; *Room at the Top*, 369, 370; *Waiting for Sheila*, 371.

Brautigan, Richard, 373-379; *The Abortion*, 375-376; *A Connecticut General from Big Sur*, 374-375; *The Hawkline Monster*, 376-377; *In Watermelon Sugar*, 375; *So the Wind Won't Blow It All Away*, 377-379; *Trout Fishing in America*, 377.

Brave New World (Huxley), 1681-1682, 3798.

Bread of Time to Come, The (Malouf), 2291-2292.

Breakfast at Tiffany's (Capote), 559-560.

Breast, The (Roth), 2900-2901.

Breathing Lessons (Tyler), 3344-3345.

Brendan (Buechner), 452.

Brewsie and Willie (Stein), 3148-3149.

Bridegroom's Body, The (Boyle, K.), 342-343.

Brideshead Revisited (Waugh), 3465-3466.

Bridge of Lost Desire, The (Delany), 854.

Bridge of San Luis Rey, The (Wilder), 3572, 3573.

Bridge of Years, The (Sarton), 2962-2963.

Bridges at Toko-Ri, The (Michener), 2372-2373

Briefing for a Descent into Hell (Lessing), 2037.

Bright Center of Heaven (Maxwell), 2342-2343.

Bright Day (Priestley), 2715-2716.

Brighton Rock (Greene), 1443-1445.

British Museum Is Falling Down, The (Lodge), 2091.

Broken Gun, The (L'Amour), 1935.

Broken Water (Hanley), 1473.

Brontë, Charlotte, 380-389; *Jane Eyre*, 385-386; *The Professor*, 384-385; *Shirley*, 386-387; *Villette*, 387-388.

Brontë, Emily, 390-396; *Wuthering Heights*, 390-396.

Brook Kerith, The (Moore, G.), 2409.

Brookner, Anita, 397-406; *The Debut*, 399-400; *Family and Friends*, 404-405; *Hotel du Lac*, 402-404; *Look at Me*, 401-402; *Providence*, 400-401.

Brotherly Love (Fielding, G.), 1114.

Brothers and Sisters (Compton-Burnett), 694-695.

Brothers in Confidence (Madden), 2233, 2236-2237.

Brown, Charles Brockden, 407-419; *Arthur Mervyn*, 411; *Edgar Huntly*, 415-419; *Wieland*, 410-415, 418.

Buccaneers, The (Wharton), 3540.

Buchan, John, 420-433; *Castle Gay*, 429; *The Courts of the Morning*, 427; *The Dancing Floor*, 429-430; *Greenmantle*, 427-428; *The House of the Four Winds*, 429; *Huntingtower*, 428-429; *John Macnab*, 429-430; *Mr. Standfast*, 426-427; *The Power-House*, 428-430; *Sick Heart River*, 429-430; *The Thirty-Nine Steps*, 427; *The Three Hostages*, 427-428; *Witch Wood*, 425.

Buck, Pearl S., 434-442; *Dragon Seed*, 440-441; *The Good Earth*, 435, 437-439; *The Mother*, 439-440; *Of Men and Women*, 434-435.

Budding Prospects (Boyle, T.), 350.

Buechner, Frederick, 443-453; *The Book of Bebb*, 449-451; *Brendan*, 452; *The Entrance to Porlock*, 449; *The Final Beast*, 448-449; *Godric*, 451-455; *A Long Day's Dying*, 444, 446-447; *The Return of Ansel Gibbs*, 447-448; *The Season's Difference*, 444, 447.

Bugles in the Afternoon (Haycox), 3852.

Bull from the Sea, The (Renault), 2811.

Bullet Park (Cheever), 621-623.

Bunyan, John, 454-461, 3726; *Grace Abounding to the Chief of Sinners*, 456-458; *The Life and Death of Mr. Badman*, 458-459; *The Pilgrim's Progress*, 458, 3726.

Burger's Daughter (Gordimer), 1389-1391.

Burgess, Anthony, 462-471; *A Clockwork Orange*, 468-469; *Earthly Powers*, 467; *Nothing Like the Sun*, 467; *The Right to an Answer*, 465-466; *Tremor of Intent*, 466-467.

Buried Land, A (Jones, M.), 1813-1814.

Buried Treasure, A (Roberts), 2874-2875.

Burmese Days (Orwell), 2593-2594.

Burney, Fanny, 472-481, 3738; *Camilla*, 479; *Cecilia*, 478-479; *Evelina*, 476-478; *The Wanderer*, 479-480.
Burning (Johnson, D.), 1773.
Burning World, The. See *Drought, The*.
Burr (Vidal), 3374.
Burroughs, Edgar Rice, 3868.
Burroughs, William S., 482-492; *Cities of the Red Night*, 489-490; *Exterminator!*, 489; *Junkie*, 486; *The Naked Lunch*, 486, 487; *Nova Express*, 486-487; *The Place of Dead Roads*, 490; *The Soft Machine*, 486, 488; *The Ticket That Exploded*, 486-487, 488-489; *The Western Lands*, 490; *The Wild Boys*, 489.
Bushwhacked Piano, The (McGuane), 2199.
Busman's Honeymoon (Sayers), 2978.
Butler, Octavia, 493-500; *Adulthood Rites*, 498-499; *Clay's Ark*, 497; *Dawn*, 497, 498-499; *Imago*, 498-499; *Kindred*, 495; *Mind of My Mind*, 496; *Patternmaster*, 496; *Survivor*, 495-496; *Wild Seed*, 496-497.
Butler, Samuel, 501-509; *Erewhon*, 503-505; *Erewhon Revisited*, 505-506; *The Fair Haven*, 506; *The Way of All Flesh*, 506-508.
Buyer's Market, A (Powell, A.), 2677.
By Love Possessed (Cozzens), 768-769.
Bye-Bye, Blackbird (Desai), 875-876.

Cab at the Door, A (Pritchett), 2724.
Cabala, The (Wilder), 3572-3573.
Cabell, James Branch, 510-520; *The Biography of the Life of Manuel*, 515-516; *Figures of Earth*, 516-517; *Jurgen*, 513, 517-519.
Cable, George Washington, 521-530; *The Grandissimes*, 526-527; *Madame Delphine*, 527-529.
Cabot Wright Begins (Purdy), 2746.
Cadillac Jack (McMurtry), 2224.
Caesar's Column (Donnelly), 3866.
Caine Mutiny, The (Wouk), 3667-3669.
Cakes and Ale (Maugham), 2336-2337.
Caldwell, Erskine, 531-539; *God's Little Acre*, 536-537; *Tobacco Road*, 534-536.
Caliban's Filibuster (West, P.), 3524-3525.
Call for the Dead (Le Carré), 1985-1986.

Call Girls, The (Koestler), 1915-1916.
Call of the Wild, The (London), 2098-2099.
Callaghan, Morley, 540-551; *Close to the Sun Again*, 543, 548-550; *The Loved and the Lost*, 543, 546-548; *Such Is My Beloved*, 542, 544-545.
Camera Obscura. See *Laughter in the Dark*.
Camilla (Burney), 479.
Can You Forgive Her? (Trollope), 3312-3313.
Cannibal, The (Hawkes), 1561-1562.
Cannibals and Missionaries (McCarthy, M.), 2155-2156.
Capote, Truman, 552-563; *Answered Prayers*, 555; *Breakfast at Tiffany's*, 559-560; "La Côte Basque: 1965," 561-562; *The Grass Harp*, 558-559; *In Cold Blood*, 560-561; "Mojave," 561; *The Muses Are Heard*, 556; *Other Voices, Other Rooms*, 556, 557-558; "Unspoiled Monsters," 561.
Captain of the Gray Horse Troop (Garland), 1290-1291.
Captains Courageous (Kipling), 1904.
Caravans (Michener), 2373-2374
Carnival (Harris, W.), 1531.
Carnival, The (Prokosch), 2734.
Carpenter's Gothic (Gaddis), 1230, 1234-1236.
Carrie (King), 1886-1887.
Carter, Angela, 564-570; *Heroes and Villains*, 568; *The Infernal Desire Machines of Doctor Hoffman*, 568; *The Magic Toyshop*, 566-567; *Nights at the Circus*, 569-570; *The Passion of New Eve*, 568-569; *Several Perceptions*, 567-568.
Cary, Joyce, 571-584; *The African Witch*, 574, 576; *Aissa Saved*, 574, 575; *An American Visitor*, 574, 576; *Castle Corner*, 576; *Charlie Is My Darling*, 577-578; *Cock Jarvis*, 574, 575; *Except the Lord*, 581-582; *A Fearful Joy*, 578; *Herself Surprised*, 578-579; *The Horse's Mouth*, 578, 580; *A House of Children*, 577-578; *Mister Johnson*, 574, 576-577; *The Moonlight*, 578; *Not Honour More*, 581, 582; *Prisoner of Grace*, 581; *To Be a Pilgrim*, 578, 579-580.

Casanova's Chinese Restaurant (Powell, A.), 2678.
Cassandra Singing (Madden), 2235-2236.
Castaway (Cozzens), 765-766.
Castle Corner (Cary), 576.
Castle Gay (Buchan), 429.
Castle of Otranto, The (Walpole), 3736, 3782, 3783, 3823, 3826-3827, 3874.
Castle Rackrent (Edgeworth), 1022-1023, 1024-1026.
Castles of Athlin and Dunbayne (Radcliffe), 2778-2779.
Casualties of Peace (O'Brien, E.), 2545-2546.
Cat and Shakespeare, The (Rao), 2792-2793.
Cat Man (Hoagland), 1630.
Catcher in the Rye, The (Salinger), 2932, 2934-2939, 3808.
Catch-22 (Heller), 1588-1590, 3808.
Cather, Willa, 585-597, 3762; *Death Comes for the Archbishop*, 595; *A Lost Lady*, 590, 593-594; *Lucy Gayheart*, 592; *My Ántonia*, 589-590, 592-593; *O Pioneers!*, 591; *One of Ours*, 590, 593; *The Professor's House*, 594-595; *Shadows on the Rock*, 595-596; *The Song of the Lark*, 591-592.
Catherine Carmier (Gaines), 1240-1242.
Catholic, The (Plante), 2647.
Catholics (Moore, B.), 2397.
Cat's Cradle (Vonnegut), 3382-3384.
Cat's Eye (Atwood), 141.
Cecilia (Burney), 478-479.
Cefalu. See Dark Labyrinth, The.
Celebration (Settle), 3004-3005, 3010-3011.
Celestial Navigation (Tyler), 3338-3339.
Centaur, The (Updike), 3351-3352.
Cervantes, Miguel de, 3873.
Challens, Mary. *See* **Renault, Mary.**
Chandler, Raymond, 598-612, 3845-3846; *The Big Sleep*, 605, 606-607, 3846; *Farewell, My Lovely*, 603; *The High Window*, 604, 606; *The Little Sister*, 604; *The Long Goodbye*, 604, 608-611; "The Simple Art of Murder," 602-603, 605.
Changing Places (Lodge), 2091-2092.
Chant of Jimmie Blacksmith, The (Keneally), 1843.
Character, **3881.**

Charioteer, The (Renault), 2809-2810.
Charlie Is My Darling (Cary), 577-578.
Charlotte Temple (Rowson), 2909-2912.
Charmed Circle, A (Kavan), 1835.
Charmed Life, A (McCarthy, M.), 2153.
Château, The (Maxwell), 2345.
Cheever, John, 613-628; *Bullet Park*, 621-623; *Falconer*, 623-625; *Oh What a Paradise It Seems*, 625-626; *The Wapshot Chronicle*, 617-619; *The Wapshot Scandal*, 619-621.
Chesapeake (Michener), 2374-2375
Chesnutt, Charles Waddell, 629-638; *The Colonel's Dream*, 637; *The Conjure Woman*, 629; *The House Behind the Cedars*, 634-636; *The Marrow of Tradition*, 636-637; *The Wife of His Youth*, 629.
Chessmaster and His Moves, The (Rao), 2794-2795.
"Child by Fever" (Foote), 1161-1162.
"Child in the House, The" (Pater), 2602.
Child of God (McCarthy, C.), 2144-2145.
Childermass, The (Lewis, W.), 2082-2083.
Children at the Gate, The (Wallant), 3421-3422.
Children of Light (Stone), 3202.
Children of the Albatross (Nin), 2516, 2518.
Children of the Ash-Covered Loam (Gonzalez), 1359.
Children of Violence (Lessing), 2035.
Child's Play (Malouf), 2291.
Childwold (Oates), 2537-2538.
Chill, The (Macdonald), 2174-2175.
Chilly Scenes of Winter (Beattie), 250-251.
Choirboys, The (Wambaugh), 3429-3430.
Chopin, Kate, 639-649; *At Fault*, 643-645; *The Awakening*, 645-648; *A Night in Acadie*, 640.
Chosen, The (Potok), 2660-2661.
Christie, Agatha, 650-660, 3844-3845; *Agatha Christie*, 651; *The Body in the Library*, 657; *A Daughter's a Daughter*, 653; *Death Comes in the End*, 655-656; *The Murder of Roger Ackroyd*, 656-657, 3844; *The Mysterious Affair at Styles*, 655, 656; *N or M? The New Mystery*, 658; *The Secret Adversary*, 657-658; *Sleeping Murder*, 658-659; *Ten Little Indians*, 3845; *Unfinished Portrait*, 652.
Christine (King), 1889-1890.

Cider House Rules, The (Irving, J.), 1702-1703.
Circle Home, The (Hoagland), 1630-1631.
Citadel, The (Cronin), 786, 789-791, 794.
Cities of the Interior (Nin), 2516-2518.
Cities of the Red Night (Burroughs), 489-490.
Citizen Tom Paine (Fast), 3838
City and the Pillar, The (Vidal), 3372.
City Boy, The (Wouk), 3667.
City of Illusions (Le Guin), 2009-2010.
City of Trembling Leaves, The (Clark), 664, 667.
Civil War, The (Foote), 1152.
Clam Shell, The (Settle), 3004, 3008.
Clarissa (Richardson, S.), 2841-2842, 3816.
Clark, Walter Van Tilburg, 661-671;
    The City of Trembling Leaves, 664, 667; *The Ox-Bow Incident*, 662, 663, 666-667; *The Track of the Cat*, 663, 667-669.
Classical tragedy, 774.
Classicism, **3881.**
Claudius the God (Graves), 1424-1425.
Clayhanger (Bennett), 298-299.
Clay's Ark (Butler, O.), 497.
Clea. See *Alexandria Quartet, The*.
Clear Light of Day (Desai), 873, 877-878.
Clemons, Samuel Langhorne. See **Twain, Mark.**
Cleveland, Grover, 1218-1219.
Climax/Crisis, **3881.**
Clock Winder, The (Tyler), 3337-3338.
Clock Without Hands (McCullers), 2168.
Clockwork Orange, A (Burgess), 468-469.
Close Quarters (Golding), 1356.
Close to the Sun Again (Callaghan), 543, 548-550.
Closed Harbour, The (Hanley), 1478.
"Cloud, The" (Fowles), 1211.
Coat of Varnish, A (Snow), 3090.
Cock and Anchor, The (Le Fanu), 1998.
Cock Jarvis (Cary), 574, 575.
Cock Pit (Cozzens), 764.
Coetzee, J. M., 672-679; *Dusklands*, 673-674; *In the Heart of the Country*, 674-675; *Life & Times of Michael K*, 676-678; *Waiting for the Barbarians*, 675-676.
Collages (Nin), 2520-2521.

Collector, The (Fowles), 1205-1207.
Collins, Wilkie, 680-690, 3788, 3843; *Man and Wife*, 684-685; "Miss Dulane and My Lord," 688; "Mrs. Zant and the Ghost," 686-687; *The Moonstone*, 687-688, 3843; *Poor Miss Finch*, 685; *The Woman in White*, 683-684, 687-688.
Collins, William, 680-681.
Colonel Jack (Defoe), 824.
Colonel Mint (West, P.), 3525-3526.
Colonel's Daughter, The (Aldington), 55-56.
Colonel's Dream, The (Chesnutt), 637.
Color Purple, The (Walker), 3407-3408, 3412-3414.
Colossus of Maroussi, The (Miller), 2381.
Comfort Me with Apples (De Vries), 887.
Comforters (Spark), 3105, 3106-3108.
Coming Up for Air (Orwell), 2594-2595.
Comment c'est. See *How It Is*.
Companions of the Day and Night (Harris, W.), 1531.
Company (Beckett), 263.
Complication, **3881.**
Compton-Burnett, Ivy, 691-701; *Brothers and Sisters*, 694-695; *A Family and a Fortune*, 697-698; *A God and His Gifts*, 699; *Manservant and Maidservant*, 698-699; *More Women Than Men*, 695-696.
Comrade Kirillov (Rao), 2793-2794.
Comte, Auguste, 3788.
Concrete Island (Ballard), 195.
Condor Passes, The (Grau), 1410-1411.
Confession (Simms), 3044.
Confessions of Nat Turner, The (Styron), 3244-3245, 3251-3253, 3839-3840.
Conflict, **3881.**
Conjure Woman, The (Chesnutt), 629.
Connecticut General from Big Sur, A (Brautigan), 374-375.
Connecticut Yankee in King Arthur's Court, A (Twain), 3325-3326, 3860.
Connell, Evan S., Jr., 702-712; *The Connoisseur*, 709-710; *The Diary of a Rapist*, 707-708; *Double Honeymoon*, 710-711; *Mr. Bridge*, 708-709; *Mrs. Bridge*, 705-706; *The Patriot*, 706-707.
Connoisseur, The (Connell), 709-710.
Conrad, Joseph, 713-731, 2821-2822, 3756-3757, 3789, 3875-3876; *The*

Arrow of Gold, 716; *Heart of Darkness*, 714, 718-722, 3756, 3875-3876; *Lord Jim*, 714, 722-726; *The Secret Agent*, 3789; *Victory*, 726.

Conservationist, The (Gordimer), 1387-1389.

Consider Her Ways (Grove), 1450.

Conspirators, The (Prokosch), 2739-2740.

Contextualist criticism, **3881.**

Conventions, **3882.**

Conversation (Aiken), 31, 35-36.

Cool Million, A (West, N.), 3516-3517.

Cooper, James Fenimore, 732-747, 3700, 3748, 3753-3754, 3800; *The American Democrat*, 732; *Home as Found*, 736-737; *The Last of the Mohicans*, 736, 741-743; Leatherstocking Tales, 736, 3748, 3749; *The Pioneers*, 737-741; *The Prairie*, 743-745.

Coover, Robert, 748-758, 3878-3879; "The Babysitter," 3879; *Gerald's Party*, 756-757; *The Origin of the Brunists*, 751-752; *The Public Burning*, 754-756; *The Universal Baseball Association*, 752-754.

Cornwell, David John Moore. *See* **Le Carré, John.**

Corridors of Power (Snow), 3089.

Cosmic Rape, The (Sturgeon), 3237-3238.

"Côte Basque: 1965, La" (Capote), 561-562.

Count Belisarius (Graves), 1422-1423.

Counterlife, The (Roth), 2900, 2904.

Country, The (Plante), 2645-2646.

Country Doctor, A (Jewett), 1743-1746.

Country Girls, The (O'Brien, E.), 2544.

Country of the Pointed Firs, The (Jewett), 1746-1748.

Coup, The (Updike), 3357-3358.

Couples (Updike), 3355-3356.

Courts of the Morning, The (Buchan), 427.

Cousin Phillis (Gaskell), 1304.

Cozzens, James Gould, 759-770; *Ask Me Tomorrow*, 763, 766-767; *By Love Possessed*, 768-769; *Castaway*, 765-766; *Cock Pit*, 764; *Guard of Honor*, 767-768; *The Just and the Unjust*, 762, 767; *The Last Adam*, 765; *Men and Brethren*, 766-767; *Michael Scarlett*, 763; *Morning, Noon, and Night*, 769-770; *The Son of Perdition*, 764; *S.

S. San Pedro, 764-765.

Crane, Stephen, 771-780, 3769, 3876; *Active Service*, 777-778; "The Blue Hotel," 3876-3877; *George's Mother*, 774; *Maggie*, 773-774; *The Monster and Other Stories*, 778-779; *The O'Ruddy* (with Barr), 779; *The Red Badge of Courage*, 774-776, 3769; *The Third Violet*, 776-777.

Cranford (Gaskell), 1301, 1303.

Crash (Ballard), 194-195.

Crazy Hunter (Boyle, K.), 342.

Crazy in Berlin (Berger), 307.

Creation (Vidal), 3374.

Crochet Castle (Peacock), 2622-2623.

Crome Yellow (Huxley), 1676-1677.

Cronin, A. J., 781-795; *The Citadel*, 786, 789-791, 794; *The Green Years*, 786, 792-794; *Hatter's Castle*, 781, 783-784, 785-786, 787-788, 794; *The Keys of the Kingdom*, 786, 791-792, 794; *The Stars Look Down*, 786, 788-789, 794.

Crossing to Safety (Stegner), 3134-3135.

Cruikshank, George, 45.

Cruise of the Breadwinner, The (Bates), 246.

Cry of Absence, A (Jones, M.), 1815-1816.

Cry, the Peacock (Desai), 872, 873-874.

Crying Game, The (Braine), 366-367.

Crying of Lot 49, The (Pynchon), 2765, 2768-2770, 3771, 3777.

Crystal Age, A (Hudson), 1660-1661.

Crystal World, The (Ballard), 194.

Cujo (King), 1889.

"Custom House, The" (Hawthorne), 1575-1576.

Custom of the Country, The (Wharton), 3539-3540.

Dahomean, The (Yerby), 3696-3698.

Dain Curse, The (Hammett), 1465.

Daisy Miller (James, H.), 1721-1722.

Daisy's Necklace and What Came of It (Aldrich), 65.

Dalkey Archive, The (O'Brien, F.), 2557-2558.

Dalton, James, 3858.

Dalva (Harrison), 1546.

Damballah. See *Homewood Trilogy, The*

Damnation of Theron Ware, The (Frederic), 1222-1226.

Dance to the Music of Time, A (Powell, A.), 2673-2675, 3773.

Dancing Floor, The (Buchan), 429-430.

Dandelion Wine (Bradbury), 360-361.

Dangerous Acquaintances (Laclos), 3819-3822.

Dangling Man (Bellow), 277.

Daniel Deronda (Eliot), 1043-1045.

Daniel Martin (Fowles), 1211-1212.

Dannay, Frederic A., 3845.

Dar. See *Gift, The*.

D'Arblay, Madame. *See* **Burney, Fanny**.

Dark Carnival (Bradbury), 357-358.

Dark Dancer, The (Prokosch), 2740-2741.

Dark Flower, The (Galsworthy), 1261.

Dark Half, The (King), 1894-1895.

Dark Labyrinth, The (Durrell), 1011.

Dark Laughter (Anderson), 116.

Dark Places of the Heart (Stead), 3123-3124.

Dark Sisters, The (Kavan), 1835.

Darkness at Noon (Koestler), 1912-1913.

Darkness Visible (Golding), 1355-1356.

Da Silva da Silva's Cultivated Wilderness and Genesis of the Clowns (Harris, W.), 1531.

Daughter of the Legend (Stuart), 3228-3229.

Daughter's a Daughter, A (Christie), 653.

Davies, Robertson, 796-804; *Fifth Business*, 799, 800; *The Lyre of Orpheus*, 802-803; *The Manticore*, 798, 799, 800-801; *The Rebel Angels*, 798-799, 801-802; *What's Bred in the Bone*, 801, 802; *World of Wonders*, 799, 800, 801.

Davis, H. L., 805-813; *Beulah Land*, 809-810; *The Distant Music*, 807, 811-812; *Harp of a Thousand Strings*, 808-809; *Honey in the Horn*, 807-808; *Winds of Morning*, 810-811.

Davita's Harp (Potok), 2661, 2665-2666.

Dawn (Butler, O.), 497, 498-499.

Dawn's Left Hand (Richardson, D.), 2832-2833.

Day of the Locust, The (West, N.), 3517-3519.

Daybreakers, The (L'Amour), 1933-1934.

Dead Babies (Amis, M.), 102-103.

Dead Father, The (Barthelme), 235-236.

Dead Hand series, 3046-3047.

Dead Man Leading (Pritchett), 2726-2728.

Dead of Spring, The (Goodman), 1372-1373.

Deadlock (Richardson, D.), 2831-2832.

De Alfonce Tennis (Donleavy), 950-951.

Dealings with the Firm of Dombey and Son, Wholesale, Retail, and for Exportation. See *Dombey and Son*.

Dean's December, The (Bellow), 286-287.

Death at Sea (Prokosch), 2734.

Death Comes for the Archbishop (Cather), 595.

Death Comes in the End (Christie), 655-656.

Death in the Family, A (Agee), 26.

Death Is a Lonely Business (Bradbury), 361-362.

Death of a Hero (Aldington), 54-55.

Death of an Expert Witness (James, P.), 1733-1734.

Death of the Fox (Garrett), 1296-1297.

Death of the Heart, The (Bowen), 322-323.

Death of William Posters, The (Sillitoe), 3030.

Death Under Sail (Snow), 3084.

Debut, The (Brookner), 399-400.

Decameron, The (Boccaccio), 3873.

Deception (Roth), 2904.

Decision (Boyle, K.), 343.

Decline and Fall (Waugh), 3462-3463.

Deconstruction, **3882.**

Deep Sleep, The (Morris), 2418.

Deephaven (Jewett), 1741-1743.

Deer Park, The (Mailer), 2251-2252.

Defamiliarization, **3882.**

Defoe, Daniel, 814-830, 3727, 3731-3732, 3781, 3806; *Colonel Jack*, 824; *A Journal of the Plague Year*, 819-821; *Moll Flanders*, 824, 826-827, 3728-3729, 3731-3732, 3806; *Robinson Crusoe*, 821-824, 3727-3728, 3733; *Roxana*, 824-828.

De Forest, John William, 831-840; "The Great American Novel," 834-835; "The 'High-Toned Gentleman,'" 834-835; *Honest John Vane*, 838; *Kate Beaumont*, 837-838; *A Lover's Revolt*, 835; *Miss Ravenel's Conversion from Secession to Loyalty*, 834-835; *Seacliff*, 833-834; "Two Girls," 834-835; *Witching Times*, 833-834, 836.

de la Mare, Walter, 841-847; *Memoirs of a Midget*, 844, 845-846; *The Return*,

844-845; *The Three Mulla-Mulgars*, 843-844.
Delany, Samuel R., 848-861; *Babel-17*, 853-854; *The Bridge of Lost Desire*, 854; *Dhalgren*, 853, 855-857; *The Einstein Intersection*, 854; *Flight from Nevèrÿon*, 854; *Nova*, 854; *Stars in My Pocket Like Grains of Sand*, 855, 859-860; *Tales of Nevèrÿon*, 854; *Triton*, 855, 857-859.
DeLillo, Don, 862-870; *Americana*, 863-864; *End Zone*, 864; *Great Jones Street*, 864-865; *Libra*, 868-869; *The Names*, 866-867; *Ratner's Star*, 865-866; *White Noise*, 866, 867-868; *Deliverance* (Dickey), 916-917.
Deloney, Thomas, 3723-3724; *Jack of Newbury*, 3723-3724; Thomas of Reading, 3723, 3724.
Delta Wedding (Welty), 3491-3492, 3494-3495.
Democracy (Didion), 931-932.
Depression, The, 3155.
Dépeupleur, Le. See *Lost Ones, The*.
Deptford trilogy. See *Fifth Business*, *Manticore, The*, and *World of Wonders*.
Desai, Anita, 871-880; *Baumgartner's Bombay*, 878-879; *Bye-Bye, Blackbird*, 875-876; *Clear Light of Day*, 873, 877-878; *Cry, the Peacock*, 872, 873-874; *Fire on the Mountain*, 872, 873, 876-878; *Voices in the City*, 872, 873, 874-875; *Where Shall We Go This Summer?*, 876.
Destinies of Darcy Dancer, Gentleman, The (Donleavy), 950.
Destry Rides Again (Faust), 3851-3852.
Detective fiction, 598-600.
Detective novel, **3842-3848.**
Detective story, **3882.**
Determinism, **3882.**
Devices and Desires (James, P.), 1736-1737.
Devil on the Cross (Ngugi wa Thiong'o), 2508.
Devil's Diary, The (McGinley), 2191, 2192-2194.
Devil's Stocking, The (Algren), 81.
De Voto, Bernard, 3630.
De Vries, Peter, 881-891; *The Blood of the Lamb*, 887-888; *Comfort Me with Apples*, 887; *The Glory of the*

Hummingbird, 889; *The Mackerel Plaza*, 886-887; *Peckham's Marbles*, 889, 890; *The Prick of Noon*, 889-890; *Reuben, Reuben*, 888-889; *Sauce for the Goose*, 889; *Slouching Towards Kalamazoo*, 889; *The Tents of Wickedness*, 887; *The Tunnel of Love*, 885-886.
Dhalgren (Delany), 853, 855-857.
Dharma Bums (Kerouac), 1868-1869.
Dialect, 3211.
Dialogue, **3882.**
Diana of the Crossways (Meredith), 2366-2367.
Diaries of Jane Somers, The (Lessing), 2039-2040.
Diary of a Rapist, The (Connell), 707-708.
Diary of Anaïs Nin, The (Nin), 2510, 2512.
Dick, Philip K., 892-900; *Do Androids Dream of Electric Sheep?*, 893, 897; *Eye in the Sky*, 894-895; *Flow My Tears, the Policeman Said*, 898; *The Man in the High Castle*, 895-896; *Martian Time-Slip*, 896; *The Penultimate Truth*, 896; *Solar Lottery*, 894; *The Three Stigmata of Palmer Eldritch*, 896-897; *Time Out of Joint*, 895; *Ubik*, 897; *Valis*, 898-899.
Dick Gibson Show, The (Elkin), 1049.
Dickens, Charles, 901-914, 3740-3741, 3786-3787, 3806-3807, 3838, 3843; *Bleak House*, 3786-3787, 3843; *Dombey and Son*, 909-910, 3787; *Hard Times*, 3787; *Little Dorrit*, 910-911, 3787; *Martin Chuzzlewit*, 907-909; *Nicholas Nickleby*, 906-907; *Oliver Twist*, 3786; *Our Mutual Friend*, 912-913; *Pickwick Papers*, 906, 3786, 3806-3807; *A Tale of Two Cities*, 3838.
Dickens, John, 902.
Dickey, James, 915-921; *Alnilam*, 917-919; *Deliverance*, 916-917.
Didion, Joan, 922-933; *A Book of Common Prayer*, 928-931; *Democracy*, 931-932; *Play It As It Lays*, 927-928; *Run River*, 924-926.
Dinner at the Homesick Restaurant (Tyler), 3343-3344.
Displacement, **3882.**
Dispossessed, The (Le Guin), 2011-2012.
Distant Horns of Summer, The (Bates), 245-246.
Distant Music, The (Davis), 807, 811-812.

Distant Trumpet, A (Horgan), 1639-1640.
Diviners, The (Laurence), 1943-1944, 1947-1949.
Do Androids Dream of Electric Sheep? (Dick), 893, 897.
Do, Lord, Remember Me (Garrett), 1295-1296.
Doctor Copernicus (Banville), 203-204.
Doctorow, E. L., 934-943; *Big as Life*, 935; *Billy Bathgate*, 939-942; *The Book of Daniel*, 935-937; *Loon Lake*, 938; *Ragtime*, 937-938; *Welcome to Hard Times*, 935; *World's Fair*, 938-939.
Documents Relating to the Sentimental Agents in the Volyen Empire (Lessing), 2039.
Dodsworth (Lewis, S.), 2076.
Dog Soldiers (Stone), 3200-3201, 3202.
Dombey and Son (Dickens), 909-910, 3787.
Dominant, **3883.**
Donleavy, J. P., 944-952; *The Beastly Beatitudes of Balthazar B.*, 948-979; *De Alfonce Tennis*, 950-951; *The Destinies of Darcy Dancer, Gentleman*, 950; *A Fairy Tale of New York*, 949-950; *The Ginger Man*, 946-947; *Leila*, 950; *The Onion Eaters*, 949; *The Saddest Summer of Samuel S.*, 948; *Schultz*, 950; *A Singular Man*, 947-948.
Donnelly, Ignatius, 3866.
Don't Stop the Carnival (Wouk), 3673.
Doolittle, Hilda. *See* H. D.
Doomsters, The (Macdonald), 2172-2173.
Doppelgänger, **3883.**
Dos Passos, John, 953-963, 3763, 3766; *The Big Money*, 961-962; *The 42nd Parallel*, 958-960; *Manhattan Transfer*, 957-958; *1919*, 960-961; *Three Soldiers*, 956-957, 3763; *U.S.A.* trilogy, 958-962, 3766.
Double, Double (Yglesias), 3705-3707.
Double Honeymoon (Connell), 710-711.
Double Vision, 1137-1138.
Down the Long Hills (L'Amour), 1935-1936.
Doyle, Arthur Conan, 964-978, 3861, 3788-3789, 3843; *The Hound of the Baskervilles*, 974; *The Lost World*, 974-975, 3861; *Micah Clarke*, 972; *The Parasite*, 975; *The Poison Belt*, 974; *The Sign of the Four*, 973-974; *A Study in Scarlet*, 974, 3843; *The White Company*, 972-973.
Drabble, Margaret, 979-993; *The Ice Age*, 990-991; *Jerusalem the Golden*, 982-985; *The Needle's Eye*, 986-988; *The Realms of Gold*, 988-990; *A Summer Bird-Cage*, 982; *The Waterfall*, 985-986.
Dracula (Stoker), 3831-3832, 3863.
Dragon Can't Dance, The (Lovelace), 2109.
Dragon Seed (Buck), 440-441.
Drama in Muslin, A (Moore, G.), 2406-2407.
Draper, Eliza, 3176.
Dream Journey, A (Hanley), 1478-1477.
Dream Life of Balso Snell, The (West, N.), 3515.
Dreaming Jewels, The (Sturgeon), 3233-3236.
Dred (Stowe), 3212.
Dreiser, Theodore, 994-1006, 3757, 3758-3759; *An American Tragedy*, 1002-1004, 3759; *The Financier*, 1001-1002; *Jennie Gerhardt*, 999-1001; *Sister Carrie*, 997-999, 3759.
Driver's Seat, The (Spark), 3106, 3111-3113.
Drought, The (Ballard), 193.
Drowned World, The (Ballard), 192-193.
Dubliners (Joyce), 1820.
"Dulcima" (Bates), 246.
Dumas, Alexandre, *père*, 3837-3838.
Dunne, John Gregory, 923-924.
Dunyazadiad (Barth), 3878.
Durrell, Lawrence, 1007-1017; *The Alexandria Quartet*, 1011-1014; *The Avignon Quintet*, 1014-1015; *The Black Book*, 1011; *The Dark Labyrinth*, 1011; *Nunquam*, 1014; *Tunc*, 1014.
Dusklands (Coetzee), 673-674.
Dusty Answer (Lehmann), 2017-2018.
Dutiful Daughter, A (Keneally), 1846-1847.

Each Man's Son (MacLennan), 2214-2215.
Eagles' Nest (Kavan), 1836-1837.
Earthbreakers, The (Haycox), 3853.
Earthly Possessions (Tyler), 3340-3341.
Earthly Powers (Burgess), 467.
Earthsea series, The (Le Guin), 2013-2014.
East Is East (Boyle, T.), 352-353.
"Ebony Tower, The" (Fowles), 1209-1210.
Ebony Tower, The (Fowles), 1209-1211.

Eddison, E. R., 3861.
Edgar Huntly (Brown), 415-419.
Edgeworth, Maria, 1018-1031, 3739; *The Absentee*, 1022, 1026-1028; *Castle Rackrent*, 1022-1023, 1024-1026; *Ormond*, 1023-1024, 1028-1029.
Edgeworth, Richard Lovell, 1020.
Edmonds, Helen (Wood). *See* **Kavan, Anna**.
Egoist, The (Meredith), 2365-2366.
Eight Men (Wright), 3679.
1876 (Vidal), 3375-3376.
Eighth Day, The (Wilder), 3576-3577.
Einstein Intersection, The (Delany), 854.
Eliot, George, 1032-1045, 3741, 3743; *Adam Bede*, 1035-1038; *Daniel Deronda*, 1043-1045; *Middlemarch*, 1040-1043; *The Mill on the Floss*, 1038-1039; *Silas Marner*, 1039-1040.
Elkin, Stanley, 1046-1052; *A Bad Man*, 1048; *Boswell*, 1047-1048; *The Dick Gibson Show*, 1049; *The Franchiser*, 1049; *George Mills*, 1049-1050; *The Magic Kingdom*, 1050; *The Rabbi of Lud*, 1050.
Ellison, Ralph, 1053-1064, 3776, 3808; *Invisible Man*, 1055-1063, 3776, 3808.
Elmer Gantry (Lewis, S.), 2074-2076.
Embezzler, The (Auchincloss), 152-153.
Emma (Austen), 164-166.
Empire (Vidal), 3376.
Empire City, The (Goodman), 1369-1374.
Empire of the Sun (Ballard), 197.
End and a Beginning, An. See Fury Chronicle.
End of the Battle, The (Waugh), 3470.
End of the Road, The (Barth), 223-224.
End Zone (DeLillo), 864.
Enemies (Singer), 3064-3065.
English Teacher, The (Narayan), 2483-2484.
"Enigma, The" (Fowles), 1210-1211.
Enigma of Arrival, The (Naipaul), 2477-2478.
Entered from the Sun (Garrett), 1298.
Entrance to Porlock, The (Buechner), 449.
Epic, **3883**.
Episodic narrative, **3883**.
Epistolary novel, **3810-3822, 3883**.
Equations of Love, The. See Tuesday and Wednesday and *Lilly's Story*.
Erdrich, Louise, 1065-1072; *The Beet Queen*, 1068-1070; *Love Medicine*, 1066-1068; *Tracks*, 1070-1071.
Erewhon (Butler, S.), 503-505.
Erewhon Revisited (Butler, S.), 505-506.
Esmond in India (Jhabvala), 1754-1755.
Estate, The (Singer), 3061-3063.
Esther Waters (Moore, G.), 2402, 2407-2408.
Ethan Frome (Wharton), 3537.
Euphues, the Anatomy of Wit (Lyly), 3722.
Euphuism, 3722, **3883**.
Europeans, The (James, H.), 3750.
Eustace and Hilda (Hartley), 1554.
Eustace Chisholm and the Works (Purdy), 2746-2747.
Eustace Diamonds, The (Trollope), 3313-3315.
Eva Trout (Bowen), 324.
Evans, May Ann. *See* **Eliot, George**.
Evelina (Burney), 476-478.
Evelyn Innes (Moore, G.), 2408.
Evidence of Love (Grau), 1411-1413.
Excellent Women (Pym), 2757-2759.
Except the Lord (Cary), 581-582.
Executioner's Song, The (Mailer), 2258-2260.
Exile, An (Jones, M.), 1814-1815.
Existentialism, 1586, 2438, 2628-2630.
Expedition of Humphrey Clinker, The. See Humphrey Clinker.
Expensive People (Oates), 2535-2536.
Exposition, **3883**.
Exterminator! (Burroughs), 489.
Eye in the Sky (Dick), 894-895.
Eye of the Scarecrow, The (Harris, W.), 1530-1531.
Eye of the Storm, The (White), 3554-3555.
Eyeless in Gaza (Huxley), 1682-1683.
Eyes of Darkness (Highwater), 1625.
Eyes of the Dragon, The (King), 1893.

Fahrenheit 451 (Bradbury), 360.
Fair Blows the Wind (L'Amour), 1934.
Fair Game (Johnson, D.), 1771.
Fair Haven, The (Butler, S.), 506.
Fair Jilt, The (Behn), 272.
Fairly Good Time, A (Gallant), 1252-1253.
Fairly Honourable Defeat, A (Murdoch), 2444-2448.
Fairy Tale of New York, A (Donleavy), 949-950.

Faith and the Good Thing (Johnson, C.), 1763-1765.
Falconer (Cheever), 623-625.
Falkner (Shelley), 3020, 3022-3023.
"Fall of the House of Usher, The" (Poe), 3830-3831.
Falling in Place (Beattie), 251-252.
Family, The (Plante), 2643-2644.
Family and a Fortune, A (Compton-Burnett), 697-698.
Family and Friends (Brookner), 404-405.
Family Arsenal, The (Theroux), 3285-3286.
Family Madness, A (Keneally), 1847.
Family Moskat, The (Singer), 3061-3063.
Fanshawe (Hawthorne), 1574-1576.
Fantasia of the Unconscious (Lawrence), 1957.
Fantastic, **3883.**
Fantasy novel, **3857-3864.**
Far Cry from Kensington, A (Spark), 3116.
Far from Cibola (Horgan), 1638-1639.
Far from the Madding Crowd (Hardy), 1500-1502.
Far Journey of Ouidin, The (Harris, W.), 1529.
Far Tortuga (Matthiessen), 2308-2309, 2312, 2313, 2316-2318.
Farewell, My Lovely (Chandler), 603.
Farewell to Arms, A (Hemingway), 1601-1603, 3763, 3769.
Farmer (Harrison), 1537-1539.
Farrell, James T., 1073-1081, 3770; The Bernard Carr trilogy, 1079; The O'Neill-O'Flaherty series, 1077-1079; *Studs Lonigan: A Trilogy*, 1076-1077, 3770.
Farrell, J. G., 1082-1087; *The Siege of Krishnapur*, 1085-1086; *The Singapore Grip*, 1086; *Troubles*, 1084-1085.
Fast, Howard, 3838.
Fat Woman's Joke, The. See *. . . And the Wife Ran Away*
Fatal Revenge (Maturin), 2325-2326.
Father's Words, A (Stern), 3169-3170.
Faulkner, William, 1088-1111, 3766, 3771-3772, 3832-3833, 3840, 3875; *Absalom, Absalom!*, 1102-1106, 3772, 3832, 3840-3841; *As I Lay Dying*, 1096-1097, 3832; "The Bear," 3874; *Go Down, Moses*, 1106-1109, 3766, 3771; *Light in August*, 1098-1102, 3772;

Sanctuary, 1097-1098; *The Sound and the Fury*, 1092-1096, 3766, 3771, 3832; *The Wild Palms*, 3776.
Faust, Frederick Schiller, 3851-3852.
Fearful Joy, A (Cary), 578.
Feast of Lupercal, The (Moore, B.), 2392-2394.
Fellowship of the Ring, The. See *Lord of the Rings, The*.
Ferdinand, Count Fathom (Smollett), 3074.
Ferguson, Helen. *See* **Kavan, Anna.**
Feud, The (Berger), 315.
Fielding, Gabriel, 1112-1118; *The Birthday King*, 1113, 1114-1115; *Brotherly Love*, 1114; *Gentlemen in Their Season*, 1113, 1114, 1115-1116; *In the Time of Greenbloom*, 1113, 1114.
Fielding, Henry, 1119-1134, 3734, 3782, 3806, 3814-3815; *Amelia*, 3782; *Jonathan Wild*, 1130-1131; *Joseph Andrews*, 1128-1130, 3815; *Shamela*, 1124, 1126-1128, 3814-3815; *Tom Jones*, 1131-1132, 3732, 3733, 3782, 3806.
Fields, The (Richter), 2865.
Fifth Business (Davies), 799, 800.
Fifth Child, The (Lessing), 2040.
Fifty-two Pickup (Leonard), 2027, 2028.
Fight Night on a Sweet Saturday (Settle), 3007-3008.
Figures of Earth (Cabell), 516-517.
Final Beast, The (Buechner), 448-449.
Financial Expert, The (Narayan), 2485-2486.
Financier, The (Dreiser), 1001-1002.
Finished Man, The (Garrett), 1295.
Finishing School, The (Godwin), 1344-1345.
Finnegans Wake (Joyce), 1829-1831, 3765-3766.
Fire and the Sun, The (Murdoch), 2441, 2452.
Fire Down Below (Golding), 1356-1357.
Fire-Dwellers, The (Laurence), 1947.
Fire from Heaven (Renault), 2813.
Fire on the Mountain (Desai), 872, 873, 876-878.
First Deadly Sin, The (Sanders), 3847.
First Fast Draw, The (L'Amour), 1933.
First Men in the Moon, The (Wells), 3482.
Fitzgerald, F. Scott, 1135-1150, 3768-3769, 3796; *The Beautiful and the Damned*, 1141-1144; *The Great Gatsby*,

1138, 1143-1146, 3768, 3796, 3799;
Tender Is the Night, 1146-1148; *This Side of Paradise*, 1140-1141, 1142.
Fitzgerald, Zelda, 1137.
Fixer, The (Malamud), 2273-2275.
Flag for Sunrise, A (Stone), 3201-3203.
Flame of Life, The (Sillitoe), 3031.
Flashback, **3884.**
Flaubert, Gustave, 3874, 3875.
Flaubert's Parrot (Barnes), 212-213.
Fleming, Ian, 3774.
Flight from Nevèrÿon (Delany), 854.
Flight to Canada (Reed), 2804.
Floating Opera, The (Barth), 221-223.
Flow My Tears, the Policeman Said (Dick), 898.
Foggage (McGinley), 2191, 2192.
Folded Leaf, The (Maxwell), 2344.
Follow Me Down (Foote), 1157-1158.
Fong and the Indians (Theroux), 3283-3284.
Food of the Gods, and How It Came to Earth, The (Wells), 3482.
Foote, Shelby, 1151-1164; "Child by Fever," 1161-1162; *The Civil War,* 1152; *Follow Me Down*, 1157-1158; "The Freedom Kick," 1162; *Jordan County*, 1160-1162; *Love in a Dry Season*, 1158-1160; "A Marriage Portion," 1161; "Pillar of Fire," 1162; "Rain Down Home," 1161; "Ride Out," 1161; "The Sacred Mound," 1162; *September September*, 1162-1163; *Shiloh*, 1160; *Tournament*, 1156-1157.
For Love Alone (Stead), 3122-3123.
For Whom the Bell Tolls (Hemingway), 1604-1605.
Ford, Ford Madox, 52, **1165-1174,** 2821-2822, 3761; *The Good Soldier*, 1168-1171; *Parade's End*, 1171-1172.
Ford, Richard, 1175-1180; *A Piece of My Heart*, 1176-1177; *The Sportswriter*, 1178-1179; *The Ultimate Good Luck*, 1177-1178; *Wildlife*, 1179-1180.
Foreign Affairs (Lurie), 2128-2130.
Foreigner, The (Plante), 2646-2647.
Foreshadowing, **3884.**
Forest of the Night (Jones, M.), 1812-1813.
Foretaste of Glory (Stuart), 3227.
Formalist criticism, **3884.**
Forster, E. M., 1181-1198, 3761;
Howard's End, 1191-1193; *The Longest Journey*, 1187-1189; *Maurice*, 1193-1194; *A Passage to India*, 1194-1196, 3761; *A Room with a View*, 1189-1191; *Where Angels Fear to Tread*, 1186-1187.
Fortunes and Misfortunes of the Famous Moll Flanders. See *Moll Flanders.*
Fortunes of Colonel Torlogh O'Brien, The (Le Fanu), 1998-1999.
Fortunes of Perkin Warbeck, The (Shelley), 3020.
42nd Parallel, The (Dos Passos), 958-960.
Four-Chambered Heart, The (Nin), 2516, 2518-2519.
Four-Gated City, The (Lessing), 2035, 3833.
Fowles, John, 1199-1215; *The Aristos*, 1199; "The Cloud," 1211; *The Collector*, 1205-1207; *Daniel Martin*, 1211-1212; "The Ebony Tower," 1209-1210; *The Ebony Tower*, 1209-1211; "The Enigma," 1210-1211; *The French Lieutenant's Woman*, 1207-1209; *A Maggot*, 1213-1214; *The Magus*, 1203-1205; "Poor Koko," 1210.
Foxes of Harrow, The (Yerby), 3693-3694.
Foxprints (McGinley), 2191, 2192.
Foxybaby (Jolley), 1793-1794.
Fragments (Armah), 124-126.
Franchiser, The (Elkin), 1049.
Francoeur Novels, The (Plante), 2643-2646.
Frankenstein (Shelley), 3016-3017, 3831.
Fraternity (Galsworthy), 1260-1261.
Freaky Deaky (Leonard), 2029.
Freddy's Book (Gardner), 1279-1280.
Frederic, Harold, 1216-1227; *The Damnation of Theron Ware*, 1222-1226; *Gloria Mundi*, 1220; *In the Valley*, 1218, 1220; *The Lawton Girl*, 1220; *Seth's Brother's Wife*, 1221-1222.
Free Fall (Golding), 1353.
Free-Lance Pallbearers, The (Reed), 2801-2802.
"Freedom Kick, The" (Foote), 1162.
French Lieutenant's Woman, The (Fowles), 1207-1209.
French Vulgate Cycle, 2279.
Freudianism, 1959-1960, 2438.
Fringe of Leaves, A (White), 3555-3556.
From a View to a Death (Powell, A.), 2676.

From Here to Eternity (Jones, J.), 1797, 1802-1804.
Fruits of the Earth (Grove), 1456-1457.
Full Moon (Wodehouse), 3612.
Funeral Games (Renault), 2815.
Fury Chronicle, The (Hanley), 1475-1477.
Furys, The. *See* Fury Chronicle, The.
Future Is Ours, Comrade, The (Kosinski), 1920.

Gaddis, William, 1228-1237; *Carpenter's Gothic*, 1230, 1234-1236; *JR*, 1230, 1233-1234; *The Recognitions*, 1230, 1231-1233.
Gaines, Ernest J., 1238-1247; *The Autobiography of Miss Jane Pittman*, 1243-1244; *Catherine Carmier*, 1240-1242; *A Gathering of Old Men*, 1245-1246; *In My Father's House*, 1244-1245; *Of Love and Dust*, 1242-1243.
Gala (West, P.), 3526.
Gallant, Mavis, 1248-1255; *A Fairly Good Time*, 1252-1253; *Green Water, Green Sky*, 1251-1252; *Home Truths*, 1251; *Its Image on the Mirror*, 1252; *The Other Paris*, 1250-1251; *The Pegnitz Junction*, 1253.
Galsworthy, John, 1256-1266, 3760, 3791; *The Dark Flower*, 1261; *Fraternity*, 1260-1261; *In Chancery*, 1263-1264; *The Man of Property*, 1261-1263; *A Modern Comedy*, 1264; *To Let*, 1264.
Galton Case, The (Macdonald), 2173-2174.
Garden of Adonis, The (Gordon), 1399-1400.
Gardner, Erle Stanley, 3846-3847.
Gardner, John, 1267-1285; *Freddy's Book*, 1279-1280; *Grendel*, 1273-1274; *Mickelsson's Ghosts*, 1281-1282; *Nickel Mountain*, 1276-1278; *October Light*, 1278-1279; *On Moral Fiction*, 1269-1271; *The Resurrection*, 1271-1272; *Shadows*, 1282-1283; *Stillness*, 1282; *The Sunlight Dialogues*, 1274-1276; *The Wreckage of Agathon*, 1272-1273.
Garland, Hamlin, 1286-1293; *Captain of the Gray Horse Troop*, 1290-1291; *A Little Norsk*, 1289-1290; *Rose of Dutcher's Coolly*, 1290; *A Spoil of Office*, 1288-1289.

Garrett, George, 1294-1299; *Death of the Fox*, 1296-1297; *Do, Lord, Remember Me*, 1295-1296; *Entered from the Sun*, 1298; *The Finished Man*, 1295; *Poison Pen*, 1297; *The Succession*, 1297.
Gaskell, Mrs. Elizabeth, 1300-1310; *Cousin Phillis*, 1304; *Cranford*, 1301, 1303; *Mary Barton*, 1302, 1306; *North and South*, 1303-1304, 1305, 1307-1308; *Ruth*, 1301, 1306-1307; *Sylvia's Lovers*, 1304; *Wives and Daughters*, 1308-1309.
Gass, William H., 1311-1317, 3878-3879; "In the Heart of the Heart of the Country," 1312; *In the Heart of the Heart of the Country and Other Stories*, 1312; *Omensetter's Luck*, 1312-1315; *Willie Masters' Lonesome Wife*, 1315-1316, 3878.
Gaston de Blondeville (Radcliffe), 2777, 2779.
Gaston de Latour (Pater), 2612-2613.
Gathering of Old Men, A (Gaines), 1245-1246.
Gaudy Night (Sayers), 2977-2978.
Generation Without Farewell (Boyle, K.), 344.
Generous Man, A (Price), 2700, 2703-2704.
Genius and the Goddess, The (Huxley), 1685-1686.
Genre, **3884.**
Genre fiction, **3884.**
Gentlemen, I Address You Privately (Boyle, K.), 341-342.
Gentlemen in England (Wilson, A. N.), 3584-3585.
Gentlemen in Their Season (Fielding, G.), 1113, 1114, 1115-1116.
George Mills (Elkin), 1049-1050.
George's Mother (Crane), 774.
Gerald's Party (Coover), 756-757.
Geronimo Rex (Hannah), 1482-1483.
Get Ready for Battle (Jhabvala), 1756.
Get Shorty (Leonard), 2029-2030.
Ghost Horse Cycle, The (Highwater), 1625-1626.
Ghost in the Machine, The (Koestler), 1916.
Ghost Writer, The (Roth), 2901-2902, 3877-3878.
Ghostly Lover, The (Hardwick), 1492.
Gift, The (Nabokov), 2463-2464.
Gift of Asher Lev, The (Potok), 2666-2667.

Gilded Age, The (Twain), 3795.
Giles Goat-Boy (Barth), 227-229.
Gilman, George, 3855.
Ginger Man, The (Donleavy), 946-947.
Ginger, You're Barmy (Lodge), 2090-2091.
Girls in Their Married Bliss (O'Brien, E.), 2544-2545.
Gissing, George, 1318-1326; *New Grub Street*, 1323-1324; *The Private Papers of Henry Ryecroft*, 1325; *The Unclassed*, 1322-1323; *Workers in the Dawn*, 1322.
Gladiators, The (Koestler), 1911-1912.
Glance Away, A (Wideman), 3562-3563.
Glasgow, Ellen, 1327-1336, 3762; *Barren Ground*, 1332-1333; *The Romantic Comedians*, 1333-1334; *The Sheltered Life*, 1334-1335; *Vein of Iron*, 1330; *Virginia*, 1331-1332.
Glass Key, The (Hammett), 1467-1468.
Glass of Blessings, A (Pym), 2757, 2759.
Glass People (Godwin), 1339, 1340-1341.
Glidden, Frederick Dilley, 3853-3854.
Gloria Mundi (Frederic), 1220.
Glory of Hera, The (Gordon), 1402.
Glory of the Hummingbird, The (De Vries), 889.
Glory's Course (Purdy), 2750.
Go-Between, The (Hartley), 1555-1556.
Go Down, Moses (Faulkner), 1106-1109, 3766, 3771.
Go Tell It on the Mountain (Baldwin), 178-181, 3776.
God and His Gifts, A (Compton-Burnett), 699.
God Knows (Heller), 1592-1593.
Godric (Buechner), 451-455.
God's Grace (Malamud), 2275.
God's Little Acre (Caldwell), 536-537.
Godwin, Gail, 1337-1347; *The Finishing School*, 1344-1345; *Glass People*, 1339, 1340-1341; *A Mother and Two Daughters*, 1343-1344; *The Odd Woman*, 1341-1342; *The Perfectionists*, 1339-1340; *A Southern Family*, 1345-1346; *Violet Clay*, 1342-1343.
Goethe, Johann Wolfgang von, 3736, 3817-3819, 3873-3874.
Going Abroad (Macaulay), 2139.
Golden Apples of the Sun, The (Bradbury), 359.
Golden Bowl, The (James, H.), 3755-3756.

Golden Fleece, The. See *Hercules, My Shipmate*.
Golden Notebook, The (Lessing), 2036.
Golden Spur, The (Powell, D.), 2687-2688.
Golding, William, 1348-1358, 3768; *Close Quarters*, 1356; *Darkness Visible*, 1355-1356; *Fire Down Below*, 1356-1357; *Free Fall*, 1353; *The Inheritors*, 1351-1352; *Lord of the Flies*, 1350- 1351, 3768; *The Paper Men*, 1357; *Pincher Martin*, 1352-1353; *The Pyramid*, 1354-1355; *Rites of Passage*, 1356; *The Spire*, 1353-1354.
Goldsmith, Oliver, 3736, 3782.
Golk (Stern), 3164-3165.
Gone with the Wind (Mitchell), 3836-3837.
Gonzalez, N. V. M., 1359-1365; *The Bamboo Dancers*, 1363-1364; *Children of the Ash-Covered Loam*, 1359; *Look, Stranger, On This Island Now*, 1359-1360; *A Season of Grace*, 1362-1363; *Seven Hills Away*, 1359; *The Winds of April*, 1362.
Good Apprentice, The (Murdoch), 2455-2456.
Good as Gold (Heller), 1592.
Good Companions, The (Priestley), 2714-2715.
Good Day to Die, A (Harrison), 1537.
Good Earth, The (Buck), 435, 437-439.
Good Morning, Midnight (Rhys), 2819.
Good Soldier, The (Ford, F.), 1168-1171.
Good Spirit of Laurel Ridge, The (Stuart), 3227-3228.
Good Terrorist, The (Lessing), 2040.
Goodman, Paul, 1366-1377; *The Dead of Spring*, 1372-1373; *The Empire City*, 1369-1374; *The Grand Piano*, 1369-1371; *The Holy Terror*, 1373-1374; *Making Do*, 1374-1376; *The State of Nature*, 1371-1372.
Goosefoot (McGinley), 2191, 2192.
Gordimer, Nadine, 1378-1394; *Burger's Daughter*, 1389-1391; *The Conservationist*, 1387-1389; *A Guest of Honor*, 1386-1387; *July's People*, 1391-1392; *The Late Bourgeois World*, 1385- 1386; *The Lying Days*, 1381-1382; *Occasion for Loving*, 1384-1385; *A Sport of Nature*, 1392-1393; *A World of Strangers*, 1382-1384.

Gordon, Caroline, 1395-1404; *Aleck Maury, Sportsman*, 1398; *The Garden of Adonis*, 1399-1400; *The Glory of Hera*, 1402; *Green Centuries*, 1400; *The Malefactors*, 1402; *None Shall Look Back*, 1398-1399; *Penhally*, 1397-1398; *The Strange Children*, 1401; *The Women on the Porch*, 1400-1401.

Gossip from the Forest (Keneally), 1841-1842.

Gothic novel, 42-44, 46, 166-167, 409-410, 2055, 2057, 2329, 2774-2775, 2777-2778, 2781-2783, 3015-3016, **3823-3834, 3885.**

Gothic romance, 408-409.

Goy, The (Harris, M.), 1517-1518.

Grace Abounding to the Chief of Sinners (Bunyan), 456-458.

Grain of Wheat, A (Ngugi wa Thiong'o), 2504-2506.

Grand Piano, The (Goodman), 1369-1371.

Grandissimes, The (Cable), 526-527.

Grandmothers, The (Wescott), 3505-3507.

Grapes of Wrath, The (Steinbeck), 3158-3159, 3770.

Grass Harp, The (Capote), 558-559.

Grass Is Singing, The (Lessing), 2034-2035.

Grateful to Life and Death. See *English Teacher, The.*

Grau, Shirley Ann, 1405-1414; *The Condor Passes*, 1410-1411; *Evidence of Love*, 1411-1413; *The Hard Blue Sky*, 1408; *The House on Coliseum Street*, 1408; *The Keepers of the House*, 1409-1410.

Graves, Caroline, 683-684.

Graves, Robert, 1415-1429, 3838-3839; *The Antigua Stamp*, 1419; *Claudius the God*, 1424-1425; *Count Belisarius*, 1422-1423; *Hercules, My Shipmate*, 1425; *Homer's Daughter*, 1426; *I, Claudius*, 1424, 3838-3839; *The Islands of Unwisdom*, 1420-1421; *King Jesus*, 1425-1426; *My Head! My Head!*, 1418; *No Decency Left*, 1418-1419; *Sergeant Lamb's America*, 1420; *The Story of Marie Powell, Wife to Mr. Milton*, 1421-1422; *They Hanged My Saintly Billy*, 1419-1420; *Watch the North Wind Rise*, 1426.

Graveyard for Lunatics, A (Bradbury), 361-362.

Gravity's Rainbow (Pynchon), 2765, 2770-2771, 3771, 3777.

"Great American Novel, The" (De Forest), 834-835.

Great American Novel, The (Roth), 2900.

Great Circle (Aiken), 30-31, 32-33.

Great Gatsby, The (Fitzgerald), 1138, 1143-1146, 3768, 3796, 3799.

Great Jones Street (DeLillo), 864-865.

Great Meadow, The (Roberts), 2873-2874.

Great Victorian Collection, The (Moore, B.), 2397-2398.

Great World, The (Malouf), 2293.

Greek literature, 2808-2815.

Green, Henry, 1430-1438; *Blindness*, 1433-1434; *Loving*, 1434-1436; *Nothing*, 1436-1437.

Green Centuries (Gordon), 1400.

Green Man, The (Amis, K.), 94-95.

Green Mansions (Hudson), 1661-1663.

Green Water, Green Sky (Gallant), 1251-1252.

Green Years, The (Cronin), 786, 792-794.

Greene, Graham, 1439-1449, 3768, 3771; *Brighton Rock*, 1443-1445; *The Heart of the Matter*, 1445-1446; *The Human Factor*, 1446-1447; *The Power and the Glory*, 1447; *The Quiet American*, 1447.

Greene, Robert, 3722.

Greenmantle (Buchan), 427-428.

Grendel (Gardner), 1273-1274.

Grey, Zane, 3850-3851.

Griffin's Way (Yerby), 3694-3695.

Griffith, George, 3866-3867.

Grimmelshausen, H. J. C. von, 3805.

Grimus (Rushdie), 2919.

Grotesque, **3885.**

Group, The (McCarthy, M.), 2153-2154.

Grove, Frederick Philip, 1450-1459; *Consider Her Ways*, 1450; *Fruits of the Earth*, 1456-1457; *A Search for America*, 1454-1456; *Settlers of the Marsh*, 1452-1454.

Groves of Academe, The (McCarthy, M.), 2152-2153.

Gryll Grange (Peacock), 2623-2624.

Guard of Honor (Cozzens), 767-768.

Guerillas (Naipaul), 2475-2476.

Guest of Honor, A (Gordimer), 1386-1387.

Guffey, George, 270.
Guiana Quartet, The (Harris, W.),
    1526-1530.
Guide, The (Narayan), 2484-2485.
Guilleragues, Gabriel, 3811.
Gulliver's Travels (Swift), 3262-3264.
Guy Rivers (Simms), 3042.
Guzmán de Alfarache (Alemán), 3804.

Hacker, Marilyn, 850-851.
Haggard, H. Rider, 3860.
Hail and Farewell (Moore, G.),
    2402-2403.
Hall of Mirrors, A (Stone), 3200.
Hall-Stevenson, John, 3174.
Hammett, Dashiell, 1460-1470, 3771,
    3845-3846; *The Dain Curse*, 1465; *The
    Glass Key*, 1467-1468; *The Maltese
    Falcon*, 1465-1466, 3846; *Red Harvest*,
    1462-1463, 1464-1465; *The Thin Man*,
    1463-1464, 1468-1469, 3846.
Handful of Dust, A (Waugh), 3463-3465.
Handmaid's Tale, The (Atwood), 140-141.
Handy, Lowney, 1799-1800.
Hanley, James, 1471-1480; *Boy*,
    1474-1475; *Broken Water*, 1473; *The
    Closed Harbour*, 1478; *A Dream
    Journey*, 1478-1477; *The Fury
    Chronicle*, 1475-1477; *Hollow Sea*, 1471;
    Levine, 1478; *The Ocean*, 1477-1478;
    Sailors Song, 1478.
Hannah, Barry, 1481-1488; *Boomerang*,
    1487; *Geronimo Rex*, 1482-1483; *Hey
    Jack!*, 1487; *Nightwatchmen*, 1483-1484;
    Ray, 1484-1485; *The Tennis Handsome*,
    1485-1486.
Happy Valley (White), 3546-3547.
Hard Blue Sky, The (Grau), 1408.
Hard Life, The (O'Brien, F.), 2557.
Hard Times (Dickens), 3787.
Hardwick, Elizabeth, 1489-1494; *The
    Ghostly Lover*, 1492; *The Simple Truth*,
    1492-1493; *Sleepless Nights*, 1493.
Hardy, Thomas, 1495-1513, 3742, 3743,
    3757-3758, 3788; *Far from the Madding
    Crowd*, 1500-1502; *Jude the Obscure*,
    1510-1512, 3758, 3788; *The Mayor of
    Casterbridge*, 1506-1507, 3758; *The
    Return of the Native*, 1504-1506; *Tess of
    the D'Urbervilles*, 1507-1510, 3758; *The
    Woodlanders*, 1502-1503.
Harknett, Terry. *See* Gilman, George.

Harland's Half Acre (Malouf), 2292.
Harness Room, The (Hartley), 1553.
Harp of a Thousand Strings (Davis),
    808-809.
Harris, Mark, 1514-1523; *The Goy*,
    1517-1518; *Something About a Soldier*,
    1519-1521; *The Southpaw*, 1518-1519;
    Wake Up, Stupid, 1521-1522.
Harris, Wilson, 1524-1533; *The Angel at
    the Gate*, 1531; *Ascent to Omai*, 1531;
    Black Marsden, 1531; *Carnival*, 1531;
    Companions of the Day and Night, 1531;
    *Da Silva da Silva's Cultivated
    Wilderness and Genesis of the Clowns*,
    1531; *The Eye of the Scarecrow*,
    1530-1531; *The Far Journey of Ouidin*,
    1529; *The Guiana Quartet*, 1526-1530;
    Heartland, 1530; *Palace of the Peacock*,
    1526-1529; *The Secret Ladder*, 1530;
    The Tree of the Sun, 1531-1532;
    Tumatumari, 1531; *The Waiting Room*,
    1530-1531; *The Whole Armour*,
    1529-1530.
Harrison, Jim, 1534-1549; *Dalva*, 1546;
    Farmer, 1537-1539; *A Good Day to Die*,
    1537; *Legends of the Fall*, 1541-1542;
    The Man Who Gave Up His Name,
    1540-1541; *Revenge*, 1539-1540;
    Sundog, 1544; *Warlock*, 1542-1544;
    Wolf, 1536-1537; *The Woman Lit by
    Fireflies*, 1546-1548.
Hartley, L. P., 1550-1557; *The Boat*,
    1554-1555; *Eustace and Hilda*, 1554;
    The Go-Between, 1555-1556; *The
    Harness Room*, 1553; *The Shrimp and
    the Anemone*, 1553; *The Sixth Heaven*,
    1553-1554.
Hatter's Castle (Cronin), 781, 783-784,
    785-786, 787-788, 794.
Hawkes, John, 1558-1568; *The Blood
    Oranges*, 1562-1564; *The Cannibal*,
    1561-1562; *The Passion Artist*,
    1565-1567; *Travesty*, 1564-1565.
Hawkline Monster, The (Brautigan),
    376-377.
Hawthorne, Nathaniel, 1569-1584,
    3749, 3798, 3831; *The Blithedale
    Romance*, 1579-1580, 3798; "The
    Custom House," 1575-1576; *Fanshawe*,
    1574-1576; *The House of the Seven
    Gables*, 1577-1579, 3831; *The Marble

Faun, 1580-1583; *The Scarlet Letter*, 1575-1577, 3831.
Haycox, Ernest, 3852-3853.
Hazard of New Fortunes, A (Howells), 1652-1654.
H. D., 51-52.
He Sent Forth a Raven (Roberts), 2877-2878.
Headlong Hall (Peacock), 2617-2618.
Healers, The (Armah), 129-130.
Healing Art, The (Wilson, A. N.), 3582-3583.
Hearing Secret Harmonies (Powell, A.), 2681.
Heart for the Gods of Mexico, A (Aiken), 31, 34-35.
Heart Is a Lonely Hunter, The (McCullers), 2163-2164.
Heart of Darkness (Conrad), 714, 718-722, 3756, 3875-3876.
Heart of Midlothian, The (Scott), 2995-3000.
Heart of the Matter, The (Greene), 1445-1446.
Heartland (Harris, W.), 1530.
Heat and Dust (Jhabvala), 1757.
Heat of the Day, The (Bowen), 323-324.
Heaven's My Destination (Wilder), 3574-3575.
Hebraic/Homeric styles, **3885.**
Heller, Joseph, 1585-1594, 3808; *Catch-22*, 1588-1590, 3808; *God Knows*, 1592-1593; *Good as Gold*, 1592; *Picture This*, 1593-1594; *Something Happened*, 1591-1592.
Hellman, Lillian, 1461-1462.
Hello, America (Ballard), 196.
Héloise and Abélard (Moore, G.), 2409.
Hemingway, Ernest, 1595-1607, 3763, 3769-3770, 3797, 3799, 3875; "Big Two-Hearted River," 1597-1598, 3763, 3769; *A Farewell to Arms*, 1601-1603; *For Whom the Bell Tolls*, 1604-1605; *The Old Man and the Sea*, 1605-1607, 3769-3770, 3875; *The Sun Also Rises*, 1598-1601, 3769.
Hemlock and After (Wilson, Angus), 3590-3591.
Henderson the Rain King (Bellow), 280-282, 3775.
Hercules, My Shipmate (Graves), 1425.
Heritage of the Desert, The (Grey), 3850.

Heroes and Villains (Carter), 568.
Herself Surprised (Cary), 578-579.
Hersey, John, 1608-1616; *A Bell for Adano*, 1610, 1613-1614; *Hiroshima*, 1610-1611; *Into the Valley*, 1610; *Men on Bataan*, 1610; *The Wall*, 1614-1615.
Herzog (Bellow), 282-283.
Hetty Dorval (Wilson, E.), 3602.
Hey Jack! (Hannah), 1487.
Hiding Place. See *Homewood Trilogy, The*
High Rise (Ballard), 195.
High Road, The (O'Brien, E.), 2548.
" 'High-Toned Gentleman,' The" (De Forest), 834-835.
High Window, The (Chandler), 604, 606.
Highwater, Jamake, 1617-1627; *Anpao*, 1619-1620; *Eyes of Darkness*, 1625; *The Ghost Horse Cycle*, 1625-1626; *I Wear the Morning Star*, 1625-1626; *Journey to the Sky*, 1620-1622; *Legend Days*, 1625; *The Sun, He Dies*, 1622-1624.
Hilda Lessways (Bennett), 299.
Hind's Kidnap (McElroy), 2183-2184.
Hiroshima (Hersey), 1610-1611.
Historical criticism, **3885.**
Historical novel, **3835-3841, 3885.**
History and Remarkable Life of the Truly Honorable Col Jacque, Commonly Call'd Col Jack, The. See *Colonel Jack*.
History of Henry Esmond, Esquire, The (Thackeray), 3274-3276.
History of the Adventures of Joseph Andrews, and of His Friend Mr. Abraham Adams. See *Joseph Andrews*.
History of the Life of the Late Mr. Jonathan Wild the Great, The. See *Jonathan Wild*.
History of Mr. Polly, The (Wells), 3483-3484.
History of Pendennis, The (Thackeray), 3273-3274.
History of the Nun, The (Behn), 271.
History of the World in 10½ Chapters, A (Barnes), 215.
History of Tom Jones, a Foundling, The. See *Tom Jones*.
H. M. Pulham, Esquire (Marquand), 2302-2303.
Hoagland, Edward, 1628-1635; *Cat Man*, 1630; *The Circle Home*, 1630-1631; *Peacock's Tail*, 1631-1632; *Seven Rivers West*, 1632-1633.
Hobbit, The (Tolkien), 3298-3299, 3862.

Hoffman, E. T. A., 3874.
Hogg, James, 3858.
Hollow Sea (Hanley), 1471.
Holy Grail, The, 2284.
Holy Terror, The (Goodman), 1373-1374.
Home as Found (Cooper), 736-737.
Home Place, The (Morris), 2412.
Home Truths (Gallant), 1251.
Homer's Daughter (Graves), 1426.
Homewood Trilogy, The (Wideman), 3561-3562, 3565-3567.
Hondo (L'Amour), 1932, 3854.
Honest John Vane (De Forest), 838.
Honey in the Horn (Davis), 807-808.
Honourable Schoolboy, The (Le Carré), 1990-1991.
Horgan, Paul, 1636-1643; *A Distant Trumpet*, 1639-1640; *Far from Cibola*, 1638-1639; *Things as They Are*, 1640; *Whitewater*, 1640-1641.
Horse and His Boy, The (Lewis, C.), 2049.
Horseman, Pass By (McMurtry), 2220.
Horse's Mouth, The (Cary), 578, 580.
Hotel, The (Bowen), 320.
Hotel du Lac (Brookner), 402-404.
Hotel New Hampshire, The (Irving, J.), 1700-1702.
Hound of the Baskervilles, The (Doyle), 974.
House Behind the Cedars, The (Chesnutt), 634-636.
House by the Churchyard, The (Le Fanu), 1999-2000.
House for Mr. Biswas, A (Naipaul), 2473-2474.
House in Paris, The (Bowen), 321-322.
House of Children, A (Cary), 577-578.
House of Five Talents, The (Auchincloss), 147-148.
House of Incest (Nin), 2514-2515.
House of Mirth, The (Wharton), 3534, 3535-3536.
House of the Four Winds, The (Buchan), 429.
House of the Prophet, The (Auchincloss), 153-154.
House of the Seven Gables, The (Hawthorne), 1577-1579, 3831.
House of the Solitary Maggot, The (Purdy), 2747, 2748-2749.
House on Coliseum Street, The (Grau), 1408.

Householder, The (Jhabvala), 1757.
How Far Can You Go? (Lodge), 2092.
How It Is (Beckett), 262-264.
Howard, Robert E., 3862.
Howard's End (Forster), 1191-1193.
Howells, William Dean, 1644-1655, 3751, 3757, 3795; *A Hazard of New Fortunes*, 1652-1654; *A Modern Instance*, 1649-1651; *The Rise of Silas Lapham*, 1651-1652, 3757, 3795.
Hudson, W. H., 1656-1664; *A Crystal Age*, 1660-1661; *Green Mansions*, 1661-1663; *A Little Boy Lost*, 1663; "Marta Riquelme," 1659; "Ombú, El," 1659; *The Purple Land*, 1658- 1660.
Huge Season, The (Morris), 2419-2420.
Human Age, The (Lewis, W.), 2085-2086.
Human Comedy, The (Saroyan), 2946, 2951-2952.
Human Factor, The (Greene), 1446-1447.
Human Season, The (Wallant), 3419-3420.
Human Vibration (Richter), 2860-2861.
Humboldt's Gift (Bellow), 285-286.
Humor, 882-883.
Humphry Clinker (Smollett), 3075-3076.
Hunters, The (Salter), 2940-2941.
Huntingtower (Buchan), 428-429.
Hurry Home (Wideman), 3563-3564.
Hurry on Down (Wain), 3395-3397, 3808.
Hurston, Zora Neale, 1665-1673; *Jonah's Gourd Vine*, 1669, 1670-1671; *Moses, Man of the Mountain*, 1669; *Mules and Men*, 1668; *Seraph on the Sewanee*, 1669; *Their Eyes Were Watching God*, 1669, 1671-1673.
Huxley, Aldous, 1674-1689, 3767, 3798, 3868; *After Many a Summer Dies the Swan*, 1683-1684; *Antic Hay*, 1677-1678; *Ape and Essence*, 1684-1685; *Brave New World*, 1681-1682, 3798; *Crome Yellow*, 1676-1677; *Eyeless in Gaza*, 1682-1683; *The Genius and the Goddess*, 1685-1686; *Island*, 1686-1687; *Point Counter Point*, 1679-1681; *Those Barren Leaves*, 1678-1679; *Time Must Have a Stop*, 1684.

I Am Elijah Thrush (Purdy), 2747-2748.
I Am Mary Dunne (Moore, B.), 2396-2397.
I, Claudius (Graves), 1424, 3838-3839.

I Hardly Knew You (O'Brien, E.), 2547-2548.
I Wear the Morning Star (Highwater), 1625-1626.
Ice (Kavan), 1837-1838.
Ice Age, The (Drabble), 990-991.
Ida, A Novel (Stein), 3148.
Ides of March, The (Wilder), 3575-3576.
If Morning Ever Comes (Tyler), 3334.
Ill Seen Ill Said (Beckett), 263.
Illustrated Man, The (Bradbury), 359.
I'm Expecting to Live Quite Soon (West, P.), 3523-3524.
Imaginary Friends (Lurie), 2128-2133.
Imaginary Life, An (Malouf), 2290-2291.
Imagist poetry, 51.
Imago (Butler, O.), 498-499.
Implied author, **3885.**
Impressionism, 580, 771.
In a Free State (Naipaul), 2475.
In A Shallow Grave (Purdy), 2749.
In Any Case (Stern), 3165-3166.
In Chancery (Galsworthy), 1263-1264.
In Cold Blood (Capote), 560-561.
In Dubious Battle (Steinbeck), 3155-3156, 3770.
In My Father's House (Gaines), 1244-1245.
In Search of Love and Beauty (Jhabvala), 1754.
In the Beginning (Potok), 2663-2664.
In the Days of the Comet (Wells), 3483.
In the Heart of the Country (Coetzee), 674-675.
"In the Heart of the Heart of the Country" (Gass), 1312.
In the Heart of the Heart of the Country and Other Stories (Gass), 1312.
In the Hollow of His Hand (Purdy), 2750-2751.
In the Time of Greenbloom (Fielding, G.), 1113, 1114.
In the Valley (Frederic), 1218, 1220.
In Their Wisdom (Snow), 3090.
In Watermelon Sugar (Brautigan), 375.
Industrialism, 115-116.
Infernal Desire Machines of Doctor Hoffman, The (Carter), 568.
Inhabitants, The (Morris), 2412.
Inheritors, The (Golding), 1351-1352.
Ink Truck, The (Kennedy), 1851-1852.
Innocent, The (Jones, M.), 1810-1812.
Innocent Blood (James, P.), 1734-1735.

Innocent Traveller, The (Wilson, E.), 3603.
Innommable, L'. See *Unnamable, The*.
Inside, Outside (Wouk), 3674-3677.
Insular Possession (Mo), 3793.
Interior monologue, **3885.**
International theme, 1719-1720, 1723-1725.
Interpreters, The (Soyinka), 3094-3097.
Into the Valley (Hersey), 1610.
Invisible Man (Ellison), 1055-1063, 3776, 3808.
Invisible Man, The (Wells), 3482.
Invitation to the Waltz (Lehmann), 2018-2020.
Irish literary revival, 2553.
Iron Heel, The (London), 2101.
Ironweed (Kennedy), 1855-1856.
Irrealism, **3886.**
Irving, John, 1690-1705; *The Cider House Rules,* 1702-1703; *The Hotel New Hampshire,* 1700-1702; *The 158-Pound Marriage,* 1697-1698; *A Prayer for Owen Meany,* 1703-1704; *Setting Free the Bears,* 1694-1696; *The Water-Method Man,* 1696-1697; *The World According to Garp,* 1698-1700.
Irving, Washington, 3799-3800.
Ishiguro, Kazuo, 1706-1712, 3792-3793; *An Artist of the Floating World,* 1708-1709, 3793; *A Pale View of Hills,* 1707-1708, 3793; *The Remains of the Day,* 1709-1711, 3793.
Island (Huxley), 1686-1687.
Island of Dr. Moreau, The (Wells), 3482.
Islands of Unwisdom, The (Graves), 1420-1421.
Isolation, 1573-1574.
It (King), 1892-1893.
Italian, The (Radcliffe), 2781-2782.
Its Image on the Mirror (Gallant), 1252.

Jack of Newbury (Deloney), 3723, 3724.
Jacob's Room (Woolf), 3648-3649.
James, Henry, 1713-1730, 3743, 3750, 3751, 3755-3757, 3763, 3791-3792, 3800, 3874-3875; *The Ambassadors,* 1715, 1727-1728; *The American Scene,* 1714; *The Bostonians,* 1725-1727; *Daisy Miller,* 1721-1722; *The Europeans,* 3750; *The Golden Bowl,* 3755-3756; *The Portrait of a Lady,* 1722-1725; *The Turn of the Screw,* 3874-3875; *Washington Square,* 1720.

James, P. D., 1731-1738; *Death of an Expert Witness*, 1733-1734; *Devices and Desires*, 1736-1737; *Innocent Blood*, 1734-1735; *Shroud for a Nightingale*, 1732-1733; *A Taste for Death*, 1735-1736; *An Unsuitable Job for a Woman*, 1733.
James, William, 3763.
Jane Eyre (Brontë, C.), 385-386.
Jealous God, The (Braine), 369, 370-371.
Jeeves and Wooster novels, (Wodehouse), 3613-3615.
Jennie Gerhardt (Dreiser), 999-1001.
Jeremy's Version (Purdy), 2747.
Jerusalem the Golden (Drabble), 982-985.
Jest of God, A (Laurence), 1946-1947.
Jewett, Sarah Orne, 1739-1751; *A Country Doctor*, 1743-1746; *The Country of the Pointed Firs*, 1746-1748; *Deephaven*, 1741-1743; *The Tory Lover*, 1748-1750.
Jhabvala, Ruth Prawer, 1752-1759; *Amrita*, 1753-1754; *A Backward Place*, 1756; *Esmond in India*, 1754-1755; *Get Ready for Battle*, 1756; *Heat and Dust*, 1757; *The Householder*, 1757; *In Search of Love and Beauty*, 1754; *The Nature of Passion*, 1754; *Travelers*, 1756-1757.
Jingling in the Wind (Roberts), 2877.
John Brown (Warren), 3438.
John Macnab (Buchan), 429-430.
Johnno (Malouf), 2289-2290.
Johnson, Charles, 1760-1769; *Faith and the Good Thing*, 1763-1765; *Middle Passage*, 1766-1768; *Oxherding Tale*, 1765-1766.
Johnson, Diane, 1770-1777; *Burning*, 1773; *Fair Game*, 1771; *Loving Hands at Home*, 1771-1773; *Lying Low*, 1774-1775; *Persian Nights*, 1775-1776; *The Shadow Knows*, 1773-1774.
Johnson, Samuel, 1778-1789, 3734, 3735; *Rasselas*, 1783-1787.
Jolley, Elizabeth, 1790-1796; *Foxybaby*, 1793-1794; *Milk and Honey*, 1793; *Miss Peabody's Inheritance*, 1793; *Mr. Scobie's Riddle*, 1792-1793; *Palomino*, 1791-1792; *The Well*, 1794-1795.
Jonah's Gourd Vine (Hurston), 1669, 1670-1671.
Jonathan Wild (Fielding, H.), 1130-1131.
Jones, James, 1797-1807; *From Here to Eternity*, 1797, 1802-1804; *The Thin Red Line*, 1804-1805; *Whistle*, 1805-1806.
Jones, Madison, 1808-1819; *A Buried Land*, 1813-1814; *A Cry of Absence*, 1815-1816; *An Exile*, 1814-1815; *Forest of the Night*, 1812-1813; *The Innocent*, 1810-1812; *Last Things*, 1818; *Passage Through Gehenna*, 1816-1817; *Season of the Strangler*, 1817-1818.
Jordan County (Foote), 1160-1162.
"Joscelyn" (Simms), 3040-3041.
Joseph Andrews (Fielding, H.), 1128-1130, 3815.
Joshua Then and Now (Richler), 2849, 2852-2854.
Journal of the Plague Year, A (Defoe), 819-821.
Journey to the Sky (Highwater), 1620-1622.
Joyce, James, 1820-1832, 3765-3766, 3807; *Dubliners*, 1820; *Finnegans Wake*, 1829-1831, 3765-3766; *A Portrait of the Artist as a Young Man*, 1824-1826, 3765; *Ulysses*, 1826-1829, 3765, 3807.
JR (Gaddis), 1230, 1233-1234.
Jude the Obscure (Hardy), 1510-1512, 3758, 3788.
Judgment of Paris, The (Vidal), 3372-3373.
Judith Hearne (Moore, B.), 2391-2393.
Julian (Vidal), 3373-3374.
Julie: Or, The New Heloïse, Letters from Two Lovers (Rousseau), 3816-3817.
July's People (Gordimer), 1391-1392.
Jungle, The (Sinclair), 3050-3052, 3761, 3797.
Junkie (Burroughs), 486.
Jurgen (Cabell), 513, 517-519.
Just Above My Head (Baldwin), 183-188.
Just and the Unjust, The (Cozzens), 762, 767.
Justine. See *Alexandria Quartet, The*.
Juxtaposition, 1092.

Kafka, Franz, 3877.
Kamera obskura. See *Laughter in the Dark*.
Kanthapura (Rao), 2788-2790.
Kate Beaumont (De Forest), 837-838.
Kate Vaiden (Price), 2701-2702.
Kavan, Anna, 1833-1839; *A Charmed Circle*, 1835; *The Dark Sisters*, 1835; *Eagles' Nest*, 1836-1837; *Ice*, 1837-1838;

Let Me Alone, 1835; *A Scarcity of Love*, 1836; *Who Are You?*, 1837.
Keep the Change (McGuane), 2204-2205.
Keepers of the House, The (Grau), 1409-1410.
Keneally, Thomas, 1840-1849; *Blood Red, Sister Rose*, 1843-1844, 1846; *The Chant of Jimmie Blacksmith*, 1843; *A Dutiful Daughter*, 1846-1847; *A Family Madness*, 1847; *Gossip from the Forest*, 1841-1842; *Passenger*, 1844, 1845; *Schindler's List*, 1841; *Season in Purgatory*, 1841, 1842; *Three Cheers for the Paraclete*, 1845; *To Asmara*, 1847-1848; *A Victim of the Aurora*, 1844-1845.
Kennedy, William, 1850-1858; *The Albany Cycle*, 1852-1856; *Billy Phelan's Greatest Game*, 1854; *The Ink Truck*, 1851-1852; *Ironweed*, 1855-1856; *Legs*, 1852-1854; *Quinn's Book*, 1856-1857.
Kepler (Banville), 204-205.
Kerouac, Jack, 1859-1870, 3808; *Dharma Bums*, 1868-1869; *On the Road*, 1865-1867, 3808; *The Subterraneans*, 1867-1868; *The Town and the City*, 1863-1865.
Kesey, Ken, 1871-1882, 3808; *One Flew over the Cuckoo's Nest*, 1877-1879, 3808; *Sometimes a Great Notion*, 1879-1881.
Key to the Door (Sillitoe), 3029-3030.
Key to Uncle Tom's Cabin, A (Stowe), 3209, 3210.
Keys of the Kingdom, The (Cronin), 786, 791-792, 794.
Kidnapped (Stevenson), 3194.
Kill Price, The (Yglesias), 3707-3708.
Killing Ground, The (Settle), 3009-3010.
Killing Time (Berger), 308-309.
Killshot (Leonard), 2026, 2029.
Kim (Kipling), 1904-1906, 3789.
Kindly Ones, The (Powell, A.), 2678-2679.
Kindred (Butler, O.), 495.
King, The (Barthelme), 236-237.
King, Stephen, 1883-1897, 3863; *Carrie*, 1886-1887; *Christine*, 1889-1890; *Cujo*, 1889; *The Dark Half*, 1894-1895; *The Eyes of the Dragon*, 1893; *It*, 1892-1893; *Misery*, 1893-1894; *Pet Sematary*, 1890-1892; *'Salem's Lot*, 1887-1888; *The Shining*, 1888; *The Stand*, 1888-1889.

King Coal (Sinclair), 3053-3054.
King Coffin (Aiken), 30-31, 33-34.
King Jesus (Graves), 1425-1426.
King Must Die, The (Renault), 2811-2812.
King of the Fields, The (Singer), 3065-3066.
King, Queen, Knave (Nabokov), 2462.
Kipling, Rudyard, 1898-1907, 3789; *Captains Courageous*, 1904; *Kim*, 1904-1906, 3789; *The Light That Failed*, 1903; *The Naulahka*, 1903-1904.
Kipps (Wells), 3483.
Kiss of Kin, The (Settle), 3004, 3006, 3010.
Kit Brandon (Anderson), 116.
Kittredge, G. L., 2280-2281.
Know Nothing (Settle), 3006-3007.
Koestler, Arthur, 1908-1917; *The Age of Longing*, 1914-1915; *Arrival and Departure*, 1913-1914; *The Call Girls*, 1915-1916; *Darkness at Noon*, 1912-1913; *The Ghost in the Machine*, 1916; *The Gladiators*, 1911-1912; *Thieves in the Night*, 1914; *The Yogi and the Commissar and Other Essays*, 1910.
Korol', dama, valet. See *King, Queen, Knave.*
Kosinski, Jerzy, 1918-1928; *Being There*, 1925-1926; *Blind Date*, 1926-1928; *The Future Is Ours, Comrade*, 1920; *No Third Path*, 1920; *The Painted Bird*, 1921-1923; *Steps*, 1923-1925.
Kuntsnmakher fun Lublin, Der. See *Magician of Lublin, The.*

Labyrinthine Ways, The. See *Power and the Glory, The.*
Laclos, Pierra Choderlos de, 3819-3822.
Ladders to Fire (Nin), 2516, 2518.
Lady, The (Richter), 2864.
Lady Chatterley's Lover (Lawrence), 1974-1977, 3767.
L'Amour, Louis, 1929-1939, 3854; *Bendigo Shafter*, 1936; *The Broken Gun*, 1935; *The Daybreakers*, 1933-1934; *Down the Long Hills*, 1935-1936; *Fair Blows the Wind*, 1934; *The First Fast Draw*, 1933; *Hondo*, 1932, 3854; *Last of the Breed*, 1936; *Last Stand at Papago Wells*, 1932-1933; *The Lonesome Gods*, 1936; *Sackett's Land*, 1934; *Shalako*,

3854; *Sitka*, 1933; *The Walking Drum*, 1936.
Lancelot (Percy), 2635-2637.
Land of Spices, The (O'Brien, K.), 2564-2565.
Lanny Budd series, 3055.
Last Adam, The (Cozzens), 765.
Last Battle, The (Lewis, C.), 2050.
Last Days of Louisiana Red, The (Reed), 2803-2804.
Last Gentleman, The (Percy), 2633-2634.
Last Man, The (Shelley), 3018-3020.
Last of the Breed (L'Amour), 1936.
Last of the Mohicans, The (Cooper), 736, 741-743.
Last of the Wine, The (Renault), 2811.
Last Picture Show, The (McMurtry), 2221-2222.
Last September, The (Bowen), 320-321.
Last Stand at Papago Wells (L'Amour), 1932-1933.
Last Things (Jones, M.), 1818.
Late Bourgeois World, The (Gordimer), 1385-1386.
Late George Apley, The (Marquand), 2302.
Laughing Matter, The (Saroyan), 2953-2954.
Laughter in the Dark (Nabokov), 2462-2463.
Laurence, Margaret, 1940-1950; *The Diviners*, 1943-1944, 1947-1949; *The Fire-Dwellers*, 1947; *A Jest of God*, 1946-1947; *The Prophet's Camel Bell*, 1942; *The Stone Angel*, 1944-1946; *This Side Jordan*, 1944.
Lawd Today (Wright), 3683-3684.
Lawrence, D. H., 1951-1980, 3766-3767; *Fantasia of the Unconscious*, 1957; *Lady Chatterley's Lover*, 1974-1977, 3767; *The Plumed Serpent*, 1958, 1970-1974; *The Rainbow*, 1962-1964, 3767; *Sons and Lovers*, 1958-1962, 3767; *Women in Love*, 1964-1969.
Lawrence, Frieda von Richthoven, 1954-1955.
Lawrence L'Imposteur (Aldington), 53.
Lawton Girl, The (Frederic), 1220.
Lazarillo de Tormes, 3803-3804.
Leatherstocking Tales (Cooper), 736, 3748, 3749, 3849.
Le Carré, John, 1981-1994, 3774, 3789; *Call for the Dead*, 1985-1986; *The*

Honourable Schoolboy, 1990-1991; *The Little Drummer Girl*, 1992-1993; *The Looking Glass War*, 1988-1989; *A Murder of Quality*, 1986; *A Perfect Spy*, 1993; *The Russia House*, 1993; *A Small Town in Germany*, 1989; *Smiley's People*, 1991-1992; *The Spy Who Came in from the Cold*, 1986-1988; *Tinker, Tailor, Soldier, Spy*, 1989-1990.
Lee, Manfred B., 3845.
Le Fanu, Joseph Sheridan, 1995-2004, 3859; *The Cock and Anchor*, 1998; *The Fortunes of Colonel Torlogh O'Brien*, 1998-1999; *The House by the Churchyard*, 1999-2000; *Uncle Silas*, 2001-2002; *Willing to Die*, 2002-2003; *Wylder's Hand*, 2000-2001.
Left Hand of Darkness, The (Le Guin), 2010-2011.
Legend Days (Highwater), 1625.
"Legend of Sleepy Hollow, The" (Irving, W.), 3800.
Legends of the Fall (Harrison), 1541-1542.
Legs (Kennedy), 1852-1854.
Le Guin, Ursula K., 2005-2015, 3870; *City of Illusions*, 2009-2010; *The Dispossessed*, 2011-2012; The Earthsea series, 2013-2014; *The Left Hand of Darkness*, 2010-2011; *Rocannon's World*, 2008-2009; *Tehanu*, 2013-2014.
Lehmann, Rosamond, 2016-2024; *The Ballad and the Source*, 2020-2023; *Dusty Answer*, 2017-2018; *Invitation to the Waltz*, 2018-2020.
Leiden des jungen Werthers, Die. See *Sorrows of Young Werther, The*.
Leila (Donleavy), 950.
Leonard, Elmore, 2025-2031; *Fifty-two Pickup*, 2027, 2028; *Freaky Deaky*, 2029; *Get Shorty*, 2029-2030; *Killshot*, 2026, 2029; *Swag*, 2028-2029.
Le Sage, Alain René, 3805.
Less Than Angels (Pym), 2756.
Lessing, Doris, 2032-2042, 3774, 3775, 3833; *Briefing for a Descent into Hell*, 2037; *Children of Violence*, 2035; *The Diaries of Jane Somers*, 2039-2040; *Documents Relating to the Sentimental Agents in the Volyen Empire*, 2039; *The Fifth Child*, 2040; *The Four-Gated City*, 2035, 3833; *The Golden Notebook*, 2036; *The Good Terrorist*, 2040; *The*

Grass is Singing, 2034-2035; *The Making of the Representative for Planet 8*, 2039; *Marriages Between Zones Three, Four, and Five*, 2038; *The Memoirs of a Survivor*, 2037-2038; *Shikasta*, 2038; *The Sirian Experiments*, 2038; *The Summer Before the Dark*, 2037.

Let It Come Down (Bowles), 329-330.

Let Me Alone (Kavan), 1835.

LETTERS (Barth), 229-231.

Letting Go (Roth), 2898-2899.

Lettres pesanes, Les. See *Persian Letters*.

Lettres portugaises. See *Portugese Letters*.

Letty Fox (Stead), 3119, 3122.

Levine (Hanley), 1478.

Lewes, George Henry, 1034-1035.

Lewis, C. S., 2043-2054, 3860; *The Horse and His Boy*, 2049; *The Last Battle*, 2050; *The Lion, the Witch, and the Wardrobe*, 2048-2049; *The Magician's Nephew*, 2049; *Out of the Silent Planet*, 2046; *Perelandra*, 2046-2047; *Prince Caspian*, 2049-2050; *The Silver Chair*, 2050; *That Hideous Strength*, 2047- 2048; *Till We Have Faces*, 2050-2051; *The Voyage of the Dawn Treader*, 2050.

Lewis, Matthew Gregory, 2055-2063, 3783, 3824-3825; *The Monk*, 2057-2061, 3824, 3828-3829.

Lewis, Sinclair, 2064-2078, 3761-3762; *Arrowsmith*, 2073-2074; *Babbitt*, 2071-2073; *Dodsworth*, 2076; *Elmer Gantry*, 2074-2076; *Main Street*, 2068-2071.

Lewis, Wyndham, 2079-2087, 3860; *The Apes of God*, 2082-2083; *The Childermass*, 2082-2083; *The Human Age*, 2085-2086; *Mrs. Dukes' Million*, 2083; *The Revenge for Love*, 2084; *Self Condemned*, 2084-2085; *Snooty Baronet*, 2083; *Tarr*, 2082.

Liaisons dangereuses, Les. See *Dangerous Acquaintances*.

Libra (DeLillo), 868-869.

Lie Down in Darkness (Styron), 3243, 3247-3249.

Life and Adventures of Martin Chuzzlewit, The. See *Martin Chuzzlewit*.

Life and Adventures of Nicholas Nickleby, The. See *Nicholas Nickleby*.

Life and Death of Mr. Badman, The (Bunyan), 458-459.

Life and Loves of a She-Devil, The (Weldon), 3475-3476.

Life and Opinions of Tristram Shandy, Gent., The. See *Tristram Shandy*.

Life and Strange Surprizing Adventures of Robinson Crusoe of York, Mariner, The. See *Robinson Crusoe*.

Life & Times of Michael K (Coetzee), 676-678.

Life Before Man (Atwood), 136-138.

Light in August (Faulkner), 1098-1102, 3772.

Light That Failed, The (Kipling), 1903.

Light Years (Salter), 2941-2942.

Lilly's Story (Wilson, E.), 3604-3606.

Lincoln (Vidal), 3375.

Linden Hills (Naylor), 2492.

Lindsay, David, 3860.

Lion Country. See *Book of Bebb, The*.

Lion, the Witch, and the Wardrobe, The (Lewis, C.), 2048-2049.

Literary impressionism, 1168, 2822-2823.

"Literature of Exhaustion, The" (Barth), 217.

"Literature of Replenishment, The" (Barth), 217.

Little Big Man (Berger), 307-308.

Little Boy Lost, A (Hudson), 1663.

Little Dorrit (Dickens), 910-911, 3787.

Little Drummer Girl, The (Le Carré), 1992-1993.

Little Norsk, A (Garland), 1289-1290.

Little Sister, The (Chandler), 604.

Living and the Dead, The (White), 3547.

Living, The Dying, and the Dead, The (Gilman), 3855.

Liza of Lambeth (Maugham), 2333.

Local colorists, **3886.**

Lockwood Concern, The (O'Hara), 2587-2589.

Locusts Have No King, The (Powell, D.), 2686-2687.

Lodge, David, 2088-2095; *The British Museum Is Falling Down*, 2091; *Changing Places*, 2091-2092; *Ginger, You're Barmy*, 2090-2091; *How Far Can You Go?*, 2092; *Nice Work*, 2093-2094; *Out of the Shelter*, 2091; *The Picturegoers*, 2090; *Small World*, 2092-2093.

Lodore (Shelley), 3020-3022.
Loitering with Intent (Spark), 3105, 3113-3115.
Lolita (Nabokov), 2465-2466.
London, Jack, 2096-2105; *The Call of the Wild*, 2098-2099; *The Iron Heel*, 2101; *Martin Eden*, 2101-2102; *The Sea-Wolf*, 2099-2100; *The Valley of the Moon*, 2103; *White Fang*, 2100.
London Fields (Amis, M.), 104-106.
Loneliness of the Long-Distance Runner, The (Sillitoe), 3028-3029.
Lonely Girl, The (O'Brien, E.), 2544.
Lonely Passion of Judith Hearne, The. See *Judith Hearne*.
Lonesome Dove (McMurtry), 2225-2228.
Lonesome Gods, The (L'Amour), 1936.
Long and Happy Life, A (Price), 2700, 2702-2703.
Long Day's Dying, A (Buechner), 444, 446-447.
Long Dream, The (Wright), 3688-3689.
Long Goodbye, The (Chandler), 604, 608-611.
Long March, The (Styron), 3249-3250.
Long Storm (Haycox), 3853.
Longest Journey, The (Forster), 1187-1189.
Look at Me (Brookner), 401-402.
Look Homeward, Angel (Wolfe), 3631, 3632-3634.
Look, Stranger, On This Island Now (Gonzalez), 1359-1360.
Looking Backward: 2000-1887 (Bellamy), 3866.
Looking Glass War, The (Le Carré), 1988-1989.
Lookout Cartridge (McElroy), 2184-2186.
Loon Lake (Doctorow), 938.
Lord Jim (Conrad), 714, 722-726.
Lord of the Flies (Golding), 1350-1351, 3768.
Lord of the Rings, The (Tolkien), 3299-3300, 3862.
Losing Battles (Welty), 3497-3498.
Lost Empires (Priestley), 2716-2717.
Lost Lady, A (Cather), 590, 593-594.
Lost Ones, The (Beckett), 262-263.
Lost World, The (Doyle), 974-975, 3861.
Love Always (Beattie), 252.
Love Among the Cannibals (Morris), 2420.
Love and Friendship (Lurie), 2127-2130.
Love and Work (Price), 2702.

Love Eaters, The (Settle), 3004, 3005-3006.
Love Feast. See *Book of Bebb, The*.
Love for Lydia (Bates), 244-245.
Love in a Dry Season (Foote), 1158-1160.
Love in the Ruins (Percy), 2634-2635.
Love Medicine (Erdrich), 1066-1068.
Loved and the Lost, The (Callaghan), 543, 546-548.
Loved One, The (Waugh), 3466-3467.
Lovelace, Earl, 2106-2111; *The Dragon Can't Dance*, 2109; *The Schoolmaster*, 2108; *While Gods Are Falling*, 2107-2108; *The Wine of Astonishment*, 2109-2110.
Lover's Revolt, A (De Forest), 835.
Love's Pilgrimage (Sinclair), 3053.
Loving (Green), 1434-1436.
Loving Hands at Home (Johnson, D.), 1771-1773.
Lowell, Robert, 1491.
Lowry, Malcolm, 2112-2125; *Under the Volcano*, 2116-2125.
Lowry, Margerie Bonner, 2115.
Luck of Ginger Coffey, The (Moore, B.), 2394-2395.
Lucky Jim (Amis, K.), 89-91, 3775, 3808.
Lucy Church Amiably (Stein), 3147.
Lucy Gayheart (Cather), 592.
Lurie, Alison, 2126-2134; *Foreign Affairs*, 2128-2130; *Imaginary Friends*, 2128-2133; *Love and Friendship*, 2127-2130; *The Nowhere City*, 2129-2130; *Only Children*, 2128, 2130-2132; *Real People*, 2128, 2130; *The War Between the Tates*, 2128, 2129.
Lying Days, The (Gordimer), 1381-1382.
Lying Low (Johnson, D.), 1774-1775.
Lyly, John, 3722.
Lynchers, The (Wideman), 3564-3565.
Lyre of Orpheus, The (Davies), 802-803.

Macaulay, Rose, 2135-2141; *Going Abroad*, 2139; *Orphan Island*, 2138; *Potterism*, 2137-2138; *The Shadow Flies*, 2139; *Told by an Idiot*, 2138; *The Towers of Trebizond*, 2140; *The World My Wilderness*, 2139-2140.
McBain, Ed, 3847.
McCarthy, Cormac, 2142-2148; *Blood Meridian*, 2146-2147; *Child of God*, 2144-2145; *The Orchard Keeper*, 2144;

Outer Dark, 2145; *Suttree*, 2145-2146.

McCarthy, Mary, 2149-2157; *Birds of America*, 2154-2155; *Cannibals and Missionaries*, 2155-2156; *A Charmed Life*, 2153; *The Group*, 2153-2154; *The Groves of Academe*, 2152-2153; *The Oasis*, 2152.

McCullers, Carson, 2158-2169, 3877; *The Ballad of the Sad Café*, 2165-2167, 3877; *Clock Without Hands*, 2168; *The Heart Is a Lonely Hunter*, 2163-2164; *The Member of the Wedding*, 2167; *Reflections in a Golden Eye*, 2164-2165.

Macdonald, Ross, 2170-2179; *The Blue Hammer*, 2177-2178; *The Chill*, 2174-2175; *The Doomsters*, 2172-2173; *The Galton Case*, 2173-2174; *The Underground Man*, 2176-2177; *The Zebra-Striped Hearse*, 2174.

McElroy, Joseph, 2180-2189; *Hind's Kidnap*, 2183-2184; *Lookout Cartridge*, 2184-2186; *Plus*, 2186-2187; *A Smuggler's Bible*, 2182-2183; *Women and Men*, 2187-2188.

McGinley, Patrick, 2190-2196; *Bogmail*, 2190-2191; *The Devil's Diary*, 2191, 2192-2194; *Foggage*, 2191, 2192; *Foxprints*, 2191, 2192; *Goosefoot*, 2191, 2192; *The Red Men*, 2194; *The Trick of the Ga Bolga*, 2191, 2192-2193.

McGuane, Thomas, 2197-2206; *The Bushwhacked Piano*, 2199; *Keep the Change*, 2204-2205; *Ninety-Two in the Shade*, 2199-2200; *Nobody's Angel*, 2200-2202; *Panama*, 2200; *Something to Be Desired*, 2202-2204; *The Sporting Club*, 2198-2199.

Mackerel Plaza, The (De Vries), 886-887.

MacLennan, Hugh, 2207-2218; *Barometer Rising*, 2213-2214; *Each Man's Son*, 2214-2215; *Oxyrhynchus*, 2210; *The Precipice*, 2214; *Return of the Sphinx*, 2215-2216; *Two Solitudes*, 2208, 2214; *Voices in Time*, 2216-2217; *The Watch That Ends the Night*, 2215.

McMurtry, Larry, 2219-2229; *All My Friends Are Going to Be Strangers*, 2223-2224; *Anything for Billy*, 2220; *Cadillac Jack*, 2224; *Horseman, Pass By*, 2220; *The Last Picture Show*, 2221-2222; *Lonesome Dove*, 2225-2228;

Moving On, 2222-2223; *Texasville*, 2222.

McTeague (Norris), 2527-2529.

Madame Delphine (Cable), 527-529.

Madden, David, 2230-2242; *The Beautiful Greed*, 2233-2235; *Bijou*, 2237-2238; *Brothers in Confidence*, 2233, 2236-2237; *Cassandra Singing*, 2235-2236; *On the Big Wind*, 2239; *Pleasure-Dome*, 2238-2239; *The Poetic Image in Six Genres*, 2232; *The Suicide's Wife*, 2233-2234, 2238.

Maggie (Crane), 773-774.

Maggot, A (Fowles), 1213-1214.

Magic Kingdom, The (Elkin), 1050.

Magic Toyshop, The (Carter), 566-567.

Magician of Lublin, The (Singer), 3063-3064.

Magician's Nephew, The (Lewis, C.), 2049.

Magus, The (Fowles), 1203-1205.

Maid Marian (Peacock), 2621-2622.

Mailer, Norman, 2243-2263, 3773; *An American Dream*, 2252-2254; *Ancient Evenings*, 2260-2261; *The Armies of the Night*, 2256-2258; *Barbary Shore*, 2250-2251; *The Deer Park*, 2251-2252; *The Executioner's Song*, 2258-2260; *Marilyn*, 2258; *The Naked and the Dead*, 2246-2250, 3773; *Of Women and Their Elegance*, 2258; *Tough Guys Don't Dance*, 2261-2262; *Why Are We in Vietnam?*, 2254-2256.

Main Street (Lewis, S.), 2068-2071.

Making Do (Goodman), 1374-1376.

Making of a Saint, The (Maugham), 2333-2334.

Making of Americans, The (Stein), 3141-3142.

Making of the Representative for Planet 8, The (Lessing), 2039.

Mal vu mal dit. See Ill Seen Ill Said.

Malamud, Bernard, 2264-2277, 3775-3776; *The Assistant*, 2266, 2271-2273, 3775; *The Fixer*, 2273-2275; *God's Grace*, 2275; *The Natural*, 2266, 2268-2271; *The People*, 2275-2276.

Malcolm (Purdy), 2744-2745.

Malcontents, The (Snow), 3089-3090.

Malefactors, The (Gordon), 1402.

Malign Fiesta. See Human Age, The.

Malone Dies (Beckett), 260-261.

Malone meurt. See *Malone Dies.*
Malory, Sir Thomas, 2278-2287; *Le Morte d'Arthur,* 2282-2287.
Malouf, David, 2288-2295; *The Bread of Time to Come,* 2291-2292; *Child's Play,* 2291; *The Great World,* 2293; *Harland's Half Acre,* 2292; *An Imaginary Life,* 2290-2291; *Johnno,* 2289-2290.
Maltese Falcon, The (Hammett), 1465-1466, 3846.
Mama Day (Naylor), 2492-2493.
Man and Boy (Morris), 2417-2418.
Man and Wife (Collins), 684-685.
Man from the North, A (Bennett), 295.
Man in the High Castle, The (Dick), 895-896.
Man of Property, The (Galsworthy), 1261-1263.
Man of the People, A (Achebe), 6, 12-14.
Man Who Gave Up His Name, The (Harrison), 1540-1541.
Man Who Killed the Deer, The (Waters), 3451-3453.
Man Who Loved Children, The (Stead), 3120-3122.
Man Who Was There, The (Morris), 2416-2417.
Man with the Golden Arm, The (Algren), 76-80.
Manassas (Sinclair), 3050.
Mandala, 3552-3553.
Mangan Inheritance, The (Moore, B.), 2398-2399.
Manhattan Transfer (Dos Passos), 957-958.
Manichaean vision, 465.
Manservant and Maidservant (Compton-Burnett), 698-699.
Mansfield Park (Austen), 162-164.
Manson, M.D. See *Citadel, The.*
Manticore, The (Davies), 798, 799, 800-801.
Many Marriages (Anderson), 116.
Marble Faun, The (Hawthorne), 1580-1583.
Marcel, Gabriel, 2629.
March Moonlight (Richardson, D.), 2833.
Marching Men (Anderson), 112-113.
Marilyn (Mailer), 2258.
Marius the Epicurean (Pater), 2605-2612.
Marjorie Morningstar (Wouk), 3669-3671.
Marquand, John P., 2296-2307; *B. F.'s Daughter,* 2303; *H. M. Pulham, Esquire,* 2302-2303; *The Late George Apley,* 2302; *Melvill Goodwin, U.S.A.,* 2304; *North of Grand Central,* 2303; *Point of No Return,* 2304; *Repent in Haste,* 2303; *Sincerely, Willis Wayde,* 2303, 2304-2305; *So Little Time,* 2303; *Wickford Point,* 2302; *Women and Thomas Harrow,* 2305.
"Marriage Portion, A" (Foote), 1161.
Marriages Between Zones Three, Four, and Five (Lessing), 2038.
Marrow of Tradition, The (Chesnutt), 636-637.
Marry Me (Updike), 3356.
"Marta Riquelme" (Hudson), 1639.
Martian Chronicles, The (Bradbury), 358-359.
Martian Time-Slip (Dick), 896.
Martin Chuzzlewit (Dickens), 907-909.
Martin Eden (London), 2101-2102.
Martin Faber (Simms), 3044.
Mary (Nabokov), 2462.
Mary Barton (Gaskell), 1302, 1306.
Mary Lavelle (O'Brien, K.), 2563-2564.
Mashen'ka. See *Mary.*
Mask of Apollo, The (Renault), 2812-2813.
Masked Gods (Waters), 3447.
Master of Ballantrae, The (Stevenson), 3194-3195.
Masters, The (Snow), 3088-3089.
Matthiessen, Peter, 2308-2320; *At Play in the Fields of the Lord,* 2308-2309, 2311, 2312-2316; *Far Tortuga,* 2308-2309, 2312, 2313, 2316-2318; *Partisans,* 2310, 2312; *Race Rock,* 2309-2310, 2312
Maturin, Charles Robert, 2321-2330, 3825; *The Albigenses,* 2328; *Bertram,* 2321; *Fatal Revenge,* 2325-2326; *Melmoth the Wanderer,* 2322, 2327-2328, 3825, 3829; *The Milesian Chief,* 2326-2327; *The Wild Irish Boy,* 2326; *Women,* 2327.
Maugham, W. Somerset, 2331-2340; *Cakes and Ale,* 2336-2337; *Liza of Lambeth,* 2333; *The Making of a Saint,* 2333-2334; *The Moon and Sixpence,* 2335-2336; *The Narrow Corner,* 2338-2339; *Of Human Bondage,* 2334-2335; *The Razor's Edge,* 2337-2338.
Maurice (Forster), 1193-1194.

Maxwell, William, 2341-2347; *Bright Center of Heaven*, 2342-2343; *The Château*, 2345; *The Folded Leaf*, 2344; *So Long, See You Tomorrow*, 2345-2346; *They Came Like Swallows*, 2343-2344; *Time Will Darken It*, 2344-2345.

Mayor of Casterbridge, The (Hardy), 1506-1507, 3758.

Meet Me in the Green Glen (Warren), 3443-3444.

Mefisto (Banville), 206-207.

Melincourt (Peacock), 2618-2620.

Mellichampe (Simms), 3039, 3041.

Melmoth the Wanderer (Maturin), 2322, 2327-2328, 3825, 3829.

Melville, Herman, 2348-2358, 3745, 3795, 3875-3876; "Bartleby the Scrivener," 3875-3876; *Billy Budd, Foretopman*, 2354-2356; *Moby Dick*, 2352-2354, 3745, 3795, 3799; *Omoo*, 2351-2352; *Typee*, 2351.

Melville Goodwin, U.S.A. (Marquand), 2304.

Member of the Wedding, The (McCullers), 2167.

Memoirs of a Midget (de la Mare), 844, 845-846.

Memoirs of a Survivor, The (Lessing), 2037-2038.

Men and Brethren (Cozzens), 766-767.

Men at Arms (Waugh), 3468-3469.

Men on Bataan (Hersey), 1610.

Mentoria (Rowson), 2912-2913.

Mercier and Camier (Beckett), 259-260.

Meredith, George, 2359-2369, 3788; *Beauchamp's Career*, 2363-2365; *Diana of the Crossways*, 2366-2367; *The Egoist*, 2365-2366; *The Ordeal of Richard Feverel*, 2361-2363.

Meridian (Walker), 3407, 3410-3412.

Merritt, Abraham, 3861.

Messiah (Vidal), 3373.

Metafiction, **3886.**

Metamorphosis, The (Kafka), 3877

Metroland (Barnes), 211.

Metropolis, The (Sinclair), 3052.

Micah Clarke (Doyle), 972.

Michael Scarlett (Cozzens), 763.

Michener, James A., 2370-2377; *The Bridges at Toko-Ri*, 2372-2373; *Caravans*, 2373-2374; *Chesapeake*, 2374-2375; *Poland*, 2376; *Space*, 2375-2376; *Tales of the South Pacific*, 2372; *Texas*, 2376-2377.

Mickelsson's Ghosts (Gardner), 1281-1282.

Middle Age of Mrs. Eliot, The (Wilson, Angus), 3592-3593.

Middle Passage (Johnson, C.), 1766-1768.

Middlemarch (Eliot), 1040-1043.

Midnight's Children (Rushdie), 2919, 2920-2922, 3793.

Miguel Street (Naipaul), 2473.

Milesian Chief, The (Maturin), 2326-2327.

Military Philosophers, The (Powell, A.), 2677-2678, 2680.

Milk and Honey (Jolley), 1793.

Mill on the Floss, The (Eliot), 1038-1039.

Miller, Henry, 2378-2388; *The Colossus of Maroussi*, 2381; *Tropic of Cancer*, 2383-2385; *Tropic of Capricorn*, 2380.

Mimic Men, The (Naipaul), 2471.

Mind of My Mind (Butler, O.), 496.

Mind of the Maker, The (Sayers), 2973-2974.

Minister's Wooing, The (Stowe), 3213-3214.

Misery (King), 1893-1894.

Misfortunes of Elphin, The (Peacock), 2622.

"Miss Dulane and My Lord" (Collins), 688.

Miss Lonelyhearts (West, N.), 3515-3516.

Miss Peabody's Inheritance (Jolley), 1793.

Miss Ravenel's Conversion from Secession to Loyalty (De Forest), 834-835.

Missolonghi Manuscript, The (Prokosch), 2741.

Mr. Beluncle (Pritchett), 2728-2732.

Mr. Blettsworthy on Rampole (Wells), 3484-3485.

Mr. Bridge (Connell), 708-709.

Mr. Britling Sees It Through (Wells), 3484.

Mr. Bullivant and His Lambs. See *Manservant and Maidservant*.

Mr. Gallion's School (Stuart), 3229.

Mister Johnson (Cary), 574, 576-577.

Mr. Sammler's Planet (Bellow), 283-285.

Mr. Scobie's Riddle (Jolley), 1792-1793.

Mr. Standfast (Buchan), 426-427.

Mr. Stone and the Knights Companion (Naipaul), 2474-2475.

Mrs. Bridge (Connell), 705-706.

Mrs. Dalloway (Woolf), 3650-3652.

Mrs. Dukes' Million (Lewis, W.), 2083.

Mrs. Stevens Hears the Mermaids Singing (Sarton), 2965-2966.
"Mrs. Zant and the Ghost" (Collins), 686-687.
Mitchell, Margaret, 3836-3837.
Mo, Timothy, 3793.
Moby Dick (Melville), 2352-2354, 3745, 3795, 3799.
Modern Comedy, A (Galsworthy), 1264.
Modern Instance, A (Howells), 1649-1651.
Modern Lover, A (Moore, G.), 2406.
"Modern novel," 2909.
Modernism, **3886.**
"Mojave" (Capote), 561.
Moll Flanders (Defoe), 824, 826-827, 3728-3729, 3731-3732, 3806.
Molloy (Beckett), 260.
Monday Night (Boyle, K.), 343.
Money (Amis, M.), 104.
Money Changers, The (Sinclair), 3052-3053.
Monk, The (Lewis, M.), 2057-2061, 3824, 3828-3829.
Monkey King, The (Mo), 3793
Monster and Other Stories, The (Crane), 778-779.
Monstre Gai. See *Human Age, The.*
Montesquieu, Charles de, 3811.
Month of Sundays, A (Updike), 3358.
Moon and Sixpence, The (Maugham), 2335-2336.
Moonlight, The (Cary), 578.
Moonstone, The (Collins), 687-688, 3843.
Moore, Brian, 2389-2401; *An Answer from Limbo*, 2395-2396; *Catholics*, 2397; *The Feast of Lupercal*, 2392-2394; *The Great Victorian Collection*, 2397-2398; *I Am Mary Dunne*, 2396-2397; *Judith Hearne*, 2391-2393; *The Luck of Ginger Coffey*, 2394-2395; *The Mangan Inheritance*, 2398-2399; *The Temptation of Eileen Hughes*, 2399.
Moore, George, 2402-2411; *Aphrodite in Aulis*, 2409-2410; *The Brook Kerith*, 2409; *A Drama in Muslin*, 2406-2407; *Esther Waters*, 2402, 2407-2408; *Evelyn Innes*, 2408; *Hail and Farewell*, 2402-2403; *Héloïse and Abélard*, 2409; *A Modern Lover*, 2406; *A Mummer's Wife*, 2406.
Morality, 1715-1716.

Moran of the Lady Letty (Norris), 2527, 2529-2530.
More Die of Heartbreak (Bellow), 287.
More Than Human (Sturgeon), 3234, 3236-3239.
More Women Than Men (Compton-Burnett), 695-696.
Morgan's Passing (Tyler), 3341-3342.
Morning, Noon, and Night (Cozzens), 769-770.
Morning Watch, The (Agee), 22-26.
Morris, Wright, 2412-2423; *A Bill of Rites, a Bill of Wrongs, a Bill of Goods*, 2413; *The Deep Sleep*, 2418; *The Home Place*, 2412; *The Huge Season*, 2419-2420; *The Inhabitants*, 2412; *Love Among the Cannibals*, 2420; *Man and Boy*, 2417-2418; *The Man Who Was There*, 2416-2417; *My Uncle Dudley*, 2416; *Plains Song, for Female Voices*, 2419, 2420-2421; *The Works of Love*, 2418.
Morrison, Toni, 2424-2435; *Beloved*, 2433; *The Bluest Eye*, 2425-2426; *Song of Solomon*, 2427-2431; *Sula*, 2426-2427; *Tar Baby*, 2431-2433.
Morrow, James, 3871.
Morte d'Arthur, Le (Malory), 2282-2287.
Morte d'Urban (Powers), 2692-2695.
Moses, Man of the Mountain (Hurston), 1669.
Mosquito Coast (Theroux), 3286-3287.
Mother, The (Buck), 439-440.
Mother and Two Daughters, A (Godwin), 1343-1344.
Mother Night (Vonnegut), 3381-3382.
Motif, **3886.**
Motivation, **3886.**
Mountain Dialogues (Waters), 3447.
Mountolive. See *Alexandria Quartet, The.*
Mourners Below (Purdy), 2750.
Movement poets, 84-85.
Moviegoer, The (Percy), 2631-2633.
Moving On (McMurtry), 2222-2223.
Mules and Men (Hurston), 1668.
Mulford, Clarence Edward, 3852.
Mumbo Jumbo (Reed), 2800, 2802-2803.
Mummer's Wife, A (Moore, G.), 2406.
Murder of Quality, A (Le Carré), 1986.
Murder of Roger Ackroyd, The (Christie), 656-657, 3844.

"Murders in the Rue Morgue, The" (Poe), 3842.

Murdoch, Iris, 2436-2457; *An Accidental Man*, 2441, 2448-2452; *The Black Prince*, 2452; *A Fairly Honourable Defeat*, 2444-2448; *The Fire and the Sun*, 2441, 2452; *The Good Apprentice*, 2455-2456; *The Sea, the Sea*, 2452-2455; *Under the Net*, 2441-2444.

Murphy (Beckett), 258.

Muses Are Heard, The (Capote), 556.

My Ántonia (Cather), 589-590, 592-593.

My Head! My Head! (Graves), 1418.

My Heart and My Flesh (Roberts), 2877.

My Life as a Man (Roth), 2900.

My Name Is Aram (Saroyan), 2946, 2951.

My Name Is Asher Lev (Potok), 2662-2663.

My Next Bride (Boyle, K.), 341.

My Secret History (Theroux), 3287.

My Uncle Dudley (Morris), 2416.

My Wife and I (Stowe), 3216.

Myra Breckenridge (Vidal), 3376-3377.

Mysteries of Udolpho, The (Radcliffe), 2780-2781, 3783, 3824, 3827-3828.

Mysteries of Winterthurn (Oates), 2538-2539.

Mysterious Affair at Styles, The (Christie), 655, 656.

Mystery and Manners (O'Connor), 2574.

"Mystery of Marie Roget, The" (Poe), 3842.

Mystic Masseur, The (Naipaul), 2472.

Myth, 3886.

Myth criticism, 3887.

N or M? The New Mystery (Christie), 658.

Nabokov, Vladimir, 2458-2468; *Bend Sinister*, 2464-2465; *The Gift*, 2463-2464; *King, Queen, Knave*, 2462; *Laughter in the Dark*, 2462-2463; *Lolita*, 2465-2466; *Mary*, 2462; *Pale Fire*, 2466; *The Real Life of Sebastian Knight*, 2464.

Naipaul, V. S., 2469-2479; *A Bend in the River*, 2476-2477; *The Enigma of Arrival*, 2477-2478; *Guerillas*, 2475-2476; *A House for Mr. Biswas*, 2473-2474; *In a Free State*, 2475; *Miguel Street*, 2473; *The Mimic Men*, 2471; *Mr. Stone and the Knights Companion*, 2474-2475; *The Mystic Masseur*, 2472; *The Suffrage of Elvira*, 2473.

Naked and the Dead, The (Mailer), 2246-2250, 3773.

Naked Lunch, The (Burroughs), 486, 487.

Names, The (DeLillo), 866-867.

Narayan, R. K., 2480-2488; *The Bachelor of Arts*, 2483; *The English Teacher*, 2483-2484; *The Financial Expert*, 2485-2486; *The Guide*, 2484-2485; *The Painter of Signs*, 2486; *Swami and Friends*, 2483.

Narrative, 3887.

Narrative of Jacobus Coetzee, The. See *Dusklands*.

Narratology, 3887.

Narrator, 3887.

Narrow Corner, The (Maugham), 2338-2339.

Narrow Rooms (Purdy), 2749-2750.

Nashe, Thomas, 3724-3725, 3806.

Native Son (Wright), 3684-3686, 3776.

Natural, The (Malamud), 2266, 2268-2271.

Natural Shocks (Stern), 3168-3169.

Naturalism, 3887.

Nature of Passion, The (Jhabvala), 1754.

Naulahka, The (Kipling), 1903-1904.

Naylor, Gloria, 2489-2495; *Linden Hills*, 2492; *Mama Day*, 2492-2493; *The Women of Brewster Place*, 2491-2492.

Needle's Eye, The (Drabble), 986-988.

Negritude, 2496.

Neighbors (Berger), 312-313.

Nephew, The (Purdy), 2745-2746.

Neutral territory, 1572.

Never Come Morning (Algren), 76-78.

New Centurions, The (Wambaugh), 3427-3428.

New Criticism. See Formalist criticism.

New Grub Street (Gissing), 1323-1324.

New Heloïse, The. See *Julie: Or, The New Heloïse, Letters from Two Lovers*.

New Lives for Old (Snow), 3084.

Newcomes, The (Thackeray), 3271, 3276-3277.

Newton Letter, The (Banville), 205-206.

Ngugi, James. See Ngugi wa Thiong'o.

Ngugi wa Thiong'o, 2496-2509; *Devil on the Cross*, 2508; *A Grain of Wheat*, 2504-2506; *Petals of Blood*, 2506-2508;

The River Between, 2498, 2501-2504; *Weep Not, Child*, 2498, 2500-2501.
Nice Work (Lodge), 2093-2094.
Nicholas Nickleby (Dickens), 906-907.
Nickel Mountain (Gardner), 1276-1278.
Nigger Heaven (Van Vechten), 3366.
Night (O'Brien, E.), 2547.
Night and Day (Woolf), 3647-3648.
Night in Acadie, A (Chopin), 640.
Night of the Poor (Prokosch), 2740.
Night Rider (Warren), 3439-3440.
Nightmare Abbey (Peacock), 2620-2621.
Nights at the Circus (Carter), 569-570.
Nightspawn (Banville), 201-202.
Nightwatchmen (Hannah), 1483-1484.
Nin, Anaïs, 2381, **2510-2522**; *Children of the Albatross*, 2516, 2518; *Cities of the Interior*, 2516-2518; *Collages*, 2520-2521; *The Diary of Anaïs Nin*, 2510, 2512; *The Four-Chambered Heart*, 2516, 2518-2519; *House of Incest*, 2514-2515; *Ladders to Fire*, 2516, 2518; *Seduction of the Minotaur*, 2516, 2519-2520; *A Spy in the House of Love*, 2516, 2519; "*Stella*," 2515-2516; "*The Voice*," 2515-2516; *Winter of Artifice*, 2515-2516.
Nine Days to Mukalla (Prokosch), 2738-2739.
Nine Tailors, The (Sayers), 2975-2977, 3844.
Nineteen Eighty-Four (Orwell), 2597-2599.
1919 (Dos Passos), 960-961.
1939 (Boyle, K.), 344.
Ninety-Two in the Shade (McGuane), 2199-2200.
No Decency Left (Graves), 1418-1419.
No Laughing Matter (Wilson, Angus), 3594-3595.
No Longer at Ease (Achebe), 6, 8-10.
No Third Path (Kosinski), 1920.
Nobody's Angel (McGuane), 2200-2202.
None Shall Look Back (Gordon), 1398-1399.
Nonfiction novel, 1608-1609.
Noon Wine (Porter), 2653-2654, 3876-3877.
Norris, Frank, 2523-2532, 3797; *McTeague*, 2527-2529; *Moran of the Lady Letty*, 2527, 2529-2530; *The Octopus*, 2527, 2530, 3797, 3799; *The Pit*, 2527, 2530-2531; *Vandover and the Brute*, 2527.
North and South (Gaskell), 1303-1304, 1305, 1307-1308.
North of Grand Central (Marquand), 2303.
Northanger Abbey (Austen), 166-167.
Not Honour More (Cary), 581, 582.
Not to Disturb (Spark), 3106.
Nothing (Green), 1436-1437.
Nothing Like the Sun (Burgess), 467.
Nouveau roman, 3112-3113.
Nouvelle Héloïse, La. See *Julie: Or, The New Heloïse, Letters from Two Lovers*.
Nova (Delany), 854.
Nova Express (Burroughs), 486-487.
Novel, **3887**.
Novel of manners, 145-146, **3888**.
Novella, **3873-3879, 3888**.
Nowhere City, The (Lurie), 2129-2130.
Nun, The (Behn), 271.
Nunquam (Durrell), 1014.

O Beulah Land (Settle), 3006-3007.
O Pioneers! (Cather), 591.
O-Zone (Theroux), 3287.
Oasis, The (McCarthy, M.), 2152.
Oates, Joyce Carol, 2533-2541; *Bellefleur*, 2538; *Childwold*, 2537-2538; *Expensive People*, 2535-2536; *Mysteries of Winterthurn*, 2538-2539; *With Shuddering Fall*, 2534-2535; *Wonderland*, 2536-2537.
O'Brien, Edna, 2542-2550; *August Is a Wicked Month*, 2545; *Casualties of Peace*, 2545-2546; *The Country Girls*, 2544; *Girls in Their Married Bliss*, 2544-2545; *The High Road*, 2548; *I Hardly Knew You*, 2547-2548; *The Lonely Girl*, 2544; *Night*, 2547; *A Pagan Place*, 2546; *Zee & Co.*, 2547.
O'Brien, Flann, 2551-2559; *At Swim-Two-Birds*, 2553, 2554-2555; *The Dalkey Archive*, 2557-2558; *The Hard Life*, 2557; *The Poor Mouth*, 2554, 2556-2557; *The Third Policeman*, 2554, 2555-2556.
O'Brien, Kate, 2560-2566; *The Land of Spices*, 2564-2565; *Mary Lavelle*, 2563-2564; *That Lady*, 2565; *Without My Cloak*, 2562-2563.
Occasion for Loving (Gordimer), 1384-1385.

Ocean, The (Hanley), 1477-1478.

O'Connor, Flannery, 2567-2575, 3874, 3875; *Mystery and Manners*, 2574; *The Violent Bear It Away*, 2569, 2572-2573; *Wise Blood*, 2569, 2570-2572, 3874, 3875.

October Light (Gardner), 1278-1279.

Octopus, The (Norris), 2527, 2530, 3797, 3799.

Odd Woman, The (Godwin), 1341-1342.

Odor of Sanctity, An (Yerby), 3695-3696.

Of Human Bondage (Maugham), 2334-2335.

Of Love and Dust (Gaines), 1242-1243.

Of Men and Women (Buck), 434-435.

Of Mice and Men (Steinbeck), 3156.

Of the Farm (Updike), 3352.

Of Time and the River (Wolfe), 3630-3631, 3634-3636.

Of Women and Their Elegance (Mailer), 2258.

Officers and Gentlemen (Waugh), 3469.

Oh What a Paradise It Seems (Cheever), 625-626.

O'Hara, John, 2576-2590; *Appointment in Samarra*, 2581-2583; *The Lockwood Concern*, 2587-2589; *Sermons and Soda Water*, 2586-2587; *Ten North Frederick*, 2583-2586; *We're Friends Again*, 2587.

Old Devils, The (Amis, K.), 90, 95-98.

Old Man and the Sea, The (Hemingway), 1605-1607, 3769-3770, 3875.

Old Men at the Zoo, The (Wilson, Angus), 3593-3594.

Old Mortality (Porter), 2652-2653.

Old Mortality (Scott), 2989-2991.

Old Saint Paul's (Ainsworth), 45-46.

Old Wives' Tale, The (Bennett), 296-297.

Oldtown Folks (Stowe), 3215-3216.

Oliver Twist (Dickens), 3786.

"Ombú, El" (Hudson), 1659.

Omensetter's Luck (Gass), 1312-1315.

Omniscient narrator, 980.

Omoo (Melville), 2351-2352.

On Moral Fiction (Gardner), 1269-1271.

On the Big Wind (Madden), 2239.

On the Road (Kerouac), 1865-1867, 3808.

Once and Future King, The (White, T.), 3862

One Flew over the Cuckoo's Nest (Kesey), 1877-1879, 3808.

158-Pound Marriage, The (Irving, J.), 1697-1698.

One of Ours (Cather), 590, 593.

O'Neill-O'Flaherty series, The (Farrell, James), 1077-1079.

Onion Eaters, The (Donleavy), 949.

Only Children (Lurie), 2128, 2130-2132.

Only Problem, The (Spark), 3115-3116.

O'Nolan, Brian. *See* **O'Brien, Flann.**

Open Door, The (Sillitoe), 3031-3032.

Open Heart. See Book of Bebb, The.

Optimist's Daughter, The (Welty), 3491-3492, 3498-3499.

Oral storytelling tradition, 2230-2231, 2232-2233, 2238-2240.

Orchard Keeper, The (McCarthy, C.), 2144.

Ordeal of Richard Feverel, The (Meredith), 2361-2363.

Orderly Life, An (Yglesias), 3703-3705.

Origin of the Brunists, The (Coover), 751-752.

Orley Farm (Trollope), 3310-3312.

Ormond (Edgeworth), 1023-1024, 1028-1029.

Oroonoko (Behn), 270, 272, 3727.

Orphan Island (Macaulay), 2138.

Orrie's Story (Berger), 315.

O'Ruddy, The (Crane with Barr), 779.

Orwell, George, 2591-2601, 3798; *Animal Farm*, 2595-2597, 3789; *Burmese Days*, 2593-2594; *Coming Up for Air*, 2594-2595; *Nineteen Eighty-Four*, 2597-2599.

Other Men's Daughters (Stern), 3167-3168.

Other Paris, The (Gallant), 1250-1251.

Other People (Amis, M.), 103-104.

Other Voices, Other Rooms (Capote), 556, 557-558.

Our Gang (Roth), 2900.

Our Mutual Friend (Dickens), 912-913.

Our Time Is Gone. See Fury Chronicle, The.

Out of the Shelter (Lodge), 2091.

Out of the Silent Planet (Lewis, C.), 2046.

Outer Dark (McCarthy, C.), 2145.

Outsider, The (Wright), 3686-3688.

Overholser, Stephen D., 3855.

Ox-Bow Incident, The (Clark), 662, 663, 666-667.

Oxherding Tale (Johnson, C.), 1765-1766.

Oxyrhynchus (MacLennan), 2210.

Pagan Place, A (O'Brien, E.), 2546.
Painted Bird, The (Kosinski), 1921-1923.
Painter of Signs, The (Narayan), 2486.
Palace of the Peacock (Harris, W.), 1526-1529.
Pale Fire (Nabokov), 2466.
Pale Horse, Pale Rider (Porter), 2654-2655.
Pale View of Hills, A (Ishiguro), 1707-1708, 3793.
Palomino (Jolley), 1791-1792.
Pamela (Richardson, S.), 2839-2840, 3721, 3732, 3781-3782, 3814, 3816.
Panama (McGuane), 2200.
Paper Men, The (Golding), 1357.
Parade's End (Ford, F.), 1171-1172.
Paradise (Barthelme), 236.
Parasite, The (Doyle), 975.
Pardoner's Tale, The (Wain), 3395, 3399-3401.
Parties (Van Vechten), 3366-3367.
Partisan, The (Simms), 3041.
Partisans (Matthiessen), 2310, 2312.
Passage Through Gehenna (Jones, M.), 1816-1817.
Passage to India, A (Forster), 1194-1196, 3761.
Passenger (Keneally), 1844, 1845.
Passion Artist, The (Hawkes), 1565-1567.
Passion of New Eve, The (Carter), 568-569.
Pastoral novel, 1499.
Pater, Walter, 2602-2614; "The Child in the House," 2602; *Gaston de Latour*, 2612-2613; *Marius the Epicurean*, 2605-2612.
Patriot, The (Connell), 706-707.
Patternmaster (Butler, O.), 496.
Pawnbroker, The (Wallant), 3420-3421.
Peacock, Thomas Love, 2615-2625, 3739; *Crochet Castle*, 2622-2623; *Gryll Grange*, 2623-2624; *Headlong Hall*, 2617-2618; *Maid Marian*, 2621-2622; *Melincourt*, 2618-2620; *The Misfortunes of Elphin*, 2622; *Nightmare Abbey*, 2620-2621.
Peacock's Tail (Hoagland), 1631-1632.
Pearl, The (Steinbeck), 3159-3160.
Peckham's Marbles (De Vries), 889, 890.
Pegnitz Junction, The (Gallant), 1253.
Penhally (Gordon), 1397-1398.
Penultimate Truth, The (Dick), 896.
People, The (Malamud), 2275-2276.

People of the Valley (Waters), 3450-3451.
Percy, Walker, 2626-2641; *Lancelot*, 2635-2637; *The Last Gentleman*, 2633-2634; *Love in the Ruins*, 2634-2635; *The Moviegoer*, 2631-2633; *The Second Coming*, 2637-2638; *The Thanatos Syndrome*, 2638-2640.
Peregrine Pickle (Smollett), 3073-3074.
Perelandra (Lewis, C.), 2046-2047.
Perelman, S. J., 3514.
Perfect Spy, A (Le Carré), 1993.
Perfectionists, The (Godwin), 1339-1340.
Persian Boy, The (Renault), 2813-2814.
Persian Letters (Montesquieu), 3811, 3812-3814.
Persian Nights (Johnson, D.), 1775-1776.
Persuasion (Austen), 167-168.
Pet Sematary (King), 1890-1892.
Petals of Blood (Ngugi wa Thiong'o), 2506-2508.
Peter Whiffle (Van Vechten), 3363-3365.
Phenomenological criticism, **3888.**
Philby, Kim, 1443.
Picaresque novel, **3803-3809, 3888.**
Picaro, 3803.
Pickwick Papers (Dickens), 906, 3786, 3806-3807.
Picture of Dorian Gray, The (Wilde), 3862-3863.
Picture Palace (Theroux), 3286.
Picture This (Heller), 1593-1594.
Picturegoers, The (Lodge), 2090.
Piece of My Heart, A (Ford, R.), 1176-1177.
Pikes Peak (Waters), 3450, 3455-3457.
Pilgrim Hawk, The (Wescott), 3507-3509.
Pilgrimage (Richardson, D.), 2828-2833, 3764.
Pilgrim's Progress, The (Bunyan), 458, 3726.
"Pillar of Fire" (Foote), 1162.
Pincher Martin (Golding), 1352-1353.
Pioneers, The (Cooper), 737-741.
Pit, The (Norris), 2527, 2530-2531.
Place of Dead Roads, The (Burroughs), 490.
Place to Come To, A (Warren), 3443.
Plagued by the Nightingale (Boyle, K.), 340.
Plains Song, for Female Voices (Morris), 2419, 2420-2421.
Plante, David, 2642-2648; *The Catholic*,

2647; *The Country*, 2645-2646; *The Family*, 2643-2644; *The Foreigner*, 2646-2647; *The Francoeur Novels*, 2643-2646; *The Woods*, 2644-2645.

Plato, 2452-2453, 2808-2810.

Play It As It Lays (Didion), 927-928.

Player Piano (Vonnegut), 3380-3381.

Pleasure-Dome (Madden), 2238-2239.

Plot/Story, **3888.**

Plotting, 2212.

Plumed Serpent, The (Lawrence), 1958, 1970-1974.

Plus (McElroy), 2186-2187.

Poacher, The (Bates), 243.

Poe, Edgar Allan, 3830-3831, 3842-3843.

Poetic Image in Six Genres, The (Madden), 2232.

Poganuc People (Stowe), 3216-3217.

Point Counter Point (Huxley), 1679-1681.

Point of No Return (Marquand), 2304.

Point of view, **3888.**

Pointed Roofs (Richardson, D.), 2830-2831.

Poison Belt, The (Doyle), 974.

Poison Pen (Garrett), 1297.

Poland (Michener), 2376

Political Romance, A (Sterne), 3175, 3177.

Ponder Heart, The (Welty), 3491-3492, 3495-3497.

"Poor Koko" (Fowles), 1210.

Poor Miss Finch (Collins), 685.

Poor Mouth, The (O'Brien, F.), 2554, 2556-2557.

Poor White (Anderson), 109, 115-116.

Poorhouse Fair, The (Updike), 3350-3351.

Poppa John (Woiwode), 3623-3624.

Popular literature, 40, 41-42, 47.

Porter, Katherine Anne, 2649-2658, 3876-3877; *Noon Wine*, 2653-2654, 3876-3877; *Old Mortality*, 2652-2653; *Pale Horse, Pale Rider*, 2654-2655; *Ship of Fools*, 2655-2657.

Portnoy's Complaint (Roth), 2899-2900.

Portrait in Brownstone (Auchincloss), 149-150.

Portrait of a Lady, The (James, H.), 1722-1725.

Portrait of the Artist as a Young Man, A (Joyce), 1824-1826, 3765.

Portuguese Letters (Guilleragues), 3811-3812.

Posthumous Papers of the Pickwick Club,

The. See *Pickwick Papers*.

Postmodernism, 234, **3889.**

Postures. See *Quartet*.

Potok, Chaim, 2659-2668; *The Book of Lights*, 2660, 2664-2665; *The Chosen*, 2660-2661; *Davita's Harp*, 2661, 2665-2666; *The Gift of Asher Lev*, 2666-2667; *In the Beginning*, 2663-2664; *My Name Is Asher Lev*, 2662-2663; *The Promise*, 2661-2662.

Potterism (Macaulay), 2137-2138.

Powell, Anthony, 2669-2682, 3773; *The Acceptance World*, 2677; *Afternoon Men*, 2675-2676; *Agents and Patients*, 2676; *At Lady Molly's*, 2678; *Books Do Furnish a Room*, 2680; *A Buyer's Market*, 2677; *Casanova's Chinese Restaurant*, 2678; *A Dance to the Music of Time*, 2673-2675, 3773; *From a View to a Death*, 2676; *Hearing Secret Harmonies*, 2681; *The Kindly Ones*, 2678-2679; *The Military Philosophers*, 2677-2678, 2680; *A Question of Upbringing*, 2676-2677; *The Soldier's Art*, 2679-2680; *Temporary Kings*, 2677, 2680-2681; *The Valley of Bones*, 2679; *Venusberg*, 2676; *What's Become of Waring*, 2676.

Powell, Dawn, 2683-2689; *Angels on Toast*, 2685-2686; *The Golden Spur*, 2687-2688; *The Locusts Have No King*, 2686-2687; *The Wicked Pavilion*, 2687.

Power and the Glory, The (Greene), 1447.

Power-House, The (Buchan), 428-430.

Powers, J. F., 2690-2698; *Morte d'Urban*, 2692-2695; *Wheat That Springeth Green*, 2695-2697.

Prague Orgy, The (Roth), 2903-2904.

Prairie, The (Cooper), 743-745.

Praise Singer, The (Renault), 2814.

Prayer for Owen Meany, A (Irving, J.), 1703-1704.

Precipice, The (MacLennan), 2214.

Present-tense narration, 577.

Price, Reynolds, 2699-2709; *A Generous Man*, 2700, 2703-2704; *Kate Vaiden*, 2701-2702; *A Long and Happy Life*, 2700, 2702-2703; *Love and Work*, 2702; *The Source of Light*, 2707; *The Surface of the Earth*, 2704-2707.

Prick of Noon, The (De Vries), 889-890.

Pride and Prejudice (Austen), 161-162.

Priestley, J. B., 2710-2719; *Angel Pavement*, 2715; *Bright Day*, 2715-2716; *The Good Companions*, 2714-2715; *Lost Empires*, 2716-2717.

Prime of Miss Jean Brodie, The (Spark), 3105, 3108-3111.

Primer for Combat (Boyle, K.), 349.

Prince and the Pauper, The (Twain), 3323.

Prince Caspian (Lewis, C.), 2049-2050.

Prince of Abissinia, The. See Rasselas.

Principles in Bio-Physics (Richter), 2860-2861.

Prisoner of Grace (Cary), 581.

Prisons (Settle), 3008.

Pritchett, V. S., 2720-2733; *A Cab at the Door*, 2724; *Dead Man Leading*, 2726-2728; *Mr. Beluncle*, 2728-2732.

Private Memoirs and Confessions of a Justified Sinner, The (Hogg), 3858.

Private Papers of Henry Ryecroft, The (Gissing), 1325.

Professor, The (Brontë, C.), 384-385.

Professor's House, The (Cather), 594-595.

Prokosch, Frederic, 2734-2742; *Age of Thunder*, 2740; *The Asiatics*, 2737; *The Assassins*, 2734; *A Ballad of Love*, 2739; *The Carnival*, 2734; *The Conspirators*, 2739-2740; *The Dark Dancer*, 2740-2741; *Death at Sea*, 2734; *The Missolonghi Manuscript*, 2741; *Night of the Poor*, 2740; *Nine Days to Mukalla*, 2738-2739; *The Seven Sisters*, 2739; *The Seven Who Fled*, 2737-2738; *The Skies of Europe*, 2739; *Storm and Echo*, 2740; *A Tale for Midnight*, 2740; *The Wreck of the "Cassandra,"* 2741.

Promise, The (Potok), 2661-2662.

Promise of Love (Renault), 2809.

Prophet's Camel Bell, The (Laurence), 1942.

Protagonist, **3889.**

Protocol of reading, 852-853.

Providence (Brookner), 400-401.

Prudence Palfrey (Aldrich), 68-70.

Psmith novels, (Wodehouse), 3615.

Psychological criticism, **3889.**

Psychological novel, **3889.**

Psychological realism, 1715.

Public Burning, The (Coover), 754-756.

Public Image, The (Spark), 3105.

Purdy, James, 2743-2752; *Cabot Wright Begins*, 2746; *Eustace Chisholm and the Works*, 2746-2747; *Glory's Course*, 2750; *The House of the Solitary Maggot*, 2747, 2748-2749; *I Am Elijah Thrush*, 2747-2748; *In A Shallow Grave*, 2749; *In the Hollow of His Hand*, 2750-2751; *Jeremy's Version*, 2747; *Malcolm*, 2744-2745; *Mourners Below*, 2750; *Narrow Rooms*, 2749-2750; *The Nephew*, 2745-2746.

"Purloined Letters, The" (Poe), 3842.

Purple Land, The (Hudson), 1658-1660.

Purposes of Love. See Promise of Love.

Pym, Barbara, 2753-2762; *Excellent Women*, 2757-2759; *A Glass of Blessings*, 2757, 2759; *Less Than Angels*, 2756; *Quartet in Autumn*, 2757, 2759-2760; *An Unsuitable Attachment*, 2753-2754.

Pynchon, Thomas, 2763-2773, 3777; *The Crying of Lot 49*, 2765, 2768-2770, 3771; *Gravity's Rainbow*, 2765, 2770-2771, 3771; *V.*, 2766-2768; *Vineland*, 2771-2772, 3771.

Pyramid, The (Golding), 1354-1355.

Quality of Mercy, A (West, P.), 3521-3522.

Quartet (Rhys), 2819.

Quartet in Autumn (Pym), 2757, 2759-2760.

Queen, Ellery, 3845.

Quest for Karla, The. See Honourable Schoolboy, The, Smiley's People, and *Tinker, Tailor, Soldier, Spy.*

Question of Upbringing, A (Powell, A.), 2676-2677.

Quiet American, The (Greene), 1447.

Quinn's Book (Kennedy), 1856-1857.

Quod Erat Demonstrandum (Stein), 3144-3145.

Rabbi of Lud, The (Elkin), 1050.

Rabbit at Rest (Updike), 3354-3355.

Rabbit Is Rich (Updike), 3354.

Rabbit Redux (Updike), 3353-3354.

Rabbit, Run (Updike), 3352-3353, 3806, 3808.

Race Rock (Matthiessen), 2309-2310, 2312

Rachel Papers, The (Amis, M.), 102.

Radcliffe, Mrs. Ann, 2774-2784, 3783, 3824; *Castles of Athlin and Dunbayne*, 2778-2779; *Gaston de Blondeville*, 2777, 2779; *The Italian*, 2781-2782; *The*

Mysteries of Udolpho, 2780-2781, 3783, 3824, 3827-3828; *The Romance of the Forest*, 2779-2780; *A Sicilian Romance*, 2779.

Raditzer (Matthiessen), 2310-2311. 2312.

Ragged Dick (Alger), 3795.

Ragtime (Doctorow), 937-938.

"Rain Down Home" (Foote), 1161.

Rainbow, The (Lawrence), 1962-1964, 3767.

Rao, Raja, 2785-2796; *The Cat and Shakespeare*, 2792-2793; *The Chessmaster and His Moves*, 2794-2795; *Comrade Kirillov*, 2793-2794; *Kanthapura*, 2788-2790; *The Serpent and the Rope*, 2790-2792.

Rasselas (Johnson, S.), 1783-1787.

Rat Man of Paris (West, P.), 3527-3528.

Ratner's Star (DeLillo), 865-866.

Ray (Hannah), 1484-1485.

Razor's Edge, The (Maugham), 2337-2338.

Real Life of Sebastian Knight, The (Nabokov), 2464.

Real People (Lurie), 2128, 2130.

Realism, **3889.**

Realms of Gold, The (Drabble), 988-990.

Rebel Angels, The (Davies), 798-799, 801-802.

Recapitulation (Stegner), 3133-3134.

Reception aesthetics, **3889.**

Reckless Eyeballing (Reed), 2804-2805.

Reckoning, A (Sarton), 2966-2967.

Recognitions, The (Gaddis), 1230, 1231-1233.

Rector of Justin, The (Auchincloss), 150-152.

Red Badge of Courage, The (Crane), 774-776, 3769.

Red Harvest (Hammett), 1462-1463, 1464-1465.

Red Men, The (McGinley), 2194.

Red Pony, The (Steinbeck), 3156-3157.

Reed, Ishmael, 2797-2806; *Flight to Canada*, 2804; *The Free-Lance Pallbearers*, 2801-2802; *The Last Days of Louisiana Red*, 2803-2804; *Mumbo Jumbo*, 2800, 2802-2803; *Reckless Eyeballing*, 2804-2805; *The Terrible Twos*, 2804; *Yellow Back Radio Broke-Down*, 2802.

Reef, The (Wharton), 3538.

Reflections in a Golden Eye (McCullers), 2164-2165.

Regiment of Women (Berger), 309-310.

Regional novel, **3890.**

Reinhart in Love (Berger), 307, 314.

Reinhart's Women (Berger), 313-314.

Rejected Guest (Aldington), 59-60.

Religious fiction, 616, 617.

Remains of the Day, The (Ishiguro), 1709-1711, 3793.

Renault, Mary, 2807-2816; *The Bull from the Sea*, 2811; *The Charioteer*, 2809-2810; *Fire from Heaven*, 2813; *Funeral Games*, 2815; *The King Must Die*, 2811-2812; *The Last of the Wine*, 2811; *The Mask of Apollo*, 2812-2813; *The Persian Boy*, 2813-2814; *The Praise Singer*, 2814; *Promise of Love*, 2809.

Repent in Haste (Marquand), 2303.

Resurrection, The (Gardner), 1271-1272.

Return, The (de la Mare), 844-845.

Return of Ansel Gibbs, The (Buechner), 447-448.

Return of the King, The. See *Lord of the Rings, The*.

Return of the Native, The (Hardy), 1504-1506.

Return of the Sphinx (MacLennan), 2215-2216.

Reuben (Wideman), 3567.

Reuben, Reuben (De Vries), 888-889.

Revenge (Harrison), 1539-1540.

Revenge for Love, The (Lewis, W.), 2084.

Rhetorical criticism, **3890.**

Rhys, Jean, 2817-2824; *Good Morning, Midnight*, 2819; *Quartet*, 2819; *Wide Sargasso Sea*, 2819-2823.

Riceyman Steps (Bennett), 300.

Richard Hurdis (Simms), 3042-3043.

Richardson, Dorothy, 2825-2834, 3764; *Dawn's Left Hand*, 2832- 2833; *Deadlock*, 2831-2832; *March Moonlight*, 2833; *Pilgrimage*, 2828-2833, 3764; *Pointed Roofs*, 2830-2831.

Richardson, Samuel, 2835-2845, 3721, 3732, 3781, 3811; *Clarissa*, 2841-2842, 3816; *Pamela*, 2839-2840, 3721, 3732, 3781-3782, 3814, 3816; *Sir Charles Grandison*, 2842-2843.

Richler, Mordecai, 2846-2856; *The*

Acrobats, 2848; *The Apprenticeship of Duddy Kravitz*, 2849-2851; *Joshua Then and Now*, 2849, 2852-2854; *St. Urbain's Horseman*, 2849, 2851-2852; *Solomon Gursky Was Here*, 2854-2855.

Richter, Conrad, 2857-2868; *The Fields*, 2865; *Human Vibration*, 2860-2861; *The Lady*, 2864; *Principles in Bio-Physics*, 2860-2861; *The Sea of Grass*, 2861-2862; *A Simple Honorable Man*, 2860, 2866-2867; *Tacey Cromwell*, 2862-2864; *The Town*, 2865-2866; *The Trees*, 2864-2865; *The Waters of Kronos*, 2866.

"Ride Out" (Foote), 1161.
Riders in the Chariot (White), 3551-3552.
Riders of the Purple Sage (Grey), 3851.
Riding, Laura, 1417, 1422.
Right to an Answer, The (Burgess), 465-466.
Riotous Assembly (Sharpe), 3847-3848.
"Rip Van Winkle" (Irving, W.), 3800.
Rise of Silas Lapham, The (Howells), 1651-1652, 3757, 3795.
Rites of Passage (Golding), 1356.
River Between, The (Ngugi wa Thiong'o), 2498, 2501-2504.
Rob Roy (Scott), 2991-2995.
Robber Bridegroom, The (Welty), 3493-3494.

Roberts, Elizabeth Madox, 2869-2879; *Black Is My Truelove's Hair*, 2874, 2875-2876; *A Buried Treasure*, 2874-2875; *The Great Meadow*, 2873-2874; *He Sent Forth a Raven*, 2877-2878; *Jingling in the Wind*, 2877; *My Heart and My Flesh*, 2877; *The Time of Man*, 2876-2877.

Robinson Crusoe (Defoe), 821-824, 3727-3728, 3733.
Rocannon's World (Le Guin), 2008-2009.
Rock Wagram (Saroyan), 2952-2953.
Roderick Random (Smollett), 3072-3073, 3735, 3782, 3806.
Roger's Version (Updike), 3358.
Roman à clef, **3890.**
Romance, **3890.**
Romance of Casanova, The (Aldington), 60.
Romance of the Forest, The (Radcliffe), 2779-2780.

Romantic Comedians, The (Glasgow), 1333-1334.
Romantic movement, 3014.
Romanticism, **3890.**
Rookwood (Ainsworth), 43-44.
Room at the Top (Braine), 369, 370.
Room with a View, A (Forster), 1189-1191.
Rose of Dutcher's Coolly (Garland), 1290.

Ross, Sinclair, 2880-2894; *As for Me and My House*, 2882, 2883-2884, 2885-2887; *Sawbones Memorial*, 2885, 2891-2893; *The Well*, 2884, 2887-2889; *Whir of Gold*, 2883-2884, 2889-2891.

Roth, Philip, 2895-2905, 3877; *The Anatomy Lesson*, 2903; *The Breast*, 2900-2901; *The Counterlife*, 2900, 2904; *Deception*, 2904; *The Ghost Writer*, 2901-2902, 3877-3878; *The Great American Novel*, 2900; *Letting Go*, 2898-2899; *My Life as a Man*, 2900; *Our Gang*, 2900; *Portnoy's Complaint*, 2899-2900; *The Prague Orgy*, 2903-2904; *Zuckerman Unbound*, 2902-2903.

Rousseau, Jean-Jacques, 3737, 3816-3817.

Rowson, Susanna, 2906-2916; *Charlotte Temple*, 2909-2912; *Mentoria*, 2912-2913; *Trials of the Human Heart*, 2913-2914.

Roxana (Defoe), 824-828.
Run River (Didion), 924-926.

Rushdie, Salman, 2917-2928, 3777, 3793; *Grimus*, 2919; *Midnight's Children*, 2919, 2920-2922, 3793; *The Satanic Verses*, 2919, 2925-2927, 3777, 3793; *Shame*, 2919, 2922-2925, 3793.

Russia House, The (Le Carré), 1993.
Ruth (Gaskell), 1301, 1306-1307.

S. (Updike), 3358-3359.
Sackett's Land (L'Amour), 1934.
"Sacred Mound, The" (Foote), 1162.
Saddest Summer of Samuel S., The (Donleavy), 948.
Sailors Song (Hanley), 1478.
Saint Jack (Theroux), 3284-3285.
St. Urbain's Horseman (Richler), 2849, 2851-2852.
Saintsbury, George, 2279.
'Salem's Lot (King), 1887-1888.
Salinger, J. D., 2929-2938, 3808; *The*

Catcher in the Rye, 2932, 2934-2939, 3808.

Salter, James, 2939-2944; *The Hunters*, 2940-2941; *Light Years*, 2941-2942; *Solo Faces*, 2942-2943.

Sanctuary (Faulkner), 1097-1098.

Sanders, Lawrence, 3847.

Sandman, The (Hoffman), 3874.

Saroyan, William, 2945-2957; *The Adventures of Wesley Jackson*, 2946, 2952; *Boys and Girls Together*, 2954-2955; *The Human Comedy*, 2946, 2951-2952; *The Laughing Matter*, 2953-2954; *My Name Is Aram*, 2946, 2951; *Rock Wagram*, 2952-2953.

Sarton, May, 2958-2968; *The Birth of a Grandfather*, 2963-2965; *The Bridge of Years*, 2962-2963; *Mrs. Stevens Hears the Mermaids Singing*, 2965-2966; *A Reckoning*, 2966-2967.

Satan in Goray (Singer), 3060-3061.

Satanic Verses, The (Rushdie), 2919, 2925-2927, 3777, 3793.

Satire, 3177, 3462.

Saturday Night and Sunday Morning (Sillitoe), 3029.

Sauce for the Goose (De Vries), 889.

Sawbones Memorial (Ross), 2885, 2891-2893.

Sayers, Dorothy L., 2969-2981, 3844; *Busman's Honeymoon*, 2978; *Gaudy Night*, 2977-2978; *The Mind of the Maker*, 2973-2974; *The Nine Tailors*, 2975-2977, 3844; *Whose Body?*, 2974-2975.

Scapegoat, The (Settle), 3009-3010.

Scarcity of Love, A (Kavan), 1836.

Scarlet Letter, The (Hawthorne), 1575-1577, 3831.

Scene, **3890.**

Schindler's List (Keneally), 1841.

School novels, The (Wodehouse), 3611-3612.

Schoolmaster, The (Lovelace), 2108.

Schultz (Donleavy), 950.

Science fiction, **3890.**

Science fiction novel, **3865-3872.**

Scott, Sir Walter, 2982-3002, 3739, 3784-3785, 3835; *The Heart of Midlothian*, 2995-3000; *Old Mortality*, 2989-2991; *Rob Roy*, 2991-2995; *Waverley*, 2984-2989, 3739, 3835.

Scout, The (Simms), 3041.

Sea of Grass, The (Richter), 2861-2862.

Sea, the Sea, The (Murdoch), 2452-2455.

Sea-Wolf, The (London), 2099-2100.

Seacliff (De Forest), 833-834.

Search, The (Snow), 3084-3085.

Search for America, A (Grove), 1454-1456.

Searching for Caleb (Tyler), 3339-3340.

Season in Purgatory (Keneally), 1841, 1842.

Season of Anomy (Soyinka), 3097-3099.

Season of Grace, A (Gonzalez), 1362-1363.

Season of the Strangler (Jones, M.), 1817-1818.

Season's Difference, The (Buechner), 444, 447.

Second Coming, The (Percy), 2637-2638.

Secret Adversary, The (Christie), 657-658.

Secret Agent, The (Conrad), 3789.

Secret Journey, The. See Fury Chronicle, The.

Secret Ladder, The (Harris, W.), 1530.

Secret Sharer, The (Conrad), 3876.

Seduction by Light (Young), 3717-3719.

Seduction of the Minotaur (Nin), 2516, 2519-2520.

Seize the Day (Bellow), 278-280.

Self Condemned (Lewis, W.), 2084-2085.

Semiotics, **3890.**

Sensation novel, 46-47.

Sense and Sensibility (Austen), 160-161.

Sent for You Yesterday. See Homewood Trilogy, The

Sentimental Journey, A (Sterne), 3178, 3182-3185.

Sentimental novel, **3891.**

September September (Foote), 1162-1163.

Seraph on the Sewanee (Hurston), 1669.

Sergeant Lamb of the Ninth. See Sergeant Lamb's America.

Sergeant Lamb's America (Graves), 1420.

Serialization, 47.

Sermons and Soda Water (O'Hara), 2586-2587.

Serpent and the Rope, The (Rao), 2790-2792.

Set This House on Fire (Styron), 3244, 3250-3251.

Seth's Brother's Wife (Frederic), 1221-1222.

Setting, **3891.**

Setting Free the Bears (Irving, J.), 1694-1696.

Setting the World on Fire (Wilson, Angus), 3596.

Settle, Mary Lee, 3003-3012; *Blood Tie*, 3004, 3008-3009, 3010; *Celebration*, 3004-3005, 3010-3011; *The Clam Shell*, 3004, 3008; *Fight Night on a Sweet Saturday*, 3007-3008; *The Killing Ground*, 3009-3010; *The Kiss of Kin*, 3004, 3006, 3010; *Know Nothing*, 3006-3007; *The Love Eaters*, 3004, 3005-3006; *O Beulah Land*, 3006-3007; *Prisons*, 3008; *The Scapegoat*, 3009-3010.

Settlers of the Marsh (Grove), 1452-1454.

Seven Against Reeves (Aldington), 59.

Seven Hills Away (Gonzalez), 1359.

Seven Rivers West (Hoagland), 1632-1633.

Seven Sisters, The (Prokosch), 2739.

Seven Who Fled, The (Prokosch), 2737-2738.

Several Perceptions (Carter), 567-568.

Shadow Flies, The (Macaulay), 2139.

Shadow Knows, The (Johnson, D.), 1773-1774.

Shadows (Gardner), 1282-1283.

Shadows on the Rock (Cather), 595-596.

Shalako (L'Amour), 3854.

Shame (Rushdie), 2919, 2922-2925, 3793.

Shamela (Fielding, H.), 1124, 1126-1128.

Sharpe, Tom, 3847.

Shelley, Mary Wollstonecraft, 3013-3025, 3831; *Falkner*, 3020, 3022-3023; *The Fortunes of Perkin Warbeck*, 3020; *Frankenstein*, 3016-3017, 3831; *The Last Man*, 3018-3020; *Lodore*, 3020-3022; *Valperga*, 3017-3018.

Shelley, Percy Bysshe, 2618, 2620, 3014-3015.

Sheltered Life, The (Glasgow), 1334-1335.

Sheltering Sky, The (Bowles), 328-329.

Shikasta (Lessing), 2038.

Shiloh (Foote), 1160.

Shining, The (King), 1888.

Ship of Fools (Porter), 2655-2657.

Shirley (Brontë, C.), 386-387.

Shosha (Singer), 3065.

Shoten an Goray. See Satan in Goray.

Shrapnel Academy, The (Weldon), 3476-3477.

Shrimp and the Anemone, The (Hartley), 1553.

Shroud for a Nightingale (James, P.), 1732-1733.

Sicilian Romance, A (Radcliffe), 2779.

Sick Heart River (Buchan), 429-430.

Sidney, Sir Philip, 3722.

Siege of Krishnapur, The (Farrell, J. G.), 1085-1086.

Sign of the Four, The (Doyle), 973-974.

Silas Marner (Eliot), 1039-1040.

Sillitoe, Alan, 3026-3033, 3808; *The Death of William Posters*, 3030; *The Flame of Life*, 3031; *Key to the Door*, 3029-3030; *The Loneliness of the Long-Distance Runner*, 3028-3029; *The Open Door*, 3031-3032; *Saturday Night and Sunday Morning*, 3029; *A Tree on Fire*, 3031.

Silmarillion, The (Tolkien), 3295-3298.

Silver Chair, The (Lewis, C.), 2050.

Silverberg, Robert, 3871.

Simenon, Georges, 3848.

Simms, William Gilmore, 3034-3045; *Beauchampe*, 3043; *Confession*, 3044; *Guy Rivers*, 3042; "Joscelyn," 3040-3041; *Martin Faber*, 3044; *Mellichampe*, 3039, 3041; *The Partisan*, 3041; *Richard Hurdis*, 3042-3043; *The Scout*, 3041; *Woodcraft*, 3041-3042; *The Yemassee*, 3043.

"Simple Art of Murder, The" (Chandler), 602-603, 605.

Simple Honorable Man, A (Richter), 2860, 2866-2867.

Simple Truth, The (Hardwick), 1492-1493.

Simplicissimus the Vagabond (Grimmelshausen), 3805.

Sincerely, Willis Wayde (Marquand), 2303, 2304-2305.

Sinclair, May, 3765.

Sinclair, Upton, 3046-3057, 3761, 3797; *Boston*, 3054-3055; Dead Hand series, 3046-3047; *The Jungle*, 3050-3052, 3761, 3797; *King Coal*, 3053-3054; Lanny Budd series, 3055; *Love's Pilgrimage*, 3053; *Manassas*, 3050; *The Metropolis*, 3052; *The Money Changers*, 3052-3053.

Singapore Grip, The (Farrell, J. G.), 1086.

Singer, Isaac Bashevis, 3058-3067; *Enemies*, 3064-3065; *The Estate*, 3061-3063; *The Family Moskat*, 3061-3063; *The King of the Fields*,

3065-3066; *The Magician of Lublin*, 3063-3064; *Satan in Goray*, 3060-3061; *Shosha*, 3065.

Singular Man, A (Donleavy), 947-948.

Sir Charles Grandison (Richardson, S.), 2842-2843.

Sir Launcelot Greaves (Smollett), 3074-3075.

Sirian Experiments, The (Lessing), 2038.

Sister Carrie (Dreiser), 997-999, 3759.

Sitka (L'Amour), 1933.

Sitting Pretty (Young), 3715-3716.

Sixth Heaven, The (Hartley), 1553-1554.

Skies of Europe, The (Prokosch), 2739.

Slaughterhouse-Five (Vonnegut), 3384-3388.

Sleeping Murder (Christie), 658-659.

Sleepless Nights (Hardwick), 1493.

Slipping-Down Life, A (Tyler), 3336-3337.

Slouching Towards Kalamazoo (De Vries), 889.

Small Town in Germany, A (Le Carré), 1989.

Small World (Lodge), 2092-2093.

Smiley's People (Le Carré), 1991-1992.

Smith, June Edith, 2380-2381.

Smollett, Tobias, 3068-3077, 3734, 3735, 3782, 3806; *Ferdinand, Count Fathom*, 3074; *Humphry Clinker*, 3075-3076; *Peregrine Pickle*, 3073-3074; *Roderick Random*, 3072-3073, 3735, 3782, 3806; *Sir Launcelot Greaves*, 3074-3075.

Smuggler's Bible, A (McElroy), 2182-2183.

Snakes (Young), 3712-3714.

Snapshots, 1948.

Sneaky People (Berger), 310-311.

Snooty Baronet (Lewis, W.), 2083.

Snow, C. P., 3078-3091, 3766; *A Coat of Varnish*, 3090; *Corridors of Power*, 3089; *Death Under Sail*, 3084; *In Their Wisdom*, 3090; *The Malcontents*, 3089-3090; *The Masters*, 3088-3089; *New Lives for Old*, 3084; *The Search*, 3084-3085; *Strangers and Brothers* series, 3085-3086, 3766; *Time of Hope*, 3087-3088.

Snow Leopard, The (Matthiessen), 2311.

Snow White (Barthelme), 235.

So Little Time (Marquand), 2303.

So Long, See You Tomorrow (Maxwell), 2345-2346.

So the Wind Won't Blow It All Away (Brautigan), 377-379.

Soft Machine, The (Burroughs), 486, 488.

Solar Lottery (Dick), 894.

Soldier's Art, The (Powell, A.), 2679-2680.

Solid Mandala, The (White), 3552-3553.

Solo Faces (Salter), 2942-2943.

Solomon Gursky Was Here (Richler), 2854-2855.

Solzhenitsyn, Aleksandr, 3839.

Something About a Soldier (Harris, M.), 1519-1521.

Something Happened (Heller), 1591-1592.

Something to Be Desired (McGuane), 2202-2204.

Something Wicked This Way Comes (Bradbury), 361.

Sometimes a Great Notion (Kesey), 1879-1881.

Son of Perdition, The (Cozzens), 764.

Song of Solomon (Morrison), 2427-2431.

Song of the Lark, The (Cather), 591-592.

Sonim de Geshichte fun a Liebe. See *Enemies*.

Sons and Lovers (Lawrence), 1958-1962, 3767.

Sophie's Choice (Styron), 3253-3255.

Sorrows of Young Werther, The (Goethe), 3736, 3817-3819.

Sot-Weed Factor, The (Barth), 225-227.

Sound and the Fury, The (Faulkner), 1092-1096, 3766, 3771, 3832.

Sour Sweet (Mo), 3793

Source of Light, The (Price), 2707.

Southern Family, A (Godwin), 1345-1346.

Southern literature, 3332-3334.

Southpaw, The (Harris, M.), 1518-1519.

Soyinka, Wole, 3092-3101; *The Interpreters*, 3094-3097; *Season of Anomy*, 3097-3099.

Space (Michener), 2375-2376

Spark, Muriel, 3102-3117; *Comforters*, 3105, 3106-3108; *The Driver's Seat*, 3106, 3111-3113; *A Far Cry from Kensington*, 3116; *Loitering with Intent*, 3105, 3113-3115; *Not to Disturb*, 3106; *The Only Problem*, 3115-3116; *The Prime of Miss Jean Brodie*, 3105, 3108-3111; *The Public Image*, 3105; *Symposium*, 3116; *Territorial Rights*, 3105.

Spatial form, **3891.**

Spella Ho (Bates), 243-244.
Spider's House, The (Bowles), 330-331.
Spillane, Mickey, 3846.
Spire, The (Golding), 1353-1354.
Spoil of Office, A (Garland), 1288-1289.
Sport of Nature, A (Gordimer), 1392-1393.
Sporting Club, The (McGuane), 2198-2199.
Sportswriter, The (Ford, R.), 1178-1179.
Spy in the House of Love, A (Nin), 2516, 2519.
Spy Who Came in from the Cold, The (Le Carré), 1986-1988.
S. S. San Pedro (Cozzens), 764-765.
Stand, The (King), 1888-1889.
Staring at the Sun (Barnes), 213-215.
Stars in My Pocket Like Grains of Sand (Delany), 855, 859-860.
Stars Look Down, The (Cronin), 786, 788-789, 794.
State of Nature, The (Goodman), 1371-1372. See also *Empire City, The*.
Stead, Christina, 3118-3126; *Dark Places of the Heart*, 3123-3124; *For Love Alone*, 3122-3123; *Letty Fox*, 3119, 3122; *The Man Who Loved Children*, 3120-3122.
Stegner, Wallace, 3127-3136; *Angle of Repose*, 3130, 3131-3133; *The Big Rock Candy Mountain*, 3130-3131; *Crossing to Safety*, 3134-3135; *Recapitulation*, 3133-3134.
Stein, Gertrude, 3137-3150; *Brewsie and Willie*, 3148-3149; *Ida, A Novel*, 3148; *Lucy Church Amiably*, 3147; *The Making of Americans*, 3141-3142; *Quod Erat Demonstrandum*, 3144-3145; *Three Lives*, 3145; *The World Is Round*, 3147-3148.
Steinbeck, John, 3151-3162, 3770; *The Grapes of Wrath*, 3158-3159, 3770; *In Dubious Battle*, 3155-3156, 3770; *Of Mice and Men*, 3156; *The Pearl*, 3159-3160; *The Red Pony*, 3156-3157.
"Stella" (Nin), 2515-2516.
Steps (Kosinski), 1923-1925.
Sterling, John, 3858.
Stern, Richard G., 3163-3171; *A Father's Words*, 3169-3170; *Golk*, 3164-3165; *In Any Case*, 3165-3166; *Natural Shocks*, 3168-3169; *Other Men's Daughters*,

3167-3168; *Stitch*, 3166-3167.
Sterne, Laurence, 3172-3187, 3733, 3782; *A Political Romance*, 3175, 3177; *A Sentimental Journey*, 3178, 3182-3185; *Tristram Shandy*, 3179-3182, 3733, 3782.
Stevenson, Robert Louis, 3188-3197, 3790, 3876; *The Black Arrow*, 3192; *Kidnapped*, 3194; *The Master of Ballantrae*, 3194-3195; *The Strange Case of Dr. Jekyll and Mr. Hyde*, 3193, 3876; *Treasure Island*, 3190-3192.
Stillness (Gardner), 1282.
Stillwater Tragedy, The (Aldrich), 70-71.
Stitch (Stern), 3166-3167.
Stoker, Bram, 3831-3832, 3863.
Stone, Robert, 3198-3204; *Children of Light*, 3202; *Dog Soldiers*, 3200-3201, 3202; *A Flag for Sunrise*, 3201-3203; *A Hall of Mirrors*, 3200.
Stone Angel, The (Laurence), 1944-1946.
Storm and Echo (Prokosch), 2740.
Story of a Bad Boy, The (Aldrich), 66-68.
Story of a Novel, The (Wolfe), 3634.
Story of Marie Powell, Wife to Mr. Milton, The (Graves), 1421-1422.
Stowe, Harriet Beecher, 3205-3218, 3750; *Dred*, 3212; *A Key to Uncle Tom's Cabin*, 3209, 3210; *The Minister's Wooing*, 3213-3214; *My Wife and I*, 3216; *Oldtown Folks*, 3215-3216; *Poganuc People*, 3216-3217; *Uncle Tom's Cabin*, 3209-3211, 3750; *We and Our Neighbors*, 3216.
Strange Case of Dr. Jekyll and Mr. Hyde, The (Stevenson), 3193, 3876.
Strange Children, The (Gordon), 1401.
Strangers and Brothers series, 3085-3086, 3766.
Stream of consciousness, **3891.**
Strike the Father Dead (Wain), 3395, 3397-3398.
Structuralism, **3891.**
Stuart, Jesse, 3219-3230; *Daughter of the Legend*, 3228-3229; *Foretaste of Glory*, 3227; *The Good Spirit of Laurel Ridge*, 3227-3228; *Mr. Gallion's School*, 3229; *Taps for Private Tussie*, 3225-3227; *Trees of Heaven*, 3224-3225.
Studs Lonigan: A Trilogy (Farrell, James), 1076-1077, 3770.

Study in Scarlet, A (Doyle), 974, 3843.
Sturgeon, Theodore, 3231-3240; "Baby Is Three," 3236; *The Cosmic Rape*, 3237-3238; *The Dreaming Jewels*, 3233-3236; *More Than Human*, 3234, 3236-3239; *Venus Plus X*, 3234, 3238-3239.
Style, 1490, 1715, 2212-2213.
Styron, William, 3241-3256, 3839-3840; *The Confessions of Nat Turner*, 3244-3245, 3251-3253, 3839-3840; *Lie Down in Darkness*, 3243, 3247-3249; *The Long March*, 3249-3250; *Set This House on Fire*, 3244, 3250-3251; *Sophie's Choice*, 3253-3255.
Subterraneans, The (Kerouac), 1867-1868.
Success (Amis, M.), 103.
Succession, The (Garrett), 1297.
Such Is My Beloved (Callaghan), 542, 544-545.
Suffrage of Elvira, The (Naipaul), 2473.
Suicide's Wife, The (Madden), 2233-2234, 2238.
Sula (Morrison), 2426-2427.
Summary, **3891.**
Summer (Wharton), 3537-3538.
Summer Before the Dark, The (Lessing), 2037.
Summer Bird-Cage, A (Drabble), 982.
Sun Also Rises, The (Hemingway), 1598-1601, 3769.
Sun, He Dies, The (Highwater), 1622-1624.
Sundog (Harrison), 1544.
Sunlight Dialogues, The (Gardner), 1274-1276.
Surface of the Earth, The (Price), 2704-2707.
Surfacing (Atwood), 135-136.
Surrealism, 2515.
Survivor (Butler, O.), 495-496.
Suttree (McCarthy, C.), 2145-2146.
Swag (Leonard), 2028-2029.
Swami and Friends (Narayan), 2483.
Swamp Angel (Wilson, E.), 3606.
Sweets of Pimlico, The (Wilson, A. N.), 3581-3582.
Swift, Jonathan, 3257-3265, 3857; *Gulliver's Travels*, 3262-3264; *A Tale of a Tub*, 3259-3261; *Verses on the Death of Dr. Swift*, 3259.
Sword of Honour (Waugh), 3467-3468.
Sylvia's Lovers (Gaskell), 1304.

Symbolism, 2513, 3504-3505.
Symposium (Spark), 3116.
Synthetic Man, The. See *Dreaming Jewels, The*.

Tacey Cromwell (Richter), 2862-2864.
Take a Girl Like You (Amis, K.), 89, 91-92, 97-98.
Tale for Midnight, A (Prokosch), 2740.
Tale of a Tub, A (Swift), 3259-3261.
Tale of Two Cities, A (Dickens), 3838.
Tales of Nevèrÿon (Delany), 854.
Tales of the South Pacific (Michener), 2372
Taps for Private Tussie (Stuart), 3225-3227.
Tar Baby (Morrison), 2431-2433.
Tarr (Lewis, W.), 2082.
Taste for Death, A (James, P.), 1735-1736.
Tate, Allen, 1396.
Tattooed Countess, The (Van Vechten), 3365-3366.
Tehanu (Le Guin), 2013-2014.
"Tell-Tale Heart, The" (Poe), 3831.
Temple, Mary (Minny), 1717.
Temporary Kings (Powell, A.), 2677, 2680-2681.
Temptation of Eileen Hughes, The (Moore, B.), 2399.
Ten Little Indians (Christie), 3845.
Ten North Frederick (O'Hara), 2583-2586.
Tenants of Moonbloom, The (Wallant), 3422-3423.
Tender Is the Night (Fitzgerald), 1146-1148.
Tenement of Clay (West, P.), 3522-3523.
Tennis Handsome, The (Hannah), 1485-1486.
Tents of Wickedness, The (De Vries), 887.
Terrible Twos, The (Reed), 2804.
Territorial Rights (Spark), 3105.
Tess of the D'Urbervilles (Hardy), 1507-1510, 3758.
Texas (Michener), 2376-2377.
Texasville (McMurtry), 2222.
Thackeray, William Makepeace, 3266-3280, 3787; *The History of Henry Esmond, Esquire*, 3274-3276; *The History of Pendennis*, 3273-3274; *The Newcomes*, 3271, 3276-3277; *Vanity Fair*, 3270-3273, 3787; *The Virginians*, 3271, 3277-3279.
Thanatos Syndrome, The (Percy), 2638-2640.

That Hideous Strength (Lewis, C.), 2047-2048.
That Lady (O'Brien, K.), 2565.
Theft, A (Bellow), 287.
Their Eyes Were Watching God (Hurston), 1669, 1671-1673.
Thematics, **3892.**
Theophilus North (Wilder), 3577-3578.
Theroux, Paul, 3281-3289; *The Family Arsenal*, 3285-3286; *Fong and the Indians*, 3283-3284; *Mosquito Coast*, 3286-3287; *My Secret History*, 3287; *O-Zone*, 3287; *Picture Palace*, 3286; *Saint Jack*, 3284-3285.
These Twain (Bennett), 299-300.
They Came Like Swallows (Maxwell), 2343-2344.
They Hanged My Saintly Billy (Graves), 1419-1420.
Thieves in the Night (Koestler), 1914.
Thin Man, The (Hammett), 1463-1464, 1468-1469, 3846.
Thin Red Line, The (Jones, J.), 1804-1805.
Things as They Are (Horgan), 1640.
Things Fall Apart (Achebe), 6, 7-8.
Third Life of Grange Copeland, The (Walker), 3407, 3408-3410.
Third-person narration, 577.
Third Policeman, The (O'Brien, F.), 2554, 2555-2556.
Third Violet, The (Crane), 776-777.
Thirty-Nine Steps, The (Buchan), 427.
This Side Jordan (Laurence), 1944.
This Side of Paradise (Fitzgerald), 1140-1141, 1142.
Thomas of Reading (Deloney), 3723, 3724.
Those Barren Leaves (Huxley), 1678-1679.
Three Cheers for the Paraclete (Keneally), 1845.
Three Hostages, The (Buchan), 427-428.
Three Lives (Stein), 3145.
Three Mulla-Mulgars, The (de la Mare), 843-844.
Three Musketeers, The (Dumas), 3838.
Three Soldiers (Dos Passos), 956-957, 3763.
Three Stigmata of Palmer Eldritch, The (Dick), 896-897.
Ticket That Exploded, The (Burroughs), 486-487, 488-489.
Till We Have Faces (Lewis, C.), 2050-2051.

Time Machine, The (Wells), 3481-3482, 3867.
Time Must Have a Stop (Huxley), 1684.
Time of Hope (Snow), 3087-3088.
Time of Man, The (Roberts), 2876-2877.
Time Out of Joint (Dick), 895.
Time Will Darken It, 2344-2345.
Tin Can Tree, The (Tyler), 3334-3335.
Tinker, Tailor, Soldier, Spy (Le Carré), 1989-1990.
To Asmara (Keneally), 1847-1848.
To Be a Pilgrim (Cary), 578, 579-580.
To Let (Galsworthy), 1264.
To the Lighthouse (Woolf), 3652-3655, 3764.
To the North (Bowen), 321.
Tobacco Road (Caldwell), 534-536.
Told by an Idiot (Macaulay), 2138.
Tolkien, J. R. R., 3290-3303, 3862; *The Hobbit*, 3298-3299, 3862; *The Lord of the Rings*, 3299-3300, 3862; *The Silmarillion*, 3295-3298.
Tom Jones (Fielding, G.), 1131-1132, 3732, 3733, 3782, 3806.
Tone, **3892.**
Tono-Bungay (Wells), 3483.
Tory Lover, The (Jewett), 1748-1750.
Tough Guys Don't Dance (Mailer), 2261-2262.
Tournament (Foote), 1156-1157.
Tower of London, The (Ainsworth), 44-45.
Towers of Trebizond, The (Macaulay), 2140.
Town, The (Richter), 2865-2866.
Town and the City, The (Kerouac), 1863-1865.
Toynbee Convector, The (Bradbury), 362.
Track of the Cat, The (Clark), 663, 667-669.
Tracks (Erdrich), 1070-1071.
Tradition, 1572-1573.
Tragedy of Puddn'head Wilson, The (Twain), 3326.
Tragic novel, 1499.
Tragicomic, 883.
Travelers (Jhabvala), 1756-1757.
Travels into Several Remote Nations of the World . . . See Gulliver's Travels.
Travesty (Hawkes), 1564-1565.
Treasure Hunt. See Book of Bebb, The.
Treasure Island (Stevenson), 3190-3192.
Tree of Man, The (White), 3550.

Tree of the Sun, The (Harris, W.), 1531-1532.

Tree on Fire, A (Sillitoe), 3031.

Trees, The (Richter), 2864-2865.

Trees of Heaven (Stuart), 3224-3225.

Tremor of Intent (Burgess), 466-467.

Trent's Last Case (Bentley), 3843.

Trials of the Human Heart (Rowson), 2913-2914.

Trick of the Ga Bolga, The (McGinley), 2191, 2192-2193.

Triple Echo, The (Bates), 246.

Tristram Shandy (Sterne), 3179-3182, 3733, 3782.

Triton (Delany), 855, 857-859.

Trollope, Anthony, 3304-3316, 3742-3743, 3787, 3788; *Barchester Towers*, 3309-3310; *Can You Forgive Her?*, 3312-3313; *The Eustace Diamonds*, 3313-3315; *Orley Farm*, 3310-3312.

Tropic of Cancer (Miller), 2383-2385.

Tropic of Capricorn (Miller), 2380.

Trouble on Triton. See *Triton*.

Troubles (Farrell, J. G.), 1084-1085.

Trout Fishing in America (Brautigan), 377.

Truth About Them, The (Yglesias), 3705.

Tuesday and Wednesday (Wilson, E.), 3603-3604.

Tumatumari (Harris, W.), 1531.

Tunc (Durrell), 1014.

Tunnel of Love, The (De Vries), 885-886.

Turn of the Screw, The (James, H.), 3874-3875.

Twain, Mark, 3317-3328, 3745, 3750, 3751, 3795, 3807, 3860; *The Adventures of Huckleberry Finn*, 3318-3319, 3323-3325, 3745, 3750, 3807; *The Adventures of Tom Sawyer*, 3318-3319, 3321-3323; *A Connecticut Yankee in King Arthur's Court*, 3325-3326, 3860; *The Gilded Age*, 3795; *The Prince and the Pauper*, 3323; *The Tragedy of Puddn'head Wilson*, 3326.

Two Deaths of Christopher Martin. See *Pincher Martin*.

"Two Girls" (De Forest), 834-835.

Two Solitudes (MacLennan), 2208, 2214.

Two Thousand Seasons (Armah), 128-129.

Two Towers, The. See *Lord of the Rings, The*.

Twyborn Affair, The (White), 3556-3557.

Tyler, Anne, 3329-3346; *The Accidental Tourist*, 3343-3344; *Breathing Lessons*, 3344-3345; *Celestial Navigation*, 3338-3339; *The Clock Winder*, 3337-3338; *Dinner at the Homesick Restaurant*, 3343-3344; *Earthly Possessions*, 3340-3341; *If Morning Ever Comes*, 3334; *Morgan's Passing*, 3341-3342; *Searching for Caleb*, 3339-3340; *A Slipping-Down Life*, 3336-3337; *The Tin Can Tree*, 3334-3335.

Typee (Melville), 2351.

Ubik (Dick), 897.

Ultimate Good Luck, The (Ford, R.), 1177-1178.

Ulysses (Joyce), 1826-1829, 3765, 3807.

Unclassed, The (Gissing), 1322-1323.

Uncle Silas (Le Fanu), 2001-2002.

Uncle Tom's Cabin (Stowe), 3209-3211, 3750.

Unconditional Surrender. See *End of the Battle, The*.

Under the Net (Murdoch), 2441-2444.

Under the Volcano (Lowry), 2116-2125.

Underground Man, The (Macdonald), 2176-2177.

Underground Woman, The (Boyle, K.), 345-346.

Unfinished Portrait (Christie), 652.

Unfortunate Traveller: Or, The Life of Jack Wilton, The (Nashe), 3725, 3806.

Universal Baseball Association, The (Coover), 752-754.

Unlimited Dream Company, The (Ballard), 196.

Unnamable, The (Beckett), 261.

Unreliable narrator, **3892.**

"Unspoiled Monsters" (Capote), 561.

Unsuitable Attachment, An (Pym), 2753-2754.

Unsuitable Job for a Woman, An (James, P.), 1733.

Untamed, The (Faust), 3851.

Unvanquished, The (Fast), 3838

Up Above the World (Bowles), 331-332.

Updike, John, 3347-3360, 3808; *Bech*, 3357; *Bech Is Back*, 3357; *The Centaur*, 3351-3352; *The Coup*, 3357-3358; *Couples*, 3355-3356; *Marry Me*, 3356; *A*

Month of Sundays, 3358; *Of the Farm*, 3352; *The Poorhouse Fair*, 3350-3351; *Rabbit at Rest*, 3354-3355; *Rabbit Is Rich*, 3354; *Rabbit Redux*, 3353-3354; *Rabbit, Run*, 3352-3353, 3806; *Roger's Version*, 3358; *S.*, 3358-3359; *The Witches of Eastwick*, 3356-3357.
U.S.A. trilogy (Dos Passos), 958-962, 3766.

V. (Pynchon), 2766-2768.
Valis (Dick), 898-899.
Valley of Bones, The (Powell, A.), 2679.
Valley of the Moon, The (London), 2103.
Valperga (Shelley), 3017-3018.
Van Dine, S. S., 3845.
Van Vechten, Carl, 3361-3368; *Nigger Heaven*, 3366; *Parties*, 3366-3367; *Peter Whiffle*, 3363-3365; *The Tattooed Countess*, 3365-3366.
Vandover and the Brute (Norris), 2527.
Vanity Fair (Thackeray), 3270-3273, 3787.
Vein of Iron (Glasgow), 1330.
Venus Plus X (Sturgeon), 3234, 3238-3239.
Venusberg (Powell, A.), 2676.
Verne, Jules, 3866, 3867.
Verses on the Death of Dr. Swift, 3259.
Very Heaven (Aldington), 58-59.
Very Rich Hours of Count von Stauffenberg, The (West, P.), 3526-3527.
Vicar of Wakefield, The (Goldsmith), 3736.
Victim, The (Bellow), 277-278.
Victim of the Aurora, A (Keneally), 1844-1845.
Victorian novel, **3892.**
Victory (Conrad), 726.
Vidal, Gore, 3369-3378, 3839; *Burr*, 3374; *The City and the Pillar*, 3372; *Creation*, 3374; *1876*, 3375-3376; *Empire*, 3376; *The Judgment of Paris*, 3372-3373; *Julian*, 3373-3374; *Lincoln*, 3375; *Messiah*, 3373; *Myra Breckenridge*, 3376-3377; *Washington, D.C.*, 3376.
Vietnam Project, The. See Dusklands.
Villette (Brontë, C.), 387-388.
Vineland (Pynchon), 2771-2772, 3771, 3777.
Violent Bear It Away, The (O'Connor), 2569, 2572-2573.
Violet Clay (Godwin), 1342-1343.

Virginia (Glasgow), 1331-1332.
Virginian, The (Wister), 3849.
Virginians, The (Thackeray), 3271, 3277-3279.
Vital Parts (Berger), 309.
Vivisector, The (White), 3553-3554.
"Voice, The" (Nin), 2515-2516.
Voices in the City (Desai), 872, 873, 874-875.
Voices in Time (MacLennan), 2216-2217.
Vonnegut, Kurt, Jr., 3379-3389, 3870, 3878; *Cat's Cradle*, 3382-3384; *Mother Night*, 3381-3382; *Player Piano*, 3380-3381; *Slaughterhouse-Five*, 3384-3388.
Vorticism, 2081.
Voss (White), 3550-3551.
Voyage of the Dawn Treader, The (Lewis, C.), 2050.
Voyage Out, The (Woolf), 3646-3647.
Voyage to Arcturus, A (Lindsay), 3860.
Vraisemblance/Verisimilitude, **3892.**

Wain, John, 3390-3403, 3808; *Hurry on Down*, 3395-3397, 3808; *The Pardoner's Tale*, 3395, 3399-3401; *Strike the Father Dead*, 3395, 3397-3398; *A Winter in the Hills*, 3395, 3398-3399.
Waiting for Sheila (Braine), 371.
Waiting for the Barbarians (Coetzee), 675-676.
Waiting Room, The (Harris, W.), 1530-1531.
Wake in Ybor City, A (Yglesias), 3701-3703.
Wake Up, Stupid (Harris, M.), 1521-1522.
Waldo, Edward Hamilton. *See* **Sturgeon, Theodore.**
Walk on the Wild Side, A (Algren), 80-81.
Walker, Alice, 3404-3415; *The Color Purple*, 3407-3408, 3412-3414; *Meridian*, 3407, 3410-3412; *The Third Life of Grange Copeland*, 3407, 3408-3410.
Walking Drum, The (L'Amour), 1936.
Wall, The (Hersey), 1614-1615.
Wallant, Edward Lewis, 3416-3424; *The Children at the Gate*, 3421-3422; *The Human Season*, 3419-3420; *The Pawnbroker*, 3420-3421; *The Tenants of Moonbloom*, 3422-3423.
Walpole, Horace, 3736, 3782, 3823, 3874.

Wambaugh, Joseph, 3425-3431; *The Black Marble*, 3430; *The Blue Knight*, 3428-3429; *The Choirboys*, 3429-3430; *The New Centurions*, 3427-3428.

Wanderer, The (Burney), 479-480.

Wapshot Chronicle, The (Cheever), 617-619.

Wapshot Scandal, The (Cheever), 619-621.

War and Remembrance (Wouk), 3673-3674, 3837.

War Between the Tates, The (Lurie), 2128, 2129.

War of the Worlds, The (Wells), 3482.

Warlock (Harrison), 1542-1544.

Warren, Robert Penn, 3432-3446, 3772; *All the King's Men*, 3440-3441, 3772; *At Heaven's Gate*, 3443; *John Brown*, 3438; *Meet Me in the Green Glen*, 3443-3444; *Night Rider*, 3439-3440; *A Place to Come To*, 3443; *Wilderness*, 3443; *World Enough and Time*, 3441-3443.

Washington, D.C. (Vidal), 3376.

Washington Square (James, H.), 1720.

Watch That Ends the Night, The (MacLennan), 2215.

Watch the North Wind Rise (Graves), 1426.

Water-Method Man, The (Irving, J.), 1696-1697.

Water Music (Boyle, T.), 349-350.

Waterfall, The (Drabble), 985-986.

Waters, Frank, 3447-3459; *The Man Who Killed the Deer*, 3451-3453; *Masked Gods*, 3447; *Mountain Dialogues*, 3447; *People of the Valley*, 3450-3451; *Pikes Peak*, 3450, 3455-3457; *The Woman at Otowi Crossing*, 3453, 3454-3455; *The Yogi of Cockroach Court*, 3453-3454.

Waters of Kronos, The (Richter), 2866.

Watt (Beckett), 258-259.

Waugh, Evelyn, 3460-3472, 3767, 3768; *Brideshead Revisited*, 3465-3466; *Decline and Fall*, 3462-3463; *The End of the Battle*, 3470; *A Handful of Dust*, 3463-3465; *The Loved One*, 3466-3467; *Men at Arms*, 3468-3469; *Officers and Gentlemen*, 3469; *Sword of Honour*, 3467-3468.

Waverley (Scott), 2984-2989, 3739, 3835.

Waves, The (Woolf), 3655-3656.

Way of All Flesh, The (Butler, S.), 506-508.

We and Our Neighbors (Stowe), 3216.

Web and the Rock, The (Wolfe), 3636-3637.

Weep Not, Child (Ngugi wa Thiong'o), 2498, 2500-2501.

Weil, Simone, 2447.

Weinstein, Nathan. *See* **West, Nathanael.**

Welcome to Hard Times (Doctorow), 935.

Weldon, Fay, 3473-3479, 3871; *. . . And the Wife Ran Away*, 3475; *The Life and Loves of a She-Devil*, 3475-3476; *The Shrapnel Academy*, 3476-3477.

Well, The (Jolley), 1794-1795.

Well, The (Ross), 2884, 2887-2889.

Wells, H. G., 3480-3487, 3791, 3866, 3867, 3869; *Ann Veronica*, 3484; *The Autocracy of Mr. Parham*, 3485; *The First Men in the Moon*, 3482; *The Food of the Gods, and How It Came to Earth*, 3482; *The History of Mr. Polly*, 3483-3484; *In the Days of the Comet*, 3483; *The Invisible Man*, 3482; *The Island of Dr. Moreau*, 3482; *Kipps*, 3483; *Mr. Blettsworthy on Rampole*, 3484-3485; *Mr. Britling Sees It Through*, 3484; *The Time Machine*, 3481-3482, 3867; *Tono-Bungay*, 3483; *The War of the Worlds*, 3482;

Welty, Eudora, 3488-3500; *Delta Wedding*, 3491-3492, 3494-3495; *Losing Battles*, 3497-3498; *The Optimist's Daughter*, 3491-3492, 3498-3499; *The Ponder Heart*, 3491-3492, 3495-3497; *The Robber Bridegroom*, 3493-3494.

We're Friends Again (O'Hara), 2587.

Wescott, Glenway, 3501-3511; *Apartment in Athens*, 3509; *The Apple of the Eye*, 3503-3505; *The Grandmothers*, 3505-3507; *The Pilgrim Hawk*, 3507-3509.

West, Nathanael, 3512-3519; *A Cool Million*, 3516-3517; *The Day of the Locust*, 3517-3519; *The Dream Life of Balso Snell*, 3515; *Miss Lonelyhearts*, 3515-3516.

West, Paul, 3520-3529; *Alley Jaggers*, 3523; *Bela Lugosi's White Christmas*, 3524; *Caliban's Filibuster*, 3524-3525; *Colonel Mint*, 3525-3526; *Gala*, 3526; *I'm Expecting to Live Quite Soon*,

3523-3524; *A Quality of Mercy*, 3521-3522; *Rat Man of Paris*, 3527-3528; *Tenement of Clay*, 3522-3523; *The Very Rich Hours of Count von Stauffenberg*, 3526-3527.
Western Lands, The (Burroughs), 490.
Western novel, **3849-3856, 3892.**
Wharton, Edith, 3530-3542, 3762; *The Age of Innocence*, 3536-3537; *The Buccaneers*, 3540; *The Custom of the Country*, 3539-3540; *Ethan Frome*, 3537; *The House of Mirth*, 3534, 3535-3536; *The Reef*, 3538; *Summer*, 3537-3538.
Wharton, Edward (Teddy) Robbins, 3533.
What I'm Going to Do, I Think (Woiwode), 3621-3622.
What's Become of Waring (Powell, A.), 2676.
What's Bred in the Bone (Davies), 801, 802.
Wheat That Springeth Green (Powers), 2695-2697.
Where Angels Fear to Tread (Forster), 1186-1187.
Where Shall We Go This Summer? (Desai), 876.
While Gods Are Falling (Lovelace), 2107-2108.
Whir of Gold (Ross), 2883-2884, 2889-2891.
Whistle (Jones, J.), 1805-1806.
White, Patrick, 3543-3559; *The Aunt's Story*, 3548-3549; *The Eye of the Storm*, 3554-3555; *A Fringe of Leaves*, 3555-3556; *Happy Valley*, 3546-3547; *The Living and the Dead*, 3547; *Riders in the Chariot*, 3551-3552; *The Solid Mandala*, 3552-3553; *The Tree of Man*, 3550; *The Twyborn Affair*, 3556-3557; *The Vivisector*, 3553-3554; *Voss*, 3550-3551.
White, Ruth Withycomb, 3544.
White, T. H., 3862.
White Company, The (Doyle), 972-973.
White Fang (London), 2100.
White Noise (DeLillo), 866, 867-868.
Whitewater (Horgan), 1640-1641.
Who Are You? (Kavan), 1837.
Who Is Angelina? (Young), 3714-3715.
Who Is Teddy Villanova? (Berger), 311.
Who Was Oswald Fish? (Wilson, A. N.), 3583-3584.

Whole Armour, The (Harris, W.), 1529-1530.
Whose Body? (Sayers), 2974-2975.
Why Are We in Vietnam? (Mailer), 2254-2256.
Why Are We So Blest? (Armah), 126-128.
Wicked Pavilion, The (Powell, D.), 2687.
Wickford Point (Marquand), 2302.
Wide Sargasso Sea (Rhys), 2819-2823.
Wideman, John Edgar, 3560-3569; *A Glance Away*, 3562-3563; *The Homewood Trilogy*, 3561-3562, 3565-3567; *Hurry Home*, 3563-3564; *The Lynchers*, 3564-3565; *Reuben*, 3567.
Wieland (Brown), 410-415, 418.
Wife of His Youth, The (Chesnutt), 629.
Wild Boys, The (Burroughs), 489.
Wild Irish Boy, The (Maturin), 2326.
Wild Palms, The (Faulkner), 3766, 3776.
Wild Seed (Butler, O.), 496-497.
Wilde, Oscar, 3743, 3862-3863.
Wilder, Thornton, 3570-3579; *The Bridge of San Luis Rey*, 3572, 3573; *The Cabala*, 3572-3573; *The Eighth Day*, 3576-3577; *Heaven's My Destination*, 3574-3575; *The Ides of March*, 3575-3576; *Theophilus North*, 3577-3578; *The Woman of Andros*, 3573-3574.
Wilderness (Warren), 3443.
Wildlife (Ford, R.), 1179-1180.
Williams, Charles, 3860.
Willie Masters' Lonesome Wife (Gass), 1315-1316, 3878.
Willing to Die (Le Fanu), 2002-2003.
Wilson, A. N., 3580-3586; *Gentlemen in England*, 3584-3585; *The Healing Art*, 3582-3583; *The Sweets of Pimlico*, 3581-3582; *Who Was Oswald Fish?*, 3583-3584; *Wise Virgin*, 3583.
Wilson, Angus, 3587-3597; *Anglo-Saxon Attitudes*, 3591-3592; *As if by Magic*, 3595; *Hemlock and After*, 3590-3591; *The Middle Age of Mrs. Eliot*, 3592-3593; *No Laughing Matter*, 3594-3595; *The Old Men at the Zoo*, 3593-3594; *Setting the World on Fire*, 3596.
Wilson, Ethel, 3598-3607; *Hetty Dorval*, 3602; *The Innocent Traveller*, 3603; *Lilly's Story*, 3604-3606; *Swamp Angel*,

3606; *Tuesday and Wednesday*, 3603-3604.
Wind from Nowhere, The (Ballard), 192.
Winds of April, The (Gonzalez), 1362.
Winds of Morning (Davis), 810-811.
Winds of War, The (Wouk), 3673-3674, 3837.
Windy McPherson's Son (Anderson), 110, 112.
Wine of Astonishment, The (Lovelace), 2109-2110.
Winesburg, Ohio (Anderson), 113-115, 116.
Winter in the Hills, A (Wain), 3395, 3398-3399.
Winter of Artifice (Nin), 2515-2516.
Winter Song. See Fury Chronicle, The.
Wise Blood (O'Connor), 2569, 2570-2572, 3874, 3875.
Wise Virgin (Wilson, A. N.), 3583.
Wister, Owen, 3849.
Witch Wood (Buchan), 425.
Witches of Eastwick, The (Updike), 3356-3357.
Witching Times (De Forest), 833-834, 836.
With Shuddering Fall (Oates), 2534-2535.
Without My Cloak (O'Brien, K.), 2562-2563.
Wives and Daughters (Gaskell), 1308-1309.
Wodehouse, P. G., 3608-3618; The Blandings novels, 3612-3613; *Full Moon*, 3612; The Jeeves and Wooster novels, 3613-3615; The Psmith novels, 3615; The School novels, 3611-3612.
Woiwode, Larry, 3619-3626; *Beyond the Bedroom Wall*, 3622-3623; *Born Brothers*, 3624-3625; *Poppa John*, 3623-3624; *What I'm Going to Do, I Think*, 3621-3622.
Wolf (Harrison), 1536-1537.
Wolfe, Thomas, 3627-3640; *Look Homeward, Angel*, 3631, 3632-3634; *Of Time and the River*, 3630-3631, 3634-3636; *The Story of a Novel*, 3634; *The Web and the Rock*, 3636-3637; *You Can't Go Home Again*, 3636, 3637-3638.
Woman at Otowi Crossing, The (Waters), 3453, 3454-3455.
Woman in White, The (Collins), 683-684, 687-688.
Woman Lit by Fireflies, The (Harrison), 1546-1548.

Woman of Andros, The (Wilder), 3573-3574.
Women (Maturin), 2327.
Women and Men (McElroy), 2187-2188.
Women and Thomas Harrow (Marquand), 2305.
Women in Love (Lawrence), 1964-1969.
Women Must Work (Aldington), 57-58.
Women of Brewster Place, The (Naylor), 2491-2492.
Women on the Porch, The (Gordon), 1400-1401.
Wonderland (Oates), 2536-2537.
Woodcraft (Simms), 3041-3042.
Woodlanders, The (Hardy), 1502-1503.
Woods, The (Plante), 2644-2645.
Woolf, Virginia, 3641-3662, 3763-3764; *Between the Acts*, 3658-3661; *Jacob's Room*, 3648-3649; *Mrs. Dalloway*, 3650-3652; *Night and Day*, 3647-3648; *To the Lighthouse*, 3652-3655, 3764; *The Voyage Out*, 3646-3647; *The Waves*, 3655-3656; *The Years*, 3656-3658.
Workers in the Dawn (Gissing), 1322.
Works of Love, The (Morris), 2418.
World According to Garp, The (Irving, J.), 1698-1700.
World Enough and Time (Warren), 3441-3443.
World Is Round, The (Stein), 3147-3148.
World My Wilderness, The (Macaulay), 2139-2140.
World of Strangers, A (Gordimer), 1382-1384.
World of Wonders (Davies), 799, 800, 801.
World's End (Boyle, T.), 351-352.
World's Fair (Doctorow), 938-939.
Worm Ourobouros, The (Eddison), 3861.
Wouk, Herman, 3663-3678, 3837; *Aurora Dawn*, 3666-3667; *The Caine Mutiny*, 3667-3669; *The City Boy*, 3667; *Don't Stop the Carnival*, 3673; *Inside, Outside*, 3674-3677; *Marjorie Morningstar*, 3669-3671; *War and Remembrance*, 3673-3674, 3837; *The Winds of War*, 3673-3674, 3837; *Youngblood Hawke*, 3671-3673.
Wreck of the "Cassandra" (Prokosch), The 2741.
Wreckage of Agathon, The (Gardner), 1272-1273.
Wright, Richard, 3679-3690, 3776;

Black Boy, 3679-3680; *Eight Men*, 3679; *Lawd Today*, 3683-3684; *The Long Dream*, 3688-3689; *Native Son*, 3684-3686, 3776; *The Outsider*, 3686-3688.
Wright, Willard Huntington. *See* Van Dine, S. S.
Wuthering Heights (Brontë, E.), 390-396.
Wylder's Hand (Le Fanu), 2000-2001.

Yankee Ranger. See *Tory Lover, The*.
Year Before Last (Boyle, K.), 340-341.
Years, The (Woolf), 3656-3658.
Yellow Back Radio Broke-Down (Reed), 2802.
Yemassee, The (Simms), 3043.
Yerby, Frank, 3691-3698; *The Dahomean*, 3696-3698; *The Foxes of Harrow*, 3693-3694; *Griffin's Way*, 3694-3695; *An Odor of Sanctity*, 3695-3696.
Yerkes, C. T., 1001.
Yglesias, José, 3699-3709; *Double,*

Double, 3705-3707; *The Kill Price*, 3707-3708; *An Orderly Life*, 3703-3705; *The Truth About Them*, 3705; *A Wake in Ybor City*, 3701-3703.
Yogi and the Commissar and Other Essays, The (Koestler), 1910.
Yogi of Cockroach Court, The (Waters), 3453-3454.
Yorke, Henry Vincent. *See* **Green, Henry**.
You Can't Go Home Again (Wolfe), 3636, 3637-3638.
Young, Al, 3710-3720; *Ask Me Now*, 3716-3717; *Seduction by Light*, 3717-3719; *Sitting Pretty*, 3715-3716; *Snakes*, 3712-3714; *Who Is Angelina?*, 3714-3715.
Youngblood Hawke (Wouk), 3671-3673.

Zebra-Striped Hearse, The (Macdonald), 2174.
Zee & Co. (O'Brien, E.), 2547.
Zoroastrianism, 2361-2363.
Zuckerman Unbound (Roth), 2902-2903.